...ford Studies in ... ...al History
...eral Editor: ...

Death, Religion,
and the Family in England,
1480–1750

Death, Religion, and the Family in England, 1480–1750

RALPH HOULBROOKE

CLARENDON PRESS · OXFORD

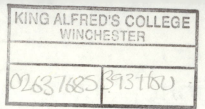

OXFORD
UNIVERSITY PRESS

Great Clarendon Street, Oxford OX2 6DP

Oxford University Press is a department of the University of Oxford.
It furthers the University's objective of excellence in research, scholarship,
and education by publishing worldwide in

Oxford New York

Athens Auckland Bangkok Bogotá Buenos Aires Calcutta
Cape Town Chennai Dar es Salaam Delhi Florence Hong Kong Istanbul
Karachi Kuala Lumpur Madrid Melbourne Mexico City Mumbai
Nairobi Paris São Paulo Shanghai Singapore Taipei Tokyo Toronto Warsaw
with associated companies in Berlin Ibadan

Oxford is a registered trade mark of Oxford University Press
in the UK and in certain other countries

Published in the United States
by Oxford University Press Inc., New York

British Library Cataloguing in Publication Data
Data available

Library of Congress Cataloging in Publication Data
Houlbrooke, Ralph A. (Ralph Anthony), 1944–
Death, religion, and the family in England, 1480–1750 / Ralph Houlbrooke.
p. cm.—(Oxford studies in social history)
Includes bibliographical references and index.
1. Funeral rites and ceremonies—England.   2. Death—Social aspects—England.
3. Funeral sermons—England—History.   4. Wills—England—History.
5. England—History—Sources.   6. England—Religious life and customs.
7. England.—Social life and customs.   I. Title.   II. Series.
GT3244A2H68   1998   393'.0942—dc21   98-3013
ISBN 0-19-821761-7 (hbk)
ISBN 0-19-820876-6 (pbk)

3 5 7 9 10 8 6 4 2

Typeset by Jayvee, Trivandrum, India
Printed in Great Britain on acid-free paper by
Biddles Ltd., Guildford and King's Lynn

In memory of our parents

C.E.B. 1915–1991
M.H.B. 1913–1993
A.H. 1902–1994
A.H. 1909–1998

ACKNOWLEDGEMENTS

Two History editors at Oxford University Press showed admirable patience during the many years which elapsed between the deadline originally set for the delivery of the text of this book and its final arrival in Great Clarendon Street. I greatly appreciated their unfailing tact and quiet encouragement. The project might have remained unfinished even now but for the award of a British Academy/Leverhulme Trust Senior Research Fellowship for the year 1993–4. This gave me relief from teaching and administration just when I most needed it. The completion of the undertaking also owes much to the fact that the History Department at the University of Reading has remained happy and harmonious despite the mounting external pressures of the last two decades. This has been due above all to the efforts of Donald Matthew and Michael Biddiss, Heads of Department during a difficult and challenging period.

This book draws on the contents of many libraries and archives. I am particularly indebted to the staffs of the Reading University Library (especially David Knott, the Rare Books Librarian), the Berkshire Record Office, the Bodleian Library, the British Library, the Norfolk Record Office, the Guildhall Library, the Somerset Record Office, the Warwick County Record Office, and the Buckinghamshire Record Office. Special words of grateful acknowledgement are due to Mrs Lorise Topliffe, the sub-librarian of Exeter College, Oxford, where I spent many peaceful hours studying the College's collection of funeral sermons, and to John Maddicott, the Fellow Librarian, for permission to use this magnificent resource.

Over the years many friends and colleagues have helped me by answering my enquiries, directing me to useful materials, or giving me offprints of their own work. They include Anthony Camp, Patrick Collinson, David Cressy, Anne Curry, Joan Dils, Mary Dobson, Anthony Fletcher, Ian Green, Vanessa Harding, Brian Kemp, Katalin Péter, Conrad Russell, Paul Slack, Peter Spufford, Stephen Taylor, Tony Walter, and Heide Wunder. It gives me particular pleasure to record the friendly interest of Clare Gittings, who is always ready to encourage workers in a field where she has made her own enduring contribution. Several passages in this book have benefited from discussion at seminars and conferences, especially the 1987 conference of the Social History Society. Earlier versions of some passages in Chapters 6 and 7 appeared in a paper on 'The Puritan Deathbed', read at the April 1993 conference on 'The Social Context of Death, Dying, and Disposal' at Mansfield College, Oxford, organized by Peter Jupp and Glennys Howarth. This paper was the basis of chapter 4 of *The Culture of English Puritanism, 1560–1700*, edited by Christopher Durston and Jacqueline Eales, and published by Macmillan in 1996.

Eamon Duffy, Margaret Houlbrooke, Stephen Taylor, Tony Walter, and Michael Biddiss kindly read the whole typescript before its final submission, Ross Wordie Chapter 1. I am indebted to the first four readers for a number of valuable suggestions. I was, alas, unable to make use of them all. Fairly extensive changes, particularly cuts made in order to avoid repetition, resulted from the scrutiny of Sir Keith Thomas, my former supervisor. The publication of this book under his general editorship gives me much happiness and satisfaction. I am very grateful to Rowena Anketell for the exemplary thoroughness of her copy-editing. It has been reassuring to have her firm yet sensitive hand on the tiller during the final passage between the mud-flats at the end of a long voyage. Many people have helped me, but it was not to be expected that they would notice all my mistakes, and the responsibility for those that remain is my own.

Tackling the chief subject of this book has sometimes been a gloomy task. A sense of my folly and presumption in confronting it has occasionally induced a certain despondency. One person, Margaret Houlbrooke, has borne the brunt of that mood and its results. To her patience and sympathy above all this book's completion is due. To her, together with Tom and Sarah Houlbrooke, my thanks for the many precious years they have given me.

R.A.H.

Reading, October 1997

CONTENTS

ABBREVIATIONS AND
NOTE ON REFERENCES

ANW	Archdeaconry of Norwich
BL	British Library, London
BMA	British Medical Association
Bod. Lib.	Bodleian Library, Oxford
Brightman, *English Rite*	F. E. Brightman, *The English Rite* (2 vols., 1915)
BRO	Berkshire Record Office, Reading
Dekker, *Plague Pamphlets*	*The Plague Pamphlets of Thomas Dekker*, ed. F. P. Wilson (Oxford, 1925)
D'Ewes, *Autobiography & Correspondence*	*The Autobiography and Correspondence of Sir Simonds D'Ewes, Bart*, ed. J. O. Halliwell (2 vols., 1845)
Duffy, *Stripping of Altars*	E. Duffy, *The Stripping of the Altars: Traditional Religion in England c.1400–c.1580* (New Haven, 1992)
EETS	Early English Text Society
EHR	*English Historical Review*
Emmison (ed.), *Elizabethan Life*, iv	F. G. Emmison (ed.), *Elizabethan Life*, iv. *Wills of Essex Gentry and Merchants Proved in the Prerogative Court of Canterbury* (Chelmsford, 1978)
Evelyn, *Diary*	*The Diary of John Evelyn*, ed. E. S. de Beer (6 vols., Oxford, 1955)
Gataker, *Certaine sermons*	T. Gataker, *Certaine sermons first preached and since published* (2 pts. in 1 vol., 1637)
GL	Guildhall Library, London
Greaves, *Society and Religion*	R. L. Greaves, *Society and Religion in Elizabethan England* (Minneapolis, 1981)

Heywood, *Autobiography, Diaries*	*The Rev. Oliver Heywood, B.A. 1603-1702: his Autobiography, Diaries, Anecdote and Event Books*, ed. J. Horsfall Turner (4 vols., Brighouse, 1882-5)
HRO	Hampshire Record Office, Winchester
Josselin, *Diary*	*The Diary of Ralph Josselin, 1616-1683*, ed. A. Macfarlane (Records of Social and Economic History, NS 3; 1976)
Kay, *Diary*	*The Diary of Richard Kay, 1716-1751, of Baldingstone, near Bury, a Lancashire Doctor*, ed. W. Brockbank and K. Kenworthy (Chetham Soc., 3rd ser. 16; 1968)
LACT	Library of Anglo-Catholic Theology (97 vols., Oxford, 1841-63)
Laud, *Works*	W. Laud, *Works*, ed. W. Scott and J. Bliss (LACT, 7 vols., 1847-60)
NRO	Norfolk Record Office, Norwich
ODCC	F. L. Cross and E. A. Livingstone (edd.), *The Oxford Dictionary of the Christian Church* (2nd edn., 1974)
Oldmayne, *Lifes brevitie*	T. Oldmayne, *Lifes brevitie and deaths debility. Evidently declared in a sermon preached at the funerall of E. Lewkenor* (1636)
Pepys, *Diary*	*The Diary of Samuel Pepys: A New and Complete Transcription* ed. R. Latham and W. Matthews (11 vols., 1970-83)
PRO	Public Record Office, London
SRO	Somerset Record Office, Taunton
STC	Short Title Catalogue (revd. edn. 1986-92)

Thomas, *Religion*	K. Thomas, *Religion and the Decline of Magic: Studies in Popular Beliefs in Sixteenth- and Seventeenth-Century England* (1971)
WCRO	Warwick County Record Office
Whitelocke, *Diary*	*The Diary of Bulstrode Whitelocke, 1605–1675*, ed. R. Spalding (Records of Social and Economic History, NS 13; 1990)

NOTE ON REFERENCES

In the Notes and Bibliography, place of publication is London unless otherwise stated.

Introduction

Death has become a fashionable subject for investigation in the last thirty years. However, the perception that the twentieth-century Western world 'deals with' it less well than previous generations and other cultures has continued to influence the way in which the topic is approached. Geoffrey Gorer expressed this idea particularly cogently in his article 'The Pornography of Death' (1955) and his book *Death, Grief and Mourning in Contemporary Britain* (1965). It bulks large in the work of Phillippe Ariès, the only writer to attempt to create a long-term historical framework for the evolution of Western attitudes to death. Ariès argued that the last thousand years have seen a gradual change from the acceptance of death as a natural part of life to its separation from the rest of everyday experience and exclusion (so far as possible) from people's minds. Ariès's explanation for this development embraces changes in religious belief and its ultimate decline, material culture, the development of medicine, increasing life expectancy, and (perhaps above all) the rise of 'individualism'. This last he sees both in an increasing preoccupation with self and in a heightened awareness of the uniqueness (and therefore irreplaceability) of loved ones. The rise of individualism is also seen as the main cause of change in *Death, Burial and the Individual in Early Modern England* (1984) by Clare Gittings, who generously acknowledges her debt to Ariès.

This study approaches the history of attitudes and behaviour in face of death by way of the history of religious change, and in particular the Protestant Reformation. Christianity offered the most comprehensive and coherent body of available guidance as to what to believe and do about death during the later Middle Ages and early modern times. It provided rites both for the dying and for survivors, explained death, pain, and bereavement in terms of God's purpose for mankind, predicted with absolute certainty a life after death, and set out very clearly the chief duties of the individual both towards the dead and in preparing for his or her own death. Changes in religious doctrine and practice during the Reformation transformed officially approved conceptions of the nature of the next life as well as the relationship between this world and the hereafter. The upheavals of the Protestant

Reformation set in train a sequence of events whose full repercussions need to be studied in a long perspective. This book investigates the effects of religious change on the social history of death between the close of the Middle Ages and the mid-eighteenth century.

Religious beliefs offer by no means the only key to late medieval and early modern attitudes to death, but certainly the most obviously important and readily accessible one. A high proportion of the written evidence that survives is set in a religious framework. Of course religion interacted with political, social, and economic developments, by which it was influenced and which in turn it helped to shape. The importance of political events is clear. To take just one example: the crown's determination to acquire adequate resources to wage war was the biggest single reason for the confiscation, in little more than a decade between 1536 and 1548, of what remained of the immense endowments invested during the Middle Ages in prayer for the souls of the dead. Much more varied, diffuse, and difficult to pin down are the connections between religion and changes in such things as social structure, the climate of family life, and attitudes to the individual. All these changes proceeded far more slowly than political or (at the official level, anyway) religious ones. Their pace, their extent, and their nature have all been subjects of controversy.

Family relationships are inextricably bound up with every aspect of the history of death considered in this book. That is why the word 'Family' appears in the title. Yet 'the Family' will not be discussed as explicitly as either 'Death' or 'Religion'. The changing causes and nature of mortality can be identified with growing confidence. The main lines of development of religious doctrine are fairly clear. However, what happened in the history of the family, and when, is far more obscure. That story is beyond the scope of this study. Nevertheless, there are good reasons for thinking that the character of the English family changed relatively slowly between the fifteenth and the eighteenth centuries, and that the appearance of change is due far more to the evolution of the media of expression than to major shifts in the institution itself. Changes in the social structure are much clearer. All sorts of rites and practices associated with death were influenced by such developments as the strengthening and decline of neo-feudalism, the growth of the urban population, especially in London, the widening gap between the middling sort and the poor, and the vast increase in the numbers of the latter. These developments have been described very fully elsewhere, and are only touched on briefly and indirectly in the account which follows, but their influence will be apparent. Much more elusive is the rise of 'individualism', partly because the concept itself is so protean, carrying so many different meanings, partly because the evidence of its existence is open to so many different interpretations.

The first two chapters are devoted respectively to the demographic and physical facts of death, and to religious beliefs concerning the hereafter. They set the stage for the account which follows. Chapters 3–7 focus on various aspects of preparation for death, including the making of wills and the last rites. The rest are concerned with what followed death: grief, mourning, funerals, burial, and commemoration. The main respect in which this book differs from previous works on the social history of death in England is the attention which it pays to preparation for death. Some other accounts have focused on funeral rites above all. (This is not true of two important surveys of other countries, however. David Stannard and John McManners, writing about Puritan New England and eighteenth-century France respectively, both tackled such matters as the deathbed experience.) Throughout this study I have drawn heavily on the work of other scholars. My debt will be most apparent in the first two chapters, in the discussion of the contents of wills, and the analysis of changing funeral customs. Much less work has been done on such subjects as will-making, the deathbed, grief, consolation, and the funeral sermon.

There are various important aspects of the social history of death that this book does not tackle. First, and most importantly, it is not concerned with the history of medical theory and practice, though they are at various points briefly taken into account. Secondly, it does not attempt a thorough survey of popular beliefs and customs connected with death. The majority of the population may have assimilated Christian teaching only partially or superficially. It seems unlikely, on the basis of what is known, that there was a body of folk beliefs which came anywhere near rivalling Christianity in its coherence, consistency, or comprehensiveness. Rather there was an immensely rich variety of ideas and practices, varying from place to place and time to time. Some of these ideas and practices may have developed independently of Christianity or even have had roots which antedated its establishment, but others were borrowed from it or were (particularly after the Reformation) adapted remnants of proscribed rites. It will be an immense task to unearth and analyse all surviving evidence of 'unofficial' death beliefs and customs with the requisite thoroughness.

Lack of time and space has prevented me from drawing on the huge wealth of relevant imaginative literature as fully as I would have liked to do. However, it is worth emphasizing that the boundaries between 'fact' and 'fiction' are especially difficult to define and map in the territory covered by this study. For our knowledge of the behaviour of the dying and those around them (for example) we are heavily dependent upon sources such as funeral sermons which used judicious selection and literary art to present deceased individuals in the best possible light. Preachers were further influenced in their choice of what to lay before their audiences by ideal models of the good death which matched their own churchmanship. If we seek to correct our impressions of the early modern deathbed by examining other ostensibly more factual accounts such as those contained in depositions taken during the course of testamentary litigation, we shall find that such evidence is in many ways equally selective, though governed by a different set of priorities and conventions. Ascertaining testators' last intentions with regard to the disposal of their worldly goods casts no more than a fitful and incidental light on their other preoccupations. The scheming and quarrelling recalled during disputes over wills and the exemplary faith and fortitude depicted in funeral sermons and biographies of the godly may have been equally atypical. Epitaphs and kindred sources present different and even more obvious problems of interpretation. All too often we do not know who wrote them or at whose behest they were inscribed, let alone what was the true relationship between the picture they presented and the lives or feelings they purport to describe. Letters and diaries often appear to offer the most direct access to intimate personal feelings and private opinions. However, letters were subject to a variety of conventions, and were moreover written with a particular audience in view. Nowhere, perhaps, is this more evident than in the complex multimedia performance by means of which Sir Kenelm Digby sought to project an image of himself as a grieving widower after the death of his wife Venetia in 1633.[1] Diaries sometimes appear to be exceptionally frank in their exposure of individual attitudes and experience—Samuel Pepys's is the prime example—but the very fact that their authors were exceptional in this respect compels the historian to ask how atypical they were in others. Securely founded generalizations are especially difficult to make in dealing with a subject like this. Perhaps the most that one can hope to do is to present, like a Chinese painter, the outlines of a landscape in which some features stand out while the greater part of the view is shrouded in mist.

---

[1] C. Gittings, 'Venetia's Death and Kenelm's Mourning', in A. Sumner (ed.), *Death, Passion and Politics: Van Dyck's Portraits of Venetia Stanley and George Digby* (1995), 54–68.

1

The Face of Death

'He increaseth the nations, and destroyeth them: he enlargeth the nations, and straiteneth them again' (Job 12: 23). Until the recent past, the belief that the growth and decline of populations were due to God's protective or destructive actions helped to make sense of fluctuations in climate and disease which were beyond human understanding or control. The fourteenth century had seen a demographic catastrophe. The population of the country had possibly been halved, largely as a result of a series of outbreaks of plague which began in 1348. Estimates of its size around 1300 range between a minimum of just over 4 million and a maximum of just over 6 million. By 1377 it had fallen to 3 million or less, and went on falling for some time after that. In the early 1520s the population was probably between 2.25 and 2.75 million. It was not until the 1590s that it rose above 4 million (the lowest estimate generally regarded as reasonable for 1300), not until the 1750s that it reached the 6 million mark (the highest estimate). So for much, possibly most, of this period the population of England was less than it had been before the famines and plagues of the fourteenth century.[1]

Fluctuations in mortality exercised a strong influence over population trends between the fifteenth century and the mid-eighteenth. Assessments of the respective contributions of mortality and fertility to the course of late medieval demographic change remain speculative. There are no sources for this period which provide a basis for statistics of sufficient chronological or geographical scope; however,

[1] J. Hatcher, *Plague, Population and the English Economy, 1348-1530* (Basingstoke, 1977), 68-9, 71; E. A. Wrigley and R. S. Schofield, *The Population History of England, 1541-1871: A Reconstruction* (1981), 531-3, 736-8; R. M. Smith, 'Population and its Geography in England 1500-1730', in R. A. Dodgshon and R. A. Butlin (edd.), *An Historical Geography of England and Wales* (1978), 200. L. Clarkson's *Death, Disease and Famine in Pre-Industrial England* (Dublin, 1975), is a helpful and accessible introduction to the topics of this chapter but subsequent advances, particularly in historical demography, have made considerable changes in the picture he drew.

figures from certain monastic communities (a small sample, but of exceptionally reliable accuracy) show that life expectancy declined there during the fifteenth century. At Westminster Abbey, a sharp fall in the second half of the fifteenth century was followed by a marked recovery early in the sixteenth. According to the best available estimates, national population, stagnant in the mid-fifteenth century, began to rise gently from *c.*1470, and more strongly from *c.*1520. It is 'surely hard to deny pride of place to mortality' among the variables which produced these changes.[2] Parish registers of baptisms, marriages, and burials enable demographers to identify the causes of population change during the period after their inception in 1538 with greater confidence. During the next two centuries, taken as a whole, the effects of mortality and fertility fluctuations were roughly equal. Mortality fell markedly during the 'golden period' of the later sixteenth century, between 1691 and 1706, and after 1731. It rose, however, between 1611 and 1676, and between 1706 and 1731.[3]

Today, death rates in developed countries are comparatively stable from year to year. They generally stand at around 10 per thousand. In medieval and early modern times, however, they were not only far higher, but they also fluctuated markedly. Even smoothed-out five-year average national figures could vary sharply: between just under 22 per thousand and just over 33 per thousand in the second half of the sixteenth century, for example. Variations from year to year and in particular places could be much more pronounced. Sharp and irregular oscillations in mortality perhaps contributed to anxiety about death through their scale and unpredictability. The incidence of 'mortality crises' during which the numbers of deaths rose well above the prevailing trend has been measured by historical demographers. In the period 1540–1750 there were eleven national crisis years when mortality rose at least 30 per cent above trend. By far the worst were 1557–9. There was another cluster of three years in 1727–30. The other six crises fell in 1625/6, 1638/9, 1657/8, 1665/6,

[2] Hatcher, *Plague, Population and the English Economy*, 72–3; Wrigley and Schofield, *Population History*, 736; B. Harvey, *Living and Dying in England 1100–1540: The Monastic Experience* (Oxford, 1993), 128, 144–5. Some historians emphasize the role of restrained fertility: see P. J. P. Goldberg, *Women, Work, and Life Cycle in a Medieval Economy: Women in York and Yorkshire c.1300–1520* (Oxford, 1992), 7, 324–61; L. R. Poos, *A Rural Society after the Black Death: Essex, 1350–1525* (Cambridge, 1991), 111–29. An excellent survey of the question is M. Bailey's 'Demographic Decline in Late Medieval England: Some Thoughts on Recent Research', *Economic History Review*, 49 (1996), 1–19.

[3] Wrigley and Schofield, *Population History*, 240–4.

1680/1, and 1741/2. In all there were twenty-one years when mortality rose at least 20 per cent above trend. All but five of these crises occurred in the years up to 1666. Save for the abnormally severe mortality of the 1720s, major crises were tending to become less frequent in the course of time. This impression is confirmed by the pattern of local crisis mortality.[4]

'The days of our age are threescore years and ten; and though men be so strong that they come to fourscore years: yet is their strength then but labour and sorrow; so soon passeth it away, and we are gone.' So Psalm 90. Since pre-classical times there has been an idea of man's natural lifespan (but the existence of some people who lived beyond this span has been reported in most epochs since then). Recent estimates have tended to be more optimistic than the Psalmist's. One has extended the span to eighty-five years.[5] However, the cells of the human body wear out and die with the process of natural ageing, and only techniques not yet developed could interfere with this process. So far, what has been achieved for the inhabitants of developed countries is an average life expectancy slightly exceeding the biblical span. This has been done by controlling or eliminating the diseases which caused premature death in past generations. (The notion of 'premature' death, too, is a long established one. St Isidore of Seville (c.560–636) distinguished three kinds of death. The deaths of children were bitter, and those of younglings came too soon, but those of the old were natural.)[6]

Historical demographers now estimate with a fair degree of confidence the likely average life expectancy of past generations at birth. For most of this period, the national figure probably fluctuated between 30 and 40 years. Low points of 27.77, 28.47, and 27.88 have been calculated for 1561, 1681, and 1731 respectively, and peaks of 40.26, 41.68, and 40.82 for 1576, 1581, and 1606.[7] The first year of life was much the most dangerous, and it saw by far the largest numbers of deaths. Calculations based on the registers of thirteen parishes suggest that between one in six and one in five of all babies born died

---

[4] *1992 Demographic Yearbook* (New York, 1994), 500–3; Wrigley and Schofield, *Population History*, 311–20, 332–5, 528, 650, 531–3.

[5] *The Times*, 30 July 1980, 16d, summarizing work by J. F. Fries originally published in *New England Journal of Medicine* (1980).

[6] *On the Properties of Things: John Trevisa's Translation of Bartholomaeus Anglicus De Proprietatibus Rerum. A Critical Text*, ed. M. C. Seymour (3 vols., Oxford, 1975–88), i. 293.

[7] Wrigley and Schofield, *Population History*, 528–9. These are averages for the quinquenniums centred on the years mentioned.

before reaching the age of 1. However, the list includes none of the unhealthiest places, where the proportion was as high as a quarter or a third. Furthermore, infant mortality rates seem to have worsened between the early seventeenth and the early eighteenth century.[8] Contemporaries were well aware of the waste of infant life, and may even have been inclined to overestimate it. 'How many are carried from the *wombe* to the *tombe*, (as *Iob* speaketh) from birth immediately to *buriall?*', demanded Thomas Gataker, a famous Puritan minister, in 1627. 'How many come only to suck a Bib, or shake a Ratle, and returne again to earth?', asked John Toy, preaching in 1642. 'I dare say the third part of mankind do not attaine to a moneth.'[9]

Because of the very high level of infant mortality (i.e. deaths before the first birthday), life expectancy at the age of 1 year was higher than at birth. In British peerage families, life expectancy was between five and ten years higher at the age of 5 than it had been at birth in every quarter-century from 1550 to 1750. Male life expectancy at age 5 improved from 44.4 (1550–74) to 47.5 (1725–49), female from 43.7 to 45.3, though between those periods both sexes experienced a fall in life expectancy during the seventeenth century. A mean figure based on the experience of twelve parishes with very good registers suggests that over much of provincial England adults who reached the age of 30 could look forward to another twenty-eight or thirty years of life in early modern times.[10]

Anybody who survived the hazardous years of early childhood had a reasonable chance of reaching middle age, but it remains true that mortality at every stage of life before old age was higher than it is today. It fell increasingly sharply after the first year, reaching its lowest level in the 10–14 age group. Thereafter, the death rate climbed sharply. The majority of those who had survived childhood died before they reached 60.[11] Only a very small minority of those

[8] R. A. Houston, *The Population History of Britain and Ireland 1500–1750* (Basingstoke, 1992), 50–1; T. R. Forbes, 'By what Disease or Casualty: The Changing Face of Death in London', in C. Webster (ed.), *Health, Medicine and Mortality in the Sixteenth Century* (Cambridge, 1979), 124, 139; J. Landers, *Death and the Metropolis: Studies in the Demographic History of London, 1670–1830* (Cambridge, 1993), 183–93.

[9] Gataker, *Certaine sermons*, ii. 296; J. Toy, *A Sermon preached . . . at the funerall of M^{ris} Alice Tomkins wife unto Mr Thomas Tomkins one of the Gentlemen of his Majesties Chappell Royall* (1642), 4.

[10] T. H. Hollingsworth, 'The Demography of the British Peerage', suppl. to *Population Studies*, 18 (1964), 56–7; Wrigley and Schofield, *Population History*, 250.

[11] Forbes, 'By what Disease or Casualty', 124; Landers, *Death and the Metropolis*, 100.

born, therefore, were left to die in old age, whereas today that is when most people die. Contemporaries were well aware of this state of affairs. The weekly summaries of London deaths usually contained more 'dead Children than aged men', as Nathaniel Hardy remarked in 1653. God took multitudes out of the world before their natural term, the minister Timothy Cruso correctly observed in 1688. Very few reached the age of 70.[12]

'Anyone can stop a man's life, but no one his death; a thousand doors open on to it.'[13] Thus Seneca (d. AD 65), in an epigram which underwent innumerable adaptations in medieval and early modern times. Then, the experience of death differed fundamentally from that of the developed world at the present day. The great killers in countries with a high standard of living are now cancer and disorders of the heart and circulatory system. Then, a host of communicable diseases ravaged the populations of Europe. Some of these caused widespread fear of a sort almost forgotten in the wealthier countries before the appearance of Aids in the 1980s. The fall in the incidence of communicable diseases has been attributed to a variety of causes. Disagreement among historical demographers centres on the weight to be given each one. Outside human control were a decline in the virulence of the micro-organisms which cause disease, and immunological adjustments by the human body. The most direct means of combating such micro-organisms have been inoculation (the practice of inducing a mild form of a given disease in order to make the subject immune to it), the use of antibiotics to destroy them, and antiseptic measures to prevent the infection of wounds and surgical incisions. A great range of drugs have played an auxiliary role in combating diseases by alleviating their symptoms, such as pain, fever, nausea, and looseness. Measures have been taken to check the spread of diseases (e.g. by quarantine) and to eliminate the conditions in which they thrive (by improving water supplies and sanitation, draining swamps, building better houses, and encouraging personal hygiene). Higher standards of nutrition have raised individuals' resistance to disease. The importance of each of these causes

---

[12] N. Hardy, *Death's Alarum: or, Security's Warning-Piece. A Sermon preached ... at the Funerall of M*[rs]*. Mary Smith* (1654), 12; T. Cruso, *The Period of Humane Life determined by the Divine Will. A Funeral Sermon on the Death of Mr. Henry Brownsword* (1688), 7–8.

[13] Seneca, *Phoenissae*, 152, cited in *The Oxford Dictionary of Quotations* (3rd edn., Oxford, 1979), 420; R. Eaton, *A sermon preached at the funeralls of Thomas Dutton of Dutton, esquire* (1616), 12.

has varied from one disease to another, but most of them had major effects only after 1750.[14]

Although broad differences between early modern and contemporary patterns of mortality are clear, the precise cause of most early modern deaths remains uncertain. Diagnosis was relatively primitive. Even where causes are assigned for relatively large numbers of deaths (as in the London Bills of Mortality, and certain unusually detailed parish registers), the terminology employed now appears hopelessly vague, muddled, and inaccurate. Furthermore, the precise role of a specific disease in causing a person's death is often far from clear. Infectious disease can certainly result in death, especially when it attacks populations or individuals (particularly infants) who have developed no immunity against it. However, the majority of individuals undergo a series of weakening insults from disease, faulty diet, and environmental toxins before finally succumbing to the effects of a disease from which they might earlier have recovered.[15] No full account of the causes of death could neglect the earlier insults, but in the case of pre-modern populations there is no chance of recovering more than a minuscule minority of life histories. Attention perforce focuses on the terminal episode.

The study of early modern burial records in relation to the ages of the deceased and the months of the year has revealed some basic patterns. In northern countries, including England, the winter and early spring months saw the heaviest mortality, with a peak in March and April when resistance may have reached its lowest point after prolonged cold. During the colder half of the year, two groups in particular suffered: infants (rather earlier) and the older members of the population (rather later). It was then that airborne respiratory diseases wrought the greatest havoc. The summer saw the peak of diseases affecting the digestive tract, such as dysentery, which were especially lethal for children. These were associated with contaminated food and water supplies. Infants, who were largely protected against gastric infection by maternal breastfeeding, lost that immunity when weaned, or to the extent that they were fed artificially.[16]

[14] N. L. Tranter, *Population and Society, 1750-1940: Contrasts in Population Growth* (1985), 64–88; Landers, *Death and the Metropolis*, 7–39; P. Razzell, *Essays in English Population History* (1994), 219–29, esp. 220.

[15] G. Alter and J. C. Riley, 'Frailty, Sickness, and Death: Models of Morbidity and Mortality in Historical Populations', *Population Studies*, 43 (1989), 25–45.

[16] Wrigley and Schofield, *Population History*, 293–8; R. S. Schofield and E. A. Wrigley, 'Infant and Child Mortality in England in the Late Tudor and Early Stuart Period', in Webster (ed.), *Health, Medicine and Mortality*, 81, 89–91.

Medical science distinguishes between endemic diseases, habitually prevalent in particular areas, and epidemics whose prevalence is
intermittent. Some diseases may become endemic as local conditions
change. Thus smallpox is thought to have become endemic in
London during the later seventeenth century, but remained epidemic
elsewhere.[17] It caused very high mortality among children and adolescents, often carrying off several members of the same family.
Bubonic plague was endemic in London and some other cities until
the seventeenth century, but 'broad tides of infection' from the con-
tinent were necessary to produce epidemics which spread the disease more widely through the country.[18]

Of the epidemic diseases, the most notorious experienced in late
medieval and early modern times was bubonic plague, a disease of the
summer and early autumn months. The chief agent in the terrifying
fourteenth-century culling of the population, plague was taking a
much smaller toll by 1500. During the sixteenth century it seems to
have continued to recede gradually from the countryside, becoming
concentrated in the poorer areas of towns. Major outbreaks took
place in London in 1513, 1543, 1563, 1578, 1593, 1603, 1625, 1636,
and 1665. The 1665 outbreak, the last and now the best remembered,
killed far more people than any of the others, but this was because
London had grown so fast. It carried off a smaller proportion of the
population than three earlier outbreaks: 12.2 per cent compared with
the 20.5 per cent of 1563, the 17.8 per cent of 1603, and the 12.8 per
cent of 1625. Three provincial towns are known to have lost around
a third of their populations in a major epidemic: Norwich (1579),
Newcastle (1636), and Colchester (1666). Plague was either certainly
or probably involved in seventeen out of twenty-five outbreaks of epidemic disease known to have hit a number of English towns between
1485 and 1665–6. Yet it probably caused a fairly small fraction of all
deaths nationally: 15 per cent in London between 1580 and 1650, not
nearly so large a percentage elsewhere.[19]

One other disease, the sweating-sickness, inspired a dread similar
to that caused by the plague. It claimed the lives of rich as well as
poor, and in fatal cases brought death very swiftly, but its outbreaks
were far rarer and shorter than the plague's. It struck in 1485, 1507–8,

---

[17] Wrigley and Schofield, *Population History*, 656 n. 28, 668–9; Landers, *Death and the Metropolis*, 121–2.

[18] P. Slack, *The Impact of Plague in Tudor and Stuart England* (Oxford, 1985), 13–14, 68–9, 147, 151.

[19] Ibid. 8–9, 15–17, 60–2, 65, 129–130, 151, 194–5; Houston, *Population History*, 55.

1517, and 1551. In 1551, the year of the best documented attack, high mortality was limited to the months of July and August. The sweating-sickness passed very quickly and had a comparatively small effect on overall death rates.[20]

The most serious early modern upsurge in mortality, and the one whose causes were most complex, was not due to plague. Spread over the years 1557-9, and over a much larger area of the country than any other comparable episode, it was exceptional in temporarily reducing the national population during a period of strong growth. There were two phases. In 1556-7 there were outbreaks of 'burning' or 'spotted' fevers (possibly including typhus), followed in 1558-9 by a 'new ague', possibly 'a virulent viral infection, a variety of influenza'. The harvests of 1555-6 were exceptionally poor. The impact of the diseases of the first phase may have been enhanced by the fact that the population had been weakened by malnutrition. They may also have been spread by the unusually active traffic in foodstuffs needed to meet the needs of communities hard hit by the harvest shortfall.[21] The link between poor harvests and subsequent mortality crises in 1586-8, 1596-8, and 1622-3 seems clear. All three crises were most severe in the pastoral areas of the north which were dependent on imports of grain from outside the region, but the first two were experienced in many southern pastoral areas as well. Typhus, dysentery, and tuberculosis were probably among the diseases which followed these deficient harvests. Markedly increased mortality followed such harvests on at least eight other occasions between 1501-2 and 1630. After that, improvements in agricultural productivity and grain supplies greatly reduced the impact of poor harvests. During the 1690s, a decade which saw several of them, England did not share the heavy mortality suffered by many of its neighbours.[22]

Typhus was probably carried to many different parts of the country by the rival armies during the 1640s. After 1650 crisis mortality was less common, though there was a higher general level of mortality in the later seventeenth century. Exceptionally severe crises occurred in 1657-9, 1665-6 (the year of the last great plague outbreak in

[20] Slack, *Impact of Plague*, 70-1; J. A. H. Wylie and L. H. Collier, 'The English Sweating Sickness (Sudor Anglicus): A Reappraisal', *Journal of the History of Medicine*, 36 (1981), 425-45.

[21] P. Slack, 'Mortality Crises and Epidemic Disease in England, 1485-1610', in Webster (ed.), *Health, Medicine and Mortality*, 27-32.

[22] Slack, *Impact of Plague*, 73-4; Wrigley and Schofield, *Population History*, 340-1, 664-7, 670-3, 675-9; J. Walter and R. Schofield (edd.), *Famine, Disease and the Social Order in Early Modern Society* (Cambridge, 1989), esp. 1-73.

London), and in 1680-1. No one disease was responsible for the episodes of 1657-9 and 1680-1, it is thought, but probably a combination of disorders, including smallpox, gastric illnesses such as typhoid and dysentery, and, in the south-eastern marshes, malaria. The years 1727-30 saw by far the worst mortality since the 1550s. Then again, a number of diseases combined to raise the general level of mortality, including smallpox, whooping-cough, malaria, and a 'putrid fever'. The last great crisis of this period, in 1741-2, was formerly attributed to typhus in particular, but dysentery was probably more important. Smallpox was perhaps the most feared killer of the century 1650-1750. Relatively mild and infrequent before 1600, it seems to have become much more common and lethal by the later seventeenth century. As early as 1629 it was claimed that scarcely one family in the Isle of Wight escaped it, and that many people died. In larger eighteenth-century towns most children were exposed to it. Smallpox claimed adult victims among those who encountered it in epidemic form outside its main urban centres or who were infected when visiting a big town. A disease commonly confused with smallpox, at least until the 1670s, was measles, which occurred as a cold-weather disease in phases of different levels of virulence. Two epidemics in the town of Bolton in the 1640s probably killed 20 per cent or more of the children aged between 6 months and 3 years.[23]

The incidence of disease varied from place to place. Big cities where long-distance contacts were most numerous, and which also contained densely populated areas of poor housing, suffered worst. The enormous growth of London (far faster than that of the national population in the early modern period) created, in the capital's poorer suburbs and the more congested of its inner parishes, an especially unhealthy environment. In London and some larger towns, disease seems for much of this period to have been linked above all with insanitary conditions, producing a later summer and early autumn mortality peak, although in London the peak occurred during the winter after 1700. Long-established gastric diseases seem to have declined, but smallpox, typhus, and tuberculosis contributed to an increasing death rate. The 'metropolitan penalty' was at its heaviest in childhood. Between 1680 and 1750 the infant mortality rate possibly hovered for most of the time between 350 and 380 per thousand,

[23] Wrigley and Schofield, *Population History*, 332-6, 663-4, 667-70; *The Oglander Memoirs: Extracts from the MSS of Sir J. Oglander Kt.*, ed. W. H. Long (1888), 54; A. Dyer, 'Epidemics of Measles in a Seventeenth-Century English Town', *Local Population Studies*, 34 (1984), 35-45; Landers, *Death and the Metropolis*, 121-2.

peaking around 390 per thousand in about 1740. Estimated life expectation at birth in the 1740s was as low as 17.6. However, conditions worsened in the early eighteenth century for adults too. A 30-year-old London Quaker male's life expectation was 28 in the period 1650–99 (very close to the average calculated for twelve provincial parishes). Yet in 1700–49 it was nearly two years lower, whereas the corresponding figure for the twelve parishes had risen by two years. Provincial towns, especially industrial centres with a large proportion of poor workers, also experienced high death rates. Henry Newcome, a young Presbyterian minister, came to Manchester in 1657 from a rural parish where in one year, 1652, not one person had died. He recorded in a famous passage the depressing effect of urban mortality upon his spirits. There he visited three or four sick persons a day, and saw several burials in a week. Yet in time he grew accustomed to these conditions.[24]

There were considerable variations in levels of mortality outside the towns. Some relatively isolated communities which received few disease-bearing visitors from the outside world enjoyed high life expectancies. Certain areas were notably unhealthy: fens, marshes, and low-lying estuarial tracts. Vivax malaria was widespread in fens and marshes from the sixteenth century, and seems to have reached its peak morbidity during the seventeenth. The northern uplands, and particularly those parts where population had grown rapidly as a result of the development of rural industry, suffered worst in the aftermath of sixteenth- and early seventeenth-century dearths. After the mid-seventeenth century south-east England experienced very high levels of mortality. Various developments tended to facilitate infectious contacts in an age of economic expansion: increased personal mobility, growing traffic in and out of the unhealthy metropolis, trade with overseas sources of disease, and the growth of livestock herds, creating more dirt in which flies throve. These were coupled with worsening malaria in many south-eastern coastal areas.[25]

---

[24] J. Landers and A. Mouzas, 'Burial Seasonality and Causes of Death in London 1670–1819', *Population Studies*, 42 (1988), 62, 76–9; Landers, *Death and the Metropolis*, 94–8, 152–61, 170–1, 203–41; Wrigley and Schofield, *Population History*, 250; *The Autobiography of Henry Newcome, M.A.*, ed. R. Parkinson (Chetham Soc., os 26 and 27; 1852), 42–3, 73.

[25] Wrigley and Schofield, *Population History*, 679–81; M. J. Dobson, 'The Last Hiccup of the Old Demographic Regime: Population Stagnation and Decline in Late Seventeenth- and Early Eighteenth-Century South-East England', *Continuity and Change*, 4 (1989), 395–428; ead., 'History of Malaria in England', *Journal of the Royal Society of Medicine*, suppl. no. 17, vol. 82 (1989), 3–7; ead., 'Malaria in England:

Such were the chief killers and the main elements of the chronology and geography of death during this period. So far as individual experience was concerned, the biggest differences distinguishing the period under review from that of the present day were first the much greater likelihood of dying young, and secondly that of succumbing to a fever-inducing malady which killed comparatively quickly. High temperature, often accompanied by delirium in severe cases, is a feature common to many of these diseases. Death is frequently due to exhaustion or to complications. Of them all, influenza is the one which remains most familiar today. It is caused by an adaptable family of viruses. (Viruses are the smallest known type of pathogen or infectious agent, ranging from one-half to one-hundredth of the size of the smallest bacteria, the micro-organisms which caused most of the diseases described here. Viruses are much simpler than bacteria in their structure and method of multiplication.) An infection of the respiratory tract spread by infected droplets coughed or sneezed into the air, influenza generally claims its heaviest toll in winter. The classic symptoms of the 'A' and 'B' types are chills, fever, headache, muscular aches, loss of appetite, and fatigue, usually followed by a cough, sore throat, and itching nose. Severe forms of influenza cause an acute pneumonia which may be fatal even to healthy young adults within a day or two.[26]

Among the diseases of the digestive tract, dysentery and typhoid fever are spread by flies, polluted food and water, and contact with human carriers. In the form of dysentery familiar in early modern England, pain in the abdomen is followed by diarrhoea, the stools consisting mainly of mucus and blood, hence the name 'bloody flux' then commonly applied to it. It is accompanied by fever, and often by nausea, aches in the limbs, and shivering. Both dysentery and typhoid fever can result in ulceration of the intestine, with a risk of perforation and haemorrhage, but the likelihood is greater in typhoid fever. Its onset is much more gradual than that of dysentery. The early symptoms include headache, tiredness, and nocturnal sleeplessness and feverishness. The temperature rises gradually during the first week to a plateau of 102 to 104 °F. Diarrhoea is a common symptom, but constipation is an alternative in mild cases. Spots often appear on the abdomen, chest, and back in the second week. The patient frequently

A Geographical and Historical Perspective', *Parassitologia*, 36 (1994), 35–60. I am grateful to Mary Dobson for giving me offprints of the last two articles.

[26] T. Smith (ed.), *The BMA Complete Family Health Encyclopaedia* (London, 1990), 152, 584, 1055.

suffers delirium and tremors during the third week, after which, if he
has survived that long, the fever begins to subside.[27]

Some formidable killers were communicated to human beings by
insect-bites: typhus (most commonly in winter, especially where
people huddled together for warmth), malaria, and plague (predom-
inantly in summer and autumn). 'Typhus' is a generic term for a group
of infectious diseases spread by rickettsiae, micro-organisms intermediate in size between bacteria and viruses. Epidemic typhus is
spread between human beings by body lice and introduced into the
bloodstream by scratching the skin, while endemic or murine typhus
is spread from rats to humans by fleas. The symptoms of epidemic
typhus develop suddenly and include severe headache, pain in the
back and limbs, followed by high fever and a rash. Malaria is spread by
the Anopheles mosquito. The period between being bitten and the
onset of symptoms is usually a week or two. Uncontrollable shivering
is followed by a hot stage in which the temperature may reach 105 °F,
and finally a drenching sweat which brings the temperature down,
leaving the patient exhausted. The fever recurs cyclically, every other
day, for example (a 'tertian' ague in early modern reckoning) or every
third day (a 'quartan'). The *vivax* and *malariae* strains dominant in
England may have been more virulent on their first arrival than they
subsequently became. From the eighteenth century onwards 'marsh
fever' was regarded as a debilitating rather than a lethal disease.
Bubonic plague, carried from rats to human beings by fleas, killed half
its victims within eight days of infection (though some survived for
up to a month). Their temperature swiftly rose to about 104 °F. They
suffered 'headaches, vomiting, pain and delirium before sinking into
a final coma', while their skin was disfigured by swelling of the glands
of the groin or armpits and subcutaneous haemorrhages producing
black gangrenous patches.[28]

Smallpox succeeded to the plague's position as the most widely
dreaded disease. Like the plague, it caused a disfigurement which was
particularly distressing to close relatives of sufferers. Most commonly
communicated by personal contact, smallpox has been described as
'the most highly contagious of all diseases'. Its onset was marked by
sudden shivering, followed by the primary fever, during which the
temperature rose to 103 or 104 °F. Other symptoms included thirst,

---

[27] G. Macpherson (ed.), *Black's Medical Dictionary* (37th edn., 1992), 176–7,
196–7; Smith (ed.), *BMA Health Encyclopaedia*, 381.

[28] *Black's Medical Dictionary* (37th edn.), 508, 604–5; Dobson, 'Malaria in England', 35–60; Slack, *Impact of Plague*, 7–8.

constipation, intense headache, vomiting, and pain in the back. Rashes appeared on the lower abdomen and inner thighs. The fever abated on the third day, but later returned, the patient's temperature rising to its highest point on the eighth or ninth day, before falling away sharply. Meanwhile, eruptions which first appeared on the face on the third day grew in size and changed into pustules by the eighth or ninth day, with inflammation and swelling of the surrounding skin. They gave off an offensive smell, especially when they burst. The mucous membranes, particularly of the mouth and throat, were also affected. On the eleventh or twelfth day the pustules began to dry up, and eventually the scabs which formed on them dropped off, leaving permanent scars.[29]

Apart from the great fevers, a number of chronic maladies blighted many lives. Pulmonary tuberculosis throve in the crowded poorer quarters of towns, where it might easily be spread by coughing and sneezing. It may have been one of the foremost endemic diseases in early modern London.[30] Syphilis was felt to be a uniquely shameful malady, and deaths due to it were allegedly often attributed to other causes, so that its incidence is hard to estimate. Another chronic complaint which could be fatal, but with which people often lived for many years or even decades before dying of some other disease, was kidney or bladder stone. Gout, usually a hereditary disease of males, is characterized by painful inflammation of the smaller joints which can spread to the larger ones and to internal organs. Many diarists and letter-writers recorded the excruciating pain which they or their friends suffered from the stone, together with the emission of bloody urine and gravel; a smaller number the agonizing paroxysms of gout. Other debilitating diseases included rickets (first noticed in the seventeenth century), scrofula, and scurvy.[31]

[29] W. A. R. Thompson (ed.), *Black's Medical Dictionary* (31st edn., 1976), 779–80; J. F. D. Shrewsbury, *A History of Bubonic Plague in the British Isles* (Cambridge, 1970), 133.

[30] Forbes, 'By what Disease or Casualty', 125–6; Landers, *Death and the Metropolis*, 94–8.

[31] J. Graunt, *Natural and Political Observations upon the Bills of Mortality* (5th edn., 1676), repr. in *The Economic Writings of Sir William Petty*, ed. C. H. Hull (repr. New York, 1964), ii. 356–60; L. M. Beier, *Sufferers and Healers: The Experience of Illness in Seventeenth-Century England* (1987), 87–94, 136–8, 148–50, 232, 248–41. For the stone see e.g. *The Letter Book of John Parkhurst, Bishop of Norwich, 1571–1575*, ed. R. A. Houlbrooke (Norfolk Record Soc. 43; 1974–5), 69, 72, 83; Whitelocke, *Diary*, 630, 635, 639, 650, 654, 660, 668, and 670–828 *passim*; for gout see C. F. Smith, *Mary Rich, Countess of Warwick (1625–1678), her Family and Friends* (1901), 174, 216, 231.

Today's chief killers were certainly present in early modern times, though their contribution to overall mortality was proportionately far less important. Surgeons recorded attempts to amputate cancerous tumours. Diarists and biographers sometimes described apoplectic strokes which either killed their victims outright or incapacitated them with a 'dead palsy', though such strokes do not appear as one of the chief causes of death in the London Bills of Mortality. Deaths from coronary thrombosis and cardiac arrhythmia went undiagnosed, but presumably many were concealed under the general headings of 'sudden' or 'aged' or those for which no cause was assigned. Dropsy (abnormal accumulation of fluid under the skin or in the body cavities), usually a result of diseases of the heart or kidney, was quite frequently recorded as a cause of death.[32]

Before 1750 pregnancy and childbirth were roughly 150 times more dangerous than they are today, and a good deal riskier still in London and during the second half of the seventeenth century. For most of the period, a woman's risk of death in childbed was roughly 1 per cent in any one pregnancy, and 6–7 per cent during an average procreative career. The overwhelming majority of births were not dangerous, but abnormalities and complications were far more likely to be fatal than they are today.[33]

Death was inseparable from the fallen condition of mankind. The deaths of individuals were designed by God as mercies, trials, or punishments. Yet belief in divine providence did not necessarily induce a passive fatalism or exclude the possibility of human action to preserve or restore health and prolong life. Indeed this was viewed by many as a Christian duty, expressed very well by a young lady, Maria Thynne, writing to her husband in about 1607. She urged him to protect himself against the plague and to 'remember we are bound in conscience to maintain life as long as is possible, and though God's power can work miracles, yet we cannot build upon it that because

[32] Beier, *Sufferers and Healers*, 82, 84–5; Kay, *Diary*, 134, 136, 141–2, 146–9, 151; *The Diary of Samuel Newton, Alderman of Cambridge (1662–1717)*, ed. J. E. Foster (Cambridge Antiquarian Soc. 23; 1890), 106, 108; *The Diary of Robert Hooke, F.R.S., 1672–1680*, ed. H. W. Robinson and W. Adams (1935), 154, 310; Graunt, *Observations*, 351–2, 'Table of Casualties' facing 406; Forbes, 'By what Disease or Casualty', 127; Smith (ed.), *BMA Health Encyclopaedia*, 374.

[33] R. Schofield, 'Did the Mothers Really Die? Three Centuries of Maternal Mortality in "The World We Have Lost" ', in L. Bonfield, R. M. Smith, and Keith Wrightson (edd.), *The World We have Gained: Histories of Population and Social Structure, Essays presented to Peter Laslett on his Seventieth Birthday* (Oxford, 1986), 248–50, 259; cf. A. Eccles, *Obstetrics and Gynaecology in Tudor and Stuart England* (1982), 86, 125, 130; *1992 Demographic Yearbook*, 493.

He can, He will, for then He would not say He made herb[s] for the use of man'. Maria's medicine gave no protection against the plague, but convictions such as she expressed prevented religion, in England at any rate, from acting as a barrier to medical advance.[34]

Soul, mind, and body were held to be intimately connected and to act upon each other. A clear conscience, a calm mind, and a healthy lifestyle were the means to maintain the soundness of the whole person. According to the orthodox theory dominant since antiquity, the individual's physical and mental qualities and disposition were determined above all by the balance within his or her body of the four humours (blood, phlegm, black bile, and yellow bile). Their distribution differed from person to person. The observance of an appropriate regimen in terms of diet, temperature, environment, and exercise was the first prerequisite for the maintenance of good health, but advice about how best to correct humoral imbalances by more direct means, especially by purging and bloodletting, was the particular province of the physician. Humoral theory had been passed on from the late classical world above all in the works of the Greek physician Galen (*c.*AD 130–201). Since early modern times, despite some superficial continuities and similarities, ideas concerning healthy diet, temperature, and immediate environment have changed radically. Galenic conceptions of the chief means and purposes of medical intervention have been almost completely rejected. Save by recommending certain preventive precautions of rather haphazard efficacy, and offering some palliative measures, established medical theory was quite helpless in face of the overwhelming majority of the diseases considered above.[35]

Humoral theory was the basis for the prevailing orthodoxy in early modern England, but chemical medicine, designed to combat each particular malady with an appropriate remedy, rather than to correct the overall balance of the humours, had many adherents. The alchemists were particularly concerned with the quest for the substance variously

---

[34] Genesis 3: 19; *Two Elizabethan Women: Correspondence of Joan and Maria Thynne 1575–1611*, ed. A. D. Wall (Wilts, Record Soc. 38; 1982), 36; Thomas, *Religion*, 788–9; Slack, *Impact of Plague*, 22–50, 227–54; R. Porter, 'Introduction', A. Wear, 'Puritan Perceptions of Illness in Seventeenth Century England', and J. Barry, 'Piety and the Patient: Medicine and Religion in Eighteenth Century Bristol', in R. Porter (ed.), *Patients and Practitioners: Lay Perceptions of Medicine in Pre-Industrial Society* (Cambridge, 1985), 6–7, 55–99, 169–75 respectively; R. Porter, *Disease, Medicine and Society in England 1550–1860* (Basingstoke, 1987), 27–8.

[35] Ibid. 15, 25–6; W. S. C. Copeman, *Doctors and Disease in Tudor Times* (1960), 87–9; L. Pollock, *With Faith and Physic: The Life of a Tudor Gentlewoman, Lady Grace Mildmay 1552–1620* (1993), 94.

known as the 'Quintessence', 'Philosophers' Stone', or 'Elixir of Life', which (they believed) would cure 'all infirmities whatsoever' and prolong human life to its natural limit. However, they were also interested in discovering and exploiting the medicinal potential of a whole range of substances, animal, vegetable, and mineral. The alchemical tradition in England had an outstanding native representative in Friar Roger Bacon (d. 1294), but the pre-eminent iatrochemist (i.e. one who applies chemistry to medical practice) of the sixteenth century was the Swiss Theophrastus Paracelsus (1493–1541). He encouraged an experimental approach to the trial and development of new medicines. His ideas had been 'largely assimilated' in England by 1600.[36]

Medical services were offered by several different types of practitioner in early modern England. At the highest level were the physicians, with their theoretical training, present in relatively large numbers in London, but relatively thinly scattered elsewhere. In the provinces, the apothecaries, dispensers of drugs and 'unofficial' medical advice, greatly outnumbered the physicians as medical practitioners. The surgeons let blood, dressed wounds, drew teeth, manipulated dislocations, set broken bones when possible, and (if necessary) undertook amputations.[37]

Women played an important part in medicine and healing, and certain branches traditionally belonged to them. Midwives supervised the overwhelming majority of deliveries during this period. The herb garden was part of the woman's domain, and many gentlewomen collected medicinal recipes and simples. (One, Lady Grace Mildmay, had exceptionally wide expertise, and even undertook to give help and advice which might otherwise have had to be sought from a surgeon or a physician.) 'Wise women' lower down the social scale offered traditional herbal and other remedies. Countless women relied on nursing (most of them in a domestic rather than institutional context) as one of their main sources of income.[38]

Important characteristics of the realm of medical services in early modern times were the lack of hard and fast boundaries between the

[36] Pollock, *With Faith and Physic*, 94–6; C. Webster, 'Alchemical and Paracelsian Medicine', in id. (ed.), *Health, Medicine and Mortality*, 301–34, esp. 323; A. Debus, *The English Paracelsians* (1965), 13–42, 175–83.

[37] Porter, *Disease, Medicine and Society*, 18–19; Beier, *Sufferers and Healers*, 8–15.

[38] Beier, *Sufferers and Healers*, 15–19, 42–6; Eccles, *Obstetrics and Gynaecology*, 87–93, 101–3, 116–17, 119–24; A. Clark, *Working Life of Women in the Seventeenth Century* (1919; repr. 1982), 254–9, 263–81; Pollock, *With Faith and Physic*, 35, 93–4, 97–109.

sorts of expertise offered by its different branches, and the ineffect-
iveness of regulation. Cures were offered by quacks and 'empirics'
(only some of whom were licensed), while drugs were sold by gro-
cers and pedlars. Chemical remedies were offered by practitioners
outside the ranks of the physicians before the latter came gradually to
accept their value. The readiness of sufferers to seek advice from
many sources, to try various remedies, and to use their own judgement in assessing alternative prescriptions, have been repeatedly
stressed by historians of early modern medicine.[39]

Faith in the capacity of medicine and surgery to save lives persisted
despite repeated disappointments. Everybody knew that death was
inevitable, and Christians were told that it was their chief concern to
prepare for it and the eternal life which lay beyond it. Nevertheless,
contemporary sources bear abundant witness to a widespread determination to stay alive, even at the cost of submitting to highly unpleasant treatment. 'What will not a man', asked Lancelot Andrewes, 'nay
what will not a woman weak and tender, in physic, in chyrurgery,
endure, not to endure death?'[40]

During this period there were important gains in the fight against
the grim legions of death, though by no means all of them could be
attributed to medical advances. Growing agricultural productivity
and improvements in distribution dispelled the threat of famine.
Plague disappeared from England after 1666, not because contemporaries understood its nature, but possibly at least in part because
of the efficacy of measures restricting the movement of people or
goods, especially in the form of quarantine imposed on ships coming
from ports in infected areas. In this field the balance had tipped deci-
sively in favour of government intervention to control, as far as possible, the spread of disease. The eighteenth century saw a growing
concern with the improvement of the urban environment. The
biggest single medical advance was the introduction of smallpox
inoculation from Turkey in the 1720s. This measure began the conquest of the second great contagious scourge, though its main effects
were felt only after 1750. The development of a successful technique
for lithotomy brought relief to many sufferers from the stone, including Samuel Pepys, even though the outcome of such operations

[39] Porter, *Disease, Medicine and Society*, 20–1, 28–30; D. and R. Porter, *Patient's Progress: Doctors and Doctoring in Eighteenth-century England* (Cambridge, 1989), 33–114; Beier, *Sufferers and Healers*, 19–32; Pollock, *With Faith and Physic*, 95–6.
[40] L. Andrewes, *Works*, ed. J. P. Wilson and J. Bliss (LACT, 11 vols. 1841–54), iv. 309–10.

would remain uncertain until the danger of sepsis was finally under-stood. The obstetric forceps and the technique of podalic version improved the chances of maternal survival in some difficult births. Some new medicines and drugs were introduced, and the use of others was extended. Mercury was applied to the treatment of syphilis. The use of quinine, an extract of Cinchona bark or Jesuit's bark, as a febrifuge and an antiseptic drug capable of combating malaria, was introduced to Europe from Peru in 1640, and its proper-ties soon became famous in London. Opium, known since antiquity, was gradually employed more widely as a painkiller, sedative, and a means of soothing disordered bowels.[41]

Relatively small though the impact of medical innovations was before 1750, some major advances had been achieved in the observa-tion and understanding of mortality and disease. Bills of Mortality showing the deaths which had occurred in London parishes had been compiled during epidemics since the 1530s at latest. From 1603 onwards weekly and annual bills were printed, which included chris-tenings as well as burials, and specified the numbers of plague deaths. The scope of the bills was subsequently expanded to specify the parish (from 1625), the nature of the cause of death, and the numbers dying of each sex (both from 1629). It was upon these 'poor despised Bills of *Mortality*' that John Graunt made his famous *Natural and Political Observations* (1662), the foundation of subsequent demographic and statistical studies. Graunt calculated that 36 per cent of all individuals born in London died within six years, 60 per cent by the age of 17. Only 3 per cent, he believed, reached the age of 67. From such calculations it was possible to make a rough estimate of life expectancy at different ages, the essential basis of actuarial science. Graunt also estimated the proportions of deaths due to each cause over twenty years and (of these) to acute and chronic diseases. He produced rough estimates of annual death rates and attempted to work out long-term patterns of fer-tility and mortality, and to explain why burials exceeded christenings in London when the reverse was true in the country.[42]

A recent discovery of fundamental importance to which Graunt could confidently refer as accepted fact was the heart's action in

---

[41] Slack, *Impact of Plague*, 323–6; J. C. Riley, *The Eighteenth-Century Campaign to avoid Disease* (Basingstoke, 1987); P. Razzell, *The Conquest of Smallpox* (Firle, 1975); Eccles, *Obstetrics and Gynaecology*, 115–18, 122–4, 126–8; C. Creighton, *A History of Epidemics in Britain* (2 vols., 2nd edn., 1965), ii. 315–26; Pollock, *With Faith and Physic*, 136; Porter, *Disease, Medicine and Society*, 15, 63.

[42] Graunt, *Observations*, 335–7, 342, 349–52, 372–4, 376, 386–7, 390–5.

pumping the blood, published by William Harvey in 1628. Around 1687 Anton van Leeuwenhoek, using the recently invented microscope, would be the first to observe bacteria, though their connection with disease was not to be firmly established till the nineteenth century. Important advances were made during the seventeenth century in the clinical observation of disease. The first description of rickets, by Daniel Whistler, was published in 1645. Thomas Sydenham's accounts of diseases as diverse as measles, gout, and 'Sydenham's Chorea' gained him an international reputation. Thomas Willis was the first to describe diabetes mellitus and published an account of the brain and the nervous system. In an era of enquiry and experiment, a number of hypotheses and suggestions turned out to be dead ends, but very substantial net gains in understanding were nevertheless achieved.[43]

Despite improvements in food supply, the disappearance of the plague, and some medical advances, the first half of the eighteenth century saw life expectancy in London plumb a low point. Provincial infant mortality probably reached a higher level than at any other time between 1600 and the present day. Smallpox was still a widespread and terrible scourge of all classes of the population. The 1720s witnessed the highest mortality since the 1550s. Yet by this time there existed a widespread awareness that real advances had been made, and a confidence that human knowledge and action would bring further successes in the battle against disease.[44]

Some disabling or life-shortening conditions were occupational hazards inseparable from many crafts and callings. Potters, quarriers, stonecutters, millers, and a wide range of metalworkers were all exposed to dusts which could cause serious respiratory ailments. Potters and painters risked being poisoned by lead, goldsmiths by mercury. Mining and seafaring were notoriously attended by a high rate of fatal accidents.[45]

[43] W. C. Gibson (ed.), *British Contributions to Medical Science* (1971), 8–9, 23, 123, 205–7, 243, 284–5; A. G. Debus (ed.), *Medicine in Seventeenth Century England* (Berkeley and Los Angeles, 1974), 87–8, 101, 133, 155–7, 176–8, 234, 259, 263, 276, 351.

[44] Wrigley and Schofield, *Population History*, 249, 334, 660–1; Landers, *Death and the Metropolis*, 158, 171, 194.

[45] T. Oliver (ed.), *Dangerous Trades* (1902), 134–65, 282–372, 434–46; T. M. Legge, 'Industrial Diseases under the Medieval Trade Guilds', *Journal of Industrial Hygiene*, 1 (1920), 475–83; D. Hunter, *The Diseases of Occupations* (1955 edn.); D. Levine and K. Wrightson, *The Making of an Industrial Society: Whickham 1560–1765* (Oxford, 1991), 202.

The casualties of war, a uniquely dangerous occupation, were few compared with 'natural' mortality, but death rates among participants were high. According to one estimate, between 20 and 25 per cent of soldiers in the French armies of the seventeenth century died in service (though not all of them in combat: many succumbed to disease). Another suggests that that 25 per cent died each year. The Civil Wars, the only prolonged bouts of military activity to take place on England's soil, almost certainly exacted a far higher toll than any other wars of this period in which she was involved. According to the most recent and thorough calculations, nearly 85,000 individuals died in combat in England and Wales during the Civil Wars. The incidence of war losses was geographically unequal. Battle casualties in East Anglia during the Civil Wars are calculated to have been less than a third the number for the West Country. England was exceptionally fortunate in experiencing so little fighting on her own territory, but she was engaged in foreign warfare in about one year in three during this period. Between 1589 and 1594 some 20,000 men were sent to France, of whom about half returned, while 37,000 of the 50,000 English troops drafted abroad during the 1620s (74 per cent) may have died abroad. In all wars, a high proportion of fatalities was due to disease. On some notorious expeditions, like those to Guienne in 1512, to Le Havre in 1562–4, or Count Mansfeld's in 1624, huge numbers of soldiers died without ever engaging in combat.[46]

Accidents were much less important causes of death compared with disease in the early modern period than they are today. Drownings headed the list of fatal accidents, proportionally much more important than they are today, largely because of the far greater dependence on boats to transport people and goods. Falls also caused many deaths. Fatalities involving horses and vehicles were proportionally much less significant than road accidents are in the late twentieth century. Among the less important causes of accidents were burns and scalds, whose victims were mostly old people and little children.[47]

Crime and punishment claimed few victims compared with diseases and accidents. Four hundred indictments for homicide and

[46] F. Tallett, *War and Society in Early-Modern Europe 1495–1715* (1992), 105; C. Carlton, *Going to the Wars: The Experience of the British Civil Wars, 1638–1651* (1992), 14, 17, 204–5, 211; Wrigley and Schofield, *Population History*, 497–8; J. B. Black, *The Reign of Elizabeth 1558–1603* (Oxford, 2nd edn., 1959), 61, 416.

[47] Graunt, *Observations*, 351; Forbes, 'By what Disease or Casualty', 133; P. E. H. Hair, 'Deaths from Violence in Britain: A Tentative Secular Survey', *Population Studies*, 25 (1971), 12–15.

infanticide are known from the records of the Middlesex sessions covering the years 1550–1625, or just over five a year. Graunt's consolidated table of fatalities showed eighty-six people murdered in twenty years in mid-seventeenth-century London—little more than a tenth of the number accidentally drowned. In various jurisdictions the incidence of recorded homicide fell between the later Middle Ages and the eighteenth century. By then lethal interpersonal violence was quite a rare occurrence in England.[48]

The imposition and public implementation of capital punishment for a whole range of felonies are widely and rightly regarded as deep marks of difference between our modern society and that of England before 1750. Execution took horrifying forms. Hanging was bad enough, especially if the condemned felon danced in the agony of strangulation. Burning alive was the penalty for heresy and certain other offences. Rarely employed against heretics after 1558, it nevertheless remained until the late eighteenth century the punishment for women found guilty of murdering their husbands. Hanging, drawing of the bowels, and quartering of the body, was the punishment for treason, commuted to decapitation in the case of specially favoured or high-born offenders. Capital punishment was a public spectacle which attracted huge crowds. It inspired sadistic pleasure, righteous satisfaction, or sympathetic sorrow, according to the spectator, but above all the onlookers were drawn by curiosity. How would a fellow creature face the universal fate of mankind under exceptional conditions which exposed him to the searching gaze of the multitude? In the 'theatre of punishment', human powers deliberately took into their hands something which was normally a divine prerogative. The infliction of death served a number of purposes: retribution, deterrence, even (by a wonderful concentration of his mind upon essential things) the salvation of the offender's soul. The bodies of criminals were sometimes left exposed to teach their grim lesson to passers-by long after the execution. The corpses of local highwaymen were hung up on Shooter's Hill till their bones fell to the ground.[49]

The numbers of those who suffered capital punishment fell sharply between the sixteenth and eighteenth centuries. Ever smaller proportions of those indicted of felonies reached the gibbet, largely because of the imposition of alternative penalties (whipping,

[48] J. A. Sharpe, *Crime in Early Modern England, 1550–1750* (Harlow, 1984), 55, 57–8; Graunt, *Observations*, 351, 354; Carlton, *Going to the Wars*, 9–10; Hair, 'Deaths from Violence', 17–19.

[49] Pepys, *Diary*, ii. 72–3.

branding, or transportation) and the granting of pardons. Studies of various counties suggest that around a quarter of those so indicted were executed in Elizabeth's reign, about a tenth in the early eighteenth century.[50] The fascination of the spectacle of capital punishment in the eighteenth century may have been partly due to the fact that it was much less common than it had once been.

Self-murder was widely regarded as the worst death of all. Yet it was not a rare offence. Estimates for various jurisdictions and different spans of time within the early modern period range from a rate similar to today's to a third or a half as high. In Graunt's twenty year *Table of Casualties* suicides by hanging were over 2½ times as numerous as murders. The suicides recorded in the Bills of Mortality reached their highest level between 1720 and 1740, when there were often more than fifty a year. In London, the leading historian of early modern suicide remarks, this was a time 'when all the measures of social degradation peaked . . . as the city expanded faster than its economy or its amenities could readily bear'.[51]

To kill oneself was to despair of God's mercy, or to ignore all religion's warnings and promises about the future, eternal life. Who would suffer all the trials of human existence, Hamlet asked, if he could be sure of subsequent oblivion? Who would bear the burdens of a weary life,

> But that the dread of something after death,
> The undiscover'd country from whose bourn
> No traveller returns, puzzles the will,
> And makes us rather bear those ills we have,
> Than fly to others that we know not of?[52]

Religion, though indeed it provided no maps of the 'undiscover'd country', described in some detail what individuals might expect in the afterlife, and it is to that prospectus that we must now turn. In the Christian scheme, it was the life after death which was real, permanent, solid, all-important; life on earth was full of illusions, transitory, insubstantial, and of little worth. Death is ready to seize upon us wherever we are, and whatever our age: this was the message of countless sermons. Preachers drew on a great store of biblical metaphors of the frailty of human life: it is as grass, a shadow, smoke, a bubble, a

---

    [50] Sharpe, *Crime in Early Modern England*, 63–9.
    [51] M. MacDonald and T. R. Murphy, *Sleepless Souls: Suicide in Early Modern England* (Oxford, 1990), 240, 245–6, 272; Graunt, *Observations*, table facing 406.
    [52] *Hamlet*, III, i. 80–4.

weaver's shuttle, a spider's web, a cloud, a flower, vapour, or wind. Our destiny lies beyond death, which is like a midwife who delivers us from the womb into the land of the living.[53] Nevertheless Hamlet's words provide a salutary reminder of the uncertainties concerning the afterlife which flourished in a time of religious strife and change.

---

[53] See e.g. J. Preston, *A sermon preached at the funerall of J. Reynel* (1615), sig. B3, C3; J. Warren, *Domus ordinata. A funerall sermon, preached in Bristoll, at the buri- all of mistresse Needes* (1618), 35[*sic*]-34.

2

The Hereafter

Death loomed far larger in everybody's lives in later medieval and early modern times than it does today. Ties of family and friendship were far more likely to be severed before old age. The possibility of losing parents, spouse, children, friends, colleagues, employer, or servants was an ever-present one. Individual life expectancy was lower at every age than it is today. However, death, Christian religion taught, is not the end of the story. Life on earth is a mere prelude to an eternal life beyond the grave. How well orthodox teaching was communicated to the majority of the population, and how widely and thoroughly it was assimilated and believed, we cannot say. It is nevertheless clear that Christian beliefs informed and coloured what was written about the life after death by all sorts of literate lay people in media of expression as diverse as poetry, letters, diaries, epitaphs, and preambles to wills.

A belief in a life after this is one which Christianity shares with other important world religions, but ideas concerning the future life or lives vary greatly. In Buddhism, the goal is liberation of the self from the cycle of cosmic existence and the realization of its identity with the principle of true reality. The self and its negative karma are loads ultimately to be shed. The conceptions shared by the two main monotheistic religions, Christianity and Islam, are different. Each individual will be rewarded or punished after this life for his or her obedience or disobedience towards God in this one. Soul and body, separated at death, will ultimately be reunited, to experience an eternity of bliss or torment. In the Christian scheme individuals retain their essential identity in the next life. Shared contemplation and adoration of God will be the eternal reward of the saved, who will enjoy full communion with him in heaven, but this is not the same as Buddhist union with an ultimate reality.[1]

---

[1] S. G. F. Brandon, *The Judgment of the Dead: An Historical and Comparative Study of a Post-Mortem Judgment in the Major Religions* (1967), chs. 5, 6 and 8; C. McDannell and B. Lang, *Heaven: A History* (New York, 1990), 43–4, 59, 88–92.

In ancient Mesopotamia, early Israel, and Homeric Greece, the dead were thought to survive only as faint ghostly residues of their earthly selves. However, in ancient Egypt there developed from as far back as the third millennium BC two important beliefs: first, that rites performed by the living might assist the survival of the 'vital being' of the dead; and secondly, that an individual's fate after death might be influenced by his or her behaviour in this life. Later there emerged a conception of post-mortem judgement, and of the weighing of good deeds against bad. Of all the ancient religions it was the Zoroastrianism of Persia which most closely anticipated the Christian scheme of the afterlife. Zoroastrian beliefs included two judgements of the dead, one upon each individual immediately after death, followed by a period of reward or punishment, the other a general one, immediately preceded by a general resurrection.[2]

Death, according to the Book of Genesis, was, along with unavoidable suffering in life, the punishment of all mankind for Adam's and Eve's disobedience in eating the fruit of the forbidden tree. Early Jewish writers said little about a life after death. Job uttered what seemed, in medieval and early modern translations, the most resonant of all declarations of faith in the resurrection of the body.

For I know that my redeemer liveth, and that he shall stand at the latter day upon the earth:
And though after my skin worms destroy this body, yet in my flesh shall I see God: (19: 25-6)

However, more cautious modern translators no longer accept that this passage refers to bodily resurrection in the original Hebrew.[3] The prophet Ezekiel, reflecting the influence of Zoroastrian ideas during the sixth century BC, was the first Jewish prophet to describe a bodily resurrection. God took Ezekiel to a valley full of the dry and scattered bones of the children of Israel, which he assembled together, clothed with flesh, and revived with the breath of new life. The Book of Daniel (c.165 BC) foresaw the deliverance of the people of God, and the awakening of many of those who slept in the dust. Daniel's was the first biblical book to distinguish different fates for the resurrected dead: eternal rewards for the good, and punishments for the wicked.[4]

---

[2] Brandon, *Judgment of the Dead*, chs. 1–4, 7.
[3] *The New English Bible* (Oxford, 1970), 581.
[4] McDannell and Lang, *Heaven*, 12–13; A. E. Bernstein, *The Formation of Hell: Death and Retribution in the Ancient and Early Christian Worlds* (1993), 173–5.

Around the time of Christ there were three main Jewish views about what would happen after death. The Pharisees looked forward to a resurrected and purified Jewish nation. The individual soul would receive 'either the reward of a new life in another body or eternal punishment in the underworld'. Their opponents, the Sadducees, rejected belief in the resurrection of the body and the immortality of the soul. The Essenes believed in the immortality of the soul, already strongly emphasized by certain Greek thinkers who believed in different fates for the souls of the good and the wicked.[5]

Jesus Christ presented a vivid picture of future rewards and punishments in the parable of Dives and Lazarus in St Luke's Gospel. The parable implies that the two men experienced their very different fates immediately after death, i.e. before resurrection. Dives was a rich man, who feasted in opulence and neglected Lazarus, the beggar at his gate. After their deaths, Lazarus was carried away by the angels to be with the patriarch Abraham, but Dives went to a place (variously translated as hell, or Hades) where he suffered agonies in fire. In response to Dives's pleas for relief, Abraham pointed out the justice of his punishment and explained also that there was an impassable chasm between Lazarus's place of felicity and Dives's place of torment. Other warnings of punishment by hellfire were given in various places in the Gospels of Mark and Matthew.[6]

Jesus also confronted the issue of resurrection.[7] Questioned by Sadducees, he answered that those accounted worthy of resurrection and eternal life would not marry (Luke 20: 27–40). When Martha told him that her brother Lazarus had died, Jesus assured her both of the immortality and of the resurrection of those who believed in him.

Jesus said unto her, I am the resurrection, and the life: he that believeth in me, though he were dead, yet shall he live:
And whosoever liveth and believeth in me shall never die. (John 11: 25–6)

He proceeded to raise Lazarus from the dead. Later he himself rose from the dead on the third day after the Crucifixion. However, though these events, and more especially Christ's own resurrection, confirmed his followers' faith in him, they were exceptional and miraculous happenings.

Jesus ascended into heaven forty days after his resurrection, but

[5] McDannell and Lang, *Heaven*, 19–22; Bernstein, *Formation of Hell*, 179.
[6] Luke 16: 19–31; Matthew 3: 12; 5: 22; 13: 42; 25: 41; Mark 9: 43–8 (all discussed in Bernstein, *Formation of Hell*, 228–47).
[7] McDannell and Lang, *Heaven*, 25–7.

before his arrest he had foretold his coming again after a time of terrible upheavals and tribulations. He would appear in the clouds with great power and glory and gather together his chosen ones from the uttermost parts of heaven and earth. Members of the present generation would still be present on earth. The second coming would be soon. This was a forecast which in various respects resembled the prophecies of Jewish Messianic tradition. When he returned in his glory, Jesus would sit in judgement, separating those who had given charitable succour to his brethren from those who had not, inviting the former to inherit the kingdom prepared for them from the foundation of the world, and despatching the latter to the everlasting fire prepared for the devil and his angels.[8]

St Paul's Epistles, mostly written before the surviving versions of the Gospels, contain the earliest written evidence of Christian beliefs. On his second coming (1 Thessalonians 4: 16), the Lord would descend from heaven 'with a shout, with the voice of the archangel, and with the trump of God'. Then dead Christians would rise. (Paul's Epistles refer to the dead as sleepers on a number of occasions. He may not have shared the belief in immediate rewards and punishments underlying the parable of Dives and Lazarus.) After the dead had risen, those Christians who were still alive would join them, caught up in the clouds to meet the Lord in the air. Paul also described the nature of the resurrected body, especially in 1 Corinthians 15. There were different sorts of flesh, he explained, and different sorts of body, earthly and heavenly. The body was buried mortal, ugly, and weak; it would be raised immortal, beautiful, and strong. 'It is sown a natural body; it is raised a spiritual body.' Paul clearly expected the resurrected body to be utterly different in nature from the buried corpse. This transformation of the body went far beyond the revival of mortal remains of which Ezekiel had written. In 2 Corinthians 5: 10 it was foreseen that all would appear before Christ's judgement seat to receive their just deserts. The wicked would receive punishment, but Paul's references to this punishment were vague. He was probably inclined to envisage the annihilation of the wicked rather than their perpetual suffering.[9]

The Book of Revelation, possibly dating from the late first century AD, supplies the most detailed picture of early Christian conceptions of the Last Judgement. It would follow Christ's thousand-year reign

8 Mark 13: 14–31; Matthew 24: 15–41; 25: 31–46.
9 McDannell and Lang, *Heaven*, 33–5; Bernstein, *Formation of Hell*, 205–24.

on earth, and Satan's final defeat. All who had lived would assemble before the divine throne, to be judged according to their deeds. All those who were not written in the book of life would be cast into a lake of fire. There, they would, like Satan, presumably be 'tormented day and night for ever and ever'. Meanwhile, the first heaven and the first earth would have passed away. God would dwell with his people in a new Jerusalem of gold and precious stones, shining with a brilliant light. He would wipe away all tears from their eyes. There would be no more death, sorrow, or pain. God's servants would worship him, see him face to face, and reign for evermore.[10]

There was sufficient imprecision and variety in the New Testament accounts of resurrection and the afterlife to allow eschatological ideas considerable scope for change and development during late antiquity and the Middle Ages. St Augustine (354–430), the foremost theologian of the late Roman West, formulated while still a young man a conception of a heavenly existence which would be utterly unlike earthly life. Each soul would enjoy its vision of God alone. Entirely focused on God, the souls of the saved would not communicate with each other. Their transformed bodies would have no material qualities. Later on, however, and especially in *The City of God*, his last great work, Augustine depicted the experience of heaven as a social one. It would be shared with friends. However, the love of God would be paramount, and the love of friends would be but one way of apprehending him. There would be no exclusive affection in heaven: the fellowship of love would be all-embracing. The spiritual body, Augustine now thought, would be like the resurrected body of Christ, a tangible body of flesh and bones, but also unblemished and in the flower of youth.[11]

Some subsequent theologians inclined to a rigorously theocentric view, others to one which allowed the inhabitants of heaven the joys of a celestial society. During the high Middle Ages new ideas emerged about the location and nature of heavenly space. Augustine had considered such questions theologically irrelevant, but the medieval schoolmen sought to achieve a synthesis of Christian theology and Aristotelian conceptions of the universe. Differing in matters of detail, the scholastic theologians agreed about the main outlines of a new picture of heaven. Beyond the firmament, the outermost sphere of the material universe, lay the empyrean, a region of pure light where, after the resurrection, the glorified and shining bodies of the

---

[10] Revelation 20: 10–22: 5.   [11] McDannell and Lang, *Heaven*, 54–66.

blessed would live together with the angels. Here their occupation would be the perfect contemplation of God, who would dwell higher yet, in the heaven of heavens. His presence would always be felt, but he would be visible only in the person of Jesus. St Thomas Aquinas (*c.*1225–74) insisted that the enjoyment of God was the only source of eternal happiness, though the saints would rejoice in their shared fellowship in God. Other theologians took different views. Giles of Rome (1247–1316) insisted that the saints' ability to speak to each other would contribute to their perfect social life. St Bonaventure (1221–74) held that the saints in heaven would be united by a bond of universal love of which only the closest earthly friendship gave some intimation. Certain mystic writers also believed that the essence of heavenly bliss would lie in the achievement of a passionate union of love with God. This way of envisaging the relationship between the saints and God stood in contrast with the scholastic theologians' emphasis on knowledge.[12]

Late antiquity and the Middle Ages also elaborated the picture of hell as a place of everlasting torment. The schoolmen placed this eternal prison in the centre of the earth. The suffering of the damned lay both in their complete exclusion from God's presence and in physical pain. The torments of hell were pictured in vivid detail in the early second century *Apocalypse of Peter*. The idea of some differentiation within hell developed quite early. The late fourth-century *Apocalypse of Paul* distinguished between an upper and a lower hell. St Augustine speculated that there might be a less painful hell for those who were not wholly bad. The scholastic theologian Peter Lombard (d. 1160) believed that God would distinguish between different degrees of wickedness and administer punishment accordingly. A number of descriptions of the infernal scene noted that each mortal sin was matched by its own appropriate punishments. From the eleventh century onwards, the theme of the Last Judgement became very popular in art. The sufferings of the damned and the tortures which awaited them were depicted with a relish and a vividness of imagination which were seldom equalled in the representations of heaven.[13]

[12] Ibid. 80–4, 88–110.
[13] *ODCC* 630–1; Bernstein, *Formation of Hell*, 282–305; J. Le Goff, *The Birth of Purgatory* (1984), 69, 149; Brandon, *Judgment of the Dead*, ch. 5; T. S. R. Boase, *Death in the Middle Ages: Mortality, Judgment and Remembrance* (1972), 18–37; vivid representations of hell and Last Judgement in A. K. Turner, *The History of Hell* (1995), 72, 75, 78, 87, 88, 96, colour pls. 1–15. P. Binski, in *Medieval Death: Ritual and Representation* (1996), 188–99, comments on the paucity of representations of purgatory in medieval art.

The fate of souls between death and the resurrection of the body attracted an increasing amount of theological interest, especially because the second coming, once expected within the lifetime of the Apostles, seemed to have been indefinitely postponed. Most theologians agreed that departed souls went to a place of happiness or suffering, but that the full intensity of eternal bliss or anguish would only be experienced after the resurrection. The elaboration of the idea of purgatory, a state or place of punishment of sin, was the Middle Ages' most important contribution to conceptions of the afterlife. Only those who had died in the grace of God could be admitted to it. They were clearly separate from the damned, but, though saved, had not merited immediate admission to heaven. The scriptural evidence for the existence of purgatory was slender. The passage on which most reliance was placed is 2 Maccabees 12: 39–45. It describes how Judas Maccabaeus (d. 161 BC) ordered an atoning sacrifice on behalf of certain Jews who were found to have worn idolatrous amulets under their tunics after they had died fighting for their country. This passage seemed to show two things: the possibility of atonement after death, and the effectiveness of action taken by the living on behalf of the dead. In Matthew 12: 32 Jesus is described as saying that anyone who speaks against the Holy Spirit will not be forgiven either in this world or the world to come. So it appeared that forgiveness in the world to come, that is after death, was possible. St Paul's First Epistle to the Corinthians, 3: 11–15, says that whatever each man builds on Jesus Christ, the only possible foundation, will be tested by fire. If a man's building survives, he will be rewarded. 'If any man's work shall be burned, he shall suffer loss: but he himself shall be saved; yet so as by fire.' This passage pointed to the possibility that those who had lived, albeit inadequately, on a basis of Christian faith, might undergo a process of purging.[14]

Clement of Alexandria (d. before 215 AD) believed that those who repented on their deathbeds but had no time to perform penance would be sanctified by fire after their deaths. This doctrine was accepted by a number of Western theologians in the fourth century, St Augustine among them. It was not until the late twelfth century, however, that the existence of purgatory as a distinct place of punishment was definitely established. The word itself was probably first used some time during the 1170s. In 1254 Innocent IV was the first pope to authorize a definition of purgatory. It was the place for those

---

[14] Le Goff, *Birth of Purgatory*, 41–4.

guilty of venial sins and those who, after confessing mortal sins, had not had time to complete penance.[15]

In practice, very few Christians could hope to escape purgatory altogether. It would contain many souls whose lives had been good by earthly standards, and many others who had only very narrowly escaped hell—even a deathbed repentance could save the sinner from damnation. If purgatory was not to seem a soft option for the rapidly swelling numbers of prospective inhabitants, it had to be depicted as a fearsome place. Later medieval writing tended to dwell on its infernal characteristics rather than the positive aspects of hope and rehabilitation emphasized in Dante's early fourteenth-century *Divina commedia*. Some insisted that the only difference between the tortures suffered in purgatory and in hell was that the latter were eternal. Depictions of purgatory commonly included horrific physical mutilations administered by devils. Yet the souls in purgatory knew that they were saved. This knowledge alone made their sufferings tolerable. This was the orthodox mainstream view, clearly laid down by St Thomas Aquinas, but, according to a minority of writers, there were some grave sinners in purgatory who remained in doubt of their salvation. Even venial sins could earn decades or centuries of punishment. However, purgatorial time, or at least the experience of it, differed from earthly time. Souls might be released after what seemed rather a short time on earth, though the soul had already suffered for centuries in purgatory. Terms of punishment varied. Many souls would be released from purgatory long before the Day of Judgement.[16]

The development of the doctrine of purgatory influenced society, the Church, and the relationship between them in very important ways. The notion that the actions of the living can help the dead is not logically dependent upon belief in a specific purgatorial process or place, but the more concrete the conception of the purgatorial punishments undergone by the dead, the more focused and purposeful such actions could be. St Augustine distinguished three main ways of assisting the souls of the dead: masses, prayers, and alms. St Thomas Aquinas agreed that the most effective forms of suffrage (i.e. help, support, or assistance) were those singled out by Augustine. He discussed

[15] *ODCC* 1144–5; Le Goff, *Birth of Purgatory*, 163, 283–4, 362–6; C. Burgess, ''A Fond Thing vainly invented'': An Essay on Purgatory and Pious Motive in later Medieval England', in S. J. Wright (ed.), *Parish, Church and People: Local Studies in Lay Religion 1350–1750* (1988), 62–4.

[16] Le Goff, *Birth of Purgatory*, 273, 334–55; Duffy, *Stripping of Altars*, 343–8.

other ways in which the dead could be helped. The Church might remit the penalties of their forgiven sins by means of indulgences, drawing on its store of 'common merits'. The quantity of remission later came to be precisely measured. Funeral ceremonies might be useful to the dead by encouraging the living to do good works for them. Burial near a saint might secure his or her aid. Suffrages varied in their potency, but a sufficient accumulation of them could drastically curtail the period of purgatorial punishment.[17]

The number of benefactions and meritorious deeds which might assist souls in purgatory was immense, ranging from the foundation of a monastery to the lighting of a candle before the image of a saint, or the gift of a penny to a beggar. However, the most popular in late medieval England, among the sufficiently well-off, was the endowment of intercessory masses celebrated on behalf of departed souls. Medieval funerals normally included a mass or masses. Those who could make further provision; some of the wealthiest purchasers established endowments to support the celebration of masses for several decades, or even in perpetuity. There were special masses closely associated with the souls of the dead which were highly favoured. The cycle of masses making up the trental of St Gregory (named for the efforts which the saint had made for his mother's soul) spanned ten major feasts. A papal indulgence was attached to requiem masses said at the church of St Mary at Scala Coeli near Rome, where St Bernard had seen the souls for whom he prayed ascending a heavenly ladder. From 1500 onwards indulgences of Scala Coeli were purchased for requiem masses celebrated in certain English churches, the first by Henry VII for the chapel he had built in Westminster Abbey.[18]

On the eve of the Reformation there were in England thousands of chantries, as long-term intercessory foundations were called. A multitude of institutions had intercession for the founder's soul as one of their purposes, including hospitals, almshouses, and colleges of priests. Many foundations which were principally designed to support a chantry priest also included endowments intended for such 'charitable uses' as education, poor relief, and the maintenance of roads and bridges. Closely related to chantries, and sometimes impossible to distinguish from them, were religious confraternities. One parish might contain several of them, but the more celebrated con-

---

[17] Le Goff, *Birth of Purgatory*, 81–2, 274–7.
[18] Duffy, *Stripping of Altars*, 368–76; Burgess, 'A Fond Thing', 71–7.

fraternities drew their members from a much larger area. The chief purposes of these brotherhoods included the observation of members' funeral rites and the support of prayers and masses for their souls. Many of them maintained lights on certain altars or before particular images. Chantries could develop into confraternities, and confraternities could also act as trustees for the chantry foundations of individual members. Some confraternities were endowed with land, others were maintained by members' subscriptions or bequests. The wealthiest employed several priests; many supervised the disbursement of charitable bequests. The poorest ones, often comparatively short-lived, have left few traces of their existence.[19]

Departed members of their own families headed the list of people whom living Christians were bound to help with their suffrages. Tales of dramatic apparitions of neglected souls in purgatory which came back to threaten or to plead with survivors commonly involved their closest relatives, especially sons and widows. The solicitous widow, as depicted just before the Reformation, took good care of her husband's soul. The children of the dead, according to *Dives and Pauper*, an early fifteenth-century exposition of the Ten Commandments which was printed three times between 1493 and 1536, were bound to help their parents' souls with holy prayer and alms deeds. Confraternities encouraged individuals to contribute to and share in the benefits of suffrages paid for by larger groups of Christian people.[20]

Belief in purgatory and in the efficacy of the suffrages of the living to help the souls of the departed played a central part in the religious and social life of the later Middle Ages. It channelled personal and communal religious practice, shaped some of the most characteristic institutions of the epoch, and provided the chief stimulus and motive for an enormous investment in prayer, masses, and multifarious charitable works.

The Reformation began with Martin Luther's attack on indulgences. His doctrine of salvation by faith alone dealt a lethal blow to belief in purgatory among his followers, and in 1530 he 'declared war' on the doctrine. By then, in 1529, Simon Fish, in his *Supplicacyon for the Beggers*, had already opened the English polemical attack upon its

---

[19] A. Kreider, *English Chantries: The Road to Dissolution* (Cambridge, Mass., 1979), 5–37, 58–70; J. J. Scarisbrick, *The Reformation and the English People* (Oxford, 1984), 19–39.

[20] Duffy, *Stripping of Altars*, 348–54; R. Copland, *The seuen sorowes that women haue when theyr husbands be deade* (c.1565), sig. C1r–v, cited in Greaves, *Society and Religion*, 706; *Dives and Pauper*, ed. P. H. Barnum (EETS 275, 280; 1976, 1980), vol. i. pp. ix–xi, 328; Scarisbrick, *Reformation and English People*, 19–21.

supposed abuses, and especially the clergy's exploitation of it for their own gain. In *A Disputacion of Purgatorye* (1531), John Frith insisted that it had no scriptural foundation. The sacrifice of Christ, whose merits could not be disposed of by the clergy, was the only source of satisfaction for sins.[21]

After the break with Rome, belief in purgatory was one of the first Roman Catholic tenets to be cautiously abandoned by the Church of England. The last of the Ten Articles of 1536 strongly commended prayers for departed souls, which might relieve 'some part of their pain'. However, it pointed out, Scripture left uncertain the place where they were, its name, and the pains suffered there. It condemned abuses promoted 'under the name of purgatory', including papal indulgences, and masses at Scala Coeli, in any other particular place, or before any image. The article thus abandoned certain key elements of late medieval religion: a definite purgatorial location, imaginable pains, and calculable remissions. By 1538 Henry VIII had accepted the view that the Books of Maccabees, containing the chief scriptural basis for prayers for the dead, were uncanonical, although he refused to reject their authority altogether. The King's Book of 1543 prohibited the use of the very term 'purgatory', and avoided any reference to pains suffered by the dead. In future, masses were to be performed for 'the universal congregation of Christian people' even if intended for the benefit of particular individuals. An Act of 1545, only partially implemented before the king's death, empowered Henry to dissolve most of the more substantial intercessory institutions.[22]

In 1547 a new Act confiscated all endowments designed to fund lights or intercessory masses. Its preamble denounced 'vain opinions of purgatory and masses satisfactory, to be done for them which be departed'. However, the last trace of intercession for the departed was not eliminated from the English Communion service till 1552, and even then an element of implicit prayer for the dead survived in the burial service. More explicit prayers were included in the Primer of 1559.[23]

Those leading Elizabethan churchmen who expressed an opinion on the subject were nevertheless hostile to prayers for the dead. John

---

[21] Kreider, *English Chantries*, 96-9.

[22] *Documents of the English Reformation*, ed. G. Bray (Cambridge, 1994), 173-4; Kreider, *English Chantries*, 122-4, 135, 151-2, 179-80.

[23] *Documents Illustrative of English Church History*, ed. H. Gee and W. J. Hardy (1896), 328; Brightman, *English Rite*, ii. 858-60, 872-6; *The First and Second Prayer Books of Edward VI* (1910), 222, 277; R. J. E. Boggis, *Praying for the Dead: An Historical Review of the Practice* (1913), 177-80.

Jewel condemned them in the *Homily concerning Prayer* published in 1563. They were useless, because there were only two destinations for those departing from this life. They went straight away to either heaven or hell. During the seventeenth century, however, there was a strong current of opinion within the Church in favour of such prayers. These views were not restricted to anti-Calvinists or High Churchmen, even though such men were amongst their clearest exponents. Richard Field, John Overall, James Ussher, and Jeremy Taylor all argued that such prayers were justified by the ancient practice of the Church, while also insisting that they did not necessarily imply belief in purgatory. Lancelot Andrewes included several prayers for the dead in his private devotions. John Cosin went so far as to describe the Eucharist as a sacrifice propitiatory for the sins of the whole world, for the benefit of both the living and the dead. After the Restoration, a number of churchmen, including Cosin, directed that the words 'requiescat in pace' or an explicit request for prayer from the reader should be inscribed on their gravestones. Bishop Wilson of Sodor and Man kept during the early eighteenth century a list of deceased friends and relatives, concluding with a prayer that their names might be found written in the book of life.[24]

The evidence concerning praying for the dead among the laity after the Reformation is thinly scattered yet fairly extensive. The ringing of bells on the eve of All Souls' Day, a powerful reminder to offer prayers for departed friends and kinsfolk, was a recurrent episcopal concern. 'Our vulgar seldome pray for friends till dead', claims a printed marginal note in the published version of a funeral sermon preached by Robert Harris in 1614. William Wentworth, John Evelyn, and John Aubrey all prayed for mercy or peaceful rest for at least one friend or relative. A rhyming inscription of *c*.1714 in the church of Northmoor (Oxon.) commemorates Richard Lydall's provision of a new bell and bell-loft and records his request that future ringers should pray for him. Samuel Johnson not only prayed for his wife and mother, but was also inclined to believe that there was after death a 'middle state', akin to purgatory. Even more surprising is the fact that a young Lancashire Nonconformist, Richard Kay, should have prayed with fervour for a cousin of his shortly after hearing of his death in 1749.[25]

---

[24] *Certain Sermons or Homilies*, ed. G. E. Corrie (Cambridge, 1850), 337–40; Boggis, *Praying for the Dead*, 216–24, 227–8; J. W. Legg, *English Church Life from the Restoration to the Tractarian Movement* (1914), 316–17.

[25] W. P. M. Kennedy, *Elizabethan Episcopal Administration: An Essay in Sociology and Politics* (Alcuin Club Collections, 26–7; 1924), ii. 72, 93, 118;

Meanwhile, the English Catholic community continued to cele-
brate masses for the dead. A story told by the missionary priest John
Gerard vividly illustrates the comfort survivors might derive from
them. A flickering light appeared every night in the room of a Staffordshire lady whose husband had died a convert to Catholicism, but
before a confessor could reach him. It was a sign that her husband still
needed prayers said for him. After the last mass of a customary trental
had been offered on his behalf, three lights appeared instead of the
usual one, and seemed to rise heavenwards. The lady interpreted the
vision as showing that her husband's soul had been carried to heaven
by angels. Apparitions of the dead returning from purgatory had
played a part in religious instruction before the Reformation. Such
visions nurtured a popular belief in ghosts which the Protestant
reformers sought to combat by insisting that God never allowed the
dead to return to earth. Hamlet, seeing a ghost in his father's form, was
the victim of a debilitating uncertainty. Was this apparition truly his
father's spirit, or simply a diabolical illusion? In a sermon published in
1619, John Preston firmly reproved those who claimed to have seen
and heard ghosts seeking more masses to shorten their time in purgatory. Such apparitions were either popish frauds or evil spirits.[26]

The soul's journey to heaven or hell took place immediately after
death, according to the majority of leading Protestant theologians.
The belief that the soul slept between death and the resurrection was
nevertheless quite widespread among Protestants. It was shared by
Martin Luther himself, even though it was never included in any
Lutheran creed. Both John Frith and William Tyndale inclined
towards this notion. The more radical view that the soul died with the
body was held by Edward Wightman, the last heretic burnt in England
(1612), and by many of the English General Baptists, whose existence
in England can be traced back to James I's reign. One of them, Richard
Overton, argued in his *Mans Mortalitie* (1643) that there was no such
thing as a separate soul. Man died until the resurrection, and only

---

R. Houlbrooke, *Church Courts and the People during the English Reformation
1520-1570* (Oxford, 1979), 249; R. Harris, *Samuels funerall. Or A Sermon preached
at the funerall of sir Anthonie Cope*, in id., *The workes . . . Revised, and in sundrie
places corrected. With an addition of two sermons, not formerly extant. As also two
tables* (1635), 220; Legg, *English Church Life*, 316, 319, 329–30; *Wentworth Papers
1597–1628*, ed. J. P. Cooper (Camden 4th ser. 12; 1973), 33; Evelyn, *Diary*, v. 497;
Kay, *Diary*, 146.

[26] *John Gerard: The Autobiography of an Elizabethan*, trans. P. Caraman (1951),
38–9; Duffy, *Stripping of Altars*, 351–4; Thomas, *Religion*, 701–5; J. Preston, *A sermon
preached at the funerall of M^r. Arthur Upton* (1619), 33.

thereafter became immortal. John Milton shared this belief. Both men felt that the doctrine of the soul's continuous existence tended to diminish the importance of the resurrection.[27]

The doctrine of the separation of the soul and body at death was based on three texts in particular. 'Then shall the dust return to the earth as it was: and the spirit shall return unto God who gave it,' says Ecclesiastes 12: 7. Luke 16: 22 tells how the angels carried Lazarus into Abraham's bosom, while Luke 23: 43 contains Christ's promise to the penitent thief: 'To day shalt thou be with me in paradise.' Numerous references to eternal life could not (it seemed) be applied to the body. The life envisaged must have been that of the soul. The return of all souls to God did not mean that the souls of all men were saved, but that each soul would appear before God immediately after death. He would reward or punish them according to their deeds in the body. This was a 'privy Sessions' for every particular soul, as distinct from the 'general Assize' of the universal judgement.[28]

The happiness of the saved would not be complete till after the resurrection, but most Protestants were reluctant to dwell on this fact, probably fearing that to do so might encourage a reopening of the question of the existence of purgatory. The majority of English Protestants agreed upon certain fundamental points. The faithful soul would be perfected in holiness immediately after death, but the glory would not be complete until body and soul were reunited. The souls of the saved would enjoy the presence of God, but would also look forward to reunion with their bodies and the consummation of glory. Jeremy Taylor, a divine who was prepared to give a relatively full account of the intermediate state, described paradise in 1657 as 'a region of rest, of comfort, and holy expectations' for the souls of the saved. In the state of separation, the souls of the blessed would see God from afar, but not until after the resurrection face to face. Only then would their joy be complete. Some Protestants, including Jeremy Taylor and Thomas Ken, believed that the virtuous dead were concerned about the welfare of their friends on earth and prayed for

---

[27] N. T. Burns, *Christian Mortalism from Tyndale to Milton* (Cambridge, Mass., 1972), 27–35, 90–183.

[28] J. Chardon, *A comfortable sermon for all such as thirst to be ioined with Jesus Christ. Preached at the funerals of syr Gawen Carew in Exeter the two and twentieth of April 1584* (Oxford, 1586), unpaginated; Baxter, *The Saints' Everlasting Rest* (1887), i. 180–4; R. Pricke, *A verie godlie and learned sermon, treating of mans mortalitie and of the estate both of his bodie, and soule after death* (1608), sig. E; W. Dillingham, *A Sermon at the Funeral of the Lady Elizabeth Alston, wife of Sir Thomas Alston, . . . Septemb. 10, 1677* (1678), 37–8.

them. Taylor was sure that their affection towards such survivors was greater than it had ever been on earth.[29]

The predominant view among Protestants was that the souls of the damned would be tormented by knowledge of their eternal exclusion from God's love and presence, but only suffer the physical agonies of hellfire after the reunion of soul and body. The experience of the damned, like that of the saved, would therefore become far more intense after the resurrection. The change would be like that undergone by a prisoner haled forth from a horrible dungeon to a neverending execution.[30]

The awesome process of the resurrection encouraged preachers to broach two issues in particular: the omnipotence of God, and the nature of the resurrected body. It was, they often conceded, difficult for human intellects to comprehend how corporal elements thoroughly dispersed and seemingly transformed might be reassembled in a living body. However, it was impossible that anything which had once existed should perish into nothing. Each part of the world would yield up 'each part of every man' at the resurrection. God had all the materials to hand, and the miracle of reassembly was easier to understand than the initial creation of all out of nothing. The process of bringing together the scattered elements of bodies inspired some vivid imaginative writing, but there was some tension between this emphasis on concrete, corporal reconstitution and the Pauline theme of the transformation of the body's essential nature.[31]

The Middle Ages had bequeathed the belief that the saved would be resurrected free of all blemishes, enjoying the use of all their senses. The doctrine that they would be 'in that vigour of age' enjoyed by a 'perfect man' at about 33, Christ's age at the time of the Crucifixion, regardless of their own age at death, was widely accepted. Some held

---

[29] Baxter, *Saints' Rest*, i. 180–4; Dillingham, *Sermon*, 37; J. Bayes, *A Funeral Sermon occasioned by the Death of the late Reverend Mr. Christopher Taylor* (1723), 17; *The Sermons of John Donne*, ed. G. R. Potter and E. M. Simpson (10 vols., Berkeley and Los Angeles, 1953–62), viii. 92; Oldmayne, *Lifes brevitie*, 75; *The Whole Works of the Right Reverend Jeremy Taylor, D.D.* ed. C. P. Eden (10 vols., 1847–54), viii. 435, 551–9.

[30] Oldmayne, *Lifes brevitie*, 50; P. C. Almond, *Heaven and Hell in Enlightenment England* (Cambridge, 1994), 93–5.

[31] J. Toy, *A Sermon preached . . . at the funerall of M^{ris} Alice Tomkins wife unto Mr Thomas Tomkins one of the Gentlemen of his Majesties Chappell Royall* (1642), 13–15; J. Barlow, *Hieron's last fare-well. A sermon* (1618), 25–6; G. Ferebe, *Lifes farewell. Or a funerall sermon. At the funerall of John Drew gentleman* (1615), 22–3; E. Cooke, *A Sermon Preach'd . . . at the Funeral of William Ives Esq.* (2nd edn., 1719), 16; Chardon, *Comfortable sermon*, leaf following sig. B4; *ODCC* 1178–9.

that the bodies even of the reprobate would be made more excellent, John Barlow remarked in 1618, so that they might undergo the greater torment. However, opinions differed concerning this point. Others believed that the state of the souls of the damned would be appropriately reflected in the loathsome appearance of their resurrected bodies.[32]

The nature of the resurrected body would be very different from that of the mortal body consigned to the grave. 'It is sown a natural body; it is raised a spiritual body,' St Paul had written in 1 Corinthians 15: 44. Flesh and blood, he had insisted, could not inherit the kingdom of heaven. It would indeed be the same body, wrote Thomas Brooks in 1657, but it would be like the glorious body of Christ, seven times brighter than the sun, free from all types of suffering, capable of moving as fast as a thought, and completely responsive to the spirit of God. Bodies which were in their earthly state frail and brittle, heavy and unwieldy burdens, claimed Edward Cooke in 1719, would be raised 'impassible as Angels, subtile as a Ray of Light, bright as the Sun, and nimble as the Wings of Lightning'. To think in terms of bodies so utterly different from the ones made familiar by earthly experience perhaps made the idea of a resurrection more readily credible but inevitably weakened the notion of corporal continuity. Reason showed, wrote William Sherlock in 1689, that gross earthly bodies could no more live in the pure regions of light and glory inhabited by God than a stone could be lodged in the air. He concluded 'that when we once put off these Bodies, we shall ever after live without them'.[33]

A final judgement would be passed on all mankind soon after the resurrection. Each individual's life's record would be laid open to all. God's wisdom and justice would be made manifest. After the awful solemnities of this colossal general session, all those who had lived would take up their eternal residence, the saved in heaven, the damned in hell.

The main themes of countless descriptions of heaven were the nature of the heavenly environment, the beatific vision, the occupations of the saved, and their relationship with other members of the

---

[32] Boase, *Death in Middle Ages*, 21; L. Bayly, *The practise of pietie: directing a christian how to walke* (11th edn., 1619), 120; Barlow, *Hieron's last fare-well*, 26; E. Calamy, *The Doctrine of the Bodies Fragility: with A Divine Project, discovering how to make these vile bodies of ours glorious by getting gracious Souls* (1655), 11.

[33] T. Brooks, *A String of Pearles: Or, The best things reserved till last. Discovered, In a Sermon Preached . . . At The Funeral of . . . Mris. Mary Blake, . . . with an Elegy on her Death* (1657), 84–90; Cooke, *Sermon*, 20; W. Sherlock, *A Practical Discourse concerning Death* (23rd edn., 1739), 43.

heavenly host. Heaven, all agreed, was a realm of brilliant light. The Revelation vision was widely held to be an imperfect metaphor. In truth, the perfection of heaven was beyond human experience and comprehension. As St Paul had written, paraphrasing the words of the prophet Isaiah, 'Eye hath not seen, nor ear heard, neither have entered into the heart of man, the things which God hath prepared for them that love him' (1 Corinthians 2: 9).

The chief joy of heaven was, however, certain: the immediate experience of God. The saved would be joined with him in a union of perfect love, their natures would be assimilated to his, and they would be granted full understanding of the divine plan, including all God's most mysterious actions.[34] Earthly intimations of the power, wisdom, and love of God were the highest forms of human happiness, but they were mere dim foreshadowings of the joy of the heavenly state. 'For now we see through a glass, darkly; but then face to face: now I know in part; but then shall I know even as also I am known' (1 Corinthians 13: 12). The everlasting work of the saints would be to praise God, their eyes and hearts being filled with his knowledge, love, and glory. Yet though this constant activity sounded strenuous, the other, superficially paradoxical characteristic of heavenly experience was the deep calm and peace which the saved would enjoy.[35]

The heavenly existence would be a perfect one, completely free from sin, doubts of God's love, temptations, the inherent shortcomings of the world and the flesh, of persecution, doctrinal dissension, mental or physical suffering, the burdens of duty, and the sense of God's absence. In 1677 Dr William Bates, a famous Presbyterian divine, dared to allude to the sneaking fear that such an existence might eventually cloy. He raised the notion only to dismiss it

---

[34] Gataker, *Certaine sermons*, ii. 248; Baxter, *Saints' Rest*, i. 15–29; J. Cosin, *Works*, ed. J. Sansom (LACT, 5 vols., 1843–55), i. 40–1; H. Parsley, *A Sermon Preached at the Funeral of M*. *Thomas Whitchurch. October the 15ᵗʰ 1691* (1692), 13; E. Griffith, *A Sermon preached . . . At the Funerall of Sir Matthew Hale Kᵗ Late Chief Justice of His Majestie's Court of the King's Bench* (1677), 19–20; M. Clarke, *A Funeral Sermon on the Death of the Late Reverend Mr. Thomas Michell* (1722), 24; P. Belbin, *A Sermon Preach'd at the Funeral of Mr. George Elliott of Reading* (1730), 29–30.

[35] *Certain Sermons or Homilies*, 97–100; Baxter, *Saints' Rest*, i. 20, 89–91; E. Dent, *Everlasting Blessedness. A Sermon preached at the Funerall of . . . Mr. William Baker, who . . . was received to Heavenly Joyes, the 14ᵗʰ. Day of October, 1691* (1692), 24–8; C. Scott, *The Saints Priviledge, or Gain by Dying* (1673), 7; G. Stanhope, *Death just Matter of Joy to good Men. A Sermon Preach'd . . . At the Funeral of Mr. Richard Sare, of London, Bookseller* (2nd edn., 1724), 11–14; Bayes, *Funeral Sermon*, 16; Griffith, *Sermon*, 13–14.

emphatically. The impossibility of enduring satisfaction in this life was a natural consequence of the imperfections of all earthly things.[36]

There would nevertheless be social interaction in heaven, most divines believed. Jesus had said that many should sit down with Abraham, Isaac, and Jacob in the kingdom of heaven. At the Transfiguration, some of the disciples had seen Moses and Elias together with Jesus (Matthew 8: 11; 17: 3). These texts suggested that the great men of Israel would be individually recognizable in heaven. It was generally held that the faithful departed would meet many other members of the celestial company, including the Apostles, saints, and martyrs. Robert Harris, preaching in 1614, looked forward to meeting all the famous and godly men who had ever lived. There, conversation with angels and the spirits of just men made perfect would be, thought John Scott in 1689, 'a perpetual intercourse of wisdom and love, fidelity and truth, without jealousy or design, caution or reserve, but all frank and open, Heart with Heart, and Soul with Soul'.[37]

The reunion of the saved with their closest earthly friends was a consolation for many on or by the deathbed, and a theme of countless epitaphs. 'Oh what a comfortable thing is this, that we shall know one another in the life to come: Talke one with another, loue one another: and praise God one with another, and all together worlde without ende:' thus the 19-year-old Katherine Stubbes, dying shortly after the birth of her only child in 1590. This was one of the most eloquent of several such deathbed declarations. Preachers of all shades of churchmanship encouraged belief in the heavenly reunion of close friends and relatives. By death God divided man from wife, mother from child, friend from friend, but he gave them the consolation of knowing that they would all meet at the resurrection. Rising in the same bodies, the saints would have a 'perfect, particular, personal knowledge . . . one of another'.[38]

---

[36] W. Bates, *A Funeral Sermon preached Upon the Death of . . . Dr. Thomas Manton* (1678), 34–40.

[37] Harris, *Workes*, 220; Dekker, *Plague Pamphlets*, 216; Cosin, *Works*, i. 41; Baxter, *Saints' Rest*, i. 61–4; J. Scott, *A Sermon Preached at the Funeral of Sir John Chapman Late Lord Mayor of London* (1689), 19–21; T. Allet, *The Christian's Support under the Loss of Friends. A Sermon Occasion'd by the Death of Mr. Henry Clements, of London Bookseller* (1720), 19–20; Bates, *Funeral Sermon*, 28–30; Parsley, *Sermon*, 15–17.

[38] P. Stubbes, *A christal glasse for christian women. Contayning an excellent discourse, of the life and death of Katherine Stubbes* (1592 edn.), sig. C2; S. Clarke, *The Marrow of Ecclesiastical History* (3rd edn., 1675), 449; id., *The Second Part of the Marrow of Ecclesiastical History* (2 bks. in 1 vol., 2nd edn., 1675), ii. 55; I. Walton, *The Lives of Dr John Donne, Sir Henry Wotton, Mr Richard Hooker, Mr George Herbert and Dr Robert Sanderson* (Oxford, 1824), 252; D'Ewes, *Autobiography &*

A number of churchmen nevertheless thought it dangerous to place too much emphasis on the pleasures of heavenly society. John Calvin went so far as to say that the inhabitants of heaven would neither speak to nor hear each other, but only enjoy the company of God. Some hedged their predictions concerning the reunion of friends with words of caution. Edmund Layfielde told a funeral congregation in 1631 that it was impossible to forecast its precise nature, and he rebuked those '*curious* and inquisitive heads' who busied themselves to understand it. The mutual knowledge which the saints would enjoy in the state of glory would of course be very different from earthly recognition, Richard Baxter asserted: not 'by stature, voice, colour, complexion, visage, or outward shape', nor by worldly distinctions or relationships, nor (he thought) by sex. There was general agreement that earthly relationships, hierarchies, and social organizations could not subsist in heaven. Above all there could be no exclusive friendships or marriage. Sir Ralph Verney, devastated by the loss of his wife in 1650, was properly cautious in hoping that they would at least be known to one another in heaven despite the fact that there was no marriage in the resurrection.[39]

The worst fear of all was seldom mentioned: that loved ones might be consigned to hell. Richard Baxter imagined how deeply the saved would be affected by the spectacle of the damnation of their neighbours and closest relatives. The Scriptures provided a vivid picture of the main features of hell. Fire was depicted as the appointed medium of infernal punishment. Yet hell was also a place of darkness, Milton's 'darkness visible'. Early commentators had added extremes of cold as well as heat, and all sorts of exquisite torment. Every sense would be assaulted. The devils, themselves undergoing torture, would savage their victims without conscience and without mercy. As in the

Correspondence, ii. 281; *Memoirs of the Life of Mr. Ambrose Barnes, late Merchant and sometime Alderman of Newcastle upon Tyne*, ed. W. H. D. Longstaffe (Surtees Soc. 50; 1867), 254; Donne, *Sermons*, viii. 62; T. Becon, *The Sicke mannes Salue . . .*, in id., *Prayers and other Pieces of Thomas Becon, S.T.P.*, ed. J. Ayre (Parker Soc. 1844), 152–3; Pricke, *Verie godlie and learned sermon*, sig. A2ᵛ; Taylor, *Works*, viii. 436; Cooke, *Sermon*, 7; Stanhope, *Death just Matter of Joy*, 20; G. Lewis, *A Sermon Preach'd . . . on the Occasion of the Death of Mrs. Paynter, Wife of Robert Paynter, Esq.* (1726), 20; Brooks, *String of Pearles*, 81; J. Dunton, *An Essay Proving We shall Know our Friends in Heaven* (1698).

[39] McDannell and Lang, *Heaven*, 154–5; E. Layfielde, *The soules solace. A sermon preached at the solemn funerall of William Fawcit Gent.* (1632), 30; Baxter, *Saints' Rest*, i. 63; L. Andrewes, *Works*, ed. J. P. Wilson and J. Bliss (LACT, 11 vols., 1841–54), v. 347; Evelyn, *Diary*, v. 607–8; Matthew 22: 30; F. P. Verney and M. M. Verney, *Memoirs of the Verney Family during the Seventeenth Century* (2nd edn., 1907), i. 475.

parable of Dives and Lazarus, so in early modern images of heaven and hell, the contrast between the two was often heightened by having the good removed from a life of suffering, the wicked from one of ease. The latter would face the horrifying reality of eternal torture which they had previously refused to contemplate. The damned would suffer never-ending torments of the soul: grief, envy, resentment, futile regret, gnawing conscience, and an excruciating despair. According to a widely accepted interpretation, it was to these torments that Isaiah's prophecy 'their worm shall not die' had referred.[40]

As the highest happiness of the saved would be to enjoy the fullness of God's presence and love, so the worst torment of the damned would be utter deprivation of them. Their sentence was irreversible, their damnation eternal. They would wish in vain that they might be given one more chance. It would have been better for reprobates had they never been born, and their greatest unhappiness was that, being immortal, they could not die completely, like an animal. Their punishment would never end: they were excluded from happiness for ever. Some writers imagined God laughing at the sufferings of the damned. They would know that although they were for ever excluded from God's presence, he was the judge who had condemned them to perpetual misery. They would react with grief and anger, with 'weeping and gnashing of teeth' (Matthew 8: 12). On earth, sorrow might have been the beneficial prelude to contrition and repentance, but in hell punishment could have no such ameliorative function. The damned would be inescapably riveted in sin; if anything, some judged, the experience of hell would make them worse. They would 'fret and fume against the providence of *God*', and even curse him for afflicting them.[41]

In early modern times, orthodox Protestant eschatology envisaged heaven and hell as two utterly separate and immutable realms. Yet these facts, it was widely held, did not exclude awareness in one of what was happening in the other, or some variety in the conditions experienced by the inhabitants of each realm. St Augustine, and after

---

[40] Baxter, *Saints' Rest*, i. 60; Bernstein, *Formation of Hell*, 284–90; Almond, *Heaven and Hell*, 81–95; *Paradise Lost*, I. 62; J.D., *A Sermon Preached at the Funeral Of that incomparable Lady, the Honourable, the Lady Mary Armyne* (1676), 4; Scott, *Saints Priviledge*, 16–18; Isaiah 66: 24; Mark 9: 44.

[41] J. Barlow, *The true guide to glory. A sermon preached at Plympton Mary in Devon, at the funerals of the lady Strode of Newingham* (1619), 31–2; Gataker, *Certaine sermons*, ii. 246; Almond, *Heaven and Hell*, 97–9; E. Warren, *No Praeexistence* (1667), 44, cited in Almond, *Heaven and Hell*, 69–70.

him St Thomas Aquinas, inferred from the story of Dives and Lazarus
that part of the happiness of the saved would consist in contemplating the torments of the damned. This was still accepted by some early
modern writers, especially those who imagined the triumph of Christians over those who had despised or persecuted them in the world.
The suffering of the wicked would be sharpened by the spectacle of
the bliss of the saved. Worst of all would be to find oneself eternally
shut out from the bliss enjoyed in heaven by those who had been
one's nearest and dearest relatives on earth, a predicament imagined
by John Bunyan among others.[42]

Many Catholics and Protestants agreed that there were degrees of
punishment in hell. They believed that some mitigation of the pains
of the damned resulted both from their refraining from doing evil
and from their doing good. Jesus, sending out his disciples to preach
and heal in Israel, had told them that it would be more tolerable in
the Day of Judgement for the land of Sodom and Gomorrha than for
a house or city which refused to receive them or hear their words
(Matthew 10: 15). This was the main basis for the doctrine of different degrees of severity of punishment in the afterlife. The longer the
wicked lived, John Scott declared in 1689, the hotter would be the
furnace of their future torment. But what of different rewards in
heaven? In his Sermon on the Mount, Jesus had specified different
rewards for different works, and distinguished between those who
would be called great and least in the kingdom of heaven according
to their different degrees of fidelity to God's commandments
(Matthew 5: 19). There were other possibly pertinent passages in the
New Testament, though they were less clear and more open to different interpretations. The Church had upheld the doctrine of different rewards since the fourth century. The majority of Protestants
who discussed it accepted it. However, not all did so, and there were
disagreements concerning the meaning of the texts traditionally
adduced in its support. Orthodox Protestants held that different
degrees of glory in heaven stemmed from God's free and entirely
unmerited bounty. They were indeed distinctions accorded to those
who had performed good deeds, but these good deeds were the
automatic results of a faith conferred by means of God's grace. Furthermore, the transcendent joy of the beatific vision would make all

---

[42] Almond, *Heaven and Hell*, 97–8; D. P. Walker, *The Decline of Hell: Seventeenth-
Century Discussions of Eternal Torment* (1964), 29–32; Barlow, *Hieron's last farewell*, 27; Baxter, *Saints' Rest*, i. 43–4; R. Sparke, *A Sermon preached . . . at the Funeral
of that Pious and Worthy Gentlewoman, Mrs Frances Fenn* (1679), 22.

the saints equally happy, despite the fact that they shone with unequal degrees of glory.[43]

Besides heaven and hell, medieval eschatology had envisaged one other permanent realm in the afterlife. This was the limbo of unbaptized children. St Augustine held that all who died unbaptized would suffer damnation. His harsh doctrine was modified by the medieval Church, which taught that unbaptized children would enjoy full natural happiness in limbo, even though they would be excluded from the supernatural beatitude of heaven. The chief Protestant reformers agreed in rejecting limbo, yet differed in their views about baptism. The Church of England, open to various continental influences, expressed its belief in different ways in its liturgy and its articles of faith respectively. Opinions expressed within the Church after the Reformation ranged from Thomas Becon's claim in his *Catechism* (1560) that the baptism of water was only a seal or token of God's promise to receive the children of Christian parents into everlasting life, to William Laud's insistence that baptism was essential to ensure infants' salvation. John Bramhall, a protégé of Laud's (d. 1663), conceded that God had not limited his grace to his outward ordinances and sacraments. The Protestants (he wrote) believed that little infants who had not been baptized might be saved, but, Bramhall concluded, it was possible that while some of them were crowned in heaven, others were tormented in hell, according to God's good pleasure. English parents therefore faced some uncertainty about the fate of children who died unbaptized, but the gradual lengthening of the gap between birth and baptism during the two centuries following the Reformation points to an increasingly relaxed attitude towards the performance of the rite.[44]

After the Reformation there was a broad consensus of opinion among Protestants on important aspects of the afterlife. Differences

---

[43] E. Disley, 'Degrees of Glory: Protestant Doctrine and the Concept of Rewards Hereafter', *Journal of Theological Studies*, NS 42 (1991), 77–105, esp. 98–105; Bates, *Funeral Sermon*, 20(ii); D. Featley, *A sermon preached at the funerall of sir Humphrey Lynd. . . . June the 14th 1636*, in H. Lynde, *A case for the spectacles, or, a defence of Via tuta, together with Stricturae in Lyndomastygem* (1638), 184; Scott, *Sermon Preached*, 13–14; T. Bray, *The good Fight of Faith, in the Cause of God against the Kingdom of Satan, Exemplified, in a Sermon Preach'd . . . on the 24th of March, 1708/9, at the Funeral of Mr. John Dent* (1709), 11–13.

[44] *ODCC* 126–8, 823–4; T. Becon, *The Catechism of Thomas Becon, S.T.P. . . . with other pieces written by him in the Reign of King Edward the Sixth*, ed. J. Ayre (Parker Soc., 1844), 216–17; Laud, *Works*, ii. 64–6; J. Bramhall, *Works*, ed. A. W. Haddan (LACT, 5 vols., 1842–5), v. 171–80; B. M. Berry and R. S. Schofield, 'Age at Baptism in Pre-Industrial England', *Population Studies*, 25 (1971), 456–63; R. Houlbrooke, *English Family Life 1576–1716* (Oxford, 1988), 129–30.

there certainly were concerning such matters as the middle state, mutual knowledge in heaven, and the fate of the unbaptized. However, outside the mainstream, various more radical opinions were held. Denials of the resurrection, of the existence of the soul, of heaven and hell, or of a devil within hell, were reported from time to time. The collapse of censorship and ecclesiastical control in the 1640s allowed unorthodox ideas to be expressed more freely. All the main heresies mentioned above appeared in the compendious catalogue of misbelief which the Presbyterian Thomas Edwards published in 1646.[45]

From around 1650 onwards, almost every aspect of belief concerning the afterlife gave rise to speculation or debate among scholars in Britain. The fear of damnation was seen as the chief buttress of morality, and divine justice as the foundation of its earthly counterpart. Any challenge to traditional doctrines concerning hell and everlasting punishment was thought to have potentially serious implications for society as well as religion. Yet several eschatological thinkers considered, with varying degrees of confidence, one of two alternative possibilities: the ultimate redemption of all mankind or the annihilation of obdurate sinners.

One loose grouping of like-minded thinkers can be discerned among the friends and admirers of the Neoplatonist Henry More (1614–87), fellow of Christ's College, Cambridge. More set out in his *Immortality of the Soul* (1659) the hypothesis that the souls of the wicked would have another chance of salvation in a new life on earth. An anonymous tract published in 1661 which (among other things) defended the doctrine of universal salvation propounded by Origen of Alexandria (*c*.185–*c*.254), was possibly written by George Rust, a pupil of More's. Lady Conway, a close friend of More's, and Baron Van Helmont, her confidant during the 1670s, wrote treatises in which they presented all God's punishments as reformative. Another fellow of Christ's College strongly influenced by More's ideas was Thomas Burnet (d. 1715). His main interest was the interpretation of the scriptures in the light of modern science. His final known opinion concerning the fate of the damned was that they would have a chance of reformation: their punishment would not be eternal. The time would come when the notion of eternal torments would be 'reckon'd as absurd and odious' as transubstantiation was in England in his day.

---

[45] Houlbrooke, *Church Courts*, 229; Thomas, *Religion*, 198–206; T. Edwards, *Gangraena: or a . . . Discovery of Many Errours, Heresies, Blasphemies and Pernicious Practices* (1646), 26–7.

Yet Burnet himself believed that orthodox doctrine was the only means of preventing the people from running 'headlong into vice'. His treatise was not published until after his death: in Latin in 1720, in English in 1727.[46]

Two Cambridge Neoplatonists outside the More connection, Peter Sterry (d. 1672) and his disciple Jeremy White (d. 1707), believed in a God whose overpowering love would burn away evil in the purifying fires of hell until all souls were saved. White's defence of universal salvation, 'certainly the most convincing' written in early modern England, was published in 1712 with a preface by Richard Roach (1662–1730) of St John's College, Oxford, and rector of St Augustine's in Hackney. In 1704 Roach became leader of the Philadelphian Society, a small group of chiliastic mystics. Mrs Jane Lead, his predecessor as leader, had set out the doctrine of universal salvation in her *Enochian Walks with God* (1694). Universalist ideas expounded by the Philadelphians probably inspired Marie Huber, a Swiss woman who was the first to challenge the 'abominable fancy' that the pleasures of the saved are enhanced by the sufferings of the damned.[47]

Another possibility was that the torments of the wicked might be cut short by their annihilation rather than their ultimate redemption. This doctrine, held by the Arians in particular, was taught during the interregnum by John Biddle and Samuel Richardson. Thomas Hobbes came to believe that the wicked would finally suffer this fate after a period of punishment. John Locke expressed a basically similar view in a tract which was not to be published till long after his death. Locke's ideas may have influenced William Whiston (d. 1752), who foresaw that the wicked, including even Satan himself, would have an opportunity of repentance before the Last Judgement. Then the incorrigible would be resurrected for a proportionate time of torment before their ultimate annihilation.[48]

Speculations about heaven centred on the nature of its social life, the activities of its inhabitants, and the possibility of further progress within it. Henry More envisaged the possibility of a refined ethereal love and family relationships, and imagined that the denizens of heaven would pass their time in 'study and philosophical debate'. William Assheton, rector of Beckenham (d. 1711), forecast that

---

[46] Walker, *Decline of Hell*, 122–6, 133–46, 156–66; Almond, *Heaven and Hell*, 4–37, 119–23; T. Burnet, *A Treatise Concerning the State of Departed Souls Before, and At, and After the Resurrection* (1733).

[47] Walker, *Decline of Hell*, 104–21, 218–30, 260–2.

[48] Ibid. 93–103; Almond, *Heaven and Hell*, 50–1, 147, 150.

heaven would be a highly organized society with 'laws and statutes and governors and subjects'. The essayist Joseph Addison looked forward in 1711 to a heaven of continuing individual development and improvement in self-control, virtue, and knowledge. Isaac Watts, hymn-writer and Independent pastor, foresaw in 1722 a heaven whose inhabitants would still be differentiated by individual personality traits. There would always be new activities besides contemplation and worship, and 'businesses and joys' would alternate throughout eternity. The soul would be engaged in a constant process of improvement. An assimilation of heavenly existence to earthly had commenced which would reach its fullest development during the nineteenth century.[49]

The Neoplatonists argued that there were different vehicles of the soul, appropriate to each sphere of existence: terrestrial, aerial, and ethereal. The great natural philosopher Robert Boyle denied the necessity of the restoration of every particle of the body at the resurrection, pointing out that its composition changed greatly even during an individual's lifetime. There were also various suggestions concerning the possible natural causes which might bring about the destruction and renewal of the earth forecast in various places in the New Testament. A combination of volcanic and meteoric action was perhaps the favourite.[50]

The freedom to speculate about the hereafter in mid-eighteenth-century England is well illustrated by a vigorous correspondence in the *Gentleman's Magazine* in 1739–40. Its subjects were the fate of infants after death and the role of baptism. Wouldn't God be acting unreasonably if he admitted infants to the happiness of the life to come? Did infants have souls? What use was baptism to infants who had not yet arrived at the use of reason? Would not God treat all beings in the same circumstances in the same manner, since he couldn't be 'imposed upon by worthless external Rites and unavailing Ceremonies'? Some correspondents dealt with these questions by invoking the authority of Scripture. Jesus Christ had said that the kingdom of heaven was of such as little children. It was God's infinite goodness which led him to bring creatures into existence for the purpose of admitting them to heavenly bliss. There were no scriptural grounds for thinking that anyone not guilty of actual sin would suffer eternal damnation. Clearly infants had souls, for the archangel Gabriel

---

[49] McDannell and Lang, *Heaven*, 206–12.
[50] Almond, *Heaven and Hell*, 29–32, 111–30, 133–43.

had declared that John the Baptist should be filled with the Holy
Ghost from his mother's womb. More than one writer thought it perfectly just that parents who obeyed God's ordinance and had their
children baptized should gain them advantages in the future life.
A public discussion of this sort could not have taken place in any
century before the eighteenth. All the participants sought to
conduct their arguments 'rationally'. They varied, of course, in the
extent of their reliance upon free 'rational' speculation. One relatively conservative contributor recalled that another correspondent
had expressed a desire to 'hear reason . . . By which, I hope, he meant
Reason guided by Revelation.' However, even those protagonists
who cited Scripture in their support tended to interpret it optimistically and in the light of what they considered it reasonable to expect
of a benign providence. Some of what they wrote was frankly hetero-
dox. One of them, for example, argued that infants would undergo
a trial of their virtue in the next life before being raised to a more
perfect state of bliss.[51]

The wider effects of the questioning of the inherited eschatological
scheme between 1650 and 1750 are hard to assess. William Dodwell
claimed in 1743 that since men had learnt to 'wear off' the fear of
eternal punishment, 'Impiety and Immorality' had made great
progress. A pessimistic conviction that disbelief and atheism were
undermining morals was often expressed after the Restoration. The
pernicious influence of one man, Thomas Hobbes, was especially
blamed. Yet Hobbes's views concerning the future punishment
and ultimate annihilation of the wicked, though unorthodox, were
hardly calculated to encourage sinners to abandon all restraint.[52] Most
writers who questioned orthodox doctrines concerning hell and
eternal punishment did so anonymously, obliquely, or with major
provisos. Many of them emphasized the severity of the torments
which the wicked would have to endure before ultimate redemption
or annihilation.

Complaints that many people preferred not to think about
their eternal fate were common long before philosophers began
to question orthodox eschatology. There were people, claimed

---

[51] *Gentleman's Magazine*, 9 (1739), 177–9; 10 (1740), 3–4, 52–4, 167–8, 245–6,
341–2, 441–2.

[52] W. Dodwell, *The Eternity of future Punishment asserted and vindicated. In
answer to Mr Whiston's late Treatise on that Subject* (Oxford, 1743), 85; on Hobbes's
alleged influence see e.g. R. Parsons, *A Sermon preached at the Funeral of the . . . Earl
of Rochester* (Oxford, 1680), 26; Almond, *Heaven and Hell*, 47–51.

Robert King in Edward VI's reign, who expressed doubt about the very existence of a future life.

We knowe (say they) what we haue here, but we know not what we shall haue ther. Who dothe know, whether ther be any other life after this life? Who wil chaunge (that wise is) the certentie of thinges that we be suer of here in this worlde, for the vncertentie of thynges that be to come in a nother (to vs vnkowen [*sic*]) worlde. Ther is none (say they) that will do thus except a few of momishe mopers whiche can do none other thyng else, but mope vppon ther bookes, to make vs afraied of shadowes and buggeberes.

Hugh Latimer, preaching before the king, referred to a saying that many people in England did not believe in the soul, in heaven, or in hell.[53]

The official repudiation of purgatory might have been expected to cause serious difficulties of adjustment for a large proportion of the population. The doctrine of purgatory had met what might be thought important psychological needs. It held out to the repentant sinner the prospect of expiation after death. It assured him that his trials might be shortened by the prayers of the faithful. It offered what seemed a just and reasonable alternative to the great majority of Christians who felt themselves neither good enough to go straight to heaven nor bad enough to be consigned to hell. After the Reformation, such people found themselves confronted by a stark alternative: heaven or hell. Yet there is little firm evidence that this caused a serious or widespread psychic crisis. Strict Protestants and Catholics were almost certainly vastly outnumbered by those who reassured themselves with the simple reflection that God was too loving and merciful to send them to hell. Hell was an unthinkable destination, so popular expectation widened the entrance to heaven to accommodate those who might previously have gone to purgatory. The last recorded words of Samuel Pepys's brother Tom perfectly express this expectation. He had lived a disordered life. Samuel, belatedly anxious to give him some spiritual assistance, asked Tom which way he thought he would go when he died. He answered 'in distracted manner':

Why, whither should I go? there are but two ways: If I go to the bad way I must give God thanks for it, and if I go the other way I must give God the more

---

[53] *A funerall sermon that was prepared to have bene preched, by Robert King doctour in divinite for a certein honourable Lady then almoste deade, but afterward recovered* (1552), sig. Fiiii[r-v], *Sermons by Hugh Latimer*, ed. G. E. Corrie (Parker Soc., 1844), 187. Cf. Dudley North's view in Charles II's reign, cited in Thomas, *Religion*, 204.

thanks for it; and I hope I have not been so undutifull and unthankfull in my life but I hope I shall go that way.[54]

Preachers repeatedly warned their audiences that God was not as merciful as people liked to imagine. In 1581 the Puritan George Gifford poured scorn on the 'Countrie diuinitie' of the rustic 'Atheos' who believed that 'the mercy of God must saue all'. Nearly seventy years later, after giving a vivid picture of God's delight in punishing the wicked in hell, Richard Baxter pictured the reaction of a 'sensual unbeliever' to his description. 'It is incredible. How can this stand with the infiniteness of His mercy? I would not thus torment the worst enemy that I have in the world, and yet my mercifulness is nothing to God's.' Anthony Horneck, preaching in 1677, derided the wishful thinking of the generality of men who imagined God to be somebody just like themselves, 'childishly merciful', and tolerant of their own frailty and weakness. God did not make souls to damn them, Edward Dent imagined a poor uneducated person telling the minister who urged his or her salvation. Marie Huber was almost certainly describing a long-established state of affairs when she wrote (c.1731) that although Christians imagined they believed in hell 'everyone is persuaded that he himself is not of the number of the wicked, whose Portion shall be in the Lake of Fire and Brimstone'.[55]

Famine, disease, and war might create superficially hellish conditions in certain areas and for a limited time. Horrible judicial punishments might seem to mimic divine vengeance. Nevertheless, the sustained cruelty of eternal torment of body and soul was hard to comprehend. Purgatory had been easier to come to terms with. By elaborating a doctrine characterized by what its leading historian has described as 'subtlety, justice, accuracy and measure',[56] the later medieval Church probably made the afterlife play a larger role in society, and brought it closer to most people's everyday consciousness,

---

[54] Pepys, *Diary*, v. 87.

[55] G. Gifford, *A briefe discourse of certaine points of the religion, which is among the common sort of christians which may be termed the countrey divinitie. With a confutation of the same, after the order of a dialogue* (1581), 66ʳ; Baxter, *Saints' Rest*, i. 224–9; A. Horneck, *A Sermon, Preached at the Solemnity of the Funeral of Mʳˢ. Dorothy St. John, Fourth Daughter of the late Sir Oliver St. John* (1677), 31; Dent, *Everlasting Blessedness*, 8–9; M. Huber, *The World Unmask'd* (1736), 290, quoted by Walker, *Decline of Hell*, 41. Elizabeth Livingston thought, c.1664, when she was 14, that 'there are but few who will not sooner be alured with his [God's] mercy's then frighten'd by his judgement's'; she did not believe, despite her sins, that she would be condemned to hell: *The Meditations of Lady Elizabeth Delaval, written between 1662 and 1671*, ed. D. G. Greene (Surtees Soc. 190; 1978), 49.

[56] Le Goff, *Birth of Purgatory*, 360.

than has been the case at any time before or since. The denial of purgatory by the reformers enormously widened the gap between this life and the next. In the eighteenth century, however, reading revelation in the light of 'reason', philosophers and divines took an increasingly optimistic view of the divine plan. In terms of the stricter theodicy of the seventeenth century, they were refashioning God in their own image. A gradual and uneven 'decline of hell' was under way. Heaven, meanwhile, was envisaged by a growing minority not as an utterly different realm, but as a perfect version of earth, a place of useful activity, of refined social pleasures, and of landscapes of surpassing beauty.

3

Preparation for Death

Given the probable brevity of life, preparation for death could hardly begin too soon. Indeed, it was the most important business of earthly existence. This was a view shared by most preachers and writers of Christian advice literature between the Middle Ages and the early eighteenth century. In medieval times, the message was reinforced by large numbers of paintings of the Last Judgement over chancel arches. The motif of the dance of death, into which men and women of every age and degree were drawn by skeletal partners, first appeared in England in the pardon churchyard of St Paul's in London in the 1440s. In woodcuts and engravings its portrayal continued long after the Reformation. The skull and the animated skeleton as a personification of death, sometimes armed with a spear, were very popular motifs in every conceivable medium: paintings, engravings, sculptures, and woodcut broadside pictures. The fifteenth century saw the introduction of the 'cadaver tomb' and the portrayal of corpses and skeletons on memorial brasses. All such monuments were designed to remind passers-by of the fate they would soon share. Some of those who commissioned cadaver tombs did so for their own edification as well as to show their equanimity in face of the body's dissolution.[1]

St John Fisher kept a skull near him both when he dined and when he celebrated mass. Once portrait-painting had become established in England in the 1530s, sitters sometimes had prominent reminders

[1] T. S. R. Boase, *Death in the Middle Ages: Mortality, Judgment and Remembrance* (1972), 49, 104–5; Duffy, *Stripping of Altars*, 303–10; A. Caiger-Smith, *English Medieval Mural Paintings* (Oxford, 1963), 31–43; P. M. King, 'The Cadaver Tomb in England: Novel Manifestations of an Old Idea', *Church Monuments*, 5 (1990), 26–38; T. Watt, *Cheap Print and Popular Piety 1550–1640* (Cambridge, 1991), 113, 163, 164; B. R. Kemp, *English Church Monuments* (1980), 160–5. The memorial inscription to Agnes Halke, the first person to be buried in a new churchyard at St Alpheges in Canterbury, 1502, recorded that it 'was soe hir chavnce . . . Afore alle others to begynne the dans': T. F. Ravenshaw, *Antiente Epitaphes (from A.D. 1250 to A.D. 1800) collected and set forth in Chronologicall Order* (1878), 17.

of death included in their pictures. The best known of such representations is perhaps the mysterious tableau known as *The Judd Memorial*, painted in 1560, in the aftermath of the worst mortality crisis of the sixteenth century. It depicts a husband and wife, each of whom has a hand resting on a skull which sits between them: directly behind it are the words 'We behowlde ower Ende'. In front of the couple lies a corpse, to which the husband points with his right hand. They are united for the moment, but not for long: the verses 'The Worde of God | Hathe knit vs twayne | And Death shall vs | Devide agayne' tell us so. The largest and most prominent text in the whole picture appears in the foreground: 'Lyve to dye and dye to lyve etarnally'. Sir Edward Grimston, gaunt and severe, holds a skull in his 1590 portrait; John Evelyn, rapt in contemplative melancholy, caresses one in a picture painted in 1648, the year after his marriage. Evelyn's young friend Mrs Godolphin (d. 1678) ordered that she be drawn in a '*Lugubrous Posture*, Sitting on a *Tombstone*, supporting a *Sepulchral-Urne*'. She loved to be in the company of mourners, which reminded her of her end.[2]

Elizabeth Joceline (d. 1622) secretly ordered a new winding-sheet as soon as she realized that she was pregnant. Some people kept a coffin near them in order to familiarize themselves with the prospect of death. In 1717 a young Northumberland curate, John Thomlinson, recalled 'The story of [his] grandfather's keeping his coffin in his bedchamber for six years; applauded as a piece of extraordinary christian courage'. In 1750 the *Gentleman's Magazine* reported the death of a Mrs Reed of Kentish Town, at the age of 81. She had kept a mahogany coffin and shroud near her for six years, but then, 'thinking she should not soon have occasion for them she sold them, and dy'd suddenly the same evening'.[3]

Funeral ceremonies served among many other things to remind the living of their own mortality. The tolling of bells, the black garments, pall, and hangings, and the solemn gait of the mourners, all helped to focus the attention of a receptive passer-by upon his own end. 'And

---

[2] Duffy, *Stripping of Altars*, 303; N. Llewellyn, *The Art of Death: Visual Culture in the English Death Ritual c.1500–c.1800* (1991), 6, 9–12, 24; R. Strong, *The English Icon: Elizabethan & Jacobean Portraiture* (1969), 39–40, 174, 232, 324; J. Evelyn, *The Life of Mrs Godolphin*, ed. H. Sampson (Oxford, 1939), portrait opposite frontispiece and 71–2.

[3] E. Joceline, *The mothers legacie, to her unborne childe* (6th impression, 1632; repr. 1894), 'The Approbation', by Thomas Goad, unpaginated; *The Diary of the Rev. John Thomlinson*, in *Six North Country Diaries*, ed. J. C. Hodgson (Surtees Soc. 118; 1910), 66; *Gentleman's Magazine*, 20 (1750), 188.

therefore never send to know for whom the *bell* tolls; It tolls for *thee*.' A custom which originated before the Reformation but grew in popularity for two centuries after it was the distribution of memorial rings at funerals. Favoured designs included a skull, and helpful messages such as 'Learn to die' were often engraved on them. To what end, asked the godly minister Robert Pricke, rhetorically, in 1606, 'serue so many Funeralls of all sorts, olde, young, rich, poore, noble, and base? To what ende, so many Graues and Sepulchers, in the places of buriall? so many drie bones cast out of the Graues? but to set forth visiblie before our eyes, the mortall estate of mankinde.' Various pagan peoples had disposed of their dead in ways which would leave no reminders behind, observed Richard Werge in 1683. 'But surely it will be Christian prudence to have death always before your eyes, and to look at those things, that might put you in mind of Death.'[4]

Books, tracts, and sermons designed either to arm readers against the fear of death or to tell them how to prepare for it poured from the presses between the late fifteenth and early eighteenth centuries. The printed word, in this as in other fields, took over much of the didactic function of pictures and symbols, without ever replacing them entirely. Many of the key arguments and maxims of this literature can be found set out with particular eloquence and succinctness in a relatively early work: Erasmus's *Preparation to deathe* (1538). Erasmus occupies a pivotal place in Philippe Ariès's thesis that the literature of long-term preparation for death tended to devalue the last moments of life, which had come to assume paramount importance during the later Middle Ages. He claims that 'the sense of death that had formerly been concentrated on the historical reality of the moment itself was henceforth diluted and distributed over the whole of the life, and in this way lost all its intensity'. The thesis may contain some truth, but nevertheless seems overstated. Erasmus sought both to help the Christian make long-term preparation and to comfort and strengthen the dying. He did indeed claim that 'good lyuynge gyueth a great imboldyng agaynst the dyuell' on the deathbed, but he also saw the experience of dying as a crucial trial upon whose outcome

---

[4] J. Donne, *Devotions upon Emergent Occasions*, ed. A. Raspa (New York, 1987), 87; Llewellyn, *Art of Death*, 19, 86, 95–6; R. Pricke, *A verie godlie and learned sermon, treating of mans mortalitie and of the estate both of his bodie, and soule after death* (1608), sig. Cl[v]; R. Werge, *A Sermon preached . . . at the Funeral of George Johnson, Gent.* (1683), 20–1; T. Hall, *A Sermon Preached . . . At the Funeral of Robert Huntington Esq.* (1684), sig. A2.

the individual's eternal fate depended. This view was only very gradually abandoned over the following two hundred years.[5]

There were differences of emphasis among writers on preparation
for death between Catholics and Protestants, and within Protestantism between (for example) Calvinists and anti-Calvinists. However, what such writers shared was more important than the issues
which divided them. Neither the importance of trusting to God's
grace rather than one's own good works (already stressed by Erasmus), nor the Calvinist doctrines of election and predestination,
diminished the urgency of the task of preparation. The belief that salvation is finally the work of God alone did not remove the individual's
duty to make ready for death. William Perkins, foremost of Puritan
practical theologians, emphasized the co-action of God and man in
this as in other Christian duties.[6]

Certain basic themes stand out in this literature. The life after death
is what matters. It will be without end, whereas this life is short. Yet it
is by what happens in this life that our fate is decided for all time thereafter. Our chances of winning salvation end with death. It is certain,
but its time is uncertain. God leaves human beings in ignorance of the
precise time of their death to encourage them to make themselves
ready for it every day, rather than postpone their preparations as they
might well do if they knew when it would occur.[7] Death is often a terrible experience even for good men and women. Only a well-grounded
faith and the knowledge that we have tried to live our lives in accordance with God's commandments can arm us against its terrors. Preparation must therefore start without delay. John Warren, dedicating a
funeral sermon in 1618, expressed the hope that it would be like a
death's head in the reader's hand, helping to ensure that he would have
a joyful deathbed while others were senseless, or yelled and howled.[8]

---

[5] P. Ariès, *The Hour of our Death* (Harmondsworth, 1983), 297–305, 314–15; D.
Erasmus, *Preparation to deathe, a boke as deuout as eloquent* (1538), sig. Aii, Dv[v].
For the prominence of death and the need to prepare for it in the 'godly chapbooks' of
17th-cent. England, see M. Spufford, *Small Books and Pleasant Histories: Popular Fiction and its Readership in Seventeenth Century England* (1981), 200–8.

[6] D. W. Atkinson, 'The English ars morendi [*sic*]: Its Protestant Transformation',
Renaissance and Reformation, NS 6, OS 18 (1982), 3–5; Erasmus, *Preparation*, sig. Fiii.
For themes common to both Catholic and Protestant texts about preparation for death,
see also J. Delumeau, *Sin and Fear: The Emergence of a Western Guilt Culture
13th–18th Centuries* (New York, 1990), 505–22.

[7] Erasmus, *Preparation*, sig. D; W. Kennett, *A Sermon Preach'd at the Funeral of
the . . . Duke of Devonshire. . . . on Friday Septemb. 5th. MDCCVII* (1708), 14–16.

[8] J. Warren, *Domus ordinata. A funerall sermon, preached in Bristoll, at the buriall of mistresse Needes* (1618), sig. A2[v].

A common complaint was that people refused to face up to what lay ahead. Some, asserted Robert Pricke in 1606, beguiled by the pleasures of the world, thought no more of death than a brute beast; others could talk about it, yet without applying the remembrance of it to their hearts by serious meditation. Others again quaked and trembled at the thought of it, yet took no steps to enable themselves to die well. Instead of praying God to teach them to remember death, Richard Eaton grumbled in 1616, 'teach vs to forget death, to prolong life, is the common language of our times'. Timothy Hall claimed in 1684 that those who had the greatest reason to dread death diverted their thoughts from the 'formidable prospect' of their ends, 'couzening themselves as far as they can, with that vain Opinion, *That the way to escape the sting of death, is not to think of it*'. Even when saddened by the deaths of friends or relations, Richard Eyre lamented in 1726, people turned their reflections on these events away from themselves, so that they were no use to them. The way to lessen their fear of death, he insisted, was to think about it more frequently.[9]

Some of the most vivid passages in this sort of literature evoked the experience of dying. Thomas More, in his treatise on the four last things (*c*.1522), invited the individual to imagine himself on his deathbed, feeling pain or weakness in every part of his body, his throat rattling and his mouth gaping. William Perkins's *Death's Knell*, frequently reprinted as a penny chap-book in the early seventeenth century, called on the reader to imagine how much he would give 'for a dayes contrition, an houres repentance, or a minutes amendment of life' if he lay panting and sweating on his deathbed. Robert Sparke claimed in 1679 that it was 'the most dreadful astonishing spectacle on this side Hell, to see a graceless wretch, an unbelieving and prophane worlding [*sic*] breathing out his last. . . . O miserable case, when suddenly the senses fail, the body languisheth; when thou shalt feel the sting of thy sins tormenting thy soul, and see the flames of Hell slashing in thy face,' he continued. 'O', Henry Read exclaimed towards the end of a funeral discourse in 1737, 'the Horror of an awakened Sinner, that finds his Life ending, before his great Work of Preparation is begun! who feels he cannot live, and yet dare not die; but die he must!'[10]

[9] Pricke, *Verie godlie and learned sermon*, sig. C2; R. Eaton, *A sermon preached at the funeralls of Thomas Dutton of Dutton, esquire* (1616), 14–15; Hall, *Sermon*, 8–9; R. Eyre, *A Sermon preached . . . At the Funeral of Thomas Pitt Esq.* (1726), 26–7.

[10] 'A Treatise (unfinished) upon these Words of Holy Scripture. Memorare novissima, & in aeternum non peccabis. "Remember the last things, & thou shalt never sin"—Ecclus. 7', in id., *The English Works of Sir Thomas More*, ed. W. E. Campbell,

True meditation on death was the essential basis of preparation. Thomas More believed that such meditation would make the seven deadly sins seem both futile and repugnant, Christopher Sutton similarly argued, *c.*1600, that thinking of death would curb temptations to covetousness, pride, or oppression. A 'well-guided and bounded' fear of death, according to Timothy Hall, weakened pride, strengthened faith, and acted as a stimulus to preparation. He who lives under a constant sense of death, claimed William Sherlock, author of the immensely popular *A Practical Discourse concerning Death* (1689), 'has a perpetual Antidote against the Follies and Vanities of this World, and a perpetual Spur to Virtue'.[11]

Death was only to be faced with confidence by those armed with a sure faith and a clear conscience. Preachers and writers emphasized one or the other according to their own theological leanings and the nature of their audience. Some writers pointed out that pagan sages, too, had found meditation on death to be the best philosophy, but the believing Christian possessed a sure prospect of eternal salvation of which Plato and Seneca could have had but a dim intimation. Sound faith was the essential basis of effective preparation for death, the earl of Manchester emphasized in his widely read tract on death and immortality (1633). All admirers of pagan antiquity needed to remember what their master Aristotle had said when he died: 'I lived uncertain, I die doubtful: O thou Being of beings, have mercy upon me!'[12] However, it was useless to ask for mercy then. Some Puritan writers in particular ridiculed those people who counted on their own good

A. W. Reed, R. W. Chambers, and W. A. G. Doyle-Davidson (2 vols., 1927, 1931), i. 468; W. Perkins, *Death's knell or the sicke mans passing-bell* (9th edn., 1628), sig. A5, cited by Watt, *Cheap Print and Popular Piety*, 313; R. Sparke, *A Sermon preached ... at the Funeral of that Pious and Worthy Gentlewoman, Mrs Frances Fenn* (1679), 21–2; H. Read, *Be Ye also ready. A Funeral-Discourse. Occasion'd by the Much lamented Death of Mr Thomas Adams, Who Died in the 23d Year of his Age* (2nd edn., 1737), 26. A work of advice about preparation for death written by a friend of Thomas More's has recently been analysed by M. Collins in 'A Little Known "Art of Dying" by a Brigittine of Syon: *A Daily Exercise and Experience of Death* by Richard Whitford', in J. H. M. Taylor (ed.), *Dies Illa: Death in the Middle Ages* (Vinaver Studies in French, 1; 1984), 179–93. Whitford distinguished between a vain fear of death and a beneficial one, playing down physical pain.

[11] More 'Treatise', 476–94 (which breaks off before it gets to lust); C. Sutton, *Disce Mori; Learn to Die* (1843, repr. from 1st edn. of 1600), 25; T. Hall, *Sermon*, 20–2; W. Sherlock, *A Practical Discourse concerning Death* (23rd edn., 1739), 92.

[12] H. Montagu, *Death and Immortality*, ed. E. Waterhouse (1906), 99–103, 122–3; cf. Erasmus, *Preparation*, sig. A5ᵛ and following unfoliated leaves; A. Horneck, *A Sermon, Preached at the Solemnity of the Funeral of Mʳˢ. Dorothy St. John, Fourth Daughter of the late Sir Oliver St. John* (1677), 29–30; J. Scott, *A Sermon Preach'd at the Funeral of Sir John Buckworth ... December 29, 1687* (1688), 3.

works and a vague expectation of God's mercy. Those who died without saving faith would be excluded from heaven.[13]

Repentance and renewal of life were not to be postponed.
'Who would venture the infinite Hazards of a Death-bed Repentance?', asked William Sherlock. Was it likely that 'after a Long Life of
Sin and Wickedness, a few distracted, confused, and almost despair-
ing Sighs and Groans' would carry the tardy penitent to heaven?
Repentance needed to be followed up by a process of continual and
regular self-monitoring. Jeremy Taylor, recalling that all the individual's thoughts and actions would be scrutinized at the Day of Judgement, advised a nightly personal scrutiny of one's moral accounts.
Advice like this encouraged the habit of keeping diaries and meditation books which spread gradually among pious people of all shades
of religious opinion from the late sixteenth century onwards. The
diary carefully kept by the devout minister John Janeway (d. 1657)
helped him keep a constant watch over himself and 'left a sweet calm
upon his Spirit, because that every Night he made his accounts even,
so that had his Sheet proved his Winding Sheet, it had been all one
to him'.[14]

Consciousness of the shortness of his earthly sojourn would
instil in the Christian a sense of urgency in doing all possible service
in the time that remained to him: 'the night cometh, when no
man can work' (John 9: 4). Good works of charity were the most
important of all. They should begin early. That alms given during a
person's lifetime were more meritorious than those bequeathed by
will was a theme inherited from the Middle Ages. A lifetime gift,
unlike a testamentary bequest, involved an immediate sacrifice.
Special promises had been made in respect of works of charity in
Scripture both for this life and the next. Jesus had told his disciples to
sell their possessions and give alms, thereby providing themselves
with an unfailing treasure in heaven (Luke 12: 33). The rich should be
told to be ready to share their wealth, Paul had advised Timothy,
'Laying up in store for themselves a good foundation against the time

[13] G. Gifford, *A briefe discourse of certaine points of the religion, which is among
the common sort of christians which may be termed the countrey divinitie. With a
confutation of the same, after the order of a dialogue* (1581), 20, 31–3, 68ᵛ; E. Dent,
*Everlasting Blessedness. A Sermon preached at The Funerall of . . . Mr. William
Baker, who . . . was received to Heavenly Joyes, the 14ᵗʰ. Day of October, 1691*
(1692), 8–9.

[14] Sherlock, *Discourse*, 222, 240–72; Erasmus, *Preparation*, sig. Cᵛ; J. Taylor, *The
Rule and Exercises of Holy Dying* (London, 1929), 39–41; S. Clarke, *The Lives of
Sundry Eminent Persons in this Later Age* (2 pts. in 1 vol., 1683), i. 74.

to come, that they may lay hold on eternal life' (1 Timothy 6: 17–19). In 1687 John Scott presented the message in terms appropriate for the funeral sermon of a great Turkey merchant. By doing good with our wealth, he said, 'we shall transmit it into the Eternal World, as it were, by Bill of Exchange, there to be repaid us, Ten Thousand fold in Glory and Honour and Immortality'.[15] The ability to wean one's heart from earthly goods was a measure of the sincerity of a person's belief in the future life. 'Thou fool,' God said to the rich man who rejoiced in his abundant possessions, 'this night thy soul shall be required of thee: then whose shall those things be, which thou hast provided?' This was the question to be asked of all those who laid up treasure for themselves and were not 'rich towards God' (Luke 12: 16–21).

Christians had to avoid excessive involvement in even essential earthly business, and set aside regular hours of retirement and withdrawal during which their secular activities might be put in their proper perspective. We must not, the famous Puritan minister Thomas Gataker reminded his hearers in 1626, allow our affections to be glued to the things of this life. Let them instead hang loose about us, so that when we are stripped of them they may slip off easily rather than stick like clothes to an ulcerous body, making the inevitable parting as painful as if our skin were being pulled from our flesh, or flesh torn from our bones. It is impossible, the High Churchman Francis Atterbury asserted in 1706, for a man to have a lively hope in another life, and yet be deeply immersed in the enjoyments of this one.[16]

Mortification of the flesh was recommended by some writers on the task of preparing for death. In the case of that exemplary Catholic layman Thomas More, this meant a measure of physical self-punishment as well as self-denial. Such practices smacked for many Protestants of the 'arrogancy and impiety' attached to works of supererogation by the fourteenth of the Thirty-Nine Articles. They preferred more moderate measures, such as occasional fasting. 'All the Severities of Mortification, Abstinence from bodily Pleasures, Watchings, Fastings, hard Lodgings, when they are Instruments of a real Virtue, not the Arts of Superstition' were nevertheless valuable

---

[15] *A funerall sermon that was prepared to have bene preched, by Robert King doctour in divinite for a certein honourable Lady then almoste deade, but afterward recovered* (1552), sig. Fiiᵛ; Scott, *Sermon*, 14.

[16] Gataker, *Certaine sermons*, ii. 277–0 (*recte* 278); F. Atterbury, *Sermons and Discourses on Several Subjects and Occasions* (2 vols., 1820), i. 248–9.

means of refining the body in preparation for its resurrection in glory, according to the High Churchman William Sherlock.[17]

For many writers, the best tests of true Christian fortitude were the trials which God sent. They were to be borne meekly, patiently, and gratefully. William Perkins advised his readers to prepare for the greatest crosses by willingly bearing the small ones such as bodily sicknesses, anxiety, loss of goods, friends, and good name. Such sufferings were signs of God's love for the believing Christian. A solicitous parent, he chastised his children for their own good. Their earthly sufferings served to wean their hearts from transient pleasures and set them instead on the heavenly life to come. God seldom gave his people so sweet a foretaste of their future rest as in their deep afflictions, Richard Baxter asserted.[18]

Setting their hearts on heaven was the most important thing for believers to do. The commonest of all metaphors for the life course were those of journey or pilgrimage. The Christian was a traveller through a barren land where he pitched his tent but had 'no continuing city' (Hebrews 13: 14), or a seafarer crossing a stormy sea. Heaven was his true home, but the quest for it was an arduous task. 'We must sweat, and labour, and seek after it, as we do for our daily bread,' Richard Kidder insisted in 1686. 'We must seek as for silver, and search as for hid treasures.'[19]

Thomas Wilson, an exemplary bishop (of Sodor and Man, 1698–1755), set out things which a wise man should do in expectation of death under eight heads: settlement of his worldly concerns; timely repentance; faithful discharge of the duties of his calling; weaning his affections from temporal things; crucifying the affections and lusts of the flesh; acts of justice, mercy, charity, and alms; the acquisition of habits of patience and resignation to the will of God; and a 'constant practice of devotion preparatory for death'.[20] Generations of previous writers would have agreed with this prescription. In the end all must trust in the saving merits of Jesus Christ. No man

---

[17] W. Roper, *The Life of Sir Thomas More*, in *Two Early Tudor Lives*, ed. R. S. Sylvester and D. P. Harding (New Haven, 1962), 224; Erasmus, *Preparation*, sig. Cii^v; Sherlock, *Discourse*, 55.

[18] W. Perkins, *A salue for a sicke man, or, a treatise containing the nature, differences, and kindes of death: as also the right manner of dying well* (edn. of c.1638, STC 19747.3), 80–2; R. Baxter, *The Saints' Everlasting Rest* (2 vols., 1887), ii. 60; Sutton, *Disce Mori*, 75–6; Sherlock, *Discourse*, 278.

[19] Erasmus, *Preparation*, sig. Aiiii^v; R. Kidder, *A Sermon Preached at the Funeral of Mr William Allen* (1686), 15.

[20] T. Wilson, *Works* (LACT, 7 vols.; 1847–63), v. 254–5.

could rely on his own good works. However, it was proper to warn
the careless sinner and the 'cold formalist' that they were less likely to
experience saving faith in their hour of need, more likely to suffer
indifference or despair, than the person who had long sought Christ.

Some of those who urged their readers to contemplate the
prospect of death recognized that it could not be an all-absorbing preoccupation. William Sherlock conceded that 'we cannot live as if we
were immediately to die,' which would put an end 'not only to all
innocent Mirth, but to all the necessary Business of the World'. Even
the great sinner should spend his whole time in penance and mortification only until he had in some measure subdued his love of sin,
regained self-control, and recovered his hopes of divine forgiveness.[21]
The Presbyterian Benjamin Grosvenor, in his *Observations on Sudden Death* (1720), thought that he who had once properly prepared
for death might say to himself: 'In the mean Time, I will enjoy my self
. . . I will enjoy my God, my Friend, and my Comforts of Life, and that
with so much the greater Pleasure, and sweeter relish, than others
can do, in as much, as it is without the fears of *Death*, or the Danger
of Damnation.' In Grosvenor's eyes the process of preparation for
death was thoroughly compatible with 'Day labour, Merchandise, or
any Business of Life'.[22] From Luther onwards, Protestant divines had
taught that worldly callings were compatible with Christian duty. Yet
there was a tension between earlier Puritan insistence on the need to
preserve a measure of detachment from earthly pleasures, and
Grosvenor's assurance that the Christian, once prepared, could enjoy
them with the greater relish. The idea that the believer who had once
thoroughly digested the lesson of mortality did not need frequent
reminders of it marks an important change of emphasis in Christian
advice literature. Guides to preparation for death still sold very well
during the early eighteenth century. John Hayward's *The horrors
and terrors of the hour of death* and *Hell's everlasting flames
avoided*, both first published in the 1690s, are good examples of such
works. It was Sherlock's *Discourse*, however, that was by far the most
successful essay in the genre. Though not perhaps the last of its line,
it had no successor of equal stature. In 1733, forty years after its first
appearance, it was still the standard work on its subject. In that year
Lord Chesterfield in his light-hearted poem '*To a Lady on Reading
Sherlock Upon Death*' advised her

---

[21] Sherlock, *Discourse*, 95, 182.
[22] B. Grosvenor, *Observations on Sudden Death. Occasion'd by the late frequent
Instances of it, both in City and Country* (1720), 22, 37.

MISTAKEN fair, lay *Sherlock* by,
His doctrine is deceiving;
For, whilst he teaches us to die,
He cheats us of our living.[23]

The level of receptivity to warnings to prepare for death depended in large part upon age, sex, personal character, and individual experience. It was thought especially appropriate that the aged should make themselves ready. Indeed, they sometimes looked forward to it, like the old man in Chaucer's Pardoner's Tale, who knocked on Mother Earth to let him in. Having tasted enough of both the sweet and the sour of the world to make him weary of life, Lord Burghley desired nothing but death for some time before his demise in 1598. Sir John Oglander claimed that he would be a happy man if only he were able to leave the world when he wanted to without offence to God's laws or man's. In 1734, the year before his death, Dr John Arbuthnot wrote that euthanasia was his friends' kindest wish for him.[24]

The desire to devote the last years of life to religious duties and preparation for the coming change was described as an important reason for the retirement of several men active in government, business, or politics. One of them was William Allen, a London merchant (d. 1686), who left off trading some time before his death in order to devote himself more fully to religion and good works. 'He wisely considered that it was fit there should be a considerable space of time allowed between the hurries of life and the great work of dying well.'[25] Pious members of the upper classes whose lives had long been free from toil might mark their passage of a milestone on life's slope with a change of gear. John Evelyn was a classic example. In 1680, having reached the age of 60, he began a 'more solemn survey' of his whole life, in order to make and confirm his peace with God.[26] The elderly were sometimes given personal exhortations to prepare for death. In the epistle dedicatory prefaced to his funeral sermon for

[23] I am grateful to Prof. Ian Green for references to Hayward's works; *The New Oxford Book of Eighteenth Century Verse*, ed. R. Lonsdale (Oxford, 1984), 275.

[24] *Pardoner's Tale*, ll. 729–31; F. Peck, *Desiderata Curiosa; or, a Collection of divers Scarce and Curious Pieces, relating chiefly to Matters of English History* (2 vols., 1779), i. 40; *A Royalist's Notebook. The Commonplace Book of Sir John Oglander Kt of Nunwell*, ed. F. Bamford (1936), 133; G. A. Aitken, *The Life and Works of John Arbuthnot* (Oxford, 1892), 148.

[25] Kidder, *Sermon*, 31. See also C. Wren, *Parentalia* (1750), 344; W. Wynne, *The Life of Sir Leoline Jenkins . . . and a Compleat Series of Letters . . .* (2 vols, 1724), vol. i. p. xlix; *The Whole Works of the Right Reverend Jeremy Taylor, D.D.*, ed. C. P. Eden (10 vols., 1847–54), viii. 567.

[26] Evelyn, *Diary*, iv. 223.

her husband (d. 1614) Robert Harris reminded Lady Anne Cope that
parents, children, and husbands had gone before her. The time would
shortly come when she too must yield to the stroke of death. He therefore advised her, 'husband your soule well, sow much, worke much,
give much, pray much, and you and we shall speed the better at that
Harvest'. In 1629–31 an aged Puritan widow, Lady Barrington,
received copious spiritual counsel from both clergy and laymen.
They repeatedly alluded to the fact that her death could not be far distant. 'Forgett not that your time cannot be long,' Ezekiel Rogers wrote
in July 1631, 'and therefore be a good huswife in plying your
worke.'[27]

In earlier life, women in their childbearing years had more frequent occasion than men to contemplate the possibility of death.
Seventeenth-century diaries show that some expectant mothers
looked forward to childbirth with considerable anxiety. Jane Josselin
'dreaded her confinements for months before the baby was due'. Alice
Thornton recorded a series of pregnancies marked among other things
by a dangerous fall, a terrifying dream of a blood-sprinkled sheet, 'five
great trialls and hazards of miscarige', and 'a weake and sickely time in
breeding'. Childbirth itself was sometimes like an excruciatingly
painful dress rehearsal for death. It was natural, therefore, to make
some spiritual preparations. Receiving Communion before being
brought to bed was regarded as an appropriate preparatory step by
some expectant mothers. Various women experienced a premonition
that they would not survive a childbirth. One of them, Elizabeth
Joceline (d. 1622), used the time left to her to write *The Mothers
Legacie, To her vnborne* CHILDE as a means of discharging, as far as
possible, her maternal duty of giving her child religious training.[28]

Women were more likely than men to be intimate spectators of
death because nursing (including support at childbirth) was regarded
as one of their special responsibilities. Visiting other people's

[27] R. Harris, *The workes . . . Revised, and in sundrie places corrected. With an
addition of two sermons, not formerly extant. As also two tables* (1635), 210; *Barrington Family Letters*, ed. A. Searle (Camden 4th ser. 28; 1983), 199; cf. 65, 68, 167.
[28] L. M. Beier, 'In Sickness and in Health: A Seventeenth Century Family's Experience', in R. Porter (ed.), *Patients and Practitioners: Lay Perceptions of Medicine in
Pre-Industrial Society* (Cambridge, 1985), 104; *The Autobiography of Mrs Alice
Thornton, of East Newton, Co. York*, ed. C. Jackson (Surtees Soc. 62; 1875), 95, 123,
139, 140, 164; NRO DN/ACT 4/4B, fo. 97ʳ; Evelyn, *Mrs Godolphin*, 79; Stubbes,
Christal glasse, repr., with some omissions in *Philip Stubbes's Anatomy of the Abuses
in England in Shakspere's Youth, A.D. 1583*, ed. F. J. Furnivall (New Shakspere Soc.,
6th ser. 4, 6, 12; 1877–82), 200; Joceline, *Mothers legacie*, 'The Letter to her Husband'.

deathbeds was a charitable work and a helpful means of reminding oneself of what lay ahead. It was one appropriately performed by either men or women, but probably more popular among women in practice. Lady Margaret Beaufort kept twelve poor folk in her house to whom she ministered in their sickness with her own hands, and at whose deathbeds she attended in order that she might learn how to die. Deathbed visiting was also a favoured charitable activity of some of the pious ladies of Restoration England.[29]

Illness, at any time of life, might be seen as a warning to prepare for death. In 1550 a young single man called Edmund Cooke of Gorleston (Suffolk), feeling 'not well at ease', though still up and about, was found sitting on the cliff-top by a headless cross on Ascension Day reading the Word of God in English. He was probably preparing spiritually for his end, having already made his will. Gilbert Davies, a young Devon gentleman (d. 1620), meditated daily on mortality after being visited with a serious illness, and set his house in order so that if sickness suddenly returned he might be free from worldly cares and so more cheerfully prepare himself for God. Crosses of physical ailments and illnesses were gifts for which the pious Christian thanked God. 'Long health', Sir Thomas Browne told his son Edward in 1682, 'is apt to begett security & god mercifully interposeth some admonitions & rubbes to make us consider our selves, & to carry a warie hand in our affayres of all kinds.' Chronic poor health might be regarded in Christian terms as a blessing in disguise, making the sufferer readier to leave the world. Mrs Mary Gunter (d. 1622) had been prepared for her 'last combate' by her weak and sickly state for many years beforehand; her approaching death had been 'the principal, and almost only subject of her discourses' for six months before it happened. The behaviour of Lady Cranborne, who in 1674 continued to play at dice and cards and dress herself in the latest fashions despite being half-paralysed by a stroke, met with the severe disapproval of pious observers. So 'loude a summons from Heauen to prepare for her dissolution' was not to be ignored.[30]

Individuals' reactions to illness varied according to their temperaments, their education, and the strength of their religious convictions.

[29] *The English Works of John Fisher*, ed. J. E. B. Mayor (EETS extra ser. 27; 1876), 297; Evelyn, *Mrs Godolphin*, 11–12, 105–6; *The Meditations of Lady Elizabeth Delaval, written between 1662 and 1671*, ed. D. G. Greene (Surtees Soc. 190; 1978), 94–6.

[30] NRO DN/DEP 4/4B, fos. 35–6, 80; W. Miller, *A sermon preached at the funerall of Gilbert Davies esquire* (1621), sig. D3ᵛ; Sir Thomas Browne, *Works*, ed. G. Keynes (4 vols., 1964), iv. 202; Clarke, *Eminent Persons*, ii. 139; BL Add. MS 27356, fo. 233ᵛ.

Christian teaching encouraged each person to see his or her health in both spiritual and physical terms. A malady of the body might be the outward symptom of a sickness of the soul, a punishment from God, a salutary reminder of mortality, or a test of individual fortitude. In each of these cases, it was the sick person's duty to seek God through self-examination, confession, and prayer. However, all sickness had secondary causes as well as God's providence. It was open to physical as well as spiritual treatment. The patient was expected to use medical remedies while invoking God's blessing upon them. Many ministers of religion offered their parishioners medical as well as spiritual counsel. Many physicians, for their part, were devout Christians who believed that there were links between their patients' spiritual and corporal infirmities. In so far as there was a shift in the course of time from providential to natural explanations of disease, it was a very gradual and rather uneven one. There were still many people in the eighteenth century who interpreted illness in religious terms, and emphasized the interaction of body, mind, and soul.[31]

Some diaries and autobiographies throw considerable light on the writers' own experience of sickness. In one of the earliest English autobiographies, the musician Thomas Whythorne (1528–96) described how he suffered during his early twenties from a prolonged attack of ague. He repined against 'Dame Fortune' for leaving him at the bottom of her wheel. He remembered that God's power, far superior to Fortune's, was where he should place all his hope. However, he ruefully admitted, young folk were soon forgetful of troubles when they were past. Whythorne took the good luck which he had previously enjoyed less for granted after his illness, but his humorous account suggests that his experience did not have a profound effect on him.[32]

Two of the fullest Puritan diaries of the seventeenth century, those of Bulstrode Whitelocke (1605–75), lawyer, diplomat, and politician, and Ralph Josselin, minister of Earl's Colne in Essex (1617–83), reveal attitudes to sickness very different from those of Whythorne. They both relied in serious illness on God first and foremost, but also on human and natural means. They attributed recovery to divine mercy, but this often worked through an identifiable treatment or

---

[31] A. Wear, 'Puritan Perceptions of Illness in Seventeenth Century England', and J. Barry, 'Piety and the Patient: Medicine and Religion in Eighteenth Century Bristol', in Porter (ed.), *Patients and Practitioners*, 55–99 and 145–75 respectively.

[32] *The Autobiography of Thomas Whythorne*, ed. J. M. Osborn (Oxford, 1961), 35–7.

medicine. Whitelocke took a close interest in the treatments he received. Josselin read a medical work concerned, as its subtitle indicated, with the *Right Course of Preserving Life and Health unto Extream Old Age*. Both men had a strong will to live which survived even into later life, when both of them suffered for many years from chronic ill health and Whitelocke in particular from a whole range of distressing symptoms. Shortly before the end, when he was 66, Josselin was still hoping that he might survive. During a critical illness in 1670, Whitelocke was not as terrified by the prospect of death as he had feared he might be. He was willing to surrender his soul into God's hands. He nevertheless prayed God to prolong his life for the sake of his wife and children, and so that he might do him further service.[33]

There were differences between the two men's attitudes to illness, though these were less important than the similarities. Whitelocke received medical advice from several physicians and surgeons, as well as spiritual comfort from ministers. Josselin rarely consulted a physician. Yet he was 'unusually preoccupied with his symptoms, major and minor', largely because he saw his health as a barometer of divine favour whose smallest movements had to be read with care. He had an acute sense of personal sinfulness, and a strong tendency to see illness as corrective. Whitelocke seems to have been much less inclined to explain his sufferings in terms of his need to undergo purging and punishment.[34]

Samuel Pepys was a young man when he kept his diary during the 1660s, and his outlook was far more secular than Josselin's or Whitelocke's. He was grateful to God for the improvement in his health effected by a successful operation for the stone in 1658, but he explained his comparatively minor ailments during the diary years in natural terms. His health sometimes caused Pepys anxiety, but he never faced an immediately life-threatening illness during this period or made serious spiritual preparations for death. This is not to say that he never thought of it; he was concerned about his posthumous reputation. At Christmas 1664 he decided to review his private papers

[33] Whitelocke, *Diary*, esp. 661, 690–2, 763–6, 808–9, 822, 829; Josselin, *Diary*, 154, 644; Josselin's attitudes to illness have been discussed by A. Macfarlane in *The Family Life of Ralph Josselin, a Seventeenth-Century Clergyman: An Essay in Historical Anthropology* (Cambridge, 1970), 168–78, and by Beier, 'In Sickness and in Health', 110–28.

[34] Beier, 'In Sickness and in Health', 110, 121–2; for Josselin's readiness to 'kiss the rod' of divine correction in illness see e.g. Josselin, *Diary*, 585, 595; cf. Whitelocke, *Diary*, 690–1, 763–5.

and destroy those which he judged unfit to be seen if it should please God to take him away suddenly.[35]

A Catholic gentleman, Nicholas Blundell of Little Crosby (1669–1737) made relatively few references to illness in the diary he kept between 1702 and 1728. However, three bouts of serious sickness in 1706, 1712, and 1724 were marked by a cluster of visits from friends, relatives, physicians, and priests. In 1706 two doctors and five priests came to see him. Rather than any spiritual counsel, however, what Blundell noted about the priests' visits was a debate between two of them concerning the height of King David, and the fact that a third brought him a 'Bottle of good Brandy'. In 1724 Blundell responded to his longest recorded spell of illness by going to Wigan to be under the closer supervision of a trusted physician. He clearly resembled the Puritan diarists in meeting serious illness with a combination of spiritual and medical measures, but he differed from them in being less spiritually autonomous and more easygoing.[36]

The loss of acquaintances, colleagues, and relatives in youth and middle life was an experience more common in early modern times than it is today. Christians were thereby warned to make timely preparation for their own ends, preachers told their congregations. 'If we saw only elder persons drop into the grave, and that death always observed the order of nature, we might possibly think, that it did not much concern us, and that our time was a great way off.' This was not the case, however.[37] It is difficult to say much about individuals' reactions to the deaths of any but their closest acquaintances before the seventeenth century. News of recent deaths (sometimes accompanied by a prayer for the departed soul) was often reported in very laconic fashion by later medieval letter-writers. Margaret Paston took unusual advantage of the loss of two friends to remind her son John of the need to know God and serve him better than he had done hitherto. In one of the earliest English diaries (1576–7), Nicholas Carnsew of Bokelly recorded without expression of personal feeling

[35] Pepys, *Diary*, i. 97–8; ii. 60; iii. 53; iv. 86, 332–7; v. 98, 360; vi. 16, 66–7; vii. 129–30; x. 172–80 (see esp. p. 177 for M. H. Stein's suggestion that in 1665 and 1666, the years of the Plague and Fire, Pepys 'responded to the fear of death by urgent sexuality').

[36] *The Great Diurnal of Nicholas Blundell of Little Crosby, Lancashire*, ed. F. Tyrer and J. J. Bagley (Record Soc. of Lancashire and Cheshire, 110, 112, 114; 1968, 1970, 1972), i. 124–5; ii. 12–14; iii. 140–1, 143, 145–6.

[37] W. Harris, *Funeral Discourses, In Two Parts: containing, I. Consolations on the Death of our Friends. II. Preparations for our Death* (1736), i. 61–2.

well over twenty deaths, among them those of his brother and several neighbours.[38]

More intimate seventeenth-century diaries point to the predictable conclusion that individuals' reactions to death depended upon their age, personality, and piety. Samuel Pepys registered many deaths without comment. Sometimes he pitied the dead, or regretted an untimely death. Rather more often he expressed sympathy with the bereaved or those who had lost the services of the deceased. Occasionally, however, he frankly admitted some pleasure in the news of a death which brought or might bring him some financial advantage, such as that of his uncle Robert in 1661, or that of his predecessor as clerk of the acts in 1665. On the latter occasion he blessed God from the bottom of his heart for this unexpected providence. When his cousin Dr Tom Pepys died in January 1665, Samuel was 'but little sorry' because Tom was a shame to his family and profession. On one occasion, however, other people's indifference to a death made a deep impression on Pepys. Sir William Compton, 'one of the worthyest men and best officers of state' in England died in late youth in 1663. Pepys found 'the sober men of the Court troubled for him', but not enough to disturb their usual pleasures.[39]

Ralph Josselin's diary records a wide variety of responses to the many deaths which appear in it. Quite often, especially when the dead person was somebody of no great importance to him, Josselin did not comment. Bad ends moved him to moralizing reflection, for example 'sin brings forth death'. Particularly distressing ones might elicit a prayer. When in July 1656 he buried 'old Reyner', who had suddenly fallen dead at his work, leaving a widow and nine children, he made the conventional, but no doubt heartfelt, request 'the lord sanctifie his hand unto us, and give us wisely daily to provide against our latter end'. The death of an important parishioner, Mr Cressener, in July 1677, 'impressed on mee to live more to god', as Josselin put it. He sometimes thought that deaths might be disguised mercies, removing the people concerned from coming troubles. On other occasions, he hoped that a death would move the hearts of his intractable flock. When in 1677 a servant died after after a drinking bout, Josselin prayed 'god awaken persons by it'. The need to prepare for his own

---

[38] *Paston Letters and Papers of the Fifteenth Century*, ed. N. Davis (2 vols., Oxford, 1971, 1976), i. 346; N. J. G. Pounds, 'William Carnsew of Bokelly and his Diary, 1576–7', *Journal of the Royal Institution of Cornwall*, NS 8/1 (1978), 29, 30, 31, 37–9, 42, 43, 44, 48, 49, 50, 51, 57.

[39] Pepys, *Diary*, ii. 73, 132; iv. 113, 338–9; v. 157; vi. 16, 33; viii. 273; ix. 32–4.

end was prominent among the reflections which other people's deaths inspired in Josselin, but by no means the only one. Mortality was so much on his mind that he needed no reminding of it.[40]

The Nonconformist doctor Richard Kay (1716–51) started to keep a diary in 1737. Practising near Bury, in populous East Lancashire, Kay frequently encountered death among the young and middle-aged, including his own relatives, and was still a young man when he died himself. His sense of sin seems to have been strong, his personality timid and gloomy. These considerations help to explain why his reflections on mortality are more numerous than one might expect to find in an eighteenth-century diary. Deaths, funerals, and even the extraction of a decayed tooth, prompted him to pray that God would help him and others to prepare for their own ends.[41]

Not surprisingly, many young people found it more difficult to keep their minds on death and what lay beyond it. A teenager in the 1660s, Elizabeth Livingston repeatedly tried through the medium of her meditation book to concentrate her thoughts on mortality and the transitoriness of the world. However, her natural *joie de vivre* and 'foleish mirth' proved hard to contain. After hearing a funeral sermon preached for an acquaintance of his in 1716, Dudley Ryder, a young law student, remarked in his diary that it was a strange thing how very little people thought about their own death, though daily warned of it by the decease of their friends, neighbours, or acquaintances. 'I wish with all my heart', he continued, 'I could bring myself more to think of it.' A few days later he had to confess that the immortality of the soul and the next world made no impression upon him. He was too strongly attached to this one. In August reflection on the recent deaths of some young men he had known temporarily focused his thoughts on mortality. However, when on 30 September he actually witnessed a death (that of his grandmother) for the first time, he found that the spectacle did not shock him nearly as much as he should have expected. He seems to have been quite untroubled by any gloomy reflections.[42]

No reminder of mortality made a more powerful impression on contemporaries than did the plague. Its seemingly inexorable advance instilled a unique dread. Thousands of anxious letters and diary entries monitored its progress. Those who could fled from the

[40] Josselin, *Diary*, 375, 378, 393, 395, 405, 442, 599, 601, 603.
[41] Kay, *Diary*, 9, 10, 19, 20, 28, 44, 46, 47, 142, 145–6.
[42] Delaval, *Meditations*, 48–50, 55–6, 82, 86–7, 155–7; *The Diary of Dudley Ryder, 1715–1716*, ed. W. Matthews (1939), 258, 266, 291–2, 339.

cities where it struck hardest. All his friends were in the country by reason of the plague, wrote John Husee to Lord Lisle in August 1537, one of countless letter-writers to send similar reports.[43] Fear of plague made many turn to God, if only for a time. Thomas Whythorne had to stay in London during the great plague of 1563, probably the worst outbreak of the early modern period. He was greatly troubled by the fear of death, and reflected that plagues were often sent by God as punishments for sin, but reading a sermon and comfortable passages in Scripture helped to reassure him. He persuaded himself of the divine love and willingness to do him good, and wrote a song of thanksgiving based on Psalm 138. The plague of 1563 seems to have affected Whythorne much more profoundly than his earlier bout of ague.[44]

Among pious Christians fear of plague inspired heartfelt prayers for preservation, forgiveness, and greater closeness to God. Between August and October 1603, as the plague spread to northern York-shire, prayers mingled with reports of its near approach in the diary of Lady Margaret Hoby. During the outbreak of 1625, the Puritan London woodturner Nehemiah Wallington and his family heard the continual tolling of bells, saw coffins pass almost every day, and heard how whole families and vast numbers of children had been swept away. They marvelled at being spared, but they could not relax their vigilance, Wallington insisted. Every one of them must prepare for death. In 1665 Ralph Josselin followed the steady progress of the epidemic with growing apprehension, interspersing his notes with prayers such as 'lord brake our hearts and then stepp in, save and deliver us for thy mercy sake'. He thanked God for sparing his parish, especially when so many places round about had been infected.[45]

Terrible though the plague was, it called forth examples of daunt-less courage. In London some magistrates, doctors, and clergy remained at their posts. Some people calmly prepared for death on experiencing the first symptoms. (At Malpas in Cheshire one man dug his own grave in 1625.) William Mompesson, rector of Eyam (Derby.), showed great coolness and heroism as well as a 'hard-headed' realism in his efforts to sustain the morale of his flock and

[43] *The Lisle Letters*, ed. M. St Clare Byrne (6 vols., Chicago, 1981), iv. 376; *Paston Letters*, i. 156.

[44] Whythorne, *Autobiography*, 145–62.

[45] *Diary of Lady Margaret Hoby, 1599–1605*, ed. D. M. Meads (1930), 204–8; R. Houlbrooke (ed.), *English Family Life, 1576–1716: An Anthology from Diaries* (Oxford, 1988), 141; Josselin, *Diary*, 518–22.

prevent them from spreading the infection into neighbouring parishes when plague reached the village in 1666.[46] The strength of the impression left by the plague depended upon individuals' personalities and circumstances. Its effects were sometimes relatively superficial or transitory. In 1665 Elizabeth Livingston, preserved from death despite the infection of her father's house, had to admit that the distress caused by many thousands of plague deaths had had little effect on her life of 'gayety and pleasures'. Despite losing several acquaintances, Samuel Pepys wrote that he had never lived so merrily or made such gains as he had during that plague time.[47]

This uniquely terrifying disease nevertheless cast a widespread pall of anxiety outside the areas of its immediate impact. Its disappearance may have helped to change the psychic climate of Europe.[48] The end of plague in England made little difference to the overall death rate, but urban crisis mortality never again reached the forbidding peaks experienced during the plague centuries. The final cessation of these terrible visitations lifted a recurrent shadow from people's lives.

Life-threatening illnesses were conventionally regarded in the Christian scheme as reminders of mortality and calls to repentance. In popular lore there were a host of omens and portents of coming death or misfortune. John Aubrey collected a number of these. They included a hare crossing one's path, stumbling at the threshold, the spilling of salt towards a person sitting at table, and the spontaneous falling of a tree near somebody's house. 'A Screech-Owl at Midnight has alarm'd a Family, more than a Band of Robbers,' wrote Joseph Addison in 1711; 'nay, the Voice of a Cricket hath struck more Terrour, than the Roaring of a Lion.' Some omens were more specific. A cracking sound made by a pot was a sign of coming death in a family. So at any rate Sarah Harrold, a Lancashire wigmaker's wife, was told in July 1712. She died the following December. Despite Addison's scepticism, various other early eighteenth-century sources record omens which presaged death. Before the tragic accidental death in 1718 of a young married woman of Rothbury in Northumberland, strange moanings and groanings were heard. She and her husband supposedly saw a stream of fire rise from a well and go down their chimney. In 1723, before the deaths of Richard Haworth of Wymond-

---

[46] P. Slack, *The Impact of Plague in Tudor and Stuart England* (Oxford, 1985), 79, 246, 257–66, 268–9, 286–7; Dekker, *Plague Pamphlets*, 161; NRO DN/DEP 48/52, fos. 28ᵛ–29ʳ.

[47] Delaval, *Meditations*, 85–6, 91–2; Pepys, *Diary*, vi. 342.

[48] P. Chaunu, *La Mort à Paris: 16ᵉ, 17ᵉ, 18ᵉ siècles* (Paris, 1978), 187, 454–6.

houses in Lancashire and his child, there were 'several remarkable warnings from the invisible world' including 'knockings or workings as of a carpenter', the calling of Richard's name two or three times, and the repeated opening and shutting of the pantry doors on the night of his death.[49]

Well-attested dreams and visions of death were common. Particularly vivid and odd was John Dee's 1582 dream of talking to various people after his corpse had been disembowelled. They included Lord Burghley, who had come to Dee's house to burn his books. In 1635 William Laud dreamt that a servant of his, whom he knew to be ill, came to receive his blessing. When he woke up, he felt certain that the man was dead or about to die. One of Ralph Josselin's parishioners 'received the sentence of death in her selfe from dreams' in 1656. When the young Lancashire doctor Richard Kay dreamt in 1737 that his beloved father was dead, he was almost overwhelmed by the problems involved in carrying on their practice.[50]

Omens, portents, and dreams cannot be fitted into any consistent pattern. Many of them lacked a precise or obvious meaning. Some dreams came true, others did not. Some dreams of death and loss were rooted in rational apprehensions, others were not. Individuals' reactions to omens and dreams were shaped by their own beliefs, experience, and personalities. A Christian could interpret them as warnings from God, snares set by the devil, or (in many cases) natural phenomena devoid of special significance. All such seeming messages were to be treated with caution. To disregard them could be considered a mark of courage, but the anxious, the superstitious, and those weighed down by a sense of their own sin often took serious notice of them. In November 1740, for example, Richard Kay dreamt that he was shut up in hell, where he imagined he 'kept sinking in a dark and stenchy Place'. The gloomy and introspective Kay was especially susceptible to the influence of such a dream. Waking up, he immediately knelt down to thank God that it was only a dream and that he was still in position to pray. He begged God to undertake his salvation.[51]

Men who faced the danger of death as soldiers and sailors left many

[49] Thomas, *Religion*, 747–51; J. Aubrey, *Remaines of Gentilisme and Judaisme*, in id., *Three Prose Works*, ed. J. Buchanan-Brown (Fontwell, 1972), 216–24; *The Spectator*, ed. D. F. Bond (5 vols., Oxford, 1965), i. 33; Houlbrooke (ed.), *Family Life*, 96–8; Thomlinson, *Diary*, 143; *The Note Book of the Rev. Thomas Jolly, A.D. 1671–1693*, ed. H. Fishwick (Chetham Soc., NS 33; 1894), 149.

[50] *The Private Diary of Dr John Dee*, ed. J. O. Halliwell (Camden OS 19; 1842), 17–18; Laud, *Works*, iii. 224–5; Josselin, *Diary*, 380; Kay, *Diary*, 11–12.

[51] Thomas, *Religion*, 747–8; Kay, *Diary*, 39.

descriptions of their experiences, but relatively few dispassionate analyses of the states of mind of themselves and their comrades. In 1711 Richard Steele, himself a former professional soldier, sought to explain through the imaginary character of Captain Sentry how soldiers overcame the fear of death. Sentry distinguished between a 'certain mechanick Courage' of ordinary men and the habitual resolution of men 'formed for Command'. The former behaved as members of a crowd, trusting in their luck, inured to the loss of even their closest friends, their fear pushed aside by the pressures of immediate business and the prospect of gratification and reward. The latter had convinced themselves that the outcome, whether life or death, must be a good one so long as they did their duty. They were inspired by their cause, the thirst for glory, and the fellowship of danger, among other things. They felt bonds of friendship and brotherhood with their fellow officers and men and a concern for their welfare. The crucial element in the contrast was perhaps the difference between men who had overcome their fear of death by reason and philosophy, and those who had acquired a 'certain Habit of being void of Thought'.[52]

The recorded experience of men who fought in the British Civil Wars bears out Steele's analysis to some extent, though it reveals a more finely shaded range of motives and attitudes. In the first place men were induced to fight by conviction, duty, loyalty, the preservation of honour, and the lure of adventure, or driven to do so by unemployment, conscription, or the threat of eviction. Once part of a company or regiment, soldiers had to subsume their individual personalities and aspirations within those of the larger unit. This sense of being part of a bigger whole helped diminish the individual's fear of death. Training played a crucial part in establishing this larger identity, reinforced by effective leadership, comradeship, and shared experience. Soldiers going into battle were largely inspired by expectations of victory, hope of booty and revenge, alcohol, and relief that the waiting time was over. Some were pushed forward at sword's point. It has been said that troops entering combat were imprisoned in a 'moving box', psychologically by 'the iron laws of tradition, military justice and self-respect', physically by their closed ranks.[53]

The outlook which Steele attributed to the common soldier left little room for religion. On the face of it, the plunder, rapine, and brutal slaughter which accompanied early modern war were fatally

---

[52] *Spectator*, ii. 96–9.
[53] C. Carlton, *Going to the Wars: The Experience of the British Civil Wars, 1638–1651* (1992), 44–69, 74–7, 82, 101–2, 111, 126, 128–9, 174, 255.

inimical to the practice of Christian virtues. The Protestant cause nevertheless produced its own version of the godly hero, above all in the person of Philip Sidney. During the British Civil Wars, there were some men who prayed long and earnestly before joining one of the two armies. Religion played some part in sustaining the morale of the common soldier on both sides. This was particularly true of the parliamentary forces, whose resistance to the armies of their earthly sovereign was largely justified by their higher duty to God. Religious preparation focused on earthly victory rather than heavenly rewards. *The Souldier's Pocket Bible* (1643) drew nearly all its extracts from the Old Testament, where the accounts of Israel's wars and heroes are to be found. Speeches and sermons by officers and chaplains sharpened the resolve to fight by stirring up hatred of the enemy and depicting the parliamentary cause as a good and godly one. Major-General Skippon ended a speech to his men before Turnham Green in November 1642 with the words 'Come, my honest brave boys, pray heartily and fight heartily and God will bless us.' At Edgehill, the parliamentary chaplains were said to have been in the thick of the fight, exhorting the soldiers to fight for their religion and laws. The parliamentary armies were famous for their practice of singing psalms as they marched into battle.[54]

Religion played a less well-documented yet important part on the royalist side. Individuals made their private prayers. 'O Lord! thou knowest how busy I must be this day,' prayed the royalist major-general Sir Jacob Astley before Edgehill, in the best known of all these supplications, 'if I forget thee, do not thou forget me.' The earl of Derby, a High Churchman, made his confession before going into battle in 1651. In January 1643 Sir Ralph Hopton had prayers said throughout the army before the battle of Braddock Down. Before Marston Moor, Prince Rupert's chaplain preached on a text suitably hostile to rebellion. In 1643 one royalist chaplain ran among the troops, encouraging them with 'fearful oaths'.[55]

The smashing-open of a unit by enemy action, or the foundering of a ship, marked a psychological turning-point. Then solidarity all too

---

[54] R. Howell, *Sir Philip Sidney, the Shepherd Knight* (1968), 258–64; Carlton, *Going to the Wars*, 61–4, 80, 86–7, 127; C. H. Firth, *Cromwell's Army* (1902; 4th edn. 1962), 312–13, 318–19, 327–34.

[55] Carlton, *Going to the Wars*, 93, 127; Firth, *Cromwell's Army*, 311–12; Sir Philip Warwick, *Memoires of the Reign of King Charles I . . . Together with A Continuation to the Happy Restauration of King Charles II* (1702), 252; T. T. Carter, *The Doctrine of Confession in the Church of England* (1865), 199.

often disappeared, leaving every man to look after himself. Some died defiantly; others lost their nerve in face of the hitherto unimaginable. Those men whose seeming courage was based upon their being 'more apt to think they shall escape than another man in fight', as Lord Fitzharding put it in conversation with Samuel Pepys in 1665, were 'as much troubled and apprehensive of it as any man else' when death stared them in the face.[56]

A vivid description of the behaviour of some men of action when helpless in the face of extreme danger appears in Bulstrode White-locke's account of how the ship carrying him back from Sweden in 1654 ran aground in the North Sea in stormy weather. All, he wrote, were in great terror and amazement. Some on the ship who had formerly boasted most when there was no danger were now most dejected; 'the sighs & tears & waylings in the ship would have melted a stony heart into pitty'. His sense of duty kept the captain on his bridge. Whitelocke recalled that his own faith had kept him cool in the face of danger. He had encouraged others, and particularly his two sons, to submit to the will of God. If they must die, he told them, they would shortly meet together in heaven. However, the man who showed the most positive courage was the boatswain. It had been revealed to his spirit that God would deliver them. Sure enough, the ship soon floated free. On this occasion the men who behaved best were those whose faith was strong enough to allow them to trust God completely.[57]

Accounts of the vicissitudes of war and seafaring present the seeming paradox that those who exposed their lives to the greatest risks were often surprised and downcast by the immediate prospect of death. One sign of recognition of the dangers faced by soldiers and sailors was to make a will before they left home. In practice few seem to have done so, either because the majority had too little property or because Steele's estimate of their psychology was correct. To make one's will in health was a good sign of readiness to contemplate the worst. However, as we shall shortly see, will-making long remained associated with the nearer approach of death.

[56] Carlton, *Going to the Wars*, 131, 137, 142–5, 195; Pepys, *Diary*, vi. 12.
[57] Whitelocke, *Diary*, 384–6.

4

The Making of Wills

'We brought nothing into this world, and it is certain we can carry nothing out' (1 Timothy 6: 7). The solemn act of making a will is a recognition of the inevitability of death, yet it also declares an individual's wishes concerning the disposal of the worldly goods he or she will leave behind. 'A last wil, is a lawfull disposing of that which anie would haue done after death', wrote Henry Swinburne (d. 1623), one of the foremost civil lawyers of early modern England.[1] He went on to explain that a testament was a form of last will perfected by the appointment of an executor. The executor was responsible for proving the will and fulfilling its provisions. The probate of testaments came within the jurisdiction of the Church courts during the Middle Ages. Medieval landowners often distinguished between the testament, disposing of personal property, and a separate document concerning real property (with which the Church courts could not interfere) by calling the latter the 'last will'. However, the distinction was not always observed, and the term 'last will and testament' came into general usage during early modern times to describe an instrument disposing of either land or goods or both.

The Church played a key part in developing and upholding the right to make a testament. Indeed it taught that it was as much a duty as a right, an expected part of the Christian's preparation for death, and a powerful means of helping the soul. A medieval testament was among other things a means of accomplishing duties of which visiting priests were supposed to remind the sick. Indeed, statutes promulgated in certain dioceses tried to ensure that a priest was present at the making of all testaments.[2] They began with a committal of the soul

---

[1] H. Swinburne, *A briefe treatise of testaments and last willes* (1590), fo. 11.

[2] M. M. Sheehan, *The Will in Medieval England: From the Conversion of the Anglo-Saxons to the End of the Thirteenth Century* (Toronto, 1963), 11–12, 68, 180–1, 231–3, 258–63; *Manuale ad vsum percelebris ecclesie Sarisburiensis*, ed. A. J. Collins (Henry Bradshaw Soc. 91; 1960), 101–3; *John Mirk's Instructions for Parish Priests*, ed. G. Kristensson (Lund Studies in English, 49; 1974), 163–5.

into the keeping of the Almighty and the body for burial in consecrated ground. They usually contained pious bequests to the Church,
and sometimes released debtors from payment. The duty of making a
testament was naturally most important for people of property.
Those who had little to bequeath, or who were debarred from
making a testament by law, could discharge all their most important
Christian duties by word of mouth, without a legal instrument:
declare their faith, dispose of their souls and bodies, seek reconciliation, and forgive their enemies.[3]

The Church also encouraged lifetime giving. A fairly common
theme of later medieval sermons and advice books was the unwisdom
of relying upon executors to fulfil pious bequests. The best way of
making sure that one's intentions were implemented was to carry
them out during one's lifetime. 'That thow geueth wyth thin hond
that shal thow fynd | For wydowes be sloful & chyldren beth vnkynd
| Executors be couetos and kep al that they fynd'.[4]

However, not until the Reformation was it laid down, in the 1549
Book of Common Prayer, 'that menne must be ofte admonished that
they sette an ordre for theyr temporall goodes and landes, whan they
be in health'. The attempt to remove will-making from its traditional
deathbed setting was new. The thoroughgoing reformer John
Hooper, visiting his dioceses of Gloucester and Worcester in 1552,
issued a carefully explained injunction to this effect. All ministers
were to exhort their parishioners, four times a year, to make their last
wills while they were in good health and perfect memory, so that
when sickness came they might be concerned only with such things
as were proper to those certain or likely to die. Such a precaution
would not only give them quietness of mind, but also ensure their
own control over their will-making and lessen the risk of disputes
after their deaths. (A sermon which Hooper had preached in 1550
shows that he was particularly hostile to certain sorts of 'supersti-

---

[3] For a case concerning a choice of burial-place made *in extremis* by a married
woman (who would have been debarred from making a will by the common law), see
Norwich Consistory Court Depositions, 1499-1512 and 1518-1530, ed. E. D. Stone
(Norfolk Record Soc. 10; 1938), no. 125.

[4] *Dives and Pauper*, ed. P. H. Barnum (EETS 275, 280; 1976, 1980), ii. 277-8; *The
Book of the Knight of the Tower*, ed. M. Y. Offord (EETS, suppl. ser. 2; 1971), 179-81;
Peter Idley's Instructions to his Son, ed. C. D'Evelyn (Modern Language Association of
America, Monograph Ser. 6; 1935), 185-9, 191; S. Powell and A. J. Fletcher, ' "In Die
Sepulture Seu Trigintali": The Late Medieval Funeral and Memorial Sermon', *Leeds
Studies in English*, NS 12 (1981), 198; T. F. Ravenshaw, *Antiente Epitaphes (from A.D.
1250 to A.D. 1800) collected and set forth in Chronologicall Order* (1878), 15 (from
St Edmund, Lombard St, c.1500).

University of Winchester

Customer ID: ****0722

Items that you have borrowed

Title: Death, religion, and the family in
England, 1480-1750 /
ID: 9602637685
Due: 02 November 2022

Total items: 1
Account balance: £0.00
05/10/2022 12:12
Borrowed: 1
Overdue: 0
Hold requests: 0
Ready for collection: 0

tious' deathbed bequest, once believed to benefit the soul, but now proscribed or severely discouraged.)[5] Hooper's example was seldom imitated by later bishops, but the advice was taken up in sermons and other works of Christian counsel which called for the settlement of worldly affairs well before death or praised those who had freed their minds of temporal concerns on their deathbeds by making wills in good time. William Gouge pointed out in his especially popular book *Of Domesticall Duties* (1622) that the fit time for making a will was when a man's understanding was still good, and his memory perfect, so that he might call to mind what goods he had to bestow, 'and with discretion and wisdome order his estate'. Yet ancient habits changed only slowly. 'That which should be the *living* Mans care,' complained Timothy Hall in 1684, 'is too often the *dying* Man's task: The ending of our Accounts with Men, and the beginning of our Accounts with God, are both of them generally put off to the inconvenient season of a Death-bed! To reckon with God and Man at once, is too hard a Province for a sick and languishing sinner.'[6]

Various legal restrictions on the freedom to dispose of property by will or testament were removed during early modern times. Acts of 1540 and 1543 allowed the free devise of land by will unless the testator held of the king by knight service, in which case his freedom of disposal was limited to two-thirds of his lands. This remaining limitation disappeared with the abolition of tenure by knight service in 1660. During this period an earlier medieval rule reserving one-third of a man's goods for his widow and another for equal distribution among his children survived only in the ecclesiastical province of York (till 1693), in London (till 1725), and in certain other towns and cities. Only if a man died intestate were reasonable shares of his goods allocated to his widow and children. A widow had a common law right of dower for her life in a third of her husband's lands, but this right was increasingly waived in favour of a settled jointure.[7]

The medieval Church wished the right to make a will to be widely shared. Girls were held to have gained sufficient discretion to do so by the age of 12, boys at 14, but the 1540 statute of wills forbade the

[5] Brightman, *English Rite*, ii. 828; *Visitation Articles and Injunctions of the Period of the Reformation*, ed. W. H. Frere and W. P. M. Kennedy (Alcuin Club Collections, 14–16; 1910), ii. 288; *A Funerall Oratyon*, in *Early Writings of John Hooper*, ed. S. Carr (Parker Soc., 1843), 870–1.

[6] W. Gouge, *Of domesticall duties eight treatises* (1622), 570–1; T. Hall, *A Sermon Preached . . . At the Funeral of Robert Huntington Esq.* (1684), 28.

[7] Short summary of the scope and development of the will in R. A. Houlbrooke, *The English Family 1450–1700* (Harlow, 1984), 229–31.

devise of land by those under the age of 21. The common law insisted that a wife could make a will only with her husband's consent, over-ruling the Church's support for the rights of married women in this regard. The proportion of surviving wills made by wives fell markedly between the mid-fourteenth and mid-sixteenth centuries, when very few were being proved.[8] In summary, the scope of wills was consid-erably increased between the later Middle Ages and the early eight-eenth century. However, property-holding adult males were the chief beneficiaries. Furthermore, wills, though very important in arranging the transmission of wealth, were far from being the only instruments for this purpose. Any property-owning family could use a variety of means besides wills, including settlement agreements and other sorts of transfer between living people.[9]

How many of those free to make wills actually did so? Did will-making become more widespread or less common in the long run? An answer to these questions depends in the first place on the counting of wills proved before the Church courts and entered in their regis-ters. It has been estimated that at least 18 per cent of the adult inhab-itants of the province of Canterbury (which contained a substantial majority of the English population) made wills in the 1560s, at least 19 per cent in the 1620s. In both periods almost exactly a third of adult males left wills; in the 1620s perhaps 5 per cent of women did so.[10] Besides these testators many intestates (people who, though legally capable of making a will, did not do so) came within the net of the Church courts when administration of their estates was granted, usually to the widow or next of kin. About half the men buried in the Kentish Wealden parish of Staplehurst between 1566 and 1601 are covered by extant wills or inventories of their property.[11]

Will registration seems to have been far less systematic during the

---

[8] M. M. Sheehan, 'The Influence of Canon Law on the Property Rights of Married Women in England', *Mediaeval Studies*, 25 (1963), 109-24.

[9] L. Bonfield, 'Normative Rules and Property Transmission: Reflections on the Link between Marriage and Inheritance in Early Modern England', in id., R. M. Smith, and K. Wrightson (edd.), *The World We have Gained: Histories of Population and Social Structure, Essays presented to Peter Laslett on his Seventieth Birthday* (Oxford, 1986), 155-76.

[10] M. Takahashi, 'The Number of Wills proved in the Sixteenth and Seventeenth Centuries', in G. H. Martin and P. Spufford (edd.), *The Records of the Nation* (Wood-bridge, 1990), 212-13. Between c.1560 and 1750 the Prerogative Court of Canterbury took a rapidly increasing share of probate business: see ibid. 190, 198.

[11] M. L. Zell, 'The Social Parameters of Probate Records in the Sixteenth Century', *Bulletin of the Institute of Historical Research*, 57 (1984), 110-11; D. K. Coldicott, *A Long Sutton Miscellany, including a Study of the Wills (1502-1856) and Probate Inventories (1558-1709) from the Parish of Long Sutton and Well, Hampshire*

later Middle Ages than it was during the century after the Reformation. However, will-making appears to have been very widespread during the fifteenth century, as indeed the Church's emphasis on its importance might have led one to expect. In 1407–8 alone, no fewer than eighty-two wills made by inhabitants of two of the thirteen deaneries of the relatively sparsely inhabited diocese of Hereford were proved in the bishop's court. It has been calculated that some 70 per cent of males older than 25 who died in mid-fifteenth-century Suffolk were probably listed by the Church courts as will-makers or intestates.[12]

There are some signs that the proportion of the population making wills fell during and after the seventeenth century. This at any rate is what studies of such different places as Banbury (Oxon.), Long Sutton (Hants), and Terling (Essex) all suggest. In Powick (Worcs.), the percentage of those buried who were testators fell from just over 11 to just over 7 between the last quarter of the seventeenth century and the last quarter of the eighteenth.[13] If a decline did indeed take place, it probably had two main causes: a growth of the proportion of the population which had no property worth bequeathing, and the diminishing authority of the Church.

Most studies of will-making in local communities have shown that the poor were far less likely to come to the notice of the probate courts than were the better-off. Wills or inventories survive for four out of five of the men of Elizabethan Staplehurst described as 'householders', for fewer than one in ten of the 'poor householders', and for none of the 'poor men'. Nearly half the will-makers of sixteenth-century Grantham have been described as 'middling rich'. In Banbury during the years 1700–23 gentlemen, yeomen, and the practitioners of some of the most respected crafts and trades, were all well represented among testators. However, relatively few members of the poorer crafts, a handful of labourers, and none of those described in the burial register as poor left wills which have survived. In some communities the will-making fraction of the population shrank in the

(1979), 3; R. T. Vann, 'Wills and the Family in an English Town: Banbury, 1550–1800', *Journal of Family History*, 4 (1979), 352–3.

[12] Takahashi, 'Number of Wills', 200; R. S. Gottfried, *Epidemic Disease in Fifteenth-Century England* (Leicester, 1978), 22–3, 33.

[13] Coldicott, *Long Sutton Miscellany*, 3; Vann, 'Wills and Family', 352 (this trend was, however, partially reversed at Banbury, 1700–23); K. Wrightson and D. Levine, *Poverty and Piety in an English Village: Terling, 1525–1700* (1979), 34–5, 92, 96; J. A. Johnston, 'The Probate Inventories and Wills of a Worcestershire Parish 1676–1775', *Midland History*, 1 (1971–2), 21.

long term, largely because the numbers of the poor and propertyless grew much faster than those of the better off. In sixteenth- and seventeenth-century Terling (Essex), substantial property-holders 'seem always to have been inclined to make wills'; cottagers and labourers very rarely did so. There, the numbers of wills known to have been made in each succeeding fifty-year period between 1550 and 1699 remained almost exactly the same. The numbers of wealthier and middling villagers increased very little between 1524/5 and 1671, but those of the poor nearly three times over.[14]

Religious change and the diminution of clerical influence may also have resulted in some decline in will-making. After the Reformation there was probably a long-term decline in the administration of the last rites, and the proportion of wills written by clergy fell sharply. In the long run, especially in the eighteenth century, the will lost its former religious character.[15] The decision whether or not to make one became increasingly a matter of convenience rather than a duty. Our knowledge of wills largely depends on their having been registered by the Church courts. After the mid-seventeenth century those courts lost much of their authority and coercive power.[16] In a majority of

---

[14] Zell, 'Social Parameters', 111; S. Coppel, 'Wills and the Community: A Case Study of Tudor Grantham', in P. Riden (ed.), *Probate Records and the Local Community* (Gloucester, 1985), 79; Vann, 'Wills and Family', 355-6; Wrightson and Levine, *Poverty and Piety*, 34-6, 92, 96-7; Coldicott, *Long Sutton Miscellany*, 2; J. A. Johnston, 'Social Change in the Eighteenth Century: The Evidence in Wills from Six Lincolnshire Parishes, 1661-1812', *Lincolnshire History and Archaeology*, 27 (1992), 27-8, 32. 'Making a will was a status symbol rather like marrying by licence was for some': Johnston, 'Social Change', 28. Prof. M. Spufford long ago argued that the need to provide for dependent children was a more important consideration than their level of wealth when individuals decided whether or not to make wills. However, it was of course necessary to have some property worth bequeathing. See M. Spufford, 'Peasant Inheritance Customs and Land Distribution in Cambridgeshire from the Sixteenth to the Eighteenth Centuries', in J. Goody, J. Thirsk, and E. P. Thompson (edd.), *Family and Inheritance in Western Europe 1200-1800* (Cambridge, 1976), 169-73; for excellent short review of this question see E. J. Carlson, 'The Historical Value of the Ely Consistory Probate Records', in C. and D. Thurley (comp.), E. Leedham-Green and R. Dodd (edd.), *Index of the Probate Records of the Consistory Court of Ely 1449-1858*, i. *A-E* (Index Library, 103: British Record Soc. 1994), pp. xxiv-xxv. Prof. Carlson remarks, 'Historical Value', p. xxx, that over half the surviving labourers' wills proved in the diocese of Ely (1449-1858) date from the sixty years 1581-1640. The numbers of labourers can hardly have decreased over the following two centuries.
[15] See below, Ch. 5.
[16] The courts themselves did not always demand the probate of poorer testators' wills. The will of Mary Honial of Great Snoring (Norfolk) was 'exhibited the 5th April 1746 but not Proved the dec[ease]ds effects being und[e]r 5¹' (NRO ANW Wills 97, 1746-7, p. 3). As early as c.1542, when Elizabeth Barett of St Sepulchre's parish in London made her will, the curate 'put yt not in wrytyng then by [cause?] the value of the goodes was so small but resorted [to?] Mr Chaunsler & shewyd hym the matter. And

cases, seeking a grant of probate or administration may have been a sensible or necessary step, but the prospect of action to enforce probate by the courts themselves was now far smaller. The provisions of most early modern wills were fairly simple. If family members and other beneficiaries of wills could agree among themselves, they might be able to do without probate or letters of administration. Against the greater security which the courts' authority afforded had to be set the cost of even the shortest and least contentious court proceedings.

We should note in passing that the proportion of testators among women who were at liberty to make wills (spinsters and widows) was far smaller than among their male counterparts. Only a tenth of female potential testators of Banbury actually made use of their freedom, while about a quarter of the men did so. One-tenth of the potential female testators of Staplehurst came to the notice of the probate courts, compared with about half the men.[17] Why did so few women avail themselves of their right to make wills? The question concerns widows in particular, since few young single people of either sex made them in any case. The most important reason was probably the limited control over the property entrusted to them which most widows enjoyed. Many of them had only a life interest in any land held by their husbands. The scale and nature of provision for the children of a marriage had often been laid down by a husband in his own will. Most widows will have been considerably poorer than their husbands.[18]

Only a minority of those who died in England during this period left wills which survive today. Wills are nevertheless immensely vivid and illuminating documents. Furthermore, they represent— albeit unequally—all ranks save the poorest. There was no clearly defined social borderline between those who made wills and those who did not. Nor was there a hard-and-fast distinction between wills and other, more informal arrangements. The conventional testament was but one of the means by which people passed on their property. Many of the documents filed in probate archives record the oral or nuncupative dispositions which individuals made, sometimes long

Mr Chaunceler willyd hym to put yt in wrytyng and so he dyd' (GL MS 9065A/1, fo. 54ᵛ). Expert advice was not so readily available in most English parishes.

[17] Vann, 'Wills and Family', 352; Zell, 'Social Parameters', 110–11; N. Evans, 'Inheritance, Women, Religion and Education in Early Modern Society as revealed by Wills', in Riden (ed.), *Probate Records*, 55.

[18] A. L. Erickson, *Women and Property in Early Modern England* (1993), 204–7, nevertheless suggests that 'those women who were eligible to do so were more likely than most men to make wills'.

before they died. It is highly unlikely that all such declarations came
to the attention of the courts. The ones which have come down to us
are often extremely simple; many of them are rather clumsily
expressed. One example is a crudely spelt memorandum of the 'will
and mynde of Elizabeth Dowse Widdowe late of the parishe of Kings
Langley deceased made & declared in or about September Anno
domini 1637': 'the said widow douse gave too thomas bigg too the
marage of her daughter All such goods for the present which shee
Could spare from her one nesserey use and All the Rest after her
desese.' Widow Douse was buried on 9 February 1640. An inventory
drawn up three months later valued her few possessions (her clothes,
a few pieces of old furniture, one ewe, and three hens) at £4. 7*s*. 2*d*.[19]
The first part of Widow Douse's dispositions was a gift made in her
lifetime, rather than a will. Written instruments recording such gifts
were 'deeds of gift', which were often made in consideration of some
such benefit as care for the donor during his life. Although such deeds
were not wills at all, some of them were entered in the Church court
registers, probably as a result (in most cases) of action taken by a relative claiming an interest in the deceased's estate.[20] It is likely that only
a small fraction of the nuncupative directions made and the deeds of
gift drawn up were permanently recorded. Very many of those who
left no known will may have made some sort of arrangement to pass
on their possessions before their deaths.

PATTERNS OF WILL-MAKING:
CONTINUITY AND CHANGE

A will indubitably written or subscribed in the testator's hand was
valid even if it had not been witnessed during his lifetime. The valid-
ity of other wills depended upon the presence of two sufficient witnesses. An oral or 'nuncupative' will written down only after the
testator's death on the basis of the concordant testimony of two such
witnesses was acceptable. The exception to the admissibility of nuncupative wills was the rule (laid down by statute in 1540) that all wills
of land must be in writing. The law relating to such wills was made
more stringent by the Act of Frauds of 1677, which required three
credible witnesses and the signature of the testator, or that of his

---

[19] L. M. Munby (ed.), *Life & Death in Kings Langley: Wills and Inventories
1498–1659* (Kings Langley, 1981), 102–3.

[20] BRO D/A1/ (prefix for all probate file and bundle numbers) 37/44, 47; 43/136a,
192; 45/41; 53/145; 54/104, 107; 55/25a; 62/45; 64/74a (a selection dating from 1600
to 1721).

authorized deputy, writing in his presence. The will accepted for probate had to be the testator's last will—hence the conventional term 'last will and testament' normally employed by testators. The last will superseded all previous wills. An alteration in the provisions of an existing will created a new one, though additions could be made to a will by means of a codicil, so long as it was not contrary to anything in the will. The last will presented for probate might be the product of quite a lengthy process of revision and addition. Lord Burghley, for example, reviewed or reformed his will on numerous occasions between first drawing it up in 1579 and his death nineteen years later, including no fewer than seven times between 1586 and 1598. The Lancashire squire Nicholas Blundell signed his sixth will in 1724, when he was 55, over twelve years before his death.[21]

Between the Reformation and the eighteenth century, the previously close connection between will-making and death was loosened. The will became a more secular document and its making more private. Two main sources can be used to chart these developments: wills themselves, and the testimony of witnesses concerning them. A will normally included in its first few lines the date on which it was made, together with a brief description of the testator's state of mind, and very often of his physical health as well. A declaration of 'perfect memory', considered the key indicator of mental health, was common form, though it was not of course sufficient to protect a will against a challenge based on good evidence of mental incapacity. The date of probate, very often entered at the foot of the will, indicates the maximum length of time which can have elapsed between the making of the will and the death of the testator. (A more accurate indication is provided by the date of the compilation of an inventory, where one exists, or the date of burial.) At the end of the will come the witnesses' names. Those named might not have been the only people present. Sometimes the writer of the will recorded his identity by putting a note such as 'scr' or 'writer thereof' after his name.

The testimony of witnesses gives us a fuller picture in that minority of cases in which it is available. The examination of witnesses was an integral part of probate 'in solemn form of law', a procedure which

---

[21] Swinburne, *Briefe treatise*, fos. 23, 185ᵛ–188ʳ, 191ʳ–192ʳ; 29 Charles II c. 2; A. Collins, *The Life of William Cecil Lord Burghley* (1732), 80; *The Great Diurnall of Nicholas Blundell of Little Crosby, Lancashire*, ed. F. Tyrer and J. J. Bagley (Record Soc. of Lancashire and Cheshire, 110, 112, 114; 1968, 1970, 1972), iii. 145. Samuel Pepys made his fourth recorded will on 13 June 1667: Pepys, *Diary*, i. 90; viii. 266; xi. 313. John Evelyn 'new made' his will after a tertian ague in 1682, twenty-four years before his death: Evelyn, *Diary*, iv. 271–2.

gave additional protection to a will which might possibly be open to challenge from interested parties.[22] However, most surviving depositions were probably made in the course of litigation. Disputes arose for various reasons: because the testator had made more than one will, for example; because he was alleged to have been of unsound mind at the time of making his will; or because he had supposedly been subjected to undue pressure by those around him. Yet when due allowance has been made for the exceptional circumstances which often produced them, witnesses' depositions can still yield much vivid and valuable information. Such testimony allows us to go much further than do wills themselves towards setting will-making in its social context and pinpointing the influences of law, religion, customary practice, professional expertise, and individual expectations.

Some of the elements which were characteristic of the process of will-making on the eve of the Protestant Reformation can be illustrated from unusually full and vivid testimony given in a London case of 1544. It involved the will or wills of a Londoner, George Isatson, about which the testator's widow Elizabeth and his son George, the child of an earlier marriage, seem to have been in dispute. Elizabeth's witnesses told their story first.[23] On 11 November 1544, a few days before his death, Isatson, then lying sick in bed, made his confession at his own request to Sir Adam Garrett, a chaplain serving in his parish church of St Alfege, London Wall, and two or three hours later received from Garrett the sacrament of the altar. Afterwards, Garrett reminded Isatson of the shortness and uncertainty of time, recalled that he had been 'a greate Travelor . . . busye with many matters', and advised him to make his testament. Isatson agreed, and Garrett asked him whom he would have present. He named three neighbours, two of whom came to him at once. Isatson began to declare his will, which the parish clerk wrote down on a piece of paper. After a short time, the clerk first asked Isatson what he would give his son George, and then, when Isatson made no answer, said that he would put something down himself. This suggestion upset Isatson, and the attempt to get him to make his will was thereupon given up for the time being.

Two days later, on 13 November, Isatson sent once more for Garrett and for his previous witnesses to hear his will made. His wife and another woman were also present. He then recited the simple provisions of his will, which included legacies to his sister, to a servant boy,

[22] R. A. Marchant, *The Church under the Law: Justice, Administration and Discipline in the Diocese of York, 1560–1640* (Cambridge, 1969), 88–91.
[23] GL MS 9065A/1, fos. 84^r–85^r, 88^v–94^r.

and to the poor women who had tended him during his sickness. He made his wife his executrix. He left his lands to her, and after her death to his son George and his heirs, on condition that George paid half his debts, and did not trouble or vex Elizabeth. Garrett wrote the will down, and then read it to Isatson. Was he content that it should stand for his last will? Isatson answered 'yea', and, holding up both his hands, desired those present to bear witness. His wife allegedly wanted Isatson to let his son George be executor with her, but Isatson told her to hold her peace, saying that she was interceding for a man who would never do her any good.

George produced four witnesses: Sir John Maris, curate of the parish of St Nicholas by the Shambles, and three lay inhabitants of the same parish.[24] They had met each other on the way to Isatson's house during the afternoon of 15 November. Maris was coming at Isatson's request, brought to him by his son. One of the other witnesses, a scrivener and linendraper, urged Isatson to see that he died in charity, giving both his wife and his son what was due to them by the custom of the City of London. He was not to reduce his wife's part because of love for his son, or his son's part for love of his wife. Isatson proceeded to tell the witnesses the main provisions of his will, even though his wife pointed out that this was unnecessary because he had declared it sufficiently already. His son George seems to have objected to being saddled with half his father's debts. He may have thought that he had succeeded in changing his father's mind about this point, but that outcome is not indicated by the surviving testimony.

The witnesses of George Isatson's will described especially fully a number of recurrent features of early sixteenth-century testamentary cases: the close association of the will with impending death, the prominent part played by priests, the comparatively large number of people present, and the manner of the will's declaration. By far the commonest known way of making a will during the first part of our period was to give oral instructions to a scribe who read the will to the testator after writing it down. Both the giving of instructions and the reading very often took place in the presence of witnesses. The gradual and uneven erosion and disappearance of some of these features will be the subject of the analysis which follows. More enduring were the underlying causes of litigation. Personal enmities, especially within the testator's immediate family circle, but also involving

---

[24] Ibid., fos. 102ᵛ–106ʳ (depositions taken in Feb. 1545).

remoter kinsfolk and unrelated acquaintances, have always been responsible for much testamentary litigation. They still are today. The Isatson case seems to present a classic instance of a discordant step-relationship.

The openness of will-making encouraged witnesses to intervene, as the Isatson case shows. The process was one in which others besides the testator could play an active part, reminding him of what was expected of him, seeking to influence him by request, advice, and exhortation. The very act of making a will was often the result of an initiative taken by somebody other than the testator: the priest, friends, or neighbours.[25]

Reluctance to make a will because of the fear that it would bring death closer, or weaken one's control of one's possessions, was widespread. Writers of Christian counsel from Erasmus in the 1530s to William Assheton in the 1690s repeatedly complained of it.[26] Some men shied away from the dread formalities which heralded the end of mortal life. William Naggyngton of West Ham, visited by the curate of the parish two days before his death in 1544, adamantly refused to make his will or receive the sacrament of the altar. In 1570 William Kirkus of Kirk Merrington (Co. Durham) complained that the vicar wanted him to make a will 'with great circumstanc; and many maks a will that he repentith all the daies of his life'. The vicar had only performed his prescribed duty. Kirkus's words betray not only his dread of a formality associated with death but also a seeming belief that a will would be hard to revoke once made even if he survived. It may be that his remark reflects an illiterate man's awe of the written word. In about 1590 two fellow widows of Hinksey (Berks.) urged Joan Bond to appoint what should be done with her goods 'for quietnes sake', and in order to remove any cause for dispute between her children after her death. One of the two neighbours felt sure that Joan would

---

[25] These generalizations are principally based on an analysis of witnesses' depositions in eighty-nine cases concerning wills in the Norwich consistory court (1519–46) and twenty-five cases in the London consistory court (1537–45), in NRO DN/DEP 2/3; 3/4A; 4/4B; GL MS 9065A/1. Cf. the discussion of will-making in D. Levine and K. Wrightson, *The Making of an Industrial Society: Whickham 1560–1765* (Oxford, 1991), 288–90.

[26] D. Erasmus, *Preparation to deathe, a boke as deuout as eloquent* (1538), next folio after sig. C^v (unfoliated); W. Perkins, *A salue for a sicke man, or, a treatise containing the nature, differences, and kindes of death: as also the right manner of dying well* (edn. of c.1638, STC 19747.3), 147; Swinburne, *Briefe treatise*, fo. 24; L. Bayly, *The practise of pietie: directing a christian how to walke* (11th edn., 1619), 639; Gataker, *Certaine sermons*, ii. 224; W. Assheton, *A Theological Discourse of Last Wills and Testaments* (1696), 7–9; S. Coppel, 'Willmaking on the Deathbed', *Local Population Studies*, 40 (1988), 40.

not recover, but nevertheless assured her that she would not die 'any whit the sooner' by settling her affairs. Joan would 'by no meanes' do so, according to one witness, though she did declare her wish that her two children should share her goods equally. Some testators clearly thought that those who pressed them to make a will did so for their own selfish ends. In 1713 Joan Frances, landlady of The Bell public house in Hosier Lane, London, was advised by her brother-in-law to make her will and settle matters, which might prevent a great deal of trouble if she died. She complained angrily that he seemed to want her property before she was gone.[27]

As people tried to make their wills in the face of sickness and approaching death, friends and kinsfolk were all too ready to remind them of their supposed obligations, or to question their decisions. Three examples illustrate the sorts of pressure which were brought to bear. Alison Chambers of Darlington (Co. Durham) was an unmarried woman who lived with her brother John and his wife. When she fell ill in 1588, she wanted to make a will precisely in order avoid trouble between her brothers. After her burial had been paid for and twenty shillings had been given to the poor, the residue of her goods was to go to John. Yet once various people had asked her whether she would give anything to her remaining brother and sister, her resolution seems to have wavered, and 'she said some tyme that they shold have somewhat'. (However, she firmly rebuffed a similar enquiry on his own behalf from a young labourer, remarking that he had never given her anything.) Three years later, in 1591, when Peter Sandford of Garford (Berks.), wished to make his will, some of his children tried to prevent him from doing so, claiming that he was not in his right mind. When Sandford made a second attempt eight weeks later, a local gentleman suggested that he give portions of corn to his children and grandchildren 'where he knewe was neede'. The curate of Fifield, who wrote this second will, put in a word for a neighbour of his, one of Sandford's daughters, whose legacy was enhanced as a result. When Mary Chute of Pawlett in Somerset, probably the widow of a small or middling farmer, set about making her will in 1630, she had to contend with the efforts of her son and son-in-law to influence her decisions

---

[27] GL MS 9065A/1, fos. 74^v, 76, 77^v-78^r; MS 9065A/11, fos. 50^r, 52^r, 108^r-109^v; *Depositions and other Ecclesiastical Proceedings from the Courts of Durham, extending from 1311 to the Reign of Elizabeth*, ed. J. Raine (Surtees Soc. 21; 1845), 214; BRO D/A2/c155, fos. 96^r-97^v; see GL MS 9065A/1, fo. 43^v (1542), for James Walwyn, a London testator who was uncertain whether he might make a new will. A scrivener assured him that he might make as many as he wished.

and even countermand some of her instructions to the scribe. Finally, she lost patience, and insisted that she would make a new will the following day. She could see, she said, that what had been written down so far accorded with her son-in-law's wishes, not her own.[28]

The scribe, often chosen because he possessed a modicum of expertise beyond the mere ability to write, was the person best placed to influence the form and contents of the will. As he was writing down Marion Marham's will (*c*.1536), Stephen Close discussed several of her intended bequests with her, and also asked her various questions, both about her own goods and about the debts that she owed. She reduced the endowment of an obit which Close thought too costly, but even then had finally to insist that the reduced bequest be put in the will, saying 'go to, so lett yt bee, sett ytt in'. A number of writers 'moved' testators to leave something to particular members of their families or asked what they intended to do for them. In 1703 Thomas Craven, a Whitechapel scrivener, informed James Talford of the custom of the City of London when he received Talford's oral instructions, 'and told him t'would be proper to pursue it in the design of making his will'. However, Talford refused to follow his advice. (In 1745 one testator sought guidance from the writer of his will as to whether it was necessary to 'cut off' certain relatives he disliked by leaving them small legacies. They had no right to a customary portion of his goods, but were presumably among his heirs at law. The intended bequests would have shown that they had not simply been forgotten, an oversight which might have called his soundness of mind in question.)[29]

The preamble, with its committal of soul and body, was one of the elements of the will most open to scribal influence. Some writers subsequently admitted that they had supplied preambles themselves. Thus in 1595 Thomas Yate, a gentleman of Fernham (Berks.), described how Thomas Trulocke of Sutton Courtney had dictated his will to him 'savinge the preamble [and] forme of it', which Yate had supplied. In 1596, when Robert Robertes of Maidenhead lay dying, the writer of his will began it with a 'proheme' expressing his trust that he would be saved at the Last Day by the merits of Christ's passion. Only then did he read the preamble to Robertes, 'and desired the said Robert Robertes to speake and declare what goodes, and to

---

[28] *Durham Proceedings*, 328–30; BRO D/A2/c154, fos. 73–6; SRO D/D/Cd 71 (unfoliated).

[29] GL MSS 9065A/1, fos. 6ᵛ–8ʳ; 9182/1 (iv) (loose papers); NRO DN/DEP 61/65, Woolston and Bateman against Rising and Tilney, deposition of William Varden (unfoliated).

whom, he would bequeath or give them'. John Packwood, a gentleman of Wapping who came to write Andrew Ashford's will on the day
of his death early in 1665, described how he went over to the window
of the dying man's chamber to write the preamble while Ashford discussed his dispositions with his wife. When witnesses gave what they
claimed to be a verbatim account of testators' own words, they commonly recalled the simplest of committal formulas or none at all. Such
accounts give the impression that many testators were more interested in the disposal of their bodies than the bequest of their souls.
Alison Chambers, the Darlington woman whose will-making has
already been described, began 'I will that I be honestlie brought forth,
like an honest man's barne, and laid beside my father'.[30]

A competent scribe would make sure that an executor had been
named. He might think it prudent to include a declaration that all previous testaments had been revoked. Edmund Bryghte, a London
scrivener, readily admitted in 1544 that he had added a revocation
clause to James Mounford's will without his knowledge, because it
was the custom among London scriveners to include such a clause
without being required to do so by the testator. Will-writers might
also remind testators, if necessary, of some other formalities, such as
bequests to the high altar for tithes forgotten (customary down to the
Reformation), or to the poor (commonest between the Reformation
and the Civil War). In about 1542 Anthony Levenson of St Andrew's
by the Wardrobe in London began his will with a simple preamble.
Then the scrivener asked what he would give to the high altar.
'"Nothing", quod the said Anthony, "I haue payd my dutie to God"'.
Increasing awareness of the Church's diminished authority would
before long make a hitherto customary payment a thing of the past.[31]

THE REFORMATION AND ITS EFFECTS

The most obvious effect of the Reformation upon the traditionally
dominant pattern of will-making was to diminish the previously high
level of priestly participation. Before the religious changes, local
priests probably witnessed the majority of wills. Witnesses were
named in 97 per cent of over 230 early Tudor wills from Lincoln
diocese printed in a volume which covers the years up to 1527. At
least 75 per cent of the groups of witnesses contained one priest or
more (some of them included three or even four). A priest's name

---

[30] BRO D/A2/c155, fos. 47ᵛ–50ʳ, 117ʳ; GL MS 9065A/1, fo. 101ʳ; 9065A/8, fos. 7ᵛ–8ᵛ;
NRO DN/DEP 3/4A, fos. 269ʳ, 414ʳ, 488ᵛ; *Durham Proceedings*, 329.
[31] GL MS 9065A/1, fos. 51ᵛ, 101ᵛ.

usually headed the list, which may indicate that he wrote the will. Over two-thirds of a collection of wills made in the diocese of London between 1508 and 1547 were witnessed by priests.[32]

The fact that most extant wills made before the late sixteenth century have survived in the form of registered copies means that we cannot be sure who wrote them. Nevertheless, depositions in testamentary cases indicate that priests were by far the most important single source of scribal expertise. In nearly eighty Norwich consistory court cases concerning wills which had been made between *c.*1520 and the end of Henry VIII's reign, over half the wills were clearly said to have been written by priests. Other writers included a parish clerk (almost certainly in minor orders), and a proctor of the bishop's consistory court who was also a notary public. Of some sixteen last wills written in London or its immediate environs whose making was later described by witnesses before the bishop's commissary's court between 1537 and 1545, priests wrote seven, scriveners five. Professional lay scribes were more readily available in the capital than in the mainly rural diocese of Norwich.[33]

Will-making was sometimes the result of an enquiry or a reminder by a visiting priest. Thus Robert Thew, Carmelite friar and curate of All Saints Fiebridgegate in Norwich, moved Henry Goodewyn 'to be at a staye with his wor[l]dely substance' after hearing his confession in 1536. Some priests gave testators good practical advice about the disposal of their estates. Priestly influence was sometimes thought to have been excessive. In 1546 one witness to the reading of the will of William Downes of Martlesham (Suffolk) believed that Downes had been unable to say anything 'but as he was moved by Sir John', the priest who had read his will. The same year the vicar of Honingham (Norfolk), come to give John Dobbes extreme unction, not only exhorted the dying man to give a penny to each of five people, telling him that 'oon peny now gyven was better then xx after', but took Dobbes's purse to the window to see what was in it, while the sick man cried out 'carry not aweye my purse!'[34]

---

[32] *Lincoln Wills*, i. *A.D. 1271 to 1526*, ed. C. W. Foster (Lincoln Record Soc. 5; 1914), 19–188; *London Consistory Court Wills 1492-1547*, ed. I. Darlington (London Record Soc. 3; 1967), nos. 96–245. (Most of these were made by people living in or around London, the majority of them in the 1540s.) Priests witnessed 75% of King's Langley wills, 1523–58: Munby (ed.), *Kings Langley*, 3–24.

[33] Based on analysis of NRO DN/DEP 2/3; 3/4A; 4/4B; GL MS 9065A/1. It is not clear in all cases whether the will-writer was a layman or a priest.

[34] NRO DN/DEP 3/4A, fos. 77ᵛ, 89ʳ, 94ʳ, 116ʳ, 257, 269–70, 273ʳ, 281ʳ, 312ᵛ, 384, 419ʳ, 449ʳ, 488ʳ; GL MS 9065A/1, fos. 12ᵛ–15ʳ, 19ᵛ–30ʳ, 41ᵛ–42ʳ, 54, 65ᵛ, 74ᵛ, 89ʳ.

Testimony in the Norwich consistory court books suggests that priestly participation in will-writing fell sharply after the end of Henry VIII's reign. Of the wills whose making was described by witnesses, little more than a third of those drawn up under Edward VI appear to have been written by priests, a proportion which fell to under a third during Mary I's reign, and to little more than a sixth in the first two years of Elizabeth I's.[35] The Edwardian Reformation took away some of the most important traditional functions of the priesthood—the celebration of the mass, intercession for souls in purgatory, the administration of extreme unction, and the hearing of confessions. The last rites were drastically simplified and stripped of much of their ancient power and mystery. Communion became less readily available to the sick. Only one Norwich case has been found in which witnesses mentioned the viaticum in connection with a will of Edward's reign.[36] Priestly guidance also became less readily available. The numbers of stipendiary priests were drastically reduced by the proscription of intercessory masses. Whereas the majority of clerical will-writers mentioned in the Norwich testimony of Henry VIII's reign had been stipendiaries, the greater number were incumbents of parish livings under Edward. Men of this type were now having to undertake more of the pastoral work previously shouldered by the unbeneficed. The return of Catholicism under Mary I did little to relieve this situation. Indeed, high mortality in the later 1550s helped to create a shortage of critical proportions. So although there is more evidence in the testimony concerning Marian wills of priestly initiative, advice, and celebration of the last rites[37] (which is what one might expect, given the restoration of the old religion), the overall proportion of cases in which priestly participation was described fell even lower than it had been in Edward's reign. During the 1550s there was also a sharp increase in the proportion of testimony concerning oral or nuncupative wills—one reason for which may have been a shortage of readily available expert will-writers. The dearth of clergy continued for a time after Elizabeth's accession. When in 1560 Thomas Toll of Massingham (Norfolk), was asked during his sickness whether he wished to make his will, he answered 'I would yf the parson may be hable to

---

[35] Testimony relating to some 115 wills made during the years 1547–60 has been found in the deposition books compiled during those years, running from NRO DN/DEP 3/4A to 8/7E.

[36] Below, 154–5; NRO DN/DEP 7/6A, fo. 262ʳ.

[37] NRO DN/DEP 7/6A, fos. 162ᵛ–163ʳ, 215ʳ, 227–9, 248ʳ, 262ᵛ; 8/7E, fo. 99.

com vnto me'.[38] He never did, and Toll's oral declaration was posthumously recorded. However, depositions show that other testators were turning in increasing numbers during the 1550s to lay willwriters: not only scriveners, gentlemen, and yeomen but also a husbandman, a servant, and a teenager.[39]

Will-making was commonly a somewhat open affair throughout the Reformation. Wills were declared, or read out, or both. Three or four witnesses, including the writer, were often named in depositions, though in many cases larger numbers, between five and nine, were present. The group in the testator's chamber might include the scribe, members of the testator's family, servants, neighbours, and sometimes fellow tenants who had come to take the surrender of his lands. In fewer than a fifth of the recorded Norwich cases of the years 1509-60 were testators described as declaring their wishes before only one or two people. This was often because they died before customary formalities could be completed.

A majority of testators were sick or close to death when they made their last wills. A number of them did so on the day of death, or within a few hours of it. They tended to be found either in bed or sitting near a fire. Will registers, which contain many thousands of wills, support the impression given by the detailed testimony of witnesses. When testators mentioned their physical health (something which was not everywhere customary), they usually described themselves as sick, weak, or both. During the Reformation, as beforehand, most wills were proved not long after they were made. Of course the length of time varied considerably from one jurisdiction to another: most executors had to travel further to attend a higher court than a lower one. However, in the lowest and most accessible courts, those of the archdeaconry, the proportion of wills proved within two months of their being made was nearly always over 40 per cent, and often much higher. The great majority—usually well over 70 per cent, and sometimes over 90 per cent—were proved within a year.[40]

---

[38] NRO DN/DEP 8/7B, fos. 69^v-70^r. See ibid. 8/7E, fo. 36^r, for the writing of a testament begun by a layman, but then begun anew by a priest whose services were preferred because he could write faster.

[39] Ibid. 4/4B, fos. 268^v, 284^r; 7/6A, fos. 161-2; 8/7B, fo. 18; 8/7E, fos. 46^v-47^r, 72^r.

[40] Below, App. 1; R. Houlbrooke, *Church Courts and the People, during the English Reformation 1520-1570* (Oxford, 1979), 96; Munby, *Kings Langley*, 3-24 (85% of 26 wills made between 1523 and 1558 proved within a year). Of 308 wills of 15th-cent. gentry, 50% were proved within three months of being made, a figure the more impressive in view of the fact that several were proved in the Prerogative Court of Canterbury: P. Maddern, 'Friends of the Dead: Executors, Wills and Family Strategy in

In most will registers, however, a few wills stand out because their makers described themselves as being in good health or because they were drawn up a considerable time, in some cases several years, before they were proved. A readiness to contemplate the possibility of death and to provide against it before its imminent approach was traditionally associated with certain situations: preparation for war or departure on a long journey. It was particularly appropriate for people who had substantial property to dispose of. Perhaps it was also linked with certain personal traits: providence, prudence, and independence. Those who made their wills well before death were more likely than deathbed testators to act as their own scribes (though few did so) or to make use of the best professional advice.

One of the small minority of people who wrote their own wills was Edmund Cooke, of Gorleston (Suffolk), a pensive young man in poor health. His reputedly considerable substance and lack of close relatives gave him incentives to make a will. A desire for privacy and freedom from interference was a good reason for doing so before death became imminent. Some testators dictated their wills to scribes before sending for witnesses. Agnes Woodforth of Heigham (Norfolk), was one of them. She asked a Norwich scrivener to come to her house to write her will in 1554, three years before her death, and told him that she intended to have it witnessed 'secretly'. One Norwich testator, Roland Amery, went a stage further, anticipating today's standard practice when in 1558 he had a witness sign his will without hearing it read. Such a procedure, however, seems to have been very rare at that time.[41]

FROM THE REFORMATION TO THE COMMONWEALTH

After the Elizabethan settlement, the clergy never recovered their once dominant position as will-writers, though they long remained one of the most important groups of scribes, together with yeomen and members of the lesser gentry. Scriveners were active, especially in cities like Norwich. Other writers mentioned in testamentary depositions included not only people whom one might expect to be literate, such as parish clerks, a schoolmaster, an innkeeper, and a beerbrewer, but also a joiner, a tailor, a weaver, a husbandman, and a labourer.[42]

Fifteenth-Century Norfolk', in R. S. Archer and S. Walker (edd.), *Rulers and Ruled in Late Medieval England: Essays presented to Gerald Harriss* (1995), 162.

[41] NRO DN/DEP 4/4B, fos. 35–8, 79–84; 7/6A, fos. 161–2; 8/7B, fo. 19.

[42] BRO D/A2/c40, fos. 119ᵛ–120ʳ; c154, fos. 107ᵛ, 121; c155, fos. 24, 151ʳ–153ʳ; NRO DN/DEP 28/30B, fos. 13ᵛ, 123, 273ᵛ; 36/39, fos. 131ʳ–132ʳ, 236ʳ, 311ᵛ–314ᵛ, 351ʳ, 355ᵛ;

Studies of individual communities show that the availability of will-writers varied greatly from time to time and place to place. In Bury St Edmunds fifteen writers besides the clergy are known to have been at work during Elizabeth's reign. One of these was a woman, Margaret Spitlehouse, who between 1582 and 1596 wrote at least thirteen wills, mostly for people of middling or lower rank. Men described as yeomen were the most active scribes in late Elizabethan Grantham. In Long Sutton (Hants) the curates of the parish may have influenced the preambles of wills as witnesses and scribes down to about 1605, but a blacksmith drew up or witnessed many of the village wills between 1624 and 1681. Will-writing was, then, a very widespread skill and ancillary source of income under Elizabeth and the early Stuarts.[43]

The means by which wills were ratified were also changing. The sealing of wills had been common among wealthy and high-born testators long before 1500,[44] but such manual authentication does not appear to have been widespread among less well-off medieval will-makers. Depositions recorded in testamentary cases before and during the Reformation are largely concerned with the declaration of testators' wishes and their oral confirmation of will-texts read back to them by scribes. Witnesses commonly testified to what they had heard (the contents of the will) as well as to what they had seen (the writing of the document produced in court). Large numbers of depositions in testamentary cases describe no signing or marking of wills by testators or witnesses. Extant wills which refer to the presence of witnesses commonly preface their names with some such phrase as 'these beyng witnesses' or 'byfor theis witnesse'. Unless an

---

38/43, fos. 211, 282. Cf. L. C. Attreed, 'Preparation for Death in Sixteenth Century Northern England', *Sixteenth Century Journal*, 13/3 (1982), 40.

[43] J. Craig, 'Margaret Spitlehouse, Female Scrivener', *Local Population Studies*, 46 (1991), 54–7; Coppel, 'Wills and the Community', 82–7; Coldicott, *Long Sutton Miscellany*, 8–9; C. Cross, 'The Development of Protestantism in Leeds and Hull, 1520–1640: The Evidence from Wills', *Northern History*, 18 (1982), 233; M. Spufford, *Contrasting Communities: English Villagers in the Sixteenth and Seventeenth Centuries* (Cambridge, 1974), 322, 330, 333; see Bayly, *Practise*, 638–9, for recommendation that testators take a 'religious Diuines' advice concerning their benefactions, and an 'honest Lawyers' counsel about how to give legal effect to them.

[44] Sheehan, *Will in Medieval England*, 190–5; *Wills and Inventories from the Registers of the Commissary of Bury St Edmund's and the Archdeacon of Sudbury*, ed. S. Tymms (Camden os 49; 1850), 73, 75, 81, 82–3, 95, 105, 106, 108, 113. Fewer than 5% of the *c*.250 wills printed in *The Courts of the Archdeaconry of Buckingham 1483–1523*, ed. E. M. Elvey (Buckinghamshire Record Soc. 19; 1975) contain references to seals: see ibid., nos. 30, 95, 113B, 162B, 228A, 281, 312, 323, 372.

original will survives it is impossible to tell whether such witnesses signed or marked the will.[45]

Because most wills recorded before the later years of Elizabeth's reign survive only in the form of official copies entered in registers or placed on file, they throw only a very uncertain light on the process of attestation. Nor do such copies often make clear how the testator confirmed the will—by seal, mark, signature, gesture, or word of mouth. In the diocese of Ely, whose probate archive has been very thoroughly studied, the consistory court retained the original wills from about the 1580s onwards. Only two wills made in the village of Willingham before the end of 1600 bear marks, and none bears a signature, even though forty-seven wills were made there in the 1590s alone. Not until the second quarter of the seventeenth century was a substantial majority of surviving wills signed or marked. Nearly half the surviving Berkshire wills made in 1600 were signed or marked, most of those made in 1620. Almost all King's Langley wills made after 1585 bear the testator's mark or signature, as do the surviving original wills from Long Sutton made after 1596. The texts of wills themselves, even in official copies, confirm the fact of manual authentication by the testator. An increasing proportion of the wills made from the late sixteenth century onwards end with some such phrase as 'in wytnes wheareof I have heareunto set to my hand and seal', or 'my hande'. A form of words such as 'sealed, subscribed, published and declared' was very often added. Testamentary depositions of the 1590s describe testators as having confirmed their wills with their hands, seals, or both, in a majority of cases.[46]

The reasons for what looks like a gradual shift from oral to manual confirmation are far from clear, but its consequences were certainly to be far-reaching. Attestation eventually came to focus on the testator's formal ratification of a written document, and especially on signature and sealing, rather than the contents of the will itself. This facilitated far greater privacy in will-making than had hitherto been customary.[47]

---

[45] Swinburne, *Briefe treatise*, fo. 19, makes clear that this formality was not legally necessary. It was not even necessary to ask those present to act as witnesses. However, for some cases in which signing, sealing or marking by testators or witnesses were described, see NRO DN/DEP 3/4A, fos. 235–6; 4/4B, fos. 39, 43–4, 48, 252, 268, 300; 7/6A, fos. 111–12, 129–30, 208, 258ᵛ; 8/7B, fo. 30; 8/7D, fo. 13.

[46] Carlson, 'Ely Probate Records', p. xxxiii ('Quinquennial totals of Willingham wills'), p. xlviii ('Percentage of testators signing own wills'); Spufford, *Contrasting Communities*, 199, 323; Munby (ed.), *King's Langley*, 32–146; Coldicott, *Long Sutton Miscellany*, 13; below, App. 1.

[47] The testator might 'close vp the writing, without making the witnesses priuie to the contents thereof; and shewing the same to the witnesses, . . . say vnto them: *This is my last will and testament*, or *herein is contained my wil*': this was sufficient, but

By the end of the sixteenth century, even wills which would later be read over before witnesses were increasingly often drawn up privately. In 1586 or 1587, for example, John Peien of Thatcham (Berks.) sent for three fellow parishioners to come and witness his will. Already made before their arrival, it was read to them at the testator's request. Peien then sealed and signed it, and the witnesses put their hands to it. He delivered it to his wife, whom he had named executrix. In 1596 Richard Belcher of Abingdon had his will written by the vicar before he sent for two husbandmen to witness it. He then had to send for a third man, a yeoman, to read the will to him and the other witnesses 'for that none of them could reade'. (This last witness was later to be the only one to sign his deposition.) After hearing the will read, Belcher acknowledged it and asked the witnesses to set their hands to it. Here was a testator who, while moving towards greater privacy in will-making, found that his own illiteracy limited his control of the process of ratification.[48]

Several testators wished to keep their intentions secret as long as possible. Some tried to ensure privacy by leaving their own homes for the purpose of will-making, or requesting only the minimum number of witnesses to testify. In May 1592, over eight months before her death, Joan Luckins of Abingdon went to Henry Frie's house to have her will written, so that 'her yong kinsfolke shoulde not truble her or vexe her in doeing the same'. Besides the writer, only Frie and his wife were present. William Alborowe's motive for wanting privacy was similar to Joan Luckins's. In April 1639 he came from his home in Sharrington (Norfolk) to the neighbouring village of Brinton to ask Christopher Walker, yeoman, to write his will 'and desired him to bee very priuate therein, because he would not haue his children to knowe it'. He subscribed, sealed, and delivered the will, the witnesses subscribed it, and he left with it hidden under his jerkin. Thomas Cole of Wenham in Suffolk, signing and sealing his will in 1629, was glad to hear that two witnesses were sufficient, saying 'I care not howe fewe knowe of it'.[49]

---

in order to provide subsequent proof of the identity of the writing it was expedient that all the witnesses write their names 'on the backside, or some part of the testament': Swinburne, *Briefe treatise*, fo. 23ᵛ. Secrecy, as Swinburne pointed out, was the great advantage of this procedure.

[48] BRO D/A2/c40, fos. 78–81; c154, fos. 31, 34. Bayly, *Practise*, 638, advised testators to deliver their wills locked or sealed in a box to a faithful friend in the presence of honest witnesses.

[49] BRO D/A2/c154, fos. 127–8; NRO DN/DEP 38/43, fos. 23–4; 44/48A, fos. 181ᵛ–184ʳ.

The reading before the witnesses might be omitted altogether. In 1629, not long before his death, Simon Loveledge of Acle (Norfolk) had the curate rewrite his will, read it to himself, and then subscribed his name and put his seal to both sheets in the presence of the curate and one other witness. The account underlines the way in which literacy secured the testator's control of the will-making process. A number of other testators were described as reading their wills to themselves during the early seventeenth century. Yet some testators and witnesses found the very idea of attestation without an open reading a strange one. About the middle of James I's reign, Rose Feake, a Norfolk widow, had her will drawn up by a local gentleman, who read it through to her. Her grandson Ambrose then sent for another witness, a miller. Ambrose seems to have laid her will and another 'writing' before her. 'Ambrose, Ambrose,' said the old woman, 'let the man hear them reade.' However, he answered, 'noe grandmoth[e]r you shall not neede to trouble your self so much'. So she proceeded to seal, mark, and confirm her will. In 1625 Mary Morgan, a cutler's wife of St Bride's in London 'was vnwillinge to subscribe' the will of Miles Banckes, telling him 'that she would knowe to what shee should sett her hand', though she later relented.[50]

During Elizabeth I's reign, most wills were probably made not long before death. Between 1562 and 1600 half the testators in the Lincolnshire parishes of Leverton and Grantham whose burial dates are known made their wills within a week before burial, the overwhelming majority within a year. All the Leverton testators who described their physical state were sick. Only a handful of Grantham testators were in good health. In Long Sutton (Hants) between 1562 and 1606, will-making took place under a month before burial in the majority of measurable cases, under a year in all but one.[51]

Patterns observable in the records of larger jurisdictions and over longer periods suggest that there was however a gradual movement away from will-making just before death before the Civil War. In the archdeaconry of Norwich, the proportion of wills made over a year before probate rose from 12.5 per cent to 30 per cent between 1549 and 1649. Few of the Norwich testators whose wills were proved in 1649 over a year after they were made described themselves as sick, as the great majority of Elizabethan testators who gave an account of their physical condition had done. Some were aged, but others

[50] NRO DN/DEP 36/39, fos. 387ʳ, 403ʳ; 38/43, fos. 222ᵛ–223ᵛ; GL MS 9065A/6, 15 Dec. 1625, unfoliated.
[51] Coppel, 'Willmaking on the Deathbed', 37–8; Coldicott, *Long Sutton Miscellany*, 4.

described themselves as being in good health or 'reasonable good health'. Among the testators there were also men who had good reason to make their wills long before death. Robert Greene, a mariner, showed a foresight appropriate to his hazardous occupation. He made his will in September 1638, over a decade before it was proved. In the archdeaconry of Sudbury, 24 per cent of the wills proved between the spring of 1630 and the summer of 1632 had been made more than a year beforehand. In the archdeaconry of Berkshire the interval between the making of the will and the compilation of the inventory of the deceased's estate lengthened markedly between 1600 and 1640. (The inventory was nearly always made before probate, and much closer to death.) Nine per cent of the wills were made less than a week before the inventory in 1600, 55 per cent less than a month, 5 per cent over a year beforehand. The corresponding percentages in 1640 were 4, 21, and 14.[52]

Religious teaching encouraged the move away from deathbed will-making. Its influence was reflected in the lengthy preamble to the 1647 will of Thomas Dolman Esq. of Childrey, scion of a family of wealthy Berkshire clothiers. Consideration of the frailty of human nature, the certainty of death and the uncertainty of its time, together with his desire to free his thoughts from the care of worldly affairs in case of sickness, knowing that Satan was readiest to assault and hurt the soul when his power over it was about to end, had impelled him to make his will.[53] However, whatever the role of religion, it seems likely that the practical advantages of earlier will-making, more private and less open to importunate pressures than deathbed declarations, appealed to a growing minority of testators. Increasing reliance was placed on ratification and attestation by means of seals, signatures, and marks. Together with literacy, these formalities made greater privacy possible.

FROM THE RESTORATION TO THE 1740s

After the Restoration, the emergent patterns of the pre-war decades were confirmed. Priestly participation in will-making declined even further. William Sampson, a later Stuart rector of Clayworth (Notts.), famous among historians for his detailed listings of his flock and his careful surveillance of their behaviour, wrote not a single one of their

---

[52] Below, App. 1; NRO, ANW Wills 1648–52, fos. 155^v–156^r; *The Wills of the Archdeaconry of Sudbury 1630–1635*, ed. N. Evans (Suffolk Records Soc. 29; 1987), nos. 1–450 (in a few cases one of the two relevant dates was not recorded).

[53] BRO D/A1/62/181a; cf. Munby (ed.), *King's Langley*, 128.

surviving wills. In 1681 a Norwich clergyman admitted that he was not skilful in making wills. In the long run, the dominant role in will-writing would pass to scriveners and lawyers, but depositions show that many other lay will-writers were active during this period; gentlemen, yeomen, and men of various callings, including physician, surgeon, schoolmaster, innholder, vintner, draper, grocer, maltster, and fishmonger.[54]

Women, as well as men, sometimes wrote their own wills. In about 1695 Elizabeth Witherly of Norwich gave instructions for her will to her intimate friend Mrs Canning. However, when she saw the result of her friend's efforts, she rejected it, saying that she would not put her hand to so long a preamble. She at once took pen and paper and wrote it out with her own hand. The will of Susanna Tuggy of St Giles in the Fields, widow, was discovered in a box at her lodging the morning after her death in 1705. It had not been witnessed, but she had acknowledged its existence, and her handwriting was verified by three witnesses, including two other women.[55]

The testator's initial instructions (in the majority of cases where somebody else wrote the testament) were usually addressed to the writer alone, though people subsequently produced as witnesses in court had sometimes overheard them, or, more often, the reading to the testator which commonly followed. (Many testators, however, did not have to have their wills read back to them, because they could scrutinize them for themselves.) Some people tried to ensure that their instructions were not overheard, first excluding from the room everybody except the writer.[56]

The normal form of ratification during this period was by signing, sealing, 'publishing', and declaration. Many witnesses did not know the contents of the will they saw ratified. The now standard procedure was described in 1692 by witnesses to the will of Widow Swatman of Mendham (Suffolk). Mrs Swatman sent for two of her

---

[54] *Village Life from Wills and Inventories: Clayworth Parish 1670–1710* ed. E. R. Perkins (Centre for Local History, Univ. Nottingham, Record Ser. 1; 1979), 18; R. C. Richardson, 'Wills and Will-Makers in the Sixteenth and Seventeenth Centuries: Some Lancashire Evidence', *Local Population Studies*, 9 (1972), 35–7; Coldicott, *Long Sutton Miscellany*, 9; BRO D/A1/47/123; D/A1/73/81; D/A1/90/143; GL MSS 9065A/8, fos. 33ʳ–38ʳ; 9065A/10, fos. 8ᵛ–9ʳ; NRO DN/DEP 48/52, fos. 12–14; 51/55, fos. 190–1, 297; SRO D/D/Cd/97, fos. 44–5.

[55] NRO DN/DEP 53/58A (unpaginated; depositions made 28 Nov. 1695); GL MS 9065A/10, fos. 1–5. A woman of a much higher social class, Lady Elizabeth Darcye, had written her own will as early as 1564, but this instance seems to have been exceptional: Emmison (ed.), *Elizabethan Life*, iv. 6–7.

[56] BRO D/A1/47/123 (making of will of Henry Blyth of Brimpton, 1687).

neighbours about a week before her death. She explained that a reading would not be necessary: she had already heard the will read
through to her twice. She put her hand and seal to it, 'published' it,
desired the witnesses to take notice that it was her last will and testament, and asked them to set their hands to it. (The word 'publish' as
used in the case of Mrs Swatman and countless others, meant only
that the testator published the fact that the document shown to the
witnesses was his or her will, not that its provisions were revealed.
One witness testified that the will Mrs Swatman had published was
the same as the one exhibited in court, but he had never heard the tes-
tatrix say what she had left to John Bray or anybody else 'for she was
a very private living woman'.) Some testators also entrusted their testaments physically to their executor. In 1705 Edward Dyer of Longcot
(Berks.) reportedly said 'I doe deliver this to my wife as my last will
and Testament'.[57]

Although it was by no means uncommon for only two people to
witness wills in the late seventeenth and early eighteenth centuries,
three was the more normal number. The 1677 Statute of Frauds
insisted upon three credible witnesses to all devises of land. It probably influenced customary practice even in the case of those wills
concerned with movables alone. In 1685, for example, Henry Bolt, a
Berkshire farmer, told John Hill, a yeoman in his sixties, that Hill's will
would not be good in law without three witnesses. Yet since Bolt, as
a witness to the will, later testified in court that he was not acquainted
with its contents and had never heard it read, it is hard to see what
grounds he can have had for saying so.[58] The average number of witnesses, which had fallen between the Reformation and the Civil War,
therefore rose slightly after 1677, but eighteenth-century wills were
rarely witnessed by more than three people. Subscription or marking
by witnesses was now normal practice. In 1675 Mary Cozens of Stoke
Talmage (Oxon.) was asked to witness the will of her friend Anne
Martin, but 'not knowing how to write her name desired that she
might be left out', testimony which both underlines the importance
of written attestation and points to a feeling of disadvantage on the
part of those incapable of it.[59]

The average length of time which elapsed between the making of
the last will and death or probate was tending, albeit slowly and

[57] NRO DN/DEP 53/58A (unpaginated); cf. *Sevenoaks Wills and Inventories in the
Reign of Charles II*, ed. H. C. F. Lansberry (Kent Archaeological Soc., Kent Records, 25;
1988), p. xxv; BRO D/A1/64/25c.
[58] BRO D/A1/82/68.   [59] BRO D/A1/98/137.

unevenly, to increase in the long term. A growing minority of testators made their wills over a year before they died. This may have been
due in part to a declining propensity to make wills among the less
well-off. However, the lengthening of the interval between will-
making and burial is too marked to be explicable chiefly in terms of
changes in the social composition of successive cohorts of will-
makers. Whereas the great majority of sixteenth-century testators had
described themselves as sick, those who gave some account of their
state after the Restoration employed a much wider range of terms,
including 'weak' (much more frequently used than previously), 'aged
and weak', 'infirm', 'indisposed', 'somewhat indisposed', 'in indifferent health', 'in good health', and 'in perfect health'. These descriptions suggest that many testators settled their earthly affairs in
response to an 'early warning', while others needed no such stimulus.
Yet the numbers of testators who completed their wills shortly before
death remained high in various places. In the town of Sevenoaks,
50 per cent of the testators whose dates of burial can be verified made
their wills within a month of it during Charles II's reign. In the rural
parish of Clayworth nearly two-thirds did so within twelve days of
burial between 1670 and 1710. In some parishes, the propensity to
ratify wills on the deathbed remained strong at the very end of the
period. At Horbury (Yorks.), 62 per cent of the testators of the decade
1741-50 whose dates of burial are known were interred less than a
week after their wills had been witnessed. Only one went to the grave
over a year later.[60]

NUNCUPATIVE WILLS

The informality of the nuncupative will, which depended for its
implementation on being heard by at least two witnesses, stood in
stark contrast with the formality and privacy characteristic of a growing number of written wills. However, contrary to the reported mis-
conceptions of some witnesses, properly witnessed nuncupative

[60] Coldicott, *Long Sutton Miscellany*, 4 (7% of wills made more than a year before
burial, 1562-1606; 43%, 1669-97; 71%, 1760-1810); Johnston, 'Social Change', 32
(%age of male testators making wills more than a year before burial rose from 15 in
1661-1700 to 37 in 1701-33). About half the wills registered in the archdeaconry
courts of Norwich and Berkshire in the mid-18th cent. had been made over a year
before probate. The corresponding proportions in 1600 had been 22% (Norwich) and
10% (Berkshire): see below, App. 1 for details of wills analysed. *Sevenoaks Wills*, ed.
Lansberry, p. xiv; *Village Life from Wills*, ed. Perkins, 3 (at Clayworth, 1670-1710,
nearly a third of testators made their wills over a year before burial, but nearly two-
thirds within twelve days of it); *The Will of Horbury*, ed. K. S. Bartlett, ii. *1688-1757*
(Wakefield, 1980), 102-27.

wills remained valid and continued to be admitted to probate throughout this period.

Some of them were relatively casual utterances, not (it seems) inspired by any thought of imminent death. So James Champe of Mortimer (Berks.), who died in 1607, 'walking abroade did say vnto two of his neighbors: That his three childrene should haue two kine a peice and that his wife should pay his debts out of [th]e rest and yet there wilbee some thing left for her selfe'. Other nuncupative testators were like Widow Conisby of Bray, 'haueing an intent to make hir last will & Testam[en]t in writeing but being by the suddennesse of hir death thereof surprised'. Some, such as Richard Bassett, yeoman, of the parish of Thatcham, were questioned by neighbours. Lying on his deathbed in 1644, he was asked what he would give to his son Richard, who should have his beds, and who should be his executor. Thomas Barton, husbandman, of Kingston Bagpuize, sitting upright in his deathbed in 1627, was asked by his wife whether he would give his daughter half a quarter of barley: he 'then answered yea [and] fell speechlesse shortlie after'. The onset of the plague was the occasion for the making of many nuncupative wills. The nearness of death concentrated the mind upon the most important things: essential provision for wife and children above all. Testators who died without the support of close relatives might seek to recompense those who had helped them in their hour of need. In 1741 Charles Chittester, a private soldier, was suddenly seized with yellow fever in Port Royal harbour in Jamaica. Before he was taken ashore, he borrowed from Corporal George Ellis half a guinea—probably in order to mitigate the horrors of confinement in a tropical hospital. He told Ellis that if he never saw him again, everything he had in the world should be his. In 1742 Anne Door of Kintbury (Berks.), dying of smallpox, was asked how she intended to dispose of her money and effects. She wanted Robert Adams, in whose house she had lived before she fell ill, to 'take to all and pay all . . . For She was the last of the Family & had no Brothers or Sisters or Brother or Sister's Children living'.[61]

CONCLUSION

Will-making changed in important ways between the fifteenth and the eighteenth centuries. It ceased to be something in which the clergy had an important part to play. By 1750 the attorney had

---

[61] BRO D/A1/43/122a, 123a, 156a, 157a; D/A1/45/8, 18a; D/A1/53/175a; D/A1/56/46a, 48a; D/A1/59/206a; D/A1/64/133a.

replaced the clergyman as the main source of professional expertise in matters testamentary, though the lawyer had by no means yet achieved the dominant position enjoyed by the confessor before the Reformation. The connection between death and will-making had been loosened. No longer was a close association between the will and the last rites thought to be natural and proper. Ever since the Reformation, some churchmen had been calling for worldly affairs to be settled in time of health, to allow the deathbed to be devoted to preparation for the next world. This advice was increasingly reinforced by considerations of worldly prudence in an ever more complex market economy. Will-making was now regarded as a more private affair than had generally been the case two hundred years earlier. Indeed the desire for privacy was a good reason for making one's dispositions in good time, so as to minimize the risks of pressure and interference. The move away from oral confirmation of a publicly read document to reliance on ratification by witnessed signature and seal facilitated the move to privacy. All these developments: secularization, the spread of earlier will-making, and the growth of privacy, were underpinned by the rise of literacy, which gave individuals much greater understanding of, and immediate control over, the instruments by which they disposed of their property.

The extent of change must not be overstated. Throughout this period, prudent men of property began to plan the settlement of their worldly affairs long before death. The making of the last will was often but one phase in a long process of property transfer in which other legal instruments played an important part. In many cases the 'last' will was only the final link in a series of wills, or a document prepared long beforehand but not ratified until death approached. On the other hand, very many people still made their wills on their deathbeds in the 1740s. Some wills were still delivered orally; the change from memory to written record was not yet complete. It seems likely that very many people passed on their belongings by means of brief and informal instructions, oral or written, without the help of the probate courts.

So far we have been concerned with the process of will-making and its context, but the changing significance and functions of wills cannot be understood without looking more closely at their form and contents. To these we now turn.

5

Last Wills and Testaments:
Form and Contents

The medieval will was both a religious and a secular document. It bequeathed soul, body, and worldly goods. Most testators declared their Christian faith by committing their soul to God, and left bequests both to the 'pious uses' defined by the Church and to the relatives they left behind on earth. The gradual shrinking of the religious functions of the will during the centuries following the Reformation is the main theme of this chapter. Wills have been the subject of close analysis and much controversy in recent decades. They have been studied for the light they throw upon the development of religious opinions, the changing nature of charitable bequests, and the strength of individual relationships with families and neighbours. Research has tended to focus on particular communities or topics. This survey takes a broad and long view of the evolution of the will as a document drawn up in preparation for death.

FAITH AND WORKS IN THE ENGLISH WILL

Before the Reformation

Certain elements, especially in the preamble to the will, are common to the great majority of late medieval English wills, but there were also considerable differences in patterns of pious and charitable bequests between regions, dioceses, and communities, as well as between town and countryside. There was also great variety in the choices made by individual testators, especially the wealthier ones, in accordance with their own preferences and personal loyalties. The composite picture which follows is based upon a number of local studies.[1]

The first important bequest made by the overwhelming majority of testators was that of the soul to Almighty God, the Virgin Mary, and all

---

[1] Duffy, *Stripping of Altars* is now the most comprehensive account of late medieval popular piety.

the saints in heaven. The Virgin Mary was regarded as a uniquely effective intercessor on behalf of sinful human beings. A minority chose a formula simpler or more elaborate than the usual one. Some mentioned God alone; others added their patron saint, or the saint to whom their parish church was dedicated. Nearly all testators asked that their bodies be buried in consecrated ground. Most specified the parish church or churchyard, a minority a cathedral or religious house. By the close of the Middle Ages, priests, most of the gentry, and the wealthier inhabitants of towns, were requesting burial within the church. Beneficed clergy and more important laypeople often asked to be interred near the high altar or elsewhere in the chancel. Others specified a place near the grave of a relative, before an altar or saint's image, or in the porch. However, most people were interred in the churchyard. That was where the majority of testators requested burial, as is apparent from those probate archives where the largest numbers of wills survive, covering the widest social spectrum.[2]

The place where people wished to be buried was also the main focus of their pious benefactions. The overwhelming majority of testators made some bequest, however small, to their parish church. Most of them left to the high altar, or for tithes forgotten, a sum ranging from 1*d*. to 6*s*. 8*d*. The incidence of this practice varied, however: almost universal among Norfolk testators, it was less widespread in Buckinghamshire.[3] Other bequests of money to churches were very numerous. Most were for the repair of the fabric or for new building. They ranged in value from a few pence to several pounds; some were to be paid in kind. Rood-screens, windows, porches, bells, bell-towers, and steeples were mentioned in many wills. Some

---

[2] P. W. Fleming, 'Charity, Faith, and the Gentry of Kent 1422–1529', in J. Pollard (ed.), *Property and Politics: Essays in Later Medieval English History* (Gloucester, 1984), 50; V. Harding, 'Burial Choice and Burial Location in Later Medieval London' and R. Dinn, 'Death and Rebirth in Late Medieval Bury St Edmunds', in S. Bassett (ed.), *Death in Towns: Urban Responses to the Dying and the Dead, 100–1600* (Leicester, 1992), 119–35 and 152–3 respectively; N. P. Tanner, *The Church in Late Medieval Norwich, 1370–1532* (Toronto, 1984), 11–13; M. G. A. Vale, *Piety, Charity and Literacy among the Yorkshire Gentry, 1370–1480* (Borthwick Papers, 50; 1976), 8–9; of 50 wills registered in the archdeaconry of Norwich between 1497 and 1500, 90% specified churchyard burial (below, App. 1); 61% of 83 wills registered in the archdeaconry of Buckingham, 1483–97: see *The Courts of the Archdeaconry of Buckingham, 1483–1523*, ed. E. M. Elvey (Buckinghamshire Record Soc. 19; 1975), 1–189. Many wills proved in this court were not registered, esp. those of poor testators: *Buckingham Archdeaconry Courts*, pp. xxii, 303–9, 311–14. Cf. A. D. Brown, *Popular Piety in Late Medieval England: The Diocese of Salisbury 1250–1550* (Oxford, 1995), 253.

[3] Below, App. 1; *Buckingham Archdeaconry Courts*, 1–189 (*c.*74%); Duffy, *Stripping of Altars*, 356 and n. 71; Tanner, *Church in Norwich*, 127.

testators left items of liturgical equipment. A gentleman of Windsor directed in 1519 that the substantial sum of £10 be spent on 'vestimentes copys bokes or Any other ornamentes most nedfull' under the oversight of the mayor and his brethren.[4]

A particularly popular purpose of pious bequests was the maintenance of votive lights (i.e. candles). Well over half the testators in Berkshire and Norfolk left money or gifts in kind for their upkeep. The majority of lights specified were those dedicated to saints, above all the Virgin Mary. The saints, it was hoped, would intercede for those who honoured them in such a tangible, useful, and symbolically potent fashion. Lights in honour of Christ, especially before the rood, but also before the Easter sepulchre or the sacrament of the altar, were popular as well.[5]

Religious guilds or confraternities existed in enormous numbers in pre-Reformation England. Their importance, however, varied from one part of the country to another. A substantial majority of Norfolk wills included bequests to them, but only a minority of Berkshire or Buckinghamshire ones. Over a quarter of the Norfolk testators were benefactors of two or three guilds. In 1500 James Andrews of Wiveton hoped that his legacy of four bushels of malt to St Mary's guild would both assist his soul and promote conviviality. It was to go towards a drinking of ale for the guild's profit, with the intention that his soul might be admitted to the brotherhood to be prayed for in perpetuity.[6]

Bequests for prayers and masses were numerous. A mass at the month's mind and the twelve-month's mind, a trental of thirty masses, usually sung in the first month after burial, or a combination of these, may well have formed part of the normal funeral provision for people whose estates could meet the cost. Most testators who mentioned masses requested something different, which was perhaps an addition to the basic provision. Some stipulated that celebration continue for half a year or one year. Thomas Plummer of Cublington (Bucks.) requested that the rector say a mass, preceded the day before by the office of the dead, once a week for a year. Considerable faith was placed in the concentrated power of a large number of masses said in a short time, but they were often combined with a series of services

    [4] BRO D/A1/1A, fo. 32[r–v].
    [5] Below, App. 1; Duffy, *Stripping of Altars*, 134, 146–8; Tanner, *Church in Norwich*, 84, 118 (lights increasingly popular on eve of Reformation); D. R. Dendy, *The Use of Lights in Christian Worship* (Alcuin Club Collections, 41; 1959), 110–18; J. J. Scarisbrick, *The Reformation and the English People* (Oxford, 1984), 4, 8, 54.
    [6] Scarisbrick, *Reformation and English People*, 19–39; Tanner, *Church in Norwich*, 73–82; below, App. 1; NRO, ANW Wills, Fuller alias Roper, fos. 305[v]–306[v].

spread over a longer period. Thus Edward Watson of Saham Tony (Norfolk) provided both for a hundred masses sung by 'religiowse men' all on one day and for a trental spread over a year. More substantial testators provided for terms of service lasting several years or even decades. A much cheaper alternative to a daily or weekly service over such a span of time was the anniversary, or obit, the celebration of masses on the day of the individual's death or funeral. However, only a small minority of those who endowed masses sought to establish them in perpetuity. (Many long-term chantries were not established by will, because it was prudent to start making the arrangements for their foundation well before death.)[7]

A place on the bede-roll of the parish church would ensure that one was prayed for by name at least once a year. Such inclusion had to be secured either by means of an annual payment or by a particularly generous gift to the church. The famous 'Black Book' of Swaffham (Norfolk) records over 120 benefactors, of whom nearly half were husbands and wives, about one in ten priests. The book gives a vivid impression of the wealth of precious things given to their church by the richer members of a prosperous later medieval community. Other gifts went to rebuild and furnish the church. Every Whitsunday mass was celebrated for benefactors. The following day, after a mass of requiem sung specially for John Botwright, the rector who started the book in 1454, the lengthening list of donors was recited, with an injunction to pray for each one named. Several had made lifetime gifts, a reminder that wills give only an incomplete picture of the great range of pious benefactions.[8]

One major exception to the concentration of bequests on the local parish church was the legacy of between a penny and a shilling to the cathedral church long customary in certain dioceses, such as those of Lincoln and Salisbury. Some people of substance left money to two or more churches of parishes where they held land. Outside the

---

[7] Just under half the Norwich archdeaconry wills registered in 1497–1500 included such provision, nearly all those of a wealthier group of testators registered in the archdeaconry of Berkshire, 1509–20 (below, App. 1); *Buckingham Archdeaconry Courts*, 61, 159; J. T. Rosenthal, *The Purchase of Paradise: Gift Giving and the Aristocracy 1307–1485* (1972), 27–8, 41; NRO, ANW Wills, Fuller alias Roper, fo. 312[v]; Duffy, *Stripping of Altars*, 370–1; Dinn, 'Death and Rebirth', 159–65; BRO D/A1/1A, fos. 15[v], 21, 30; C. Burgess, ' "By Quick and by Dead": Wills and Pious Provision in Late Medieval Bristol', *EHR* 102 (1987), 846–7, 855–6; Scarisbrick, *Reformation and English People*, 5–6.

[8] Duffy, *Stripping of Altars*, 334–7; F. Blomefield and C. Parkin, *An Essay towards a Topographical History of the County of Norfolk* (2nd edn., 11 vols., 1805–10), vi. 217–22.

immediate neighbourhood, the friars were probably the most favoured beneficiaries. The friaries in Norwich and other Norfolk towns attracted bequests from rural as well as urban testators. Outside the upper classes and wealthy citizenry there was relatively little support for monks. Many of the nobility and gentry inherited family connections with individual older houses which were still important. Norwich was unique among major towns in its testators' generosity towards hermits and anchorites.[9]

Material help for the poor and afflicted was one of the most important Christian duties. The prayers of the honest poor were held to be especially efficacious, and they were explicitly requested or even required by some testators. Nevertheless, bequests to the indigent were far less numerous than ones to the parish church or to priests. They were most widespread among the upper classes and wealthy townsfolk, some of whom gave large sums. Such bequests took many forms. Probably the most popular were the funeral dole, either in money or in food and drink, and the provision of mourning garb for the poor men who carried torches in the funeral procession. The total doles specified by testators of middling rank were generally rather modest, and the most favoured provision for each poor person was a penny or a penny's worth of bread.[10] Hospitals (most of them in or near towns) and contributions to the relief of prisoners and the dowries of poor maidens were also favoured by urban testators in particular. London seems to have been outstanding in the scale of testamentary support given to large civic projects. Bequests towards the repair of roads and bridges were a relatively popular form of benefaction in Buckinghamshire. The most ambitious charitable foundations,

---

[9] Scarisbrick, *Reformation and English People*, 4, 6; over a quarter of Norwich archdeaconry wills 1497–1500 included bequests to friars, nearly all to more than one house (below, App. 1); Tanner, *Church in Norwich*, 58–64, 119–25; J. A. F. Thomson, 'Piety and Charity in Later Medieval London', *Journal of Ecclesiastical History*, 16 (1965), 189–90; Fleming, 'Charity, Faith, and the Gentry of Kent', 48–9; Rosenthal, *Purchase of Paradise*, 82; Brown, *Popular Piety*, 29.

[10] Duffy, *Stripping of Altars*, 355, regards almsgiving as 'one of the two main religious preoccupations evident in the wills made before 1540'. Yet in the archdeaconries of Berkshire, Buckingham, and Norwich only a small minority of testators made explicit provision for alms (*Buckingham Archdeaconry Courts*, 449; below, App. 1). Even in London only 13.4% of wills registered in the consistory court, 1522–39, 'left money to relieve poverty'; a higher proportion of wealthy testators made such bequests: S. Brigden, *London and the Reformation* (Oxford, 1989), 41. Cf. R. Whiting, *The Blind Devotion of the People: Popular Religion and the English Reformation* (Cambridge, 1989), 6, 278 (20% of surviving Devon and Cornwall wills of non-gentry testators, who included several wealthy people, 1520s), and Brown, *Popular Piety*, 199.

such as almshouses, were often established during benefactors' lives, rather than by will.[11]

A substantial majority of testators directed their executors to dispose of the residue of their estates as might be to the pleasure of God and the best advantage of their souls: 'in dedes of charyte messes syngyng and other Almes dedes', specified Richard Broun of Alby (Norfolk) in 1499. Hardly a single testator made a will without pious provisions. The great range of possible objects of pious benefaction made for an enormous variety in the contents of individual wills. Yet every so often one encounters a testator who stands out because of the exceptionally marked individuality of his provisions. One of these was William Dagar, a Norfolk man whose will was proved in 1500. The very fact that he wrote it for himself was unusual. He left his soul to Father, Son, and Holy Ghost, with no mention of a saint. He wished to be buried in the earth, specifying no consecrated place, and left no money to the high altar. All these elements of his will suggest an independence of mind bordering on the nonconformist. Yet his request that the soul bell be rung for him at the moment of death 'in tokenyng [of] callyng to god for help', and his desire for a trental of masses on the day of his burial both seem thoroughly orthodox. His provision for 'a grave stone in tokenyng [of] my karkas' sits somewhat uneasily with the show of unconcern in his bequest of his body. The precise significance of Dagar's will is now hard to fathom, but it is clear that a thinking and literate layman could, well before the Reformation, depart from the conventional phraseology of the priestly scribe when writing his own will.[12]

A sense of the intimate interpenetration of the physical and the spiritual was a central element of the piety shown by these late medieval testators. Their generosity was centred on the church where they would be buried. While their bones rested with those of their ancestors and neighbours, their piety spoke in the light of candles, in stones, glass, and vestments, and intercessions rose in sung masses, responses to the reading of the bede-roll, and the prayers of the poor. Yet less than twenty years would suffice to destroy these long established patterns of devotion.

On the eve of the Reformation wills evinced few if any signs of an imminent collapse of support for the Catholic Church. In Norwich, for example, nearly three-quarters of all lay testators provided for

[11] Tanner, *Church in Norwich*, 132–7, 223; Thomson, 'Piety and Charity', 180–9; *Buckingham Archdeaconry Courts*, 449; Burgess, 'By Quick and by Dead', 845–7.
[12] NRO, ANW Wills, Fuller alias Roper, fos. 301^r, 305^r.

masses, prayers, or religious services between 1490 and 1517, while
no fewer than 97 per cent made bequests to parish churches. Both
proportions were higher than they had ever been before. They were
almost as high between 1518 and 1532. Bequests to hermits or
anchorites, to votive lights, and even to the cathedral church and pri-
ory, actually reached a peak after 1518. The onset of the continental
Reformation had little discernible effect. In London, the proportion
of wealthier testators endowing anniversary masses for their souls
was greater in the late 1520s than ever before.[13]

The Reformation

The Reformation brought fundamental changes in the pattern of
pious bequests. The religious houses had been dissolved by 1540. (In
the south-west, bequests were still being made to the friaries in the
year of their dissolution.) The royal injunctions of 1538 forbade lights
to be kept before any image in future, restricting them to the rood-
loft, the Easter sepulchre, and the altar. From 1547 they were permitted only on the altar; in 1549 they were ordered to be removed from
there too. In 1538 all images to which offerings or pilgrimages had
been made were ordered to be removed; in 1548 all others. Not surprisingly, bequests to images and lights collapsed during the 1530s
and 1540s.[14]

Legislation and an increasingly restrictive royal licensing policy had
made the endowment of perpetual masses all but impossible by the
mid-1530s. Successive official statements of doctrine between 1536
and 1543 undermined the doctrine of purgatory. The dissolution of
religious houses along with chantries attached to them gave an impression of brutal royal indifference to the fate of the souls of founders.
More elaborate or expensive forms of provision for longer periods
understandably declined sharply from about 1530 onwards. Yet
according to one estimate, as many as two-thirds of testators explicitly
asked for intercessory services as late as the mid-1530s. Both in north-
east England and in East Sussex, the proportion of testators providing
for prayers and masses remained high until the 1540s. People still
accepted the value of intercessory prayer, but feared that money
invested in its longer term forms would be wasted. Confraternities
were hard hit by the developing apprehension and mistrust. Both in

---

[13]   Tanner, *Church in Norwich*, 222–3; Thomson, 'Piety and Charity', 179, 192.

[14]   Whiting, *Blind Devotion*, 122; *Documents of the English Reformation*, ed.
G. Bray (Cambridge, 1994), 181, 249; *Documentary Annals of the Reformed Church
of England*, ed. E. Cardwell (2 vols., Oxford, 1844), i. 74–5..

the south-west, where they seem to have been especially popular, and in London, support for them by way of wills plummeted between the 1520s and the 1540s. There was also a sharp fall in the numbers of names added to bede-rolls. These developments were an understandable response to increasingly threatening official policies.[15]

In 1547 a long-feared blow fell: Edward VI's first parliament explicitly condemned the doctrine of purgatory and empowered the government to dissolve guilds and chantries and seize all capital devoted to the support of prayers for the dead. A few testators nevertheless continued to provide for masses after 1547. The first Book of Common Prayer, introduced in 1549, abolished special masses for the dead, but allowed Holy Communion 'commonly called the Masse' to be celebrated at funerals, and a few testators requested this service between 1549 and 1551; it too disappeared in 1552. Masses, though regarded as especially efficacious, had never been the only vehicle of intercession for the souls of the dead. During Edward's reign, a number of testators simply requested another person, not always a priest, to say prayers for them. Two Reading men, for example, making their wills in 1549 and 1550, asked their wives to do so.[16]

Royal injunctions of 1536 and 1547 tried to redirect the flow of pious benefactions from purposes now defined as superstitious to more constructive ends, above all the relief of the deserving poor, now held more conducive to the health of donors' souls. In 1547 the clergy were instructed to exhort their neighbours, especially when they made their testaments, to give money to the parish poor chest, instead of a variety of 'blind devotions'. This duty of exhorting the dying to be liberal to the poor was also emphasized in the Books of Common Prayer. It is hardly surprising that during the Reformation years the proportion of testators making bequests to the poor increased rapidly all over the country. This can be seen wherever one looks: London (where the growth in dire poverty was probably most dramatically evident), Sussex, Berkshire, the south-west, the north-east, and Norfolk. Desire to help donors' souls was an important motive. Indeed, a high proportion of them probably expected the

---

[15] A. Kreider, *English Chantries: The Road to Dissolution* (Cambridge, Mass., 1979), 78, 84–6, 93–153; Scarisbrick, *Reformation and English People*, 5; L. C. Attreed, 'Preparation for Death in Sixteenth Century Northern England', *Sixteenth Century Journal*, 13/3 (1982), 45–6; G. J. Mayhew, 'The Progress of the Reformation in East Sussex 1530–1559: The Evidence from Wills', *Southern History*, 5 (1983), 52–3; Whiting, *Blind Devotion*, 30, 277; Brigden, *London and Reformation*, 389.

[16] NRO, ANW Wills, Aleyn, 215bᵛ–216bᵛ, 219bᵛ; Mayhew, 'Progress of Reformation', 53; BRO D/A1/2, fo. 30; D/A1/5, fo. 84.

prayers of those who benefited from their charity. Many wanted their
alms dispensed in a fashion which recalled the chronological patterns
of intercessory masses. So William Ylsley of Burghfield (Berks.), provided in December 1549 for bread, cheese, and beer to be distributed
at his funeral and month's mind. In 1548 Elizabeth Fyntcham of South
Lynn (Norfolk) wanted a dole dispensed on the day of her burial and
twice a year thereafter for three years. Finally, she directed her executors to sell the residue of her goods and give the proceeds to poor
people for the wealth of her soul, her husbands' souls, and all Christian souls. Many people provided for distribution of alms to the poor
rather than the officially approved gift to the poor chest or box
'accordinge to the Kinges Iniunctions'. Some, like Nicholas Catton, a
husbandman of Barney (Norfolk) gave to both (1549). He left 1s. to
the box, but the much larger sum of £2. 6s. 8d. to be disbursed for him
to the poor of the parish in seven annual instalments by his son.[17]

All over the country there was a marked fall in bequests to the
church and to church repairs between the 1530s and the 1550s. The
small bequest for tithes negligently forgotten was on its way out during Edward's reign even in the conservative south-west, and in Norfolk, where it had once been all but universal. In the dioceses where
small offerings to the cathedral church had been customary, they fell
away sharply. Nor did other sorts of charitable gift now explicitly
encouraged by various episcopal injunctions, towards roads, bridges,
poor scholars, and poor girls' dowries, come anywhere near com-
pensating for the decline in these once popular benefactions.[18]

Some testators continued the previously very widespread practice
of giving their executors discretion to employ the residue of their
goods to the best advantage of their souls. If trusted executors used
this opportunity of paying for some form of intercessory service,
there would be no record of it. In both Norfolk and Berkshire this
type of provision usually went hand in hand with a traditional or non-
committal preamble. In August 1551 Richard Wyer of St Mary's parish

---

[17] *Documents of English Reformation*, 176, 255; Brightman, *English Rite*, ii.
828–9; 475–6; Brigden, *London and Reformation*, 481–2; Mayhew, 'Progress of Reformation', 52–3, 55; Whiting, *Blind Devotion*, 278; Attreed, 'Preparation for Death', 46;
BRO D/A1/5, fo. 102; NRO, ANW Wills, Aleyn, fos. 213b^v–214b^r, 233^v–235^v; C. Litzenberger, 'Local Responses to Changes in Religious Policy based on Evidence from
Gloucestershire Wills (1540–1580)', *Continuity and Change*, 8 (1993), 432.

[18] Whiting, *Blind Devotion*, 131–2, 276–7; Attreed, 'Preparation for Death', 46;
Brigden, *London and Reformation*, 485; Litzenberger, 'Local Responses', 431; *Visit-
ation Articles and Injunctions of the Period of the Reformation*, ed. W. H. Frere and
W. P. M. Kennedy (Alcuin Club Collections, 14–16; 1910), ii. 112, 188, 240, 266.

in Reading left his soul to Almighty God, scrupulously made the traditional offerings to Sarum cathedral and for tithes negligently forgotten, left £1 to the poor and money towards the finishing of St Mary's
church, and enjoined his wife to do for his soul and all Christian souls
as God should put in her mind.[19]

Almost every will began with the committal of the soul into the
hands of God, but the Blessed Virgin Mary and all the saints, or the
whole company of heaven, previously joined with God or named as
intercessors on the soul's behalf, disappeared from an increasing
number of wills. There were two especially popular alternatives. The
bequest of the soul into the hands of God alone, without mentioning
the saints, had prefaced some wills in the decades before the Reformation, but now became much commoner. This formula has been
interpreted in different ways. Some historians have described it as
non-traditional, others have called it neutral. At various stages of the
Reformation this discreet formula might serve to conceal very different personal opinions: incipient Protestantism in the 1530s, and a discreet conservatism in the 1560s. The second alternative was to couple
the committal of the soul into God's hands with an affirmation of faith
in Christ's merits or passion. This has been generally thought to be a
positively Protestant formula, though the Catholic Church had long
encouraged dying Christians to place their hopes of salvation in
Christ's sacrifice on the Cross. The subtlest and most cautious analyst
of will preambles is inclined to see this formula as 'neutral' unless
coupled with a more explicit indicator such as disavowal of trust in
other means of salvation. It was sometimes combined with conservative bequests. Furthermore, several testators, of whom Henry VIII was
perhaps the most outstanding example, combined elements of more
than one major type of preamble. All over the country the same broad
pattern is discernible: abandonment of the traditional form of preamble began under Henry VIII, and change accelerated under Edward
VI, culminating in the widespread adoption of declarations of faith in
Christ's saving merits. However, the pace and scale of the change
nevertheless varied greatly in different parts of England. It was most
pronounced in such places as London, Norwich, and the coastal towns
of East Sussex. In north-eastern England, on the other hand, traditional
formulas remained by far the most popular during Edward's reign.[20]

[19] BRO D/A1/4, no. 160.
[20] A. G. Dickens, *Lollards and Protestants in the Diocese of York, 1509-1558*
(1959), 171-2; Mayhew, 'Progress of Reformation', 38-9, 46, 50, 58-62; Litzenberger, 'Local Responses', 420-2, 426; *John Mirk's Instructions for Parish Priests,*

One thing seems clear. Rather than representing independent currents of thought, those who chose and wrote preambles very often
took their cue from official directives.[21] As early as 1536, the eighth of
the Ten Articles denied that 'any saint is more merciful, or will hear us
sooner than Christ', thus calling in question the invocation of saintly
intercession in wills. *An Exhortation against the Fear of Death*,
among the Homilies published in 1547, preached trust in God's
mercy through the merits of Jesus Christ. In 1549–50 the invocation
of saints was condemned together with the doctrine of purgatory in
more than one set of injunctions. The radical Bishop Hooper went further, enquiring whether anybody made or wrote wills with 'traditional' preambles, which he denounced as injurious to God, perilous
for the salvation of the dead, and dangerous to the maker. His pressure led to their abandonment in his diocese of Gloucester in the early
1550s.[22]

In choosing will preambles the majority of scribes and testators
probably sought to conform to official policy, with varying degrees of
enthusiasm, or masked their own views. Only small minorities reso-
lutely held back or moved ahead of the column, but the seeming
ambiguities of official statements often allowed some room for individual choice. The less common variants employed were extremely
numerous and finely shaded. A study of nearly 2,500 wills drawn up
in East Sussex between 1530 and 1559, the most thorough of its kind,
sets out over fifty distinct preamble formulas, many of them ex-
hibiting only small, but possibly significant, differences.[23] Whereas
the Reformation drastically curtailed the previously exuberant variety
of pious bequests, its effect on preambles was the opposite: a relative
uniformity gave way to great diversity.

Was the choice of preamble the testator's or the scribe's? If the
scribe chose the formula, did he thereby express his own opinions,
use a standard form, or offer the testator a choice from a range of such
preambles which he had memorized or copied out? Research has

ed. G. Kristensson (Lund Studies in English, 49; 1974), 164; Duffy, *Stripping of Altars*,
507–9; T. Rymer, *Foedera* (The Hague, 1739–45), vi/3 142–3; Brigden, *London and
Reformation*, 383–4, 483–6; E. Sheppard, 'The Reformation and the Citizens of Norwich', *Norfolk Archaeology*, 38 (1981–3), 56; Attreed, 'Preparation for Death', 40.

   [21] As cogently argued by Duffy, *Stripping of Altars*, 506–14.
   [22] *Documents of English Reformation*, 172; *Certain Sermons or Homilies*, ed.
G. E. Corrie (Cambridge, 1850), 102; *Documentary Annals* ed. Cardwell, i. 76, 95;
Visitation Articles and Injunctions, ii. 306; Litzenberger, 'Local Responses', 417–18,
425–6.
   [23] Mayhew, 'Progress of Reformation', 39–40, 58–61 (a far larger number of minor
variations); Litzenberger, 'Local Responses', 426.

uncovered examples of practice which suggest or illustrate all these possibilities. By itself, the analysis of will preambles offers no reliable barometer of the changing climate of belief. Even when they seem reasonably explicit, they usually give us only a very partial view of an individual's opinions. Very often their precise meaning is obscure. Yet to deny them any value as evidence of religious opinions would be even more mistaken than placing an uncritical trust in them. They need to be read in conjunction with other provisions in the will which may throw a fuller or different light upon the testator's religious preferences.[24]

Preambles are nevertheless sometimes so exceptionally full and unequivocal that they offer a clear picture of the testator's most important religious tenets. William Tracy was posthumously condemned as a heretic in 1531 because he had made his soon notorious preamble a manifesto of Lutheran belief. He explicitly disavowed trust in any mediator save Jesus Christ and any reliance on his own good works. This Gloucestershire gentleman's preamble, soon circulating in manuscript and later in print, subsequently inspired several other testators as far afield as Sussex and the West Riding. The earliest known was William Shepard of Mendlesham in Suffolk, who made his will in 1537, but Shepard's very long declaration of faith contains sufficient elements peculiar to him to show that he was a careful and discriminating borrower. He belonged to a local group of 'Christian brethren' which was to suffer persecution under Mary Tudor.[25]

Although there was a major swing back towards the use of fully traditional formulas in southern England under Mary I, they appeared in fewer than half the wills made during these years of Catholic reaction. More testators than ever before combined old and new elements in their declarations of faith. This was what one of the

---

[24] J. D. Alsop, 'Religious Preambles in Early Modern English Wills as Formulae', *Journal of Ecclesiastical History*, 40 (1989), 19–27; S. Coppel, 'Wills and the Community : A Case Study of Tudor Grantham', in P. Riden (ed.), *Probate Records and the Local Community* (Gloucester, 1985), 81–6; Litzenberger, 'Local Responses', 422–4; C. Haigh, *English Reformations: Religion, Politics and Society under the Tudors* (Oxford, 1993), 199–202; E. J. Carlson, 'The Historical Value of the Ely Consistory Probate Records', in C. and D. Thurley (comp.), E. Leedham-Green and R. Dodd (edd.), *Index of the Probate Records of the Consistory Court of Ely 1449–1858*, i. *A–E* (Index Library, 103, British Record Soc., 1994), pp. xxxvi–xlvii.

[25] J. Craig and C. Litzenberger, 'Wills as Religious Propaganda: The Testament of William Tracy', *Journal of Ecclesiastical History*, 44 (1993), 415–31; *Wills and Inventories from the Registers of the Commissary of Bury St. Edmund's and the Archdeacon of Sudbury*, ed. S. Tymms (Camden os 49; 1850), 130–3; D. MacCulloch, *Suffolk and the Tudors: Politics and Religion in an English County 1500–1600* (Oxford, 1986), 178–9.

principal architects of the Marian restoration did: Stephen Gardiner trusted to be saved 'by mediacion of [Christ's] bludde and passion . . . and by the intercession of all the companny of heaven'. In the north-east of England there was a much more pronounced resumption of older ways: nearly two-thirds of all Marian testators used the trad-itional preamble, and over three-quarters of the formulas used may be described as conservative.[26]

However, we must look to the other bequests for more solid evi-dence of readiness to return to old habits and to invest in traditional devotions. There was an encouraging rise in the number of testators making bequests to the parish church, though it is questionable whether it was proportionate to the extensive programme of restor-ation necessitated by the depredations of the previous reign. More striking, however, is the failure of bequests for masses and obits to return to the level of the later years of Henry VIII's reign. There was very little support for religious confraternities. Even lights were endowed by few testators.[27]

Wills testify above all to the conservatism or wary conformism of the great majority of English people in the face of the dramatic devel-opments of the Reformation. Testamentary provisions changed in response to the perceived or anticipated trends of government pol-icy. There was no point in investing money in forbidden practices or in pious gifts which might shortly be confiscated. Yet even after the doctrine of purgatory had been repudiated, a dwindling number of will-makers continued to ask for prayers, or to express the hope that the disposal of their earthly possessions might do their souls good. Official efforts to channel pious benefactions into alternative chan-nels, above all poor relief, met with some success. The revival of dis-tinctively Catholic benefactions under Mary Tudor was slow, partial, and patchy. The meagre scale of bequests for intercessory masses reflected lasting doctrinal doubts and uncertainties about future pol-icy. The official Reformation had done damage to the old devotions

[26] Brigden, *London and Reformation*, 629–30; Mayhew, 'Progress of Reformation', 46–7, 51; P. Clark, *English Provincial Society from the Reformation to the Revolution* (Hassocks, 1977), 100; Sheppard, 'Reformation and Citizens of Norwich', 56; Litzen-berger, 'Local Responses', 425–7; *Wills from Doctors' Commons*, ed. J. G. Nichols and J. Bruce (Camden os 83; 1862), 42; Attreed, 'Preparation for Death', 40; Duffy, *Strip-ping of Altars*, 518–23.

[27] Brigden, *London and Reformation*, 581–2, 588; Attreed, 'Preparation for Death', 46, 51–2; Mayhew, 'Progress of Reformation', 52–5; Whiting, *Blind Devotion*, 42, 68–9, 99–100, 111–12, 276–7; Duffy, *Stripping of Altars*, 551–5; L. M. Munby (ed.), *Life & Death in Kings Langley: Wills and Inventories 1498–1659* (King's Langley, 1981), p. xii; Litzenberger, 'Local Responses', 431, 434.

which was irreparable in the short term, but there is little sign that it had so far implanted the new religion in the hearts of more than a minority.

1558–1660

The old formula committing the soul to God, the Blessed Virgin Mary, and all the saints in heaven all but disappeared during Elizabeth's reign. In most areas of the country this happened quite quickly after 1558, though in some remoter areas it took rather longer. This preamble became a badge of deliberate religious conservatism or recusancy. As such, it was used well into the seventeenth century.[28]

Many testators left their souls to almighty God alone, often described as their maker, or maker and redeemer. This unrevealing formula was by far the most popular in the diocese of Exeter during the 1560s and in north-eastern England between 1558 and 1588. In the south-east, it was used by over 40 per cent of Berkshire testators in 1580, and by about 30 per cent on the eve of the Civil War. It is to be found in over a quarter of the West Suffolk wills of the early 1630s. Even in some parishes where Puritan ministers were active, like Dry Drayton in Cambridgeshire, or ones later notable for the Puritan fervour of leading parishioners, like Terling in Essex, such reticent formulas were the ones most commonly used until at least the second half of Elizabeth's reign.[29]

In the early seventeenth century preambles which invoked the merits of Christ or expressed reliance on him were the most popular, and in much of southern England were used by the majority of testators. A pithy and confident formula recommended by William West in his *Symbolaeographia* (1590), a comprehensive guide to the various forms of legal instrument—'First I commend my soule into the handes of God my maker, hoping assuredly through the onely merites

---

[28] BRO D/EBt/F43 (copy of the will of Edward Gage Esq., 1 Mar. 1614); *The Wills of the Archdeaconry of Sudbury 1630–1635*, ed. N. Evans (Suffolk Records Soc. 29; 1987), no. 841.

[29] Whiting, *Blind Devotion*, 157; Attreed, *Preparation for Death*, 40; D. M. Palliser, *Tudor York* (Oxford, 1979), 250; below, App. 1; *Sudbury Wills 1630–1635*, nos. 1–450; M. Spufford, *Contrasting Communities: English Villagers in the Sixteenth and Seventeenth Centuries* (Cambridge, 1974), 327–8; K. Wrightson and D. Levine, *Poverty and Piety in an English Village: Terling 1525–1700* (1979), 155; D. K. Coldicott, *A Long Sutton Miscellany, including a Study of the Wills (1502–1856) and Probate Inventories (1558–1709) from the Parish of Long Sutton and Well, Hampshire* (1979), 8; *Darlington Wills and Inventories 1600–1625*, ed. J. A. Atkinson *et al.* (Surtees Soc. 201; 1993), 10.

of Jesus Christ my Sauiour to bee made partaker of life euerlasting'[30]—was widely favoured. However, other testators preferred to begin on a humbler, suppliant note, beseeching God to receive their souls or be merciful to them for Christ's sake, and forgive their sins. The merits of God the Son were coupled with the mercy of God the Father in a number of other formulas. Some testators simply mentioned their trust or hope that they would be saved without any explicit reference to Christ, but others emphasized that they hoped to be saved, as one Berkshire testator put it, 'by grace throwe fayeth in Christ Jesus and by no other wayes meanes or merittes'.[31] Only a minority of preambles, however, dwelt upon Christ's 'death and pretious blood shedinge', his 'blody passion', or his 'passion and all sufficient sacrifice . . . offered upon the alter of the Crosse'.[32]

The focus of Christian hopes in the hereafter was variously expressed: salvation, everlasting life, eternal happiness, the kingdom of heaven, or a combination of those things. Some looked forward to entry into the glorious presence of God, or to reigning in glory with Jesus Christ for evermore. The prospect of joining the blessed saints or angels, the elect, or the chosen people of God was quite frequently mentioned. While some preambles voiced testators' hopes of acceptance into the ranks of the elect company, others expressed their confidence of belonging to it, 'assuredly trustinge to be one of [God's] saved people', for example.[33] The great majority of preambles were concerned with the destination of the soul rather than with the ultimate fate of the body. A relatively small number expressed hopes of resurrection. Fewer still were those which made explicit reference to the reunion of soul and body, or described the incorruptible nature of the risen body.[34]

---

[30] W. West, *Symbolaeographia. Which may be termed the art, description or image of instruments, covenants, contracts &c* (1590), sig. MM[v]. (West included various other formulas, terser or more prolix.)

[31] BRO D/A1/40, 92a, 141a; D/A1/41, 137a, 140a, 150a; D/A1/53, 119a; Munby (ed.), *Kings Langley*, 39, 41-3, 47, 55-62, 65, 69, 72, 74; NRO, ANW Wills, Bastard, fos. 45[r-v], 57[v].

[32] *The Will of Horbury*, ed. K. S. Bartlett, i. *1404-1688* (Wakefield, 1979), 28, 56, 59, 63, 64; *Darlington Wills and Inventories*, 11; Wrightson and Levine, *Poverty and Piety*, 158.

[33] *Will of Horbury*, i. 48; BRO D/A1/43, 44a, 48a; Coldicott, *Long Sutton Miscellany*, 8; NRO, ANW Wills, Bastard, fos. 52[r], 57[v]-58[r], 59[r]; R. C. Richardson, 'Wills and Will-Makers in the Sixteenth and Seventeenth Centuries: Some Lancashire Evidence', *Local Population Studies*, 9 (1972), 34-5; *Sudbury Wills 1630-1635*, nos. 20, 106, 120, 128, 141, 171.

[34] *Sudbury Wills 1630-1635*, no. 91; *Will of Horbury*, i. 61; Munby (ed.), *Kings Langley*, 55; *Durham Wills*, iv. 251; BRO D/A1/62, 174a; Spufford, *Contrasting Communities*, 325, 342.

Before the Reformation it had been customary to specify the resting-place of the mortal remains—church or churchyard—during their separation from the soul. However, it was not unknown even then for testators to refer the fate of their body to God's will, or simply require Christian burial or 'holy sepulture'.[35] Unconcern about the fate of the corpse was appropriate in a Christian. What mattered was the destination of the soul. The Protestant reformers saw burial in consecrated ground as a matter of respect and convenience, but it could do the dead themselves no manner of good. So the indifference about the place of burial which had hitherto been unusual gradually became conventional during the century following the Reformation. By the 1640s the majority of testators were leaving their bodies to the earth, or specifying no precise resting-place. The manner of burial was increasingly left to executors' discretion.[36]

The preambles of the later Elizabethan and early Stuart periods present fewer dramatic contrasts than do those of the years of upheaval in the mid-sixteenth century. Most of them cannot confidently be categorized as Calvinist or anti-Calvinist, but some ministers stamped the wills of a generation of parishioners with the imprint of their own distinctive combination of Protestant tenets.[37] Some of the lay scribes who were taking an increasingly large share of the business of will-writing relied on one pattern for most of their preambles. Many seemingly distinctive preambles were based on printed formularies, including the oft-reprinted *Boke of Presidents* (1543), and William West's *Symbolaeographia*. Other patterns enjoyed a wide circulation in manuscript. Yet several writers clearly experimented with a variety of formulas and may well have offered their clients a choice. The close resemblance between an elaborate and ostensibly fervent testamentary declaration of faith and a pattern in a formulary does not deprive the will of all value as

[35] *Bury Wills and Inventories*, 83, 105, 114; *Buckingham Archdeaconry Courts*, 21, 319.
[36] Greaves, *Society and Religion*, 697, 701; *Sudbury Wills 1630–1635*, p. xii; D. Levine and K. Wrightson, *The Making of an Industrial Society: Whickham 1560–1765* (Oxford, 1991), 342–3; over 60% of Berkshire wills made in 1640, 84% of those registered in the archdeaconry of Norwich in 1649, specified no particular resting-place: below, App. 1. The chronology of change varied from place to place: see Coldicott, *Long Sutton Miscellany*, 9 (churchyard burial normally specified till 1642).
[37] Munby (ed.), *Kings Langley*, p. xi; D. Beaver, '"Sown in Dishonour, raised in Glory": Death, Ritual and Social Organization in Northern Gloucestershire, 1590–1690', *Social History*, 17 (1992), 397.

evidence of individual opinions, especially if it stands out from the run of surviving local testaments.[38]

A minority of testators gave careful thought to the composition of their will preambles. Some indeed used them as manifestos for the declaration of their own view of the nature of the Church: the Northamptonshire Presbyterian Robert Smith in 1573, Edmund Wyther, Brownist of Bury St Edmunds, in 1588, and, most famously, the Coventry preacher Humphrey Fenn, who in 1631 used his will to protest against the 'ceremoniall bondage of our Church'. Less controversially, Francis Hastings (d. 1610) prefaced his draft will with a confession of faith which takes up half the document. It begins with an unusually explicit exposition of his predestinarian belief, commending his soul into the hands of God, who had chosen Hastings to be his child before he had done either good or evil. Only after setting out the responsibilities which his election placed upon him did Hastings acknowledge God's gift of his only son Jesus Christ, by whose death men's life had been restored. The faith which enabled men to grasp 'this unspeakable mercy' was produced by the grace of the Holy Ghost inwardly working in them.[39] Eloquently expressive of the opposite pole of opinion within the Church from that represented by this famous Puritan is the will which William Laud made in the Tower early in 1644. Its second and third paragraphs contain prayers for forgiveness and remission of sins. It places hope in the merit and mediation of Jesus Christ, the merciful compassion of God the Father, and the love of the Holy Ghost. Not for Laud any confidence of election or happy anticipation of entry into the heavenly company, but a humble prayer that God might prepare him for, and preserve him in, the hour of his dissolution, and receive him 'to that rest which He prepared for all them that love and fear His name'. He sought the forgiveness of all those whom he had offended, and claimed that he died a true member of the Catholic

---

[38] Spufford, *Contrasting Communities*, 320 and n. 4, 325-6, 331-2, 334-44; B. Capp, 'Will Formularies', *Local Population Studies*, 14 (1975), 49-50; E. Poole, 'Will Formularies', *Local Population Studies*, 17 (1976), 42-3; Coppel, 'Wills and the Community', 82-7; Alsop, 'Religious Preambles', 19-27.

[39] Craig and Litzenberger, 'Wills as Religious Propaganda', 418-20; *The Letters of Sir Francis Hastings, 1574-1609*, ed. C. Cross (Somerset Record Soc. 69; 1969), 116-19 (dated 'Before *c*.1596', and preceded by an incomplete earlier draft will consisting entirely of an even longer preamble). In 1608 George Abbot warmly commended the unusual preamble in which the earl of Dorset, while mentioning his confident belief that he was one of the elect, also acknowledged that he was bound to do as many good works as he could: G. Abbot, *A sermon preached at Westminster May 26, 1608. At the funerall solemnities of Thomas earle of Dorset* (1608), 19-20.

Church 'within the communion of a living part thereof, the present Church of England'.[40]

Some testators omitted the customary religious preamble altogether. Among them were the makers of 14 per cent of the wills proved in the archdeaconry of Sudbury in 1630–2. Most of these wills were either nuncupative or very simple documents disposing of rather small estates. The bequest of the soul and body seems to have been regarded as an inessential formality by many of those who disposed of their worldly belongings without the benefit of expert advice.[41]

Bequests to the parish church and the cathedral declined still further after 1558. As late as 1620 both sorts of bequest were still being made by over a quarter of Berkshire testators, but they dwindled rapidly thereafter. In West Suffolk church bequests had all but disappeared by the 1630s. Almost all these legacies were small sums of money for repairs or unspecified uses. The bequest made by Elizabeth Jenyson of Walworth (Co. Durham) in 1605 of a carpet for the Communion table, a pulpit cloth, and cushions of green velvet, was exceptional.[42]

Many of the wealthier testators provided for funeral sermons. In Elizabethan Essex, more than one in six merchants provided for them, and one in eight esquires, but only one in ten of the mere gentlemen, and few members of the middling ranks of society.[43] Some of these bequests recall the patterns of intercessory provision. As late as 1590 Margaret Rampston of Chingford (Essex) provided for funeral and 'month's' sermons. In 1579 Margaret Ayloffe left money for twenty sermons to be preached at Runwell (Essex); at every one five shillings were to be distributed to the poor.[44]

---

[40] Laud, *Works*, iv. 441–2.

[41] *Sudbury Wills 1630–1635*, nos. 1–450. Cf. Munby (ed.), *Kings Langley*, pp. x, 37, 52, 56, 67, 83, 93, 102–3. However, some nuncupative wills *did* include a bequest of the soul, see Beaver, 'Sown in Dishonour', 397, and *Sudbury Wills 1630–1635*, no. 696.

[42] Below, App. 1; *Sudbury Wills 1630–1635*, 467 (seven bequests for repairs in 894 wills); Beaver, 'Sown in Dishonour', 410–12 (bequests to parish, including church, but excluding poor relief, appear in 35% of 1590–1615 wills, 13% of 1616–40 wills); Coldicott, *Long Sutton Miscellany*, 10, 58 (last bequest to Winchester cathedral, 1624); *Wills and Inventories from the Registry at Durham*, pt. iv, ed. H. M. Wood (Surtees Soc. 142; 1929), 6.

[43] Emmison (ed.), *Elizabethan Life*, iv. 1–321; cf. *Sudbury Wills 1630–1635*, 468 (17 out of 894 mostly non-gentle testators made bequests for funeral sermons). Funeral sermons (paid for by executors) were, however, almost certainly far commoner than these figures suggest.

[44] Emmison (ed.), *Elizabethan Life*, iv. 25, 26, 53–4, 70, 96, 176, 185, 213, 230, 242, 274, 281, 300; *Sudbury Wills 1630–1635*, nos. 514, 563, 580, 612, 818; *Durham Wills*, iv. 234; C. Cross, 'The Development of Protestantism in Leeds and Hull, 1520-1640: The Evidence from Wills', *Northern History*, 18 (1982), 234.

Gifts to the poor were the commonest type of pious bequest during this period, and probably more numerous than at any other time. The proportion of testators making specific provision for alms was highest among the wealthy. Among West Suffolk testators of identifiable social status in the early 1630s, over half the gentlemen and clergy made bequests to the poor, nearly half the clothiers, just under one-third of the yeomen, but only 4 per cent of the husbandmen.[45] Bequests were most commonly in money, but were also distributed in the form of food, fuel, or clothing. Some of the bequests were directed to the poor box, but the great majority were intended for distribution. Some benefactors' instructions had a distinctively conservative flavour, especially during the early years of Elizabeth's reign, stipulating payment at the month-day as well as the funeral. Several wills provided for a series of distributions: on twenty successive Sunday mornings after service, on a number of feast-days, or annually for a few years, several decades, or even in perpetuity. But some testators, while continuing the long-established custom of the dole, sought to avoid giving the impression that they wanted intercessions in return for their largesse. So in 1573 Thomas Franck Esq. stipulated that the recipients of his alms on the day of his funeral or the morrow were 'to be thankful and give praise to God for the departing of my soul'. It nevertheless seems likely that very many testators hoped that their legacies would yield spiritual benefit.[46]

The very substantial sums laid out in some doles could have attracted large numbers of vagrant poor. House-to-house distribution, or the careful distinction of certain categories of recipient, such as the poorest householders in the parish, poor widows, and elderly people, or poor employees of the benefactor, were means of excluding the undeserving. The poor of the parish or neighbourhood were the commonest objects of charitable munificence, but some testators bequeathed money to poor prisoners and the inmates of hospitals and almshouses. Such 'true works of mercy', listed in some Elizabethan episcopal articles of enquiry, as the marriages of poor maidens, the maintenance of the ministry and schools, and the repair of highways, attracted support from relatively few people.[47]

---

[45] *Sudbury Wills 1630-1635*, nos. 1-450; Munby (ed.), *Kings Langley*, p. xiii.

[46] Emmison (ed.), *Elizabethan Life*, iv. 19, 73, 85, 102, 159; Munby (ed.), *Kings Langley*, 29; *Durham Wills*, iv. 59; *Sudbury Wills 1630-1635*, nos. 514, 529, 849; I. W. Archer, *The Pursuit of Stability: Social Relations in Elizabethan London* (Cambridge, 1991), 169; *Darlington Wills*, 141.

[47] Emmison (ed.), *Elizabethan Life*, iv. 31, 74, 93, 102, 111, 123, 126, 130, 156, 190, 196, 241, 249, 272-3, 278; *Essex Wills, 1558-1603*, ed. F. G. Emmison (Chelmsford,

The middling ranks of society whose wills dominate diocesan and archdeaconry probate archives had charitable aspirations much more limited and conservative than those of the great merchants and gentry who bulk so large in Professor W. K. Jordan's eloquent account of the rise of the secular charitable impulse. That account emphasizes the great capital investments required to establish such institutions as schools, colleges, almshouses, and lectureships. Only a minority of testators could afford the necessary outlays. Since Professor Jordan was concerned above all with sums laid out rather than with numbers of donors, 'a relatively small group of rich, aggressive, and generous men' dominate the picture he presented. Yet although only a small minority of benefactors by will seem to have been caught in Professor Jordan's net, the great majority, even of his donors, made quite modest gifts. Over three-quarters of Jordan's 2,714 Norfolk donors made benefactions which were very small on average, for immediate use rather than capital endowment. In England as a whole, the aspirations of smaller donors changed much more gradually than did those of the merchants and the gentry. Over half of the gifts made by the yeomen, the largest group of donors, during the period 1480–1660, were for poor relief, most of it to be paid directly to recipients. Husbandmen, representing one of the largest English social groups, were also the most conservative donors, giving almost half of their trickle of small donations to the church, most of the rest in direct alms to the poor. Jordan noted that in Norfolk it was not until about 1580 that men of this class 'began to shed the habit of leaving small and customary bequests for church uses and instead to give tiny outright sums for doles for poor men'.[48]

The charitable aspirations of the vast majority of donors changed slowly between 1558 and 1660, but pious giving never recovered from the shocks administered by the Reformation. It has long been clear that Professor Jordan's figures for total charitable donations, including those of the merchants and gentry, show a sharp decline in

1982–), vol. vii. pp. xiv, 228; vol. viii. pp. xxi, 273; vol. ix. pp. ix, 271; *Durham Wills*, iv. 18–19, 295; W. P. M. Kennedy, *Elizabethan Episcopal Administration: An Essay in Sociology and Politics* (Alcuin Club Collections, 26–7; 1924), ii. 97, 120, 132; iii. 213, 291, 348.

[48] W. K. Jordan, *Philanthropy in England, 1480–1660* (1959), 18, 241, 322, 345–6, 380–1; id., *The Charities of Rural England 1480–1660* (1961), 91, 95, 207–8; cf. Levine and Wrightson, *Making of Industrial Society*, 341. Only a tiny fraction of the extant Norfolk wills of 1480–1660 are represented in Prof. Jordan's statistics for that county. It is hard to believe that his survey of benefactions was anywhere near complete. I am grateful to Paul Slack for discussing this point with me.

real terms between the Reformation and the early seventeenth century. Even after that the peak level of pre-Reformation giving was not regained. The donations of the majority of testators of modest means declined in nominal as well as real terms, and never approached in variety, number, or value the gifts attracted by the late medieval Church. Certainly the proportion of testators leaving bequests to the poor increased during and after the Reformation. This increase offset to some extent the decline in other forms of pious gift, but, after reaching a peak at a date within a few decades of 1558 (which varied from one part of the country to another), this giving fell away in the long term. Even in towns, where the problem of poverty was most immediately obvious, the majority of testators were not very generous. Between 1560 and 1640 fewer than half the testators of Hull gave to the poor, fewer than a third of those of Leeds. At Worcester, bequests declined sharply after the 1560s. In London, the proportion of testators making bequests for poor relief reached its highest known level in the early 1570s. A little more twenty years later, the proportion of less well-off testators leaving such bequests had already declined from just over a third to just under a quarter.[49]

Of the various possible reasons for the stagnation of pious giving after the Reformation two stand out. The most popular types of late medieval bequest had yielded results which were satisfyingly tangible while also benefiting the testator's soul. Protestant theology denied that good works could themselves help the benefactor. More importantly, some of the principal good works (church fabric maintenance, upkeep of the highways, and poor relief) were increasingly financed by compulsory local rates after the Reformation. Many ratepayers of modest means may have seen little reason for charitable donations on top of the payments they had already made. This attitude was succinctly expressed by William Kirkus of Kirk Merrington (Co. Durham) in 1570. Asked by the vicar who had come to write his will what he would give to the poor man's box, Kirkus answered 'I gyve dayly to the poore, as other neighbours doith; and therefore I will nothing to the poore man box.'[50]

---

[49] W. G. Bittle and R. T. Lane, 'Inflation and Philanthropy in England: A Re-Assessment of W. K. Jordan's Data', *Economic History Review*, 2nd ser. 29 (1976), 203–10; Comments by J. F. Hadwin, D. C. Coleman, and J. D. Gould, and Bittle and Lane, 'A Re-Assessment Reiterated', ibid. 31 (1978), 105–28; Cross, 'Development of Protestantism', 236–7; A. D. Dyer, *The City of Worcester in the Sixteenth Century* (Leicester, 1973), 241–3; Archer, *Pursuit of Stability*, 167–74. For 17th-cent. decline in Gloucestershire, see Beaver, 'Sown in Dishonour', 411, table 4.

[50] *Depositions and other Ecclesiastical Proceedings from the Courts of Durham, extending from 1311 to the Reign of Elizabeth*, ed. J. Raine (Surtees Soc. 21; 1845), 214.

From the Restoration to 1750

In 1696 William Assheton, rector of Beckenham in Kent, explained in his *Theological Discourse of Last Wills and Testaments* that it was important to use the will as an opportunity of making a declaration of faith and vindicating its maker against suspicions of irreligion. Too many wills, he remarked, broke off abruptly after the commendation of the soul into the hands of God its creator. Yet this was not enough. Why did the testator thus commend his soul to God? What were the grounds of his hope? Only the merits of Jesus Christ: and a failure to mention him was the highest presumption as well as a careless omission. Assheton believed that the testator should make clear his reliance on Christ's merits and mediation alone in casting himself upon God's mercy for the pardon of his sins and hopes of eternal life. The suppliant tone of Assheton's recommended preamble was of a piece with his High Churchmanship.[51]

The bare commendation of the soul to God the Creator was, despite Assheton's strictures, still limited to a minority of wills at the time when he wrote. Most late seventeenth-century preambles look forward to the forgiveness of sins, to salvation, to eternal life, to the kingdom of heaven, or to a combination of these things. They rely upon the merits, or the death and passion, of Jesus Christ, some of them upon his mediation or intercession. There were distinct local and denominational differences. The phraseology favoured by many of the testators of a town such as Great Yarmouth, long in the vanguard of Norfolk Protestantism, was far in spirit from that of High Church preambles. Their wills express an assured trust in the prospect of salvation and anticipate the body's joyful resurrection to everlasting glories. Yet even in strongholds of Puritanism, the religious language of most wills had become conventional. Despite the survival of different local patterns and innumerable smaller differences of phrasing or word-order, there are few surprises among the soul commendations of the typical will register of this period, few truly individual ideas arrestingly expressed.[52] After the Restoration, only a small and dwindling number of wills specified a particular place of burial, in many cases because the testator wanted to be buried near a relative, or left money to pay for a

---

[51] W. Assheton, *A Theological Discourse of Last Wills and Testaments* (1696), 15–19.

[52] NRO, ANW Wills 1699–1700, fos. 19^v, 72, 106^v, 114, 143, 178^v (Mrs Margaret Yates, who left a legacy to the pastor of the Congregational church). Cf. R. T. Vann, 'Wills and the Family in an English Town: Banbury, 1550–1800', *Journal of Family History*, 4 (1979), 360; Spufford, *Contrasting Communities*, 332, 343.

monument. Even the north, where old custom survived longest, saw rapid change in the later seventeenth century.[53]

During the first three decades of the eighteenth century these conventional formulas of the years since the Civil War remained dominant. Then, after about 1730, a remarkable change set in quite quickly. In widely separate areas of England, in Berkshire, the Midlands, Norfolk, the West Riding, and the north-east, the previously normal type of preamble was rapidly abandoned by an increasing number of testators who simply entrusted their souls into the hands of 'allmighty God that Gave it me' or 'Almighty God my Maker' or just to 'Almighty God'. Such a simple and unrevealing formula had been the natural choice of the wary or uncertain during a previous period of transition—in that case from Catholicism to Protestantism—but now its adoption heralded a withdrawal from the making of any sort of religious statement in the last will. This was not necessarily a sign of indifference. Some sincere Christians may have disliked a convention which had come to seem hackneyed and empty.[54]

Amateur scribes, writing wills of the simplest sort, distinguished by sprawling, misshapen characters and erratic spelling, had tended to omit religious preambles ever since the sixteenth century. However, their abandonment in the eighteenth century even by professional will-writers marked a fundamental change of practice. The commendation of the soul and body, the heart of the preamble, disappeared first. In many wills expressions of gratitude to God for soundness of mind lasted a while longer. The preliminary invocation of the name of God, the last remaining element of religious solemnity, survived longest.

Around 1700 printed will forms for use by soldiers and sailors began to appear. The preamble of one such form explains that the testator, 'considering the Perrils and Dangers of the Seas and other uncertainties of this Transitory Life', is making his will so as to avoid controversies after his decease. 'First', it continues, 'I recommend my

---

[53] *Selby Wills*, ed. F. Collins (Yorkshire Archaeological Soc. Record Ser. 47; 1912), 1–199 (over 60% specified place of burial in 1660s; none did so after 1700); *Will of Horbury*, ii. *1688–1757* (Wakefield, 1980), 53–126.

[54] Berkshire 1740: 35 wills, 37% no bequest of soul, 29% to God; Norwich archdeaconry 1746: 50 wills, 52% no bequest of soul, 20% to God (below, App. 1); Durham: 30 wills proved Aug.–Oct. 1750, 63% no bequest of soul (Durham, Prior's Kitchen, will register 1734–52, fos. 223–54; E. Parry, 'Helmdon Wills 1603–1760', *Northamptonshire Past and Present*, 5 (1975), 240; Coldicott, *Long Sutton Miscellany*, 9; *Will of Horbury*, ii. 53–126. For an early example of a pious Christian who included no bequest of soul or body in his will, see Sir Thomas Browne, *Works*, ed. G. Keynes (4 vols., 1964), iv. 403.

Soul to God that gave it, and my Body I commit to the Earth or Sea, as it shall please God to Order'. It is a very simple instrument which bequeaths the whole estate to one person.[55] This sort of brief and impersonal form, the prototype of those sold by stationers today, was used in the early eighteenth century by many of those who faced death on active service in the kingdom's wars to bequeath their meagre belongings to mothers, wives, or sweethearts.

The flow of charitable bequests from wealthier testators, recorded on benefaction boards in parish churches, or detailed in later returns to national enquiries concerning charitable endowments, continued through the later seventeenth and eighteenth centuries. Yet a diminishing proportion of affluent testators made charitable bequests during the century following the Restoration. Fewer than a third of middle-class Londoners with children to provide for made such bequests in the years 1665–1720, and even those who did so left sums small in relation to their wealth. William Assheton felt obliged to defend charitable benefactions against several imagined pleas to divert a covetous miser from doing good. The first of them was that to urge charity was a 'Popish Trick', the second that the laws of the land had taken care of the poor. 'Shall not our Friends Dispose of their Estates and make their wills as they please,' a hostile critic would say, 'but these Men in Black must pretend to Direct, and bring in their Items for the Poor, and the Church?' Some of the more spectacular testamentary benefactions of the early eighteenth century attracted unfavourable comment. The men concerned were criticized for their supposedly self-glorifying motives or for neglecting the rights of heirs. The preacher at the funeral of the great Bristol benefactor Edward Colston in 1721 felt bound to emphasize that Colston had given during his lifetime as well as by will, knowing that to give by will is to give things we can no longer possess. The Mortmain Act of 1736 forbade the charitable donation of land less than a year before death. The widespread belief that many endowments entrusted to the stewardship of parish officials had been mismanaged or misapplied encouraged the quest for new methods of donation. An increasing proportion of charitable giving by wealthy people was accomplished by regular lifetime subscription to deserving causes rather than by will.[56]

[55] BRO D/A1/59/245; D/A1/64/132.
[56] Assheton, *Theological Discourse*, 77–96; P. Langford, *Public Life and the Propertied Englishman, 1689–1798* (Oxford, 1991), 491–2; J. Harcourt, *A Sermon Preach'd . . . Upon the Death of Edward Colston, Esq* (1721), 27–30, 39–44; D. T. Andrew, *Philanthropy and Police: London Charity in the Eighteenth Century* (Princeton, 1989), 46–9; P. Earle, *The Making of the English Middle Class: Business,*

The great majority of testators made no charitable bequests.[57] These were infrequent after the Restoration, rare by the middle of the eighteenth century. The middling ranks of rural society came to feel that testamentary philanthropy was not for them. In 1685 John Hill, a prosperous yeoman of Basildon (Berks.), told the minister that he had not given anything to the poor because there were several gentlemen and freeholders in the parish who were better able to give than he. Even in 1739 it was possible to find a gentleman like Samuel Bever of Mortimer (Berks.), who left £10 to the poor of the parish, of which £3 were to be spent on bread to be distributed among them, and £7 were to pay for six strong grey coats for the six poor men who should carry him to church. However, such provision looked distinctly old-fashioned by that date.[58]

The Reformers kept the bones of the pious will while animating them with new theology. The 'superstitious' objects of medieval devotion were replaced by different charitable priorities, but by the eighteenth century testamentary charity and piety, once expressed in a myriad small bequests, had become the preserve of a substantial but dwindling minority of the rich. The will finally slipped out of the realm of the spiritual and the sacred. It remained a means of transmitting property to family and friends.

THE FAMILY AND THE LAST WILL

The medieval Church had tried to maintain and extend testamentary freedom above all in order to enable individuals to devote part of their property to the performance of good works. There was a tension between the Church's aspirations on the one side and family expectations on the other. Indeed, it was in order to prevent the alienation of patrimonies by deathbed penitents that the king's judges had first prohibited the devise of lands by will.[59]

Society and Family Life in London, 1660-1730 (1989), 316-19, 394-5; P. Slack, *The English Poor Law, 1531-1782* (Basingstoke, 1990), 50-1.

[57] Beaver, 'Sown in Dishonour', 411; Coldicott, *Long Sutton Miscellany*, 10; Parry, 'Helmdon Wills', 238; J. A. Johnston, 'The Probate Inventories and Wills of a Worcestershire Parish, 1676-1775', *Midland History*, 1 (1971-2), 32; id., 'Social Change in the Eighteenth Century: The Evidence in Wills from Six Lincolnshire Parishes, 1661-1812', *Lincolnshire History and Archaeology*, 27 (1992), 32. Norwich archdeaconry 1699: 16% of wills made bequests to poor; 1746, 6%; only 4% of Berkshire wills of years 1680-1740 did so (below, App. 1).

[58] BRO D/A1/82/68; D/A1/49/221a. Cf. the description of the very old-fashioned will and funeral of Sir Roger de Coverley in *The Spectator*, ed. D. F. Bond (5 vols., Oxford, 1965), iv. 340-1.

[59] Sir F. Pollock and F. W. Maitland, *The History of English Law before the Time of Edward I* (2 vols., 2nd edn., reissued, Cambridge, 1968), ii. 327-9.

Throughout this period, provision for their closest relatives was testators' main earthly concern. This was a duty. When the reformer Thomas Becon wrote that 'whosoever provideth not for his hath denied the faith, and is worse than an infidel',[60] he was expressing with especial force a point with which both Catholic and Protestant would have agreed. However, before the Reformation, bequests to pious uses often took a sizeable chunk out of the estates of people who had wives and children to provide for. The end of investment in the welfare of the dead, and the later decline in pious bequests of all sorts, benefited the surviving members of testators' families first and foremost. As the will became less important as a vehicle for spiritual and other-worldly concerns, it became a more significant means of expressing earthly affections and attachments. Of these the bond between husband and wife was the strongest.

Before the Reformation, many of those who provided for intercessory prayers planned to share their benefits with particular individuals. William Dormer of High Wycombe, endowing a twenty-year obit in 1487, drew up an exceptionally long list: his parents, wives, brothers, sisters, sons, daughters, kinsfolk, friends, benefactors, and all the faithful dead.[61] The sequence probably reflects the order of priority of personal duty. Parents and spouses were the individuals most frequently designated as beneficiaries of intercessory prayers. Brothers and sisters were seldom mentioned, children rarely, people outside the first degree of relationship (apart from benefactors) hardly at all. Survivors and descendants were expected to provide for the souls of those who had gone before them. A large proportion of these charitable bequests was intended to help the souls of dead relatives.[62]

Another way of acknowledging the importance of deceased relatives was to ask to be buried near them, though such requests, always relatively infrequent, grew rarer in the long run. Members of the nobility and gentry were the most likely to require burial near another person. In Elizabethan Essex nearly 42 per cent of the peers and

---

[60] T. Becon, *The Sicke mannes Salue . . .*, in id., *Prayers and other Pieces of Thomas Becon, S.T.P.*, ed. J. Ayre (Parker Soc., 1844), 117.

[61] *Buckingham Archdeaconry Courts*, 1–189, esp. 57.

[62] Wills specified in App. 1, below; cf. Rosenthal, *Purchase of Paradise*, 16, for similar pattern revealed by licences to nobility to alienate in mortmain. Many testators mentioned friends or benefactors in general terms, but few named them individually. Dinn, 'Death and Rebirth', 157–8, presents some important exceptions to the generalizations sketched here; neither of his tables 11.4 or 11.5 mentions wives, and only 11.4 mentions parents, but the large and ambiguous category 'friends' may have been understood to include relatives.

knights and their wives did so, 21 per cent of the esquires, 11 per cent of the mere gentry, and 3 per cent of the merchants. However, such requests were by no means limited to the upper classes, and they occasionally appeared in the wills of quite humble people. In and around Selby (Yorks.), they were made by nearly one in every ten testators between 1633 and 1680. Well over 80 per cent of testators specifying the person or persons near whom they wished to be buried mentioned individual members of their elementary families of origin or marriage. Most named one person: above all a husband or wife. A number chose to be interred near to parents. Siblings were seldom mentioned, and even then tended to be coupled with other members of the family. Despite the high levels of infant and child mortality, requests for burial next to deceased children were rare. Grandparents, uncles, and aunts were seldom specified. Relatively few testators wanted simply to be buried among ancestors, kinsfolk, or friends. Some testators, especially after 1600, underlined their affection for a 'late dear husband', a 'loving' or 'dear' wife, a 'loving mother', or 'beloved parents'. In 1738 William Heron of Horbury (Yorks.) directed that he be buried in Hoyland church 'as near to the ashes of my late Dear Grandmother as may be'.[63]

The fulfilment of the testator's wishes depended upon the appointment of reliable executors. In 1600 Avis Harper of Billingford (Norfolk) pithily summarized the duties of her own executors. They were, as she put it, to 'paye my debtes, discharge my Legacies, Christianly to see me buryed, And to p[er]forme other such good deedes of Mercie, as it shall please god to move them'.[64] After the Reformation, the customary instruction to use the residue to the best advantage of the testator's soul gradually disappeared. By 1600 a reference to 'good deeds of Mercie' looked distinctly conservative. It became customary to appoint executors residuary legatees. Nomination as executor, with the concomitant bequest of the residue, was clearly regarded by many testators as a mark of favour as well as trust.

Married men relied first and foremost upon their wives, whom (at various times and in different jurisdictions) between 63 and 96 per cent of them chose. Before the Reformation women were much more

---

[63] Harding, 'Burial Choice', 126–7; Emmison (ed.), *Elizabethan Life*, iv. 1–321; *Selby Wills*; *Will of Horbury*, ii. 92; Munby (ed.), *Kings Langley* (c.5% of testators requested burial near a specified person). In the archdeaconries of Norwich and Berkshire, the % age of wills in which requests for burial near a particular person were made never rose above 5% after the Reformation.
[64] NRO, ANW Wills, Bastard, fo. 59ᵛ.

often appointed jointly with a man or men than as sole executrix. Afterwards such joint appointments became much less common. Wives were chosen sole executrix in between 49 and 80 per cent of married men's wills proved in most jurisdictions so far studied.[65] When deciding whether or not to make his wife executrix, a married man was probably influenced by his social standing, the nature of his occupation, his wife's age, and the availability of alternative candidates. The proportion of testators making their wives executrices was smallest among the upper classes and merchants, largest among husbandmen, craftsmen, retailers, and labourers. Running a farm, shop, or small workshop could more readily be entrusted to a wife, commonly a close partner in the business, than could the oversight of widely scattered estates or the management of a sizeable trading enterprise. The wife's age and the stage reached in the marriage cycle were also important. Men with dependent children, or no children at all, were far more likely to choose their wives than were those who had adult children or grandchildren. An elderly wife might prefer to be spared the burdens of executorship. There were several practical reasons for not appointing wives executrices. They were probably far more important than any personal dislike. Among those who did not name their wives, expressions of love and affection were far more common than signs of mistrust.

A large majority of those men who named another person executor, with or without their wives, turned to their children. Widows and widowers who had children showed the same preference. Sons were appointed far more often than daughters, though widows were readier than widowers to choose daughters.[66] After their own children, testators most often nominated sons-in-law and daughters-in law. Brothers and sisters were seldom entrusted with executorship; grandchildren were chosen almost as often. Remoter kinsfolk such as cousins, nephews, and nieces were rarely nominated.

Testators often sought to provide their inexperienced executors with additional support or supervision by nominating overseers. Many of those chosen for what could be onerous responsibilities were friends or neighbours, frequently distinguished as 'loving' or 'beloved'. Clergymen were sometimes asked to take on the responsibility, especially before the Reformation. Overseers were often of

[65] A. L. Erickson, *Women and Property in Early Modern England* (1993), 156–60, esp. table 9.1 on p. 158; S. D. Amussen, *An Ordered Society: Gender and Class in Early Modern England* (Oxford, 1988), 81–5.
[66] Erickson, *Women and Property*, 220; Amussen, *Ordered Society*, 92.

higher status than the testators who asked them to act, some of them probably landlords or former employers. Among kinsfolk, brothers and brothers-in-law seem to have been the most frequently chosen, followed by sons-in-law.

Wealthier testators of higher standing were more likely to request the services of overseers than were those of little substance and low status. Nominations seem to have grown more frequent after the Reformation. They were commonest under Elizabeth and the early Stuarts, and in the south of England. The shift away from the practice of coupling other executors together with the testator's wife was therefore offset by the more frequent appointment of overseers. After about the middle of the seventeenth century, this practice declined very markedly. To some extent trustees took over the responsibilities once discharged by overseers. The practice of appointing them spread downwards through the gentry and by the early eighteenth century was being adopted by some of the middling sort.[67]

The support and comfort of their widowed partners seems to have been a major concern of most husbands. Dying men were sometimes reported to have said that they would have given all they had to their wives even if it had been far more than they actually possessed, or to have refused to give anything away from them.[68] Wills often fail to reveal the full extent of provision for widows, because it was not strictly necessary to mention in them either the customary widow's right to a third of her husband's land or an income already arranged for her by means of a marriage settlement. However, the widow's interest in lands left her by will was probably for her life in the majority of cases. Most widows received money or movable goods, including explicit bequests of the residue of the estate made to executrices. In the ecclesiastical province of York, custom reserved to his widow

---

[67] Erickson, *Women and Property*, 159–61; Coldicott, *Long Sutton Miscellany*, 13, Dr Erickson points to major regional variations in the propensity to appoint overseers, and says that in Yorkshire, though always rare, they were becoming more common during the 17th cent. However, the figures from Selby (4% of testators appointed overseers, 1634–1710), are too small and thinly scattered to reveal much of a trend. Of the selected wealthy and middling testators represented in *Durham Wills*, iv. 1–48, 231–84, 41% named overseers 1604–10, while 21% did so 1631–40. The appointment of overseers reached a peak in 1600 in the archdeaconries of both Berkshire (90% of wills) and Norwich (38%).

[68] BRO D/Al/56/46a; NRO DN/DEP 3/4A, fo. 282^r; ANW Wills 1699–1700, fo. 45; *Sudbury Wills, 1630–1635*, nos. 108, 374, 513; V. Brodsky, 'Widows in Late Elizabethan London: Remarriage, Economic Opportunity and Family Orientations', in L. Bonfield, R. M. Smith, and K. Wrightson (edd.), *The World We have Gained: Histories of Population and Social Structure, Essays presented to Peter Laslett on his Seventieth Birthday* (Oxford, 1986), 147.

a third of a man's goods (the 'reasonable part' once customary in the southern province too) until 1693, but English widows very often, perhaps generally, received more than the 'reasonable' third. The provision made for widows was usually sufficiently generous to obviate the need to specify that they were to be given maintenance or accommodation. Most husbands aimed to provide for their widows in a way which would give them more freedom of choice, but some hoped that their widows and children would continue to live together after their deaths.[69]

Many men faced the prospect of their widows' remarriage, especially in London, where many people married two or three times before reaching old age. Yet most husbands made no reference to such an eventuality in their wills. In those places where custom insisted upon the loss of widows' rights in their husbands' holdings on remarriage, this would have been a more powerful disincentive than any testamentary stipulations. It seems clear that the material interests of children were the overriding concern of most of that small minority of testators who did attempt to guard against the results of remarriage.[70]

Because so many will-makers of both sexes were widowed, the proportion of wills mentioning children in any particular place or period was often higher than that mentioning a spouse. In all will samples children make up by far the biggest single category of legatee,[71] but wills nevertheless present a very partial picture of provision for children. Lands descending according to the terms of the lease often do not appear in them. Even more importantly, many testators made their wills when some of their children had already married or had children of their own. Fathers who left young children commonly left the responsibility of their material provision to their wives. The latter were sometimes specifically empowered to reward children

[69] Erickson, *Women and Property*, 66–7, 162–71. Over two-thirds of the testators in the archdeaconry of Norwich (see below, App. 1) who bequeathed some or all of their land to their widows made bequests for life; nearly a quarter did so outright (but some of these 'outright' bequests may have been of leases which did not have long to run). The use of wills in this context is beset with problems. It is often difficult to tell whether a widow's bequest included all a testator's landholdings or only part of them. A number of widows were left land, part of it to be held for their lives, part of it without limitation.

[70] Brodsky, 'Widows in London', 144–6; Erickson, *Women and Property*, 166–9.

[71] W. Coster, *Kinship and Inheritance in Early Modern England: Three Yorkshire Parishes* (Borthwick Papers, 83; 1993), 9; D. Cressy, 'Kinship and Kin Interaction in Early Modern England', *Past and Present*, 113 (1986), 55, 57; Johnston, 'Probate Inventories and Wills', 32.

according to their obedience and good behaviour.[72] The care of minor children was usually entrusted to the mother by those testators who named a guardian. Brothers-in-law, brothers, or eldest sons were the most frequent alternatives, the likeliest to be named by widowers.

In the sixteenth and early seventeenth centuries many testators of rank or standing expressed the hope that their children would be brought up virtuously and in the fear of God, or given a good and godly education. After the Restoration, the care they desired was described in more urbane and secular terms: 'convenient and decent', 'handsome and fitting', 'handsome . . . & genteel'. Explicit references to attendance at school or university, or to the skills to be acquired, such as reading and writing in the case of boys, or reading and sewing in that of girls, were relatively rare. Few will-makers at any time specified what professions or occupations their sons should follow. An expectation was, however, implicit in some of the bequests made, of tools or equipment in particular. Some townsmen or more substantial rural testators mentioned the possibility of their sons' being apprenticed, or left money for that purpose. Concern about the marriages of children (usually daughters) was shown in a very small minority of wills. The full payment of legacies was occasionally made conditional upon marriage with the approval of mothers or other close kinsfolk.[73]

Bequests were concentrated above all within the circles of the individual's nuclear family of birth or marriage and direct descendants. A large proportion of the wills registered in the Norwich and Berkshire archdeaconry courts, perhaps not far short of half, made no bequests at all to other relatives. Kinsfolk often occupied quite an important place in the lives of individuals in early modern England, but the first duties of the dying were to their immediate family. Progress through the life cycle brought with it the assumption and relinquishment of responsibilities, the severance of some old ties, the making of new ones, successive phases of expansion and contraction in individual networks of kinship and acquaintance. The unmarried, the widowed,

---

[72] BRO D/Al/1A, fos. 203, 221; D/Al/4l/142a; NRO ANW Wills: Fuller alias Roper, fos. 295ᵛ, 311ᵛ; Aleyn, fos. 238ᵛ, 262ʳ; Bastard, fos. 32ᵛ, 37ᵛ; 1648-52, fo. 138ᵛ; Munby (ed.), *Kings Langley*, xix-xx; *Durham Wills*, iv. 305.

[73] BRO D/Al/1, fo. 29ʳ; D/Al/1A, fo. 282ᵛ; D/Al/35/262; D/Al/37/25; D/Al/40/90a; D/Al/4l/138a; D/Al/47/56a; D/Al/53/119a; D/Al/56/12; D/Al/61/214a; D/Al/62/159a; NRO ANW Wills: Aleyn, fo. 243ᵛ; Bastard, fos. 33ᵛ, 37ᵛ, 47ʳ; 97 (1746-7), fo. 41ᵛ; Munby (ed.), *Kings Langley*, 31, 144; Emmison (ed.), *Elizabethan Life*, iv. 55-6, 113, 136, 158, 168; *Durham Wills*, iv. 25, 35, 42, 62, 73, 143, 178, 190, 203, 207, 223, 243, 266, 268, 292, 307, 310-11.

and the childless were free to be more diffuse in their bequests than those with dependants to provide for. More distant relatives might occupy some of the emotional space which would normally have belonged to wife and children. Wealthy people were always better able to maintain contacts with a comparatively wide circle of kinsfolk and to leave them bequests than were people of lesser means. Friends and kinsfolk outside the immediate family could be recognized in tangible ways, above all perhaps by according them places in the funeral ceremony, and by giving them tokens of remembrance such as rings. However, wills give only a few glimpses of such arrangements, which must often have been made by executors by virtue of oral instructions or in the light of their own knowledge of testators' social networks.[74]

Young unmarried will-makers were understandably more likely than other people to mention parents, uncles, and aunts. Sometimes they named intended spouses. In 1540 John Davye of Shalbourne (Berks.), 'yong man', left twenty sheep and twenty shillings to 'Maryone Jhoynys the wyche schulde hayue beyne my wyffe', and the rest of his sheep to his mother. The widowed, the single, and the childless were the most likely to mention brothers, sisters, nephews, and nieces. Grandparents showed the highest prospensity to make bequests to sons-in-law (or, much less often, daughters-in-law); in many cases they seem to have lost the child who had made the link in the first place, but the interests of their grandchildren maintained it. Rarely did testators show a sense of obligation to a larger body of kinsfolk. John Frenche of Ridgewell (Essex), seemingly a childless bachelor or widower, was an exception. In 1576 he bequeathed £20 to be distributed among twenty of his poor kinsfolk, who bore as many as fourteen different names and lived in eleven parishes. However, of all the countless small bequests to the poor made between the Reformation and the Civil War, only a very small proportion gave any sort of preference to poor kindred. Nor does the subsequent decline of pious bequests appear to have benefited testators' more distant kinsfolk.[75]

---

[74] Johnston, 'Inventories and Wills', 31–2; Vann, 'Wills and the Family', 363–5; Munby (ed.), *Kings Langley*, p. xv; Coldicott, *Long Sutton Miscellany*, 10–11; Cressy, 'Kinship and Kin Interaction', 53–9; Brodsky, 'Widows in London', 148–50; Erickson, 'Women and Property', 212–17; Coster, *Kinship and Inheritance*, 9–21; Levine and Wrightson, *Making of an Industrial Society*, 284–6; NRO ANW Wills 1699–1700, 45^v–52^v, 70–1, 96–9 (a very unusual nomination of her pallbearers by Margaret Payne, widow); below, Ch. 8.

[75] BRO D/A1/2/158; *Essex Wills*, ix. 71.

Godparents were chosen for children from among relatives (especially grandparents), friends, neighbours, employers, and land-lords. Spiritual and natural kinship overlapped. The commonest bequests to godchildren were small sums of money, a bushel of grain, or a young animal. Only rarely did godparents allude to their religious duties. (However, in 1590 one Essex gentleman, Robert Cheeke, bequeathed £3, to be paid to his godson when he could read the New Testament and recite his catechism.) References to godchildren in wills were quite common until the Civil War in many parts of the country. Only thereafter did they fall away markedly. This develop-ment may have had something to do with the gradual secularization of the will or a decline in the perceived importance of godparent-hood, but it still awaits a satisfactory explanation.[76]

After relatives, servants made up the largest and most easily distin-guishable category of legatee. (Some of them may indeed have been relatives as well, though beneficiaries were usually described as one or the other, seldom as both.) Bequests to servants were most numer-ous in the sixteenth and seventeenth centuries, and became less common thereafter. People who were or had been in service them-selves sometimes left bequests to employers or fellow servants.[77] Lodgers who maintained no household of their own (unmarried or 'retired' people) sometimes showed their appreciation of their hosts' kindness. Some testators made bequests to people who had cared for them during their final illness, including kinswomen, servants, land-ladies, and hired nurses, and such nursing was occasionally men-tioned with especially warm gratitude.[78]

Wills contain one further indicator of the strength and importance of personal relationships: the use of adjectives expressive of affection given or received, especially 'loving' and 'beloved'. Such terms

---

[76] Coster, *Kinship and Inheritance*, 9, 22–3; Emmison (ed.), *Elizabethan Life*, iv. 179; *Durham Wills*, iv. 234, 273, 284; Munby (ed.), *Kings Langley*, xvi; Cressy, 'Kin-ship and Kin Interaction', 55, 57: contrast table 3 (Elizabethan) with table 1 (1680s). In Berkshire archdeaconry wills, %ages of testators mentioning godchildren fluctuated between 37 (1560) and 14 (1540) before the Civil War; between 7 and 0 afterwards. Overall, 22%, 1509–1640; 3%, 1660–1740.

[77] Coster, *Kinship and Inheritance*, 9, 21–2; Vann, 'Wills and the Family', 364–5; Johnston, 'Inventories and Wills', 32; Munby (ed.), *Kings Langley*, p. xvi; *Sevenoaks Wills and Inventories, in the Reign of Charles II*, ed. H. C. F. Lansberry (Kent Archaeological Soc., Kent Records, 25; 1988), p. xxx; *Sudbury Wills 1630–1635*, nos. 536, 696, for two striking examples of gratitude to employers.

[78] NRO ANW wills: Bastard, fo. 29ʳ; 1648–52, fo. 107ᵛ; 1699–1700, fos. 71, 96–9, 178ᵛ–181ʳ; BRO D/A1/36/75a; D/A1/44/155a; D/A1/47/81a; D/A1/54/68a; D/A1/56/62a; *Sudbury Wills 1630–1635*, nos. 159, 174, 356, 749; Emmison (ed.), *Elizabethan Life*, iv. 6, 102, 108, 130, 154, 242.

clearly have to be treated with great caution, but they never became simply a matter of form. They were never applied consistently to all the people in a given category. Marriage partners were more often distinguished in this way than any other type of relative. The range of adjectives used to describe spouses was wider, and more often emphasized in such combinations as 'Dear and truly loving', dearly beloved', and 'dear and tender'. As early as 1472 Sir Thomas Cobham's widow Anne directed that she be interred 'where the body of my dere hert and late husband restith buried', but it was not until the late seventeenth or eighteenth century that the majority of marriage partners (never all of them) were described in affectionate terms. By Elizabeth's reign the use of such terms was already common among the gentry; it was another century or so before it became widespread among the middling sort. The secularization of the will, and the growth of testamentary privacy, encouraged the use of more intimately affectionate language. Some testators paid warm tributes to well-loved spouses' affection, fidelity, and steadfastness.[79]

A parental blessing, or invocation of God's blessing, was an eloquent means of expressing love and good will. In 1647 Thomas Davy, a yeoman of Swanton Morley (Norfolk) recorded his hope that his son William might by God's blessing and with his supervisors' help spend the rest of his life to God's glory, his friends' comfort, his country's good, and his own eternal felicity.[80] Such expectations were, however, seldom expressed in wills. More frequently exposed was a persistent vein of anxiety about the future behaviour of children. Some testators enjoined surviving members of their families to live together in love and harmony, or reminded eldest sons of their duty to look after their brothers and sisters.[81]

During the sixteenth and seventeenth centuries last messages of

---

[79] G. E. C(okayne), *The Complete Peerage*, rev. and ed. V. Gibbs *et al.* (13 vols., 1910–59; rep. 6 vols., Gloucester, 1987), x. 239, n. (i); for other examples from 1528 and 1531 see Munby (ed.), *Kings Langley*, 8–9, 11. In the archdeaconry of Norwich wives were described in affectionate terms in a third of husbands' wills proved in 1649, three-quarters of those proved in 1699, 81% of those proved in 1746. Overseers and executors were very often described in such terms as 'trusty and well beloved', but as Dr Erickson observes, this 'could have been meant to encourage the overseer to do right, rather than by way of affectionate remembrance', *Women and Property*, 161.

[80] *Buckingham Archdeaconry Courts*, 138; *Durham Wills*, iv. 83, 268; Emmison (ed.), *Elizabethan Life*, iv. 298; NRO, ANW Wills, 1648–52, fo. 151ᵛ.

[81] Emmison (ed.), *Elizabethan Life*, iv. 293; *Durham Wills*, iv. 136–7; Munby (ed.), *Kings Langley*, xii–xiii; *Sudbury Wills 1630–1635*, 157, 192, 272, 394; BRO D/A1/43/53a; D/A1/44/128a; D/A1/49/221a; D/A1/59/184; G. A. Aitken, *The Life and Works of John Arbuthnot* (Oxford, 1892), 159.

advice which complemented the material provisions of the will were drawn up by several parents in upper-class and professional families. Dr Robert Harris, a famous divine, quite explicitly intended his 'advice and counsel' to his family as a supplement to his will. He seems to have envisaged it as a sort of moral testament or bequest which (he wrote) he divided amongst them all. Never very free in speech, and fearing that the onset of sickness might prevent his delivering a suitable deathbed discourse, Harris wanted his family to hear him speaking in his writing. Last parental messages varied enormously in length. Some fathers summed up their most important concerns in a few pithy lines. Sir Henry Slingsby's lengthy instructions to his sons, written in 1658 while he awaited execution for his part in a royalist plot, run to well over thirty pages in print.[82]

Among the many and various themes of parental advice were obedience to God, to earthly superiors and to surviving mothers; wisdom in choosing spouses, friends, and careers; avoidance of bad company; self-governance, sobriety, and temperance; love and fidelity to spouses; and the careful upbringing of children. Eldest sons were often entrusted with the care of younger brothers and sisters. One particularly strong paternal concern was that children should love one another. Robert Harris was especially emphatic in his 'request and charge' that his children live together in an 'undivided bond of love'. He adjured them to 'know one another, visite . . . each other, comfort, counsel, relieve, succour, help, admonish one another'. They were to meet together at least once a year, or, if that were impossible, to keep in touch with each other. (One Essex gentleman was so concerned that the unity of his family should survive his death that in about 1577 he left £4 a year for the specific purpose of allowing his wife and children to meet together at Christmas and Whitsuntide.)[83]

Wives and mothers may have left written advice less often, though Elizabeth Joceline's *The mothers legacie, to her unborne childe* (1624) was one of the longest and most famous published examples of this sort of text. Outstanding in its combination of dignity and unintended pathos is the last letter Margaret Godolphin sent to her hus-

---

[82] 'The Advice and Counsel of Dr Harris to his Family, annexed to a Will made by him', in S. Clarke, *A Collection of the Lives of Ten Eminent Divines* (1662), 322–8; *The Diary of Sir Henry Slingsby, of Scriven, Bart*, ed. D. Parsons (1836), 197–230; N. Williams, *Thomas Howard Fourth Duke of Norfolk* (1964), 239–46; G. Burnet, *A Sermon Preached at the Funeral of Mr. James Houblon . . .* (1682), 28–30.

[83] 'Advice of Dr Harris', 326–7; Emmison (ed.), *Elizabethan Life*, iv. 167.

band shortly before her death in 1678. 'Deare, Believe me', she began, 'That of all Earthly-things, you were, and are the most deare to me; and I am Convinc'd, that no body ever had a better, or half so good an Husband'. After apologizing for her shortcomings, she said goodbye, with a prayer that God would bless him, and an injunction not to grieve too much for her. She sought his leave to make some specified bequests among relatives, friends, and servants and requested burial among his family. She also asked him to look after her unborn child, and to settle upon it the 'little Fortune' she had brought him if he married again. Finally she bade her child farewell, and gave it the blessing with which the Communion service ends.[84]

CONCLUSION

The will had developed during the Middle Ages as a means of expressing Christian faith and making pious bequests as well as providing for close relatives, but by 1750 it had largely lost its religious character. The reformers condemned a whole range of bequests to pious uses previously thought to assist the soul's health. Nothing replaced the parish church with its images, lights, and bede-rolls as the focus of widely shared aspirations. Reforming governments sought to divert charitable giving to the needy of this world. However, an impressive rise in bequests to the poor during and immediately after the Reformation was followed in the longer term by a decline which was especially marked in the case of middling and smaller testators. As the religious and charitable elements of wills disappeared, their importance as a means of providing for testators' families stood out all the more clearly. A fine recent study based on large numbers of later seventeenth- and eighteenth-century wills concludes that they confirm 'the consolidation of the family unit as the dominating core of English emotional life',[85] but this 'consolidation' had been a very long process. It was due not so much to changes within the family itself, which always played a central part in people's lives, as to the transformation or decline of other social focuses, especially the Church. Wills underline the pivotal importance of the marriage partnership in the English family. Wives were commonly entrusted with

---

[84] E. Joceline, *The mothers legacie, to her unborne childe* (1624); J. Evelyn, *The Life of Mrs Godolphin*, ed. H. Sampson (Oxford, 1939), 79–81.

[85] Johnston, 'Social Change in the Eighteenth Century', 27, 32. Table 1, p. 29, shows an increasing concentration of bequests within the immediate family, largely attributed to earlier and longer lasting marriages; table 6, p. 32, suggests that a dramatic fall in bequests to the poor of the parish played a considerable part.

the weightiest responsibilities and referred to in the terms of the warmest appreciation. Men with wives and children made rather limited use of the opportunity presented by will-making to acknowledge the importance of friendship, neighbourhood, or wider kinship. As they prepared for their departure from the world, the future of their closest relatives was their paramount temporal concern.

6

Last Rites and the Craft of Dying

The last moments of life were believed to be crucially important during the later Middle Ages. Each person's eternal fate, salvation or damnation, was settled when the soul left the body. Edifying stories could still be told of souls saved from damnation by the devotion of surviving relatives or because they were allowed to return as ghosts and make known their need for help. However, these were quite exceptional instances. The normal expectation was that eternal judgement would be passed on the individual immediately after death. The establishment of purgatory made plausible a very widely shared expectation of salvation, but the possibility of purgatorial re-habilitation was closed to those who died in mortal sin.[1] The final moment of life was also the last chance of repentance. At this critical juncture, the Church offered help generally regarded as indispensable in making a safe departure from the world: comfort, guidance, and above all the sacraments of penance, the altar, and extreme unction.

The time immediately before death was often depicted as a trial. The dying Christian was assailed not only by the pain of terminal illness but also by an agony of uncertainty about God's judgement. No man could know for sure whether he was in a state of grace. If the possibility of mercy and salvation was open to the repentant sinner, so was that of damnation for the Christian who fell from grace at the last. If the righteous man had lived never so virtuously and at last committed one deadly sin and so died, all his previous righteous dealing would not defend him from damnation, while if the sinful man at the

---

[1] P. Ariès, *Western Attitudes towards Death: From the Middle Ages to the Present* (Baltimore, 1974), 36–9; R. Wunderli and G. Broce, 'The Final Moment before Death in Early Modern England', *Sixteenth Century Journal*, 20 (1989), 259–75; J. Le Goff, *The Birth of Purgatory* (1984), 283–4; C. Burgess, ' "A Fond Thing vainly invented": An Essay on Purgatory and Pious Motive in later Medieval England', in S. J. Wright (ed.), *Parish, Church and People: Local Studies in Lay Religion 1350–1750* (1988), 61–4; Duffy, *Stripping of Altars*, 353; R. C. Finucane, *Appearances of the Dead: A Cultural History of Ghosts* (1982), 60–5.

end of his life returned to God, all his wickedness would not prevent his being saved. So taught John Fisher, paraphrasing the prophet Ezekiel, in his funeral sermon for Henry VII. On this last act of the play of man's life hung either everlasting bliss or eternal damnation. As the tree fell, so would it lie. How far the majority of people internalized the notion of the hour of death as an arduous trial it is impossible to say. Evidence such as that contained in testamentary depositions suggest that the making of wills and the reception of the sacraments had, for all their solemnity, a certain routine character, almost like taking out a passport for the hereafter. However, such material offers us only a partial glimpse into the mind of the dying. It is clear that the importance of the final moments, arduous or not, was widely accepted. John Aubrey, born in 1626, would remember in later life how, before the Civil Wars, 'ancient people, when they heard the Clock-strike, were wont to say, "Lord grant, that my last howre may be my best howre" '.[2]

Towards the close of the Middle Ages it was above all the last rites which shaped the process of Christian dying. Only their most important elements are described here. It is hard to believe that the long, elaborate chain of prayers and exhortations set out in the Sarum Manual, the most widely used service book of the English Church, could have been recited in its entirety when time was short. The Visitation of the Sick, extreme unction, and the Communion of the Sick, were each in principle of benefit to people likely to recover as well as to the mortally ill. In practice, people were reluctant to undergo extreme unction till death was all but certain. If it had already been carried out, the dying might receive Communion (the viaticum, or food for their last journey) without being anointed again.

The priest, preceded by his clerk with candle and bell, entered the sick person's house with a blessing, and sprinkled him with holy water. He exhorted him to be grateful to God, to accept illness patiently, and to be firm in faith. Was the sick person's belief sound? An interrogation suited to his or her capacity followed. The Sarum Manual also contains reminders of the need for charity and hope. Charity included the sharing of one's earthly goods, restitution, and forgiveness. The sick person was then exhorted to make a full confession, though this was not always possible. After receiving

---

[2] *The English Works of John Fisher*, ed. J. E. B. Mayor (EETS extra ser. 27; 1876), 270 (cf. Ezekiel 18: 26–7); D. Erasmus, *Preparation to deathe, a boke as deuout as eloquent* (1538), sig. Aii'; Ecclesiastes 11: 3; J. Aubrey, *Remaines of Gentilisme and Judaisme*, in id., *Three Prose Works*, ed. J. Buchanan-Brown (Fontwell, 1972), 157.

absolution, he kissed the crucifix placed by the bedside as a reminder of the passion which Jesus had suffered for the salvation of sinners.[3]

Anointing the sick with oil is described in Mark 6: 13 and enjoined in James 5: 14. Practised by the Church for the good of soul and body from ancient times, it was during the Middle Ages increasingly seen as one of the last rites for the dying. The eyes, ears, lips, nostrils, hands, feet, and back were anointed in turn. After unction, the priest gave the sick person another chance to confess previously forgotten sins and affirm his belief that the body and blood of Christ were present in the sacrament in form of bread. Administration of the viaticum might then take place. If the sick man seemed unlikely to be able to swallow the bread, he was to be told that his true faith and good will sufficed. One more rite, the commendation of the soul at the point of death, completed the series of services for the dying. When the soul seemed to be leaving the body, the passing bell reminded the faithful to pray for it. The *Commendatio Animae* in the Sarum Manual includes the Creed, the seven penitential psalms, pleas for the intercession of all the saints, seventy-seven of whom are named, a litany, the valediction 'Go, Christian soul, out of this world', and a plea to God to receive his servant into his shining abode.[4]

During the later Middle Ages there developed a literature of instruction for the benefit of the dying and their helpers which complemented the assistance given by the priest in the last rites. The most important example was translated into English as *The Book of the Craft of Dying* during the fifteenth century.[5] Of the book's six

---

[3] Brightman, *English Rite*, ii. 818–30; *Manuale ad vsum percelebris ecclesie Sarisburiensis*, ed. A. J. Collins (Henry Bradshaw Soc. 91; 1960), 97–107; J. Mirk, *John Mirk's Instructions for Parish Priests*, ed. G. Kristensson (Lund Studies in English, 49; 1974), 164, 170–3.

[4] *ODCC* 1406–7; *Manuale*, 107–18; Mirk, *Instructions*, 162–5. A recent study of the early development of the last rites is F. S. Paxton's *Christianizing Death: The Creation of a Ritual Process in Early Medieval Europe* (Ithaca, NY, 1990).

[5] M. C. O'Connor, *The Art of Dying Well: The Development of the Ars Moriendi* (New York, 1942), 1–60, 101–10; N. L. Beaty, *The Craft of Dying: A Study in the Literary Tradition of the* Ars Moriendi *in England* (New Haven, 1970), 1–53; Duffy, *Stripping of Altars*, 316–17. Text in *Yorkshire Writers: Richard Rolle of Hampole and his Followers*, ed. C. Horstmann (2 vols., London, 1895–6), ii. 406–20; trans. into modern English with comments by R. N. Swanson, *Catholic England: Faith, Religion and Observance before the Reformation* (Manchester, 1993), 94–5, 125–47. O'Connor, *Art of Dying Well*, 164–7, thinks that the abridged version published by Caxton, *Here begynneth a lityll treatise shorte and abredged spekynge of the arte & crafte to knowe well to dye* (1490), a fresh trans. from French, is inferior to the earlier English MS version. The importance of lay help for the dying in an emergency is well illustrated by advice given by the bishop of Bath and Wells in 1349. If the dying could not secure the services of a priest, they were to confess their sins 'to any lay person, even to a

chapters, the first offers reassurance. Bodily death is dreadful, the death of the soul far more horrible. However, all who die in God are blessed, it tells us: not only the good, but also the wicked who die in a state of true repentance and contrition, and in the true faith, unity, and charity of the Church. (Yet since one must die when God decides, every man who wishes to die well ought to live in such a way as to be ready to depart at any moment.) The second chapter deals with the temptations especially characteristic of terminal sickness: unbelief, despair, impatience, spiritual pride, and excessive attachment to worldly things. The frequent sinner, for example, is especially prone to despair. Yet even if a person has committed as many heinous sins as there are drops of water in the sea or stones on the shore, and been prevented by sickness or loss of speech from confessing or doing penance, he or she must never despair. In such a case true inner contrition, and the will to be shriven, are sufficient for salvation. The third chapter contains questions concerning such matters as the sick man's belief, repentance, and will to amend his life in case of recovery, which may be put to him by a lay person in the absence of a priest. Christ crucified, dying for sinners, is repeatedly recommended as a focus for the meditations of the dying man: as a shield against despair, as a barrier between him and his sins, and, in the fourth chapter, where the Crucifixion is the major theme, as an example of prayer and willing submission.[6]

The fifth chapter tells those attending the deathbed how best to help the sick person to die well. Only after taking immediate steps to improve spiritual health (which may remove the cause of physical sickness), should one send for the physician. It is difficult for a repentance deferred to the very end to be a true one sufficient for salvation: this warning tempers the hopes earlier conveyed by the writer's efforts to counter despair. So the first duty of a sick person's friends is to induce him to make his peace with God. They should encourage him to resist temptations, read him salutary texts, present him with a crucifix or the image of a saint, and sprinkle him with holy water to keep the fiends at bay. Prayers, above all to Jesus, are the most important help rendered to a dying man, especially when time is short. (The whole of the sixth chapter is devoted to them.) Near the end, no earthly things, including wife or children, should be brought to his mind or discussed in his presence, but the role of other helpers is of

woman if a man is not available' (quoted by C. Platt, *King Death: The Black Death and its Aftermath in Late-Medieval England* (1996), 98).

[6] Swanson, *Catholic England*, 125–39.

crucial importance.[7] The last rites, pivotal though they were, occupied a comparatively short time. The *Book* told the long-term lay
attendants of the dying how best to assist them.

A series of eleven illustrations, ten of them devoted to the five
temptations and the corresponding inspirations which enable the
dying to resist them, were repeatedly republished in the fifteenth and
sixteenth centuries under the title *Ars Moriendi*. Concrete images
convey a sense of diabolical presence much more emphatically and
vividly than the text of the book itself. In the picture illustrating the
temptation to despair, horrible devils crowd in round the bedside,
between the dying man and his family, reminding him of all his sins.
Illustrating the attachment to earthly things, one devil points to the
wife, children, and friends of the dying man. In the picture of the corresponding protective inspiration provided by the figure of Christ on
the Cross, an angel spreads a sheet to conceal the dying man's children from his eyes. The final illustration pictures the moment of
death. The soul is received by waiting angels. A vision of the Crucifixion dominates the background, while the frustrated devils dance
round the bed in impotent rage.[8]

The liturgy and the literature of advice and devotion give us a very
clear and full picture of the ideal of the good death which was held up
before Christian people before the Reformation. The most eloquent
surviving account of its practice is the skilfully wrought sermon
which John Fisher preached at the funeral of Henry VII on 10 May
1509. The king's behaviour on his deathbed showed that he was well
aware that he had been a great sinner. His worldly achievements were
but smoke and shadow to him now. However, Fisher remarked,
four things showed that Henry had made a virtuous end. The first was
the true turning of his soul from the world to God, revealed in
promises of amendment after making his Lenten confession. The second was Henry's trust in prayer. Thirdly, he had shown steadfast
belief in God, the Church, and the sacraments. Twice, shortly before
he died, at mid-Lent and again on Easter Day, he had crept bareheaded
on his knees to receive the sacrament of the altar, and only two days
before his death had kissed with the utmost veneration the mon-
strance containing the consecrated host. He eagerly sought extreme
unction, offering each part of his body for anointing in turn. On the

---

[7] Ibid. 139–47.

[8] *The Ars Moriendi. Editio Princeps, c.1450. A Reproduction of the copy in The
British Museum*, ed. W. H. Rylands (Holbein Society's Facsimile Reprints, 1881);
O'Connor, *Art of Dying Well*, 113–33.

day of his death he had heard the mass of the Virgin, to whom he had always had a special devotion. He had shown intense reverence for the crucifix. Finally, Henry had diligently sought mercy and turned to God with vigorous repentance in the appropriate time of Lent. Suffering agony in soul and body, he had sent up a lamentable cry for God's help.[9]

At the month's mind of the Lady Margaret Beaufort, the king's mother, who died just over two months after Henry himself, Fisher preached a very different sermon. He said relatively little about her painful deathbed. She had affirmed Christ's presence in the sacrament held before her, placing her whole trust in him, and received extreme unction. The two sermons complement each other closely. Henry's is a classic account of the protracted ordeal of a penitent sinner. His mother tells of a woman whose exemplary life of abstinence, self-discipline, diligent religious observance, abundant charitable works, and numerous pious benefactions had well prepared her for the hour of death. In the accounts of these two exemplary, if very different, deathbeds there bulk large the main elements of the late medieval 'way of death' as described in the liturgy and the *ars moriendi*. Prayer by, with, and for the dying, confession, sincere repentance, declarations of faith, devotion to the Saviour's image or his body in the consecrated host, administration of the sacrament of the altar and extreme unction: all these were described in one or both sermons.[10]

A more dispassionate account is the one which George Cavendish, Thomas Wolsey's gentleman usher, wrote of his master's death in November 1530. When Wolsey arrived at Leicester abbey under three days before his death, he was seriously ill. He told the monks that he had come to lay his bones among them. Yet the day before he died, he responded crossly to the suggestion that he be shriven, and had to be pacified by his chaplain. By the following morning, he had decided to make his confession and thus prepare himself for God. He spent an hour on the task. He probably received the viaticum. Among his last recorded words was a solemn warning to beware of heresy. Then, as his speech and sight failed, his servants reminded him of Christ's passion, and sent for the abbot to anoint him.[11]

Depositions taken during testamentary cases before the Church courts throw some light on the deathbed preparations made by

---

[9] Fisher, *English Works*, 271–6, 279.
[10] Ibid. 289–310, esp. 308–9.
[11] G. Cavendish, *The Life and Death of Cardinal Wolsey*, in *Two Early Tudor Lives*, ed. R. S. Sylvester and D. P. Harding (New Haven, 1962), 178–86.

people from the middling ranks of society in Henry VIII's reign.[12] Of all the services performed by the visiting priest, the hearing of confessions was the one mentioned most frequently, probably because it was when hearing confession that many priests did their prescribed duty of reminding sick people to make their wills. However, a number of testators were also said to have received the sacrament of the altar. James Mounford of St George, Botolph Lane (London), eloquently expressed in 1544 his sense of spiritual sustenance. He thanked God, now that he had received his maker. He asked all the world forgiveness, and prayed those present to bear witness that he died a true Christian man, both to God and to his prince. Very different was the timid reluctance of William Naggyngton of West Ham, who refused to receive the sacrament and make his testament when the curate advised him to do so, saying 'I trust I shall not dy at this tyme'.[13]

The most vivid description of a deathbed given during a testamentary case concerned the last days of Alice Gysby or Geysby in September 1538, an 'olde mayden' of London who died as the result of the rupture of a tumour on her face or neck. Although she asked 'shall I haue my maker?' (i.e. the viaticum) after the writing of her will had been finished, the two priests who were with her put it off until it was too late. By the time it was brought to her early in the morning of the following day, she was incapable of receiving it. The priest and the women in the room repeatedly urged Alice at least to look at it, and knocked her breast, but she showed no sign of realizing that it was there. The women asked her 'what, wyll ye dye lyke a hellhound and a beaste, not remembering your maker?', but it did no good. At last, after midnight, she recovered some consciousness. Her carers urged her to remember the passion of Christ, and this time she responded by knocking herself on the breast, looking upwards, and holding up her hands. This testimony vividly conveys the potent efficacy attributed to the sacrament of the altar as preparation for the Christian's last journey, and the importance of Christ's suffering as a focus of deathbed devotion. Alice was not the only person too ill to make confession or receive the sacrament when the priest finally brought the host. Complaints of priests' failure to visit the sick, or of their conducting the last rites without due decorum, are, though uncommon, occasionally encountered in surviving bishops' and archdeacons' visitation records.[14]

---

[12] See above, Ch. 4 n. 34.   [13] GL MS 9065A/1, fos. 77^v, 86^r, 95^r.

[14] Ibid., fos. 12^v–15^v, 19^v–26^v; (the Gysby case has also been noticed and described by S. Brigden, *London and the Reformation* (Oxford, 1989), 22–3, and Wunderli and Broce, 'Final Moment', 268–9). *Visitations in the Diocese of Lincoln, 1517–1531,*

Some of the Lollards denied the value of the last rites. In about 1514 John Morden, an inhabitant of the Lollard stronghold of Chesham (Bucks.), lay dying of the plague. He sent for his son-in-law Richard Ashford, and after his arrival excluded everybody else from the chamber so that he might deliver his last message. The sacrament of the altar was nothing more than bread and wine, images were but stocks and stones, and the only true pilgrimage in the world was the journey of brothers in the unity and law of God. All this and more was to be found in a book, hidden in his barn, to which the dying man directed Richard. Morden's rejection of sacramental help and his solemn dying words foreshadowed the behaviour of radical Protestants after the Reformation.[15]

The task of immediate preparation for death remained important after the Protestant Reformation. However, the Reformers, while never rejecting wholesale the practical advice given to the dying by their Catholic predecessors, took a very different view of the last hour. The faith of the dying individual, already emphasized in Catholic liturgy and advice literature, but linked with the sacraments and with the fruits of repentance and good works, now assumed overriding importance. The value of sacramental helps was called in question or altogether denied. Reformed Protestants believed that each individual belonged to the ranks either of the elect or the damned. In this sense, the outcome was not decided at a deep level by anything that happened on the deathbed, but this did not prevent the dying or those around them from seeking assurance or suffering doubt. Protestant advice literature was largely designed to buttress the former and remove the latter. The comportment of the dying was very often interpreted as an indicator of their elect status. God had decreed their fates long before, yet it might only be in the last hour that his grace manifested itself in moving a sinner to repentance.[16]

Although the medieval liturgical inheritance of the Church of England was never entirely rejected before the 1640s, far-reaching changes were made. The orders for the Visitation and Communion of the Sick in the Books of Common Prayer of 1549 and 1552 were based on the Sarum rite. However, several psalms and collects were

ed. A. Hamilton Thompson (Lincoln Record Soc. 33, 35, 37; 1940, 1944, 1947), i. 67, 133, 138, 139; ii. 13, 50; Duffy, *Stripping of Altars*, 312.

[15] Winchester, Hampshire Record Office, Winchester Diocesan Records, Register Fox iv. fo. 18.

[16] Wunderli and Broce, 'Final Moment', 265; Beaty, *Craft of Dying*, 153–5; D. W. Atkinson, 'The English ars morendi [*sic*]: Its Protestant Transformation', *Renaissance and Reformation*, NS 6, OS 18 (1982), 1–9.

removed, as were (more importantly) the sprinkling of the sick person with holy water, and the offering of the crucifix for him to kiss. On the other hand, the element of exhortation in the service was confirmed. The priest's address to the invalid emphasized that illness came from God. Such chastisement was a sign of his love, giving the Christian the opportunity of showing Christ-like patience. The possible purposes of this visitation (trial of faith, punishment of sins) were spelt out. The sick person's faith was to be examined. He was to be exhorted to forgive all who had offended him, to make amends to all whom he had wronged, and to be liberal to the poor. The priest was to require him to examine himself, so that he might condemn himself for his faults, but he was to make a 'speciall confession' only if he felt 'his conscience troubled with any weightie matter'. Extreme unction survived in 1549 only in a drastically simplified form and vanished altogether in 1552.[17]

The Books of Common Prayer discouraged both the expectation that the consecrated sacrament would be available at short notice and superstitious reverence towards it. The clergy were to exhort their parishioners to partake of Holy Communion frequently, so that in case of sudden illness, they should have no reason to feel anxious for lack of it. If the sick person wanted to communicate at home, he had to give the priest 'convenient warning', preferably the day before. The 1552 Book of Common Prayer assumed the presence of a 'good nombre' to receive with the sick person. If for any reason he did not receive the sacrament, the curate was to assure him that he ate and drank the body and blood of Christ if he genuinely repented of his sins and steadfastly believed that Christ had suffered death on the cross for him.[18] By 1552, then, the last rites had been transformed. Of the sacraments which had been sources of comfort in the last hours, one, extreme unction, had disappeared. Whatever the communicant received in Holy Communion now depended on the inner resource of faith, not the process of transubstantiation. The new requirements concerning the celebration of Communion may have discouraged many people from seeking it. No longer were confession and absolution essential elements of deathbed preparation.

A rare glimpse of the celebration of a Communion for a sick man in Elizabeth's reign is offered by depositions about a will made by William Kirkus of Kirk Merrington (Co. Durham) in October 1570.

---

[17] Brightman, *English Rite*, ii. 818–36, but see also below, n. 19.
[18] Brightman, *English Rite*, ii. 842–3, 846–7.

Notice was given beforehand to both the vicar and the parish clerk by one of Kirkus's maidservants. When the vicar arrived the following day, he first performed the duty prescribed in the Prayer Book by advising Kirkus to make his will. He then proceeded to the Communion. Afterwards, the clerk left the vicar drinking together with Kirkus and his wife. The giving of Communion to the sick, preceded in one instance by religious advice, was mentioned incidentally in other cases of this period, but post-Reformation testamentary depositions throw relatively little light on the clergy's deathbed ministrations. Royal and episcopal visitation articles and injunctions issued from 1547 onwards emphasize their duty of comforting invalids, especially by means of suitable texts of Scripture, rather than the celebration of Communion. The separatist Henry Barrow nevertheless claimed that a 'private communion or housling of the sick' took place with only the priest and the sick man participating when the invalid could find no friends to join him. Every 'prophane glutton and wicked atheist' could be absolved for money at the hour of death. (The form of absolution in the Prayer Book order for the Visitation of the Sick was in fact a translation of the key elements in the corresponding Sarum absolution.) From his point of view, too much of the old order had been retained.[19]

The ringing of the passing-bell to call for prayers for the dying survived the Reformation. There were no theological objections to it, unlike the tolling of bells for the dead. Even that stalwart reformer John Hooper permitted the practice. A number of Elizabethan bishops enquired about it. In one Lincolnshire village around the end of Elizabeth's reign, the bell brought a dying woman's neighbours hastening to her bedside.[20]

---

[19] *Depositions and other Ecclesiastical Proceedings from the Courts of Durham, extending from 1311 to the Reign of Elizabeth*, ed. J. Raine (Surtees Soc. 21; 1845), 212–15, 233, 266; NRO DN/DEP 28/30B, fos. 122, 135ᵛ, 140, 258, 272; *Visitation Articles and Injunctions of the Period of the Reformation*, ed. W. H. Frere and W. P. M. Kennedy (Alcuin Club Collections, 14–16; 1910), ii. 123–4; iii. 14, 62–3, 378; W. P. M. Kennedy, *Elizabethan Episcopal Administration: An Essay in Sociology and Politics* (Alcuin Club Collections, 26–7; 1924), ii. 56, 115; iii. 162, 213, 321; H. Barrow, *A Brief Discoverie of the False Church* (1590), in id., *The Writings of Henry Barrow 1587–1590*, ed. L. H. Carlson (Elizabethan Nonconformist Texts, 3; 1962), 421, 458, 461. Dr Eamon Duffy thinks that the preservation of the medieval absolution formula in the 1552 Prayer Book was 'extraordinary', and, given Cranmer's own theological development, only explicable in terms of popular demand and need (personal communication).

[20] *Visitation Articles and Injunctions*, ii. 287; iii. 62; Kennedy, *Episcopal Administration*, ii. 93, 118, 132; iii. 190, 213, 228, 293; PRO STAC 5/A29/20, deposition of Elizabeth Shillington.

Meanwhile, the clandestine practice of the ancient last rites survived in the Catholic community. The Jesuit missionary priests John Gerard and William Weston both recorded some instances. In 1589, soon after Gerard's landing in England, he found Lady Wodehouse, a Catholic convert, seemingly on the point of death after a difficult labour. Shortly after being anointed and receiving the viaticum, she made an unexpected recovery which completed her husband's conversion. Two stories illustrate the sometimes crucial part played by the expert confessor in helping sinners to die well. Gerard saved a 'rich and dissipated gentleman' from a bad end. The man made two confessions with Gerard's help, drew up his will, and received extreme unction. Round his neck during his last days was a crucifix which Gerard had lent him to kiss. He vigorously exhorted all his visitors to set their lives straight with God without delay. Questioned by Gerard, he affirmed his trust in the merits of Christ and the mercy of God and his belief in every article of the Creed. He received the viaticum a few hours before his death. William Weston once faced a seemingly desperate case. The dying man whose confession he had come to hear told him that he had arrived too late: judgement had already taken place and he had been handed over to the devil. This was nonsense, Weston told him. God's mercy was infinite. No one could say that he was cut off from His goodness as long as there was life left in him. Did not Weston see, the man asked, that the room was full of fearsome devils? (Their presence could have been terrifyingly real for a fever-stricken man familiar with the woodcuts of the *Ars Moriendi*.) Weston's patient, methodical interrogation concerning his possible breaches of the Ten Commandments gradually soothed the man. The devils hung back, and finally fled. 'The next day, in great tranquillity and peace of soul, he received the Holy Sacrament, and a very few hours later, without any disturbance, he breathed forth his soul and gave it back to God.'[21]

There was a big difference between the Catholic ideal exemplified by these stories and the way of dying developed by the stricter sort of Protestants. The first outstandingly influential English Protestant guide to the *ars moriendi* was *The Sicke mannes salue*, written during Edward VI's reign by Thomas Becon, chaplain to Thomas Cranmer, but possibly not published before 1561. By 1632 eighteen further editions had appeared. It is cast in the form of a dialogue

---

[21] *John Gerard: The Autobiography of an Elizabethan*, trans. P. Caraman (1951), 19–20, 181–3; *William Weston: The Autobiography of an Elizabethan*, trans. P. Caraman (1955), 141–4.

between a wealthy invalid, Epaphroditus, and four friends who come to comfort and encourage him. One of them, Philemon, fulfils a pastoral role. The dying man holds centre stage for much of the time. He dictates his will, gives his wife, son, and daughters spiritual and temporal advice, delivers a lengthy declaration of faith, and says farewell to his family. He fervently bewails his sins, though without specific details. Philemon comforts him at length, assuring him that God has freely forgiven him, and that he is one of the elect. In a series of exhortations, Philemon seeks to fortify Epaphroditus against the fear of death, against attachment to temporal friends and possessions, and against despair. He helps him to cope with a sudden spiritual crisis during which he is so troubled in conscience that he almost wishes there were no afterlife. In a powerful passage, Philemon asserts that no genuine repentance or conversion in this world is too late. He assures Epaphroditus once again that his repentance is evident testimony that he is one of those predestined to be saved. Philemon insists that a man can be sure of his salvation. The opposite doctrine of the papists is wicked and damnable; it makes faith useless and opens a path to desperation and hell. Epaphroditus, finally ready to die, sinks towards his end with prayers and exhortations in his ears.[22]

The organization of the treatise corresponds very loosely with that of the new order for the Visitation of the Sick. Philemon, fulfilling abundantly the requirement that all ministers stand ready to comfort the sick with suitable scriptural texts, provides the sick man's chief support. Epaphroditus confesses that he has sinned (though without details), and he declares his faith. Philemon's assures him that he has been forgiven, but no Communion of the Sick takes place. Means commonly used by Catholics to ward off Satan's attacks on the dying, such as sprinkling holy water about the chamber, and ringing a hallowed bell, are firmly rejected. There are some powerfully comforting and reassuring passages in the *Salue*, as its title suggests, but all sacramental help has been removed. Epaphroditus knows that his soul must go straight to heaven or to hell.[23] The temptation to despair

[22] T. Becon, *The Sicke mannes Salue, wherein the faithfull Christians may learne both how to behaue themselues paciently and thankefully in the tyme of sickenes, and also vertuously to dispose their temporall goods, and finally to prepare themselues gladly and godly to dye*, in *Prayers and other Pieces of Thomas Becon, S.T.P.*, ed. J. Ayre (Parker Soc., 1844), esp. 108, 114–20, 124–5, 130–53, 155–78, 189–90; D. S. Bailey, *Thomas Becon and the Reformation of the Church in England* (1952), 22, 144.

[23] Becon, *Salue*, 100, 108, 156, 159–60, 172; Beaty, *Craft of Dying*, 154. For another treatise similar in orientation to Becon's see Miles Coverdale's trans. (1st pub. 1555), of

is a powerful one. Certainly he receives much expert help, but he is not encouraged to disburden himself of his sins by a detailed confession. They are a matter between him and God. The autonomy of the individual Christian is enhanced, but the price is a heavy one. It is not surprising that individual deathbed performance was of such absorbing interest to many English Protestants during the following 150 years.

In 1595 appeared *A salue for a sicke man*, by William Perkins. The title may have been intended as a tribute to Becon's earlier work, but Perkins's tract is altogether pithier and more forcefully expressed. In Perkins's account of particular preparations for death, the doctrine of the papists is set out as the yardstick of what must be avoided. They require (he claimed) a comprehensive sacramental confession, reception of the Eucharist, and extreme unction. However, there is no scriptural warrant for any of these. The minister may declare that God pardons a man's sins without hearing all of them rehearsed. 'For hee which soundly and truly repents of one or some few sinnes, repents of all.' To urge dying men to make confession is to burden them more heavily than ever God appointed. The Supper of the Lord should only be celebrated in the assembly of God's people. The anointing with oil mentioned by James was not the same as the 'greasie sacrament of the Papists' but a ceremony whose justification had been lost with the Apostles' gift of miraculous healing.[24]

The sick person's afflictions come from God. The right response to them is to seek reconciliation with him by means of fresh examination of heart and life, a confession to him of recent and particular sins, and renewed prayer. If the sick man cannot perform these things unaided he must (as St James recommended) seek the help of the elders of the Church. Such assistance is not the responsibility of ministers alone, but also of others who know God's Word and have the gift of prayer. Indeed it should be the duty of every Christian man to comfort his brother in sickness. The sick man may make a confession of any sins which lie particularly heavy upon his conscience, but not necessarily to a minister. His foremost duties towards other people are to forgive, seek forgiveness, and leave his family well provided

a work by the Swiss Protestant Otto Werdmüller, repr. as *Treatise on Death*, in *Remains of Myles Coverdale, Bishop of Exeter*, ed. G. Pearson (Parker Soc., 1846), esp. 81, 86–7, 99–100, 103–8.

[24] W. Perkins, *A salue for a sicke man, or, a treatise containing the nature, differences, and kindes of death: as also the right manner of dying well* (edn of c.1638, STC 19747.3), 84–94.

for not only materially but (by means of religious exhortations) spiritually also.[25]

Three things are expected of the Christian as he finally draws close to death. First, that he die in faith, placing his whole reliance on God's special love and mercy, focusing his inward eye on Christ crucified. This inner faith is to be expressed by the outward signs of prayer or thanksgiving, or at least the sighs, sobs, and groans of a repentant and believing heart. Last words may proclaim faith with especial power. The second duty is to die readily, in submission to God's will, and the third to render up his soul into God's hands. In a sort of postscript, Perkins pointed out that the last combat with the devil in the pangs of death is often the most dangerous of all. He advised the dying Christian not to answer Satan, but simply to close his eyes and commend his cause to God.[26]

Would-be practitioners of a Puritan *ars moriendi* were thus well armed with advice, but not until 1645 did their brief and partial triumph give the Puritans the opportunity of replacing the Book of Common Prayer with a pattern of their own devising in *A Directory for the Publique Worship of God*. The Communion of the Sick now disappeared. The section of the *Directory* concerned with the Visitation of the Sick takes the shape of a set of instructions or guidelines for the minister. He is to explain to the sick person that his affliction comes from God, investigate his religious knowledge if he suspects him of ignorance, supply any necessary instruction, and exhort him to carry out a thorough self-examination. The pastor must on the one hand give comfort and support, especially to those broken in spirit, but on the other awaken the unrepentant to their danger, and warn the complacent not to rely on their own merits. There is a scheme of prayer confessing and bewailing sins in general terms and seeking God's mercy and help. However, it was not intended to be followed exactly, nor is there any suggestion that the dying person should make a confession of particular sins. Here, then, is some helpful pastoral advice for ministers who would attend the deathbeds of all sorts and conditions of people, but there is no longer any liturgical

---

[25] Ibid. 94–108, 140–52, 191–4.

[26] Ibid. 153–71. Perkins's work has received relatively little recent comment or analysis. However, see D. W. Atkinson, '*A Salve For A Sicke Man*: William Perkins' Contribution to the *ars moriendi*', *Historical Magazine of the Protestant Episcopal Church*, 46 (1977), 409–18. Id., 'English ars morendi', 3, 5, mentions a number of other writers not discussed here, such as James Cole, John Moore, Robert Hill, and George Shawe. See also his anthology *The English* ars moriendi (New York, 1992).

framework, and the pastor's task is by his advice and exhortation to encourage and focus the sick person's own spiritual efforts.[27]

Descriptions of deathbeds survive in very large numbers from late sixteenth- and seventeenth-century England, in biographies, auto-biographies, diaries, letters, and, above all, funeral sermons. Although these descriptions concern individuals of every shade of religious opinion, Puritans are particularly well represented. Good deaths offered examples for other godly Christians to emulate. The most important purposes of deathbed accounts were encouragement and reassurance. Their ability to show Christian faith and patience was a valuable indication of the likely destination of the dying. Some accounts were clearly written to dispel fears or rumours of deathbed apostasy or despair. The dying could be well aware that their comportment would be weighed up by both friends and foes. As Mrs Mary Gunter approached death in 1622, she remarked that she knew what the world would conclude if she said anything foolish or idle through pain or want of sleep: *'This is the end of all your precise Folks, they die mad, or not themselves, &c.'*[28]

Godly Protestants were usually described as playing an active role in the drama of their own deathbeds, especially by means of good advice and exhortations, declarations of faith, devout prayers, and the ready acceptance of death itself. Sir James Whitelocke's death in 1632, succinctly described by his son Bulstrode, was exemplary in all these respects. 'In the afternoon, he lay downe uppon his bed, gave good Counsell to those about him, expressed fully his assurance of the love of God to him, & of his eternall happiness through the merits of Christ, & so recommending his soul to God, and fetching two or three little groanes, his breath expired on the 22. day of June. 1632.'[29]

Valedictory exhortations and discourses to family, friends, and neighbours occupied a prominent place in many accounts. The Puritan clergy furnished some outstanding examples. 'Stand fast in the faith,' the famous minister John Carter told his family in 1635, 'and love one another.' Most of the duties reportedly urged upon their relatives and parishioners by dying pastors fell under one or both of these heads. Reading of the Scriptures was one of the most frequently mentioned. Prayer, participation in common worship,

---

[27] *A Directory for the Publique Worship of God, Throughout the Three Kingdoms* (1645), 64–72.

[28] S. Clarke, *The Lives of Sundry Eminent Persons in this Later Age* (2 pts. in 1 vol., 1683), ii. 140.

[29] Whitelocke, *Diary*, 65–6.

mutual spiritual help, and solidarity often appeared on the list. John Bruen (d. 1625), a model of the godly layman, encouraged his eldest son to be constant in religion and exhorted him to uphold God's worship both in public and in his own household. This was a high point in a long series of godly speeches, for in the days before his death, so long as he could move about his house 'he would drop some wholesome words of counsell or comfort, amongst such as he met withall, and never cease speaking of holy, or of heavenly things amongst the rest of his family'. John Preston similarly testified in his sermon for Arthur Upton in 1615 that his 'talke for the most part in his sicknesse was of heauenly matters, and such as came to comfort him, might receiue comfort from him'.[30]

Godly women, too, delivered exhortations and advice. Simonds D'Ewes recalled that his mother, lying on her deathbed in 1618, had charged her older children to remember their duties towards God and to further her younger children in the knowledge and fear of him. Elizabeth Whitelocke spent much of the last day of her life discoursing with her son Bulstrode against the fear of death. It was, she said, but a passage to a better life for those who trusted in God. They would meet again in heaven. Parents were sometimes described as giving each of their children in turn salutary advice specially suited to their ages and capacities.[31]

Puritans were expected to be strong in faith and to know what they believed. The lively faith of the dying Puritan might be expected to manifest itself to those around the deathbed. The recorded utterances are often fairly concise: heartfelt testimonies of belief and assurance rather than rehearsals of points of doctrine. They were especially important in giving spectators their most tangible evidence of the happy state of the dying person and examples to fortify them when they faced their own time of trial. Those of famous ministers were heard with particular eagerness. When Edward Dering lay dying in 1576, it was his friends who prompted him to say something for their edification and comfort. The sun shining in his face gave added force to his assertion that there was but one righteousness in the world, one communion of saints. He insisted that all his hopes of salvation rested

---

[30] S. Clarke, *A Collection of the Lives of Ten Eminent Divines* (1662), 19; *The Journal of Nicholas Assheton of Downham, in the County of Lancaster, Esq.*, ed. F. R. Raines (Chetham Soc., os 14; 1848), 130–1; J. Preston, *A sermon preached at the funeral of M'. Arthur Upton* (1619), 35.

[31] D'Ewes, *Autobiography & Correspondence*, i. 115; Whitelocke, *Diary*, 62–3; Clarke, *Eminent Persons*, i. 39; S. Ashe, *Gray Hayres crowned with Grace, A Sermon Preached at . . . the Funerall of . . . Mr. Thomas Gataker* (1655), 60–1.

only on the righteousness of Jesus Christ. He blessed God for the fact that he felt 'so much inward joy and comfort' in his soul, that if put to a choice between death and life, he would a thousand times rather choose death, if it were consistent with God's will.[32]

Godly laypeople also expressed their faith in memorable fashion. In 1584 Sir Gawen Carew, a leading Devon Protestant, allegedly spoke of his creation, redemption, sanctification, and justification as zealously and succinctly as the most perfect divine could have done. The third earl of Huntingdon, surprised by a sudden turn for the worse in his fatal illness shortly before his death in 1595, was reminded by two of his chaplains of the duty of declaring his perseverance in the faith. Though speaking with difficulty, he rose to the occasion with what one chaplain called a 'worthy, briefe, pithy and well studied speach'. 'I professe Jesus Christ God and man to be my onely saviour. And so must you doe too: and iff I shold speak this twelvemonth I could say no more.' According to Philip Stubbes, his wife Katherine made an exceptionally full confession of faith before her death in 1590, though it is hardly credible that somebody dying of fever should have delivered a declaration as fluent and coherent as the one which Philip Stubbes wrote down. Another pious woman, Rebecka Crispe, showed a readiness to seek advice which may have been thought appropriate in a woman. At the beginning of her last sickness in 1620, she made a profession of her faith before the famous London preacher Thomas Gataker and some other friends, but she wished to be better informed if necessary, or to have it further confirmed. She wanted to be continually engaged in this work, 'forgetting her paines and weakenesse when she was about it, and neglecting her naturall rest, to attend it'.[33]

Fervent prayer occupies a prominent place in many Puritan deathbed accounts. It typically wove together scriptural phrases, sentences, and verses in extemporary combinations. It took many forms: praise for blessings bestowed, and a variety of petitions (for mercy, for a sense of God's love and forgiveness, for strength to bear the trials of sickness, and for help for those left behind). In the later

---

[32] S. Clarke, *The Marrow of Ecclesiastical History* (3rd edn., 1675), 354–5.

[33] J. Chardon, *A comfortable sermon for all such as thirst to be ioined with Jesus Christ. Preached at the funerals of syr Gawen Carew in Exeter the two and twenteth of April, 1584* (Oxford, 1586), unpaginated; M. C. Cross, 'The Third Earl of Huntingdon's Deathbed: A Calvinist Example of the *Ars Moriendi*', *Northern History*, 21 (1985), 97–9; P. Stubbes, *A christal glasse for christian women. Contayning an excellent discourse, of the life and death of Katherine Stubbes* (1592 edn.), sig. B–C2ᵛ; Gataker, *Certaine sermons*, ii. 215.

stages, such pleas as 'Lord Jesus come quickly, come quickly' were common. The godly often committed their souls into God's hands with their last breath.[34]

Compared with godly exhortations, firm and manifest faith, and devout prayers, certain other elements of the traditional craft of dying, such as the confession of sins, reconciliation, forgiveness, and seeking forgiveness, play a relatively small part in the surviving narratives. As we have seen, the writers of the Puritan *ars moriendi* encouraged a general acknowledgement of sins rather than a specific account of them. Some of the godly were described as repentant. 'In his sicknesse he was very penitent and sorrowfull, confessed his sinne, desiring God to forgiue him,' wrote John Preston of the Devon gentleman Arthur Upton, though he added that Upton assured himself that his sins had been forgiven him for Christ's sake. Upton also forgave all wrongs done to him. The young Suffolk gentleman Edward Lewkenor was commended for the 'exact surveigh' which he took of his former life during his illness. He was much troubled by the sight of his former weaknesses and infirmities, even though they were not damnable sins; his repentance was true and hearty.[35]

Some Puritan narratives, like Bulstrode Whitelocke's accounts of his parents' deaths, make no mention of any assistance which the dying may have received from ministers of the Church. However, in other cases pastoral help was clearly important. The clergy attending upon the earl of Huntingdon in 1595 are described in an exceptionally full account as having tried to help him above all by means of prayer with him and for him, reassurance, exhortation, and comfortable readings from Scripture, especially on the great themes of God's mercy, remission of sins and justification by faith. These ministrations, especially prayer and encouraging words, appear in many other shorter accounts. John Bruen and the mother of Sir Simonds D'Ewes (d. 1618) were among those who were comforted by the prayers of ministers while they lay dying. One gentleman had with

---

[34] Stubbes, *Christal glasse*, repr. with some omissions in *Philip Stubbes's Anatomy of the Abuses in England in Shakspere's Youth, A.D. 1583*, ed. F. J. Furnivall (New Shakspere Soc., 6th ser. 4, 6, 12; 1877–82), i. 201; Chardon, *Comfortable sermon*, unpaginated; R. Eaton, *A sermon preached at the funeralls of Thomas Dutton of Dutton, esquire* (1616), 25; Oldmayne, *Lifes brevitie*, 35; Preston, *Sermon*, 35; J. Warren, *Domus ordinata. A funerall sermon, preached in Bristoll, at the buriall of mistresse Needes* (1618), pref.; T. Wilson, *The practise of the saints* (1609), 66; R. Kilbie, *A sermon preached . . . in Oxford at the funeral of Thomas Holland* (Oxford, 1613), 19; J. Chadwich, *A sermon preached at Snarford at the funerals of sir George Sanct-Paule. Together with a briefe relation of his life and death* (1614), 27.

[35] Preston, *Sermon*, 35; Oldmayne, *Lifes brevitie*, 27, 32–3.

him during his last days 'divers reuerend Ministers, in whose godly speeches, and deuout prayers, and good companie he much reioyced'. According to her epitaph at North Cadbury (Som.), Lady Magdalen Hastings (d. 1596) had three preachers with her during her last illness who took it in turns to give her weekly stints of instruction and support.[36]

In their accounts of the deaths of the godly, Puritan ministers mentioned relatively seldom any attempts they might have made to prompt an examination of conscience or an acknowledgement of faults. Dr John Chadwich asked Sir George St Paul shortly before his death in 1613 whether he remembered dealing hardly with any man, and whether, if so, he had made restitution? St Paul answered cheerfully that he had never gained any goods unlawfully or uncharitably. Since St Paul was a man so scrupulous that he had once asked Chadwich whether he might lawfully kneel on a cushion when making his private prayers, the answer is hardly surprising, but Chadwich may have been rather bolder than most ministers in asking the question.[37]

The majority of the most graphic English deathbed descriptions written between about 1580 and the Restoration belong to a pattern which may be broadly described as Puritan. However, the Prayer Book order for the Visitation of the Sick probably remained in very widespread use among contentedly conforming members of the Church of England, especially those of a conservative outlook. Spiritual athletes may have achieved the sorts of deathbed performance celebrated by the Puritan writers, but the successful practice of their *ars moriendi* was beyond most of the population. From the closing years of Elizabeth's reign at latest there was a growing belief that the Prayer Book framework needed to be developed and strengthened, and that the minister should take a more active role. There was a renewed emphasis on a thorough confession of sins, and on the Communion of the Sick. The imposition of the *Directory* only strengthened the reaction among some supporters of the old Church order and sharpened their perception of what they had lost. This helps to explain why Jeremy Taylor's *Holy Dying*, the work which best encapsulated the spirit of the *ars moriendi* within the post-Reformation sacramental tradition, appeared in 1651.

[36] Cross, 'Huntingdon's Deathbed', 94–103; Assheton, *Journal*, 133; D'Ewes, *Autobiography & Correspondence*, i. 111; Chadwich, *Sermon*, 25–7; Oldmayne, *Lifes brevitie*, 34; *The Letters of Sir Francis Hastings, 1574–1609*, ed. C. Cross (Somerset Record Soc. 69; 1969), 66.

[37] Chadwich, *Sermon*, 24–5, 27.

Already in the 1590s Lancelot Andrewes, then vicar of St Giles Cripplegate, was using in his Visitation of the Sick a manual of prayers and sickbed duties of his own devising. In an Ash Wednesday sermon delivered in 1625, Andrewes emphasized that repentance required expert guidance. It was, however, a matter studied by very few, because this approach had grown quite 'out of request'. Instead the task was being put off until it was impossible to do anything. 'And then must one come, and as we call it, speak comfortably to us, that is, minister to us a little Divinity laudanum, rather stupefactive for the present, than doing any sound good.' Andrewes's *Manual of Directions for the Sick* draws the sick person by careful interrogation first to a general acknowledgement of sinful life and then to the confession of any special sin lying so heavy on his conscience that he might need absolution. The invalid is to be questioned about his belief, and about his readiness both to forgive and to seek forgiveness. The collection also contains many carefully chosen texts of Scripture designed to comfort the infirm, explain their illness in terms of divine providence, and remind them of their duties. There are several prayers to be said for or by the sick, a 'Litany for the Sick Person in danger of Death', and a *Commendatio Animae* or 'Recommending the Soul to God'. William Laud drew up a detailed Latin questionnaire to be put to the sick which for the most part closely resembles questions in the *Manual*. John Cosin also included in his *Private Devotions* (1627) a commendation of the soul at the moment of death and other prayers corresponding to ones in Andrewes's collection. Cosin interpreted the order for the Visitation of the Sick to mean that the Church required the invalid's confession of mortal sins to a priest.[38]

Detailed advice for ministers was incorporated in Christopher Sutton's *Disce Mori* (1600), one of the most popular English works about the craft of dying to appear since Becon's *Salue*. Sutton was inspired to write it by his experience at the deathbed of his patron Sir Robert Southwell, son-in-law of Charles Howard, earl of Nottingham. He emphasized that the sick needed careful spiritual direction to strengthen them against the terrors of death and troubles of conscience to which they were peculiarly prone. The first priority was to bring the sick person to do five things: confess all his sins most sincerely and humbly; accept God's will contentedly; resolve to make a

[38] L. Andrewes, *Works*, ed. J. P. Wilson and J. Bliss (LACT, 11 vols., 1841–54), i. 450–1; *A Manual of Directions for the Sick*, ibid. xi. 177–222, esp. 183–7; Laud, *Works*, iii. 91–3; J. Cosin, *Works*, ed. J. Sansom (LACT, 5 vols., 1843–55), ii. 309–21, v. 164.

hearty reconciliation with the world, desiring and giving forgiveness of all offences; take his illness in good part as a preparation for death; and wholly commend himself to God's mercy through the mediation of Christ his Saviour. He was to affirm the Creed and ask God's forgiveness. Sutton also suggested suitable prayers and scriptural readings, and included a form of commendation at the hour of death.[39]

An ideal picture of the 'Parson Comforting', in accordance with Sutton's recommendations, appears in George Herbert's *A Priest to the Temple* (1652). Herbert's parson stands ready to visit the sick armed with 'all the points of consolation' concerning such things as God's providence, Christ's example, the benefits of affliction, and the disparity between earthly griefs and heavenly joys. He persuades his suffering parishioners to make a particular confession and urges them to do pious charitable works. He intimates the benefits of the Holy Sacrament '*how comfortable, and Soveraigne a Medicine it is to all sin-sick souls; what strength, and joy, and peace it administers against all temptations, even to death it selfe*', in such a fashion that they may desire it without his direct persuasion.[40]

Sutton's work anticipated in some respects the greater achievement of Jeremy Taylor's *The Rule and Exercises of Holy Dying* (1651). Taylor turned down the spotlight on the deathbed performance. Much of the terror of death lies in the social drama which surrounds it. Take this away, 'and then to die is easy, ready, and quitted from its troublesome circumstances'. However, a 'holy and blessed death' required long-term preparation, especially by means of watchful self-discipline, self-examination, and the exercise of charity. The onset of sickness, hard at first sight, would be salutary in its effects if it led the sick person to seek the reasons for God's punishment, to renounce sin and withdraw from the world. Taylor provided detailed guidance in combating the two chief temptations of sickness; impatience and fear of death. Sickness presented the opportunity of practising patience, faith, and repentance. A thorough and comprehensive repentance was especially important, however conscientious the individual's previous efforts to lead a good life. It was here that the help of the priest might be crucial. His enquiries needed to be clear and searching. 'If we have committed sins, the spiritual man is appointed to restore us, and to pray for us, and to receive our

---

[39] Sutton, *Disce Mori: Learn to Die* (1843; repr. from 1st edn. of 1600), pp. xxxviii–xxxix, 140–55.
[40] G. Herbert, *A Priest to the Temple*, in id., *Works*, ed. F. E. Hutchinson (Oxford, 1941), 249–50. Herbert had died in 1633.

confessions, and to inquire into our wounds, and to infuse oil and remedy, and to pronounce pardon.' Once confident that the sick person retained no 'affection to any sin' he might administer the Holy Sacrament.[41]

The desire to reinforce and develop the order for the Visitation of the Sick which was expressed by a growing number of clergy after the 1580s at last made its mark in the revised Prayer Book of 1662. The minister is here directed to ask the sick person whether he repents truly of his sins, and to move him to make a special confession of them, if he feels his conscience troubled. Absolution is to be given only 'if he humbly and heartily desire it'. The order of service includes a commendatory prayer for a sick person at the point of death. Various other special prayers are supplied for use where appropriate.[42]

There are fewer readily accessible descriptions of the sort of deathbed ministry envisaged by writers in the Andrewes–Taylor tradition than there are of the practice of the Puritan *ars moriendi*, at least from the period before 1660, but a number of accounts can be found in biographies and funeral sermons. According to Izaak Walton, Richard Hooker visited his sick parishioners unsent for, and brought them to confess their sins. They received the Communion both as a means of strengthening their resolve to forsake those sins, and as a confirmation of God's mercies to their souls in the event of their deaths. The day before his own death, Hooker was given absolution (presumably after confession), and then received the sacrament together with some of his friends. The following day, he expressed his hope of forgiveness on account of Christ's death, and then, finally, the joy which sprang from his assurance of being at peace with God and men.[43]

The narrative of the last days of Robert Cecil, earl of Salisbury, by his chaplain John Bowle, later bishop of Rochester, gives a vivid picture of ministry to a dying penitent. Salisbury saw himself as a great sinner who stood in need of mercy. During his lingering and painful illness in 1612, as he reminded Bowle nine days before he died, he truly confessed his sins, professed his faith, forgave his enemies,

    [41] J. Taylor, *The Rule and Exercises of Holy Dying* (1929 edn.), 34–50, 56–149, 177–207 (quotations from pp. 94, 178, 203); Beaty, *Craft of Dying*, 197–270; C. J. Stranks, *Anglican Devotion: Studies in the Spiritual Life of the Church of England between the Reformation and the Oxford Movement* (1961), 86–93.
    [42] Brightman, *English Rite*, ii. 829, 839–41; T. T. Carter, *The Doctrine of Confession in the Church of England* (1865), 124–8.
    [43] I. Walton, *The Lives of Dr John Donne, Sir Henry Wotton, Mr Richard Hooker, Mr George Herbert and Dr Robert Sanderson* (Oxford, 1824), 170–1, 173–6.

made his peace with God, received absolution ('the message of mercy'), and had the seal of the Holy Sacrament. Nearly three years later, Bowle mentioned in the sermon he preached at the funeral of Henry Grey, earl of Kent, the humble private confession which the earl made to his chaplain on his deathbed. His last words were three Amens to his chaplain's prayers. Bowle presented Henry Grey as a man who preferred the '*Apostolicall discipline of the Church of England . . . before the lunacies, and Fansies of Consistorian confusion*'. In 1614 in another funeral sermon, George Ferebe, vicar of Bishop's Cannings (Wilts.), whose talent as a composer of music had recently gained him the favour of Anne of Denmark, described in a funeral sermon the deathbed of John Drew, a local gentleman. Despite the good character which Ferebe gave Drew as a landlord, friend, and neighbour, he believed that he had cause to be grateful to God for humbling him by means of a long sickness and granting him 'so large & pretious a time of repentance'. Upon Drew's desire 'to have his heart comforted with the pledge of Christs loue', the sacrament of his body and blood, Ferebe had received from him 'such a full confession of his faith, profession of his piety, detestation of his sinnes, petition & supplication for forgiuenes, that nothing more could be expected from a Christian man'. An especially eloquent description by a minister of his using the keys of absolution at the deathbed was included in John Wall's funeral sermon for John Stanhope, who died as a student at Oxford in 1623. It brought the sick man comfort and joy. These examples show that the tradition of sacramental deathbed ministry was alive and vigorous in the early seventeenth century.[44]

Canon 67 of 1604 required the clergy to visit their dangerously sick parishioners to instruct and comfort them in their distress according to the order of the Prayer Book, unless they were preachers, in which case they were allowed to exercise their discretion. A majority of the subsequent visitation articles which touched on this aspect of

---

[44] F. Peck, *Desiderata Curiosa: or, a Collection of divers Scarce and Curious Pieces, relating chiefly to Matters of English History* (2 vols., 1779), i. 206–7; J. Bowle, *A sermon preached at Flitton in the countie of Bedford, at the funerall of Henrie earle of Kent* (1615), sig. F2ᵛ, F4ʳ⁻ᵛ; G. Ferebe, *Lifes farewell. Or a funerall sermon. At the funerall of John Drew gentleman* (1615), 27–8; I. Gandy, *Round about the Little Steeple: The Story of a Wiltshire Parson 1573–1623* (Gloucester, 1989), 109–13, 133–51; J. Wall, *A sermon preached at Shelford in Nottinghamshire: on the death of M. John Stanhope* (1623), fourth unfoliated leaf after sig. C5. For John Cosin's description of the deathbed of Mrs Dorothy Holmes, sister of Richard Neile, bishop of Durham (1623), including her confession, absolution, and reception of Communion, see his *Works*, i. 28–30.

pastoral duty seem to have been based on this canon. Few were more specific. However, Bishop James Montagu of Bath and Wells enquired in 1609 whether clergy had at any time neglected to minister the sacrament to people in extremity of sickess, having been required to do so. In 1621 Theophilus Field of Llandaff asked whether ministers had visited the sick to pray with them or administer the Lord's Supper to them.[45]

A contrast has been drawn here between two models of the good death. Accounts of Puritan deathbeds give the central place to the dying man or woman, usually armed by a steadfast faith forged and burnished long before the hour of trial. It was sometimes reported of such saints that in their deaths they gave more comfort to their helpers than they received. The basic assumption of the second model is that the sick person is a sinner who needs help. The weight of sins is taken from the invalid's soul by means of confession, and he receives an absolution which assures him that God forgives the genuinely contrite. The pastor guides the sick person through a statement of belief, encourages him to forgive and seek forgiveness, and ministers to him the sacrament of the Lord's Supper. The priestly role is of pivotal importance.

However, deathbed confession and reception of the sacrament never became the exclusive property of the anti-Calvinist wing of the Church. A book which proved popular among Puritans was Lewis Bayly's *The practise of pietie* (*c*.1613), which, it has been said, 'exactly fulfilled all the requirements of those who accepted Calvin's theology without his church order'. It had already gone through eleven editions by 1619. Bayly advised the sick man to send for some godly and religious pastor to absolve him of his sins on his confession and unfeigned repentance. Bayly was at pains to show the scriptural basis for the clergy's authority to absolve as the ministers of Christ, and to cite passages in favour of private confession from Calvin, Beza, and Luther. Only lawful ministers, he insisted, could absolve, and it

---

[45] *Synodalia: A Collection of Articles of Religion, Canons, and Proceedings of Convocations*, ed. E. Cardwell (2 vols., Oxford, 1842), i. 284 (referring to the 'Communion-book', the 'libro publicae liturgiae' in the Latin text, ibid. 202); *Visitation Articles and Injunctions of the Early Stuart Church*, i, ed. K. Fincham (Church of England Record Soc. 1; 1994), 9, 18, 23, 30, 42–3, 57, 74, 84, 86, 101, 113, 127, 131, 161, 181, 198, 200. Communion was not to be administered in a private house save when somebody was dangerously sick or too weak to go to church: ibid. 74–5, 127. For a description of one minister's assiduous visitation of the sick, see J. Fell, *The Life of . . . Henry Hammond*, in *The Miscellaneous Theological Works of Henry Hammond*, ed. N. Pocock (LACT, 3 vols., 1847–50), vol. i. p. xxiv.

was dangerous for a sinner to be his own judge (as risky, he implied, as it was for a sick man to neglect the advice of a skilled physician). The Church of England had indeed abolished the tyranny of compulsory confession and the impossible requirement of an enumeration of all sins. Yet a private confession to God's minister was the best means of humbling a proud heart and raising up a humble spirit. After completing his confession, the penitent was recommended to receive the sacrament of the Lord's Supper if he had a sufficient number of Christian friends to join with him. This, Bayly insisted, was no private mass. Although Bayly commended Perkins's *Salue for a sicke man*, there is a sharp difference in spirit and emphasis between the two works.[46]

In 1636 Daniel Featley, a staunch Calvinist, but an episcopalian, preached at the funeral of Sir Humphrey Lynd. (Both men had written anti-Roman controversial works.) The eloquent deathbed narrative might almost have been written to illustrate the practical implementation of Bayly's advice. Among its high points are Lynd's humble confession of his sins, orthodox profession of his faith, absolution, and reception of 'that which the ancient Fathers fitly term *Viaticum morientium*', which he attempted to receive on his knees, with 'no lesse reverence then if Christ had been bodily present to his eyes'.[47]

Confession, absolution, and the viaticum did not bulk large in all deathbed accounts written by men of high church leanings. Preaching in commemoration of Lady Danvers in 1627, John Donne especially praised her unswerving loyalty to the Church of England. She participated in Common Prayer, joining in the responses with those around her bed, less than two hours before she died. However, if she made a particular confession or received the sacrament, Donne chose not to mention the fact. In the theatre of his own death, Donne as actor-manager rivalled, if he did not surpass, the performances of most Puritan ministers. When he preached at court on the first Friday in Lent 1631, his evident weakness, faint voice, and skeletal appearance made many of his audience say that he had given his own funeral sermon. Once he had retired to his house to die, Donne set by his bedside the painting on which his funeral monument would be based, so that he might contemplate it till his death. The story of Donne's last weeks resembles typical Puritan deathbed narratives in certain

---

[46] L. Bayly, *The practise of pietie: directing a christian how to walke* (11th edn., 1619), 755–68 (2); Stranks, *Anglican Devotion*, 36.

[47] D. Featley, *A sermon preached at the funerall of sir Humphrey Lynd. . . . June the 14th 1636*, in H. Lynde, *A case for the spectacles, or, a defence of Via tuta, together with Stricturae in Lyndomastygem* (1638), 217–18.

respects: his voicing 'inexpressible joy' at his intimations of election, his solemn farewells to his friends, his constant readiness to die, and his experience of 'some revelation of the beatifical vision' just before death. Izaak Walton mentioned no particular confession made by Donne after his return to London to die, and no participation in Communion while on his deathbed.[48]

Within the Church of England, the ideal pattern of the loyal conformist's deathbed survived long after the Restoration, to be celebrated in a number of eloquent funeral sermons. One of the fullest and most memorable of such accounts is the one which Richard Wroe gave of the last days of Sir Roger Bradshaigh of Haigh, Bt., at his funeral in 1684. Sir Roger had been retrieved, through the care of the earl of Derby, from the errors of popery in which the rest of his relatives had been brought up, and he had been a true Protestant of the Church of England. Yet Wroe's account brings out precisely those elements of the Church's practice which were best calculated to make a gentleman of Catholic background feel at home in it. Sir Roger had received Holy Communion for the last time, at his own earnest request, on Easter Day, the day before he died. In answer to questions, he had given a 'very satisfactory account' of the state of his soul. He said that he 'hoped that he had made his peace with God: that he was heartily sorry, and truly penitent for all his Sins, and put his whole trust in Gods mercy: that he freely and heartily forgave all men, and as heartily desired forgiveness at their hands'. He requested absolution and received it with great humility and comfort. He participated in the service with concentrated devotion, and continued in prayer till his death, which happened immediately after prayers had been offered up for him in church at his request. 'A Comfortable end', Wroe remarked, 'when the Soul expires in pious raptures, and ardent ejaculations, and ascends up [*sic*] in the incense of devout Prayers to the place of rest and repose.'[49]

Of the various elements of this model Anglican deathbed account, the one most frequently mentioned in other descriptions is the reception of Communion. Preachers referred to the sacrament itself and to its effects on the communicant in vivid and eloquent terms. Lady

    [48] *The Sermons of John Donne*, ed. G. R. Potter and E. M. Simpson (10 vols., Berkeley and Los Angeles, 1953–62), viii. 90–1; Walton, *Lives*, 47–53; N. Tyacke, *Anti-Calvinists: The Rise of English Arminianism c.1590–1640* (Oxford, 1986), 182, 261.
    [49] R. Wroe, *Righteousness Encouraged and Rewarded with an Everlasting Remembrance. In a Sermon at the Funeral of the Right Worshipful Sir Roger Bradshaigh of Haigh, Knight and Baronet* (1684), 17–20.

Paget (d. 1672) tasted in this 'Coelestial banquet' a happy anticipation of heaven. Thomas Ken recalled in 1682 how Lady Margaret Mainard's reception of her viaticum, 'the most holy Body, and Blood of her Saviour', had seemed to give her a new transfusion of grace. Despite her exhausted condition and perpetual drowsiness, she had made herself stay awake in order to continue praying and focus her thoughts on heaven. It was, Ken remarked, as if she had been teaching her soul to act independently of her body, anticipating the imminent state of separation. Sir Henry Johnson blessed God for the refreshment the sacrament gave his soul during the long and tedious sickness which preceded his death in 1683. The famous judge Sir Matthew Hale declined the suggestion that he receive Communion in his own house during his long last illness in late 1676, saying that he would go to his heavenly father's house to receive the feast which he had prepared for him. He received it with the greater devotion 'because he apprehended it was to be his last, and so took it as his viaticum and provision for his journey'.[50]

Confession and absolution also appear in descriptions of Restoration deathbeds, but less prominently than the Communion to which some writers considered them the indispensable preliminary. Surviving accounts are not always very explicit. In 1689, for example, Sir John Chapman, a former lord mayor of London, 'heartily lamented the Failings of his Life, and bound himself in new Resolutions of Amendment'. It is difficult to know in this case whether the dying man simply expressed his contrition in general terms or admitted specific sins. The penitent earl of Rochester (d. 1680) was said to have been 'very large and particular' in acknowledging his devotion to sin, but he was an extraordinary sinner. In 1694 Thomas Ken reproached Archbishop Thomas Tenison for failing to bring the dying Queen Mary to admit that she had wronged her father, James II. The value of private confession was strongly emphasized by the non-juror Nathaniel Spinckes in his exposition of the duties of *The Sick Man visited* (1712), a sort of High Church counterpart of Becon's *Salue*. Here, the sick man Anchithanes reveals to his friend Theophilus that at first he found it hard to expose his shame to the minister

[50] J. Jenny, *A Sermon preached At the Funeral of ... Lady Frances Paget...* (1673), 24; T. Ken, *At the Funeral of the Right Honourable the Lady Margaret Mainard*, in C. H. Sisson (ed.), *The English Sermon*, ii. *1650–1750* (Cheadle, 1976), 187–8; S. Peck, *A Sermon preached at the Funeral of Sir Henry Johnson K^t.* (1684), 28; G. Burnet, *The Lives of Sir Matthew Hale, Knight...; Wilmot, Earl of Rochester...; and Queen Mary* (1774 edn.), 55–6.

Theodorus. Theophilus assures the sick man that Theodorus's esteem for him will be increased, not reduced, by this testimony of repentance and renunciation of his sins.[51]

The duty of reconciliation was closely associated with that of confession. Some people forgave or sought forgiveness in general terms. The loyal churchman Thomas Whitchurch of Hedgerley in Buckinghamshire (d. 1691) declared that he was in perfect charity with all the world, forgiving all who had offended him, and desiring forgiveness from any to whom he had given offence. Others gave specific details or sought reconciliation with individuals. The earl of Rochester showed his readiness to make restitution to the utmost of his power to all those whom he had injured. He forgave all injuries done him 'some more particularly mention'd, which were great and provoking'. Shortly before her death in 1664, Lady Anne Harcourt took her woman servant by the hand and shook it, as a sign that she was heartily reconciled with her 'notwithstanding some tart words, that had some dayes before passed betwixt them'. An eminent physician, Dr Wharton (d. 1673), sent for the antiquary Elias Ashmole after suffering a fatal stroke. There had been differences between them, and Wharton wished to be reconciled with Ashmole. The description of the death of Colonel Edward Phelips in 1680 conveys something of the emotional cost and purging effect of the act of forgiveness. Our being forgiven, he was told by the minister who attended him, depends on our forgiving others. With tears in his eyes, Phelips said that he heartily forgave those who had done him evil, although he had found it very hard for flesh and blood to bear the wrongs he had received.[52]

An eighteenth-century trend towards reticence about the details of the deathbed experience is first and most clearly apparent in descriptions of the deaths of members of the Established Church. But we can sometimes catch a glimpse of the devotion to the Lord's Supper which continued to play an important part in the preparations of the

[51] Ken, *At the Funeral of Lady Mainard*, 188; J. Scott, *A Sermon Preach'd at the Funeral of Sir John Buckworth . . . December 29, 1687* (1688), 32; R. Parsons, *A Sermon preached at the Funeral of the . . . Earl of Rochester* (Oxford, 1680), 24; 'Ken's Letter to Archbishop Tenison', in E. H. Plumptre, *The Life of Thomas Ken* (2nd edn., 1890), ii. 86–94; N. Spinckes, *The Sick Man visited: And Furnish'd with Instructions, Meditations, and Prayers* (1712), 142, 147–9; cf. Carter, *Doctrine of Confession*, 196–8.

[52] H. Parsley, *A Sermon Preached at the Funeral of Mr Thomas Whitchurch. October the 15th 1691* (1692), 26–7; Parsons, *Sermon*, 29; E. Hall, *A Sermon Preached at Stanton-Harcourt Church, . . . At the Funerall of the Honourable the Lady Ann Harcourt* (Oxford, 1664), 60–1; *The Diary and Will of Elias Ashmole*, ed. R. T. Gunther (Oxford, 1927), 94; SRO DD/PH/238, fo. 199ᵛ.

pious. Lady Elizabeth Hastings, a famous benefactress, finally died of cancer in 1739 after a long illness bravely borne. Once she could no longer go to church, she received the sacrament at home every Sunday. Just before her death, she gave her parting words of advice to her assembled household and then received the last rites from the vicar of the parish. Her friend Thomas Wilson, bishop of Sodor and Man (1697–1755) attached great importance to the Visitation of the Sick and the encouragement of confessions.[53]

The Puritan way of dying continued as a distinct tradition after the Restoration. Richard Baxter's 'Directions for the Sick' in his *Christian Directory* (1673) offer a particularly effective guide to it. Baxter was concerned to advise both the sick and their friends. Rigorous self-examination, renewal of one's faith in Christ, readiness to see sickness as a mercy which weans one from the world, ability to focus one's mind on God, his mercies, and the heavenly kingdom: these, for Baxter, were among the key elements of good dying. He was especially concerned to arm the sick against five chief temptations: unbelief, despair, spiritual pride, fear, and attachment to worldly things. (Save for the substitution of fear for impatience, these were the same as the temptations listed in the *Book of the Craft of Dying*.) Baxter called upon his readers to review their lives, repenting anew of all their sins, particularly the most serious ones. Satisfaction of wrongs, reconciliation, restitution, and seeking of forgiveness were all strongly pressed. The dying could do good to others in their sickness, perhaps above all by showing that they took the life to come for a reality which they were confident of enjoying. Urgent exhortations against sin and encouragement to suffer for Christ were among the serious counsels of dying men which might make their sickness more fruitful than their health.[54]

A long first section of Baxter's 'Directions' is addressed to the unconverted sinner. He is urged to begin judging himself speedily and seriously and to humble his soul before the Lord. When thoroughly humbled, he is to remember that Jesus Christ has given himself as a sacrifice for his sins. Christ is so sure and all-sufficient a saviour that nothing can hinder his salvation but his own impenitence and unbelief. It is also necessary to love God, inspired by thoughts of the divine love and of all that God has been and will be for his soul.[55]

---

[53] T. Wilson, *Works*, with life by J. Keble (LACT, 7 vols., 1847–63), i. 909–12; vii. 53–71.

[54] *The Practical Works of the Rev. Richard Baxter*, ed. W. Orme (23 vols., 1830), iv. 412–43.

[55] Ibid. 403–12, esp. 406–10.

The chief resource of sanctified people in face of death was their faith, but Baxter expected them to receive human assistance. He advised them to test their sincerity with the help, if necessary, of a faithful, judicious minister or friend. The help of such a person was even more important for unconverted sinners, who were advised to open all their heart and life to him. Baxter dealt at length with the duty of spiritual support incumbent upon the friends of the sick. 'Procure some able, faithful minister to be with them, to counsel them about the state of their souls: and get some holy, able Christians to be much about them, who are fit to pray with them, and instruct them.' Such friends had to be compassionate, patient, and understanding, but at the same time honest in dealing with the state of the patient's soul. How few Christians were fit for such work, Baxter reflected sadly. Friends who were not able to instruct invalids might instead read them some good book.[56]

At this point Baxter mentioned with approval certain earlier books of guidance, including those written by Perkins and Bayly, but his own special concerns and emphases distinguish his work from theirs. It does not, unlike Bayly's *Practice*, accord the *viaticum* an important part in preparation for death. It dwells at greater length than Perkins's *Salve* on the sorts of help which the dying might receive from other Christians, especially expert ministers. Baxter expected the review of past sins to be truly thorough, and he placed a high value on the contribution which a faithful pastor might make to this process.

The inner comfort which the dying felt and were able to impart to those around them are the elements of the Puritan deathbed experience which stand out most strongly from the more vivid accounts of the late seventeenth and early eighteenth centuries. The eminent pastor Henry Brownsword (d. 1688), who had been frequently buffeted by temptations during his life, found that God made death very easy by wonderfully restraining the Devil and manifesting his love. Brownsword told Timothy Cruso, the young colleague who later preached his funeral sermon, that he had received more comfort during his last sickness than during his whole life before. Having previously feared death continually, he now longed for it. Cruso declared that he had never heard 'more *awakening Counsels*, and discourses' from any pulpit than Brownsword had delivered from his deathbed to those about him. In a rather lower key than Brownsword's, yet also

---

[56] *The Practical Works of the Rev. Richard Baxter*, 407, 412–13, 433, 445–6, 448–9.

comfortable and edifying, was the death in 1710 of Ambrose Barnes, an aged merchant venturer and former lord mayor of Newcastle upon Tyne. While he could still go out, about forty days before the end, he attended the Lord's Supper for the last time. Then he accepted his growing weakness with resignation. During his last weeks, Barnes gave godly advice to those about him, and faced a trying illness with fervent prayer, quiet faith, and indomitable cheerfulness.[57]

The account of the death of Mrs Susannah Rudge given in 1716 by Benjamin Grosvenor, a well-known London Presbyterian pastor, assigned her the central place, but he too had played an important part. She had always inclined to doubts about her state, and during her last sickness she had asked him to pray (among other things) for pardon of her sins, evidence of that pardon, and acceptance by God in Jesus Christ. The nearer she approached her end, the more her assurance had grown. At length she had been able to thank God for her freedom from uncertainty and fear.

From that Time we stood round the Dying, as curious Spectators, to see, to observe, how Heaven met the travelling Soul upon its way; to learn to die; to see Religion in some of its Grandour; to catch now and then an *Ejaculation* from her Lips, and carry it on, and improve it a little, to her Comfort, and our own Edification; and finally, to see a Mortal triumph over Death, and thro' Faith and Patience, more than a Conqueror, *thro' the Blood of the Lamb.*[58]

Funeral sermons and biographies describe (albeit in a creatively edited fashion) the deathbeds of many members of the gentry, clergy, and affluent middle classes between the late sixteenth and early eighteenth centuries. However, they tell us little of the experience of the majority of the population who were neither well off nor of exemplary life. The diaries of Puritan ministers say relatively little about this aspect of their pastoral labours. The rare glimpses we get suggest that it was uphill work. In 1644 Ralph Josselin made one of his few recorded visits to a sick person, one Guy Penhacke, who was 'much troubled in minde upon his life' and strongly tempted by Satan. Josselin urged him to covenant with God to be a new man if he recovered, and reflected on the sad afflictions of the soul loaded with sin in face of death. Penhacke recovered, but within two years was credibly

[57] T. Cruso, *The Period of Humane Life Determined by the Divine Will. A Funeral Sermon on the Death of Mr Henry Brownsword* (1688), 28–9; *Memoirs of the Life of Mr Ambrose Barnes, late Merchant and sometime Alderman of Newcastle upon Tyne*, ed. W. H. D. Longstaffe (Surtees Soc. 50; 1867), 252–4.

[58] B. Grosvenor, *Precious Death. A Sermon On Occasion of the Death of M*^{rs}* Susannah Rudge* (1716), 16–17.

accused of making a fellow servant pregnant, which says little for the effectiveness of Josselin's efforts. 'I dealt as well as I could with him,' wrote the Cheshire minister Henry Newcome in 1656, after visiting a 'poor ale man' in his sickness, 'but saw with him . . . how hard it is to get within poor persons at such a time, to fasten anything on them of their danger and concernment.'[59]

Were the practitioners of deathbed ministry in the tradition of Andrewes and Taylor any more successful than the Puritans in reaching a substantial proportion of the people? The evidence is too meagre to permit any confident answers to this question, but it is clear that some of them felt they faced a hard task. 'Certainly it is no good sign in this case,' wrote Herbert Thorndike in a gloomy appraisal of the state of religion in England, published in 1662, 'that our people are so willing to have the minister pray by them, but so unwilling to hear of the communion, because they know it requires them to take account of themselves.' In practice, or so Thorndike feared, the clergyman had to forgo the hearing of confessions before he administered Communion to the sick, thus 'offering all that he is able to give, before the account is tendered'. Fifty years later Nathaniel Spinckes complained that the clergy frequently found their sick neighbours 'so intolerably Stupid, and Senseless as to the Business of Religion, that . . . little Good [was] to be done with them'. A man of this sort asked for the clergyman's prayers, but could not do his part. His grounds of hope for forgiveness were that he had lived quietly and peaceably and wronged none of his neighbours. Yet he could give only a very lame account of his faith and had neglected his Christian duties. It was a melancholy business to visit such thoughtless sinners. From 1713 we have in testamentary depositions a rare glimpse of a dying person who was too far gone for a conscientious clergyman to help her. Mr Nicholson, the minister of St Sepulchre's parish in London, declared as he came downstairs from visiting the widow Joan Frances that she was not fit to be prayed with. Later he reported that she had been very weak and had showed 'noe act of Devotion either by lifting upp her hands or eyes when hee prayed by her'. She had been incapable of rendering him an account of her past life or giving him 'that satisfaction as hee desired [or?] required'.[60]

    [59] Josselin, *Diary*, 18–19, 67; for some other examples of Josselin's ministry to the sick and dying, see ibid. 57, 67 (prayed with dying man), 164, 199–200; *The Autobiography of Henry Newcome, M.A.*, ed. R. Parkinson (Chetham Soc., os 26 and 27; 1852), i. 53.
    [60] H. Thorndike, *Just Weights and Measures* (1662), repr. in id., *Works*, ed. A. W. Haddan (LACT, 6 vols., 1844–54), v. 287–8; cf. ibid. 232 (Presbyterian failure to provide

During the century after 1650 it was the Quakers and later the Methodists who enjoyed the greatest missionary success. Both developed distinctive patterns of deathbed behaviour, or at any rate of describing and interpreting that behaviour, which gave larger meaning to the last hours of countless people of comparatively humble origin. The Quaker ideal was to die in that state of 'holy quietude and composure' with which George Fox contemplated his approaching death in 1691. From the many recorded deathbed sayings of members of the Society of Friends one theme stands out: inward peace, simply and calmly expressed. The phrase 'all is well', or a very similar one, occurs repeatedly in surviving accounts of Quaker deathbeds. 'All is well,' George Fox told those who visited him, 'the Seed of God reigns over all, and over death itself.' 'It was well with him,' said John Banks before his death in 1710, 'and [he] was assured it would be well, and that he had nothing to do but to die, and that he should end in the truth as he began.' Among the last words of Philip Eliot before his death in 1735 was his declaration to his physicians 'that there was nothing that gave him any Uneasiness on his mind but that it was in great Calmness, & Serenity'. Among all the major religious groups it was the Friends who moved furthest from reliance on sacramental help or priestly support.[61]

One result of the evangelizing work on which John Wesley and his friends embarked in 1738 was a reinvigoration of the notion of joyful dying and its diffusion through social strata then largely untouched by effective Christian ministry. It was among the poor, the sick, and condemned criminals, whom misfortune had rendered especially receptive to the message of free grace, that Wesley found some of his best opportunities of saving souls. On 24 October 1741, after visiting the victims of an epidemic on three consecutive days, he wrote 'Surely our Lord will do much work by this sickness, I do not find that it comes to any house without leaving a blessing behind it.' A celebration of Communion for condemned malefactors in Newgate (in their case a true viaticum) was the prelude to what Wesley described as the most glorious instance he had ever seen of faith triumphing

a true visitation of the sick); Spinckes, *Sick Man visited*, 293–5; GL MS 9065 A/11, fos. 52ᵛ, 55ʳ, 57ʳ.

[61] *A Memoir of the Life, Travels and Gospel Labours of George Fox* (1839), 263; *Brief Narratives of the Lives of Gilbert Latey, Christopher Storey and John Banks* (Friends' Library, 9; 1834), 411–12; GLRO Acc 1017/908a. See J. Tomkins *et al.*, *Piety Promoted, in Brief Memorials, of the Virtuous Lives, Services, and Dying Sayings, of some of the People called Quakers* (3 vols., 1789), *passim*, for similar testimonies given by Friends.

over sin and death. However, exhortation and prayer were the chief means by which Wesley 'improved' the opportunities which, he felt, God had put into his hands. In the spirit of James 5, Wesley hoped to heal the soul first, and sometimes also the body. Some of those who received the message of salvation were reinvigorated to serve God in renewed health; others died gladly. The happy deaths which Wesley described in the early years of his mission were often preceded by dramatic conversion experiences in which a hardened sinner or somebody complacently reliant upon his good works suddenly embraced free grace.[62]

Just before the end of our period, the Christian ideal of the good death was powerfully expressed in a great work of imaginative literature. Samuel Richardson's novel *Clarissa*, whose publication was completed in 1748, rapidly gained international fame. Its heroine, beguiled into an elopement by the suave and ruthless Lovelace, receives an ultimately fatal psychic shock when he rapes her. The last part of the book is dominated by accounts of the deaths of its principal characters, essays in the *ars moriendi* cast in fictional form. Perhaps the most striking characteristic of Clarissa's death is her sustained control of proceedings until very near the end. She calmly prepares for the death she now longs for. She implores her mother's blessing and forgives Lovelace. She seeks guidance from the Scriptures and has her coffin placed in her chamber. As death approaches she is full of a calm assurance of future bliss and pours out edifying speeches and blessings. Throughout, her performance exacts admiration from a sympathetic audience. Strong men turn soft with sorrow and compassion at the spectacle of this teenager's exemplary death. Parts of it recall the death of Katherine Stubbes at the same age, 19, in 1590. Yet Clarissa's death draws on the sacramental as well as the Puritan deathbed tradition. She receives Communion twice during her last sickness, and is given spiritual advice by a minister of the Church. She dies with the words 'Come—O come—Blessed Lord— JESUS' on her lips.[63]

Three other deaths described by Richardson are bad ones. They provide an instructive contrast between right and wrong ways of

---

[62] *The Journal of the Rev. John Wesley A.M., sometime Fellow of Lincoln College, Oxford*, ed. N. Curnock (8 vols., 1909–16), ii. 100, 378–9, 383, 384, 393, 405, 411–14, 416–17, 436, 437, 455–7, 481–3, 503, 511, 530–2.

[63] S. Richardson, *Clarissa or, The History of a Young Lady* (8 vols., Oxford, 1930), vii. 81–2, 135, 214–24, 267–80, 334–41, 359–61, 384–7, 399–406, 409–14, 437–9, 441–6, 454–62; viii. 1–6.

dying. Lovelace's friend Belton is paralysed by the conviction that he has been so 'very, *very* wicked' that God cannot possibly be merciful to him, and finally expires in a state of abject terror. If Belton personifies despair, the bawd Sinclair, another of Lovelace's accomplices, represents impatience, also one of the five temptations of the *Craft of Dying*. Finally, Lovelace is killed in a duel, which Richardson believed to be, after suicide, the worst sort of death.[64]

In 1500 there was one dominant model of Christian dying. None of the faithful can have wished to die without the rites of the Church. As Thomas Crabbe of Axminster remarked in 1536, every man 'must needs have a priest at his coming into the world, and a priest at his departing'.[65] However, over the two following centuries there developed a variety of Christian ways of dying. The Protestant Reformation abolished extreme unction, laid down conditions for the celebration of the Communion of the Sick, and left the sick person to decide whether to make a confession. Prayer, a guided confession of faith, and the reading of comforting Scriptures, were the chief elements left in the Visitation of the Sick. The Puritan craft of dying was much more positive in its emphasis on the autonomy of the individual in his or her relationships with human agencies. The Puritan's main resource was an inner faith given by God, which he showed not only in resisting deathbed temptations, but also in prayer, devout expressions of his assurance, godly exhortations to those around him, and the willing resignation of his soul into God's hand. He might indeed call upon the services of a godly minister, but he was also encouraged to look to lay Christians for help.

Before the end of Elizabeth's reign, the value of a special private confession to a priest was once again being emphasized by some ministers of the Church of England. During the early seventeenth century an increasing number of divines, especially but by no means only those of an anti-Calvinist persuasion, made it part of their ministry to the sick and dying. Even the best of Christians, in their view, was a sinner who stood in need of mercy, and the cathartic effect of confession was of immeasurable help in preparing for the supreme trial. Absolution and the last Communion comforted the dying and strengthened them for the ordeal ahead.

It seems unlikely that either of these ideal patterns was fully

[64] Ibid. vii. 171–84, 194, 202–9; viii. 54–69, 273–7.
[65] R. Whiting, *The Blind Devotion of the People: Popular Religion and the English Reformation* (Cambridge, 1989), 126.

accepted by the majority of the population during the later seventeenth century. The Reformation changes and the divisions which followed over the next two centuries tended to increase the freedom of individuals to choose their own way of dying if they were capable of exercising it. The absence of a universally or generally accepted way of death to replace Catholic practice also assisted the development of alternative ways of managing the deathbed.

7

Good Deaths and Bad

The Christian form of the ideal of the 'good death', rooted in the Middle Ages, survived throughout early modern times. It included certain elements which transcended confessional and denominational boundaries. The deathbed was seen as the supreme trial of faith. A successful outcome, or what appeared to be one, was widely interpreted as an indication of the individual's eternal fate. It left a good example to survivors, reconciled them to their loss, and strengthened their own Christian belief.

The achievement of such a death depended both upon the inner resources of the dying individual and the help given by other people. However, the occasion was often shaped in large measure by things beyond human control: above all the form assumed by death itself. The enduring status of a particular death as 'good' or 'bad' depended upon selective description and careful interpretation. The experience of death was probably the focus of more intense interest and scrutiny between the Reformation and the Enlightenment than at any time before or since, but in the long run this close scrutiny revealed tensions and contradictions within the ideal of the 'good death' which brought it into question.

The most important functions of deathbed narratives are graphically revealed by some letters written in 1641 by the Suffolk gentleman Simonds D'Ewes immediately after his wife Anne had died of smallpox. He had left her before the end only because he had believed that the crisis was past. He subsequently suffered a terrible anguish because he felt that he had failed her, losing precious time in persuading her that she would live instead of helping to prepare her for heaven. He wrote to one of her attendants, demanding a full account of her last days. Having heard that she had complained of a lack of assurance of God's love, D'Ewes sought evidence that those around her had encouraged and reassured her, and that she had before her death 'expressed some moore comfort' than had already been

described to him. Not, he wrote, 'that I think it can in any way con-
duce to strengthen my assurance that she is a glorious Saint in heaven;
but that it might encourage us that are remaining to follow her godlie
example'. Encouraging example and reassurance (despite D'Ewes's
claim that he didn't need it) were what the godly sought in the presentation of the deathbeds of those they loved or respected.[1]

In practice it was hard to fit the diversity of deathbed behaviour and
experience into the artificial constructs of 'good' and 'bad' death.
Many deaths (possibly the majority) included both 'good' and 'bad'
elements. Much of the surviving testimony concerning deathbeds is
highly selective, but the 'mixed' character of many deathbed experiences is apparent from the fullest and most dispassionate eyewitness
accounts. A particularly informative example describes the last days
of Robert Moore, a wealthy distiller of West Cowes in the Isle of
Wight. It was written by his brother Giles, rector of the parish of
Horstead Keynes in Sussex.

Robert first complained to Giles of his terminal illness during the
night of Sunday 31 July 1670. By the following Tuesday morning, he
felt sure that he was going to die. That day he made his will, dividing
most of his estate between his two children (he was a widower). Giles
reminded him of the needs of his poorer kindred. Bequests to relatives,
to the church of West Cowes, the poor of the parish, a maidservant,
and the wife of a tenant who had helped to nurse him, were added to
the will 'new Drawne' on 9 August. Despite receiving a reassuring
prognosis from a visiting surgeon, Robert complained much of
'anguish, Misery & paine' on 16 and 17 August, saying that Job had
never felt what he suffered. On Thursday 18 August he attempted suicide by jumping into a well. He was quickly rescued, but remained very
weak and restless during the next few days. His daughter sent for her
16-year-old brother, who on 23 August knelt before his father to beg his
pardon and blessing. The end came the following day. After a much
quieter night, Robert 'sent forth with greate earnestnesse 3 or 4 most
Divine short prayers' at 7 a.m. He died at one o'clock in the afternoon.[2]

Robert's deathbed conformed in certain respects to ancient patterns. The onset of his final illness prompted him to set his worldly
affairs in order. He left most of his estate to his closest relations, was
attended by members of his family, and was nursed in his own home.
His son sought his last blessing just before he died. Robert left
bequests to the poor and the local church, and uttered devout prayers

[1] D'Ewes, *Autobiography & Correspondence*, ii. 275–82.
[2] *The Journal of Giles Moore*, ed. R. Bird (Sussex Record Soc. 68; 1971), 285–90.

near the end. However, he lacked Christian patience. His attempted suicide, if successful, would have been the very worst sort of death a Christian could die. Giles's account mentions no spiritual counsel given to the dying man, but it reminds us of the increasing availability of medical services in later seventeenth-century England. Robert was visited by a surgeon and two different physicians. In practice there was often a tension between the medical man's desire to prolong life and maintain his patient's confidence, and the priest's duty to prepare the sick man for death. (In this case the surgeon's robustly cheerful appraisal was sadly ill-founded.) The course and nature of his illness, and the support given by members of his immediate family and household, were crucial in shaping Robert Moore's deathbed experience. His trials were severe, and he nearly failed the test. At the last, however, his passing yielded some comfort.

The practice of the Christian 'good death' was in principle open to everybody who was capable of understanding the issues involved. It was not restricted by gender. Women gave some of the best examples of it. This is made particularly clear by the works of the Puritan *ars moriendi*. The craft of dying gave each sex scope for the exercise of qualities more usually associated with the other. Men, normally expected to be active and dominant, were now called upon to submit to God's hand. In one respect, women were better trained than men for this ordeal. Most of them had gone through the trials of childbirth, a sort of rehearsal for the last act, and many had done so several times.[3]

If men were called upon to exercise virtues in which women were better schooled, women for their part had certain exceptional opportunities on the deathbed. Forbidden to speak in church, they might now utter prayers, exhortations, and statements of faith which were heard with a special respect. The Puritan way of death, which particularly encouraged the outward manifestation of individual faith, allowed women a prominent role in the drama of their own deathbeds. Several widowed husbands carefully noted down the 'speciall speaches' uttered by their wives on such occasions. Some of these women spoke their minds on public as well as private duties. In May 1661, when Elizabeth Heywood lay dying of consumption, she made a long speech to her father, John Angier, and her husband, Oliver Heywood, both eminent ministers, admonishing them to keep

---

[3] The relationship between gender and the deathbed experience is sensitively explored in J. L. McIntosh, 'English Funeral Sermons 1560–1640: The Relationship between Gender and Death, Dying, and the Afterlife', M.Litt. thesis (Oxford, 1990), 140–68.

close to God and his truth, regardless of persecution. Then she prayed fervently for the preservation of the Church. Shortly afterwards, Heywood reminded her of what she had said. She 'thought it strange that she had spoken such things, and so did others, since her modesty had formerly shut up her lips in silence: but her honoured father judged it some strange extacy wherin she was acted by a strong motion of the spirit, beyond her purpose, and above her present infirmity'. It had long been acknowledged that divine inspiration sometimes enabled women to rise above the inherent 'infirmity' of the female condition, saying and doing things that would otherwise have been socially unacceptable.[4]

Some descriptions of deathbed scenes attributed 'patriarchal' authority to women. The Bible afforded no adequate matriarchal models for them to invoke. Remembering how her mother had poured out prayers and blessings on her children (1659), Alice Thornton likened her to 'good old Jacob'. In 1716 Mrs Susannah Rudge gave 'the last Admonitions and Blessings' to her family 'with the Majesty of an ancient *Patriarch*'.[5]

Children, too, could die well. Their ability to do so depended in large measure on their developing mental capacity, but the medieval Church had held that even young children might be endowed with powers beyond their years by divine grace. Some older children or adolescents appeared among John Foxe's victims of Catholic persecution, but the best-known collection of narratives of the good deaths of children was assembled after the Restoration by James Janeway, a Dissenting minister. *A Token for Children* appeared in two parts in 1671 and 1673. Janeway pushed the threshold of religious understanding well back into early childhood. Little children, he insisted, were not incapable of the grace of God, or of going to heaven or hell. Of the thirteen children whose lives he recounted, seven were boys, six girls. Nearly all had died in later childhood, between the ages of 8 and 12, one earlier, at about 5 or 6, one later, at about 14, but all had shown a precocious interest in religion, several between the ages of 4 and 6. One boy prayed as soon as he could speak, while another was 'admirably affected with the things of God, when he was between two and three years Old'. The majority became concerned about the

<hr />

[4] *The Letters of Sir Francis Hastings, 1574-1609*, ed. C. Cross (Somerset Record Soc. 69; 1969), 63; Heywood, *Autobiography, Diaries*, i. 66-8.
[5] *The Autobiography of Mrs Alice Thornton, of East Newton, Co. York*, ed. C. Jackson (Surtees Soc. 62; 1875), 112; B. Grosvenor, *Precious Death. A Sermon On Occasion of the Death of Mrs Susannah Rudge* (1716), 17.

fate of their souls in the next life at a very early age. In the case of one boy, this concern was activated by the death of a little brother, while one of the girls experienced the fear that she might go to hell when she fell sick at the age of 7. All died willingly and happily. Some of the children tried to comfort their parents or looked forward to reunion with their families in heaven. Some expressed the essentials of their faith in lively fashion.[6]

Janeway seems to have regarded his cases as entirely credible, if somewhat exceptional. Instances recorded in diaries tend to confirm this impression. They are few, but vivid and convincing. They span the whole of childhood. John Wesley recorded the story of John Woolley, who died in 1742 at the age of 13. Previously a 'loose boy' and truant, he underwent hellish temptations followed by an ecstatic conversion experience. He entered his last illness sure of Christ and filled with gratitude for the grace freely offered to him. He confessed to his mother his worries for his father, who did not seem to know God, and promised to pray for them both in heaven. He gave his eldest sister stern warnings against idleness and vanity, and urged her not to cry for him. He prayed frequently during the last eight days of his life, and just before he died kissed his little brother, sister, and mother for the last time.[7]

John Evelyn's 5-year-old son Richard, who died in 1658, showed exceptional intellectual and religious precocity. He chose 'the most pathetical' psalms and chapters out of the Book of Job to read to the maid who attended him during his illness, telling her that all God's children must suffer affliction. He often asked his visitors to pray near him, and prayed to Jesus repeatedly himself. There is no hint in his father's account that Richard Evelyn was anxious about the future of his soul. He probably felt quite secure in the love and approval of a strict but affectionate father who still seemed an effective and convincing representative of God in his own sheltered world. The Lancashire doctor Richard Kay described more briefly his little niece 'Lippy's' death at the age of 4 in 1742. Kay considered it 'very affectively remarkable' that Lippy, when in her death agonies, should have called on those around her to pray for her. Alice Thornton's account of the death of her daughter Elizabeth in 1656 at the age of little more

---

[6] J. Janeway, *A Token for Children: being an Exact Account of the Conversion, Holy and Exemplary Lives, and Joyful Deaths, of several young Children* (1676 edn.), esp. vol. i. sig. A4, pp. 10, 19, 36–7, 43; vol. ii. 2–3, 19, 52–3, 85–7; C. J. Sommerville, *The Discovery of Childhood in Puritan England* (Athens, Ga., 1992), 31, 55–7.

[7] *The Journal of the Rev. John Wesley A.M., sometime Fellow of Lincoln College, Oxford*, ed. N. Curnock (8 vols., 1909–16), ii. 529–32.

than 18 months tests the limit of the notion of a 'good death'. She 'held up those sweete eyes and hands to her deare Father in heaven, looked up, and cried in her language, "Dad, dad, dad" with such vehemency as if inspired . . . to deliver her sweet soule into her heavenly Father's hands'. So young a child clearly lacked the understanding which was a prerequisite of the 'good' death.[8]

The achievement of a 'good' death transformed the process of dying from tragedy into triumph. Both the individual at the centre of the drama and the members of the audience might be reassured and sustained. All had some part to play in the happy outcome. 'He made a happy end, comfortable to himself and comfortable to all his friends.' Sir John Oglander's words about his father were echoed by many observers of other deathbed scenes.[9] The assistance of a sympathetic and supportive audience was of the first importance in enabling the dying to play their part in achieving a 'comfortable' death. Last farewells were recalled with particular vividness by participants. When the moment of death seemed to be approaching, urgent messages were often sent out summoning close relatives to come to the deathbed.[10] Children who had left their parents' household, often long beforehand, returned to receive a last blessing, to make sure of their bequests, and to comfort their parents with their presence.

This was the time for parents to give their most solemn advice. The delivery of deathbed counsel was occasionally mentioned in late medieval narratives, but such descriptions became much commoner later on. In 1681 William Stout, a Lancashire yeoman farmer, sitting in his chair by his house fire a few days before his death, summoned his children before him, and gave them 'exhortations to live in the fear of God and in duty and obedience to [their] mother, and brotherly kindness to each other'. These were probably the main concerns of countless men whose last advice to their families, unlike Stout's, went unrecorded. Family harmony was something especially close to the hearts of many parents, and an injunction to love one another was one of the most frequently recorded last paternal messages. Heirs had special responsibilities. 'I charge you', said John Dunch of Pusey (Berks.) to his eldest son in 1668, 'to live in the feare of god and to see yo[u]r brothers and sisters well brought up and educated in the holy

---

    [8] Evelyn, *Diary*, iii. 206–9; Kay, *Diary*, 53; Thornton, *Autobiography*, 94.
    [9] *A Royalist's Notebook: The Commonplace Book of Sir John Oglander Kt of Nunwell*, ed. F. Bamford (1936), 174; *The Recusancy Papers of the Meynell Family*, ed. J. C. H. Aveling, in *Miscellanea*, ed. E. E. Reynolds (Catholic Record Soc. 56; 1964), 8, 41.
    [10] *Two Elizabethan Women: Correspondence of Joan and Maria Thynne 1575–1611*, ed. A. D. Wall (Wiltshire Record Soc. 38; 1982), 5.

feare of god.' Sometimes the dying found themselves the centre of a
larger group of friends and kinsfolk. Joseph Baron of Bury (Lancs.)
was surrounded on the morning of his death in 1750 by relatives who
customarily used his house as their rendezvous on their way to
chapel. It was very affecting, his brother-in-law recorded, 'to hear him
speak his Concern for the Good of his Family, giving them his Counsel and proper Directions taking his Farewell with One and Another
of them and praying to God for them'.[11]

The last requests of married women gained added poignancy from
the fact that they could not legally make wills without their husbands'
consent. 'Did shee not leave some desires or requests behind her for
mee to performe,' asked Simonds D'Ewes after his wife's unexpected
death in 1641, 'either concerning her children or anie of her freinds?'
Various mothers expressed their concerns about their children's
upbringing, or gave them pious advice. John Angier's vivid account of
his wife Elizabeth's death in 1642 conveys the way in which her illness interrupted what she had to say, producing odd juxtapositions of
spiritual and worldly concerns. She asked him to take good care to
train up their children in God's fear, and not allow servants to rule
over them. Soon afterwards she said 'theres pretty good store of lin-
nen let the children haue part therof'.[12]

The parental blessing, or invocation of God's blessing, was perhaps
the most important part of the farewell scene for those children who
received it. Robert Cecil, overjoyed by the sudden and unexpected
visit of his eldest son shortly before his death in 1612, broke into an
especially heartfelt benediction. 'O my sonne, God blesse thee! The
blessinge of Abraham, Isaak, and Jacobe light upon thee!' One of the
most affectionate of all recorded last blessings was given in 1690 by
Samuel Jeake, a dissenter of Rye, to his only son: 'Farewell my Dear
Lamb, The Lord bless thee, & prosper all that thou undertakest.'
According to Daniel Defoe, one victim of the plague of 1665
entrusted his last blessing to a nurse to deliver to his family from a safe
distance. Women may have attached particular importance to this last
spiritual gift because their restricted control of property limited their
opportunities to bestow more tangible benefits on their children. In
1635 Mrs Eleanor Evelyn gave each of her children a ring with her

[11] *The English Works of John Fisher*, ed. J. E. B. Mayor (EETS extra ser. 27; 1876),
285–6; HRO A1/20, fos. 18–19; *The Autobiography of William Stout of Lancaster,
1665–1752*, ed. J. D. Marshall (Chetham Soc., 3rd ser. 14; 1967), 73; BRO D/A1/63/38;
Kay, *Diary*, 158–9.
[12] D'Ewes, *Autobiography & Correspondence*, ii. 279; Heywood, *Autobiography,
Diaries*, i. 72; Evelyn, *Diary*, ii. 13–14.

blessing, and, just before she died, laid her hand on each of them. Eleven years later, Mrs Margaret Ducke gave her blessing to each of her daughters in turn. She explained to the eldest that she herself had received this blessing from her own mother. Shortly before her death in 1659 Mrs Alice Wandesford embraced and kissed each member of the family, pouring out prayers and blessings for them.[13]

Among the most poignant recorded farewells were those in which the dying handed over their little children, Katherine Stubbes, dying of fever after her only confinement in 1590, took her baby son in her arms, and with kisses invoked God's blessing on him before bequeathing him to her husband. Just over seven years later, a widowed Berkshire yeoman, Thomas Dyar of Sutton Courtenay, called for his son to be brought to his bed three days before he died. He insisted on taking the child in his arms, despite his sister's belief that he was too weak to hold him. Then, turning to his mother-in-law, he said 'Heare Mother . . . I geve you my child francke and free, for I know you will take paines with him and use him well. It is a prety fine boye and one that I doe love with all my harte.'[14]

The last farewell was often fraught with emotion. In 1530 Sir Thomas More kissed and embraced his dying father with tears, 'commending him into the merciful hands of almighty God'. Many later descriptions echo this one. Robert Cecil and his son met in 1612 with 'mutual tears', the fruit of 'those affections that none know, but those that feel them'. The dying often sought to dispel the sadness of the farewell moments by insisting on their own happiness and the prospects of reunion. In 1659 Mrs Wandesford urged her weeping daughter Alice to give her up to God willingly, submit to his decision, and fill her heart with spiritual comfort. To very many people a death in the family brought not just emotional distress but also the prospect of the loss of their material security. The night before William Hunt

---

[13] F. Peck, *Desiderata Curiosa: or, a Collection of divers Scarce and Curious Pieces, relating chiefly to Matters of English History* (2 vols., 1779), i. 209; *An Astrological Diary of the Seventeenth Century: Samuel Jeake of Rye 1652–1699*, ed. M. Hunter and A. Gregory (Oxford, 1988), 208; D. Defoe, *A Journal of the Plague Year*, ed. A. Burgess and C. Bristow (Harmondsworth, 1966), 211; Evelyn, *Diary*, ii. 13–14; S. Clarke, *A Collection of the Lives of Ten Eminent Divines* (1662), 498; Thornton, *Autobiography*, 112–13. See also B. Young, 'Parental Blessings in Shakespeare's Plays', *Studies in Philology*, 89 (1992), 179–210.

[14] P. Stubbes, *Christal glasse*, repr. with some omissions in *Philip Stubbes's Anatomy of the Abuses in England in Shakspere's Youth, A.D. 1583*, ed. F. J. Furnivall (New Shakspere Soc., 6th ser. 4, 6, 12; 1877–82), i. 202; J. Tomkins *et al.*, *Piety Promoted, in Brief Memorials, of the Virtuous Lives, Services, and Dying Sayings, of some of the People called Quakers* (3 vols., 1789), i. 27–8, 53, 69; BRO D/A2/c155, fos. 177^v–178^r.

died in his one chamber house in Cloford (Som.) in 1633, his wife bewailed his sickness, saying that she could not tell what to do if he died. Hunt sought to comfort her, not with talk of spiritual things, but with a sober assessment of her material prospects. She might do well enough, he said. He would give her all he had, but he advised her 'to be careful of her self, and with whom she married after his death'.[15]

Sorrow was sometimes controlled by an element of stoic cheerfulness and good fellowship at the farewell moment. In about 1591 a Berkshire widow, Agnes Stevenson, invited her manservant to drink with her for the last time. She died within three hours. When John Cannon, a Somerset yeoman's son, came to visit his dying sister in 1718 she ordered a cup of ale for him, saying 'her time was come that she should not drink till she drank with her friends in the kingdom of heaven'. This small but important gesture was a means for the dying to show their equanimity in face of their fate, reach out to those around them, and hold grief at bay.[16]

In most cases, physical and moral support from other people was a prerequisite of the 'good' death. Dying within a domestic household rather than in an institution was normal during this period. The burden of terminal care for all save the poorest was usually shared by a number of people. Nursing provided essential underpinning. The wealthy were largely cared for by their servants. Somewhat further down the social scale, help would often have to be hired from outside. Family tenants were sometimes recruited. Nursing belonged to women: it was part of their work to help people out of the world as well as into it; but the less arduous task of 'watching' by the dying was often performed by men. Nursing and watching might be done for payment or for friendship's sake, perhaps in expectation of reciprocal aid. Kinsfolk sometimes gave valuable assistance during sickness, more particularly, perhaps, in the middling ranks of society. Neighbours were another source of help, and probably the most obvious one for people of little property, or those elderly persons who lived on their own. At the lowest levels of society, neighbourly nursing care was often financed by parish rates or the voluntary donations of the better-off.

Descriptions of deathbeds often give the impression that sick people received a steady succession of visitors who dropped in to see

---

[15] W. Roper, *The Life of Sir Thomas More*, in *Two Early Tudor Lives*, ed. R. S. Sylvester and D. P. Harding (New Haven, 1962), 221; Peck, *Desiderata Curiosa*, i. 209; Thornton, *Autobiography*, 113; SRO D/D/Cd 77.

[16] BRO D/A2/c154, fo. 60; SRO, MS Autobiography of John Cannon, p. 141.

'how they did', give encouragement, or perhaps read from some edifying book. For conscientious Christians, visiting the sick was a religious duty, not just an obligation of good fellowship. Believers sought not only to help the terminally ill but also to receive practical lessons in dying. Visiting indigent invalids and giving them medical help were charitable works popular among pious women throughout early modern times.[17]

The fact that most deaths took place at home, the greater size of families, the employment of servants, the dependence on the help of friends and neighbours: all these things tended to bring groups of people together round the deathbed. However, the numbers present fluctuated, increasing when kinsfolk came to visit, when there was a will to be witnessed, when clergy administered the last rites, when manorial representatives took surrender of copyhold lands, and at the very end, when the passing-bell summoned neighbours to offer their prayers for the dying. At other times, especially when the household was at work, there might be only a single watcher in the chamber. Many lonely hours would pass during a long sickness. Furthermore, the picture of the crowded bedchamber corresponds most closely with the reality of life in upper-class and wealthy households. Without servants, without sufficient property to warrant the making of a will, without a kinship network which could be activated by the hope of reciprocal services, the poor were much more likely to die alone or in the company of one or two other people.

The religious help which the dying received from family and friends took the three main forms of prayer, comforting advice, and the reading of Scripture or works of devotion. Prayer was the one most frequently described. Marriage partners were the closest and most constant sources of support. 'And now sweet-heart, no more words between you and me about any worldly thing,' said Mrs Mary Gunter to her husband thirty days before her death in 1622. Feeling increasing pain, and fearing that the Devil would take advantage of her weakened state, she begged him to help her by calling on her 'to follow the Lord with prayer and patience', and to give her 'counsel, comfort and prayers'. Her entry into the liminal period of preparation

---

[17] L. Pollock, *With Faith and Physic: The Life of a Tudor Gentlewoman, Lady Grace Mildmay 1552-1620* (1993), 97–8, 170 n. 34; L. M. Beier, *Sufferers and Healers: The Experience of Illness in Seventeenth-Century England* (1987), 172, 216, 220; A. Clark, *Working Life of Women in the Seventeenth Century* (1982 edn.), 249–55; Fisher, *English Works*, 297; J. Evelyn, *The Life of Mrs Godolphin*, ed. H. Sampson (Oxford, 1939), 11–13, 105–6; *The Meditations of Lady Elizabeth Delaval, written between 1662 and 1671*, ed. D. G. Greene (Surtees Soc. 190; 1978), 94–6.

for the hereafter did not entail the severance of the most important of earthly ties. Instead her husband became her chief human source of spiritual assistance. The distraught letters which Simonds D'Ewes wrote in 1641 in his attempts to find out more about his wife Anne's death give a clear picture of the sorts of help he would have given her had he been present: most importantly, firm assurances concerning the reality of God's love for her. Other close relatives sometimes assumed the role of principal spiritual comforter. William Janeway complained to his son John (d. 1657) about the daunting nature of the business of dying and his fears about his future state. It was John who prayed successfully that God would fill his father with 'Joy unspeakable in believing'.[18]

All too often, members of the family did not fulfil their ideal supportive role. Grief and reluctance to release the dying sometimes sharpened the latter's ordeal. In 1598 Lord Burghley's children, friends, and servants, gathered in his bedchamber, were 'praying and devising, what to give him, to hold life in him, if it were possible'. However, when they tried to give him anything, he came to himself, saying 'O ye torment me! For Godes sake, let me die quietlye!' Looking up as he neared death in 1633, George Herbert saw his wife and nieces weeping bitterly. He told them to withdraw into the next room, if they loved him, and pray for him each one on her own, 'for nothing but their lamentations could make his death uncomfortable'. In 1642 Mrs Elizabeth Angier, wife of a famous Puritan minister, willing to die after a long and trying sickness, felt that she was being held back by her husband. Reproachfully she asked him, 'Loue, why will you not let me goe?' Concern that those around them were seeking to 'hold' them is a recurrent theme in a collection of Quaker deathbed speeches.[19]

Close relatives sometimes preferred to avoid the harrowing spectacle of death. The deeply dejected James I was readily dissuaded from visiting his dying son Prince Henry in 1612. In 1640 Sir Thomas Cotton (1594–1662) and his wife left their daughter in the care of

---

[18] S. Clarke, *The Lives of Sundry Eminent Persons in this Later Age* (2 pts. in 1 vol., 1683), i. 67, ii. 139; D'Ewes, *Autobiography & Correspondence*, ii. 277–8.

[19] Peck, *Desiderata Curiosa*, i. 41; I. Walton, *The Lives of Dr John Donne, Sir Henry Wotton, Mr Richard Hooker, Mr George Herbert and Dr Robert Sanderson* (Oxford, 1824), 253; Heywood, *Autobiography, Diaries*, i. 73; J. Tomkins *et al.*, *Piety Promoted*, i. 3, 35, 43, 50; M. Penington, *A Brief Account of my Exercises from my Childhood* (Philadelphia, 1848), 33, cited by P. Delany, *British Autobiography in the Seventeenth Century* (1969), 158-9; Clarke, *Eminent Persons*, i. 77. See E. Kübler-Ross, *On Death and Dying* (1973), 155, on recent testimony concerning the difficulty of dying when the family won't let go.

servants 'that they might not see her die'. Samuel Pepys, after attending his brother Tom on the last evening of his life, 'had no mind to see him die', and left before the final moment. Even Lady Warwick, an assiduous companion to her husband (d. 1673) during the years of suffering he endured from the gout, was thankful that her sister had prevented her entering his chamber at the end.[20]

The dying all too often suffered from their relatives' greed and ill feeling rather than their grief. Kinsfolk were frequently described as hovering round the deathbed in hope of gain, or putting pressure on the dying to favour them in their wills. Many passed out of the world in an atmosphere of rancour and mistrust, troubled by the prospect of family quarrels after they were gone. Depositions in testamentary cases record several instances of parents' angry refusal to make bequests to troublesome children, one accompanied by a dying curse.[21] Absence from the deathbed could also be a source of grief and disappointment. The last hours of many parents were soured by the failure of their children to come and see them. Lady Elizabeth Delaval suffered sharp remorse for her behaviour towards her dying father in 1670. Resenting the loveless marriage he had arranged for her, she had not visited him during the last eight or ten days of his life; on some days she had even neglected to enquire about his health. She knew (she later admitted) that her undutiful behaviour would grieve him deeply, but she had let her feelings sway her, and had not tried 'to do the least servise to his decaying body, ruined fortune, or aflicted soul'.[22]

Jeremy Taylor thought that death was made more difficult by 'the women and the weepers, the swoonings and the shriekings, the nurses and the physicians, the dark room and the ministers, the kindred and the watchers'. Yet company often provided the dying not only with an audience, but also with some protection against the unscrupulous. Indeed, a private death was regarded as something of a misfortune; to choose it might be regarded as a perverse refusal of

---

[20] Peck, *Desiderata Curiosa*, i. 200–1; *A Seventeenth Century Doctor and his Patients: John Symcotts, 1592?-1662*, ed. F. N. L. Poynter and W. J. Bishop (Bedfordshire Historical Record Soc. 31; 1951), 71; Pepys, *Diary*, v. 86; BL MS Add. 27353, fo. 215.

[21] *Depositions and other Ecclesiastical Proceedings from the Courts of Durham, extending from 1311 to the Reign of Elizabeth*, ed. J. Raine (Surtees Soc. 21; 1845), 319; NRO DN/DEP 4/4B, fo. 119ᵛ; 7/6A, fo. 90; 28/30B, fo. 272ᵛ; 48/52, fos. 266–7; BRO D/A1/113/28.

[22] NRO DN/DEP 4/4B, fo. 287ᵛ; 6/5B, fos. 200–1; Wiltshire Record Office, Trowbridge, Deposition Book 61, fo. 25ᵛ; Delaval, *Meditations*, 185–6, 200–3.

social and religious duties. Sir John Oglander illustrated the point very well when he described the very different deaths in October 1648 of two Isle of Wight gentlemen. Oglander's brother-in-law Edward Cheke was well prepared. He repented of his sins and confessed his faith. Clergy were among his daily visitors. Sir William Lisle, by contrast, 'died privately . . . in a nasty chamber'. He allowed nobody to visit him 'no, not his wife and children—but would bid them be gone since their company would kill him'. He received no clergymen and hardly any physicians. Oliver Heywood, an eminent Yorkshire Dissenting minister, recorded in 1681 the sad end of 'Old Duckworth', a profane swearer and blasphemer. He died miserably in poverty, 'his toes rotting off, he slighting it, said they never did him good, he stank that nobody could abide to come into the house, in a dreadful state'. Old Duckworth's stoic courage could not compensate in Heywood's eyes for his lack of repentance and failure to make proper preparation for death.[23]

The dying person's closest social relationships constituted one of the key determinants of his or her ability to die well. Another was the nature of the terminal illness. The best sort was one which heralded the coming of death some time in advance, allowing time for the orderly settlement of worldly concerns, spiritual preparation, and full acceptance of God's will. Readiness to die was a familiar phenomenon. Individuals who felt otherwise ready to depart were described as wishing to live for a time only to complete some important task, see some expected event, or see a long absent member of their family for the last time. Final farewells were followed, in many cases, by a deliberate turning from this world and its attachments, and a process of preparation for the next one. As death drew closer, the dying sometimes estimated their remaining time with a fair degree of accuracy. William Edmundson, a Quaker, took to his bed four weeks before he died in 1712 at the age of 84. Three days later he ordered where his grave should be dug and gave necessary advice to his children. Two days after that he told his wife that he was now clear of the world and the things of it.[24]

Many dying Christians not only accepted death, but looked forward

---

[23] J. Taylor, *The Rule and Exercises of Holy Dying* (1929 edn.), 94; (many other writers had described such scenes, if not as eloquently as Taylor; cf. D. Erasmus, *Preparation to deathe, a boke as deuout as eloquent* (1538), sig. C'); Oglander, *Royalist's Notebook*, 123–5; Heywood, *Autobiography, Diaries*, ii. 281.

[24] *A Journal of the Life of William Edmundson* (Friends' Library, 4; 1833), 308–13; cf. Walton, *Lives*, 52, 176; Oglander, *Royalist's Notebook*, 174; Stubbes, *Christal glasse*, 202; Josselin, *Diary*, 249; Janeway, *Token for Children*, i. 47.

to it eagerly. The keenly anticipated prospect of heaven was often even more important for them than the desire for release from worldly affliction. Gilbert Burnet attributed the joy with which Sir Matthew Hale felt his end approaching in 1676 not only to his weariness of the world and his increasing pain, but 'his longings for the blessedness of another state'. The eminent Dissenting minister Samuel Fairclough likewise experienced in 1691, 'a longing for Death, not merely to be delivered from an Unease, but upon the hope of passing into everlasting Rest and Joy'. There is abundant similar testimony concerning people of lower social status and even children. The will to die was strong enough in some cases to lead sick Christians to reject favourable medical prognoses or supposedly life-saving medical treatment. Despite the optimism of his physicians, Lord Burghley welcomed what seemed to him the harbingers of death. Yet though his spirit was willing, some obstinate flame of life remained. 'O what a hart is this, [that] will not let me die!—Come Lord Jesu!—One dropp of death, Lord Jesu!'[25]

A long, gradually encroaching terminal illness could be thought desirable. The countess of Huntingdon (d. 1633) often prayed for death by consumption, believing that God was more likely to speak with its 'still soft voice' than in the 'whirlwinde of a convulsion' or the fire of a fever. Her prayer was granted, and although she certainly suffered pain, she found herself able to bear it, and repeatedly thanked God for not making her suffer more. In 1612 the earl of Salisbury probably died of a cancer with a multitude of unpleasant side-effects. Yet John Bowle, his spiritual adviser, saw God's mercy in the fact that his sickness, though tedious, neither gave him excruciating pain nor affected his memory or understanding. Salisbury acknowledged that God had above all been good to him in weaning him from human thoughts and cares by a lingering disease.[26]

A uniquely terrifying disease was the plague. It was sudden, its course rapid. It also brought a disfiguring, painful death and often dis-

---

[25] G. Burnet, *The Lives of Sir Matthew Hale Knt. . . .; Wilmot, Earl of Rochester; and Queen Mary* (1774 edn.), 55; N. Parkhurst, *The Redeemer's Friend; or, a Sermon . . . Preached at the Funeral of the Reverend, Learned, and Faithful Minister of the Gospel, Mr. Samvel Fairclough* (1692), 22; Peck, *Desiderata Curiosa*, i. 41, 207; Walton, *Lives*, 49; Clarke, *Eminent Persons*, i. 77.

[26] I.F., *A sermon preached at Ashby De-la-zouch at the funerall of the lady Elizabeth Stanley late wife to Henrie earle of Huntingdon* (1635), 38–9 (cf. 1 Kings 19: 11–12); Peck, *Desiderata Curiosa*, i. 206–7; cf. G. Ferebe, *Lifes farewell, Or a funerall sermon. At the funerall of John Drew gentleman* (1615), 28; D'Ewes, *Autobiography & Correspondence*, ii. 7.

rupted supportive social networks. Plague chroniclers certainly recorded instances of steadfast love and heroic loyalty within the family, in particular of maternal devotion which would move the 'hardest heart'. There were stories of stoical courage, stern self-control, and altruistic foresight. Yet dread of the plague weakened even the closest ties. When Elizabeth Church of Stepney lay dying of the plague in 1665, her recently widowed father seemingly avoided her in a vain attempt to escape infection. By the third day of her illness, when the fatal marks were upon her, Elizabeth's nurse, knowing that her death was imminent, had already summoned two other women to help strip her. Elizabeth talked 'Idly & extravagantly' and called out fruitlessly to her father to come to her 'saying that he was unnaturall [and] it should bee the worse for him'. In this condition she soon died. Multitudes died abandoned and alone. 'How manye', asked Thomas Dekker, describing the plague of 1625, 'lye languishing in the common High-wayes, and in the open Fields, on Pads of Straw, end their miserable liues, vnpittyed, vnrelieued, vnknowne?' Many had been struck with delirium 'Rauing, Raging and Rayling: yea cursing God to his face!'[27]

Many diseases tested their victims severely, accentuating one or both of two traditional deathbed temptations in particular: impatience and despair. Christian endurance of such trials was warmly admired. Indeed, contemporaries sometimes regarded the feats they witnessed as impossible without divine help. Katherine Stubbes bore for six weeks before her death in December 1590 a burning quotidian ague which never allowed her more than an hour's continuous sleep. Yet never in all that time did she show any sign of discontent or impatience. A doctor who ministered to the parliamentarian Colonel Hutchinson on his deathbed in 1664 was convinced that his extraordinary fortitude was 'evidence of a devine assistance that over-rul'd all the powers and operations of nature'. One of the dying women charitably visited by Margaret Godolphin in the early 1670s set 'an Example of Patience, under a burden that was well-nigh Insupportable'. It was observed of Susanna Noel in 1715 'that as her Misery and Pain increased, so was her Hope enlarged, and her Patience doubled; insomuch that those about her were almost induced to think, that she felt little or no Pain; a thing impossible in so bad a Malady'. Some of those racked by excruciating pain, like the royalist divine

[27] Defoe, *Journal*, 69, 104–5, 119–20, 130–1, 134–5, 211; Dekker, *Plague Pamphlets*, 36, 144–5, 148–51, 166, 184; GL MS 9065A/8, fos. 1–6.

Henry Hammond, who died of the stone in 1660, thanked God that their sufferings were no worse.[28]

Yet impatience was something to which even the godly were prone. Nehemiah Wallington remembered a note of reproach mingled with his dying mother's prayers in 1603: 'No more Lord, no more; no more, Lord, no more! Lord, is my strength the strength of stones, or is my flesh of brass that thou layest on such a load upon me?' The fourth earl of Warwick, racked by gout for several years before his death in 1673, caused his wife anguish with his 'continual scolding & chiding, swearing at and cursing her' during the last months of his life. He even interrupted the good counsels of a favoured minister with curses and oaths. Near the very end he at last responded to Lady Warwick's efforts and asked her to pray for him, but until then his deathbed performance had not been a good one.[29]

Delirium was keenly feared. It played havoc with individuals' self-control at the very moment when believers were most anxious that their outward comportment should reflect their inward faith. It was attributed to diabolical possession by Humphrey Hopper of Medomsley (Co. Durham) in about 1575, when his son Thomas, raving in a high fever, accused his father of stealing his goods. Humphrey tried to exorcize the devil which he claimed to be in possession of his son. He also urged Thomas to think of the passion of Christ. 'Thou or I have offendyd God', he said, clearly revealing his belief that his son's delirium was a punishment. In 1634 the godly gentleman Edward Lewkenor was anxious lest 'for want of sleepe, and the malignant, and fiery working of his Disease' (smallpox) he might utter 'any disorderly, impatient, or prophane speeches . . . to the dishonour of Almighty God, and griefe, and sorrow of his Friends about him'. Fiery smallpox was much dreaded. Anne D'Ewes told her husband before she died in 1641 that 'shee did not soe much feare death as that, in dying of this hott and violent disease, shee might by word and impatience dishonour God'. When his friend Margaret Godolphin sank into a delirious fever soon after the birth of her only child in 1678, John Evelyn thought it highly remarkable that she uttered not a single

---

[28] Stubbes, *Christal glasse*, 200; L. Hutchinson, *Memoirs of the Life of Colonel Hutchinson, with the Fragment of an Autobiography of Mrs Hutchinson*, ed. J. Sutherland (1973), 272–3; Evelyn, *Mrs Godolphin*, 12; S. Rogers, *A Sermon Preach'd at the Funeral Of the Honourable Susanna Noel* (1715), 15; *The Miscellaneous Theological Works of Henry Hammond*, ed. N. Pocock (LACT, 3 vols., 1847–50), vol. i. p. cvii.

[29] P. S. Seaver, *Wallington's World: A Puritan Artisan in Seventeenth-Century London* (1985), 27; BL MS Add. 27353, fos. 203[v], 207[v], 214[v].

offensive syllable, something that seldom happened during such alienations of mind.[30]

Some people were felt to have been prevented from making a good end by a state of utter lassitude like that which Mrs Godolphin suffered in the intervals of her fever, leaving their closest relatives uncertain and despondent. Samuel Woodforde's wife Alice died in January 1664, five days after the birth of their second child. Delirium set in two days later, and Alice was 'distracted with ravings'. The bout left her feeling too weak to pray. Samuel asked her whether she still loved God. She answered yes, but that she would love him more if she were better able. 'My God,' Samuel wrote in his anguish, 'thou knowest shee loves thee & I know it as far as can be iudged by the outward appearance. . . . oh my God I cannot tell what to doe.' Samuel wrote that he had never seen any living creature in so low or weak a condition as Alice was on the last day of her life. She left her husband without a shred of evidence of inner comfort.[31]

Conditions which left the dying person speechless before he or she had had time to deliver last messages or affirmations of faith were often distressing both to the dying and to family and friends. Paul Cleybrooke, a godly gentleman of Kent, suffered in 1622 a stroke which, to his great grief, prevented his friends from understanding much of what he said to them. The Staffordshire minister John Machin, dying of a malignant fever in 1664, received from his wife the reproachful plea, '*Love, thou saist nothing to me, nor to thy Children.*' When the Congregationalist minister Jeremiah Smith died of a violent convulsion in 1723, the fact that he had been cut off 'without his being able to speak one word to those about him' aggravated the sense of loss.[32]

The patient's failure to satisfy expectations of a 'good' death was sometimes blamed on a depressive personality. In 1746 Richard Kay recorded just such a case, that of the wife of his cousin, Samuel Taylor. She died of a lingering illness. 'Her melancholly Disposition rendered her not so comfortable to her Friends and Relations as cou'd have been wished for.'[33]

[30] *Durham Proceedings*, 269–70, 272–5; Clarke, *Eminent Persons*, ii. 140; Oldmayne, *Lifes brevitie*, 34; D'Ewes, *Autobiography & Correspondence*, ii. 278; Evelyn, *Mrs Godolphin*, 77.

[31] Evelyn, *Mrs Godolphin*, 77–8; Bod. Lib. MS Eng. misc. f. 381, fos. 56–62.

[32] W. Stone, *A curse become a blessing: or, a sermon preached at the funerall of Paul Cleybrooke esquire* (1623), 54–5; Clarke, *Eminent Persons*, i. 94; M. Clarke, *A Funeral Sermon occasioned by the much lamented Death Of the Reverend Mr Jeremiah Smith* (2nd edn., 1723), 9.

[33] Kay, *Diary*, 111.

A sizeable minority of deathbed accounts describe states of acute anxiety or mental anguish. Such feelings, though often exacerbated by the terminal illness, also had roots in the individual's personality, beliefs, or sense of personal sinfulness. They were sometimes accompanied by a lively sense of diabolical presence, heightened by fever. When in 1561 the wealthy religious conservative Richard Allington lay sick of smallpox, creatures like puppets gathered round his bed and tormented him almost to the point of despair. At last, in response to his appeal, Jesus showed him in a vision an account of all the sums he had received in usury, and gave instructions for their repayment. Allington's experience may have been influenced by the illustrations of the *Ars Moriendi*. The Devil appears in a number of other deathbed accounts. In 1614 the earl of Kent was tempted to imagine that God had forsaken him and given him over to the malice of sorcerers. Some pious women, possibly influenced by a traditional insistence on their sex's moral weakness and vulnerability, gave especially colourful testimony of struggle against Satan. He tempted Katherine Stubbes to believe that she would be damned for her sins and made Katherine Brettergh doubt her faith and election. Both women answered him defiantly. Katherine Brettergh told him not to reason with her, a weak woman, but with Christ her advocate. Both Erasmus and William Perkins had recommended this sort of response. Katherine Brettergh also felt Satan interrupting her prayers, and entreated those around her to help her with their own intercessions.[34]

References to diabolical assaults in deathbed narratives were much rarer by the eighteenth century. However, a sense of Satan's presence revived in the dramatic atmosphere generated by Wesley's missionary activity. The deaths of some of his converts were preceded by spiritual struggles, in which as one young woman told Wesley shortly before her death in 1742, the Devil was 'very busy' with them.[35]

Dying believers frequently experienced ecstasy or an overbrimming sense of inner peace and comfort. This often followed spiritual trials and despondency. When at last the minister William Janeway felt

---

[34] J. Stowe, *Memoranda*, in *Three Fifteenth-Century Chronicles . . .* ed. J. Gairdner (Camden NS 28; 1880), 117–21; S. Brigden, *London and the Reformation* (Oxford, 1989), 630–2; J. Bowle, *A sermon preached at Flitton in the countie of Bedford, at the funerall of Henrie earle of Kent* (1615), unpaginated; Stubbes, *Christal glasse*, 205–7; S. Clarke, *The Second Part of The Marrow of Ecclesiastical History, divided into Two Parts* (2 bks. in 1 vol., 2nd edn., 1675), ii. 54–5; W. Perkins, *A salue for a sicke man, or, a treatise containing the nature, differences, and kindes of death: as also the right manner of dying well* (edn. of c.1638, STC 19747. 3), 194.

[35] Wesley, *Journal*, ii. 524, 529, 532.

the assurance of God's acceptance after a long period of gloomy apprehension concerning his soul's prospects, he wept uncontrollably in a '*fit of overpowering Love and Joy*'. Now he was ready to die. His son John in his turn experienced supreme happiness before his death of consumption in 1657. His soul was filled with 'Joyes unspeakable', and he cried out in his ecstasy, wishing that he could communicate his experience to those around him. The Janeways may be described as Puritans. However, Sir Charles Gaudy, an 'honest Cavalier', also reportedly experienced 'a most heavenly extasie' for several hours before his death in 1650. The monument to Grace Gethin (d. 1697) at Hollingbourne (Kent) records that, having received Communion the day before she died, she spent the last two hours of her life 'in an unexpressible transport of joy'. Various people visited by John Wesley during his early missionary activity experienced intense happiness in face of death even though they were 'consumed away with pining sickness' or 'well nigh torn asunder with pain'.[36]

The states of exaltation described by many believers appear to have been the result of a complex interaction between body, mind, and spirit. The collision between faith and physical anguish produced an extraordinarily powerful psychic response. Many of those who went through these experiences had a strong sense of their own sinfulness, or had previously suffered a prostrating spiritual crisis. Taught that divine chastisement was a sign of God's paternal love, they were ready to interpret even excruciating pain as loving correction. An awareness of divine presence and receptivity to what was felt as God's love produced an overwhelming sense of release and gratitude which often found expression in ecstatic praise. These joyful states were of varying duration. Some seem to have lasted only for some minutes, others for hours, or even for months in one case. Such experiences usually seem to have taken the dying by surprise. We may speculate that the body's own chemical reactions played a part in the sudden upswing of the spirit, but belief was essential.[37]

---

[36] Clarke, *Eminent Persons*, i. 67, 76–81; F. P. and M. M. Verney, *Memoirs of the Verney Family during the Seventeenth Century* (2nd edn., 2 vols., London, 1907), i. 474; Wesley, *Journal*, ii. 383–4, 393, 409, 416–17, 455–6, 481–3, 521, 522, 525–6. I am grateful to Brian Kemp for his kindness in supplying me with a copy of his transcription of Grace Gethin's epitaph.

[37] S. B. Nuland, *How We Die* (London, 1994 edn.), 129–39, discusses the 'tranquil death phenomenon' and the possible role of endorphins in inducing a feeling of serenity in face of traumatic shock. However, this was not the sort of suffering described in the 17th-cent. deathbed accounts considered here, and the state of mind discussed by Nuland is not really an ecstatic one.

Ecstasy was sometimes accompanied by visions. Katherine Stubbes saw, immediately after her victory over Satan, millions of angels with fiery chariots, ready to carry her soul into heaven. Then, after fervent prayers and exhortations, she seemed suddenly to rejoice, as though she had seen some still more glorious sight. Rising in her bed, she stretched forth her arms to embrace and welcome death, commending her soul into God's hands with her last breath. While he was at prayer sometime before his death John Bruen saw things so wonderful and unspeakable, he later reported, that he could not tell whether he had been in the body or out of it. After receiving absolution on Whitsunday 1636, Sir Humphrey Lynd fell into a trance, and in a vision saw himself presented before God in a shining damask robe edged with gold. He was greatly comforted, even though he knew that many people were apt to slight or censure visions of this sort.[38]

Painful or tedious sicknesses tested Christian faith and fortitude. Yet many people died relatively easily, it was observed, without long or sharp pains. According to Jeremy Taylor, the countess of Carbery (d. 1650), for whom he wrote his *Holy Dying*, had been vouchsafed by God a death which had seemed to be less troublesome than two fits of a common ague 'so easy, so harmless, so painless, that it did not put her patience to a severe trial'. The oldest people were widely believed to die with the least pain and trouble. Old men usually died with much ease, remarked Thomas Gataker in 1626, like a ripe apple falling, or an empty lamp going out. Richard Baxter recorded that his old housekeeper died of 'mere decay, without considerable pain or sickness'. Death sometimes found the aged sitting in a chair with children and grandchildren nearby. One old man called for something to wet his mouth, 'opened his mouth twice, as with a Yawning, and breathed his last, without noyse or groan or struggling'.[39]

An easy death was often judged to be a good thing. Richard Shute, minister of Stowmarket (d. 1689), suffered from a scorbutic dropsy

[38] Stubbes, *Christal glasse*, 207–8, cf. 202; *The Journal of Nicholas Assheton of Downham, in the County of Lancaster, Esq.*, ed. F. R. Raines (Chetham Soc., os 14; 1848), 130; 2 Corinthians 12: 2; D. Featley, *A sermon preached at the funerall of sir Humphrey Lynd. . . . June the 14ᵗʰ 1636*, in H. Lynde, *A case for the spectacles, or, a defence of Via tuta, together with Stricturae in Lyndomastygem* (1638), 218; C. Zaleski, *Otherworld Journeys: Accounts of Near-Death Experience in Medieval and Modern Times* (New York, 1987).

[39] *The Whole Works of the Right Reverend Jeremy Taylor, D.D.*, ed. C. P. Eden (10 vols., 1847–54), viii. 448; Gataker, *Certaine sermons*, ii. 268; *Richard Baxter and Margaret Charlton: a Puritan Love Story . . . being the Breviate of the Life of Margaret Baxter*, ed. J. T. Wilkinson (1928), 62; Heywood, *Autobiography, Diaries*, i. 31; *The Diary of Dudley Ryder, 1715–1716*, ed. W. Matthews (1939), 339.

which caused a marked drowsiness towards the end. His death really was 'in a sober sence' a falling-asleep. 'And next to a safe passage hence,' concluded the preacher at his funeral, 'an easie *transitus* is very desireable.' There was some tension between this opinion and the older view, enshrined in the medieval *ars moriendi*, of the deathbed as an arena for the trial of faith. That view strongly influenced John Bowle's presentation of the death of the fifth earl of Kent in 1615. He had experienced peace of soul only after severe temptation. Without spiritual combat, Bowle insisted, there could be no spiritual peace.[40]

Those who subsequently described 'good' deaths usually felt able to describe the final moment as a quiet one. Sleep was the favourite metaphor, repeated in countless biographies and funeral sermons. The ancient idea that the soul escaped from the body with the last breath was taken up by various writers. George Herbert, according to Walton, 'breathed forth his divine soul, without any apparent disturbance'. Observers sometimes remarked that it had been impossible to tell when breathing had finally ceased. The simile of a 'kiss of God's mouth' was favoured by some authors. It may be that the final quietness was the result of total exhaustion or coma, or of what has been called de-cathexis, but those who wrote of deaths sought to present the last moments positively.[41]

The bearing of the dying person was widely interpreted as conveying some intimation of the soul's destination. Yet during the sixteenth and seventeenth centuries, when thousands of deathbeds were described in unprecedented detail, empirical observation cast increasing doubt on the reliability of deathbed comportment as a mirror of inwardly bestowed grace. Erasmus, in this as in other respects, foreshadowed the conclusions of later writers. William Perkins tried to reassure his readers concerning the idle words sometimes spoken by the dying instead of excellent and godly ones. Violent sickness, he told them, 'is usually accompanied with frensies, and with unseemely motions and gestures, which we are to take in good part, even in this regard, because wee our selves may be in the

[40] S. Hudson, *David's Labour and Rest: or, a Discourse... Preached at the Funeral of Mr Richard Shute* (1689), 22; Bowle, *Sermon*, unpaginated.

[41] e.g. 1 Kings 2: 10; 11: 43; 14: 31; 15: 8, 24; John 11: 11–13; Peck, *Desiderata Curiosa*, i. 42; Stout, *Autobiography*, 74; M. C. Cross, 'The Third Earl of Huntingdon's Death-bed: A Calvinist Example of the *Ars Moriendi*', *Northern History*, 21 (1985), 103; GLRO Acc 1017/908a; Parkhurst, *Redeemer's Friend*, 11–13; Walton, *Lives*, 254; Clarke, *Eminent Persons*, ii. 140; R. Kilbie, *A sermon preached... in Oxford at the funeral of Thomas Holland* (Oxford, 1613), 20; but cf. Nuland, *How We Die*, 140–3, 197; Kübler-Ross, *On Death and Dying*, 235, 237.

like case'. 'Ravings and other strange passions are many times rather
the effect of the disease than moving from the mind,' the earl of
Manchester remarked in his *Contemplatio mortis et immortalitatis*
(1631). 'Despair in dying may as well arise from weakness of nature as
from trouble of mind; but by neither of these can he be prejudiced
that hath lived well.' Delirium and its manifestations were certainly
feared throughout the seventeenth century. There may have been a
belief that it allowed what John Evelyn described as the 'worst
Inclynations' of the dying to rise to the surface and testify against
them. Yet in the long run, the more compassionate view gained
increasing acceptance.[42]

Some preachers felt obliged to point out that an easy death was not
necessarily a good one. In 1619 John Barlow insisted that peace at
death was no sign of a good life. This, he pointed out, was contrary to
the judgement of the common people. 'Oh say some, how quietly he
dyed? But I say; how well hath hee liued?' Men were to be judged by
their lives, not by their deaths. John Bunyan made the point forcefully
when he had his Mr Badman die 'As quietly as a Lamb' (1680). Jeremy
Taylor warned his readers to 'make no judgment concerning the dying
person, by his dying quietly or violently, with comfort or without'.[43]

Once the reliability of deathbed comportment as an indicator of
the quality of the individual's life and of the soul's likely destination
had been called in question, reduction of the pain and anxiety inseparable from dying came to seem a worthy goal. If a person's behaviour
during certain types of disease was really outside his or her control,
and told the bystander nothing about his or her spiritual state, why
not seek to curb the symptoms as far as possible? It was the acknowledged aim of Sir Henry Halford, an eminent early nineteenth-century
physician 'to undertake the management of pain, thereby overcom-
ing fear and restoring tranquillity, orchestrating an end which would
be serene and blissful'. Eighteenth-century practice to a large extent
anticipated the explicit formulation of this goal, above all by means of
the administration of opium.[44]

    [42] Erasmus, *Preparation*, sig. Dii^v-iii^r; Perkins, *Salue*, 168; H. Montagu, *Death and Immortality*, ed. E. Waterhouse (1906), 155–7; Evelyn, *Mrs Godolphin*, 77.

    [43] Erasmus, *Preparation*, sig. Dii^v-iii^r; J. Barlow, *The true guide to glory. A sermon preached at Plympton Mary in Devon, at the funerals of the lady Strode of Newing-ham* (1619), 3–4; J. Bunyan, *The Life and Death of Mr. Badman. Presented to the World in a Familiar Dialogue Between Mr. Wiseman, and Mr. Attentive*, ed. J. F. For-rest and R. Sharrock (Oxford, 1988), 157; Taylor, *Holy Dying*, 224; cf. *The Practical Works of the Rev. Richard Baxter*, ed. W. Orme (23 vols., 1830), iv. 449.

    [44] R. Porter, 'Death and the Doctors in Georgian England', in R. Houlbrooke (ed.), *Death, Ritual and Bereavement* (1989), 89–93.

The use of opium as a sedative and analgesic was well established by the middle of the seventeenth century. The Paracelsian term 'laudanum' came to describe a compound which included it. 'It taketh away all pains and grief of whatsoever it proceeds and in what part of the body soever it lieth.' During the 1630s the Bedfordshire physician John Symcotts recommended laudanum's use for a wide variety of purposes. Sir Thomas Browne referred to it as a sleeping draught. In the longer term, opium came to fulfil a particularly important role in the control of pain during terminal illness. The stages by which it achieved this role are now obscure. The demand for the alleviation of pain was clearly present. Lady Slingsby (d. 1641) 'would say she was not affraid to dye, but of the pains of Death; & to her physitian she would say, she desir'd nothing to prolong her life, so she could have any thing to ease her pains'. However, there were grave doubts about opium's use as a painkiller in life-threatening illnesses. First, if administered in large quantities, it could render the patient incapable of expressing faith or confessing sins. Secondly, it was sometimes believed to have hastened death itself. Yet once laudanum had been admitted to general medical use, it was almost impossible to prevent its employment for the alleviation of deathbed pain. The distinction between a dose large enough to subdue pain and one which made the patient unable to discharge his Christian duties or hastened his death often could not be maintained in practice.[45]

In the early eighteenth century both saints and sinners took opium on their deathbeds. The ascetic nonjuror Thomas Ken (d. 1711) was 'plied with opiates' and spent his last days in a drowsy haze. Sir Robert Walpole (d. 1745) lacerated his bladder with a powerful solvent for the stone. 'His only relief was opium, and from an apprehension of returning pain, he took such large and repeated doses, that for six weeks he was almost in a constant state of stupefaction, except for two or three hours in the afternoon, when he seemed to rouse

---

[45] J. C. Kramer, 'Opium Rampant: Medical Use, Misuse and Abuse in Britain and the West in the 17th and 18th Centuries', *British Journal of Addiction*, 74 (1979), 377–89; Pollock, *With Faith and Physic*, 136 (for reference to a laudanum containing opium which must antedate 1620); *A Seventeenth Century Doctor*, 54, 55, 56, 62–3, 66, 68, 71; *The Religio Medici & other Writings of Sir Thomas Browne* (1906), 86; *The Diary of Sir Henry Slingsby, of Scriven, Bart.*, ed. D. Parsons (1836), 74; Beier, *Sufferers and Healers*, 148, 168, 178; L. Andrewes, *Works*, ed. J. P. Wilson and J. Bliss (LACT, 11 vols., 1841–54), i. 450–1; BL MS Add 27356, fos. 211, 217; *Two East Anglian Diaries 1641–1729: Isaac Archer and William Coe*, ed. M. Storey (Suffolk Records Soc., 36; 1994), 95–6; J. Jones, *The Mysteries of Opium Reveal'd* (1700); *The New Oxford Book of Eighteenth Century Verse*, ed. R. Lonsdale (Oxford, 1984), 113, 283–5.

from his lethargy, and converse with his usual vivacity and cheerfulness.'[46]

A second important change remarked upon during the eighteenth century was the growing readiness of physicians to conceal the likelihood of impending death from their patients or even to sustain false hopes of recovery. Their aim was to lessen the distress of the dying (and sometimes their families), but another consequence was to reduce or remove the sick person's incentive to make spiritual preparations for death. It was the physician's traditional duty to tell the patient when his case was hopeless, and to warn him to prepare for death. Dr Robert Kay, a pious Nonconformist, performed this traditional duty well when in 1738 he told one of his patients, taken violently ill with a pain in his belly that 'he thought his Case was very dangerous, wou'd have him set his Heart and his House in order, and prepare for the worst'.[47]

The prognosis that a doctor was able to form was not, however, always so clear. Even the physician might be surprised by death. Reluctant to admit his ignorance, he might decide that the best course was to present a cheerful face. Wealthy patients were often attended by several different medical men, who might differ in their prognoses. The doctor's verdict might itself have an effect on the patient, destroying the will to live. Simonds D'Ewes recalled that his mother had died within an hour 'after being told plainly by a physician that there was no hope'. A doctor might well hesitate before delivering a verdict likely to have such an effect. Richard Baxter denied that it was a Christian duty to warn the sick of impending death in cases where such a warning would prejudice the patient's chances of recovery.[48] There are many reasons, then, for not positing a clear-cut transition from a traditional pattern of medical advice to a new belief in the physician's right to manage the deathbed by giving or withholding information. As early as 1640, shortly before the death of Christopher Wandesford, lord deputy of Ireland, his wife sought a true account of his condition. The attendant physicians 'would not deale truly, nor acknowledge his desperate case'.[49] Yet though the movement towards the medical management of the deathbed during the

---

[46] E. H. Plumptre, *Thomas Ken* (2nd edn., 1890), ii. 202; W. Coxe, *Memoirs of the Life and Administration of Sir Robert Walpole, Earl of Orford* (3 vols., 1798), i. 743.

[47] Porter, 'Death and the Doctors', 88–91; Kay, *Diary*, 25.

[48] D'Ewes, *Autobiography & Correspondence*, i. 110; Baxter, *Practical Works*, iv. 446.

[49] Thornton, *Autobiography*, 23.

seventeenth and eighteenth centuries may have been gradual and uneven, the argument that it took place remains persuasive.

If the traditional notion of what constituted a 'good' death was open to critical evaluation and reinterpretation during this period, the same is even more clearly true of the 'bad' death. To those convinced that a death was bad it signalled, just as surely as the 'good' death, the nature of the departed person's eternal fate. The Bible abounds with such deaths. The divisions and sufferings of the Christian Church added many more to the corpus. The miserable ends of the wicked provided a rich seam of material for medieval preachers and writers of cautionary tales. John Foxe included the deaths of many persecutors in his *Acts and Monuments*. However, the most ambitious collection of such material was Thomas Beard's *Theatre of God's Judgements*, which went through a number of editions and was considerably expanded after its first publication in 1597. During the seventeenth century a number of writers, including Nehemiah Wallington and Oliver Heywood, carefully noted instances of God's judgements upon the wicked.[50]

Three common sorts of bad death may be distinguished: failure to meet the final test despite having the chance to prepare for it; sudden death without warning; and wilful self-destruction. The misery which resulted from failure to prepare for death is a recurrent theme of seventeenth-century event books. In 1679 James Mitchel, a Halifax innkeeper, fell sick as a result of his excessive drinking. The Dissenting minister Oliver Heywood clearly thought that Mitchel had ample time for preparation, for he 'wandred about weakly 8 weeks before he dyed', but he was very angry with anybody who told him he would die. Another minister, Thomas Jolly, described in 1684 the near despair of a Mr Yates of Blackburn, formerly a member of Jolly's own congregation, who had gradually declined into 'loosness of conversation'. Yates lay on his deathbed weighed down by contemplation of the many great sins of which he had never truly repented. In about 1666, when she was 17, Elizabeth Livingston, daughter of a royalist nobleman, was deeply impressed by the spectacle of an old charcoal-burner who had frequented the alehouse and seldom come to church. He was dying, as he had lived, almost alone. Having failed to repent of his sins even in old age, he was now quite without inner comforts and overwhelmed with misery. 'With amaizement do I feare he is passing from these misery's here to far worse torment's in

---

[50] J. Foxe, *Acts and Monuments*, ed. J. Pratt (8 vols., 1877), viii. 628–71; Seaver, *Wallington's World*, 46–66, 199–208; Heywood, *Autobiography, Diaries*, ii. 237–303.

another place.' These accounts of deathbeds convey the belief of observers that the individuals concerned died unprepared, in a state of anxiety, confusion, or apathy. When their time came, they were unable to make use of the opportunities given them by a long terminal illness or the presence of would-be spiritual mentors.[51]

Sudden death came high on the list of evils in the Litany from which congregations regularly prayed deliverance. As one author remarked in 1720, the number of deaths which fell into this category was naturally large. Accidents, heart attacks, apoplectic strokes, and convulsions between them accounted for a substantial proportion of fatalities. Drink was a major cause of sudden death. Numerous examples, many of them unintentionally comic, appeared in *Woe to Drunkards*, a sermon by Samuel Ward (d. 1640), a celebrated Ipswich preacher. The appropriateness of the cause or time of sudden deaths often underlined their providential character. Punishment for sabbath-breaking sometimes came with the collapse of an overcrowded floor or scaffolding where people had gathered to watch an entertainment. William Laud noted that Lord Brooke died in the siege of Lichfield cathedral on the day of St Chad, Lichfield's patron saint.[52]

The recording of sudden deaths resulting from providential judgements continued during the eighteenth century, albeit in less systematic fashion. On 23 October 1740 John Wesley was informed of a 'poor wretch' who had done all he could to hinder Wesley's missionary work. He had boasted that he would return the following Sunday. 'But on Friday God laid his hand upon him, and on Sunday he was buried.' In 1750 the *Gentleman's Magazine* carried a report about William Leaf, a former soldier. On his being asked where he was going as he left a house in Winchester, he answered 'To hell' and dropped down dead on the spot. It was, remarked the correspondent, a proper warning to all profane persons.[53]

A gradual change nevertheless took place in attitudes towards sudden death. In the later Middle Ages, the prospect of being cut off

---

[51] Heywood, *Autobiography, Diaries*, ii. 265; *The Note Book of the Rev. Thomas Jolly, A.D. 1671–1693*, ed. H. Fishwick (Chetham Soc., NS 33; 1894), 59 (Yates was later 'somwhat affected' when Jolly wrote to him 'somthing more particularly and plainly'); Delaval, *Meditations*, 94–6.

[52] B. Grosvenor, *Observations on Sudden Death. Occasion'd by the late frequent Instances of it, both in City and Country* (1720), 3, 4, 6–7, 16–21; S. Ward, *Woe to drunkards. A sermon* (1622); T. Beard, *The Theatre of Gods Judgements* (4th edn., 1648), 150, 419–25, incorporating much material from Ward; Laud, *Works*, iii. 249; see also Jolly, *Note Book*, 31, 52, 56, 63, 66, 91, 98.

[53] Wesley, *Journal*, ii. 394; *Gentleman's Magazine*, 20 (1750), 234.

unprepared for eternity was widely regarded with fear, even though *The Book of the Craft of Dying* offers a brief word of assurance concerning the fate of righteous men who die suddenly.[54] Nearly all believing Christians approached death with sins for which they needed to be shriven. The diminished importance attached to confession after the Reformation, followed by growing doubts and disagreements concerning the interpretation of the deathbed performance, gradually made sudden death something which the well-prepared not only need not fear, but might actually welcome.

For a long time, attempts to present sudden deaths in a positive light needed to be supported with strong arguments. In 1608, for example, there was good evidence that the earl of Dorset had been well prepared, especially in the shape of a pious will, and in his own references to the prospect of his death. Yet George Abbot, preaching at Dorset's funeral, saw fit to reassure his audience with several other examples of 'good and godly men' who had died suddenly. In 1639 the preacher at the funeral of Mrs Elizabeth Hoyle of York still felt wary of the word 'sudden', with its unfortunate connotations of unpreparedness. He suggested that a death like that of Mrs Hoyle, who had been 'surprized with an Apoplexie at her private Devotion' should instead be described as a present or quick death. However, in 1672 the preacher at the funeral of the incumbent of John Evelyn's parish 'shewed how suddain Death . . . was no malediction to the prepared, & those who die in the Lord'. Sudden deaths were often also easy ones, a fact noticed by a number of preachers. The deaths of some conscientious ministers were subsequently likened by their colleagues to God's sudden translation of the patriarch Enoch. The famous author Mrs Elizabeth Rowe (d. 1737) prayed for a 'sudden Removal to the Skies' which would prevent any 'indecent Behaviour' caused by violent pain or sickbed languor in her last moments. A fatal stroke after a day of outwardly perfect health and vigour seemed under these circumstances a mark of divine favour.[55]

---

[54] R. N. Swanson, *Catholic England: Faith, Religion and Observance before the Reformation* (Manchester, 1993), 126; cf. Erasmus, *Preparation*, verso of second unfoliated leaf following sig. Cᵛ.

[55] G. Abbot, *A sermon preached at Westminster May 26, 1608. At the funerall solemnities of Thomas earle of Dorset* (1608), 19–24; *An Elegie upon The much lamented Death, of . . . Elizabeth Hoyle* (York, 1644), 13–14; Evelyn, *Diary*, iii, 604; J. Tillotson, *Sermons on several Subjects and Occasions*, in id., *Works* (12 vols., 1757), ii. 136–7; P. Doddridge, *Practical Reflections on the Character and Translation of Enoch* (Northampton, 1738), 1, 35; J. Wilford, *Memorials and Characters, together with the Lives of divers Eminent and Worthy Persons* (1741), 753; Grosvenor, *Observations*, 11–14.

The Presbyterian minister Benjamin Grosvenor pointed out in his *Observations on Sudden Death* (1720) that it was not in itself a judgement from God. It was always a miserable fate for the sinful man. However, in the case of the good, the disadvantages, such as the loss of edifying expressions of faith and hope, and exhortations to friends and family, were outweighed by substantial advantages. The dying person did not suffer the miseries of a lingering sickness or the temptations and pressures of the deathbed. Dying farewells, especially the parting words of spouses and parents (vividly imagined by Grosvenor), were distressing. 'A *sudden Death* prevents these killing formalities of Separation, under which, those that are left behind do scarce survive.' Grosvenor painted a sombre picture of the death-chamber, and concluded 'this is all ghastliness and horror—let a Man die in a Minute, or an Hour, and all this is prevented'. Grosvenor implicitly rejected the ancient belief in the value of the deathbed experience as a supreme test of individual faith and virtue and a school for spectators who must die in their turn. Furthermore, he believed that it was possible for the Christian to be prepared for death and yet enjoy life's lawful comforts to the full. His tract reflected far-reaching changes in outlook with exceptional sharpness and clarity.[56]

Suicide was the worst sort of bad death. Self-murder resulted from giving way to the diabolical temptation of despair. The desperate sinner, abandoning hope of God's mercy, condemned himself. Self-murder was a secular crime as well as the worst of sins. The goods of convicted suicides were forfeit to the crown. Much more rigorous enforcement under the Tudors produced a huge growth in recorded convictions. Before the Civil War the forcefully articulated and uniform condemnation of suicide by mutually supportive authorities in Church and State inhibited open discussion and the formulation of alternative ideas. However, even then, many people knew that suicide had been widely accepted in pagan antiquity. In chivalric and romantic contexts it was sometimes preferred to dishonour or life without a loved one. It was represented on the stage, notably by Shakespeare and Chapman. Alone among English divines, John Donne argued in his tract *Biathanatos* (unpublished during his lifetime) that suicide was not absolutely contrary to divine, natural, or civil laws.[57]

---

[56] Grosvenor, *Observations*, 11, 15, 22–31, 37.
[57] M. MacDonald and T. R. Murphy, *Sleepless Souls: Suicide in Early Modern England* (Oxford, 1990), 15–106, 360–6.

Major changes in attitudes followed the mid-seventeenth-century upheavals. The forfeiture of the suicide's goods was widely resented as an unjust penalty upon heirs. The weakening of central government supervision after the abolition of Star Chamber (the key agency in the enforcement of prerogative rights) was followed by a growth in the number of verdicts of unsound mind. During the century after the Restoration, the upper classes were increasingly sceptical about the possibility of the Devil's direct intervention in human affairs, associated as it was with the 'fanaticism' of Puritanism and the 'superstition' of popery, and discredited by arguments for 'rational' religion. They were also more tolerant of the notions of classical thinkers who thought suicide justifiable under certain circumstances. Religious toleration after the Glorious Revolution made it more difficult to curb the spread of heterodoxy and speculative philosophy. A more humane view of suicide gradually emerged in this new climate. Physicians played a part in extending the diagnosis of unsound mind, but fear that suicide might be encouraged by decriminalization delayed law reform. In this situation, an inquest verdict of *non compos mentis* was the only means of showing compassion. The proportion of such verdicts rose rapidly after 1688. They were always in the majority after 1720. However, conservative attitudes died hard. Belief in the importance of diabolical suggestion survived among Nonconformists and evangelical Anglicans, and was powerfully encouraged by the Methodists.[58]

Assessment of the goodness or badness of a death depended largely upon the standpoint of the observer. The manner of a person's departure might be interpreted in very different ways by friends and enemies, by clergy and their parishioners, or by people of differing religious persuasions. In January 1680 William Jackman of Halifax woke delirious after a heavy drinking bout, and was narrowly prevented by his daughter from cutting his own throat. He died six days later. Yet the vicar commended him at his funeral as a religious man and a good husband and neighbour. Not he, but his disease, was responsible for unbecoming words spoken during his raging sickness. Though 'he could not be actually prepared, yet he was habitually prepared in an honest conversation' and the vicar felt confident that God had received him into the arms of his mercy. Yet all confessed that he had been a sad drinker, noted Oliver Heywood, many that he had been a scoffer at goodness. Heywood's private opinion of

---

[58] Ibid. 109–216, 365. For a good example of diabolical temptation to self-murder see Wesley, *Journal*, ii. 529.

Jackman's likely destination was clearly very different from the vicar's.[59]

The possibility of dying well after a bad life or the perpetration of evil deeds was much discussed during this period. *The Book of the Craft of Dying* had insisted that the repentant and believing sinner might be saved on the deathbed, just as one who had previously led a blameless life might be damned for spiritual pride at the end. However, during the following centuries writers of the literature of preparation for death repeatedly emphasized the danger of putting off repentance till the deathbed. There were three main reasons for not relying on a late repentance: the danger of sudden death; the probability that a deathbed repentance would be superficial, inspired by fear without love of God; and the possibility of being gripped by a despair which would confuse the sinner or paralyse his will. There were many instances of deathbed repentances which observers judged inadequate or doubtful. On the other hand, Erasmus, followed by other commentators, insisted that a good life could not end in a bad death.[60]

However strong the doubts expressed concerning the value of a deathbed repentance, no section of Christian opinion ruled out such a possibility. To do so was to call in question the power or the mercy of God. The greater and more eminent the sinner and his sins, the more striking the manifestation of divine power. However, in order to gain widespread acceptance, the evidence of repentance had to be solid. The penitent needed to have done all he could to show the transformation which God had wrought in the short time which remained. The most famous instance of deathbed repentance in early modern England is that of John Wilmot, earl of Rochester (1647–80), foremost libertine of Charles II's court. The drama of Rochester's conversion was heightened not only by his personal brilliance but also by the confrontation between orthodox Christianity and open scepticism. It was, he claimed on his deathbed, the 'absurd and foolish' philosophy of Thomas Hobbes which had undone him and so many others. God, said Robert Parsons, the preacher of Rochester's funeral sermon, snatched this desperate sinner like a brand out of the fire. The powerful prophecy of Christ's suffering for sinners in Isaiah 53,

---

[59] Heywood, *Autobiography, Diaries*, ii. 261, 268.

[60] Swanson, *Catholic England*, 130, 132. For the continuing prominence of timely repentance as a sermon theme, see e.g. Evelyn, *Diary*, iv. 47, 244, 283, 298, 366; v. 137, 146–7, 162, 186, 250, 407, 437, 454, 520, 539, 569, 570–1, 605; for a sermon devoted to an individual case, see J. Ellesby, *The Great Danger and Uncertainty of a Death-Bed Repentance* (1693).

read to Rochester soon after the onset of his final illness, burst upon him as a revelation. He died assured of God's mercy through Jesus Christ and longing to be with his Saviour. Before he died, Rochester gave strict orders for the destruction of his pornographic writings and pictures, exhorted a visiting friend to repent, commanded Parsons to publish the story of his correction at God's hands, and wrote a solemn testimonial of his change of heart. Parsons concluded that there was great reason to believe that Rochester's repentance was real and his end happy.[61] Less notoriously dissolute than Rochester, and justly remembered for his part in the Glorious Revolution, William Cavendish, first duke of Devonshire (d. 1707), was another nobleman who repented of his sins on his deathbed. The behaviour of these men on their deathbeds resembled, in certain respects, that of such outstanding earlier penitents as Henry VII and Robert Cecil. Both of them participated in the last rites fully and fervently. They showed what seemed like true sorrow for their sins, determination to amend their lives, and exemplary patience in a long period of sickness which tried their faith.[62]

The well-publicized cases of Rochester and Devonshire were the products of an age when the sharp conflict between piety and morality on the one hand, and irreligion and laxity on the other, created especially favourable conditions for the dramatic repentances of great men. The moral and religious climate of early Hanoverian England was greyer and more tolerant. More importantly, there was a greater scepticism about the value and meaning of deathbed testimonies, a greater reluctance to publish them, and a growing readiness to discount or pass over the last scene when assessing the whole of an individual's life performance. In these respects, as in so many others, John Wesley confronted the spirit of his time. His journals contain dramatic examples of repentance.[63]

The scaffold was a far better publicized and documented site of late repentance than the deathbed in early modern England. The condemned person faced especially strong social pressures during the

---

[61] R. Parsons, *A Sermon preached at the Funeral of the . . . Earl of Rochester* (Oxford, 1680), 10, 24, 26, 33, 34; G. Burnet, *Some Passages of the Life and Death of the Right Honourable John Earl of Rochester* (1680); G. Greene, *Lord Rochester's Monkey* (1974 edn.), 204–21.

[62] W. Kennett, *A Sermon Preach'd at the Funeral of the . . . Duke of Devonshire, . . . on Friday Septemb. 5ᵗʰ MDCCVII* (1708), 54–6; Parsons, *Sermon*, 16, 27–32; Fisher, *English Works*, 271–6, 284; W. S. Stafford, 'Repentance on the Eve of the English Reformation: John Fisher's Sermons of 1508 and 1509', *Historical Magazine of the Protestant Episcopal Church*, 54 (1985), 297–337; Peck, *Desiderata Curiosa*, i. 206–10.

[63] e.g. Wesley, *Journal*, ii. 378–9, 505.

sixteenth and seventeenth centuries to confess and repent in public. The sentence of death confronted him with his crime and its consequences in particularly stark fashion. The prospect of certain death, usually faced when the malefactor was in full possession of his faculties, did indeed concentrate the mind much more effectively than an enfeebling terminal illness.[64]

The medieval criminal could be attended by a confessor at the foot of the gibbet, but public confessions uttered from the scaffold may first have become common through incorporation in the ritual of early Tudor executions for treason. They were soon being made by other people facing capital punishment for serious crimes, especially murders. Such a speech usually incorporated submission to earthly authority, the individual's expression of contrition and acceptance of a deserved death, and a request for the prayers of spectators. Many of the convicted held themselves up as terrible examples to be avoided. Such a ritual allowed the condemned man to seize a last opportunity of doing good and to be reintegrated into earthly society before being finally despatched from it.[65]

Ideally, the criminal, spiritually rehabilitated by divine grace, faced the next life with confidence. A story about William Perkins illustrates this well. It was his practice to accompany condemned prisoners to execution in Cambridge. One 'young lusty fellow' was so dejected when he turned to speak to the people that he seemed half-dead already. Perkins asked him whether he was afraid of death. The prisoner shook his head; the thing he feared was worse than that. Perkins had him back down from the scaffold. He prayed with him, hand in hand. After aggravating his sense of sin to the point where the tearful prisoner felt he was at the gates of hell, Perkins pressed home the saving mercy and power of Jesus, and made him imagine 'the black lines

---

[64] *Boswell's Life of Johnson*, ed. R. W. Chapman (Oxford Standard Authors, 1953 edn.), 849; Sir Thomas More gave as one reason for facing the prospect of execution with equanimity the unpleasantness of the alternative—death in sickness. 'And thoughe it be a paine to die while a man is in health yet see I very fewe that in sickenes dye with ease': *The Correspondence of Sir Thomas More*, ed. E. F. Rogers (Princeton, 1947), 543.

[65] See picture of condemned criminals with confessors at the foot of the gallows reproduced in I. Arthurson, *The Perkin Warbeck Conspiracy 1491-1499* (Stroud, 1994), 119. L. B. Smith, 'English Treason Trials and Confessions in the Sixteenth Century', *Journal of the History of Ideas*, 15 (1954), 471-98; J. A. Sharpe, ' "Last Dying Speeches": Religion, Ideology and Public Execution in Seventeenth-Century England', *Past and Present*, 107 (1985), 144-67; J. Bellamy, *The Tudor Law of Treason: An Introduction* (1979), 191-201. Bellamy observes that 'few prisoners denied all, or admitted all, of the offences with which they were charged' (p. 195).

of all his sins . . . cancelled with the red lines of his crucified Saviours precious blood'. The prisoner wept for joy, and expressed his consolation so eloquently that the spectators praised God for the change in him. His exemplary end caused great rejoicing.[66]

Here, in compressed form, was the pattern of depression followed by exaltation often reported in the dying. The rehabilitated malefactor was cut off at the height of his spiritual readiness, giving the devil no chance to return. The attendant crowd became the criminal's sympathetic supporters as he prepared to meet his maker. Simonds D'Ewes described a similar response on the part of spectators of a 1613 execution. A murderer's repentance and patient acceptance of his execution persuaded all witnesses that his soul was 'in a happy condition'.[67]

There were always some condemned people who refused to repent, or who protested their innocence to the last. Protestant 'heretics' and Catholic 'traitors' turned execution rituals inside out, becoming martyrs in the eyes of their own communities. Some criminals were not to be awed by the theatre of punishment and refused to play their expected part. Different interpretations of particular scaffold performances by the godly and their opponents further limited the integrative potential of last dying speeches. However, from the last years of the seventeenth century failure to make an edifying speech at the gallows seems to have become more common. Observers emphasized the bravado or unconcern of many convicted criminals emboldened by each other's company or the sympathy of the mob. Daniel Defoe described the prison behaviour of *Six Notorious Street-Robbers* as 'outrageously impudent, hardened, and abandoned' and showing a 'brutal, not manly courage, for that is quite of another nature; such insensibility as to their condition . . . making a sport of death, and even of hell itself'. A number of criminals planned a last convivial feast or a gallows procession with considerable care, seeking at all costs to appear cheerful and debonair. Some presented a performance of studied, stylish nonchalance. A few defied the panoply of the law. John Collington of Throwleigh in Kent, condemned for arson in 1750, insulted the judge and refused to forgive his enemies at the gallows. When their courage failed, criminals

---

[66] Clarke, *Marrow*, i. 416–17. Preaching in York minster in 1649, John Shaw recalled this episode and remarked what a 'blessed work' it would be to finance an able man to preach to and catechize 'these poor souls' (i.e. condemned malefactors): *Yorkshire Diaries and Autobiographies in the Seventeenth and Eighteenth Centuries* (Surtees Soc. 65; 1877), 407.

[67] D'Ewes, *Autobiography & Correspondence*, i. 61.

presented a deplorable spectacle. Jonathan Wild (d. 1725), widely hated as an informer, said hardly anything at the gallows 'being either dozed with the liquid laudanum which he had taken, or demented and confused by the horror of what was before him, and the reflection of what was within him'.[68]

Gone by the eighteenth century was the close alliance between magistracy and ministry and the faith in scaffold rituals as a vehicle of edification which had once underpinned last dying speeches. The breakdown in religious unity, a widespread cynicism about anything which smacked of cant, and a franker readiness on the part of reporters to titillate rather than edify, left scaffold religious observance a mere husk of what it had once been. Methodism revitalized it, but only for a minority.[69]

Descriptions of deportment at the gallows present one aspect of a far larger process. The emergence of different liturgical and doctrinal currents within the Church, the end of Protestant unity, and the subsequent growth of heterodoxy and indifference, allowed or encouraged much more variety in deathbed performance and management. A growing minority, especially those whose speculations led them to question or discard various elements of orthodox Christianity, practised their own eclectic or individualistic ways of dying. They included Lord Herbert of Cherbury (1648), who calmly forwent Communion when Archbishop Ussher declined his nonchalant request for it; Lord Shaftesbury (1683), an Arian who on his deathbed denied the doctrine of satisfaction by Christ's death; and John Locke (1704), the alleged source of Shaftesbury's ideas, who, after thanking God for his happy life, and exhorting Lady Masham to prepare for a 'better

---

[68] D. Defoe, *The King of Pirates, Being an Account of the Famous Enterprises of Captain Avery with Lives of other Pirates and Robbers*, ed. G. A. Aitken (1895), 275, 379; S. Richardson, *One Hundred and Seventy-Three Letters written for Particular Friends, on the most Important Occasions* (7th edn., 1764), 239–42; *Gentleman's Magazine*, 20 (1750), 149, 184; Sharpe, 'Last Dying Speeches', 165–6; R. Wunderli and G. Broce, 'The Final Moment before Death in Early Modern England', *Sixteenth Century Journal*, 20 (1989), 272–4. T. W. Laqueur, 'Crowds, Carnival and the State in English Executions, 1604–1868', in A. L. Beier, D. Cannadine, and J. M. Rosenheim (edd.), *The First Modern Society: Essays in English History in Honour of Lawrence Stone* (Cambridge, 1989), 305–55, esp. 319–23. Laqueur focuses attention on the unruly, festive crowd, and argues that the behaviour of the condemned was often subversive of the official purposes of executions, but most of his examples date from after 1680. See also P. Lake, 'Popular Form, Puritan Content? Two Puritan Appropriations of the Murder Pamphlet from Mid-Seventeenth-Century London', in A. Fletcher and P. Roberts (edd.), *Religion, Culture and Society in Early Modern Britain: Essays in Honour of Patrick Collinson* (Cambridge, 1994), 313–34.
[69] Wesley, *Journals*, ii. 100.

state hereafter', listened to her reading the Psalms until within a few minutes of his death.[70]

The examples of courage, equanimity, and philosophical resignation supposedly set by the great men of antiquity had an enormous appeal. The behaviour of eminent Augustan Englishmen was repeatedly likened to that of Greeks or Romans. George Monck died in 1670 'like a Roman general', Alexander Pope compared himself with Socrates among his friends not long before his death in 1744, while Sir Robert Walpole was judged by an attendant surgeon to have earned on his deathbed a renown equal to that of 'the most Remarkable Sages of antiquity'. White Kennett claimed in 1708 that the duke of Devonshire had died 'not meerly like an antient Roman, but rather like a good Christian'. The idea of combining in one's death a Roman fortitude with a Christian piety was an attractive one, but this combination was incompatible with superstitious priestcraft or fanatical enthusiasm. Equanimity and consistency were admired; violent swings from depression to ecstasy implicitly deprecated.[71]

One of the most instructive of Augustan deathbed performances was that of Joseph Addison (1719). Addison regarded the accounts of the deaths of eminent persons as uniquely improving. He had been particularly impressed by those of such men as Socrates, Cato, Augustus, and Seneca. The manner of a person's departure should be consistent with his life, and his philosophy should enable him to bear it cheerfully. Addison made no special effort to take leave of his friends, and, thinking as he reportedly did that 'there was no such thing as real conversation between more than two persons', he was probably content not to have much company with him during his last days. Just before his death, he grasped the hand of his stepson the earl of Warwick and said 'See in what peace a Christian can die'. However, his performance, largely inspired by pagan models and an ideal of natural behaviour, fitted into no orthodox pattern. Nor did everybody find it convincing. Horace Walpole's much later remark that he had died of brandy ('nothing makes a Christian die in peace like being maudlin')

---

[70] *Aubrey's Brief Lives*, ed. O. L. Dick (Harmondsworth, 1972), 217; K. H. D. Haley, *The First Earl of Shaftesbury* (Oxford, 1968), 732; P. King, *The Life of John Locke* (1829), 263.

[71] M. Ashley, *General Monck* (1977), 246; M. Mack, *Alexander Pope: A Life* (New Haven, 1985), 810; J. Ranby, *A Narrative of the Last Illness of the Right Honourable the Earl of Orford* (1745), pref., unpaginated (contrast Coxe, *Memoirs*, i. 743); Kennett, *Sermon*, 56.

was equally characteristic of a more cynical, less solemn, eighteenth-century mood.[72]

CONCLUSION

Philippe Ariès argued that whereas the later Middle Ages made the deathbed the supreme trial, upon whose outcome the individual's fate depended above all, the Renaissance saw a shift of emphasis away from the deathbed to the preceding life seen as a whole. Though there is some truth in this view, the development was a very slow one. In England, recorded interest in deathbed performance was never greater than it was during the 150 years following the Reformation. Erasmus, whose work was repeatedly quarried for maxims and aphorisms by succeeding generations, boldly asserted that no death preceded by a good life was to be thought a bad one. Yet he also claimed that a man's eternal fate depended on the last act of his life's play. There was a tension between the two statements.[73]

The literature of the *ars moriendi* placed a weight of unrealistic expectations on the dying. It set up a fragile and vulnerable ideal whose contradictions were exposed by the unprecedentedly intense experimental scrutiny of the post-Reformation century. It is doubtful whether the majority of people were ever equipped for an ideal 'good death' by the strength of their religious convictions. Lethargy, delirium, excruciating pain, and sudden death made countless thousands of people incapable of anything resembling a model deathbed performance. The interpretation and assessment of the behaviour of the dying always depended to some extent upon the standpoint and sympathies of the beholder. There was nevertheless a growing recognition that outward appearance and inner reality might be very different. Once expectations of the individual's performance were relaxed, the way was open for a more fundamental reappraisal of the value of the deathbed test. An easy death came to seem desirable, and it was then not a long step to the readiness to try to make it easy.

If the form and value of the deathbed ordeal were being questioned, so too was the nature of the 'bad death'. Sudden death, once invested with a superstitious dread, could in the early eighteenth century be presented as something positively desirable. Self-murder,

[72] P. Smithers, *The Life of Joseph Addison* (Oxford, 1954), 445–8, and 448 n. 3, referring to Walpole's letter of 16 May 1759.
[73] P. Ariès, *The Hour of our Death* (Harmondsworth, 1983), 298–305, 314–15; Erasmus, *Preparation*, sig. Aii, Dii^v; C. Fitz-Geffrey, *Death's sermon unto the living. Delivered at the funerals of the ladie Philippe, late wife unto Sir A. Rous* (1620), 29.

outcome of despair, the worst of all Christian sins, gradually came to be viewed with compassion and understanding, and largely decriminalized *de facto* if not *de jure*. Late repentance was viewed with increasing scepticism. The concepts of 'good' and 'bad' death were not obsolete in 1750, but in so far as there had ever been a consensus concerning these concepts, it had by then largely broken down. Appraisal of the individual was increasingly concerned with the balance of the life as a whole. There is a world of difference between the compilations of the seventeenth-century Puritan hagiographer Samuel Clarke and a work such as *The Lives of the Poets* written by the pious Samuel Johnson. In Clarke's narratives, as in the funeral sermons on which so many of them were based, the deathbed is often the most vividly and fully described episode of all. Johnson usually had little to say about it.[74]

It has been claimed that 'the family began to assume absolute centrality in the procedures of dying' during the eighteenth century.[75] However, the family's role at the deathbed had always been central. The individual's ability to make a 'good' end largely depended upon familial support. The poignancy of parting with friends and loved ones is apparent in much sixteenth- and seventeenth-century testimony. Yet it is true that the emphasis in earlier accounts on the religious performance of the dying sometimes obscured the family's role. Divesting the deathbed of much of its religious significance made that role more visible.

[74] See e.g. S. Johnson, *Lives of the English Poets*, ed. G. B. Hill (3 vols., Oxford, 1905), ii. 18, 25, 37, 46, 51, 62, 173, 195, 227, 281, 293, 301, 310, 314, 318 (very brief references to deaths, sometimes mentioning only the date); ibid. 31, 74, 117, 164, 252, 265 (accounts of 'good' deaths, usually very brief). Richard Savage's last recorded words indicated that he had forgotten what he wanted to say: ibid. 429.

[75] Porter, 'Death and the Doctors', 86.

8

Grief and Mourning

Grief is the suffering caused by deprivation and loss, above all of friends and loved ones. Mourning embraces all grief's outward behavioural manifestations. The melancholy induced by bereavement has often taken extreme and dramatic forms. Robert Burton illustrated this fact with abundant examples in an eloquent passage of his *Anatomy of Melancholy* (1621). Its symptoms could include loss of appetite and desire to live, 'deepe sighes and groanes, teares, exclamations, . . . howling, roaring, many bitter pangs', and an obsessive preoccupation with the dead person which sometimes caused hallucinations of his or her presence. Brave and patient men often wept like children for months, according to Burton.[1]

Grief comprises various elements. The deepest and most complex feelings may be those of personal loss. The sufferer is deprived of companionship, comfort, support, possibly the mainstay of his or her material and social life. In severe cases the loved one has been so important to the sufferer's sense of worth and identity that bereavement is like amputation. Such cruel deprivation can cause inexpressible anger against the dead person who has 'abandoned' the survivor. Alternatively it may cause the survivor to blame himself for the death.[2] Such a loss brings home forcibly the reality of death and the fact of one's own mortality. Another strand of grief is sorrow for the dead. An individual with a distinctive combination of capacities and attributes is extinguished, save in the memories of surviving friends. A living human being, perhaps strong, intelligent, and attractive, suffers pain, becomes utterly helpless, and then a lifeless corpse. Any desire to cherish this abandoned residue is savagely thwarted by the repellent processes of decomposition.

---

[1] R. Burton, *The Anatomy of Melancholy*, ed. T. C. Faulkner, N. K. Kiessling, and R. L. Blair (Oxford, 1989-), i. 356-8.

[2] C. M. Parkes, *Bereavement: Studies of Grief in Adult Life* (2nd edn., Harmondsworth, 1986), 97-104, 201-8; J. Bowlby, *Attachment and Loss*, iii. *Loss: Sadness and Depression* (Harmondsworth, 1981), 13-14, 104-5, 288-9.

This is the nature of grief today, but all the feelings and responses mentioned in this brief description were also experienced and recorded between the closing years of the Middle Ages and the early eighteenth century. There is no reason to suppose that the basic character of grief changed during that time, but the means of its expression and their availability certainly did. The exploration of personality and experience was revolutionized by new poetic forms, the introspective diary, intimate biography, the development of letter-writing skills, drama, and the novel, to name but the foremost media relevant in this context.

Human societies have a range of different ways of dealing with grief. Early modern England generally demanded a degree of control on the part of the individual, and the direction of powerful feelings into socially acceptable channels of mourning. Excessive grief was normally deprecated. To surrender to one's feelings showed a lack of faith, reason, self-control, even a perverse wilfulness. Not to feel grief at all, however, was unnatural. It suggested that the individual was something less than a full human being. In between lay moderate grief. The concepts of 'excessive' and 'moderate' grief are difficult to pin down precisely. They meant different things to different writers.

Christian teaching provided explanations for the losses which caused grief and guidance concerning appropriate conduct on the part of the bereaved. The advice of the greatest pre-Christian classical writers, especially those of the Stoic philosophers, also commanded widespread respect. Yet its role in helping people to come to terms with bereavement was ancillary to that of Christian belief. The fundamental principle of Christian explanation was that nothing can happen without God's will. 'Are not two sparrows sold for a farthing? and one of them shall not fall on the ground without your Father. But the very hairs of your head are all numbered. Fear ye not therefore, ye are of more value than many sparrows' (Matthew 10: 29–31). No single death was random or without purpose or significance. Each fitted into the divine plan.

This is not to say that the timing of any particular death could be explained with confidence, but God was known to remove human beings by death for various reasons. His purposes needed to be considered in relation both to the individual thus removed and to the survivors affected by the severance. Death was a reward to the good who were thereby delivered from the temptations, trials, and sorrows of earthly life. If the deaths of the good were often to be welcomed for their sakes, they entailed deprivation for those they left behind.

However, God always had a purpose in view for the bereaved. Bitter though their experience might be, it was salutary if they were capable of receiving it in the right spirit. 'For whom the Lord loveth, he chasteneth, and scourgeth every son whom he receiveth' (Hebrews 12: 6). When he inflicted suffering upon those whom he loved, God did so either to punish them for their sins or to test their faith and patience. In either case, he taught them that it was ultimately foolish to rely upon earthly satisfactions and human comforts. Bereavement was supposed to wean the hearts of Christians from the world and focus their aspirations more clearly upon the next life, where all the saved would be united in God. Death came as a punishment to unrepentant sinners. Hell was the destination of their souls. The friends of the wicked could draw no comfort from their deaths, but if they were capable of receiving them as warnings to turn to God, they might none the less profit from them. It was a Christian duty to accept the deaths of friends with submission and patience. Outstanding biblical examples had been set by Abraham, who had prepared to sacrifice his son Isaac at God's command (Genesis 22), and Job, who had suffered the deaths of his seven sons patiently (Job 1: 19-21).

'But I would not have you to be ignorant, brethren, concerning them which are asleep, that ye sorrow not, even as others which have no hope' (1 Thessalonians 4: 13). At the coming of the Lord, St Paul continued, those who survived on earth would be caught up together with those who had died, to meet the Lord in the air. 'Wherefore comfort one another with these words.' The earliest commentators upon the passage construed it as a prohibition of all mourning, but following St Ambrose (*c*.339-97) and St Augustine (354-430), most later writers understood it as an injunction not to indulge in a sorrow like that of people who had no hope, i.e. those who had no expectation of an afterlife. Sorrow itself was not condemned, but excessive grief was.[3] The distinction was pithily put in a frequently cited saying of St Bernard (1090-1153): 'Non culpamus affectum, sed excessum' (We do not blame the emotion, but the excess).[4]

In early modern times, the most rigorous attitudes to mourning were expressed by admirers of the ancient Stoics. Erasmus, foremost

---

[3] G. W. Pigman III, *Grief and English Renaissance Elegy* (Cambridge, 1985), 28. This is an invaluable study of the sources of the ideas concerning grief which were current in 16th-cent. England.

[4] See e.g. C. Sutton, *Disce Mori: Learn to Die* (1843, repr. from 1st edn. of 1600), 157; C. Scott, *The Saints Priviledge or Gain by Dying* (1673), 22. Grief was often portrayed in medieval art, especially in pictures of the Massacre of the Innocents, the Deposition from the Cross, and the Death of the Virgin.

of northern humanists, insisted that grief, along with other unruly passions, be curbed by reason. Christians, he suggested 'should be ashamed to be surpassed by pagans'. Views of grief influenced by such rigorism were most eloquently expressed in England during Edward VI's reign. They appear in a funeral sermon which Matthew Parker preached for Martin Bucer in 1551, in the letter which Thomas Wilson wrote to his patron, the duchess of Suffolk, on the deaths of her two sons of the sweating-sickness the same year, and in Wilson's *Arte of Rhetorique* (1553). Wilson's work, especially the *Arte*, shows the strong influence of Erasmus, and of the Stoic emphasis on reason and self-control.[5] Rigorism, it may be suggested, was one logical response to the clarity of the Protestant doctrine concerning the here-after first unequivocally propounded in England under Edward VI. Purgatory and the possibility of helping the dead by means of inter-cessory prayer had both been repudiated. 'Rigorist' Protestant hostil-ity to grief may have been due, in part at least, precisely to the fact that Catholic doctrine encouraged its sublimation in psychologically therapeutic and ostensibly constructive activity on behalf of the dead. 'Rigorists' insisted that grief and intercessory prayer were equally futile.

In the longer term, however, rigorism was not, perhaps could not, be sustained. Natural grief won general, albeit always qualified, acceptance, and Christian writers explored the ways in which it served God's purposes. Absence of grief showed the individual to be deficient in feelings normally implanted by God. To seek altogether to suppress such grief at its first appearance was perverse. 'They who misuse this testimony' wrote John Calvin, commenting on 1 Thessa-lonians 4: 13, 'to establish Stoic *apatheia*, that is, an iron insensibility, among Christians, find nothing of the kind in Paul's words.'[6] It was 'one thing to bridle our grief to submit it to God and another to harden like a stone after throwing off human sensibility'. In fact the calm *apatheia* which the Stoics and their modern disciples sought to achieve through curbing the passions by reason was not insensibility. The most serious objection was more profound. Central to Stoic pre-scriptions for dealing with grief were a reliance on human willpower and an acceptance of the inevitable which had nothing to do with

---

[5] Pigman, *Grief and Elegy*, 11–19, 27–31.
[6] *Ioannis Calvini in omnes D. Pauli Epistolas* (Geneva, 1551), 481–2, quoted by Pigman, *Grief and Elegy*, 137, n. 3; cf. R. Pearson, *A Sermon Preached at the Funeral of the Reverend Doctor Ambrose Atfield. Late Minister of St. Leonard Shoreditch* (1684), 3.

Christianity. To see grief as a sign of weakness, as the Stoics did, was to overlook its place in God's scheme and its possible salutary effects.

John Jewel (d. 1571) explained that St Paul did not forbid natural affection. Our parents and children are parts of our body which cannot be cut off without our feeling it. 'The father if he feele not the deathe of his sonne: or, the sonne if he feele not the death of his Father, and haue not a deepe feeling of it, he is vnnatural.' Those who felt no natural affection were among the targets of God's anger (Romans 1: 18, 31). 'God hath neither made us stocks nor stones, nor given us hearts which should have no feeling, when occasions offered, or times beseeming require sorrowful affections,' wrote Christopher Sutton around 1600. 'And the more tender our spirits are made by religion, the more easy we are to let in grief, if the cause be innocent, and be but in any sense twisted with piety and due affections,' Jeremy Taylor claimed. What was purely natural could not be thought unlawful 'without some reflection upon the God of Nature', remarked the London minister Richard Pearson in 1684. Without grief there could be no Christian resignation or action to subdue one's own will to that of God. 'For all Resignation seems to suppose some former Reluctancy, or a foregoing Velleity, at least, of having the thing otherwise; . . . there is no Resignation in offering up unto God of such Things only as cost us nothing.' Moderate grief inclined people towards consideration of the vanity of the world, the frailty of human nature, and their own mortality. To part with friends as if one had suffered no loss showed dullness, insensibility, and a lack of awareness rather than due submission. Early in 1679 Oliver Heywood attended the funeral of a woman who had died in childbirth. Even the people who carried the corpse talked and laughed as if they had been at a bear-baiting. The hardness of such people's hearts made it seem to Heywood that 'naturall affection together with religion' had been quite banished out of the world.[7]

Grief found its natural overflow in tears. Indeed, it might be dangerous to the individual to deny grief an outlet, 'Yf it were not for

---

[7] J. Jewel, *An exposition vpon the two epistles of the apostle Sainct Paule to the Thessalonians* (1583), 160, quoted by Pigman, *Grief and Elegy*, 34; Sutton, *Disce Mori*, 155; J. Taylor, *The Rule and Exercises of Holy Living* (1926), 122; Pearson, *Sermon*, 6, 10; Heywood, *Autobiography, Diaries*, ii. 257; anon., *The Praise of Mourning*, in, *Threnoikos. The house of mourning. Delivered in XLVII sermons, preached at funeralls* (1640), 32–3. Robert Harris, remarking in 1614 on the speed with which people forgot the loss of even their closest relatives, asked 'Now when nature dies, shal we looke for any life of grace?': *The workes . . . Revised, and in sundrie places corrected. With an addition of two sermons, not formerly extant. As also two tables* (1635), 222.

weeping the heart would burst.' Words, too allowed grief to find a vent. 'Give sorrow words. The grief that does not speak Whispers the o'erfraught heart and bids it break.' Christopher Sutton adduced numerous examples from the Scriptures to show that openly expressed sorrow was quite legitimate.[8] Immoderate grief was nevertheless condemned throughout this period. Excessive manifestations of sorrow showed lack of faith, or even sincerity. The ritual ostentation of heathen or 'ethnic' lamentations was contrasted with the quiet sobriety of Christian mourning. At pagan funerals, it was asserted, women had been hired to 'sighe, sob, houle and weepe'. The Irish were notorious for their 'howlings and lamentations' at funerals. 'To weep Irish' meant to feign sorrow. It was a commonplace axiom that those who felt the least true sorrow often made the greatest show of it. Hamlet's mother, who had followed her husband's body, 'Like Niobe, all tears', married his brother a month later. Violent, uncontrolled grief, it was observed, commonly spent itself soonest, in a rapid mood-change which spoke of inconstancy and instability. Seneca's epigram 'Small sorrows speak; great ones are silent' was repeatedly echoed in poetry, drama, and sermons during the English Renaissance. No 'shows of grief' could express what Hamlet felt in the death of his father. Long-term, irreconcilable grief was also condemned. Failure to submit to God's judgements might merit further punishment. Cautionary tales were told of the terrible things that had happened to some people who repined against the deaths of loved ones.[9]

A more compassionate attitude to grief was promoted, from the later sixteenth century onward, by a growing interest in individual psychology. Some people were held to be naturally prone to grief because of their melancholic disposition. The word 'melancholy' was variously used to describe black bile or the condition resulting from

[8] *The Oxford Dictionary of English Proverbs*, comp. W. G. Smith (3rd edn.), ed. F. P. Wilson (Oxford, 1970), 338; J. Taylor, *The Rule and Exercises of Holy Dying* (London, 1929), 100; *Macbeth*, IV. iii. 210–11; Sutton, *Disce Mori*, 156–7; Pearson, *Sermon*, 3.

[9] J. Weever, *Ancient funerall monuments within the united monarchie of Great Britaine, Ireland, and the islands adjacent* (1631), 13–17; T. Hearne (ed.), *A Collection of Curious Discourses written by Eminent Antiquaries upon Several Heads in our English Antiquities* (2 vols., 1771), i. 201, 209–11; *Oxford Dictionary of Proverbs*, 744–5, 876; *Hamlet*, I. ii. 83–6, 147–56; Heywood, *Autobiography, Diaries*, ii. 239; *Memoirs of the Life of Mr. Ambrose Barnes, late Merchant and sometime Alderman of Newcastle upon Tyne*, ed. W. H. D. Longstaffe (Surtees Soc. 50; 1867), 239; *Extracts from the Papers of Thomas Woodcock (Ob. 1695)*, ed. G. C. Moore Smith, in *Camden Miscellany*, xi (Camden, 3rd ser. 13; 1907), 69.

its excess. In the physiological theory inherited from Greek antiquity and still orthodox in late medieval and early modern times, black bile was one of the four constituent humours present in every individual. The person in whom melancholy was dominant tended to be lean, dry, taciturn, solitary, and fearful by nature. Humoral imbalance could be accentuated by passions, especially grief in the case of the person of melancholic disposition. Immoderate sorrow cooled and dried the body, constricted the heart, and deadened the spirits, producing 'a heavy, despondent lassitude in which the patient finds the world and his own life wearisome and distasteful, contemns himself, and has suicidal impulses'. The aggravation of natural melancholy by grief was a serious disease.[10]

Crucial to humoral theory was the interaction of the mental and the physical. A melancholic disposition was likely to accentuate fear and grief, and vice versa. Because grief was due to quite independent causes operating on the mind, it could not be considered solely as a disorder amenable to medical remedies. It could be countered to some extent by rational and religious arguments. Timothy Bright in his *A Treatise of Melancholie* (1586), the first English work devoted to the subject, sought to help an imaginary melancholic friend afflicted by a sense of God's displeasure to distinguish between the effects of his natural melancholy and those of God's 'fatherly frowning'.[11] Similar help, *mutatis mutandis*, could be given to the sufferer from grief. It was the Christian's duty to adopt a dual strategy in coping with melancholy, using both spiritual and medical measures where appropriate. The combination of a great loss and a melancholic temperament would help to explain the severity of an individual's grief, and even earn him sympathy, but they could not excuse a spineless or wilful failure to make any effort to surmount them.

From Italy, fountainhead of the Renaissance, came during the sixteenth century a keen interest in the nature of melancholy which was one of the distinctive formative influences upon Elizabethan and early Stuart art and literature. Moderate melancholy had been associated with profound contemplation and sharp insight both by Aristotle and (of more immediate importance) Marsilio Ficino (1433-99), the Florentine philosopher and physician. Melancholy men were held

---

[10] C. Rawcliffe, *Medicine & Society in Later Medieval England* (Stroud, 1995), 29-57 (see esp. the very negative characterization of 'Malencolicus' in a poem on p. 29); L. Babb, *The Elizabethan Malady: A Study of Melancholia in English Literature from 1580 to 1642* (East Lansing, 1951), 6-10, 21-4, 103-5.

[11] Babb, *Elizabethan Malady*, 51-4.

capable of high creative achievement; women, on the other hand, were thought to suffer the negative effects of melancholy and to be unable to sublimate it in fruitful action. Hamlet stands as the supreme embodiment in early modern English literature of the melancholy introspective visionary. A posture of contemplative melancholy became popular in portrait-painting and effigies.[12]

The seed of faith could be watered by tears, and the contemplation of immortality could follow from melancholy reflections upon death. Melancholy by temperament, and saddened by personal tragedy, John Donne offered up religious verse written in a state of 'low devout mancholie'. A vein of melancholy, tempered by Christian duty and classical restraint, ran through the poetry of the seventeenth century, but only after 1700 were the themes of sympathetic nature, the darkened grove, and the sequestered churchyard exploited to the full. Edward Young's *Night Thoughts* (1742), which sought consolation for the deaths of friends in the prospect of immortality, ironically 'became a seminal work in a secular cult of sepulchral melancholy'.[13] In some eighteenth-century poetry the hope of eternal life was marginalized by the pain of loss or the pleasure of sad reverie. Other poets, after dwelling on the pathos of bereavement, indulged in a sentimental vision of celestial reunion, but too facile a treatment of the afterlife devalued the very consolations which it offered.[14]

Yet in the same period, reason and philosophy, sometimes eclectically combined with elements of Christian consolation, were widely seen as the wise man's best means of dealing with grief. Henry Fielding, who suffered severely when his wife Charlotte died in 1744, was one of those who tried to draw on both philosophy and religion in

[12] Ibid. 58–67, 175–85; J. Schiesari, *The Gendering of Melancholia: Feminism, Psychoanalysis and the Symbolics of Loss in Renaissance Literature* (Ithaca, NY, 1992), pp. x–xi, 4–18, 19; R. Strong, *The English Icon: Elizabethan & Jacobean Portraiture* (1969), 21, 35–6, 352–3; B. R. Kemp, *English Church Monuments* (1980), 99.

[13] Babb, *Elizabethan Malady*, 177–80; J. W. Draper, *The Funeral Elegy and the Rise of English Romanticism* (New York, 1929), esp. 233–331; E. Young, *Night Thoughts*, ed. S. Cornford (Cambridge, 1989), introd., 17. Several of the favourite elements of the 18th-cent. poetry of melancholy ('pathless groves', 'A midnight knell', and 'a still gloomy valley') appear in 'Melancholy' by Thomas Middleton (1580–1627); see *The New Oxford Book of Seventeenth Century Verse*, ed. A. Fowler (Oxford, 1992), 174.

[14] Jonathan Richardson (1667?–1745), 'On My Late Dear Wife' and Aaron Hill (1685–1750), 'Alone in an Inn at Southampton, April the 25th, 1737', both in *The New Oxford Book of Eighteenth Century Verse*, ed. R. Lonsdale (Oxford, 1984), 176–7, 303–5, Contrast 'An Elegiac Poem by Mr H——, On his only Daughter, who died aged 11', *Gentleman's Magazine*, 1 (1731), 261–2.

coping with their losses. He asked himself, 'How would Socrates have acted on this Occasion?'[15]

From the sixteenth century onwards the expression of grief, as well as other personal feelings, became fuller, more explicit, and more prominent in both private writings (letters, diaries, meditations) and in more public testimonies (funeral sermons, elegies, epitaphs, and works of art). The Protestant abandonment of intercessory prayer deprived the bereaved of an important means of channelling grief into constructive action. This encouraged the fuller development of means of commemoration. As well as paying tribute to the dead, writers recorded, explored, or confronted the feelings of the bereaved. The Protestant clergy, denied the confessional, poured forth from pulpit and press a stream of practical advice on all aspects of Christian duty, including the management of grief. In this advice many of them incorporated the fruits of their own experience as husbands and fathers. Their work shows as a result a more vivid and lively awareness of the difficulties and temptations of the bereaved.

A sequential study of the stages of grief has been favoured by some twentieth-century analysts. Much early modern testimony lends itself to this approach. Grief often began in anticipation of death. Samuel Pepys, unable to attend his mother's deathbed in 1667, nevertheless knew that her end was imminent. Two nights before he received definite news, he dreamt that he was at her bedside, crying as he laid his head on hers. Called home in 1618 before his mother's expected death, Simonds D'Ewes was met by his father and cousin 'with their eyes standing full of tears'. Then, hearing of his mother's sickness from her own lips, D'Ewes 'answered her with silent tears'. Tears mingled with the prayers of those present as she lay dying in a fashion described in numerous other accounts. The spectacle of deathbed suffering often caused deep distress.[16]

The moment of death and the sight of the newly dead body were often deeply shocking. William Hutton recalled in characteristically terse fashion his reaction to his uncle's death in 1746. 'I was present, and could not bear the shock. My sister was obliged to support me.' In 1664 Samuel Pepys, entering his brother Tom's chamber immediately after his death, 'found the nurse holding his eyes shut; and he,

---

[15] D. Thomas, *Henry Fielding* (London, 1990), 233.
[16] Parkes, *Bereavement*, 27; Bowlby, *Loss*, 85; Pepys, *Diary*, viii, 129; D'Ewes, *Autobiography & Correspondence*, i. 109–11; ii. 22; J. Wilford, *Memorials and Characters, together with the Lives of divers Eminent and Worthy Persons* (1741), 755; *The Autobiography and Correspondence of Mary Granville, Mrs Delany*, ed. Lady Llanover (3 vols., 1861), i. 582.

poor wretch, lying with his chops fallen . . . still and dead and pale like a stone', which put Pepys into a 'present very great transport of grief and cries'. The shock could be fatal. The Lancashire physician Richard Kay recorded in 1749 the reaction of a bereaved mother whose life was 'bound up' with those of her husband and son. The sight of her dead son 'occasioned great Pain at her Heart which made her sick and not many Hours after died'. It is not surprising that it should have been thought appropriate to conceal a newly dead corpse from the eyes of the children of a household.[17]

It was, however, customary for adults to view the bodies of deceased relations. The sight was an expected catalyst for grief. In 1601, when Christopher Wandesford was brought to see his father's corpse, he was told 'Your father is deade, loke on him and yow must weepe'. The son of the godly minister John Carter (d. 1635) behaved in the anticipated fashion when he arrived home to find his father laid out. He 'fell upon his face and kissed him, and lift up his voice and wept, and so took his last leave of him till they should meet in a better world'. Oliver Heywood experienced 'heartbreakings' on seeing his dead brother in 1677.[18]

The deterioration of the corpse was deeply distressing. Its smell was horrible. Before Alice Woodforde died in 1664, she asked to be kept two or three days in bed before being laid out, perhaps in fear of being buried alive. However, after only a day had passed she began to smell so strongly that this proved impossible. The corpse's swollen belly was bound lest it burst open. 'Oh God', wrote her husband Samuel in his anguish, 'what things are wee when once thou callest for Our breath into thyne owne hands.'[19]

The immediate shock of bereavement played havoc with the emotions. Women sometimes went into premature labour, or suffered miscarriages. When the earl of Warwick heard in 1664 that his only son had died of smallpox, 'he cried out so terribly that his cry was heard a great way'. Going to bed a few hours after finding his brother

---

[17] *The Life of William Hutton, and the History of the Hutton Family*, ed. Ll. Jewitt (1872), 151; Pepys, *Diary*, v. 86; Kay, *Diary*, 139; PRO STAC 5A/6/37 (testimony concerning the death of Edmund Hynde of Stapleford (Herts.), Nov. 1580).

[18] *The Autobiography of Mrs Alice Thornton, of East Newton, Co. York*, ed. C. Jackson (Surtees Soc. 62; 1875), 319; S. Clarke, *A Collection of the Lives of Ten Eminent Divines* (1662), 19; Heywood, *Autobiography, Diaries*, ii. 19.

[19] Bod. Lib. MS Eng. misc. f. 381, fos. 63ᵛ–64ʳ, 66. In 1718 a cat was said to have got at the corpse of Mrs Little of Rothbury (Northumberland), a young wife who had died in a tragic accident, and to have eaten part of her face: *The Diary of the Rev. John Thomlinson*, in *Six North Country Diaries*, ed. J. C. Hodgson (Surtees Soc. 118; 1910), 141.

Tom dead, Samuel Pepys lay close to his wife for comfort, so full of 'disorder and grief' that he 'could not sleep nor wake with satisfaction'. Deciding how and when to break the news of a death was often a matter of great delicacy. After his apprentice had died in 1545, the London merchant Otwell Johnson was particularly concerned that the boy's mother should learn of her loss from her husband. In 1620 Sir Arthur Chichester trusted John Trevelyan to break the unwelcome news of his brother George's death to his father at a convenient time. He forbore to do so himself, knowing it would be grievous to the old man. In 1643, when she was about to give birth to a son, Mary Rich's father died. Her husband took care that the news should be divulged to her only when her confinement was over, and then by his mother, whose tact he presumably felt unable to match. Some ten years later, Edward Phelips of Montacute (Som.) was asked to ensure that his wife was not 'suddenly informed' of her mother's death until he had a suitable opportunity and had assembled some friends and neighbours 'to comfort her & to divert melancholy, and extremity of greife which the apprehension of so great a losse may occasion'. (As these examples suggest, softening the impact of bad news was felt to be particularly important in the case of women.)[20]

The process of mourning is a long one, from which some people never completely emerge. Within it, three main stages have been distinguished. The first, and shortest, is one of numbness. Outright disbelief is a common response to a death. A second phase of pining and searching follows, during which the bereaved remain preoccupied with the dead, but achieve intellectual grasp of the fact of departure. Finally comes a stage of apathy and depression, sometimes prolonged, in which the finality of loss sinks in, which may be followed by the beginning of successful readjustment. The whole period of mourning, but especially the second phase, is characterized by symptoms such as alarm, anger, restlessness, and insomnia as well as weeping. There is an abnormal mortality among the bereaved. The stress may activate or aggravate cancers, coronary disorders, and alcoholism.[21]

Nearly all these characteristic effects of grief are described in early modern testimony. The numbness which followed the initial shock

[20] *The Autobiography of Mary, Countess of Warwick*, ed. T. C. Croker (Percy Soc. 76; 1848), 17, 30; Pepys, *Diary*, v. 87; B. Winchester, *Tudor Family Portrait* (1955), 54–5; *Trevelyan Papers*, iii, ed. Sir W. C. Trevelyan, bart., and Sir C. E. Trevelyan (Camden os 105; 1872), 160; SRO DD/PH/224/11.

[21] Parkes, *Bereavement*, 27, 36–43, 60–76, 104–6, 214–15.

appears in various descriptions. At the end of the first month after his wife's death in 1633, Kenelm Digby referred in a letter to his 'frozen and benummed condition'. Lady Warwick spent the day after her husband's death in 1673 in a 'very stunned and astonished condition', insufficiently in control of herself to perform her spiritual duties. Two days later she was, she complained, 'dull in all I did' and, despite a chaplain's help, continued 'in that dead and stupid frame'.[22]

Writers described various symptoms now associated with the second and third phases of mourning. Two months after the death of her second husband in 1595, Margaret Sidney was complaining of pain in her eyes and head and could not yet speak of him without tears. In 1633 Kenelm Digby meditated upon his wife's death for several months, and complained of insomnia and lack of concentration. After the death of his second wife in May 1649, Bulstrode Whitelocke was repeatedly moved to tears by the sight of people and places which reminded him of her. Overcome by melancholy during a fever he suffered the following December, he often thought of joining her. In 1673 the newly widowed Lady Warwick found 'great discomposure' in her head, could not sleep, had no appetite, and was often 'pationately afected' by thoughts of her husband. After his second wife's death in 1712, Edmund Harrold, a Manchester wig-maker, drank heavily in order to drown his grief. For over two months his diary records a vicious cycle of depression, drinking, and hangovers, interrupted by efforts to pull himself together.[23]

Dreams of the dead were recorded by several writers. Most dreams of loved ones seem to have been serene and comforting. Digby, Whitelocke, and Harrold all dreamt about their dead wives. William Laud dreamt of being visited by his parents decades after their deaths. Children, too, had these dreams. Bitterly mourning his grandmother, the 8-year-old Simonds D'Ewes 'was often revived in the night by continual dreams of her being alive' and of his talking with her again.

[22] Evelyn, *Diary*, ii. 13; V. Gabrieli, *Sir Kenelm Digby: Un inglese italianato* (Rome, 1957), 238; R. Houlbrooke, *English Family Life 1576–1716* (Oxford, 1988), 85–6. Sir Kenelm Digby's exceptionally well-documented mourning has been analysed by Clare Gittings, 'Venetia's Death and Kenelm's Mourning', in A. Sumner (ed.), *Death, Passion and Politics: Van Dyck's Portraits of Venetia Stanley and George Digby* (1995), 54–68.

[23] *Diary of Lady Margaret Hoby, 1599–1605*, ed. D. M. Meads (1930), 29; Gabrieli, *Sir Kenelm Digby*, esp. 241; Whitelocke, *Diary*, 239–41, 244, 248–9; BL MS Add. 27353, fos. 215–22; Manchester, Chetham's Library, MS Mun.A.2. 137 (unfoliated); extracts in *Collectanea relating to Manchester and its Neighbourhood at Various Periods*, ed. J. Harland (Chetham Soc., os 68; 1866), 190–3.

When he was 10, in 1654, Tom Josselin dreamt that Jesus took him up into heaven, where he met his sister Mary, who had died four and a half years before at the age of 8.[24]

Periods of grief varied greatly in length. Samuel Pepys rapidly recovered from his initial distress over his brother Tom's death after discovering Tom's intrigues against him. However, in other cases, the bereaved remained obsessed by their losses for months or even years. In August 1653 John Evelyn was still trying to divert his wife from her sorrow for her mother's death nearly eleven months beforehand. Lady Fanshawe later described herself as sick with grief 'almost to death' for half a year after her octogenarian father's death in 1669. Some widows suffered especially long periods of grief. The recusant Lady Vaux barely moved out of her room for a year after her husband's death in 1595, and could not bring herself to enter the wing of the house where he had died for a further three years after that. Lady Rachel Russell admitted in April 1687 that 'a flood of tears' was 'ever ready' when she permitted herself the least thought of her husband's execution for his involvement in the Rye House Plot nearly four years before.[25]

Of all types of bereavement the loss of a marriage partner was for adults usually the most immediately and deeply disruptive. Marriage is the closest and most intimate of all ties. When in 1588 Richard Rogers, an Essex clergyman, tried to prepare himself for the possible death of his wife in childbirth, he foresaw that he would be forced to forgo a very suitable companion 'for religion, housewifery, and other comforts'. He would also suffer economically, and would have to look after the children and household affairs, neglecting his studies. He might lose the friendship of his wife's relatives. Many of the eulogistic appreciations of their wives which grief-stricken husbands wrote in their diaries and memorandum books paid tribute not only to their tact and understanding but also to their practical skills, especially in household management. Good marriages were close partnerships which operated at many levels.[26]

---

[24] Laud, *Works*, iii. 198, 234; Gabrieli, *Kenelm Digby*, 241–2; Whitelocke, *Diary*, 238–9; *Manchester Collectanea*, 202; D'Ewes, *Autobiography & Correspondence*, i. 37–8; Josselin, *Diary*, 335.

[25] Pepys, *Diary*, v. 91, 93; Evelyn, *Diary*, iii. 76, 87; *The Memoirs of Ann Lady Fanshawe*, ed. H. C. Fanshawe (1907), 210; *John Gerard: The Autobiography of an Elizabethan*, trans. P. Caraman (1951), 144; *The Letters of Lady Rachel Russell: From the Manuscript in the Library at Wooburn Abbey* (4th edn., 1792), 362–3.

[26] *Two Elizabethan Puritan Diaries*, ed. M. M. Knappen (Chicago, 1933), 74; Houlbrooke, *English Family Life*, 65, 69–70, 88–9.

Lady Russell wrote, just over two months after her husband's death, that her heart mourned and could not be comforted because she lacked the dear companion and sharer of all her joys and sorrows. 'I want him to talk with, to walk with, to eat and sleep with; all these things are irksome to me now; the day unwelcome and the night so too; all company and meals I would avoid, if it might be; . . . when I see my children before me, I remember the pleasure he took in them; this makes my heart shrink.' He had lost the better half of himself, Sir Kenelm Digby wrote, because for many years he had not had any true joy save that which had related to his wife and in which she had had a share. After his first wife's death in 1661, the Presbyterian minister Oliver Heywood wrote, 'I want her at every turne, every where, and in every worke'. Partners who died within a few hours of each other were accounted happy. John Hutchinson's grandfather, dying soon after his wife, never knew that she had predeceased him. John's wife Lucy speculated whether 'some strange sympathy in love or nature tied up their lives in one' or whether God had specially spared them both 'that bitter sorrow which such separations cause'. All these examples come from the intimate records of the upper and middle ranks of society. The casebooks kept by the Buckinghamshire astrological physician Richard Napier between 1597 and 1634 tell us something of the experiences of people lower down the social scale. Almost one-third of the episodes of illness, despair, and madness among Napier's patients were precipitated by the deaths of spouses. Vivid descriptions of grief, including anger, sudden weeping, apathy, and suicidal urges, were given by his patients of both sexes.[27]

The death of a spouse might seem a shattering, irreplaceable loss when it occurred. Yet remarriage was very frequent, in large part precisely because a marriage partner was so important if not essential. In so far as remarriage was necessary to enable the bereaved to fulfil familial and occupational functions, it could be looked upon as a social duty. Friends set to work to arrange suitable new marriages. However, many more men than women remarried, largely because

[27] Russell, *Letters*, 244; Gabrieli, *Sir Kenelm Digby*, 243; Heywood, *Autobiography, Diaries*, i. 177; L. Hutchinson, *Memoirs of the Life of Colonel Hutchinson, with the Fragment of an Autobiography of Mrs Hutchinson*, ed. J. Sutherland (1973), 20; cf. *The Autobiography of Henry Newcome, M.A.*, ed. R. Parkinson (Chetham Soc., os 26 and 27; 1852), i. 5; M. Macdonald, *Mystical Bedlam: Madness, Anxiety and Healing in Seventeenth-Century England* (Cambridge, 1981), 103–4; Anne Laurence, 'Godly Grief: Individual Responses to Death in Seventeenth-Century Britain', in R. Houlbrooke (ed.), *Death, Ritual and Bereavement* (1989), 72–4.

the sex ratio and the laws and customs relating to property were in
their favour.[28]

Children gave the survivor a reason to live, yet also complicated
and sharpened the bitterness of grief. Their presence was a constant
reminder that the partner who had shared pleasure in them and
responsibility for them was gone. There was also pathos in the incom-
prehension of young children. The fact that the eldest of their five
children was 'scarcely able to discerne they haue lost a mother' whet-
ted Sir Gervase Clifton's sense of desolation in the loss of his wife in
1627.[29]

Children's deaths were, after those of marriage partners, the ones
which left the deepest imprint on diaries and letters. However, reactions varied, above all according to the child's age and the strength of
the previous relationship between parent and child. Parental feelings
were also influenced by the numbers of survivors, and the chances of
begetting more children. In some cases the child's sex was important,
especially in the upper classes, where the desire to leave at least one
son to continue the name and line was especially strong. It was well
known that the deaths of infants and young children made up a high
proportion of all mortality, but this did not make bereavement any
less painful to an individual parent. Children's deaths were always felt
to be premature. Running through many expressions of grief at their
loss is the sense of promise cut off.

Writers said little of stillbirths or the deaths of newly born children.
The mother's survival was a blessing to be grateful for, though there
is an understandable disappointment that so much pain and effort
had come to nothing in Alice Thornton's descriptions of her unsuccessful deliveries. After babies had survived a few days their deaths
certainly caused sadness. Condoling with John and Sabine Johnson in
1546 when their first son died after some weeks, John's brother-in-
law wrote of his sorrow that they had lost their 'little, little fair summer flower', poignantly expressing the fragility of an infant's life and
the pathos of its death. When in 1633 Anne D'Ewes gave birth to
twins in the eighth month, the chances of their survival were small,
and their parents 'enjoyed them but a few hours' to their 'great grief
and sorrow'. Yet one of them survived three days, and Simonds

[28] R. A. Houlbrooke, *The English Family 1450–1700* (Harlow, 1984), 211–15. For
one eloquent tribute to a long widowhood, see J. Bowle, *A sermon preached at Flitton
in the countie of Bedford, at the funerall of Henrie earle of Kent* (1615), unpaginated
('34 yeeres hee spent, as a *mourner* of her Funerals').

[29] *Wentworth Papers, 1597–1628*, ed. J. P. Cooper (Camden 4th ser. 12; 1973),
281.

D'Ewes was 'well hoping of the continuance of the life of my little Adrian'. In 1648, when Ralph Josselin's second son was born, he recorded the baby's 10-day life anxiously. The strong attachment to the child which Josselin already felt is evident in his references to it as 'our babe', 'my sonne', 'my infant', 'my litle Ralph'. When it died, Josselin remarked that it was the youngest of his and his wife's children, and that their affections were 'not so wonted unto it'. Yet his pathetic account of the baby's funeral and anxious quest for an explanation of God's chastising him point to quite severe paternal grief. When a son of Alice Thornton's sickened and died after a fortnight in 1660, his father 'whom the child was exceding like in person' was greatly upset. The loss of her ninth child who died in 1667 when he was just under 3 weeks old was the more distressing because he was a 'lovely babe' and had seemed to thrive on her breast milk. Maternal breast-feeding strengthened attachment, as was recognized by a friend who tried to dissuade Anne Newdigate (1574–1618) from suckling her own children, on the ground that she would suffer more acutely if (as was only too likely) any of them died.[30]

The growth of attachment, together with children's acquisition of skills and distinctive individual personalities, sharpened grief. ' 'Twas as pretty and as knowing a child as they had ever seen that came to see it!', wrote Isaac Archer after his daughter Mary died in 1670, just short of her first birthday. Two parents who lost children when they were just under 2 years old, Simonds D'Ewes (1636) and the countess of Bridgewater (c.1660), particularly emphasized these children's strong affection towards themselves. The countess also mentioned her daughter's kindly, sunny temperament, nascent social skills, and docile behaviour at prayers and sermons. She had been, in short, amenable as well as loving. D'Ewes and his wife both found that their sorrow for the loss of their fourth son, on whom they had 'bestowed so much care and affection' far surpassed their grief for the deaths of his three elder brothers who had died soon after birth. Nehemiah Wallington, a London artisan, derived great pleasure from the lively and playful activity of his little children. After the death of one of his daughters in 1625, just before her third birthday, Wallington was distraught and, for some time, quite inconsolable. By the time they had

[30] *The Journal of Nicholas Assheton of Downham, in the County of Lancaster, Esq.*, ed. F. R. Raines (Chetham Soc., os 14; 1848), 81; Thornton, *Autobiography* 87–90, 95–7, 125, 166; Winchester, *Tudor Family Portrait*, 102; D'Ewes, *Autobiography & Correspondence*, ii. 88–90; Josselin, *Diary*, 111–15; V. Larminie, *Wealth, Kinship and Culture: The Seventeenth-Century Newdigates of Arbury and their World* (Woodbridge, 1995), 84.

reached the age of 4 or 5, many children had had considerable parental time and energy invested in them and their progress had given much pleasure. John Evelyn, himself a bookish man, delighted in his son Richard's insatiable intellectual curiosity. After losing a son who so perfectly matched his own hopes, Evelyn suffered 'unexpressable griefe & affliction'. There, he wrote, ended the joy of his life.[31]

Deaths in later childhood were far less frequent than in infancy and early childhood, and often harder to bear. When Ralph Josselin's eldest child Mary died in May 1650 at the age of 8, he paid effusive tribute to her exceptional wisdom, gravity, knowledge, affection, and obedience among other things. Nearly three weeks later, he still felt ready to be overwhelmed by memories of her. Josselin attributed to grief an illness which his wife suffered well over two months after Mary's death. Lady Fanshawe and her husband lost their 8-year-old daughter Ann, the eldest of five surviving children, and their 'most dearly beloved' daughter, in 1654. In her mother's view her beauty and wit had exceeded those of any other child of that age whom she had known. More important was the fact that she had been the 'dear companion' of the 'travels and sorrows' of this royalist couple. 'We both wished to have gone into the grave with her.'[32]

The deaths of adolescents and young adults, especially those who were their parents' confidants, or prospective successors to their social roles, were very deeply felt. Jeremy Taylor thought that there were parents who could bear the deaths of infants but were broken in spirit by the loss of older children who were 'hopeful and provided for', and ready to yield them comfort for all their fears and cares. When in 1632 Sir John Oglander lost his 23-year-old son George, his heir, while he was travelling in France, he lamented that most of his earthly comforts had died with this son. Oglander still had 'good and dutiful sons left'; his grief was due to the closeness of the relationship, not to any fear that his line might die out. The smallpox which claimed George Oglander and so many other young people of promise also killed Bulstrode Whitelocke's daughter Frances in 1654. It carried with her out of the world 'much of the joy & comfort of

---

[31] Houlbrooke, *English Family Life*, 128, 142, 144, 152; D'Ewes, *Autobiography & Correspondence*, ii. 145; Evelyn, *Diary*, iii. 206, 210; cf. L. A. Pollock, *Forgotten Children: Parent–Child Relations from 1500 to 1900* (Cambridge, 1983), 124–31; Laurence, 'Godly Grief', 66–70.

[32] Taylor, *Holy Living*, 124–5; Josselin, *Diary*, 203, 207, 212; Fanshawe, *Memoirs*, 84.

her father, to whom she was a companion in his widdowers estate, & refresht him by the musicke of her voice and discourse'. He was to lose two more daughters, already married, but neither death distressed him as much as Frances's. He gave the first child of his third marriage her name, which was also her mother's.[33]

The loss of more than one child in quick succession (which often happened during epidemics) was especially hard to bear. Lady Verney was prostrated by the deaths of two of her children in 1647. For two nights after hearing the news she seemed distracted, talking incoherently and sometimes failing to recognize close acquaintances. Even a week later she was barely able to go up and down her chamber. In 1680 Richard Kidder buried three children in less than three weeks. A future bishop, Kidder knew his Christian duty well, but the shock was nevertheless a devastating one. 'Perhaps another man might have born this much better than I could do; It was such an affliction to me as laid me very low.' When in 1614 three of the earl of Mulgrave's sons were drowned together while crossing the Humber, his friends 'were very solicitous how to breake it to him'. The fact that Mulgrave bore the news 'with a submissive composure' was considered an outstanding example of Christian fortitude. Mulgrave had recently told the earl of Bedford that he thought he should be able to match the patience of Job, and the gentleman who brought him the news reminded him of this conversation.[34]

The sharing of grief with a spouse equally affected by bereavement was a mitigating circumstance for parents who suffered the loss of children. One partner often comforted the other, channelling emotional energy into constructive action intimately connected with the recent loss. Henry VII and Queen Elizabeth tried to console each other when their son Arthur died in 1502. In 1636 the sight of Simonds D'Ewes's mournful face told his returning wife that their fourth son had died, and she started to weep uncontrollably. He contained his own impulse to do so, and used the best arguments he could to 'frame her to patience and moderation'. In the Wallington family it was Mrs Wallington who consoled her husband Nehemiah

---

[33] Oglander, *A Royalist's Notebook: The Commonplace Book of Sir John Oglander Kt of Nunwell*, ed. F. Bamford (1936), pp. xx–xxi, 81–3, 178–81; Whitelocke, *Diary*, 398, 407.

[34] F. P. and M. M. Verney, *Memoirs of the Verney Family during the Seventeenth Century* (2nd edn., 2 vols., London, 1907), i. 381–2; *The Life of Richard Kidder, D.D., Bishop of Bath and Wells, written by himself*, ed. A. E. Robinson (Somerset Record Soc. 37; 1924), 29; *Extracts from Woodcock Papers*, 78–9.

after the deaths of two of their children, reminding him of their duty willingly to surrender their children into God's hands.[35]

It was a commonplace that parents' love for their children was greater than that of children for their parents. Some individuals were, however, deeply affected by the deaths of parents even in adulthood. Women seem to have suffered the most severe reactions, or to have been less inhibited in describing them. When Simonds D'Ewes's grandfather died in 1611, his mother was 'almost drowned in tears for the loss of so dear and loving a father'. Two women who suffered deep grief for their mothers were Lady Anne Clifford (1617) and Alice Thornton (1659). In both women's cases their mothers had been close confidantes and sources of support in difficult circumstances. Lady Anne's experience was probably the more painful, because she was unable to attend her mother's deathbed.[36]

Men's accounts of the grief they suffered in the loss of parents, though often eloquent, were generally more contained and less intense than women's. In 1534 Francis Hall wrote to Lady Lisle, wife of the lord deputy of Calais, of the 'heaviness' which the loss of a father caused, especially severe in his case, because he could not have had one more kind, gentle, and loving. Roger Lowe, a Lancashire mercer's apprentice, could still weep on a visit to his parents' grave in 1665, some years after they had died. The poet Alexander Pope was deeply saddened by both his parents' deaths. 'It is indeed a Grief to mee which I cannot express', he wrote after his 90-year-old mother's death in 1733, 'and which I should hate my own Heart if it did not feel, & yet wish no Friend I have ever should feel.' It is clearer from men's testimony than from women's, largely because men wrote more, that individual reactions differed according to the strength of the bond with a deceased parent. Simonds D'Ewes believed that his mother

[35] *The Receyt of the Ladie Kateryne*, ed. G. Kipling (EETS 296; 1990), 80–1; D'Ewes, *Autobiography & Correspondence*, ii. 146; *The Life of Adam Martindale, written by himself*, ed. R. Parkinson (Chetham Soc., os 4; 1845), 109; Houlbrooke, *English Family Life*, 142–4. 'There is considerable evidence today', Dr Tony Walter has, however, pointed out to me, 'that loss of a child can cause great strain on a marriage, quite often contributing to marital breakdown; this is because each parent grieves in a different way, or at a different pace, and each cannot understand the other at precisely the time when they most need each other.' He cites G. Riches and P. Dawson, 'Shoring up the Walls of Heartache: Marital Relations following the Death of a Child', in D. Field, J. Hockey, and N. Small (edd.), *Death, Gender and Ethnicity* (1997).

[36] W. Gouge, *Of domesticall duties eight treatises* (1622), 429; D. Rogers, *Matrimoniall Honovr: Or The mutuall Crowne and comfort of godly, loyall, and chaste Marriage* (1642), 92–3; D'Ewes, *Autobiography & Correspondence*, i. 40; *The Diary of the Lady Anne Clifford*, ed. V. Sackville-West (1923), 30, 32, 80; Thornton, *Autobiography*, 106–16; cf. Fanshawe, *Memoirs*, 210.

was particularly solicitous of his own welfare, and suffered more severely as a result of her death than his father's. Samuel Pepys, by contrast, was a man who felt less affection for his crotchety, quarrelsome mother than for his father. Hearing of her death, and especially her last words, 'God bless my poor Sam!', precipitated a bout of weeping. Then he pulled himself together, reflecting how convenient the timing of her departure had been.[37]

Recorded responses to the deaths of siblings varied greatly, from indifference to acute distress. Some very close bonds were formed between brothers and sisters at an early stage. The Lancashire minister Adam Martindale recorded that his daughter Mary (1654–8) 'seemed utterly to despise life' after the death of her younger brother when she was nearly 3, and 'would frequently talke of heaven and being buried by him'. Such ties could remain strong well into adulthood. When the sailor Edward Barlow lost his sister Anna, her death was 'a sore grief and trouble' to him a long time afterwards. Lady Mary Wortley Montagu was deeply affected by the death of her brother in 1713. He had been a much-needed supporter when her marriage aroused her father's ire the previous year.[38]

Relationships between brothers varied greatly in quality and strength. The favoured position of the eldest son as heir sometimes set him emotionally apart from his younger brothers. An unusually strong fraternal affection united the younger sons of the fourth Lord North (d. 1681). It was Francis, the second son, ultimately lord keeper of the Great Seal, not his elder brother Charles, who acted as a 'common father' to them. Roger, the sixth and youngest son, felt that all his 'life, hope, and joys' died with Francis (1685). When the next brother, Dudley, died in 1691, Roger thought that no loss was like his. 'And sometimes I can think', he wrote, 'that sorrow hath somewhat manly in it, and reason as well as truth itself warp that way, but upon recollection, say, it is the women's prerogative, usurp it not.' In sharp contrast was the relative indifference of the Presbyterian minister Henry Newcome to his brother Stephen's death in 1678. Stephen, their

[37] *The Lisle Letters*, ed. M. St Clare Byrne (6 vols., Chicago, 1981), ii. 243; *The Diary of Roger Lowe of Ashton-in-Makerfield, Lancashire, 1663–1674*, ed. W. L. Sachse (1938), 77; M. Mack, *Alexander Pope: A Life* (New Haven, 1985), 336, 546; D'Ewes, *Autobiography & Correspondence*, i. 111–12, 117–18; ii. 9–11; Pepys, *Diary*, viii. 134.

[38] *Life of Martindale*, 109; *Barlow's Journal of his Life at Sea in King's Ships, East & West Indiamen & Other Merchantmen from 1659 to 1703*, ed. B. Lubbock (2 vols., 1934), i. 251; *The Complete Letters of Lady Mary Wortley Montagu*, ed. R. Halsband (3 vols., Oxford, 1965–7), i. 146, 183–5; R. Halsband, *The Life of Lady Mary Wortley Montagu* (Oxford, 1956), 35.

parents' second son, had helped to care for his younger siblings after they had been left orphans in 1642. Henry rebuked himself for not being 'greatly affected' by it. He also expressed his disappointment that Stephen had only left him £40 rather than the £100 he had once mentioned.[39]

The relationship between grandparents and grandchildren was often a strong one, partly because many elderly people across the social spectrum shared in looking after their children's children during their early years, Simonds D'Ewes (in 1611) and Lady Elizabeth Livingston (in 1665) suffered quite severely after the deaths of grandmothers with whom they had had especially close relationships. Henry Newcome transferred much of the love he had felt for his favourite son Daniel to Daniel's little son James after Daniel's death. When James in turn was taken from him, the loss probably hastened Newcome's own demise (1695). The accidental death of Mrs Elizabeth Freke's favourite grandson in 1705 made her want to join him in the grave.[40]

There were many circumstances which aggravated or alleviated sorrow. Deaths which happened without warning, diseases which struck down the young and healthy, and fatal but avoidable accidents, especially to children, caused much distress. Deaths preceded by marital infidelity, an unresolved quarrel, or estrangement were sometimes felt to be punishments by survivors. Inability or failure to say farewell at the deathbed was often regretted. Severe pain suffered by the dying, and impatience, anger, fear, and despair on their part left deeply uncomfortable memories for the bereaved.[41]

The belief that the deceased person had had a comfortable passage out of the world was especially important in alleviating grief. The courageous acceptance of death shown by many Christians, their affectionate last messages, and eloquent parental blessings helped survivors to come to terms with their loss. Alice Thornton felt that the words of persuasion which God put into her mother's mouth on her deathbed in 1659 did more than anything else to moderate her

[39] *The Autobiography of the Hon. Roger North*, ed. A. Jessopp (1887), 143–4, 189, 228; Newcome, *Autobiography*, ii. 226; cf. Evelyn, *Diary*, ii. 544.

[40] D'Ewes, *Autobiography & Correspondence*, i. 37–8; *The Meditations of Lady Elizabeth Delaval, written between 1662 and 1671*, ed. D. G. Greene (Surtees Soc. 190; 1978), 66–8; Newcome, *Autobiography*, ii. 253–4, 283, 286–7; Houlbrooke, *English Family Life*, 239–40.

[41] Macdonald, *Mystical Bedlam*, 103–4; Gittings, 'Venetia's Death and Kenelm's Mourning', 61; D'Ewes, *Autobiography & Correspondence*, ii. 275–87; Delaval, *Meditations*, 202–3; Barnes, *Memoirs*, 77; *Extracts from Woodcock Papers*, 72; Houlbrooke, *English Family Life*, 91; Bod. Lib. MS Eng. misc. f. 381, fos. 60–2.

sorrow in the loss of her dearly loved parent. In cases where the dying had been unable to play their part with such outstanding success, it was some consolation to the survivors to know that they at least had done what they could to help. In 1673 Lady Warwick 'found much inward comfort' in the reflection that she had done everything she could for her husband's body and soul. The knowledge that the deceased had died among friends, rather than among strangers, far from home, offered a measure of consolation. Long illness before-hand gave a warning and allowed survivors some scope for adjust-ment to loss.[42]

Those who put pen to paper in early modern times to express their grief in the face of bereavement hardly ever did so without invoking religious consolations, though with varying degrees of conviction. Religion not only offered explanations for individuals' losses by death, but also held out the possibility of positive action on the part of the bereaved. Life and death were in God's hand: it was impious to resent his decisions. 'It was a great affliction to me,' Sir John Reresby wrote of the death of his son George in 1689; 'but God gives, and God takes, and blessed be the name of the Lord.' The commonplace idea that God lends us those who become dear to us seemed especially applicable to children. Grace Wallington expressed it vividly to her husband Nehemiah when they lost their second son. Human parents were like nurses, entrusted with children only until their true parents sent for them. A parent who repined at God's summons should think how annoyed he would be if a wet-nurse refused to return his child. On another occasion Mrs Wallington reminded her husband of Abra-ham's readiness to sacrifice Isaac, the scriptural example most per-tinent to the predicament of bereaved parents. Ralph Josselin wrote in 1650 of freely resigning up his beloved daughter Mary, his and his wife's 'first fruites', and rejoiced that he had such a present for God.[43]

God had taken the dead from this unhappy world to a better; this was the standard response to loss. Confidence was often expressed about the destination of very young children, unblemished by sin. Thomas Dekker urged parents who lost their 'little darlings' in the plague to reflect that all the beauty of the world was ugliness to that sweetness which they now possessed. It was a consolation for some

[42] Thornton, *Autobiography*, 110–13; Houlbrooke, *English Family Life*, 85; Bar-low, *Journal*, i. 251; W. Stout, *The Autobiography of William Stout of Lancaster, 1665–1752*, ed. J. D. Marshall (Chetham Soc., 3rd ser. 14; 1967), 192.

[43] *Memoirs of Sir John Reresby: The Complete Text and a Selection from his Let-ters*, ed. A. Browning (Glasgow, 1936), 570; Houlbrooke, *English Family Life*, 143–4; Josselin, *Diary*, 203.

parents when they lost children who had shown precocious piety to interpret their early deaths as signs of God's special love.[44] Many grief-stricken spouses, too, sought to console themselves with the reflection that their partners were happy in heaven. Such consolations were often reinforced by the hopes or convictions which the dying themselves had expressed on their deathbeds. In other cases bereft partners struggled in the face of a distressing deathbed experience to convince themselves that the outcome had been a happy one.

The notion that the dead were happy in heaven may not always have been an easy one to assimilate at a deep emotional level, however much survivors wanted to believe it. When Alice Thornton was suddenly overwhelmed by tears some months after her husband's death in 1668, it was her 6-year-old son who, snuggling up to her, put the crucial questions. Didn't she believe that his father had gone to heaven? Would she have him come out of heaven, and endure all the sickness and sorrows he had known on earth, to comfort her? Mrs Thornton not surprisingly concluded that it was God who had put the words into his mouth as a gentle reproof for her failure in Christian duty. Some children may have found it easier than adults to believe unreservedly and literally in what they were taught concerning the afterlife.[45]

Many of the dying and the bereaved drew consolation from the prospect of reunion. Elizabeth Whitelocke used it as a strong argument against the fear of death during her last walk with her son in 1631. In 1648 Ralph Josselin expressed his certainty that he would see the soul and body of his newly dead 10-day-old son arise to enjoy God. Mrs Rowe, who wrote a famous series of imaginary letters from the dead to the living, left on her own death in 1737 letters in which she looked forward to meeting her correspondents in heaven. Others expressed their expectations more cautiously or obliquely. Sir Ralph Verney hoped that he and his newly deceased wife would 'at least be knowne to one another in Heaven'. In one of his letters, the recently widowed Sir Kenelm Digby even suggested that it was foolish to seek a sanctuary against the afflictions of this life in 'the other worlde, where we know not in what estate we shall be'.[46]

---

[44] Dekker, *Plague Pamphlets*, 214; Evelyn, *Diary*, iii. 209; *Oxford Dictionary of Proverbs*, 314, s.v. 'Gods love die young, Whom the'.

[45] Thornton, *Autobiography*, 262–3.

[46] Whitelocke, *Diary*, 62; E. Rowe, *Friendship in Death: in Twenty Letters from the Dead to the Living* (1814 edn.), pp. xviii–xxi; Josselin, *Diary*, 114; Verney and Verney, *Verney Family*, i. 475; Gabrieli, *Sir Kenelm Digby*, 251 (but contrast 252); Kay, *Diary*, 119, 145–6; Evelyn, *Diary*, iv. 151.

Teaching as it did that the prayers of the living could help the dead, the Roman Catholic Church offered the possibility of therapeutic positive action for survivors. So in 1534 Francis Hall asked Lady Lisle to remember in her prayers the soul of his father, whom he had found buried on his recent return home. The Jesuit John Gerard, seeking to heal the sorrow of his widowed hostess, Lady Vaux, in the 1590s, told her that a single prayer would do her husband more good than many tears. Sir Kenelm Digby asked various correspondents to pray for his wife in 1633. (A temporary conformist to the Church of England, he also expressed his confidence that she was a saint in heaven, a pious consolation conventional among Protestant widowers.)[47]

The bereaved often sought to understand why it was that God had laid his rod upon them. Ralph Josselin seems to have been hit hard by his first experience of death among his children. He examined his own behaviour anxiously and thoroughly, singling out certain special faults which God might have wished to correct in him. When his daughter Mary died in 1650, Josselin accepted correction more readily, confident that God would indicate which of his sins needed to be dealt with. By then, God seemed to Josselin to be a kind father in his punishments. He had carefully timed Mary's removal in such a way as to allow her parents to prepare for loss beforehand. He intimated to Josselin that he took Mary away out of love to both daughter and father, intending to do Josselin good. The Puritan gentleman Simonds D'Ewes attributed his losses above all to God's resolve to humble. Sir Ralph Verney, a staunch Protestant, but hardly a Puritan, made his uncle a sort of lay confessor to assist him in the examination of his conscience after his wife's death in 1650, drawing up a careful review of his sins in writing. A reason for their correction which occurred to some of the bereaved was precisely that they had made the loved one an idol, a focus of excessive affection. God's purpose in taking away her children, Lady Anne Halkett concluded in 1661, was to teach her not to love the world or anything in it.[48]

However bitter the deaths of loved ones seemed, Christians believed that they would benefit the bereaved if they were accepted in the right spirit. They were intended above all to wean the hearts of survivors from the world and draw them closer to God. This lesson was

[47] *Lisle Letters*, ii. 243; J. Gerard, *The Autobiography of an Elizabethan*, trans. P. Caraman (1951), 147; Gabrieli, *Sir Kenelm Digby*, 258, 260–1.
[48] Josselin, *Diary*, 114–15, 203–4; Verney and Verney, *Verney Family*, 453–5; *The Autobiography of Anne Lady Halkett*, ed. J. G. Nichols (Camden NS 13; 1875), 109–10; Laurence, 'Godly Grief', 69.

reiterated countless times in the personal writings of early modern times by individuals of all shades of religious opinion. However, the process of concentrating one's affections on God could be difficult and protracted. Only if God's grace acted on the soul distressed by bereavement was a loss transformed into a blessing. This was what Oliver Heywood felt when he lost his first wife in 1661: the affliction was more deep and cutting than any he had ever had, and the supporting, quickening, and comforting grace beyond anything he had ever experienced.[49] Chastened, cast down, and then lifted up by God's hand, some felt ultimately strengthened by the losses they had endured.

The need to explore the implications of bereavement occasionally found expression in lengthy correspondence. Two outstanding seventeenth-century examples of writers of such letters are Sir Kenelm Digby and Lady Rachel Russell. Venetia Digby's sudden death in 1633 left her husband distraught. He praised her beauty, virtue, and piety. Repeatedly he rehearsed the circumstances of her death. His own unworthiness of such a woman made him feel he deserved to suffer: he seemed to embrace the torments of sorrow, exploring the nature of his grief with almost morbid thoroughness. Stoic self-control he rejected at first with contempt. 'For what is there in this life', he asked, 'worth forcing ones selfe to master any passion for?' Instead he gave himself up to melancholy without a struggle, trusting to God and time to remove it. 'There is a kinde of sweetenesse in sorrow itselfe, when ones teares are wiped away by a frendes hande,' he told Sir John Coke. On the face of it, Lady Rachel Russell made a greater effort to fulfil her Christian duty. Her declared resolve was the very opposite of Digby's: to overcome her grief by reason and religion, 'rather than by time, or necessity, the ordinary abater of all violent passions'. However, the pull of her husband's memory and a skein of complex, unresolved feelings about the manner of his death hampered her efforts.[50]

The Reformation ended the celebration of annual obits for the dead, but during the seventeenth century anniversaries of deaths were observed by several people. William Laud recorded a special prayer for the day of his father's death, in which he looked forward to

---

[49] Heywood, *Autobiography, Diaries*, i. 177.

[50] Gittings, 'Venetia's Death and Kenelm's Mourning', esp. 60–2; Gabrieli, *Sir Kenelm Digby*, 239, 244–9, 254, 275; Russell, *Letters*, 258–60. The seemingly exceptional intensity of mourning in these two instances was due to grief complicated by the nature of death: Russell's execution, and the mysteriously sudden demise of Venetia, attributed by some to 'viper-wine' administered by Digby himself. Digby also reproached himself for infidelity: Gittings, 'Venetia's Death', 61.

reunion with his parents. After his wife's death in 1664 Samuel Wood-forde resolved to keep a fast on their wedding anniversary. Lady Rachel Russell gave up to reflection the three days of her husband's arrest, trial, and execution. William Sancroft (archbishop of Canterbury, 1678–90) wrote out 'An Office for One, that hath lost his/her dearest friend', for use on the anniversary or weekday of the death. Thomas Wilson (bishop of Sodor and Man, 1698–1755) kept a long list of anniversaries of friends and relatives. The most distinctive of all private customs of remembrance was instituted by Sir Kenelm Digby. Every Wednesday he devoted to deep meditation on his wife's death, assisted by a picture of her in her deathbed by Sir Antony Van Dyck.[51]

'My greatest relief', wrote Edward Young after his father's death in 1705, 'is making my complaint to my friends and pleasing myself with the thought that they will condole with me if they really are so.' Some friends supported the bereaved by visiting them or by giving them hospitality. More common was the despatch of a letter, customarily offering consolation (reasons for not grieving) as well as condolence (sharing in the sorrow of the bereaved person). Very broadly speaking, our period saw a growing emphasis on condolence. The most influential of sixteenth-century guides for letter-writers was Erasmus's *De Conscribendis Epistolis*. Erasmus was an admirer of the Stoics; his fundamental premiss was the irrationality of grief. In the case of people too weak to rise above their grief, the consoler should begin by appearing to condole with them. Then, however, he should explain why death is not the evil it seems to be, give examples of courage in bearing misfortune, and exhort the bereaved to show similar firmness. A well-known English epistolary manual, Angel Day's *The English Secretorie* (1586) followed Erasmus fairly closely.[52]

In the early seventeenth century there was a marked shift in some manuals towards sympathetic condolence. In *A Speedie Post With*

---

[51] Laud, *Works*, iii. 80 (marginal note records date of his mother's death as well as his father's); Bod. Lib. MS Eng. misc. f. 381, fo. 160; MS Sancroft 133, fos. 8ᵛ–10ᵛ: Russell, *Letters*, 277, 295, 339, 368; T. Wilson, *Works*, with life by J. Keble (LACT, 7 vols., 1847–63), v. 277–8; Evelyn, *Diary*, iv. 219, 256–7, 292 (Mrs Godolphin); T. Birch, *The Life of the Right Honourable Robert Boyle* (1744), 20 (earl of Cork dedicated anniversary of his wife's death to solemn mourning for it); Gabrieli, *Sir Kenelm Digby*, 246; for pictures of Venetia Digby and other individuals on their deathbeds, see Sumner (ed.), *Death, Passion and Politics*, pl. vi and pp. 55–6, 117–20; for John Dwight's stoneware representation of his daughter Lydia on her deathbed, c.1674, see N. Llewellyn, *The Art of Death: Visual Culture in the English Death Ritual c.1500–c.1800* (1991), 44.

[52] H. Forster, *Edward Young: The Poet of the Night Thoughts 1683–1765* (Harleston, 1986), 22; Pepys, *Diary*, iii. 15; Evelyn, *Diary*, iii. 57, 155, 219, 377; iv. 545; Whitelocke, *Diary*, 244; Pigman, *Grief and Elegy*, 12–16, 22, 134.

certaine New Letters (1625), two letters are explicitly devoted to con-dolence and describe the writer's distress in vivid language. Yet didactic consolations still bulk large in eighteenth-century works such as a volume of model letters by Samuel Richardson. Grief is right and natural, but must not be excessive. Nor must it blind us to God's other mercies. Richardson's consoler assures his correspondents that the departed are certainly or probably enjoying eternal happiness. Earthly evils have been averted: a son, for example, has been saved from being a disappointment to his parents. The bereaved are reminded of their duties to other family members.[53]

In practice, many expressions of condolence or offers of consola-tion were of a fairly conventional kind, but individual writers differed in the extent to which they adapted convention to the characters and needs of the bereaved, and their ability to enliven their letters with truly personal elements or infuse them with a sense of genuine sym-pathy. During the fifteenth and sixteenth centuries messages of con-dolence were often very short. George Cely in 1482 and William Paston in 1504 were both urged to take their fathers' deaths patiently, accepting something that was described either as God's will or the common lot of mankind. In 1545, writing to Christopher Breten, the newly widowed husband of his wife's sister, the London merchant John Johnson assured his kinsman that he understood his grief. God's designs were inscrutable; this bereavement should not be interpreted as a punishment. Johnson concluded with hopes that their old friend-ship would continue and that Breten would join them during the fol-lowing holidays. In 1596 Sir Francis Hastings assured his brother George, after the double loss of their elder brother and George's eldest son, that he shared his sorrow. He urged George to moderate this grief (although he himself found it hard to do so) so as to gather strength to deal with the weighty business which confronted him.[54]

Among Sir Thomas Wentworth's correspondence of the early 1620s are various letters written to friends and kinsfolk who had recently lost children. In one, he expressed his confidence that the death had been 'by this tyme Christianly dygested', which was the sort of flattering assumption of which Erasmus would have approved.

[53] Pigman, *Grief and Elegy*, 20–2, 134; S. Richardson, *One Hundred and Seventy-Three Letters written for Particular Friends, on the most Important Occasions* (7th edn., 1764), 265–72.

[54] *The Cely Letters, 1472–1488*, ed. A. Hanham (EETS 273; 1975), 128; *Paston Let-ters and Papers of the Fifteenth Century*, ed. N. Davis (2 vols., Oxford, 1971, 1976), ii. 501; Winchester, *Tudor Family Portrait*, 82; *The Letters of Sir Francis Hastings, 1574–1609*, ed. C. Cross (Somerset Record Soc. 69; 1969), 57.

In two others, Wentworth essayed a formulaic balance of condolence and consolation. In each case condolence was conveyed with a light touch. He knew that the parent's grief was greater than his own. The chief consolations he offered in both cases were the heavenly destination of the dead child and the existence of other children or the likelihood of begetting them. The element of condolence was strongest in a fourth letter, written to Lord Darcy on the death of his son. The greatest comfort he could give him for the moment, Wentworth wrote, was that he participated deeply in his just grief and sorrow, and judged his own loss, after Darcy's, the heaviest.[55]

More varied in tone and content are eight letters written to the widow of the staunchly Puritan Sir Francis Barrington after his death in 1628. All the writers recognized that she had cause for sorrow, or shared her grief. The most frequently repeated consolation was an assurance of Sir Francis's present happiness. Common too were statements that he had lived in honour and that his good name or memory survived him. Lady Barrington would follow him. Further consolations were that her husband had died in old age, in peace, after a long and fruitful marriage, and the hope that the couple's children would make up for the loss suffered by the Church in his death. Some letters reminded Lady Barrington explicitly that she must not mourn excessively. The letter from Lady Eden, friend and kinswoman, is perhaps the best judged. Simple, short, and to the point, it radiates the sympathy of one experienced woman for another. It invites Lady Barrington to stay a week, 'sumwhat' to forget the loss she has suffered. Her husband is happy, it says, and they may soon follow him.[56]

A condolence letter whose erratic spelling reinforces the impression of its sincerity and spontaneity was written by Bridget Gage to her son-in-law John Belson on the death of his son Jack in 1662. She wished her own sorrow could comfort him and his wife. She would have written sooner if she could have mastered her grief: 'I shall say nothing to you of him sins I am suer both your oune knowleg & uertw is to great to repine at the will of god.' She prayed that God would bless the Belsons' remaining children and hoped that they would live to serve him and give their parents comfort.[57]

Christian duty was still the main theme of many eighteenth-century letters. On hearing in 1729 of the death of his infant daughter Nelly,

[55] *Wentworth Papers*, 131, 134–5, 150–1, 206–7.
[56] *Barrington Family Letters, 1628–1632*, ed. A. Searle (Camden 4th ser. 28; 1983), 29–30, 32–5, 37–8.
[57] BRO D/E Bt F 68.

John Byrom, poet and stenographer, wrote his wife a letter which is affectionate but very firm. He wanted them both to take this opportunity of sacrificing their wishes to God's will by patient and cheerful resignation. He was very well satisfied with her care of Nelly. He realized that she could not help but suffer grief 'upon so tender an occasion', but trusted that she would be so moderate in it as not to prejudice her own health, 'such excess being very useless and very irrational'. After they had done the best they could for their children, they had to place their trust in God.[58]

Some other eighteenth-century correspondents, however, laid their main emphasis on sympathy, ready recognition of the distress of the bereaved, and offers of support. Alexander Pope wrote to the son of his old friend John Arbuthnot two days after the latter's death in 1735 with warmth and tact. He could find no words to express his share in young Arbuthnot's grief and loss. Pope had no doubt that his dead friend was happy, but he was concerned about the family he left behind him. He expressed his utmost readiness to help them in any way he could. Other writers dropped even the residual gesture towards religious consolation contained in Pope's reference to Dr Arbuthnot's happiness. When Lady Lansdowne wrote to her nephew on the death of his father in 1724, she told him that she knew what it was like to lose a 'tender father' having done so herself some years before, assured him of his uncle's readiness to give him paternal support, and gently reminded him of his duty to his sister and widowed mother.[59]

The most important means of showing both formal respect for the dead and a personal sense of loss was mourning-dress. It also signalled humility and submission to God's will. Special mourning garments began to be worn in the later Middle Ages. Brown was widely worn as well as black, and in royal courts a range of other colours. White long remained customary for some participants in the funerals of children and virgins. The adoption and elaboration of vestimentary rules concerning mourning began in the royal household, which tended to

---

[58] *The Private Journal and Literary Remains of John Byrom*, ed. R. Parkinson (Chetham Soc., os 32, 34, 40, 44; 1854–7), ii. 387–8; Byrom wrote to another correspondent that 'a jealousy lest a child should be lost through his neglect, is what creates the greatest concern in a parent, I believe'.

[59] G. A. Aitken, *The Life and Works of John Arbuthnot* (Oxford, 1892), 157; Delany, *Autobiography and Correspondence*, i. 88. See ibid. 264 for example of practical help offered by Mrs Delany to a recently widowed Mrs Griffiths in 1730: 'I have wrote to know how the poor woman designs to dispose of her daughters, that if it lies in my power any way to serve them I may.'

follow the example set by the most fashionable European courts. In keeping with the general goals of sumptuary legislation, the crown sought to regulate the details of mourning-dress in accordance with rank. Its adoption by people of lower status was largely due to social emulation. It was one of a number of ways of demonstrating the standing of one's family, and became increasingly important for aspirants to gentility.[60]

By the eighteenth century there were fairly clear and well-established periods of mourning for some of the closest relatives: a year for husband or wife, six months for parents or parents-in-law, and three months for a sister or brother. The widow's year of mourning went back to the Roman civil law, which had also forbidden her remarriage during that time. Medieval popes had revoked the prohibition upon remarriage, but unless it took place, the year's mourning remained customary. The periods of mourning for relatives beyond the first degree were less firmly fixed. During the eighteenth century, for example, that for an uncle or aunt varied between three months and three weeks. Within the longer periods of mourning there were distinct phases: full or first mourning, second and half-mourning. In half-mourning a wider range of colours, such as mauves and greys, was permitted.[61]

Mourning-dress allowed the widow in particular to claim freedom from social obligations and time to devote to the memory of the dead. Yet the action of donning mourning could also send out a signal of matrimonial availability. An ostentatious display could provoke cynical comment. Dorothy, widow of Sir Henry Unton, was described five months after her husband's death in 1596 as having 'very well beautified her sorrow with all the ornaments of an honourable widow', tuned her voice with a 'mournful accent', and made her chamber 'look like the house of sorrow'. In the early eighteenth century Abel Boyer thought this 'dismal and troublesome vanity'

---

[60] L. Taylor, *Mourning Dress: A Costume and Social History* (1983), 65–91; *Gentleman's Magazine*, 1 (1731), 161; P. Cunnington and C. Lucas, *Costume for Births, Marriages and Deaths* (1972), 145–7, 152–5, 270, 277. White palls and scarves were used at the funerals of bachelors in the 17th and 18th cents.

[61] R. Trumbach, *The Rise of the Egalitarian Family: Aristocratic Kinship and Domestic Relations in Eighteenth-Century England* (1978), 34–41 (for the subtlest and most perceptive short discussion of 18th-cent. mourning); Taylor, *Mourning Dress*, 56–7, 60, 102–3; H. A. Kelly, *Love and Marriage in the Age of Chaucer* (Ithaca, NY, 1975), 38 n. 19; Cunnington and Lucas, *Costume*, 244–7; Taylor, *Holy Living*, 69, wrote of the widow that 'anciently it was infamous for her to marry till by common account the body was dissolved into its first principle of earth'.

most prevalent with ambitious women who strove to 'signalize their reputation by the pageantry of an inconsolable sorrow'.[62]

The wearing of mourning depended to some extent on circumstance and personal choice. In the case of close and much-loved relatives, particularly spouses, the mourning period could be prolonged far beyond what was customarily prescribed, or even be lifelong. After his wife's death, Sir Kenelm Digby wore in his retirement a 'long mourning cloake, a high crowned hatt, his beard unshorne' and 'look't like a Hermite'. Social prescriptions had greatest force when deciding whether or how long to mourn kinsfolk of a seniority equal to, or greater than, one's own. Mourning for children was very much a matter of individual discretion. The deep grief Sir John Oglander felt on the death of his son George in France in July 1632 is reflected in his expenditure of £38 on mourning clothes. (In 1622–3 he had given his wife £20 'to find her apparel and other necessaries for the whole year'.) In other cases people might choose not to adopt mourning-dress at all, or barely comply with custom. If one lived in a part of the country where one's recently deceased relative was not known, it might be possible to avoid following the rules very closely without hurting anybody's feelings or offending their sense of propriety. A coolness between kinsfolk might be reflected in the neglect or perfunctory observance of mourning. Conventions were more relaxed in the country than in London. When Roger Jacson of Shallcross in Derbyshire died in 1743, his sister, a rector's wife, planned no elaborate mourning for her daughters. 'My Dear Girls must get something of Mourning upon this Melancholy occasion; we think neat Grey Stuff Gowns for Nancy & Kitty will do very well; Dolly we think should have somthing better, as a Grey Poplin, or some such thing; Plain caps, just what you will want and no more.'[63]

Some mourning accoutrements were customarily dispensed in very large quantities for those who attended early modern funerals. Complete mourning for longer term wear was provided (either by the deceased's special direction, or by the executors) for a much smaller

[62] R. Strong, *The Cult of Elizabeth: Elizabethan Portraiture and Pageantry* (1977), 106–7; A. Boyer, *The English Theophrastus* (1702), 65, quoted by Trumbach, *Rise of Egalitarian Family*, 40; Cunnington and Lucas, *Costume*, 264. For the opinion that 'a Widow does very well in Mourning for one Twelve-Month after she is so, both because 'tis *decent*, and because she generally looks *Prettier* in't, and 'twill the sooner get her another *Husband*', see *The Ladies' Dictionary* (1694), 97.

[63] *Aubrey's Brief Lives*, ed. O. L. Dick (Harmondsworth, 1972), 188; Oglander, *Royalist's Notebook*, 231, 237; W. H. Shawcross, 'The Owners of Shallcross', *Journal of the Derbyshire Archaeological and Natural History Society*, 28 (1906), 124; Delany, *Autobiography and Correspondence*, i. 96, 101.

group of close relatives. In 1680 Elizabeth Pierrepoint, a wealthy and childless spinster of Sevenoaks, left the considerable sum of £120 to buy mourning for about twelve relatives, but she was unique among the Sevenoaks testators of Charles II's reign in making such provision. In 1703 the childless widower Samuel Pepys bestowed complete mourning on a number of friends. Administration accounts concerning the estates of people of middling rank suggest that complete mourning even for close relatives was provided in no more than a minority of cases. The widow of Christopher Keene, a Londoner whose personal estate was valued at just over £2,000 in 1733, bought mourning only for herself and her children. She spent over £37, which included the cost of black shammy shoes and clogs, black stockings, and mourning nightgowns. One London widow, Judith Braithwaite, who presented her administration account in 1678, was loth to incur the expense of mourning. She claimed £12. 13*s*. 8*d*. 'paid by this accomptant for mourneing cloath hoodes scarfes stockings Peakes and the makeing the mourneing vpp for this accomptant and her two daughters, which this accomptant was not willing to have, but the relations of the deceased did earnestly importune her to have the same'.[64]

Failure to give full mourning or a mourning token appropriate to the closeness of a friend's or kinsman's relationship with the deceased could be perceived as a grievous slight. When Henry Ireton died in 1651, his father-in-law Oliver Cromwell failed to send mourning or even any particular invitation to the funeral to Colonel John Hutchinson, one of Ireton's closest kinsmen. To underline his sense of affront, Hutchinson appeared at the funeral in a richly laced scarlet cloak. Since Cromwell had sent mourning to many people who had no connection with Ireton, 'he was resolv'd he would not flatter so much to buy for himselfe, although he was a true mourner in his heart for his cousin, whom he had ever lov'd, and therefore would goe and take his place among his mourners'. If no mourning had been issued, or the mourner stood outside the circle of those with the strongest claims of kinship, he might 'buy for himselfe', or fetch out mourning which had already been used, in order to show his respect. By the middle of the eighteenth century, a substantial legacy might be understood to carry with it the obligation to don mourning for the testator.[65]

---

[64] *Sevenoaks Wills and Inventories in the Reign of Charles II*, ed. H. C. F. Lansberry (Kent Archaeological Soc., Kent Records, 25; 1988), 170; Evelyn, *Diary*, v. 538; GL MS 9186/1, 4.

[65] Hutchinson, *Memoirs of Life of Col. Hutchinson*, 203–4; Emmison (ed.), *Elizabethan Life*, iv. 68–9 (Thomas Colshill's 1595 revocation of bequest of rings to John

More personal to the wearer than mourning clothes, at least in the sixteenth century, were memorial rings. At that time, any messages engraved on such rings were most likely to be salutary reminders of death. Alternatively they might bear a death's head. However, even then some of them were inscribed with such messages as 'Remember me' or 'Sis memor amici'. In the longer term, personal remembrance grew more important. In Elizabethan Essex, kinsfolk were by far the largest category of recipients, including those who, while held in affectionate regard, were insufficiently close to benefit from major bequests or inheritance: in-laws, cousins, godchildren, and nephews. Friends, colleagues, and clergymen were also given them. They were a widely favoured means of showing gratitude to overseers of wills. By the eighteenth century rings were being distributed in larger numbers at the funerals of the wealthy, but those given to intimate friends or closer relatives were distinguished by superior workmanship or a more precious metal. Rings were also employed as tokens of love or affection in courtship and marriage. Other tokens sometimes mentioned in the contexts of both marriage and personal remembrance were gloves and old coins of high value. (By about 1700 gloves were being dispensed in huge quantities at grand funerals, but testators of small means sometimes left them as personal gifts.) More intimate were rings and lockets containing strands of the deceased's hair, or miniature portraits. All bear witness to the desire of those facing death or left bereft by it to sustain the life of memory.[66]

CONCLUSION

Grief was recognized throughout this period as a natural but potentially morbid, even fatal, reaction to the deaths of friends and loved ones. Opinions concerning it ranged from stern disapproval to qualified acceptance. Christian teaching called for submission to God's will and in its Catholic form encouraged the sublimation of grief in positive action on behalf of the souls of the dead. Stoic philosophy called for control of human passions. Christian and Stoic

Smith and his wife because he had heard that Smith had not remembered Colshill or his wife 'so much as with a mourning gown by his will'); Assheton, *Journal*, 77; C. Gittings, *Death, Burial and the Individual in Early Modern England* (1984), 210.

[66] Emmison (ed.), *Elizabethan Life*, iv. 15, 38, 68, 72, 88, 99, 114, 117, 124, 175, 177, 212, 222, 255, 266; Taylor, *Mourning Dress*, 224–30, 232; Cunnington and Lucas, *Costume*, 253–4; *The Diary of a West Country Physician, A.D. 1684–1726*, ed. E. Hobhouse (1934), 148 (payment of £2. 10s in 1691 for a pair of buttons with Claver Morris's wife's hair set in gold, and for a locket with her hair and his daughter's); Llewellyn, *Art of Death*, 86, 95–6.

prescriptions shaped individual comportment in face of bereavement to an extent which has created for some historians the mirage of a 'low affect' society in which personal feelings of loss were relatively weak.[67] Of course the intensity of grief varied enormously from one person to another, and was influenced by a host of variables, but there is no doubt that it was often extremely painful.

By the seventeenth century grief was being more fully and variously expressed and discussed than ever before.[68] There were probably three main reasons for this state of affairs. First, and most obviously, there was a luxuriant development of the media of expression. Secondly, the intense interest in melancholy and the melancholic personality which England had inherited from the Italian Renaissance came to exercise a powerful influence over both art and literature from the later sixteenth century onwards. Finally, several Protestant preachers made clear that the natural grief formerly channelled into intercessory prayer was not useless. By softening the heart and making the spirit malleable it could render the bereaved Christian more responsive to the divine purposes. In the long run, God's providence would come to seem more impersonal.[69] This helps to explain why consolations which emphasized his intentions for individual creatures became markedly less common in eighteenth-century condolence letters. Yet the prospect of heavenly reunion remained, despite the caveats entered by the more cautious theologians, a powerful and widely expressed source of solace.

Grief was manifested by the wearing of appropriate dress, but this was only one of the functions of such garb. It was also a means of showing solidarity with bereaved kinsfolk and respect for senior relatives and public figures for whom one might feel little inward sorrow. Public losses called for public acknowledgement. Mourning-dress, and correct observance of its increasingly complicated rules, also served to underline the status of its wearers as well as their social expertise. However, the exceptional prolongation or elaboration of mourning as a means of emphasizing personal grief was regarded as bad form: eccentric, extravagant, and ostentatious.[70]

[67] L. Stone, *The Family, Sex and Marriage in England 1500-1800* (1977), 54-60, 93-119, 206-8, 215.

[68] 'No other time has so valued the expression of feeling': B. A. Doebler, *'Rooted Sorrow': Dying in Early Modern England* (Rutherford, 1994), 241. (*'Rooted Sorrow'* focuses primarily on death as a literary theme, esp. in the work of Shakespeare, Spenser, and Donne.)

[69] Thomas, *Religion*, 126-8, 765, 773-4, 783-5.

[70] Trumbach, *Rise of Egalitarian Family*, 40.

The gap left by the abolition of Catholic intercessory rites and the inadequacy of mourning-dress as a means of expressing a personal sense of loss help to explain the growth of private rites of commemoration and the increasing popularity of personal mementoes of the dead such as rings and lockets. The former never achieved standard or widely accepted forms. The latter (intimate, tangible, and portable) went on to achieve their widest currency after the end of this period.

9

Funerals

The rites which followed death served many different purposes, including the performance of religious and social duties towards the deceased; the symbolic transfer of rights, obligations, and social position; the expression of solidarity in mourning; and the discharge of duties of hospitality and almsgiving. How far any one funeral fulfilled these functions largely depended upon the wealth and status of the deceased. Discussion of funeral rites and customs must therefore take account of social differences and distinctions. Some of the main purposes of funerals changed in the course of time. The Reformation transformed their religious basis. The Civil Wars and Interregnum undermined the neo-feudal foundations of the aristocratic public funeral. Drastic simplification of burial rites by the victorious Puritans, temporary so far as the nation at large was concerned, served as a pattern for subsequent Nonconformist practice.

BEFORE THE REFORMATION

The medieval Church provided four main rites for the newly deceased: the commendation of souls, and the office of, mass for, and burial of, the dead. All these services include reiterated pleas for God's mercy upon the soul of the recently departed person in particular and all the Christian dead in general. The antiphonal prayer beginning with the word 'Requiem' (Grant them eternal rest, O Lord; and let perpetual light shine on them) runs through these rites like a golden thread. The commendation of the departed soul was supposed to begin in the death-chamber while the corpse still lay there. A chain of psalms which speak of God's help to those who turn to him in distress, including the *De Profundis*, were to be recited. The priest sprinkled the body with holy water before its removal from the house. The corpse might be accompanied to the church by a procession singing psalms and antiphons. There the priest once more sprinkled it and scattered incense over it, asking bystanders to join him in prayer.[1]

Wealthier people's obsequies were normally spread over two days. They began with the vigils or office of the dead. This service was also known as 'Placebo and Dirige' after key words in verses of its two main elements, the vespers and mattins of the dead, or simply as 'dirge'. The psalms used in this service plead for help and mercy, speak of the soul longing for God like a thirsty hart (Psalm 42) or express the comfort imparted by a sense of his protection (Psalm 23: 'The Lord is my shepherd'). Passages from the Book of Job stand in stark contrast, expressing perplexity and near despair. Only in the penultimate passage (19: 20–7) is faith in the living redeemer triumphantly asserted and bodily resurrection confidently anticipated. But the last part of the office of the dead, lauds, abounds with praise and the love of God.[2]

The mass of requiem, the climax of the funeral services, was celebrated on the following day. In the case of wealthy people it was often preceded by two other services: a mass of Our Lady and a mass of the Trinity. Immediately before the mass of the dead the priest went to the spot chosen for the burial, made the sign of the cross over it, sprinkled it with holy water, and dug the shape of a cross of the length and breadth of the person to be buried. The text of the mass begins with the introit from which it took its name, the already mentioned plea for peace (requiem). The epistle is St Paul's prophecy concerning the resurrection in 1 Thessalonians 4: 13–18, the gospel the assurance given by Jesus to Martha in John 11: 21–7 that her brother Lazarus would rise from the dead.[3]

The burial service began once mass was over. The corpse was carried to the grave, which was opened and blessed, and then lowered into it. The priest pronounced words of absolution which he also placed on the corpse's breast written in a parchment scroll. He then cast earth into the grave in the form of a cross before it was closed. The corpse and the grave were both twice asperged and censed during the proceedings. The service includes a prayer for quiet sleep in the grave and resurrection with all the saints. Soon after the closure of the grave comes the form of commendation of the soul to God and of earth to earth, ashes to ashes, dust to dust.[4]

Some of the more detailed late medieval wills yield additional

---

[1] *Manuale ad vsum percelebris ecclesie Sarisburiensis*, ed. A. J. Collins (Henry Bradshaw Soc. 91; 1960), 118–24.

[2] Ibid. 132–42.   [3] Ibid. 124–5, 142–52.   [4] Ibid. 152–62.

information about the celebration of funerals. The directions drawn up in 1463 by John Baret, a rich and pious inhabitant of St Mary's parish in Bury St Edmunds, are a good example. The mass of Our Lady, starting at 7 a.m., was to be sung 'by note' rather than as a traditional plainsong chant. The St Mary priest was to officiate in a white vestment bearing Baret's arms and his motto, 'Grace me gouerne'. After the gospel he was to stand at the end of the altar and say the psalm *De Profundis* for Baret, his parents, and all Christian souls, rehearsing the name of John Baret openly. His kindred and executors were to offer at this Lady mass. Baret also chose a preacher to deliver a sermon at the mass of requiem. He hoped that his dirge and burial would be attended by a number of priests, parish clerks, and choirboys in surplices, the masses by a larger group of priests, organists, and clerks, all of them to be appropriately paid. At both dirge and mass there were to be five poor men in black as a sign of reverence for the five wounds of Christ, and five poor women in white symbolizing the five joys of Our Lady, each of them holding a torch of clean wax. His executors, the priest of St Mary, and all the kinsfolk, friends, and servants whom he mentioned by name in his will were also to have black gowns.

On the day of Baret's burial there was to be a dinner for the 'worshipful' folk of Bury, together with priests, his good friends, his tenants, and all those who sang or played the organs at the mass of Our Lady. Nor were the poor forgotten. On the morning before his dirge was sung, twopence was to be distributed to every bedridden man and woman in Bury to pray for his soul. Every poor man and woman present at his dirge in the evening was to have a penny for the same purpose. Money and food were also to be distributed to all the prisoners in the gaol and to the lazars, the chronically sick poor. Baret's will is unusual in its detail, but the proportion of Bury wills reflecting an interest in some aspect of the funeral was increasing during the fifty years before the Reformation. Baret's directions complement the picture given by the liturgical texts, showing the importance attached to large numbers of participants, including both clergy and poor people, dress which sent out appropriate visual messages, charitable distributions, and convivial entertainment of friends.[5]

[5] *Wills and Inventories from the Registers of the Commissary of Bury St. Edmund's and the Archdeacon of Sudbury*, ed. S. Tymms (Camden os 49; 1850), 16–18; R. Dinn, 'Death and Rebirth in Late Medieval Bury St Edmunds', in S. Bassett (ed.), *Death in Towns: Urban Responses to the Dying and the Dead, 100–1600* (Leicester, 1992), 152.

The dirge and the mass of requiem were also sung long after burial on behalf of those who could afford to pay for them. The seventh and thirtieth days, and the anniversary, were favoured times for such celebrations. Anniversary services might be repeated for several years. In 1511 £3 would pay for twelve years' anniversaries. In 1528 Elizabeth Welles, a wealthy widow of Windsor, expected her anniversary obit to be kept in grander style, at a cost of 26*s*. 8*d*. a year. Dirge was to be celebrated by eight priests, requiem mass by seven more. Besides the priests, three clerks and eight poor children were to attend. Leading town officials were to make offerings. A bedeman was to announce the services in Windsor with a bell and set up the hearse, around which eight wax-tapers were to burn. Refreshments at the dirge were to include spice cakes, beef, and ale. After requiem forty-eight loaves were to be divided among poor people.[6]

However, the great majority of testators who disposed of middling or small estates seem to have been content to leave the organization of their funerals to their executors. Their obsequies were probably comparatively short and simple. Rites which convey to the reader of the Sarum Manual an impression of sustained, strenuous, and eloquent intercession may not normally have been celebrated in their entirety, or with leisurely dignity. Huge numbers of people left money for masses and lights, to the high altar, their guild, and the church, but only a minority left instructions about funeral feasts or the participants in their services.[7]

The most elaborate funerals were those of kings and noblemen. A series of reports written by heralds from the 1460s onwards helped to build up an increasingly authoritative body of precedents. Through the royal heralds, the crown tightened its control over the display of arms as well as other aspects of aristocratic funerals. The 'order limited and prescribed in the time of King Henry VII' was later taken as the standard. A directive attributed to his reign survives in several copies. It laid down, among other things, the number of mourners and amount of cloth for liveries permitted to each rank, the fees and perquisites of the heralds, and rules concerning the wearing of hoods. The mourning apparel of different ranks of ladies was specified in regulations issued by Margaret Beaufort. Underlying all these rules was a concern to reinforce by outward and visible distinctions the

---

[6] Bassett, *Death in Towns*, 160; BRO D/A1/1A, fos. 15^v–16^r, 121.
[7] Duffy, *Stripping of Altars*, 382 (quoting William Marshall's reference in *A Prymer in Englyshe* (1535) to the psalms of the *Dirige* being 'mumbled, murmured and piteously puled forth').

hierarchy of degrees upon whose stability the the health of society was held to depend. The presence of the king's heralds signalled royal countenance and support, and gave the link between monarch and subject tangible form. The confirmation of status by the majestic formalities of a heraldic funeral was probably highly valued by many aspiring families.[8]

A magnate's funeral entailed considerable preparation.[9] A month or more might well elapse between death and burial. For many great funerals an effigy of the deceased person was made, to be placed over the coffin in a position where it would be visible to spectators.[10] The corpse waited in the magnate's chamber or chapel, which, along with other rooms and the courtyard, was hung with black cloth adorned with scutcheons of his arms. Masses were celebrated by day, and servants of the deceased kept watch by night.

The journey to the burial-place was often a long one. It might be broken by an overnight stop at a church where dirge and mass were sung. Alms were often dispensed to poor men on the way, and gifts made to parish churches. The precise composition of the funeral procession as it neared its destination varied according to the rank of the deceased, but most were preceded by conductors with black staves and included clergy and a body of poor men, often corresponding with the number of years of the dead man's age. Sundry officers and gentlemen of his household, and the officers of arms, were also in the first part of the procession. Here too were borne various flags or ensigns, each of which was allowed only to those of a certain rank or above it. The banner was permitted to peers, the standard to knights, the pennon to esquires. The officers of arms bore the dead man's helmet (with mantles and crest), target (a ceremonial shield of arms), coat of arms and sword. At the heart of the procession came the

---

[8] Sir A. Wagner, *Heralds of England: A History of the Office and College of Arms* (1967), 106–9. G. Broce and R. M. Wunderli suggest in 'The Funeral of Henry Percy, Sixth Earl of Northumberland', *Albion*, 22 (1990), 199–215, that in this instance royal control of funeral ceremonies was used to underline the eclipse of a family's power.

[9] The ensuing description of the major elements of pre-Reformation aristocratic funerals is based on the following sources: *The Receyt of the Ladie Kateryne*, ed. G. Kipling (EETS 296; 1990), 81–93 (Prince Arthur, 1502); F. Blomefield, *The History of the Ancient City and Burgh of Thetford* (Fersfield, 1739), app. viii, 38–43 (2nd duke of Norfolk, 1524); BL MS Arundel 26, fos. 35ᵛ–36ʳ (Viscount Welles, 1499); MS Harley 295, fo. 155 (13th earl of Oxford, 1513); Bod. Lib. MS Ashmole 1109, fos. 48–51, 142ᵛ–146ᵛ (Lord Cobham, 1558, and duke of Suffolk, 1545). Each of these funerals differed in detail from the others.

[10] P. Cunnington and C. Lucas, *Costume for Births, Marriages and Deaths* (1972), 143, 168, 172–5.

chariot carrying the corpse, usually covered with black cloth 'garnished with scutcheons'. Attached to a peer's chariot there might be several great bannerols (especially wide banners) showing the deceased's ancestry and marriage. Four banners 'of saints' were borne at its corners. Behind came the chief mourner, usually the heir, and normally of the same sex as the deceased, followed by the other mourners, two by two, then knights, esquires, yeomen, and all the lords' and gentlemen's servants.[11]

A rich pall was held over the corpse as it was carried into the church and placed in a hearse (not a vehicle, but a specially built framework enclosing a space round the coffin). The dimensions and elaboration of this structure depended on the rank of the deceased. Within the hearse a canopy or cloth of majesty hung over the body. The barriers surrounding the hearse, and the ground and seats for the mourners within them, were supposed to be covered with black cloth. The walls of the church itself might also be covered with black cloth adorned with scutcheons.[12]

Before the dirge, a herald proclaimed the dead man's style and asked the congregation to pray for his soul. After the service, the more important participants might go to supper. Servants of the deceased kept watch overnight. From the heraldic point of view, the chief interest of the masses next morning lay in the elaborate offertory ceremonies. At all three masses, the chief mourner or his deputy made an offering called the 'mass penny'. At the mass of requiem, his oblation was followed by the ceremonial offering of the dead man's arms. They were delivered to the senior officiating priest, who gave them to the heir, thus symbolically investing him with his predecessor's dignities. He in turn delivered them to the heralds to be offered to the church. In a dramatic ceremony accorded only to those of the rank of earl or above, a knight holding in his hand an axe with the point downwards rode through the church to the middle of the choir, where he offered the horse and axe. After this rich palls were customarily offered to the corpse.[13]

After mass, the gentlemen servants of the deceased, together with the clergy, attended his corpse to burial. Once the officiant had cast

---

[11] Useful description of funeral trophies in *The Diary of Henry Machyn, Citizen and Merchant-Taylor of London, from A.D. 1550 to A.D. 1563*, ed. J. G. Nichols (Camden os 42; 1848), pp. xxvi–xxxiii.

[12] Ibid., p. xxix. A detailed drawing of the elaborate candle-bearing hearse of Abbot Islip of Westminster (1532) is well reproduced in J. Litten, *The English Way of Death: The Common Funeral since 1450* (London, 1991), 11.

[13] Cunnington and Lucas, *Costume*, 134–7; *Receyt of the Ladie Kateryne*, 91–2.

earth over the coffin, the dead man's household officers broke their staffs of office and threw them into the grave. The offering of arms and the breaking of staffs, rites symbolic of succession and farewell, were sometimes charged with strong emotion. At the offering at Prince Arthur's funeral in 1502, the narrator remarked, 'he had a herd hert that wept not'.[14]

Of all noble funerals whose cost is known the most expensive in real terms took place under the early Tudors. An incomplete account for that of the fourth earl of Northumberland in 1489 amounted to over £1,037. Of this over 40 per cent went in cloth of five different qualities to make gowns for 576 people (over a hundred of whom were members of the nobility and gentry) and to hang the church and chapels with 400 yards of material. Over 25 per cent went on the costs of food and drink for people and horses for four days. £123. 6s. 8d. (about 12 per cent) would have sufficed to give a twopenny dole to 14,800 poor folk, many more people than lived in any English town outside London. 'Lights' (candles on the hearse, and torches) cost nearly 8 per cent of the total, payments to churches and 1,500 clergy rather more than 6 per cent, heraldic accessories and the attendance of heralds come from London over 4 per cent. Preparation and coffining of the corpse accounted for not much more than 1 per cent of recorded costs. By far the most expensive element in late medieval aristocratic funerals was the overpowering display of wealth and deference made by a cortège of several hundred black-clad figures wending its stately way through the 'country' of the deceased, manifesting not only respect for his memory, but the continuing authority of his dynasty. An even greater sum, £1,340, was spent on the second duke of Norfolk's funeral in 1524. The recipients of the dole may have been more numerous than at Northumberland's funeral.[15]

One of the few medieval gentlewomen's funerals for which accounts survive is that of Anne Fortescue, who died at Stonor (Oxon.) in June 1518.[16] It cost just over £39, a tiny fraction of what was spent on a nobleman's obsequies, but it was still an elaborate

---

[14] *Receyt of the Ladie Kateryne*, 91.

[15] F. Peck, *Desiderata Curiosa: or, a Collection of divers Scarce and Curious Pieces, relating chiefly to Matters of English History* (2 vols., 1779), ii. 246–7; Blomefield, *History of Thetford*, 43. These funerals were, because of subsequent inflation, more expensive in real terms than certain nominally more costly Elizabethan funerals, as demonstrated by L. Stone, *The Crisis of the Aristocracy, 1558–1641* (Oxford, 1965), 784–5.

[16] T. Fortescue (Lord Clermont), *A History of the Family of Fortescue in all its Branches* (1880), 280–5.

affair. Anne was buried at Pyrton, about 6 miles from Stonor. Dirge and mass were celebrated for her at Watlington, on the way to Pyrton, and at Henley. Black cloth and the work of tailors and seamstresses cost over half of the total. Over 27 per cent went on a magnificent dinner 'at the burying', at which prodigious quantities of meat and alcoholic drink were consumed. The services of priests, clerks, and choristers cost over 9 per cent of the account, a penny dole for 646 beggars 7 per cent, and torches, candles, and torch-bearers about 5 per cent. Over three hundred people attended the funeral besides the beggars.

A sum equivalent to 39 per cent of the cost of the funeral itself was spent during the following year. £3. 6s. 8d. paid a priest to sing mass for Anne's soul for six months. £8. 17s. 2½d. went on celebration of the month's mind. A lavish dinner cost nearly half as much as the great funeral feast. Some four dozen priests took part at Pyrton, along with clerks and mass-helpers. A multitude of candles once more blazed on the hearse, and there was much ringing of bells. Six priests celebrated in Stonor chapel. Fifteen masses were sung at the Savoy hospital in London. The year's mind was far less costly. £1. 6s. 8d. sufficed for services at Pyrton. The distribution of scutcheons of arms to churches in the county was apparently the only heraldic expense incurred in connection with Anne's funeral.

Henry Machyn, a London merchant tailor, recorded between 1550 and 1563 every important funeral which came to his notice. His journal conveys a vivid impression of mid-sixteenth-century Londoners' constant familiarity with funeral solemnities such as the tolling of bells, the hanging of the dead person's street with black, and the passage of the procession, sights and sounds which demanded their prayers and reminded them of their own mortality. Although certain core aspects of the funeral were regulated by rule and precedent, the amount that an executor might spend on pencels (miniature pennons) and scutcheons (if the deceased had been entitled to bear arms), on candles, gowns, and dole, was nowhere precisely laid down, and largely depended upon the dead man's wealth rather than his rank.

Machyn described several funerals of prominent London citizens. These were normally attended by their colleagues in City government. Those aldermen for whom mourning had not been provided wore violet. The arms of a man's fellowship or craft were prominently displayed, and fellow members attended in the craft's livery. The craft's hall was sometimes used for the refreshments after the dirge, and the great dinner after the mass of requiem. Members of other professional groups, too, supported the obsequies of deceased colleagues. When one of the six clerks of Chancery died in 1558, his funeral was attended by 'all they of the Chanserey'. Religious confraternities played an important part in funerals, which they attended and if necessary paid for. When Master Pynoke, fishmonger and Muscovy merchant, was buried in February 1558, twenty-four fellow members of the brotherhood of the Name of Jesus in St Paul's, the most celebrated and respected of all London's confraternities, followed the mourners in the procession and preceded the company of fishmongers in their livery.[17]

Women participated as mourners in some of the funeral processions of important London men recorded by Machyn. One of his descriptions implies that they occupied a place in the latter part of the procession, as they certainly did in a number of the more fully documented post-Reformation London funerals. (Children, too, attended some seventeenth-century funerals. The only children appearing in Machyn's funeral reports were orphans from Brideswell and Christ's Hospital who participated in the funerals of hospital masters.)[18]

Six elements of late medieval funerals of people of wealth stand out particularly clearly. First, and most important, was the elaborate, repetitious chain of intercessions for the soul of the deceased and the ritual gestures about the body. Second was the presence of light, radiated by torches and candles. 'Let there be light' had been God's first creative command amid the darkness of the void. Christ was the 'light of the world'. To light a candle could be a meritorious act of worship. A lit candle symbolized resurrection in certain contexts. The great mass of candles glowing on the hearse recalled the 'light eternal' mentioned in the introit of requiem. Recording a Carthusian monk's funeral in July 1556, Machyn noticed simply that he had been buried in his monk's habit 'with grett lyght'.[19]

Heightening the effect of the lights were the generally sombre colours of mourning: this was the third element. Poor men's 'coats'

---

[17] Machyn, *Diary*, pp. xxi–xxii, 46–7, 68, 71, 106, 111–13, 140, 166, 173, 179; Cunnington and Lucas, *Costume*, 188.

[18] Machyn, *Diary*, 99, 112, 161, 291; BL MS Add. 71131 E, p. 3 (funeral of Sir Thomas Bennet, 1627: I owe this reference to Dr Vanessa Harding); MS Harley 1368, p. 2; Bod. Lib. MS Ashmole 836, p. 289.

[19] Genesis 1: 3; John 8: 12; 9: 5; Machyn, *Diary*, 110; D. R. Dendy, *The Use of Lights in Christian Worship* (Alcuin Club Collections, 41; 1959), 100–7; Duffy, *Stripping of Altars*, 361–2.

were often of russet, but the overwhelmingly dominant colour of mourning was black: for the gowns and coats of mourners, the trappings of horses and chariots, the hangings of hearse, church, house, and street. These were by far the costliest elements of funeral pomp. Fourthly, against this sombre background, the gorgeous colours of scutcheons, pencels, banners, bannerrols, standards, shields, and tabards stood out the more brilliantly.

A fifth element was the distribution of alms to the poor. Great crowds of indigent people, old, ill, maimed, or handicapped, many doubtless undernourished and emaciated, ragged, dirty, and smelling strongly, were drawn to the most lavish funerals by the hope of alms. Testators for their part expected to benefit from the prayers of these recipients.[20] The intercessions of the poor were regarded as especially potent. Finally, the funeral dinner was like a last great exercise of hospitable largesse on behalf of the deceased. It served as a sort of reward for attending the obsequies, for the work of prayer and the display of mourning. Its alcoholic conviviality stood in sharp contrast with the sombre ceremonies of intercession and burial and offered a safety-valve, a release from the constraints of mourning; perhaps too an affirmation of life over death, of the continuity of the community in face of the breaches made by mortality.

Funerary ostentation caused widespread unease in the later Middle Ages. Sir Thomas More expressed it with particular eloquence. He imagined souls in purgatory bewailing the money fruitlessly spent on gold rings and black gowns for rich men, upon many tapers and torches, worldly pomp, and high solemn ceremonies. Some of the plaintive souls had planned quite inappropriate heraldic funerals. Finally, as if mad, they had caused men to be merry at their deaths, and to treat their burying like a bride-ale.[21] Others before and after More voiced similar concerns, but in the short term the Protestant attack on the very doctrines of purgatory and intercession which More defended caused the biggest changes in funerals.

THE REFORMATION AND AFTER

The Edwardian Prayer Books brought funeral services in English, the abolition of the rites of commendation of the soul and the dirge, and the drastic pruning of what was left. However, the 1549 Prayer Book

---

[20] Duffy, *Stripping of Altars*, 360–1.
[21] T. More, *The Supplication of Souls*, ed. G. Marc'hadour, in id., *The Complete Works of St Thomas More* (New Haven, 1963–), vii (1990), 219–20.

explicitly allowed for the celebration of a Holy Communion. Some testators specifically requested the celebration of this Communion service. It disappeared from the 1552 Prayer Book. A Communion order for use at funerals was nevertheless included in the Latin Prayer Book of 1560, and Communions in English sometimes took place at funerals after 1559 despite Protestant fears that they might resemble a mass of requiem.[22]

The curtailed order for the burial of the dead provided that the priest should accompany the corpse only from the churchyard entrance to the grave, saying or singing certain texts from Scripture expressing the transience of earthly possessions and holding out the promise of resurrection. The service also included a lesson, 1 Corinthians 15: 20–58, concerning the resurrection of the body in a transformed state. The priest's commendation of the soul to God, linked with the committal of the body to the ground in 1549, disappeared from the 1552 order along with various other elements of prayer for the dead. Bystanders, not the priest, were supposed to cast the first earth into the grave from 1552 onwards. Yet a trace of intercession remained in a prayer that God would hasten his kingdom so that those present might have their perfect consummation and bliss along with the dead person and all others who had departed in the true faith. The committal of the body to the ground was prefaced by an acknowledgement of God's mercy in taking the soul of the departed to himself, and accompanied by an expression of 'sure and certaine hope of resurreccyon to eternal lyfe'. The final collect expressed the hope that the dead person rested in God. Here were grounds enough for strict Protestants to object to the Prayer Book order. *A view of Popishe abuses yet remaining in the Englishe Church* (1572) predictably condemned the prayer for perfect consummation and bliss as a relic of prayer for the dead. Other Puritans took exception to the expression of a 'sure and certain hope', especially in the case of notorious sinners. A more radical objection was that the Church was wrong to prescribe any form of service at all at burials in the absence of precedents from apostolic times.[23]

[22] Brightman, *English Rite*, ii. 874–9; G. J. Mayhew, 'The Progress of the Reformation in East Sussex 1530–1559: The Evidence from Wills', *Southern History*, 5 (1983), 52–3; H. L'Estrange, *The Alliance of Divine Offices* (4th edn., LACT, 1846), 457–8; Peck, *Desiderata Curiosa*, ii. 254 (funeral of 5th earl of Shrewsbury, 1560); *Visitation Articles and Injunctions of the Period of the Reformation*, ed. W. H. Frere and W. P. M. Kennedy (Alcuin Club Collections, 14–16; 1910), ii. 301, iii. 88, 167; Emmison (ed.), *Elizabethan Life*, iv. 19.

[23] Brightman, *English Rite*, ii. 848–9, 858–74, 876; *An Admonition to the Parliament*, in *Puritan Manifestoes*, ed. W. H. Frere and C. E. Douglas (1954), 28; Greaves,

From 1549 onwards various bishops tried to prevent the Prayer Book service being used to express Catholic beliefs and attitudes, but customs designed to assist the departed soul survived for some time after the Reformation. Excessive ringing of bells caused persistent concern. There were repeated orders that there should be only one short peal before the burial, and one after. The superstitious misuse of candles was proscribed. Unauthorized prayers for the dead, the singing of psalms in a dirge-like manner, and the practice of setting the corpse down at wayside crosses on the way to church were also forbidden. In 1590 it was allegedly customary in Lancashire and part of Cheshire for neighbours to visit the corpse and say paternoster or *De Profundis* for the soul while the bells rang 'many a solemne Peale'. Popular rites more loosely connected with orthodox Catholic worship survived a good deal longer. In Yorkshire it was (according to John Aubrey) customary for a woman to chant a rhyming prayer at 'Country vulgar Funeralls'. This 'Lyke-wake Dirge' asked Christ to receive the soul after a hazardous journey over the Whinny Moor, the thread-broad Brig of Dread, and through purgatory fires. The Herefordshire 'sin-eater' took on himself the sins of the newly departed in return for alms, and 'freed him [or her] from Walking after they were dead'.[24]

Henry Machyn recorded the effects of liturgical change between 1550 and 1563. Protestant funerals were normally completed in one day. He said little about lights. However, his descriptions of early Elizabethan London funerals show that, as a Prayer Book rubric permitted, choral singing took place at many burials. He described with disapproval the stricter sort of Protestant funeral at which singing was reduced to a minimum. (Some of the godly certainly allowed singing at funerals. In 1590 Katherine Stubbes hoped that Psalm 103, a resounding hymn of gratitude, would be sung before her to the church.) Month's minds were still occasionally kept in London in the second half of Edward's reign. In the forms of

---

Society and Religion, 701; H. Barrow, *A Brief Discoverie of the False Church* (1590), in id., *The Writings of Henry Barrow 1587–1590*, ed. L. H. Carlson (Elizabethan Nonconformist Texts, 3; 1962), 458–60. According to Barrow it was still the priest who 'cast on the first shovel full of earth'.

[24] *Visitation Articles and Injunctions of Reformation*, ii. 301–4; iii. 62, 91, 105, 159, 166, 168, 170, 176, 256, 285–6, 289–90, 309, 383; Greaves, *Society and Religion*, 696–700; *A Description of the State, Civil and Ecclesiastical, of the County of Lancaster about the Year 1590*, ed. F. R. Raines, in *Chetham Miscellany*, v (Chetham Soc., os 96; 1875), 5; J. Aubrey, *Remaines of Gentilisme and Judaisme*, in id., *Three Prose Works*, ed. J. Buchanan-Brown (Fontwell, 1972), 176–80.

doles and feasts they survived in some other places into Elizabeth's reign.[25]

Heraldic ceremonies underwent comparatively few changes as a result of the Reformation. The offertory retained its importance. A herald no longer invited the congregation to pray for the deceased before reciting his titles and offices, but praised God for taking him out of this transitory life, or prayed for his successor. The main function of the hearse was now to display scutcheons and pencels rather than carry candles. Protestantism could only have been partially responsible for one important change: a preference for shorter processional journeys. Corpses tended to be brought 'secretly', 'privately', or with a comparatively small escort from the place of death to a starting-point much closer to the church. The perambulating display of magnate power may have come to seem too costly and less politically appropriate. The costs of returning the corpses of magnates who died far from home nevertheless remained considerable.[26]

Several Elizabethan earls' funerals cost £1,000 or more. These were colossal sums, but considerably smaller in real terms than those spent on the most expensive pre-Reformation funerals. Only in the case of the queen's favourite the earl of Leicester in 1588 may the total have rivalled expenditure on those earlier ceremonies. Money was no longer spent on masses, candles, and torches or on large offerings to churches. The payments for 'blacks', mourning attire and cloth to hang house and church, always the biggest item on the funeral account, now bulked larger as a proportion of total spending than ever before: between 66 per cent and 78 per cent of the total in the cases of four magnates who died between 1579 and 1612.[27]

[25] Machyn, *Diary*, 9, 29, 193, 199, 211–12, 244–5, 307; Stubbes, *Christal glasse*, repr. with some omissions in *Philip Stubbes's Anatomy of the Abuses in England in Shakspere's Youth, A.D. 1583*, ed. F. J. Furnivall (New Shakspere Soc., 6th ser. 4, 6, 12; 1877–82), 207; Greaves, *Society and Religion*, 706–8; Emmison (ed.), *Elizabethan Life*, iv. 150; *Essex Wills, 1558–1603*, ed. F. G. Emmison (Chelmsford, 1982–), vii. *The Commissary Court 1558–1569*, nos. 99, 177, 263.

[26] M. E. James, 'Two Tudor Funerals', *Transactions of the Cumberland & Westmorland Antiquarian and Archaeological Soc.*, NS 66 (1966), 165–78; Peck, *Desiderata Curiosa*, ii. 252–5; J. Smyth, *The Lives of the Berkeleys*, in *The Berkeley Manuscripts*, ed. J. Maclean (Gloucester, 1883), ii. 388; Cunnington and Lucas, *Costume*, 203; Broce and Wunderli, 'Funeral of Henry Percy', 214–15; BL MS Add 6303, fos. 16^v–31^v (magnificent drawings of hearses appropriate to each rank); MSS Harley 304, fo. 92^v; 4774, fo. 141; MS Lansdowne 50/88, fo. 194; Bod. Lib. MS Ashmole 818, fo. 38.

[27] Stone, *Crisis of the Aristocracy*, 784–5, excluding the funeral of the 3rd earl of Huntingdon, because the account (BL MS Harley 4774, fos. 141, 148–9) enumerates many extraneous expenses and is also incomplete.

Blacks expressed the solidarity in mourning of a number of over-lapping circles of people connected with the dead. The exceptionally detailed account for the funeral of the lord keeper Sir Nicholas Bacon (1579) shows this clearly. Over three hundred participants were given cloth. The main groups represented were Bacon's colleagues in law and government, his kinsfolk, his servants (the largest group), and the sixty-eight poor men corresponding with the years of his life. Other participants included the dean of St Paul's, two physicians, and four heralds, as well as the bearers and sixteen beadles to make way for the cortège. Different ranks were distinguished by dress. Besides the poor men in their gowns, 131 men were servants or attendants of yeoman rank or below who had cloth sufficient only for a 'coat' or tunic much shorter than a gown. The lords and gentlemen had allowances of cloth ranging from 12 yards for the foremost mourners to 3¾ yards for the junior household gentlemen. The quality of the black cloth used introduced yet another set of distinctions. Some eleven different prices are specified, ranging from 30s. a yard for the foremost mourners to 6s. 8d. for the poor men. In all, nearly 910 yards of black cloth were bought on the occasion of Bacon's funeral, cost-ing just under £669.[28]

The heralds' and painters' participation, including the heralds' fees, travelling expenses and blacks, and payments for materials used, cost between £120 and £200, or well over 10 per cent of the whole, in some well-documented instances. The feast was another expensive item, though the distinction between dinner and dole was not always a very clear one.[29] After the fifth earl of Shrewsbury's burial in 1560, meat was served at Sheffield Castle 'to all manner of people who seemed honest', that is, presumably, respectable in manners and attire. After dinner, what was left was given to the poor, with a twopenny dole and 'bread and drink great plenty'. In other instances a thousand poor people were fed, in one case well over six thousand. Doles of £100 or more were sometimes distributed, though much smaller ones were also recorded.[30]

---

[28] Bod. Lib. MS Ashmole 836, pp. 21–36. These figures do not include cloth hired for hangings and covers.

[29] Ibid. 29, 35–6; BL MSS Harley 3881, fo. 60 (4th earl of Huntingdon, 1604); 4774, fo. 141 (3rd earl of Huntingdon, 1596); MSS Lansdowne 23/67, fo. 156 (1st earl of Essex 1576); 50/88, fo. 194 (Sir Henry Sidney, 1586); 82/56, fos. 123–5 (Lord Hunsdon, 1596). It is impossible to assign precise percentages to each main category of expenditure because no two accounts are entirely consistent in their organization or the amount of detail they include.

[30] Peck, *Desiderata Curiosa*, ii. 255; Smyth, *Lives of the Berkeleys*, 391; *A true reporte of the honourable buriall and funerall solempnities, of George, earle of*

Some knights' obsequies cost several hundred pounds. Nearly £444 was spent on the funeral of Sir John Forster, warden of the East Marches, in 1602. About 60 per cent went on blacks, 22 per cent on food and drink, 13 per cent on the herald. Forster was a great office-holder. Most of the gentry had very much less costly burials. In Kent, for example, between 1581 and 1650, the median cost of the funerals of twenty-five knights and esquires for whom relevant information survives in probate accounts was £23. 15s. 0d. in 1580–90 prices. The corresponding figure for 121 gentlemen was £5. 12s. 6d. There were enormous variations either side of these median figures, but not many of these Kent gentlefolk could have been given a true heraldic funeral.[31]

Wills throw some light on the expectations of gentry testators with regard to their own funerals. In Elizabethan Essex, about 15 per cent of esquires or widows of esquires, 6 per cent of the 'mere' gentry, mentioned funeral blacks. Some wealthy Essex gentry specified that they wanted £50 or more spent on black cloth (which almost certainly accounted for the greater part of the funeral costs in each case). Close kinsfolk, friends, servants, tenants, almsfolk, and clergymen were among the people mentioned by those testators who specified the recipients of blacks, but very few of them gave mourning to members of all these groups. (Most of the blacks dispensed to individuals would have been coats or gowns, not complete sets of mourning wear.)[32] Many more testators (about 40 per cent of those of the rank of knight or esquire, a third of the mere gentry) left rings, or money to buy them. The numbers ranged from one to twenty, but in most cases fewer than ten were given. The prices of rings in Elizabeth's reign ranged from 10s. to £10; most cost 20–40s.[33] A large majority of the Essex gentry made provision for the poor in their

Shrewsburie, the thirteenth of January, 1590 (1591), 4 (I am indebted to Prof. Patrick Collinson for kindly giving me a typescript copy of this report); Greaves, *Society and Religion*, 718–19; Stone, *Crisis of the Aristocracy*, 575; references in n. 29, above.

[31] J. Raine, *The History and Antiquities of North Durham* (1852), 309 (the sums given do not include certain items on this account which were not directly connected with the funeral); C. Gittings, *Death, Burial and the Individual in Early Modern England* (1984), 239.

[32] Emmison (ed.), *Elizabethan Life*, iv. 14–268, esp. 26, 37, 39, 43, 58, 67, 96, 100, 106, 119, 120, 122–4, 127, 134, 139–40, 191, 194–5, 210, 231, 242–3. All wills in this calendar were proved in the Prerogative Court of Canterbury. An article based on an analysis of these and other Essex gentry wills is D. Cressy, 'Death and the Social Order: The Funerary Preferences of Elizabethan Gentlemen', *Continuity and Change*, 5 (1989), 99–119.

[33] Emmison (ed.), *Elizabethan Life*, iv. 15, 38, 68, 71, 72, 88, 89, 99, 114, 117, 124, 175, 177, 212, 222, 255, 266.

wills. The funeral dinner or drinking was, however, relatively seldom mentioned.[34]

A gradual but far-reaching change in attitudes towards funerals took place in the upper classes between 1580 and 1640. Whereas between 1560 and 1580 all the aristocratic testators whose wills were traced by Professor Stone desired a funeral suitable to their rank, between 1600 and 1640 two-thirds wanted one which was 'seemly, but without pomp' or 'cheap', The desire to avoid wasteful ostentation had been expressed in a number of late medieval and early Tudor wills, but it was from *c*.1590 onwards that such wishes were most clearly explained. The first earl of Dorset (d. 1608) ordered that he should be buried without blacks or great solemnity, 'but in a Christian manner as other persons are of meaner sort' because the 'usuall solemnities' required by the heralds for noblemen were good only for themselves and the drapers and very prejudicial to the children, servants, and friends of the deceased and to the poor of the neighbourhood.[35]

The change in attitudes towards funerals may have been reinforced by a new religious outlook. Some Puritans criticized the spending on blacks of money which might have been better bestowed upon the poor, the hypocrisy involved in wearing mourning without feeling grief, and the encouragement of genuine grief when those who felt it should rather be grateful for their friends' removal from the world. That archetypal Puritan gentleman John Bruen firmly opposed a 'motion of blacks' which he heard on his deathbed in 1625, insisting that so far as he was concerned there was reason to rejoice rather than mourn. However, the ideal of the conformable Puritan was moderation, well expressed in 1622 by William Gouge, a popular London preacher. In burying one's parents, he wrote, excessive parsimony and sumptuousness were both to be avoided. Outward solemnities of burial, even though unnecessary, were a good means of avoiding an anabaptistical confusion (i.e. of social ranks), wrote another stout

---

[34] Emmison (ed.), *Elizabethan Life*, 164, 242.

[35] Stone, *Crisis of Aristocracy*, 577, 786; Greaves, *Society and Religion*, 701–2; K. B. McFarlane, *Lancastrian Kings and Lollard Knights* (Oxford, 1972), 210; N. P. Tanner, *The Church in Late Medieval Norwich 1370–1532* (Toronto, 1984), 99–100; for the duke of Suffolk's 1544 stipulation that black gowns or coats should only be given to his servants and torch-bearers, and Sir Francis Walsingham's 1590 requirement that his body be buried without the ceremonies usual for a man of his position because of his debts, see *Wills from Doctors' Commons: A Selection from the Wills of Eminent Persons proved in the Prerogative Court of Canterbury, 1495–1695*, ed. J. G. Nichols and J. Bruce (Camden os 83; 1862), 28, 69.

Puritan, Robert Pricke (*c*.1606). Many moderate Puritans officiated at elaborate funerals, and when a death was widely agreed to be a great and public loss, the wearing of mourning might be seen as a legitimate gesture of sorrow and humility.[36]

Robust defences of mourning garb were not wanting. Richard Hooker insisted that it was natural to show the sorrow one felt; if it was absent 'yet the signs are meet to shew what should be'. Preaching at the funeral of Sir Thomas Thynne not long before the Civil War, the moderate Calvinist Daniel Featley drew attention to the way in which so many eminent men from different walks of life had put on blacks for Thynne, publicly testifying to their respect and sense of loss. Featley anticipated that some 'prompted by *Judas*' might ask whether the money would not have been better spent on relieving many poor. Featley's answer was that both works of charity and decent rites and ceremonies ought to be performed.[37]

The precedents governing the celebration of 'public' heraldic funerals were especially important in maintaining a high level of expenditure. In 1568 began the regular registration in the college of arms of certificates of all funerals at which heralds attended. Queen Elizabeth I and Lord Burghley believed that the celebration of funerals in a manner appropriate to the degree of the deceased was an important means of reinforcing the social hierarchy. Despite her notorious parsimony, the queen paid for lavish funerals for some of her relatives. In the critical early months of 1588 Leicester and Burghley found time to take a close interest in the funeral of the earl of Rutland. Since he was the second head of the family to die within a year, they conceded that some economies might be made, but

---

[36] Greaves, *Society and Religion*, 700; Barrow, *Discoverie*, 460; N. Assheton, *The Journal of Nicholas Assheton of Downham, in the County of Lancaster, Esq.*, ed. F. R. Raines (Chetham Soc., os 14; 1848), 133; W. Gouge, *Of domesticall duties eight treatises* (1622), 477–8; R. Pricke, *A verie godlie and learned sermon, treating of mans mortalitie and of the estate both of his bodie, and soule after death* (1608), sig. F. Most Puritans refrained from direct criticism of heraldic solemnities, but see Barrow, *Discoverie*, 459.

[37] R. Hooker, *Of the Laws of Ecclesiastical Polity*, in id., *The Works of that Learned and Judicious Divine, Mr. Richard Hooker* (2 vols., Oxford, 1841), ii. 153; D. Featley, *Iter Novissimum. Or, Man his last Progresse. A Sermon preached At the Funerall of the Right Worshipfull Sir Thomas Thinne Knight*, in *Threnoikos. The house of mourning. Delivered in XLVII sermons, preached at funeralls* (1640), 830; John 12: 5. Yet John Evelyn described how his mother on her deathbed felt that God had punished her for the pomp and expense of her daughter's funeral, and importuned her husband 'that what he design'd to bestow on her Funeral, he would rather dispose among the poore': Evelyn, *Diary*, ii. 13.

689½ yards of cloth, costing £358, had nevertheless to be sent from London.[38]

During the reign of James I, 'private' aristocratic funerals became common. The private character of many of these ceremonies was underlined by the fact that they took place at night, especially in London. Privacy in this context meant above all an escape from the obligation, attendant upon a public funeral, to obey the heralds' prescriptions and clothe hundreds of people in black in a fashion befitting one's public station. The absence of elaborate preparations obviated the need for a long delay. Some historians think that one reason for the rise of the private funeral was the desire, particularly on the part of some ladies, to avoid the mutilation of the body which embalming necessitated. The private funeral (it has been argued) also allowed greater scope for the expression of personal grief and for the participation of those closest to the dead. Heraldic funeral rules required that principal mourners be of the same sex as the defunct, but they did not govern private funerals. 'A husband could now act as chief mourner for his wife and vice versa.' However, we must not assume that all widowed spouses wished to play a prominent part in the funeral ceremonial. In 1630 Robert Willan, preacher at the funeral of the first Viscount Bayning of Sudbury, recognized in the preface to his sermon a custom 'barring noble widdowes from ceremoniall and solemne sorrow, confining them to closset mourning'. Secret grief, he continued, 'is most sharpe, and teares shed in priuate as they fall lesse visible, so lesse forced'. His words suggest that a custom which, by barring them from public solemnities, created a private space for uninhibited grief, may not have been unwelcome to most widows. In fact Lord Bayning's funeral was private. In the sermon which Willan delivered in Lady Bayning's absence, he invited his audience to distinguish between the 'priuate funerall' and a 'publike mourning' in which the great officers of state and many noble peers solemnized Bayning's farewell. (On the other hand, noble widows were not barred from all participation in heraldic obsequies. When the fourth earl of Derby was buried in 1593, the countess 'and all other Ladyes

[38] Wagner, *Heralds*, 188–97; *Cheshire and Lancashire Funeral Certificates, A.D. 1600 to 1678*, ed. J. P. Rylands (Lancashire and Cheshire Record Soc. 6; 1882), p. v; Stone, *Crisis of Aristocracy*, 578; *The Manuscripts of His Grace the Duke of Rutland, G.C.B., preserved at Belvoir Castle* (Historical Manuscripts Commission, 4 vols., 1888–1905), i. 241–3.

occupied a place in the procession not far behind the chief mourner'.)[39]

The spread of private funerals may have been due in part to a more accommodating attitude on the part of James I and Robert Cecil than that shown by Elizabeth and William Cecil. The fact that a number of James's Scots courtiers, who were not subject to the jurisdiction of the English college of arms, chose to be buried by night contributed to the rise of nocturnal funerals. Charles I was to try to put a stop to them, but by then it was too late. Meanwhile the officers of arms petitioned George Abbot, archbishop of Canterbury, complaining of nocturnal burial 'especially of the better sorte'.[40] It smacked of popery and heathenism. Previous generations had thought it fit only for malefactors. They also blamed the practice for the abandonment of funeral sermons, though some published sermons explicitly describe the funerals of the people for whom they were preached as private or nocturnal.[41] The claim that it was one cause of the neglect of the 'large relief' formerly bestowed on the poor may have been better founded. The continuing threat of disorder from casual mendicants drawn to funerals in 'swarms' may well have been one reason for privacy.[42]

Another consequence was 'great confusion amonge the gentrie of the kingdom'. The officers of arms could not make proper certificates, and all sorts of heraldic irregularities were perpetrated. (Other reasons for loss of control by the heralds included their own quarrels, the delegation of heraldic functions to licensed painters and deputy heralds, and infringement of the heralds' monopoly by craftsmen who offered heraldic services at lower prices.)[43] Finally, the heralds claimed that night funerals had damaged the sale of commodities such as cloth. Certainly the crippling cost of blacks was a good reason for seeking privacy.

In November 1618 the lords commissioners for the office of earl marshal published a table of fees to be paid out of the estates of all gentlemen and noblemen worth £666. 13s. 4d. or more who were buried

[39] Stone, *Crisis of Aristocracy*, 577–9; Gittings, *Death*, 188–95; R. Willan, *Eliah's wish: a prayer for death. A sermon preached at the funerall of viscount Sudbury, lord Bayning* (1630), sig. A3ᵛ, 43; Featley, *Iter Novissimum*, 830; *Lancashire Funeral Certificates*, ed. T. W. King (Chetham Soc., os 75; 1869), 27.

[40] Gittings, *Death*, 190, 200; BL MS Harley 1301, fo. 12.

[41] R. Chambers, *Sarahs sepulture: or a funerall sermon preached for the countesse of Northumberland* (1620), 20; Willan, *Eliah's wish*, 43.

[42] Greaves, *Society and Religion*, 720–1; *True reporte*, 4; but see Gittings, *Death*, 196, for testators anxious that the poor should not suffer as a result of their own funerals being held at night.

[43] Wagner, *Heralds*, 199–221, 236–8.

by torchlight or in the day without an officer of arms. Gentlemen's funerals where scutcheons were displayed were to be paid for at a higher rate than those where they were not. (However, most gentlemen had grown so miserly, Norroy king-of-arms was told by his deputies, writing from Lichfield in 1621, that they would not have a scutcheon of arms made for them.)[44]

Expensive funerals, John Weever claimed in 1631, were now 'accounted but as a fruitlesse vanitie'; almost all ceremonial rites were 'altogether laid aside'. Noblemen and eminent gentlemen were being buried at night 'with a Torch, a two-pennie Linke, and a Lanterne' or 'parsimoniously interred in the day-time, by the helpe of some ignorant countrey painter, without the attendance of any one of the Officers of Armes'. (Daytime privacy was no doubt easier to achieve in the depth of the countryside, far from the nearest herald's deputy, than it was in London. Yet nocturnal obsequies later became fashionable in the provinces too, probably because of the influence of metropolitan example and the aesthetic appeal of a torchlit ceremony by night.) Weever exaggerated. The heraldic funeral, though declining, was not yet dead. In 1632 the sixth earl of Rutland's funeral cost £3,544. Private funerals may have been less costly than public ones, but they were seldom the parsimonious affairs depicted by Weever. Blacks were distributed to a smaller number of mourners, especially the deceased's household, increasingly in the form of loose-fitting cloaks rather than the gowns previously required. However, blacks were replaced by a variety of other gifts to friends and guests: scarves of fine silk, knots of ribbon, gloves, and rings (which Lady Strode (d. 1619), probably had in mind when she directed that her friends should receive 'priuate gifts of remembrance' instead of blacks). The readiness of mourners to appear in their own coaches, sometimes by the score, became during the seventeenth century one of the foremost measures of the social success of fashionable funerals. Family rights to bear arms were increasingly often advertised in the form of a diamond-shaped hatchment, hung outside the house during a period of mourning, before being placed in the church.[45]

[44] R. R. Steele, *A Bibliography of Royal Proclamations of the Tudor and Stuart Sovereigns, 1485-1714*, i (Bibliotheca Lindesiana, 5; 1910), no. 1225; Bod. Lib. MS Ashmole 836, p. 537.

[45] J. Weever, *Ancient funerall monuments within the united monarchie of Great Britaine, Ireland, and the islands adjacent* (1631), 17-18; Gittings, *Death*, 189, 196-7, 199; Stone, *Crisis of Aristocracy*, 785; Cunnington and Lucas, *Costume*, 190, 192; J. Barlow, *The True guide to glory. A sermon preached at Plympton Mary in Devon, at the funerals of the lady Strode of Newingham* (1619), 49; E. L. Cutts, 'Curi-

Some gentry were given a modified form of heraldic funeral even though no heralds were present, something which the heralds' weakening control made easier in the seventeenth century. The Lancashire gentleman Thomas Ireland Esq. (d. 1639) stipulated that his funeral should take place in the day, not at night, but 'with noe more pompe then accordinge to his degree'. The order of procession specifies 'No poore at all'. His helm, crest, and coat of arms were to be carried by kinsmen. His 8-year-old daughter was to follow his corpse as head mourner, with seven ladies behind her.[46]

People without pretensions to gentility (the great majority) had no need to concern themselves with such things as hatchments and blacks. The median cost of funerals of those yeomen of Kent for whom probate accounts survive from between 1581 and 1650 was £2. 4s. 8d., about 40 per cent of the figure for the county's 'mere' gentry. The corresponding figure for husbandmen was £1. 9s. 4d. Relatively small though these sums were, they represented a considerable outlay for the people concerned. At most funerals of people of lesser rank than the gentry, the feast, dinner ('arval dinner' in Lancashire), or 'drinking', was by far the biggest single item on the bill, often accounting for half, in some cases three-quarters, of the cost. Such hospitality was important for the reputation of the deceased and his family. The idea that the dead man was the unseen host was well conveyed by Robert Waughe, a wealthy yeoman of Chester-le-Street (Co. Durham) who in 1612 left the substantial sum of £6 to be spent on 'a dynner to make my honest good neighbors welcome for my laste faire well to them out of this synfull worlde'. Richard Hooker, apologist of the established church order, defended funeral feasts in face of Puritan doubts. Solomon had said, 'Give wine unto them that have grief of heart' (Proverbs 31: 6), but usually it was beer, in substantial quantities, that solaced the guests at English funerals before the Civil War. Neighbours were the people most frequently specified. The sum of about 16s. disbursed at the funeral of a Reading widow around

ous Extracts from a MS Diary, of the time of James II and William and Mary', *Transactions of the Essex Archaeological Soc.* 1 (1858), 117–18 (for torchlit funerals at Coggeshall); *The Autobiography of the Hon. Roger North*, ed. A. Jessopp (1887), 229; *Hatchments in Britain*, v. *Kent, Surrey and Sussex*, ed. P. Summers and J. Titterton (1985), the unpaginated general introd. describes this sort of hatchment as 'a debased form of the medieval achievement—the shield, helm, and other accoutrements carried at the funeral of a noble or a knight' which originated in the Low Countries. One of the oldest surviving examples in England, Archbishop Abbot's (c.1633), is in the chapel of Abbot's Hospital in Guildford: P. Froggatt, 'Surrey', *Hatchments in Britain*, v. 92, 107–8.

[46] *Lancashire Funeral Certificates*, 52–3.

1630 bought cakes, bread, beer, and meat, including two loins of mutton. Most probate accounts do not distinguish between the sums spent on neighbours and the poor. In the relatively few Berkshire accounts which permit a comparison, the sum spent on the guests was usually, but not always, substantially larger than that given to the poor or paid for food for them.[47]

Payments to the bell-ringers figure prominently in several accounts. An Abingdon account of 1594 includes three separate payments: 4*d*. for the passing-bell, 2*s*. for the knell after death, and 5*s*. 4*d*. for ringing at the burial. It points to a reversal of the emphasis called for by episcopal injunctions, with much more ringing taking place after than before death, rising to a climax at the funeral, when the bell might be rung for several hours. Other accounts show that as many as seven men might be employed. Religious conservatives probably still treated such ringing as an invitation to pray for the dead. The tolling of the passing-bell was officially acceptable. Besides acting as a salutary reminder of the mortality common to all, it summoned Christians to pray for somebody who was dying but not yet dead, and might therefore still be helped by human intercession. According to a widespread custom, probably of medieval origin, bells were used to indicate the age and sex of a newly deceased person. It long survived the Reformation in remoter parts of the country.[48]

Gifts in memory of the deceased were rarely mentioned in accounts of expenditure at the funerals of country people of middling rank, but the distribution of ribbons and laces to young people was said in 1612 to be customary in Berkshire. In 1630 gloves, points, and laces were given out after the death of a prosperous husbandman of Wargrave in that county. Among 894 wills proved in the archdeaconry of Sudbury during the years 1630–35, only about twenty contain bequests of rings, the majority to only one or two people, and some of the testators concerned were gentry.

---

[47] Gittings, *Death*, 239; York, Borthwick Institute, PROB. EX. 1607–46, 1635/5, 1637/3, 4 (for some examples of lavish northern funeral hospitality); *Wills and Inventories from the Registry at Durham*, pt. iv, ed. H. M. Wood (Surtees Soc. 142; 1929), 57; Hooker, *Laws*, ii. 154; BRO D/A1/177/12c (account of administration of Alice Burden alias Symon, widow); generalizations based on BRO D/A1/173–7 (60 accounts, names beginning A–B, mentioning funeral meals or drinkings, 1592–1640); Gittings, *Death*, 157.

[48] BRO D/A1/175/134a; *Visitation Articles and Injunctions of Reformation*, iii. 62, 91, 170, 176, 285–6; *Popular Antiquities of Great Britain . . . from the Materials collected by John Brand F.S.A.*, ed. W. C. Hazlitt (3 vols., 1870), ii. 157–65; York, Borthwick Institute, PROB. EX. 1607–46, 1631/2 (account relating to estate of William Stanshall of Nottingham: payment for bells ringing 'all the day of his funerall').

There were three bequests of gloves, by a widow, a yeoman, and a husbandman.[49]

The corpse was 'continually attended or watched' between death and burial. The gamut of spiritually or psychologically protective measures ranged from candles, crosses, and prayers to convivial drinking and the playing of games, at least one of them with sexual overtones. Medieval bishops had tried to curb the profane convivial- ity common at these wakes; Protestant ones sought to discourage watching customs which they thought superstitious. Watching grad- ually ceased to be a major focus of ritual or conviviality except in the more remote parts of the country.[50]

From the late sixteenth century onwards, a growing number of parish overseers' accounts record disbursements for poor people's burials, especially the shroud and the grave. Additional payments were sometimes made to the bearers of the corpse. Only rarely did the overseers pay for any sort of refreshment at the funeral. However, in 1618 the 6s. 6d paid for the funeral of Elinor Wreaford of Hennock (Devon) included a groat for drink 'for them that did bring her to the ground'. At Fillongley (War.), 8d. was paid for bread and drink at a burial in 1626–7. In 1648 4s. 4d. out of a total bill of 7s. 10d. for the burial of William Lucas was 'spent of them that tooke paines aboute him & for bread & drinke & Cheese'.[51]

FROM THE CIVIL WAR TO 1750

The victorious Puritans proscribed the Prayer Book burial service which they had long disliked. The 1645 *Directory* stipulated that the corpse was to be 'decently' attended to the public burial-place. Pray- ing, reading, and singing in going to and at the grave were to be laid aside. However, it was very convenient that the Christian friends who accompanied the body should apply themselves to 'meditations and conferences' suitable to the occasion, and the minister might put them in remembrance of their duty. The *Directory* specifically sanc- tioned any 'civill respects or differences' appropriate to the rank and

[49] BRO D/A1/177/21, D/A1/213/75c; *The Wills of the Archdeaconry of Sudbury 1630–1635*, ed. N. Evans (Suffolk Records Soc. 29; 1987), nos. 44, 113, 179, 205, 212, 439, 465, 468, 488, 497, 566, 611, 667, 681, 731, 818, 839, 843, 849, 859, 864, 871.

[50] F. Tate, 'Of the Antiquity, Variety, and Ceremonies of Funerals in England' (1600), in T. Hearne (ed.), *A Collection of Curious Discourses written by Eminent Antiquar- ies upon Several Heads in our English Antiquities* (2 vols., 1771), i. 216–17; *Popular Antiquities*, ii. 166–9; Gittings, *Death*, 105–10.

[51] Exeter, Devon Record Office, Hennock Overseers' Records, 2922A/PO 1 (unfoli- ated); WCRO, Fillongley Overseers' Accounts, DR 404/87 (1626–7, 1648); Gittings, *Death*, 61 (more lavish Lincolnshire examples from 1641 and 1653).

condition of the deceased. A decent Interregnum funeral could still be a solemn and pompous occasion, though it now centred upon the procession, the sermon, and (where appropriate) the heraldic solemnities, but the Civil War and Interregnum weakened the heralds' control over the conduct of funerals. In 1667, when he was Norroy king-of-arms, William Dugdale looked back to 'the late Rebellion' as the time when the herald painters began to usurp the heralds' functions with impunity.[52]

The *Directory* established the pattern for future Nonconformist funerals, but among the conforming majority the Book of Common Prayer, occasionally employed at burials even during the Interregnum, was brought back into use soon after the Restoration. The changes to the burial service in 1662 were small ones. The inclusion of two Psalms (39 and 90) powerfully expressive of the transitoriness of human life and the might of God, either or both of which were to be read on entry to the church, went some way towards meeting the concerns of those who wanted fuller and more formal rites. However, certain words which had given offence to Puritans were removed. The body was now committed to the ground in hope of *the* resurrection to eternal life, thus clearly focusing on the congregation's shared hopes of resurrection rather than an expectation concerning the fate of the dead person in particular. Secondly, the reference to the newly deceased was removed from the clause of the final prayer in which the priest besought God to accomplish the number of his elect and hasten his kingdom.[53]

In 1668 the commissioners for the office of earl marshal agreed a detailed set of rules governing the conduct of heraldic funerals, but a bill partly designed to ensure that proper funeral certificates were returned failed to pass in 1667. William Dugdale, Norroy king-of-arms, thought this was because of fears that the court of wards might

---

[52] *A Directory for the Publique Worship of God, Throughout the Three Kingdoms* (1645), 73–4; *The Life, Diary, and Correspondence of Sir William Dugdale, Kt, sometimes Garter Principal King of Arms*, ed. W. Hamper (1827), 382; Wagner, *Heralds*, 252–62. The war doubtless made it more difficult to arrange for heralds to attend. The 5th earl of Cumberland was buried with much pomp in 1643, but no herald seems to have been present, and the total costs of rather more than £500 were relatively modest for an earl's funeral: see R. T. Spence, 'A Noble Funeral in the Great Civil War', *Yorkshire Archaeological Journal*, 65 (1993), 115–21. See also I. Gentles, 'Political Funerals during the English Revolution', in S. Porter (ed.), *London and the Civil War* (1996), 205–24, which includes descriptions of the lavish official funerals of John Pym and the earl of Essex.

[53] Evelyn, *Diary*, iii. 76 (Prayer Book burial service used in Deptford church in September 1652 for the first time in seven years at his mother-in-law's funeral); Brightman, *English Rite*, ii. 849–53, 859, 873.

be restored. If the recently abolished court of wards had been the widely hated fiscal face of neo-feudalism, its ceremonial face was seen in heraldic funerals. During Charles II's reign the heralds were still trying to keep certificates of aristocratic funerals, whether public or private, but after 1688 the system of certification collapsed.[54]

Heraldic funerals continued after the Restoration, albeit in dwindling numbers. Recorded expenditure on one of them, that of Lord Brooke, performed at Warwick in 1677, was nearly £1,191. Blacks accounted for nearly two-thirds of this sum, a proportion very much in line with Elizabethan patterns. Some notable heraldic funerals were celebrated as demonstrations of the standing of families or individuals who had special reasons to assert their position. In 1662 the horseback funeral procession of Sir John Stawell, a hero of royalist resistance in Somerset, travelled over 20 miles through the middle of the county. Among the participants were several of the gentlemen who had served under him. Here was a formal celebration of Stawell's leadership, and of the restoration of his family's fortunes as well as those of the monarchy. Another remarkable heraldic funeral, that of the Duchess Dudley (d. 1669), matched in its splendour the extraordinary life peerage conferred on her by Charles I in 1644. Some of the provisions for the poor were redolent of medieval funerals, but changes in custom and nomenclature were nevertheless evident in the fact that it was the 'stately hearse' (a vehicle, clearly, not a structure within the church) attended by a 'numerous train of coaches' for the participant nobility and gentry which made the biggest impression when the corpse left London for the duchess's burial-place at Stoneleigh in Warwickshire.[55]

Among the most lavish of all heraldic funerals staged after the Restoration were those of the dukes of Buckingham in the eighteenth century. When Edmund, seventh duke and last of the Sheffield line, died in 1735, his mother, illegitimate daughter of James II, was the duke's sole legatee. The 'haughty duchess', described by Horace Walpole as 'more mad with pride than any Mercer's wife in Bedlam', was able to divert her grief and indulge her notorious snobbery by staging a stupendous heraldic funeral for him. The corpse lay in state in

---

[54] BL MS Add. 6303, fos. 49–59; Dugdale, *Life, Diary, and Correspondence*, 381; Wagner, *Heralds*, 112 and n. 2.

[55] WCRO, Greville Accounts, CR 1886/TN 185; SRO DD/ES, Box 18; G. D. Stawell, *A Quantock Family* (Taunton, 1910), 406–11; Bod. Lib. MS Ashmole 836, p. 309; Dugdale, *Life, Diary, and Correspondence*, 387–9; G. E. Cokayne, *The Complete Peerage*, rev. and ed. V. Gibbs *et al.* (13 vols., 1910–59, repr. 6 vols., Gloucester, 1987), iv. 486–7.

Buckingham House in a suite of rooms hung with mourning and elaborately furnished with scutcheons, sconces, and candlesticks. The funeral itself was exceptionally opulent. As was appropriate at the funeral of somebody who died a minor and unmarried, the virginal white of numerous plumes and of the scarves, silk hatbands, favours, and gloves of several participants figured prominently amid the funereal black. An effigy of the deceased was placed over the body. Twelve officers of arms were present, and Garter directed the ceremonial. The procession moved through Westminster Abbey by torchlight, and choral singing played a major part in the service, which ended with Garter's proclamation of the duke's style and the traditional breaking of staves.[56]

Heraldic ceremonies could be adapted to some extent to suit individual requirements. Yet they were probably coming to seem anachronistic, excessively ostentatious, insufficiently flexible, and far too expensive. In 1670 the earl of Denbigh wanted to give his beloved wife a funeral which would to do her honour, but in the end he decided against a heraldic ceremony. He regarded the inclusion of the expected contingent of poor mourners as obsolete, preferring the family custom of giving £20 to the poor of the parish. He believed that he would be unable to find in his part of the country six peers of his own rank to keep him company in mourning robes, and was unwilling to supply blacks to other families, a respect never paid to him. In 1676 the duke of Newcastle, one of the foremost noblemen of the realm, chose to be 'privately interred without any Funeral solemnity', presumably to the disappointment of the heralds.[57]

By the eighteenth century it was possible to have a great public funeral without the heralds' participation, as is shown by the example of the enormously wealthy Blackett family of Newcastle upon Tyne. The funeral of Sir William Blackett III in 1728 was a great county and municipal event. His procession was led by twenty-four 'mutes', successors of the conductors who had formerly preceded aristocratic funeral processions. The front portion of the procession also included a mourning horse and four banners. There were two knights among the eight pallbearers. The chief mourner was

---

[56] *Historical Register*, 21/81 (1736), 70–5; Wagner, *Heralds*, 112 and n. 4; Cokayne, *Complete Peerage*, ii. 399–401.

[57] Bod. Lib. MS Ashmole 836, pp. 129–30, 133, 137–8; Denbigh also wondered whether the inclusion of six horses 'caparison'd with velvet with all the achievements of hir noble ancestors' might not 'bee thought more fitt for the sonns of Mars, then for Ladies' (ibid., p. 129); BL MS Add. 12514, fo. 100.

followed by twelve 'close mourners' in cloaks and four testamentary trustees. Behind them came the corporation of Newcastle in all their pomp, preceded by the municipal regalia, then gentry of Northumberland and Durham, and some 1,500 members of Newcastle's incorporated companies. Family, household, parish, municipality, trade, industry, and the higher ranks of society both urban and rural were all represented. The total cost must have been well over £1,000.[58]

Even the Blacketts' infant children were buried in style. Three died in the 1690s, two of them certainly under a year old. Their funerals cost between £41 and £59. Such things as scarves, hatbands, and gloves accounted for by far the greater part of the recorded expenditure. The bill for wine and spices at one of these funerals came to £6. 2s. By contrast, the funeral of John Barwis, postillion to Sir William Blackett II, cost under £4 in 1695. Over 40 per cent of this sum went on drink.[59]

Another grand funeral conducted without the participation of heralds was that of the duke of Richmond and Lennox in 1723. Its management was entrusted to upholsterers. They supplied most of the materials and accessories needed for the conduct of the service, and hired attendants to carry the requisite ducal trophies. However, nearly 36 per cent of their bill of £656. 4s. 1d. was paid for mourning furnishings for two of the duke's houses, about 17 per cent for preparation of the Jerusalem Chamber in Westminster Abbey where the corpse lay in state immediately before the funeral. The bill reflects the extent to which domestic rooms had by this time become a prime scene of funerary ostentation. As early as 1648 a prosecution for heraldic irregularities by Clarenceux centred on the improper furnishings of the rooms of the recently deceased Sir John St John's house at Battersea and the structure of the hearse on which his corpse had lain there.[60]

One of the best documented of later Stuart funerals is the comparatively inexpensive private ceremony arranged for Colonel Edward

[58] *Obsequies of Certain of the Family of Blackett of Newcastle*, ed. M. A. Richardson, in *Reprints of Rare Tracts and Imprints of Antient Manuscripts &c. chiefly illustrative of the History of the Northern Counties* (Newcastle, 1846), 31–5; cf. his father's grand funeral of 1705, ibid. 21–31. A 'Baron Hilton', perhaps Lord Hilton *de jure*, was also among the pallbearers in 1728.

[59] Ibid. 15–20, 42.

[60] F. W. Steer, 'The Funeral Account of the First Duke of Richmond and Lennox', *Sussex Archaeological Collections*, 98 (1960), 156–64; BL MS Harley 5176, fos. 191ᵛ–197ᵛ; cf. BL MS Add. 6303, fos. 49–59; *Historical Register*, 21/81 (1736), 70–2.

Phelips of Montacute in 1680 and subsequently described in great detail by his son William.[61] Phelips, head of one of the major Somerset gentry families, had suffered heavy financial loss as a result of his support for Charles I. Although his funeral was carefully planned and dignified, its scale reflected his reduced circumstances. The preparations were made secretly, and few invitations were sent out. The corpse was placed in the parlour of the Abbey farmhouse to which Phelips had retired. The bell began to ring at one o'clock on 16 February 1680. At two the corpse was carried to the church. The velvet pall with scutcheons was borne by eight gentlemen, most of them colonels, deputy lieutenants, and justices, as befitted the dead man's position in his county. The colonel's children followed him. The vicar of Montacute preached on one of the most popular funeral sermon texts, Isaiah 57: 1, beginning 'The righteous perisheth, and no man layeth it to heart'. After the burial the pallbearers went to Montacute House to have supper with the colonel's heir, Sir Edward.

The Phelips family sought to give the colonel a funeral which was orderly and relatively economical. There was no great dole or feasting; the rabble was as far as possible excluded. Mourning-dress was provided for only nine close kinsfolk and fourteen servants, not all of it newly made. This may long have been the practice of most of the middling and smaller gentry. A more recent development was the enormous growth in the number of funeral gifts, which marked overlapping hierarchies of status, kinship, friendship, and regard. The Phelips material throws much light on the nature and purpose of these gifts. Twenty-six rings were provided, 29 hatbands, 48 scutcheons, 62 scarves, and 224 pairs of gloves. All these, except the rings (every one of them 'very handsomely made'), were furnished in different qualities. There were, for example, two different types of fine silk for scarves and hatbands, 'love' (the better) and 'tiffany'. Gloves were of three sorts: shammy, cordovan leather and kid, and 'sheepes and Tanned'. The pallbearers, the most honoured guests, ended up with the largest number of these presents, all of the best quality, while the outermost circle of servants, tenants, and tradesmen supplying the funeral received only the cheapest gloves. (Mrs Phelips, the colonel's widow, sent their rings and silk scutcheons to the bearers with her personal thanks after supper on the day of the funeral.) The proportion of the Phelips funeral account spent either

[61] SRO DD/PH 238, fos. 200–6, discussed and analysed by R. Houlbrooke, ' "Public" and "Private" in the Funerals of the Later Stuart Gentry: Some Somerset Examples', *Mortality*, 1 (1996), 163–76.

on mourning or on the gloves, scarves, rings, and scutcheons which had largely replaced it as gifts to guests approached 75 per cent of the total cost of £88. 2*s*. 0*d*. Yet the numbers of items of mourning given out on this occasion were comparatively modest. At the funeral of Sir William Blackett III in 1728, 157 rings were distributed, 238 scarves, and 1,886 pairs of gloves. After Samuel Pepys's death in 1703, 123 rings of three different prices were distributed to relatives, servants, friends, and colleagues.[62]

Three gallons of sherry sack, 10 gallons of port wine, 264 cakes, and 19 pounds of 'biscake' were bought in for Colonel Phelips's funeral, but much of the food and drink was presumably produced on the estate. The skill of a herald painter of the sort whose activities the college of arms was so anxious to control was sufficient to supply scutcheons for the sum of £8. 10*s*. He also loaned the velvet pall for £2. A shilling dole was sent to the houses of fifty-eight poor persons of Montacute and Odcombe, chosen with the advice of the ministers of those parishes.

In 1707 Mrs Anne Phelips, granddaughter of the colonel, died at the age of 20. Some anonymous instructions concerning the conduct of her funeral reception are permeated with a concern for decorum even stronger than that evident on the occasion of the colonel's funeral in 1680. The tenants were to be admitted two by two, and the better sort (who were to be taken into the parlour with the bearers) were to be given wine and ale, the ordinary sort beer or cider. Drink was to be strictly rationed. The servants were instructed to be grave and composed, and as far as possible to 'hinder all indecent mirth & noise in others'. They were to 'turn out all Children & Rable'. Only two senior guests were to be allowed to smoke.[63]

Another set of very detailed private accounts relates to the Greswolds, a family of lower station than the Phelipses. A wealthy provincial clergyman, Henry Greswold, rector of Solihull (War.) lost his wife Anne, as well as a daughter and son, between 1690 and 1696. The approximate recorded costs of their funerals were £71, £40, and £52 respectively. The sum spent on Mrs Greswold's funeral matched almost exactly what Gregory King thought to be the average annual income of the families of 'eminent clergymen'. Personal mourning for the immediate family was by far the biggest single cost in each account, probably amounting to well over half the total. The next

[62] *Obsequies*, 35; *Private Correspondence and Miscellaneous Papers of Samuel Pepys, 1679–1703*, ed. J. R. Tanner (2 vols., 1926), ii. 314–17.
[63] SRO DD/PH 239.

largest (ranging from *c.*14 per cent to *c.*19 per cent) was that of rings. Sixteen were given on the occasion of Anne's funeral, similar numbers at each of the children's. Most of them went to relatives, including sisters, nephews, nieces, and cousins of Greswold's, as well as the clergy who officiated at Anne's funeral. Rather larger groups of people received gloves. £8. 3*s.* 6*d.*, quite a substantial sum, was laid out on sack, claret, and cakes at Anne's funeral. It probably sufficed to refresh at least 163 guests. Charitable provisions were made at the Greswold funerals, but their precise cost is difficult to estimate because they seem to have been in effect a mixture of dole and amnesty for bad debtors of the rector's. The accounts also include payments for a substantial amount of ringing. In his son's case, 10*s.* were paid in each parish for no fewer than seven nights' ringing at both Solihull and Yardley. The Greswold funerals were much more parish and family affairs than Colonel Phelips's. Fewer mourning gifts were distributed and no people of high rank in county society were present.[64]

A good introduction to middle-class funeral customs in London under the later Stuarts is an often quoted account by Henri Misson de Valbourg, first published in 1698. It resembles the best sociological description in its attention to details, its efforts to explain them, and its awareness of social context. Misson believed that it was among middling people that a nation's customs were 'most truly to be learn'd'. Three or four days after laying out, he thought, generally sufficed for the funeral preparations. Invitations were sent to friends and relations, sometimes by means of printed tickets. (This formality may have been due in part to a desire to discourage the attendance of casual participants drawn primarily by the hope of refreshment.) On the day of the funeral, the coffin was laid on two stools, its lid removed, and the face of the corpse uncovered, so that all might come and see it. The relations, chief mourners, and more intimate friends had a chamber to themselves, apart from the other guests. A servant handed out sprigs of rosemary, to be thrown into the grave on top of the coffin. (Symbolic of eternity, rosemary's strong scent also helped to mask the smell of putrefaction.) It was customary to give the guests something to drink, such as wine boiled with sugar and cinnamon, both before they set out for the church and after their return.

---

[64] WCRO, Greswold Family Accounts, CR 1291/289, pp. 99–112, and at the other end of the book, upside down; for Gregory King's oft-printed 'Scheme' of family incomes and expenditures for 1688 see e.g. P. Laslett, *The World We Have Lost—further explored* (1983), 32–3.

One or more beadles with their staffs of office led the procession, followed by the ministers and parish clerk. The coffin, carried by six or eight men, came next, hidden by a pall, usually hired from the parish. A white pall was used for a bachelor or maid, and for a woman who had died in childbirth. The specially invited pallbearers were generally given black or white gloves and black crepe hatbands, sometimes white silk scarves as well. The relations in close mourning, and all the guests, two and two, made up the rest of the procession.[65]

Grander London funerals, rather above the level envisaged by Misson, were distinguished by a longer lying-in-state before the funeral, the despatch of larger numbers of invitation tickets, the distribution of mourning to twenty or thirty people, and the giving of several rings and fine scarves. Many wealthy guests attended in their coaches. The livery companies to which they belonged were involved in some merchants' funerals, as in Machyn's day. Such funerals might cost £200 or more, though only a small minority of London funerals were that expensive.[66]

Surviving London and suburban probate accounts exhibited between the 1660s and 1740s allow us to penetrate below the milieu described by Misson to the lower fringe of the middling sort. The majority of the deceased were people of little property whose funerals cost under £10. Among them were a baker, a ropemaker, a victualler, a tailor, and a carpenter. The hire of a pall was frequently noted. Payments for torches or links to light people to church show that some of these funerals took place at or after dusk. Coaches and hearses, associated by Misson with the funerals of persons of quality, were sometimes hired in and around London during the early eighteenth century for funerals which cost only a few pounds. Gloves were very often given, especially to bearers and relatives, even at quite cheap London funerals. Hatbands, too, were quite frequently mentioned. However, rings and scarves were provided only at the more expensive funerals. Mourning was purchased by a small minority of probate accountants, and by them only for the immediate family. It was usually by far the most expensive item on an account, its cost sometimes exceeding that of all the other purchases. Wine, especially claret and canary, had by this period become the staple element of London funeral refreshments, as Misson's description suggests, together with biscuits and cakes. The wine was often 'burnt' and

[65] H. Misson, *Memoirs and Observations in his Travels over England* (1719), 88–93; funeral description repr. Litten, *English Way of Death*, 143–6.

[66] Misson, *Memoirs and Observations*, 93; P. Earle, *The Making of the English Middle Class: Business, Society and Family Life in London 1660–1730* (1989), 311–14.

sweetened or spiced. References to distributions for the poor are extremely rare.[67]

In 1664 the funeral of his brother Tom, an unsuccessful tailor, cost Samuel Pepys £11. 6s. Claret costing £2. 2s. 6d., a sum close to that recorded in several accounts, sufficed to refresh not far short of 150 people. Only 9s. was spent on gloves, but Samuel appears to have bought prodigious quantities of biscuit, a rather expensive confectionery, and the sizeable sum of £2. 8s. was paid in church duties because Tom was buried inside the church. The service took place in the evening, and a small group of kinsfolk and friends went back for a good supper afterwards. This was an appropriate funeral for a lower ranking member of the middling sort.[68]

London probate accounts reflect the rise of the undertakers, who appear in them in rapidly increasing numbers after about 1720. By the 1730s most funerals were wholly or partially entrusted to them. The use of the term 'undertaker' to describe somebody who made a business of supplying funerals, first noted towards the end of the seventeenth century, was sufficiently well established by 1701 for an undertaker to be made the butt of satire in Steele's *The Funeral*. Engaging an undertaker offered two principal advantages: first, provision by one supplier of goods or services previously available only from various sources; secondly, the possibility of saving time and money, above all by hiring rather than purchase. It had long been customary to hire hangings and palls. Undertakers greatly extended this principle: they came to supply, for relatively modest fees, the use of mourning-garb, of funeral coaches and hearses, and the services of a wide range of professional attendants. It was claimed as early as 1698 that undertakers enabled 'persons of ordinary rank' to have as impressive a funeral for the outlay of £50 as the upper classes had formerly done at the expense of more than £500. However, by encouraging such aspirations on the part of their clients, they probably increased the funeral expenditure of the middle ranks of society.[69]

---

[67] GL MSS 9182/2 (i); 9183; 9185/1–7; 9186/1, 4. These miscellaneous papers, mostly relating to cases in the bishop's commissary's court, unsorted at the time of examination, include nearly 150 executors' or administrators' accounts dating from between the 1660s and the 1740s and used in this analysis. All specify total funeral costs, a substantial majority specify some of the things the money was spent on or name the undertaker engaged to conduct the funeral. Further accounts survive among the records of the court of the archdeacon of London.

[68] Pepys, *Diary*, v. 90–1.

[69] R. Steele, *The Funeral: or, Grief A-la-Mode*, in id., *The Plays of Richard Steele*, ed. S. S. Kenny (Oxford, 1971), 25–9 (see p. 29 for virgins to stand around the corpse of a

The herald painter William Russell, one of the earliest undertakers, arranged in 1689 that heralds would, in return for a fee, attend funerals he organized. The coffin-makers, whose trade Russell had added to his own, also moved into undertaking. One of them, William Grinley, active in the early years of the eighteenth century, supplied 'as well the meanest as those of greater Ability' with all sorts of funeral accessories. The tradesmen who appear to have been most successful in taking over the management of large-scale funerals were, however, the upholders (upholsterers and dealers in furniture).[70]

Only gradually did London funeral fashions spread to the provinces. In later Stuart Berkshire, far less was spent on funerals than in the metropolis. The average yeoman's funeral cost about £5, a craftsman's just under £4, a husbandman's about £3. 10s. Payments for bell-ringing and sermons appear in several accounts. Beer was still a far more popular drink for funerals among husbandmen and craftsmen than the more genteel wine. It washed down bread and meat as well as cakes. It is in connection with the funerals of such people as traders, victuallers, innkeepers, and professional men, many of whom lived in towns, that we find several payments for gloves, and occasional ones for hatbands and scarves. These things, let alone mourning, seem seldom to have been mentioned in accounts relating to the funerals of members of rural society below the level of the gentry.[71]

Doles appear in very few of the Berkshire accounts of the later Stuart period. However, John Cannon (b. 1684), the son of a well-to-do Somerset yeoman, described how an older tradition of hospitality and largesse survived alongside newer fashions in the funerals of his kinsfolk in the early eighteenth century. When his uncle Walter was

woman who had died in childbirth, cf. SRO DD/PH 239); Litten, *English Way of Death*, 163.

[70] Wagner, *Heralds*, 302–3; Litten, *English Way of Death*, 17–25. Litten regards William Boyce (see his trade card, ibid. 17) as 'the first recorded person trading as an undertaker'. For the 1722 attempt to form a 'United Company of Undertakers' see ibid. 22–3. Funerals organized or largely supplied by the upholders included those of the Hon. John Egerton Esq., 1707 (BL MS Harley 1529, fo. 75), the earl of Suffolk, 1722 (Bristol Record Office, AC/F9/2a), the duke of Richmond and Lennox, 1723 (Steer, 'Funeral Account', 157), and Lord Brooke, 1727 (WCRO CR 1886/TN 234, voucher no. 3). See also P. Fritz, 'The Undertaking Trade in England: Its Origins and Early Development, 1660–1830', *Eighteenth-Century Studies*, 28 (1994–5), 241–53. Fritz argues that Randle Holme was acting as an undertaker before Russell.

[71] BRO D/A1/37; 56–8; 63; 66; 68–9; 80–1; 87; 102; 107; 113; 120–2; 128; 137; 174; 178–9; 183–4; 187–90; 192; 196–204; 206; 208–9; 211; 214–15; 218–19; 222–5 (executors' and administrators' accounts): 303 accounts which specify both the deceased's status and the cost of the funeral have been found in these files; of these 73 give further details of how the money was spent. Post-1710 Berkshire accounts are far fewer and less informative.

buried in 1715, rich and poor flocked to the funeral from all parts. The poor received alms of bread and money, besides the broth and meat they ate in the yard of the dead man's house. Hatbands and gloves were distributed to relations and special friends. 'In Short there was great Entertainment & good Management.'[72] The probate account of Katherine Browne of Charlton Mackrell (1712) provides another example of Somerset hospitality, albeit on a smaller scale. £2. 7s. 6d., well over a third of her sister's recorded disbursements on her funeral, were for food and drink, including cake, bread, cheese, meat, beer, cider, sugar, and spice.[73]

However, new fashions spread even into remoter areas. The diarist Roger Lowe noticed the serving of wine and biscuits at one Lancashire funeral as early as 1664. Oliver Heywood, attending a lady's funeral near Halifax in 1673, remarked upon the fact that the invited guests had nothing during a five-hour wait 'but a bit of cake, draught of wine, peece of Rosemary, and paire of gloues', contrary to the custom of their country. Heywood, despite his disapproval of excessive funeral conviviality, seems to have noted the displeasure of 'our people' with a certain sympathy.[74]

Much more copious evidence concerning pauper funerals survives in the overseers' accounts kept after 1660 than from earlier years. Study of their contents suggests five general conclusions. First, there was a marked tendency for the overseers to shoulder an increasing proportion of poor persons' burial expenses as time went by. Secondly, the costs of pauper burial to the ratepayers rose everywhere. During the early eighteenth century the total was likely to be between 10s. and £1, and in some places well over £1. Thirdly, however, they remained a tiny fraction of the overseers' overall disbursements. At Ashburton in Devon, where payments totalled just under £160 in 1690–1, just over £312 in 1730, burial costs rose from

---

[72] 'Doles at Funeralls were continued at Gentlemens-funeralls in the West of England till the Civil-warre' (Aubrey, *Remaines*, 180); SRO, MS autobiography of John Cannon, 129. Gloves, scarves, and rings were distributed at the funeral of his cousin Mary in 1706. When Cannon's own son died in 1718, there was a 'Small yet decent Collation'. He gave 'knotts & gloves to 6 young virgins that were the bearers & gloves to some friends' (SRO, MS autobiography of Cannon, 61, 143).

[73] SRO, Administrators' Accounts, D/D/Ct, B 66.

[74] *The Diary of Roger Lowe of Ashton-in-Makerfield, Lancashire, 1663–1674*, ed. W. L. Sachse (1938), 66 (cf. his expression of disappointment at meagre fare on p. 82); Heywood, *Autobiography, Diaries*, i. 351. Thomas Turner, a Sussex shopkeeper who acted as a supplier of funerals in the 1750s and 1760s, barely mentioned their convivial aspect: *The Diary of Thomas Turner 1754–1765*, ed. D. Vaisey (Oxford, 1985), 367 (index, s.v. 'funerals' for all references).

1.5 to 2 per cent of the whole. Fourthly, parishes always varied greatly in their generosity, especially in their readiness to meet such incidental expenses as the costs of food. Several payments for bread and beer 'for the people' were made at Fillongley in Warwickshire during the later Stuart period. In a number of cases cheese, in one butter, were also recorded, and the cost of the refreshment sometimes exceeded 6s. Two shillings' or half a crown's worth of beer was provided for some funerals at West Wycombe (Bucks.) in the 1720s. Elsewhere, however, refreshments were restricted to those directly involved in laying out, bearing, or gravedigging; or not recorded at all. The ringing of the bell for a pauper's funeral was mentioned in some accounts but not others. Finally, there are signs from around the middle of the eighteenth century that some overseers, after a period of large increases in total disbursements, were trying to curb the expense of pauper funerals along with other costs of poor relief.[75]

CONCLUSION

Intercession for the souls of the departed was the main purpose of the medieval Church's funerary rites. The manner of burial also showed appropriate solicitude for mortal remains which had until very recently housed a Christian soul and would ultimately be reunited with it. St Augustine had given a rather austere, oft-paraphrased answer to a colleague's questions about the care to be taken of the dead. Only those who had lived well could benefit from intercessory prayer. Care taken in burial was of no benefit whatever to the dead, but it comforted the living, who hoped that their bodies would receive like compassion in their turn. However, despite Augustine's

---

[75] These impressions are based on the following overseers' accounts. (The years specified are ones selected for analysis from very full accounts or the only ones for which expenditure on pauper burials is recorded in less informative ones. Document reference numbers are in bibliography.) (1) Berks.: Abingdon, 1730; Aston Tirrold, 1714–39; Beenham, 1701–9; Brimpton, 1705–51; Buckland, 1660–6, 1693–1724; Cookham, 1730–9; Cumnor, 1654–84; Shellingford, 1717–18; Woolhampton, 1714–40; (2) Bucks.: Marlow, 1648–9, 1660–1, 1665–6, 1670–1, 1677–8, 1680–1, 1690–1, 1700–1, 1706–7; West Wycombe, 1714–15, 1720–1, 1730–1; (3) Devon: Ashburton, 1680–1, 1690–1, 1700–1, 1710–11, 1720–1, 1730–1, 1741–2; Chudleigh, 1660–1, 1671–2, 1681–2, 1690–1, 1730–1, 1740–1; Hennock, 1651, 1660, 1670, 1680, 1691, 1733, 1734, 1740, 1749, 1750; (4) Norfolk: Breckles, 1649–50, 1661–2, 1705–6; Guestwick, 1664–5, 1689–90; Hilgay, 1672–3, 1679–80, 1688–9, 1704–5; Norwich St John Maddermarket, 1660–1, 1680–1, 1690–1, 1701–2, 1711–13; Wighton 1656–9, 1671–2, 1681–2, 1700–1, 1710–11, 1712–13; (5) Warwickshire: Fillongley, 1657–1712; Kenilworth, 1650–1741.

view, funerals were generally seen as a means of discharging obligations to the dead.[76]

The presence of the corpse acted as a reminder of the soul which
had inhabited it. Though hidden from view, it was physically at the
centre of the rites.[77] In great funerals its centrality was underlined by
the bed of state, the chariot, the hearse, and the offering of palls.
Catholic rites harnessed the power of the complicated feelings
aroused by mortal remains to the constructive action of intercessory
prayer. To assist this process was one purpose of the lifelike effigies
of kings and noblemen carried in funeral procession long after their
corpses had been wrapped in lead. Thus the effigy of Henry V was
raised where everybody could see it 'that by this means mourning and
grief might grow and his friends and subjects might the more kindly
beseech the Lord on his soul's behalf'.[78] In this instance, the deliberate encouragement of grief was held to be legitimate even in a Christian context, provided that it was then channelled into prayer for the
dead. Grief in bereavement was formally expressed by the dress and
comportment of mourning. These served, like so many elements of
ritual, to control and direct an excess of feeling in some people, while
making up for a lack of it in others, emphasizing the unity of those
joining in the rite.

The Reformation removed all but the slightest traces of intercessory prayer from the burial service. However, funerals still served to
discharge important duties to the dead, according to Richard Hooker:
'first to shew that love towards the party deceased which nature
requireth; then to do him that honour which is fit both generally for
man and particularly for the quality of his person'. The dead still lived
in the minds of survivors. The epistle dedicatory to a sermon delivered at a lady's funeral in 1639 could claim that 'she being dead, yet
liveth in our affections and memory'. Honouring the memory of the
dead was always acknowledged to be one of the chief functions of
funerals and explicitly justified by means of comparison with other
times and cultures. It may be that from St Augustine's own perspective, or that of modern psychology, such shows of honour met the
needs of survivors, not the dead, but this was not how it seemed to

---

[76] St Augustine, *De Cura gerenda pro Mortuis*, in id., *Œuvres*, ii. *Problèmes
Moraux*, ed. G. Combès (Paris, 1948), 464–8, 488–90.

[77] Sometimes it had to be buried before the funeral, but the ceremony was still conducted as if it were present. For the burial of Roger Cave some weeks before his funeral
at Stamford in 1586, see Bod. Lib. MS Ashmole 836, p. 111. Cf. Gittings, *Death*, 167,
230, for funerals centring on effigies when burial had already taken place.

[78] Quoted in Cunnington and Lucas, *Costume*, 143.

contemporaries. The reputation of the dead survived their physical extinction, and it was above all this, their 'credit', which was nurtured or damaged by the manner in which the funeral was performed. A Lancashire minister, Adam Martindale, wrote of his yeoman father's funeral as if it were a recompense for his paternal kindness. Considering 'how good a father he had beene', his children 'thought it convenient to bring him home handsomely out of his owne'.[79]

From the later Middle Ages to the eighteenth century there were always some testators who requested that they be buried without unnecessary pomp and expense, but ideas about what constituted a simple yet acceptable funeral varied greatly. Edward Colston, a wealthy Bristol merchant (d. 1721), requested a funeral without the least pomp yet left detailed directions which would cost well over £200 to implement. Literal fulfilment of a great person's request for a simple burial could arouse unfavourable comment, as happened when the dowager Queen Elizabeth of York was buried in 1492. Quite explicit instructions were necessary to protect the executors from a charge of parsimony. Henry Selleck, gentleman, of West Monkton (Som.) made his wishes absolutely plain when in 1741 he left instructions that none of his family were to buy or wear any mourning. He had often seen it worn 'and could not find that the Pagentry of a Funeral amounted to anything more than a Black farce'.[80]

In some societies, failure to carry out the appropriate funeral rites is held to invite retribution from the unquiet dead. Unless these rites are properly implemented the integration of the newly deceased into the community of the departed cannot take place. The medieval Church encouraged to some extent the belief that apparitions or visions of those in purgatory might haunt survivors, especially those who had shown indifference to their welfare, but there were no theological grounds for believing that the soul might be trapped in the vicinity of the body. Debased or distorted interpretations of Christian doctrines nevertheless underlay such customs as the giving of alms to the sin-eater. This was designed to benefit both the living and the dead, protecting the former from the unwanted visitations of the latter.[81]

---

[79] Hooker, *Laws*, ii. 152; *An Elegie upon The much lamented Death, of . . . Elizabeth Hoyle* (York, 1644), 8; Hearne, *Curious Discourses*, i. 205; *The Life of Adam Martindale, written by himself*, ed. R. Parkinson (Chetham Soc., os 4; 1845), 119–20.

[80] Litten, *English Way of Death*, 121–3; BL MS Arundel 26, fos. 29ᵛ–30ᵛ; SRO DD/SAS c/127 6/3.

[81] A. Van Gennep, *Rites of Passage*, trans. M. B. Vizedom and G. L. Caffee (1960), 160–4; R. C. Finucane, *Appearances of the Dead: A Cultural History of Ghosts* (1982),

Funeral solemnities helped survivors in various ways. The Protestant reformers emphasized their spiritual advantages. The living were compelled to confront the fact of death, reminded to prepare for their own ends, and given Christian hopes and consolations. Psychological benefits included the opportunity of activity, and the solace of discharging a duty to the dead. Even in the depths of her grief, Lady Warwick could write in 1673 with some satisfaction of having buried her husband 'decently and honourably'. Yet a funeral could also exacerbate grief. Around 1619 his wife's death left Sir Thomas Hutchinson 'the most desolate afflicted widower that ever was beheld'. His brother-in-law, judging that the prolongation of the household's sorrow during the preparation of the intended, presumably elaborate, funeral, 'might possibly have made them all as she' arranged a private interment for her the very next morning without Sir Thomas's knowledge. Some individuals perhaps benefited from immersion in funeral work, while others did not.[82] There was wisdom in customs which shielded a surviving marriage partner from too close an involvement.[83]

The reputation of survivors depended upon their burying the dead properly. Throughout this period, funerals which fell short of what observers thought appropriate to the status of the deceased attracted unfavourable comment. Mrs Phelips wanted to avoid vain expense when she planned her husband's funeral in 1680, but nevertheless consulted her eldest son so that his credit might be upheld. With a similar eye to both economy and reputation, Adam Martindale commented in 1658 that some funerals had cost twice as much as his father's, without being so creditable to those who paid for them. A family's ability to bury their dead in appropriate fashion helped to secure their standing in the eyes of the community.[84]

The effective fulfilment of funerals' functions usually depended upon the readiness of a sizeable group of people to take part. It was the funerals of the poor, the outcast, recluses, and misers which were attended by a handful of participants. The appearance of neighbours, kinsfolk, and members of the deceased's craft or profession at the funeral, their donning of mourning-garb or tokens, and their

---

60-82; Thomas, *Religion*, 701-24; Duffy, *Stripping of Altars*, 355-6; Aubrey, *Remaines*, 176-80.

[82] Hooker, *Laws*, ii. 152; BL MS Add. 27353, fo. 221^v; L. Hutchinson, *Memoirs of the Life of Colonel Hutchinson, with the Fragment of an Autobiography of Mrs Hutchinson*, ed. J. Sutherland (1973), 20; cf. Whitelocke, *Diary*, 239.

[83] Willan, *Eliah's wish*, sig. A3^v.

[84] SRO DD/PH 238, fo. 204^v; Martindale, *Life*, 120.

participation in funeral ritual, expressed their sharing in the bereaved's sense of loss and their support for the surviving family. It was some consolation to Adam Martindale to know that his daughter was 'so well beloved among the young women of the parish, that though she died almost a mile from the church, and the way very foule, they would not suffer any man to carrie her bodie a foote, but conveyed her on their owne shoulders to her grave'. Ralph Josselin derived a similar solace from the fact that the two 'gravest matrons' of his parish laid his infant son in the earth. Very often the attendance of appropriate numbers of participants at a funeral not only marked respect for the dead but also functioned as a means of assuring the surviving family of continued countenance or support.[85]

Those who joined the family or the household of prominent individuals in the celebration of their obsequies also received benefits. Confirmation of a continuing relationship and acknowledgement of acquaintance were high among them. Mourning-dress and gifts distinguished degrees of closeness to the dead and his or her surviving heirs. The colossal quantities of mourning-garb dispensed at the funerals of medieval magnates were symbolic of the reciprocal bond of good lordship and support between their line and their 'friends', servants, retainers, and tenants. As the desiccated husk of neo-feudal heraldic solemnities ceased to reflect social needs and realities, 'blacks' came increasingly to be replaced by other, less expensive yet finely graded tokens of friendship and regard. Such gifts made numerous and visible distinctions among the participants. It was only too easy to offend by failing to give a person the recognition which he felt appropriate to his relationship or social status. One reason for Henry Selleck's 1741 prohibition of any sort of mourning at his own funeral was his experience of funerals where 'after utmost care taken' many had felt affronted none the less.[86] Funerals increasingly came to reflect wealth and personal choice rather than the deceased individual's precise position in the social hierarchy. The private funeral of the wealthy was more readily imitable by the middling sort than heraldic obsequies had been. The rise of the undertaker facilitated imitation and fostered emulation. The pattern of the genteel funeral spread outwards from the greater towns and down the social scale.

Hospitality and charity were the other benefits dispensed at funerals. A plentiful feast and large quantities of drink to refresh those who had taken the trouble to attend were long seen as appropriate

---

[85] Martindale, *Life*, 206; Josselin, *Diary*, 114.
[86] SRO DD/SAS c/127 6/3.

recompense. The dead, through their representatives, entertained their friends for the last time. Abundant refreshment of the guests at their funerals was specifically requested by some people before they died. It was the oft-repeated wish of John Berdel (d. 1746), a member of the London Huguenot community, that 'as he was an old Batchelor his Friends should keep his Wedding and Burying together'.[87] This they did at a convivial supper.

Almsgiving at later medieval funerals was designed to assist the departed soul, both as a good work meritorious in itself and by securing the prayers of beneficiaries. The prayers of the honest poor were particularly highly valued. Despite the reformers' repudiation of intercessory prayers, funeral doles became more common among the middling ranks of society in the later sixteenth century. However, funeral charity subsequently declined as a result of a growing conviction that the soul could not benefit from funeral alms, coupled with the development of an increasingly reliable system of poor relief. The participation of poor people in the funeral procession came to seem anachronistic. Social polarization and growing concern for decorous behaviour at funerals made for the gradual separation of the poor from other participants and their ultimate exclusion. In the exchange of benefits at funerals, the poor no longer had anything to offer.[88]

[87] GL MS 9185/7 (unfoliated), 15 Jan. 1748, deposition of James Maze, answer to eighth interrogatory.

[88] SRO DD/PH 238, fo. 203ᵛ; *Historical Register*, 21/81 (1736), 75.

10

Funeral Sermons

Such Commemoration was the good old way of the Primitive Church . . . restored at the Reformation into serious and rational Discourses, still fit to be retain'd as good *Words in Season*, as the *Dead yet speaking*, when the apparent Object of Mortality strikes Awe and Impression on the Eyes and Hearts of Men; and the greater the *Object*, the greater the *Impression*. Whence then came a modern way of interring our deceased Fathers (especially those of the highest Fortune and Figure) in an affected Secrecy and Silence, with no Praises of the Dead, no Instructions to the Living? Is it, that some modest People have forbid that Office, for fear of being flatter'd? Is it, that some Preachers have exceeded in Commendations and Characters beyond Truth and Decorum? Or has not that late Omission been rather a Love of Novelty and Change; the dropping a Custom because it was antient, and the affecting new Modes, not in manner of Life only, but in that of Death and Burial? Or has it been sometimes owing to a more unhappy Cause, Mens Lives and Actions not deserving, rather dreading a Memorial of them?[1]

Thus White Kennett, future bishop of Peterborough, preaching at the funeral of the duke of Devonshire in 1707. How reliable was his account of the revival of funeral sermons? Was he right in thinking that their popularity was already declining at the time when he spoke? If so, did he hit upon a persuasive explanation of this development? Under the heading of funeral sermons are counted here all sermons preached in response to the deaths of individuals. Before the Reformation, a sermon might be delivered at a mass preceding the burial, at the month's mind, or at an anniversary. During the century after the Reformation, such sermons usually, though not invariably, formed part of the order of burial, preceding the interment itself. In the eighteenth century sermons occasioned by the deaths of Protestant Dissenters were often delivered some days after the burial. Some ministers of the Established Church favoured the following Sunday.[2]

[1] W. Kennett, *A Sermon Preach'd at the Funeral of the . . . Duke of Devonshire. . . . on Friday Septemb. 5th MDCCVII* (1708), 4–5.
[2] Elizabeth Machell's desire to be buried before the sermon because she was dying of smallpox was thought worthy of a marginal note in S. Geree, *The Ornament of*

Funeral sermons were preached in England as early as the thirteenth century, though Kennett might not have considered their contents 'serious and rational'. Encouragement of the audience to pray for the soul of the dead man and to contemplate the four last things (death, judgement, heaven, and hell) were important themes of surviving medieval examples. Sermons preached at the obsequies of important men and women included praise of the deceased.[3] The earliest English funeral sermon to be printed soon after its delivery was probably the one which John Fisher preached at Henry VII's funeral in 1509. This discourse shares all the major characteristics of later funeral sermons. It is based on a biblical text, expounds doctrines suitable to the occasion, and uses the dead man's life for edification, laying particular emphasis on the deathbed. Sermons were delivered at many other funerals on the eve of the Reformation. They often included commendation of the deceased individual. Fisher himself praised the virtuous life of Henry VII's mother, the Lady Margaret, at her month's mind.[4] The funeral of the earl of Oxford in 1514 included a sermon which 'Rehersed and Righte well declared the greate virtues and Noblenes that was in the same Nobleman'. Sir Thomas More imagined the souls in purgatory regretting their waste of time and money in arranging for a learned priest to preach to their praise at their month's minds. Many other references to funeral sermons delivered under the early Tudors survive. They very often accompanied London funerals between 1550 and 1563.[4]

Women or, *A description of the true excellency of Women, Delivered in a Sermon at the Funerall of M. Elizabeth Machell* (1639), 88. The title of a sermon preached by John Graile provides one example of 18th-cent. practice: *Vigorous Longevity: or, A good old age, And the best Way, both to Attain it: and to Improve it: consider'd in a Sermon Preach'd at Hevingham in Norfolk, Sept. 25, 1720. Being the first Sunday after the Funeral of the Reverend Mr. William Heylet, late Rector of Hevingham . . .* (1720).

    [3] S. Powell and A. J. Fletcher, '"In Die Sepulture seu Trigintali": The Late Medieval Funeral and Memorial Sermon', *Leeds Studies in English*, NS 12 (1981), 195–228; D. d'Avray, 'The Comparative Study of Memorial Preaching', *Transactions of the Royal Historical Society*, 5th ser. 40 (1990), 25–42, esp. 33–4; id., *Death and the Prince: Memorial Preaching before 1350* (Oxford, 1994), esp. 222–3; *Sermon of Dead Men*, in *Lollard Sermons*, ed. G. Cigman (EETS 294; 1989), pp. xlviii–li, 207–40; *The Sermons of Thomas Brinton, Bishop of Rochester (1373–1389)* (Camden 3rd ser. 85–6; 1954), 206–9, 260–72, 280–4, 340–3.

    [4] *The English Works of John Fisher*, ed. J. E. B. Mayor (EETS extra ser. 27; 1876), 268–310; BL MS Harley 295, fo. 156; T. More, *The Supplication of Souls*, ed. G. Marc'hadour, in id., *The Complete Works of St Thomas More* (New Haven, 1963–), vii (1990), 219–20; *The Receyt of the Ladie Kateryne*, ed. G. Kipling (EETS 296; 1990), 85; T. Fortescue (Lord Clermont), *A History of the Family of Fortescue in all its Branches* (1880), 281; Bod. Lib. MS Ashmole 1109, fos. 111ʳ, 145ᵛ; *The Diary of Henry Machyn, Citizen and Merchant-Taylor of London, from A.D. 1550 to A.D. 1563*, ed. J. G. Nichols (Camden OS 42; 1848), *passim*.

After the Reformation, militant Protestants such as John Knox, Thomas Cartwright, and Henry Barrow objected to funeral sermons because of their alleged lack of scriptural warrant, debasement at Catholic hands, supposed origins in the pagan eulogy, and the temptation of flattering sinners to which they gave rise. They were said to have taken the place of intercessory masses. Such misgivings are especially understandable when sermons were preached in a series, linked with the distribution of alms and accompanied by prayers of thanks for the benefactor's bounty. Funeral sermons appeared, like intercessory masses, to benefit the dead. The priest made the dead man a better Christian in his grave than he ever had been in his life, Henry Barrow caustically remarked. In return for payment the priest would praise the rich man and assure the people of his soul's salvation, however bad a sinner he had been. Mainstream opinion within the Church of England nevertheless continued to favour the funeral sermon as a vehicle of salutary instruction for the living. Praise was to be kept in its proper place, subordinate to the explication of doctrine. It was to be confined to the truly Christian aspects of the deceased's life and death, good things wrought by God in the individual, which would also serve as examples to others. Some preachers, especially in the sixteenth century, kept their references to the deceased to a minimum, concentrating on the exposition of their text, but most published sermons of the seventeenth century include a biographical element. The foremost practitioners of the art of funeral preaching included several Puritans. As the historian of the Elizabethan funeral sermon has remarked, they appropriated this vehicle for the purpose of exhorting the faithful to imitate the saints and patriarchs of their own emergent tradition. Despite some continuing misgivings, they were often lavish in their praise of the godly. In 1635 a famous Suffolk Puritan minister, John Carter, sternly prohibited the preaching of any sermon at his own funeral, lest falsehoods be uttered from the pulpit. His redoubtable colleague Samuel Ward of Ipswich nevertheless turned his next lecture into a funeral sermon for Carter. A few years later the English delegates at the Westminster Assembly tenaciously defended the funeral sermon against Scottish attacks.[5]

[5] Greaves, *Society and Religion*, 704–6; *A view of Popishe abuses yet remaining in the Englishe Church*, pub. with *An Admonition to the Parliament*, in *Puritan Manifestoes*, ed. W. H. Frere and C. E. Douglas (1954), 28; H. Barrow, *A Brief Discoverie of the False Church* (1590), in id., *The Writings of Henry Barrow 1587–1590*, ed. L. H. Carlson (Elizabethan Nonconformist Texts, 3; 1962), 459, 461; Emmison (ed.), *Elizabethan Life*, iv. 53, 176, 185, 213, 242; *The Diary of Thomas Crosfield*, ed. F. S. Boas (Oxford, 1935), 55, 58, 60; F. B. Tromly, ' "According to Sounde Religion": The

Many funeral sermons survive in manuscript; others were noted or summarized in such sources as chronicles, diaries, or newspapers. However, our knowledge of the genre and its development depends above all on printed examples, a small fraction of the total of those actually preached. It is alas far from easy to form an accurate impression of the quantity even of printed sermons, but well over 1,300 funeral sermons preached by Anglican or Protestant Nonconformist clergy had been published by 1750, either individually or in collections. About twenty are known to have been printed during Elizabeth I's reign; by the end of the 1630s that total had risen to well over one hundred, and possibly to nearly two hundred. In 1640 a collection of forty-seven sermons was published under the title *Threnoikos. The House of Mourning*, something of a landmark. Between the appearance of *Threnoikos* and the publication of a second, expanded edition in 1660, the printing of such sermons increased rapidly. After a brief post-Restoration dip, the trend of publication soon recovered its upward path. The number of sermons published in each decade between 1680 and 1729 was well over a hundred. However, after 1700 there was a marked decline in the numbers published in each successive decade.[6]

Only a minuscule proportion of the sermons preached found their way into print. In Kent, a majority of the detailed probate accounts of the period 1601–50 include a payment for a funeral sermon, 337 sermons in all. (The accounts from Berkshire and Lincolnshire show far smaller totals, but the percentages of them which mention funeral sermons rise with each successive decade, which broadly confirms the impression given by the printed sermons.) Between 1656 and 1664 in just one parish, Horstead Keynes in Sussex, the parson, Giles Moore, recorded thirty-six funeral sermons delivered either by him or by his deputy. A local diarist noted seventy sermons preached by two incumbents of Coggeshall in Essex in just over thirty-six years between 1663 and 1699. Between 1737 and 1750 a Nonconformist

Elizabethan Controversy over the Funeral Sermon', *Journal of Medieval and Renaissance Studies*, 13 (1983), 293–312, esp. 299–305, 307–12; W. Haller, *The Rise of Puritanism* (Philadelphia, 1938), 101–2; P. Collinson, ' "A Magazine of Religious Patterns": An Erasmian Topic transposed in English Protestantism', in id., *Godly People: Essays on English Protestantism and Puritanism* (1983), 518–24; S. Clarke, *A Collection of the Lives of Ten Eminent Divines* (1662), 20; Robert Baillie to William Spong, 6 Dec. 1644, in *The Letters and Journals of Robert Baillie A.M. Principal of the University of Glasgow* (3 vols., Edinburgh, 1841–2), ii. 245.

[6] See App. 2, below, for more detailed estimates of the numbers of published funeral sermons.

Lancashire doctor, Richard Kay, heard at least twenty-six in Bury and the surrounding area.[7]

The main currents of churchmanship were well represented among the authors of printed funeral sermons. Before the Civil War, those written by Puritans outnumbered the sermons of High Churchmen, but John Buckeridge and John Donne appear on the list alongside such famous godly ministers as Thomas Gataker and Robert Harris. During the Interregnum, when the output of published funeral sermons rapidly increased, such Presbyterian divines as Simeon Ashe, Edmund Calamy, Thomas Case, and Thomas Manton all published more than one sermon. However, several sermons written by men who preferred the old Church order, like Anthony Farindon, Edward Boteler, Nathaniel Hardy, John Pearson, and Jeremy Taylor also appeared. The period between 1660 and 1714 was the heyday of the 'Anglican' funeral sermon. Known preachers, whose ranks encompassed both future nonjurors and men of Puritan background, included Francis Atterbury, Nicholas Brady, Gilbert Burnet, William Fleetwood, Anthony Horneck, Thomas Ken, Richard Kidder, John Lake, William Lloyd, Thomas Manningham, Simon Patrick, John Scott, William Sherlock, and John Tillotson. After 1662 the flow of published sermons from the pens of Protestant Nonconformists was sharply reduced. However, well over a third of those which appeared during the thirty years after the Toleration Act of 1689 had been delivered by Dissenting ministers. Thereafter, Nonconformist sermons made up an ever-increasing majority of a shrinking total; by 1741–50 their numerical preponderance was overwhelming. So far as the Established Church was concerned, the printing of funeral sermons declined sharply after about 1720, but their delivery had by no means ceased. Several funerals attended by the Sussex diarist Thomas Turner between 1754 and 1765 included them.[8]

The social composition of the group of people commemorated in printed funeral sermons changed markedly between the era before the Civil Wars and the first half of the eighteenth century. Well over a third of the sermons printed up to 1640 had been preached at the funerals of individuals of knightly or higher status, and a similar

---

[7] C. Gittings, *Death, Burial and the Individual in Early Modern England* (1984), 240; *The Journal of Giles Moore*, ed. R. Bird (Sussex Record Soc. 68; 1971), 336–8; G. F. Beaumont, *A History of Coggeshall, in Essex with an Account of its Church, Abbey, Manors, Ancient Houses &c* (1890), 220–5 (recorded by Joseph Bufton); Kay, *Diary*, 7–163.

[8] *The Diary of Thomas Turner 1754–1765*, ed. D. Vaisey (Oxford, 1985), 7, 24, 75, 77, 99, 101, 184, 223, 278.

proportion at the funerals of women,[9] but only about 10 per cent at those of clergymen. A much larger proportion of the sermons printed between 1701 and 1750 had been preached at the funerals of clergy than had been the case up to 1640, much smaller ones at those of women and members of the upper classes. These changes were linked with the decline of the printed funeral sermon outside the Dissenting minority. The leaders of the Dissenting churches were the ministers and their lay associates, few of whom belonged to the substantial gentry. There may have been less opportunity for eighteenth-century Nonconformist women to shine with exceptional brightness than there had been in gentry families of an earlier epoch, when many ladies had assumed as their especial responsibility the task of maintaining household godliness. The funeral sermon's loss of favour among the upper classes and members of the Established Church, remarked upon by White Kennett in 1707, is increasingly apparent in eighteenth-century printed sermons.

The people for whom sermons were delivered but not printed were a far larger and socially more heterogeneous group than those whose sermons were published. At Coggeshall between 1663 and 1699 this group included several clothiers (who belonged to the upper ranks of small town society), a number of farmers, four carpenters, two lawyers, two butchers, an innholder, a maltster, a barber, a retired shopkeeper, and several wives, widows, and offspring of members of the town's upper and middle strata. The people whose funeral sermons were heard by Thomas Turner in the 1750s and 1760s belonged to the middle ranks of rural society.[10] A sermon cost money. The considerable income which the English clergy derived from funeral sermons was mentioned by one Scotsman as a reason for their reluctance to give them up in the 1640s.[11] The going rate for the gentry of Elizabethan Essex was 6s. 8d. or 10s., for later Stuart Londoners about £1, for the Berkshire middling sort of the same period 10s. Even though the price of a sermon does not seem to have kept pace with inflation, it was still a luxury for the majority of the population.[12]

The preacher of a funeral sermon was usually the minister of the parish of burial or the Dissenting congregation to which the deceased

[9] J. L. McIntosh, 'English Funeral Sermons 1560–1640: The Relationship between Gender and Death, Dying, and the Afterlife', M. Litt. thesis (Oxford, 1990), 1, 205–11.

[10] Beaumont, *History of Coggeshall*, 220–5; Turner, *Diary*, 7, 24, 99, 223, 278, 326, 334, 335, 339.

[11] Baillie, *Letters and Journals*, ii. 245.

[12] Emmison (ed.), *Elizabethan Life*, iv. 26, 53, 56*, 77, 82, 87, 102, 106*, 176, 185, 213, 230, 242*, 274, 281, 300* (bequests of £1 per sermon asterisked); GL MSS: 9185/1

person had belonged. Members of the gentry were, however, sometimes able to choose from one of several ministers happy to oblige them by discharging this important duty, and testators quite often specified favoured ministers in their wills. Edmund Hall admitted that some people had been annoyed by his being chosen to preach the Lady Anne Harcourt's funeral sermon in 1664. It was the first sermon of this kind he had ever composed. He had not sought the honour, but had been unable to refuse it. 'Many might have done it with greater skill and parts, but none with stronger affection.'[13]

Hall's words remind us that it would be a mistake to see the opportunity of preaching a funeral sermon simply as a favour bestowed upon a clergyman by a customer or patron. A warm tribute or eloquent words of consolation from a respected pastor were highly valued. Funeral sermons were paid for, but the careful composition and genuine affection for the dead which distinguish the best of them could not be bought. Many of the claims prefacing the printed versions of sermons that the writers wished to commemorate the deceased or encourage others to follow their example were no doubt sincere. While some preachers, like Edmund Hall, mentioned their admiration or affection for the dead person in especially warm terms, a desire to console a respected friend or patron was also an explicit motive of great importance. Many prefaces and epistles dedicatory expressed sympathy with the bereaved. Anthony Walker, who preached at the funeral of the earl of Warwick in 1673, described with strong feeling the countess's patience in tending her husband during his prolonged illnesses.[14]

(Joseph Fletcher, John Utting); 9186/1 (Edward Baker); BRO D/A1/174/78a; D/A1/178/109c, 167a, 193; D/A1/184/31c; D/A1/187/51c, 75a; D/A1/188/82c; D/A1/196/143c; D/A1/197/73c; D/A1/204/111a; D/A1/208/135b. £1 was paid for the sermon at Col. Edward Phelips's funeral in 1680 (SRO DD/PH 238, fo. 200), but 10 guineas (really £10.15s.) in the case of Lord Brooke in 1677 (WCRO CR 1886/TN 185, no. 4). The minister or parson's blacks may sometimes have been intended in part as recompense for the funeral sermon: see e.g. Emmison (ed.), *Elizabethan Life*, iv. 44; *Mrs Elizabeth Freke her Diary 1671–1714*, ed. M. Carbery (Cork, 1913), 69. Thomas Wilson (d. 1651) was remarkable for preaching 'at diverse Funerals, yea, though the Person interred were so poor that nothing could be expected for his pains'; S. Clarke, *The Lives of Sundry Eminent Persons in this Later Age* (2 pts. in 1 vol., 1683), i. 20.

[13] Emmison (ed.), *Elizabethan Life*, iv. 25, 26, 44, 176, 213, 242, 274, 281, 300; E. Hall, *A Sermon Preached at Stanton-Harcourt Church. . . . At the Funerall of the Honourable the Lady Ann Harcourt* (Oxford, 1664), sig. A2[r-v]; S. Ashe, *Gray Hayres crowned with Grace, A Sermon Preached . . . At the Funerall of Mr. Thomas Gataker* (1655), 39; T. Bradbury, *Winning Christ, and being found in him, considered: In two Sermons on the Death of the Reverend Mr. Robert Bragge* (1738), 26.

[14] A. Walker, *Leez Lachrymans, sive Comitis Warwici Justa: A Sermon, Delivered at the Funeral of the Right Honourable Charles, Earl of Warwick* (1673), sig. A2[v].

Most prefaces and epistles dedicatory of printed sermons for lay people were addressed to surviving close relatives of the deceased, and to widows and widowers in particular. Sermons for deceased clergymen were often dedicated to their parishioners or members of their congregations. Several writers attributed publication to the request of the dedicatees. Surviving spouses headed the list. Publication was often seen as a means of commemorating the deceased. Henry Crosse, merchant of Barnstaple, acknowledged this motive in the foreword which he wrote for the sermon preached at his wife's funeral in 1628. He pictured himself like Jacob erecting a pillar upon the grave of his beloved Rachel. Preachers were not (if we may believe their own testimony) always willing to comply with such requests. Some claimed that publication of their work had been 'wrung' or 'wrested' from them. Henry Crosse 'at length' prevailed upon the preacher of his wife's funeral sermon, 'deliuered vpon a short warning (the speaker limited both for time and Text)' to make it public.[15]

For many writers, however, the publication of their work offered a welcome opportunity of expressing gratitude to the deceased or their relatives. Thus Barnaby Potter, preacher at Totnes, acknowledged in 1613 the way in which Sir Edward Giles and his wife had fetched him from university and harboured him in their house ever since with extraordinary kindness, countenanced his ministry and continually frequented the preaching of the Word. In 1723 the Nonconformist minister Joshua Bayes published at the common request of his congregation the funeral sermon he had preached for his predecessor at Leather Lane. It was an opportunity (he wrote) of acknowledging the many favours he had received from them, and in particular their speedy and unanimous choice of him to succeed the dead man. Some preachers clearly hoped that publication would help to secure the continued favour of patrons and supporters. John Barlow, for example, dedicating a sermon to Lady Margaret Hele of Winbury (Devon) in 1618, explained that only people of her 'Worth, Ranke, and Profession' could defend the Word and ministry from the malicious attacks so often made on them. The printing of funeral sermons

---

[15] W. Crompton, *A lasting jewell, for religious woemen. In the summe of a sermon, preached at the funerall of mistris Mary Crosse of Barnestaple and now published with some additions* (1630), sig. A2; B. Spencer, *Aphonologos. A Dumb Speech, Or, A Sermon made, but no Sermon preached, at the Funerall of . . . Mrs Mary Overman* (1646), unpag. leaf of epistle dedicatory, A4^v; J. Phillips, *The way to heaven* (1625), sig. A3; J. Warren, *Domus ordinata. A funerall sermon, preached in Bristoll, at the buriall of mistresse Needes* (1618), sig. A2.

may sometimes have furthered ministers' careers by bringing their talents to the attention of a larger audience, but the strengthening of existing relationships was probably more important.[16]

Authors occasionally admitted that publication had been their own idea. Some of them had preached at the funerals of their own wives, children, or other relatives. In 1630 Thomas Williamson dedicated to his father-in-law the 'little pillar' with which he hoped to perpetuate his wife's memory. Warm friendship between colleagues was another reason for taking the initiative. In 1692 the Nonconformist minister Edward Dent declared that he himself had decided to publish his funeral sermon for 'that Faithful, Famous, Pious & Godly Christian' Mr William Baker for the use and benefit of Dent's 'dear Relations', and Baker's neighbours and friends. (Hinted at here is a desire to strengthen the morale and *esprit de corps* of Dissenting congregations which may have been the most important motive for the vast increase in the numbers of published Nonconformist sermons during the decades following the Toleration Act.) The publication of funeral sermons was also inspired to some extent by the desire to make salutary doctrine and instruction more widely available. The explicit intention of the 'Reverend Divines' who published forty-seven funeral sermons under the title *Threnoikos* in 1640 was to provide 'directions to guide' their readers and 'comforts to support' them, rather than to commemorate the individuals, few of them named, for whom the sermons had originally been preached. In 1693 James Ellesby prefaced a sermon inspired by the deathbed repentance of a dissolute young man with a letter to his Chiswick parishioners. Ill health had prevented the pastoral visits to their homes which he should have made. He hoped that his printed sermon would go some way to make good that omission. He aimed it in particular at those many parishioners who seldom or never came to church, or (if they did) took little notice of what they heard there. Other sermons were published posthumously, as a tribute to a preacher's memory, often in a collection of his works. 'He being dead, yet speaketh in his Sermon', one epistle dedicatory said of the author.[17]

---

[16] B. Potter, *The baronets buriall, or a funerall sermon at Sr Edward Seymours buriall* (Oxford, 1613), sig. A2; J. Bayes, *A Funeral Sermon occasioned by the Death of the late Reverend Mr. Christopher Taylor* (1723), pref. (unpag.); Barlow, *Hierons last fare-well. A sermon* (1618), sig. A2–3.

[17] T. Williamson, *A comfortable meditation of humane frailtie, and divine mercie: in two sermons* (1630), sig. A2^v; E. Dent, *Everlasting Blessedness. A Sermon preached at The Funerall of . . . Mr. William Baker . . . the 14th. Day of October, 1691* (1692), sig. A2; *Threnoikos. The house of mourning, Delivered in XLVII sermons,*

Published funeral sermons differed from the much greater number of unprinted ones in certain respects. A much higher proportion of those which found their way into print commemorated people distinguished by their social status or their exemplary lives and deaths. Many published sermons probably underwent revision and enlargement between delivery and publication. One preacher, Robert Harris, candidly admitted as much in respect of the sermon he preached for Sir Anthony Cope in 1614. He had been unable fully to develop his themes at the time 'by reason of haste, being tied to an houre'. (Most printed sermons of the early seventeenth century are too long to have been delivered in an hour, though eighteenth-century ones tend to be much briefer.) However, some sermons had not been revised, either because of the preacher's refusal to publish his own work or (in one case) because the only available text had been taken down 'from the Authors mouth, by the pen of a ready writer'.[18]

Some printed sermons convey a vivid impression of the circumstances of their delivery. About halfway through the eighty-seven-page text of the sermon which Anthony Anderson preached at Robert Keylwey's funeral in 1581 comes the admission that the first part of what he intended to say has taken all his allotted time. 'But in asmuch as your ciuill solemnities [i.e. the heraldic ceremonies] aske more tyme, then possibly the forenoone woulde afforde vs, I will deferre my seconde part till some other time, except I receiue your pleasures, farther to proceede.' But the herald at arms conveyed the leading auditors' 'godly desires' that Anderson continue with his discourse. He was less polite to other members of his large congregation, commenting acidly on 'this huge heape of people'. He exhorted those of 'the greater sort' to take care that they did not come to hear God's Word only for such considerations as 'ciuility or neiborly courtesie'. As for the greatest number, he continued, they had been inspired by covetousness. They had come in hope of a dole. Anderson warned those responsible to guard against the danger that the wicked might

preached at funeralls (1640), leaf following sig. A4; J. Ellesby, *The Great Danger and Uncertainty of a Death-Bed Repentance* (1693), preface (unpag.); *An Elegie upon The much lamented Death, of . . . Elizabeth Hoyle* (York, 1644), 8; R. Pricke, *A verie godlie and learned sermon, treating of mans mortalitie and of the estate both of his bodie, and soule after death* (1608), Robert Allen's pref.

[18] R. Harris, *The workes . . . Revised, and in sundrie places corrected. With an addition of two sermons, not formerly extant. As also two tables* (1635), 211; W. Beerman, *Sorrow upon Sorrow: or, The much Lamented Death of the worthy Mr. Ralph Venning* (1674), sig. A2; E. Calamy, *The Doctrine of the Bodies Fragility: with A Divine Project, discovering how to make these vile bodies of ours glorious by getting gracious Souls* (1655), sig. A2ᵛ.

'father their popish prayer for the deade' upon charitable devotion to the poor.[19]

Later preachers seldom matched the severity of Anderson's tone, but some of them showed their awareness that they were addressing audiences made up of very different sorts of people, and spoke of the majority with a certain asperity. Nathaniel Parkhurst, vicar of Yoxford in Suffolk, preaching at the funeral of his Dissenting colleague Samuel Fairclough in 1691, declared that his design was to awaken careless sinners, proffer an eyesalve to the Laodiceans (i.e. improve the sight of formal, lukewarm Christians), and encourage the progress in holiness of persons of real godliness. This bracing note was less pronounced in the urbane and reasonable atmosphere of the eighteenth century, but a striking exception can be found in a highly charged tribute to a young female parishioner delivered in 1746 by Henry Piers, vicar of Bexley and admirer of John Wesley. She had, he said, shown uncommon courage in reproving sin wherever she encountered it without respect of persons. His own sermon was a warning to those who did not know God, or who presumptuously fancied they knew him 'by the Powers of Nature and Humanity without the Teachings of His Holy Spirit' and to those whom he called 'the reputable, the honourable, the polite, the self-righteous, good Christians of this Age, who *so* love GOD and Mammon!' Probably, just as he feared, all too many of his audience dismissed his message as '*Cant, Enthusiasm, Methodism,* or *melancholy Madness*'.[20]

The main part of the funeral sermon was taken up with the explication and application of a text of Scripture. There were some five themes of outstanding importance. First, life is short. All earthly things are transient and imperfect. The Christian is a stranger in this world; his true home is elsewhere. It is here, however, that the good fight is fought, the crucial race run, faithful service performed in the face of trials and temptations. All opportunity of doing good ends with this life. Secondly, death comes to all alike, rich and poor, good and bad. It is inevitable, but its time is uncertain. Preparation for death is the great business of life. Bearing it constantly in mind will help the individual to live well. Thirdly, dying is a great trial, difficult even for

---

[19] A. Anderson, *A sermon of sure comfort, preached at the funerall of master Robert Keylwey esquire* (1581), 43–4, 47.

[20] N. Parkhurst, *The Redeemer's Friend: or, a Sermon . . . Preached at the Funeral of the Reverend, Learned, and Faithful Minister of the Gospel, Mr. Samvel Fairclough* (1692), sig. A2, pp. 3–5; H. Piers, *True Wisdom from Above: or, Christianity the Best Understanding. A Sermon Preach'd . . . at the Funeral of Mary Godden* (1746), 10, 17–18, 31.

the good, but worst of all for the unprepared sinner. God is merciful, but a deathbed repentance commonly comes too late. It is never too early to repent. A well-led life is a source of comfort at the point of death. Fourthly, the next life will certainly bring eternal bliss for the good, unending torment for the wicked. The knowledge that perfect happiness is possible only in the next life helps to wean the hearts of Christians from the fleeting attractions of this world. It makes death less terrible, or even desirable, for them, even though the happiness of the saved is not complete before the reunion of body and soul at the resurrection. Finally, the preachers of funeral sermons sought to explain the deaths of friends and to indicate how the faithful should respond to them. Through death, God summons the good to their appointed happiness, while trying, or even punishing, those who have loved them. What have survivors done to merit such chastisement? (The question was especially important in the case of public figures. Preachers sometimes sought to bring home to their hearers the magnitude of their loss, even encouraging grief in their efforts to create a receptive mood.)[21]

Some favourite scriptural texts allowed more than one of these central themes to be discussed. In the majority of cases the text was probably picked by the preacher, but several people chose for themselves the passage to be expounded at their funerals. The majority of the texts employed came from the New Testament, and especially from St John's Gospel, St Paul's Epistles, and the Book of Revelation.[22] By far the most popular text, used in over sixty printed sermons, was Revelation 14: 13:

And I heard a voice from heaven saying unto me, Write, Blessed are the dead which die in the Lord from henceforth: Yea, saith the Spirit, that they may rest from their labours; and their works do follow them.

John Hooper, preaching in 1550, used it to drive home the lesson that those who die in penitence and faith enter immediately into joy. There is no purgatory. No man can profit in any way by works performed on his behalf, such as masses, bell-ringing, lights, or

---

[21] G. Hughes, *The saints losse and lamentation. A sermon at the funerall of captaine Henry Waller* (1632), 25–6; Walker, *Leez Lachrymans*, 17–20; J. Webb, *A Sermon preach'd . . . At the Funeral of the Reverend Mr. John Hinton* (1720), 6–7.

[22] Heywood, *Autobiography, Diaries*, i. 103–4; Emmison (ed.), *Elizabethan Life*, iv. 96; A. Horneck, *Sermon Preached at the Solemnity of the Funeral of M*[rs]*. Dorothy St. John, Fourth Daughter of the late Sir Oliver St. John* (1677), pref.; J. Brine, *The Covenant of Grace open'd in a Sermon Occasioned by the Death of Mrs. Margaret Busfield* (1734), 3; indexes detailed in App. 2, below (for count of the most popular texts).

pilgrimages. Refutation of the doctrine of purgatory later became less urgent, but clarification of the relationship between faith and works remained important. Men are justified through free grace and a lively faith in Christ Jesus, Edmond Thorne pointed out in 1684. Their works are the effects and signs of the sincerity of their hearts, and the truth of their belief. However, everlasting happiness was not to be won without effort. The Christian's victory was like that of a soldier who held out till the last. The latitudinarian Bishop Hoadly focused on the importance of leading a good life in a robustly straightforward sermon which he preached in 1719. Reason and religion, he remarked, open to us a future state of stable happiness. Religion assures us that it is prepared for the good and virtuous, who persevere patiently in well-doing. Those who may truly be said to die in the Lord are those who show a sincere obedience to all God's commands.[23]

Verses 21–4 of the first chapter of St Paul's Epistle to the Philippians were also very popular, and used singly or in combination in well over thirty printed sermons. Preachers tended to choose either verse 21, 'For to me to live is Christ, and to die is gain', or verses 23–4,

For I am in a strait betwixt two, having a desire to depart, and to be with Christ; which is far better:
Nevertheless to abide in the flesh is more needful for you.

Death was an indubitable benefit for those who lived in Christ and weaned themselves from the world. Their faith made death welcome, but lack of faith and attachment to worldly things were widespread. Few could look forward to death in the Apostle's spirit. Verses 23–4 were appropriate for the funerals of pillars of the community, especially ministers. Their gain entailed loss for the congregations they left behind them.[24]

Some way behind these two outstandingly favoured texts were three passages, each of them used in well over twenty printed sermons. In 2 Timothy 4: 6–8 St Paul speaks of the good fight he has fought, his maintenance of the faith, and the crown of righteousness

[23] J. Hooper, *A funerall oratyon*, in id., *Early Writings of John Hooper, D.D.*, ed. S. Carr (Parker Soc., 1843), 560–72; E. Thorne, *A Funeral Sermon Upon the much lamented Death of Col. Edward Cook* (1684), 14, 25–6; B. Hoadly, *A Sermon Preach'd at the Funeral of Mrs. Elizabeth Howland* (1719), 3–7; cf. Dent, *Everlasting Blessedness*, 5–36; H. Parsley, *A Sermon Preached at the Funeral of Mr. Thomas Whitchurch. October the 15th 1691* (1692), 1–26.

[24] Gataker, *Certaine sermons*, ii. 217–31; Spencer, *Dumb Speech*, 1–40; T. Knaggs, *A Sermon Preach'd . . . the Sunday after the Death of . . . Dr. John Sharp, Lord Archbishop of York* (1714), 3–24; N. Marshall, *A Sermon Delivered . . . Upon Occasion Of the much Lamented Death of the Rev^d. John Rogers, D.D.* (1729), 7–28.

which God will give him and all those who have set their hearts on the Lord's appearance. Like Revelation 14: 13, these verses enabled preachers to broach three outstanding themes: faith, the strenuous nature of the Christian life, and the rewards which await those who complete their course.[25]

One Thessalonians 4: 13–14, dissuading Christians from excessive sorrow for those who sleep in Jesus, reached the height of its popularity only in the eighteenth century, but the chief lessons commonly drawn were already set out in a sermon delivered by John Chardon at the funeral of Sir Gawen Carew in 1584. Immoderate sorrow is unchristian, though it is appropriate for a good and godly man to shed moderate tears for the death of his friend. The resurrection, and what happens to the body and soul between death and judgement, are the main themes of Chardon's sermon. The word 'sleep' refers only to the body, not to the soul. The transformed body will be reunited with the soul upon the resurrection. Verse 14, declaring that God will bring with him those who sleep in Jesus, holds out the prospect of a happy reunion of those who had known each other on earth.[26]

The bleak message of Isaiah 57: 1 was particularly appropriate to times when God's judgements appeared to threaten the nation or already lay heavily upon it. It invited a resounding call to repentance. It seems to have been popular during the uncertain 1650s, but by the eighteenth century was relatively seldom chosen:

The righteous perisheth, and no man layeth it to heart: and merciful men are taken away, none considering that the righteous is taken away from the evil to come.[27]

---

[25] J. Barlow, *The true guide to glory. A sermon preached at Plympton Mary in Devon, at the funerals of the lady Strode of Newingham* (1619), 1–33; G. Burches, *A Sermon preached . . . at the Funerall of . . . Mʳⁱˢ Margaret Elmes* (1641), 1–23; W. Dillingham, *A Sermon at the Funeral of the Lady Elizabeth Alston, wife of Sir Thomas Alston, . . . Septemb. 10. 1677* (1678), 5–39; T. Harrison, *A Funeral Sermon Occasioned by the Death of Dame Mary Page* (1729), 5–24, 27 (her choice of the text for the sermon).

[26] J. Chardon, *A comfortable sermon for all such as thirst to be ioined with Jesus Christ. Preached at the funerals of syr Gawen Carew in Exeter the two and twentieth of April. 1584* (Oxford, 1586) (unpag.); R. Pearson, *A Sermon Preached at the Funeral of the Reverend Doctor Ambrose Atfield. Late Minister of St. Leonard Shoreditch* (1684), 1–20; S. Rogers, *The Comfort, Certainty, and Blessedness of the Christian Hope: in a Sermon Preach'd at the Funeral Of . . . Baptist. Earl of Gainsborough* (1714), 7–20; E. Cooke, *A Sermon Preach'd . . . at the Funeral of William Ives, Esq.* (2nd edn., 1719), 5–21.

[27] Crowe, *Catalogue* (see App. 2), lists four sermons on this verse dated 1657–8. A later example was J. Marshall, *A Sermon Preach'd . . . Opon* [sic] *Occasion of the much Lamented Death of . . . Robert Nelson Esq.* (1715). The text may have seemed particu-

Several other texts appear in at least a dozen printed sermons. That death is a happy event for the faithful Christian was the message brought home by four of them. Job's question (14: 14), 'If a man die, shall he live again?', could be answered with a resounding affirmative. Ecclesiastes 7: 1 says that the day of death is better than that of one's birth. 'O death, where is thy sting? O grave, where is thy victory?', asks 1 Corinthians. 15: 55. Two Corinthians 5: 1 speaks of the 'house not made with hands, eternal in the heavens' which the blessed will possess when their earthly houses are dissolved.

Two verses from the Psalms (90: 12, 'So teach us to number our days, that we may apply our hearts unto wisdom' and 39: 5, 'Behold, thou hast made my days as an handbreadth; and mine age is as nothing before thee: verily every man at his best state is altogether vanity') served to underline the brevity and frailty of human life on earth. Death, though inevitable, is unpredictable. God, Richard Eaton remarked in 1616, is a great landlord who keeps his tenants on uncertain leases.[28] A man cannot literally count the days left to him, and this uncertainty should encourage him to make his preparations without delay. Both texts enjoyed their greatest popularity before 1700.

A number of favoured verses invited discussion of exemplary conduct or leadership and thus allowed preachers to integrate the customary two parts of the sermon more effectively. However, great care was called for in handling Psalm 37: 37, 'Mark the perfect man, and behold the upright: for the end of that man is peace'. The minister of Farthinghoe (Northants), preaching at the funeral of Mrs Alice Bray in 1646, hedged the word 'perfect' with various qualifications. Mrs Bray, he conceded, had had her faults, but, he claimed, the text as he had interpreted it was indeed applicable to her.[29]

Hebrews 13: 7, 'Remember them which have the rule over you, who have spoken unto you the word of God: whose faith follow, considering the end of their conversation', was a text especially well suited to the funerals of godly ministers and magistrates. Acts 13: 36, 'For David, after he had served his own generation by the will of God, fell on sleep, and was laid unto his fathers, and saw corruption', underlined the inevitability of death for the leaders of communities as for other men while also allowing preachers to commend those who

---

larly appropriate in the case of a famous benefactor and supporter of the nonjurors who died soon after George I's accession.

[28] R. Eaton, *A sermon preached at the funeralls of Thomas Dutton of Dutton, esquire* (1616), 18–19.

[29] W. I., *A Sermon Preached at the Fvnerall of M*rs*. Alice Bray* (1646), 5–8, 25–8.

had rendered good service.[30] Two Samuel 3: 38, David's rhetorical question concerning the fate of Abner, 'Know ye not that there is a prince and a great man fallen this day in Israel?', was employed to justify mourning for prominent members of the community, to prod hearers into awareness of their loss, and (like Acts 13: 36) to reinforce the point that death comes to all men, high and low.[31] The words 'my father, my father, the chariot of Israel and the horsemen thereof' occur in two different places in 2 Kings. Elisha's lamentation for Elijah (2: 12) could be joined with exhortations to an heir to emulate his predecessor's example, taking on Elijah's responsibilities with his mantle, but Joash had done evil in the sight of the Lord, and deserved to lose Elisha (13: 14). This was a verse which might prompt people to consider what they had done to provoke God to remove their mentors.[32]

The brevity of earthly existence, and the reality of the afterlife and its implications for the individual's attitudes towards his own death and the deaths of others remained the most consistently important themes of funeral sermons throughout this period. Preachers attempted to wean their hearers' hearts from the world and emphasized the vanity and flimsiness of temporal blessings and ambitions. In looking to the next world, their predominant note was positive rather than negative. They encouraged their audiences to hope for fulfilment in heaven, rather than threatening them with punishment in hell. The eternal fires were glimpsed less often than heavenly bliss. Some of the bleakest and most severe sermons were delivered between the Reformation and the Civil War by preachers who regarded their audiences as partly indifferent or hostile. The known attacks on purgatory are to be found in the earlier sermons. The prevalent note tended to become less harsh with the passage of time. An urbane reasonableness was common after 1714, especially in

---

[30] G. Hickes, *The Life and Death of David. A Sermon Preached at the Funeralls of that Worthy Member of the Honourable House of Commons, William Strode Esquire* (1645), 1–26; S. Hudson, *David's Labour and Rest or, a Discourse . . . Preached at the Funeral of Mr. Richard Shute* (1689), 2–15; J(ohn) W(ebb), *The Duty of serving our Generation. Set forth in a Sermon Preached at the Funeral Of . . . Mr. Isaac Milles*, in T. Milles, *An Account of the Life and Conversation of . . . Isaac Milles* (1721), 173–84.

[31] Walker, *Leez Lachrymans*, 5–20; R. Harris, *Abners Funerall, or, A Sermon Preached at the Funerall of . . . Sir Thomas Lvcie* (1641), 1–25.

[32] C. Fitz-Geffrey, *Elisha his lamentation, for his owne, and all Israels losse, in Elijah. A sermon preached at the funeralls of sir Anthony Rous* (1622), 1–37; Hughes, *The saints losse and lamentation*, 1–48; S. Ainsworth, *A Sermon Preached . . . At the Fvnerall of Mr. Andrew Pern* (1655), 1–38. In 2 Kings 13: 14 the words are preceded by the exclamation 'O'.

Anglican sermons; Dissenting ministers addressed their congregations as friends, with an intimate confidence. Reason was invoked alongside revelation in attempts to explain the providential scheme and in speculation about the nature of the afterlife. Eighteenth-century sermons were often more concise, more fluent, and simpler in structure, than those of earlier generations.

The part of the sermon which the majority of hearers and readers probably found most interesting was the account of the deceased.[33] This usually came at the end, in what Robert Harris somewhat contemptuously described in 1618 as a 'leane-to'. It commonly took up about a quarter of the sermon, but sometimes a third. Some preachers, like Harris, laid 'all [their] stuffe upon the foundation' by including brief references to the deceased in the body of the sermon. A few, especially in the sixteenth century, omitted such an account altogether. Many of those writers who did include one made a rather abrupt transition from the main part of the sermon, but some sought to integrate the commendation more effectively by using the life of the deceased as an illustration of particular qualities exemplified in the text. An explicit justification of commendation was often felt to be necessary. Some preachers simply invoked custom or the congregation's expectations. More weighty was the example of ancient Israel and the Fathers of the Church. Various biblical texts seemed to endorse it, especially Psalm 112: 6, 'the righteous shall be had in everlasting remembrance'. Had not Christ himself praised John the Baptist? Three duties were discharged by the commendation of the dead: respect to their memory, gratitude and praise to God, and instruction of those yet living. Flattery was the greatest danger. John Fisher was probably obeying an already established convention when he assured his hearers in 1509 that he did not mean to extol the Lady Margaret beyond her merits, but to edify others by means of her example. Many later preachers claimed to be well aware that funeral sermons had been abused to flatter the dead, while insisting that they were determined to say no more than the strict truth.[34]

[33] Evelyn, *Diary*, iv. 302–3; v. 81–3, 365–6; Beaumont, *History of Coggeshall*, 226–9; Kay, *Diary*, 21, 56. Some individuals told the prospective preachers of their funeral sermons about points they wanted included in them. In 1620, preaching at the funeral of Gilbert Davies at Christow (Devon), William Miller recalled an occasion when they had been sitting together alone in the church porch. Davies had entreated Miller, when preaching his funeral sermon, to testify how willing he had been to live in peace with his enemies: W. Miller, *A sermon preached at the funerall of Gilbert Davies esquire* (1621), sig. D3.
[34] Harris, *Workes*, 211; Fitz-Geffrey, *Elisha his lamentation*, 37; R. Kidder, *A Sermon Preached at the Funeral of Mr William Allen* (1686), 21; Parsley, *Sermon*, 26;

The fullest commendations described their subjects' lives in considerable detail. Ancestry, education, public career, position in the community, almsgiving, household governance, family relationships, personal piety, and deathbed behaviour might all be dealt with. Many sermons, however, omitted some or the greater number of these topics. The range of aspects of a person's life which the preacher touched on was largely determined by the individual's sex and social status. Commendations of noblemen and gentlemen were the most likely to mention ancestry and public service. Pastoral qualities and achievements were naturally emphasized in accounts of clerical careers. Descriptions of women's lives focused upon the domestic sphere. The main aim of commendation was to set forth a pattern of Christian life and constancy in the face of death: evidence of personal piety was naturally accorded a prominent place.

Throughout the period some preachers insisted that though their subjects had been well born, their sermons were not to be concerned with high birth or ancestry, and others mentioned such things very briefly or not at all. John Bowle touched on the earl of Kent's hereditary honours in 1615. The lustre conferred on nobility by antiquity was, he remarked, but a meteor compared with the fixed stars of individual virtue. To declare a man's descent was the work of the herald, not the preacher, Timothy Hall remarked in 1684; his task was to 'blazon a more noble coat' and give his hearers the grounds for hope of his new and better birth.[35]

Accounts of participation in public life were usually concise. The tenure of office was mentioned not so much for its own sake as for the opportunities it had afforded for the exercise of such virtues as integrity, loyalty, impartiality, courage, and love of justice. Social usefulness did not depend upon the occupation of a post or place. The tribute which Charles Fitzgeffrey paid his patron Sir Anthony Rous of

Crompton, *Lasting jewell*, sig. F; R. Hooker, *The Works of that Learned and Judicious Divine, Mr. Richard Hooker* (2 vols., Oxford, 1841), ii. 153; J. Tillotson, *Works* (1757), ii. 126; Warren, *Domus ordinata*, pref.; Williamson, *Comfortable meditation*, sig. A2; J. Bowle, *A sermon preached at Flitton in the countie of Bedford, at the funerall of Henrie earle of Kent* (1615), sig. E; C. Scott, *The Saints Priviledge or Gain by Dying* (1673), 23–4; R. Wroe, *Righteousness Encouraged and Rewarded with an Everlasting Remembrance. In a Sermon at the Funeral of the Right Worshipful Sir Roger Bradshaigh of Haigh, Knight and Baronet* (1684), 1–15; Fisher, *English Works*, 293; G. Ferebe, *Lifes farewell. Or a funerall sermon. At the funerall of John Drew gentleman* (1615), 25–6; Eaton, *Sermon*, 19–20; Bradbury, *Winning Christ*, 26.

35 Bowle, *Sermon*, sig. E^v; T. Hall, *A Sermon Preached . . . At the Funeral of Robert Huntington Esq.* (1684), 40–1; Eaton, *Sermon*, 20; G. Babington, *A funerall sermon* [on 2 Sam. x. I]. *Preached by G. Babington* [at] *(the funerall of maister T. L. esquire.)* (1595), sig. A2^v–3^r.

Halton (Corn.) in 1622 mentioned that he had been vice-warden of the stannaries and twice sheriff, but his hospitality, charity, readiness to forgive injuries, and settlement of other men's quarrels were accorded greater prominence. Rous had made his house 'for many yeares . . . the center of charity and hospitality, wherein met the lines of poore and strangers, drawne from a large circumference round about him'. He had been assiduous in what Fitzgeffrey called the 'studie and industrie of making peace and reconciling differences'.[36]

Charitable assistance, often, as in the case of Sir Anthony Rous, closely associated with hospitality, was the foremost of Christian neighbourly duties. Preachers tended to attach the highest value to charitable gifts which were regular, unobtrusive, and above all carried out during the benefactor's lifetime. Much beneficent activity, especially on the part of women, took the shape of medical help, often administered in person. The great range of charitable activities mentioned in sermons included daily or weekly doles, relief provided in times of crisis such as dearth and plague, interest-free loans, and support given to hospitals, almshouses, schools, and various missionary and educational societies. A nine-page appendix to his funeral sermon was required to list in full the enormous range of benefactions financed by the wealthy Bristol merchant Edward Colston (d. 1721).[37]

Much of the testimony contained in funeral sermons concerns the household and family. A clear line cannot be drawn between them and the public sphere. For much of this period the household was a

---

[36] Fitz-Geffrey, *Elisha his lamentation*, 43–9.

[37] G. Abbot, *A sermon preached at Westminster May 26, 1608. At the funerall solemnities of Thomas earle of Dorset* (1608), 17–18; J. Chadwich, *A sermon preached at Snarford at the funerals of sir George Sanct-Paule. Together with a briefe relation of his life and death* (1614), 21–4; J.D., *A Sermon Preached at the Funeral Of . . . Lady Mary Armyne* (1676), 25–6; *The Sermons of John Donne*, ed. G. R. Potter and E. M. Simpson (10 vols., Berkeley and Los Angeles, 1953–62), viii. 89–90; Eaton, *Sermon*, 22; R. Eyre, *A Sermon Preach'd at the Funeral of . . . Sir Stephen Fox* (1716), 12; B. Grosvenor, *Precious Death. A Sermon On Occasion of the Death of M*rs *Susannah Rudge* (1716), 14; T. Hall, *Sermon*, 42–3; E. Hall, *Sermon at Stanton-Harcourt*, 55–6; J. Harcourt, *A Sermon Preach'd . . . Upon the Death of Edward Colston, Esq* (1721), 10–30, 39–47; Harrison, *Funeral Sermon*, 29; J. Dodson, *A Sermon preached at the Funeral Obsequies of Jacob Lucie Esq: Late Alderman of the City of London* (1688), 29; B. Love, *A Sermon Preach'd at the Funeral of Nathanael Symonds, Esq* (1721), 18–23; Marshall, *Sermon* [Nelson], 20–1; S. Peck, *A Sermon preached at the Funeral of Sir Henry Johnson, K*t. (1684), 27–8; J. Preston, *A sermon preached at the funeral of M*r. *Arthur Upton* (1619), 35; Walker, *Leez Lachrymans*, 22, 24; R. Willan, *Eliah's wish: a prayer for death. A sermon preached at the funerall of viscount Sudbury, lord Bayning* (1630), 39–42; C. H. Sisson (ed.), *The English Sermon*, ii. *1650–1750* (Cheadle, 1976), 183. The extent of lifetime giving had sometimes been revealed only by private accounts or the testimony of servants.

centre for dispensing charity as well as hospitality. It was within the household that individuals, whether as children or servants, received much of their training as members of the commonwealth. Indeed the family was conventionally held to be a microcosm of the common-wealth, even of the Church itself. Conscientious householders were praised for the solicitude they showed for both the physical and the spiritual welfare of their servants. Paul Cleybrooke Esq. (d. 1622) would not tolerate among his servants the all too common vices of swearing and swaggering, 'and he so gouerned, admonished, and ordered them, that some haue departed out of his house, more godly, sober, frugall, and honester men, than they were before they came vnto him'. The earl of Warwick (d. 1673) maintained the 'great *Exemplar* of best *Houshold-Discipline*', permitting no disorders under his roof. He spared no cost in treating his servants when they were ill, and left them well rewarded at his death.[38]

Parents were commended for bringing up their children in religion, training them to be useful members of society, and giving them good advice, particularly in their last messages. The especially important part played in the early education of their children by conscientious mothers was mentioned in some sermons. The ideal mother was a 'tender and affectionate . . . parent, winning by love, not ruling by rigor,' but she tempered her natural bent towards indulgence with strictness when it was required.[39]

The importance of the marriage partnership to household harmony as well as individual happiness was often recognized. Various qualities were commended in husbands and wives: solicitude, discretion, faithfulness, and (sometimes) wifely obedience. It was their mutual love, however, which called forth some of the preachers' most poignant eloquence. John Bowle held up the marriage of the earl of Kent (d. 1615) as a true union of souls, in sharp contrast with those matches 'not made to vnite *hearts*, but *houses*; nor to ioyne *affections*, but *factions*,' with fatal results. Lady Anne Harcourt, who died in 1664 when only 19, was described as 'so full of respect,

---

[38] W. Stone, *A curse become a blessing: or, a sermon preached at the funerall of Paul Cleybrooke esquire* (1623), 53; Walker, *Leez Lachrymans*, 22, 27; A. Farindon, *A Sermon Preached at the Funeral of . . . Sir George Whitmore, Knight*, in id., *LXXX Sermons preached at the Parish-Church of St Mary Magdalene Milk-street, London* (2nd edn., 2 vols., 1672), 545–6; Chadwich, *Sermon*, 18; S. Knight, *A Sermon Preached at the Funeral of . . . Laetitia, Lady Dowager Russel* (1722), 22–3.

[39] Crompton, *Lasting jewell*, sig. F^v; Scott, *Saints Priviledge*, 29; C. Fitz-Geffrey, *Death's sermon unto the living. Delivered at the funerals of the ladie Philippe, late wife unto Sir A. Rous* (1620), 27; *Elegie*, 17.

tendernesse and overflowing love to her Dear, (as she call'd her husband) that you would have deemed their whole life to have been but
one wedding day'. The marriage between the third earl of Gainsborough and his wife, cut short by his early death in 1714, was 'a prefect
Pattern of conjugal Love and Affection; . . . and they seem'd to be so
strictly united to each other, as if they breathed the same Soul,' which
ensured unbroken domestic calm and allowed no scope 'for any
designing Person whatsoever' to foment suspicion or jealousy
between them.[40]

Religious duties, like other activities, were performed upon the
public stage, within the household, and in the privacy of the closet.
Public responsibilities and Christian duty coincided most closely in
the case of the minister of religion. The work of conscientious clergy
received many heartfelt tributes from their colleagues. The variety of
such tributes may be illustrated by means of two contrasting testimo-
nials concerning different types of churchmanship. Thomas Gataker,
preaching in 1626 at the funeral of the eminent Puritan minister
Richard Stock of All Hallows Bread Street, mentioned among other
things his weekday catechizing, his successful conversions, free
speaking in reproaching sin, and efforts to reform profanation of the
sabbath. His opinion had been sought by colleagues all over the country hoping for resolution of their doubts. His clear, eloquent, and well-
founded sermons had impressed both the hearts and the minds of his
hearers. Nearly a century later, in 1720, John Hinton's work as rector
of Newbury was described by his curate. During forty years' residence he had been consistently loyal to the Church, reciting her
'incomparable Liturgy' with due clarity, devotion, and energy, never
omitting the least rite or ceremony 'in the decent, orderly, and edifying Worship of *God*, which is *the Beauty of Holiness*'. He had been a
zealous supporter of the charity schools.[41] In the pulpit he had presented no novel or singular doctrinal opinions, but concentrated on
gospel teaching concerning a good life and conversation.

People of wealth and standing of both sexes had the opportunity of
giving countenance and support to deserving ministers and financial
assistance to institutions designed to promote religion. The public
duties incumbent upon all were attendance at church to pray, partici-
pate in Holy Communion, and hear the Word preached. One or other
aspect of these duties might be emphasized, depending upon the

---

[40] Bowle, *Sermon*, next leaf after sig. E3; Hall, *Sermon at Stanton-Harcourt*, 11–13,
49, 52–3; S. Rogers, *Comfort, Certainty, and Blessedness of Christian Hope*, 22.
[41] Gataker, *Certaine sermons*, ii. 257–60; Webb, *Sermon*, 23–6.

churchmanship of the preacher and the deceased. Family duties included prayers said daily or twice daily, reading of the Scriptures, the instruction of children and servants, the repetition of sermons, and sabbath observance. The most private were the 'closet duties' of prayer, reading, and meditation, which in the case of the most devout could take up several hours a day. The keeping of diaries, meditation books, and records of personal failings or divine mercies was some-times mentioned. The conscientious performance of household and closet duties, sometimes retrospectively associated above all with the Puritans, was highly valued within the Church of England after the Restoration, and commended by a number of loyal conforming divines.[42]

The regular practice of private devotions bulked larger in descriptions of women's observance than in those of men's, probably for two main reasons. First, it was the one area of religious life where they were not subject to male leadership or supervision, and the one which gave them the most scope for self-expression. Secondly, multi-farious though women's domestic responsibilities were even among the wealthier classes, they had fewer calls upon their time outside the household than did their menfolk, and probably found it easier to make space for meditation and prayer.[43]

Many of the preachers' most attentive listeners were women. The close spiritual relationship between a number of preachers and their pious confidantes imparted a special warmth to their commendations. The female sex might in general be the weaker one, but some women enjoyed an exceptional spiritual strength. A number of preachers made the point that the goodness of members of the natur-ally inferior sex manifested especially clearly the power and the grace of God, who might choose to give some women special endowments. In 1620 Thomas Gataker claimed, perhaps somewhat optimistically, that examples of the weaker sex were the more effectual in spurring on men to emulation. Domestic examples were of all others the most powerful.[44]

[42] Walker, *Leez Lachrymans*, 27–8; J.D., *Sermon*, 23–5; Fitz-Geffrey, *Elisha his lamentation*, 40–2; Chadwich, *Sermon*, 24–5; T. Hall, *Sermon*, 41–2; Peck, *Sermon*, 26–7; G. Burnet, *A Sermon Preached at the Funeral of Mr. James Houblon* . . . (1682), 27–8; Kidder, *Sermon*, 22–3.

[43] Barlow, *True guide*, 48–9; Fitz-Geffrey, *Death's sermon*, 28–9; *Elegie*, 12–13; *The Whole Works of the Right Reverend Jeremy Taylor, D.D.*, ed. C. P. Eden (10 vols., 1847–54), viii. 445–6; J. Jenny, *A Sermon preached At the Funeral of* . . . *Lady Frances Paget* . . . (1673), 22–3; Dillingham, *Sermon*, 41; Knight, *Sermon*, 20–1; Sisson, *English Sermon 1650–1750*, 174, 180–2, 260–3.

[44] Gataker, *Certaine sermons*, ii. 212; Crompton, *Lasting jewell*, sig. E2.

The climax of the funeral sermon narrative was the account of the deathbed. In some sermons it took up nearly half, or even more than half, the space devoted to commendation of the deceased. Edifying deathbed comportment could reinforce in the most direct fashion most of the important themes chosen for the main part of the funeral sermon. Readiness to leave the world, brave acceptance of death, assurance of salvation and future bliss, confident anticipation of future reunion, exhortations to friends and loved ones not to mourn: all these gave powerful practical illustrations of the lessons which preachers sought to inculcate. They helped to teach people how to die. A sudden death, on the other hand, was useful as a means of impressing on the audience the need to be prepared for death whenever it might come.[45]

Preachers often felt able, in the end, to provide solid grounds for hope, or reasons to believe, that the deceased had gained by their deaths, or had enjoyed a happy dissolution. The departed were frequently said to be in peace, perfect happiness, sharing the glories of heaven, enjoying the crown of life or a glorious reward.[46] The survivors' loss had been the dead person's gain, and this fact should moderate understandable grief. The best course, it was often emphasized, was to imitate the virtues of the dead. That was the way to keep their memory alive and to secure the prospect of an eventual reunion. The Protestant funeral sermon could thus perform one of the most important psychological functions of the intercessory prayer abolished at the Reformation, that of making survivors feel more confident and comfortable concerning the present state of the dead. In theory, the two were utterly dissimilar in their nature and purposes. Yet the same desire for reassurance about the condition of departed souls which had been a powerful motive for the endowment of funeral masses was also one reason to hope for an eloquent valedictory tribute from a respected preacher. This was the reason for widespread misgivings about funeral sermons among militant Protestants, especially in the sixteenth century.[47]

Did preachers of funeral sermons convey reassurance too readily? In their own attempts to justify the right use of such sermons, some

---

[45] See above, Chs. 6 and 7, for the presentation of deathbeds in funeral sermons; Hooker, *Works*, ii. 154.

[46] Gataker, *Certaine sermons*, ii. 216, 261, 320; W.I., *Sermon*, 28; Spencer, *Dumb Speech*, 44–5; J. Taylor, *The Whole Works of the Right Reverend Jeremy Taylor, D.D.*, ed. C. P. Eden (10 vols., 1847–54), viii. 450; Sisson, *English Sermon*, ii. *1650–1750*, 188; Kidder, *Sermon*, 21; Graile, *Vigorous Longevity*, 31.

[47] Barrow, *Brief Discoverie*, 461.

ministers criticized the eulogistic excesses of unnamed colleagues whose bad example they were determined to avoid. It is impossible to be sure how widespread such malpractice was, for only a small fraction of the sermons delivered now survives. In the published sermons, however, at any rate before the later seventeenth century, writers usually seem to have been anxious to produce persuasive evidence of Christian life or true repentance. Sometimes they may have erred on the side of indulgence, but they usually took care to distinguish, if only unobtrusively, between more and less praiseworthy personal records. Some admitted that the deceased had had frailties. Thus Robert Willan, preaching at the funeral of Viscount Sudbury in 1629, told his audience that Sudbury had been a man subject to many infirmities. However, any curious ear desiring to hear them would be disappointed: David had not touched on Saul's errors when he had made an epitaph proclaiming the king's virtues. The outward signs that Sudbury had been a good Christian included assiduous religious observance, openness to reproof, willingness to mend his ways, and 'strong paines in sicknesse meekely borne'. Willan concluded with a positive affirmation that Sudbury had gone 'into his Masters Ioy'. Anthony Walker knew, when he preached at the funeral of the earl of Warwick in 1673, how badly his patron's excruciating gout had soured his temper and sharpened the tongue with which he had lashed his long-suffering wife. It was allowable by the best authority, said Walker, 'God's own Example, to single out the *Good*, and draw a Veile of *Silence* and *Charity* over the rest, which in this Sense, must cover a Multitude of Faults'. Some preachers omitted a final allusion to the fate of the deceased (as Walker did in this case) or couched it with great care. At the end of the sermon which he delivered at the funeral of Sir William Cokayne in 1626, John Donne spoke of the charity which inclined the assembled company 'to hope confidently of his good estate'. There is a distinct difference between this charitable hope and the conviction which he expressed, the following year, that Lady Danvers had been welcomed immediately after her death with the words '*Well done good and faithfull servant: enter into thy masters joy*'.[48]

Some of the most powerful funeral sermons, including the ones preached by John Fisher for Henry VII in 1509, and by Robert Parsons for the earl of Rochester in 1680, focused on a dramatic deathbed repentance. Fisher was confident that Henry had escaped the danger

---

[48] Willan, *Eliah's wish*, 38–40, 44; Walker, *Leez Lachrymans*, sig. A2ᵛ, 23–5; Donne, *Sermons*, vii. 278; viii. 91.

of everlasting death. Parsons could say that there was great reason to believe that Rochester's repentance had been real and his end happy. Such comforting confidence, however, was not always possible. James Ellesby, vicar of Chiswick, described in his 1692 sermon on *The Great Danger and Uncertainty of a Death-Bed Repentance* how a recently strong and lusty young man had bewailed his sins during a long and tedious sickness. It was impossible to know how far God had accepted his sighs and tears; the clergy had to warn the living not to make judgements concerning the dead.[49]

Preachers were reluctant to come to a pessimistic conclusion concerning the fate of the dead even when there seemed to be good reason to do so. Preaching at the funeral of a Mr Noble, an adulterer who had murdered his lover's husband, William Fleetwood, later bishop of Ely, refrained from any assessment of Noble's prospects. Yet by implicitly comparing Noble's case with that of King David as described in 2 Samuel 11–12, Fleetwood intimated that he might have found mercy.[50]

It was hard to speak of the dead, Gervase Babington remarked *c.*1595. Friends would think the praise too little, while enemies would think it excessive. Even the truest dispraise would be greeted with a cry that it was inhumanity; nothing but good was to be said of the dead. 'Relations will think *too little* is spoke, others *too much*', complained Timothy Hall in 1684, echoing Babington. The delicacy of the preacher's task is underlined by the negative reaction to a sermon entitled *Mathew the publican* delivered by Emmanuel Utie in St Stephen's Walbrook in 1616. The main theme of the sermon was God's endless mercy and the power he had shown in the conversion of St Matthew. The dead man had had one known sin, his proneness to drink, which Utie felt he could not pass over in silence (but, the preacher implied, none of his hearers was free of sin). God had given those around the deathbed some signs of his conversion, even though his sickness made them weak. Weak or strong, his faith had been enough to save him, if true. His prayers for mercy and forgiveness, and the promise of amendment he had made to his friends shortly before his death testified to its genuineness. Utie had carefully yet

---

[49] Fisher, *English Works*, 286; R. Parsons, *A Sermon preached at the Funeral of the . . . Earl of Rochester* (Oxford, 1680), 33, 34; Ellesby, *Great Danger and Uncertainty*, 19–21.

[50] *A Compleat Collection of the Sermons, Tracts, and Pieces of all Kinds, That were Written by . . . Dr. William Fleetwood, Late Lord Bishop of Ely* (1737), 657–66. The sermon was first published in 1713, but almost certainly preached some years before that. The text was 2 Samuel 12 : 5.

positively set out the grounds for hope. However, his reference to the dead man's sin had, as he admitted in his preface to the printed sermon, angered some who heard him.[51]

Did the preachers of funeral sermons allow themselves to become the prisoners of conventional and repetitious formulas? Were they compromised by the need to eulogize the dead in order to please their audiences? A clearly affirmative answer to either of these questions would be too harsh. Perusal of large numbers of *printed* funeral commendations leaves the reader with a strong impression of their rich variety, of the adaptation of conventional patterns to meet particular circumstances, and of the extent to which authors treasured distinctive elements of personal character. The path between controversial censure and bland eulogy was often a difficult one. The skilful preacher followed it by making the most of what was good in the individual's record, and by means of carefully judged omissions, tactfully phrased references to his subject's failings, and intimations of ultimate happiness framed with considerable circumspection. However, a minority of preachers gave fulsome praise of a rather undiscriminating sort. Among the great mass of unpublished sermons there may have been a much larger number which commended the deceased with less honesty or discretion.

So far, this discussion of commendations has emphasized elements of continuity, but important changes also took place. One of these was the tendency of an increasing number of sermons to reflect political or sectarian turbulence and even, in some cases, to manifest a strongly partisan character. In the early seventeenth century godly individuals were sometimes commended for avoiding the company of the wicked as far as possible and for cherishing that of the saints, while loyal conformists were distinguished not only from papists but also from Puritan 'novelists'. In 1629 Lord Sudbury was described as having been an exemplary subject in an age when liberty was made an idol. The Civil War created deep and open divisions. On William Strode's burial in 1645, the preacher made Strode's devotion to the godly cause his most important theme, and deliberately passed over 'the piety of his private course'. Political conflict between 1679 and 1681 and more especially in the wake of the Glorious Revolution almost certainly acted as a powerful stimulus to the printing of funeral sermons, which reached its highest levels between 1680 and 1720.

---

[51] E. Utie, *Mathew the publican. A funerall sermon* (1616), sig. A2–3, 37–40; Babington, *Funerall sermon*, sig. A3; T. Hall, *Sermon*, 39–40.

George Johnson (d. 1683), a Tory gentleman of Gateshead, was said to have shown great zeal in trying to get loyal subjects elected to parliament. White Kennett extolled the duke of Devonshire's opposition to popery and arbitrary government. Under James II he had 'stoutly blam'd, and as far as He could, opposed every illegal Step,' before finally appearing in arms as a 'most signal Instrument' in the providential Revolution. In 1719 Benjamin Hoadly applauded Mrs Elizabeth Howland's Whig principles. She had known the value to be set on the liberty of being governed by laws framed by consent, not by arbitrary will. 'And She was sensible, to the highest Degree, of how great Consequence and Necessity the present Establishment was, to make so great a Happiness lasting to Us and our Posterity.'[52]

It is refreshing to find some clergymen commended precisely on the grounds that they were not party men. It was in 1681, shortly after the Exclusion Crisis, that John Tillotson, later to be archbishop of Canterbury, praised Thomas Gouge, a man who had lamented the 'heats and differences' which had divided the country. Gouge, a man notable for his outstandingly conscientious parochial ministry, philanthropic projects, and missionary work in Wales, had left his London living over the terms of conformity not long after the Restoration. At the funeral of his Nonconformist colleague Samuel Fairclough in 1692, Nathaniel Parkhurst, vicar of Yoxford (Suffolk) voiced his opinion that 'it had been alone worth an Act of Comprehension, to have included this one so valuable a Man'.[53]

More important than the partisan character of a minority of sermons, though related to it, were two further developments: shifts of emphasis from the private to the public, and from the deathbed to the events of the life. First, there was a tendency to give fewer specific details of personal religious practice in these sermons. We read less about closet duties in particular—about prayer, meditation, and the keeping of mirrors of the soul. Either less was going on in the closet, or changing notions of privacy and good manners kept the door closed. Benjamin Hoadly, for example, praised Mrs Elizabeth

---

[52] E. Layfielde, *The soules solace. A sermon at the solemn funerall of William Fawcit Gent.* (1632), 123–4; Oldmayne, *Lifes brevitie*, 21; Bowle, *Sermon*, sig. F2ᵛ; Willan, *Eliah's wish*, 39, 42; Hickes, *Life and Death of David*, 20; R. Werge, *A Sermon preached . . . at the Funeral of George Johnson, Gent.* (1683), 25; Kennett, *Sermon*, 48–51; Hoadly, *Sermon*, 19–21.

[53] Tillotson, *Works*, ii. 127–36; Parkhurst, *Redeemer's Friend*, 23. Dr Stephen Taylor has pointed out to me that 'claims of moderation or non-partisanship' nevertheless need to be read with caution since they were 'commonly appropriated by party in this period'.

Howland in 1719 as a model of calm reasonableness rather than devout practice or spiritual fervour. She had founded her faith and conduct 'in the most rational, the most just and most certain Notions of GOD' and 'embrac'd *Christianity* with her Understanding as well as her Heart, as agreeable to the Natural Notions of the Supreme Being'. She had 'esteemed it the Glory of the Gospel, that it was worthy of a Good GOD; Plain, Practical, and Useful'. She had been truly religious without superstition, pious without any of the undue heats of enthusiasm.[54]

While good works were still praised, there was a tendency to say less about the faith which should have inspired them. The sorts of good work singled out were gradually changing. After the Restoration men were seldom commended for being forbearing landlords, or for settling their neighbours' quarrels. Fewer gentlemen and ladies were praised for maintaining household religion in the eighteenth century than in the seventeenth. Some eighteenth-century sermons also reflect the belief that one could be usefully beneficent without making sacrifices. Men such as Thomas Pitt, the fabulously wealthy ex-governor of Madras (d. 1726), were applauded for setting the poor to work by creating or improving houses and gardens.[55]

Some preachers, with a comfortable blandness which would have horrified the sterner Protestants of an earlier generation, assured their audiences that good behaviour would be rewarded in this life. In 1688 the preacher at the London funeral of Alderman Jacob Lucie interpreted the 'perfect man' of Psalm 37: 37 as 'Every sincere, good and righteous man'. Such men would not enjoy peace only after death, but also 'on this side the Grave, in their well-contented and pious Minds and Souls, at the least'. He proceeded, in an effusive panegyric, to set the alderman before his audience as a 'really excellent and worthily imitable Pattern'. An even more fulsome performance in similar vein was the sermon preached by his chaplain, Lewis Stephens, at the funeral of Charles Trimnell, the Whig bishop of Winchester, in 1723. His text was Psalm 37: 11: 'But the meek shall inherit the earth; and shall delight themselves in the abundance of peace.' The best interpretation of this verse was that God would bestow on the meek man a large share of worldly goods, and a peaceable mind

---

[54] Hoadly, *Sermon*, 16–18.
[55] Eyre, *A Sermon preached ... At the Funeral of Thomas Pitt Esq.* (1726), 21–2; cf. Cooke, *Sermon*, 25; Sir George St Paul had been commended as early as 1613 for spending money on a new house fitting his place and calling, but he had been engaged in a wide range of other charitable projects: Chadwich, *Sermon*, 23.

for the enjoyment of them. The blessings promised to some of the virtues were the natural result of those virtues themselves. Trimnell's meekness, and the 'Delicacy and Tenderness of Manners' which had recommended him to men of rank, had helped to earn him a richly deserved reward in the shape of one of the wealthiest sees in England.[56]

Greater reticence about the deathbed in eighteenth-century sermons is another sign of a sea change in attitudes. Detailed narratives of faith tested by appalling pain and spiritual doubts are rarely found in these sermons. Tributes were paid to fortitude and composure in general terms, but little was said of the changing physical symptoms, or the contents of devout prayers and godly speeches. Hoadly praised Mrs Howland for her tact and consideration; on her deathbed she had made herself as little uneasy to others as possible. Lady Onslow's death from a raging distemper was briefly described in 1731: 'But I cannot proceed' the preacher continued, 'and must beg leave to drop a Veil over this fatal and melancholy Scene.' As early as 1707 the Nonconformist minister William Tong discerned a growing unwillingness even to speak of the dead. 'I am told', he wrote to his colleague John Shower, 'it is accounted a piece of Ill Breeding now-a-days to make mention of those that are lately dead in the presence of their nearest surviving Relations.' If this was so, he went on, it was a sad sign of a degenerate age. What was this 'but for Men to study to defeat the great Designs of God in such awakening Providences, and to contrive that Death may surprise and overtake them unawares?' He felt sure that Shower was otherwise minded. Though none could question the tenderness of Shower's affection to his deceased daughter, 'yet you are willing both to speak and to hear of her, of her Sickness, and of her dying Moments, that your own Mind, and the Minds of your Friends may be the more deeply and seriously impress'd thereby'.[57]

The Nonconformists remained more faithful to old patterns and ideals, at least for a time. Furthermore, the numbers of printed Nonconformist sermons increased for about four decades after the passage of the Toleration Act. The publication of funeral sermons served to nourish the Nonconformists' sense of common purpose

[56] Dodson, *Sermon*, 12, 20, 26–31; L. Stephens, *A Sermon Preached . . . At the Funeral of . . . Dr. Charles Trimnel, Late Lord Bishop of Winchester* (1723), 4, 9, 15–24.

[57] Hoadly, *Sermon*, 23; G. Stephens, *The amiable quality of goodness as compared with Righteousness, considered. In a Sermon Preach'd . . . the Sunday after the funeral of . . . Elizabeth, Lady Onslow* (1731), 24; W. Tong, *A Funeral Sermon Upon Occasion of the Death of Mrs. Ann Warner* (1708), pp. iii–iv.

and identity during the political strife and uncertainty of the following twenty-five years and in face of the very different challenges
posed by an era of relative ease and security. However, the way in
which the Dissenting minority made use of funeral sermons, and
printed them in numbers out of all proportion to their own share of
the population, may well have contributed to the genre's seeming
loss of favour among the gentry.

The belief that some preachers had been too ready to give good
characters to the deceased had caused misgivings about funeral sermons ever since the sixteenth century. During the seventeenth, confessional or party bias was sometimes blamed when individuals
received more or less than their perceived due. That was why the
Yorkshire Presbyterian minister Oliver Heywood disliked some sermons preached by neighbouring clergy of the established Church. In
April 1679, for example, the vicar of Halifax commended Mr Horton
of Sowerby, a noted benefactor of the Nonconformists, in lukewarm
terms. Mrs Horton told Heywood she would rather the vicar had said
nothing at all. Heywood realized that Horton's generosity had not
been recognized because his charity had not 'run in the desired channel'. Yet when in July 1681 the vicar of Burstall died as a result of falls
after heavy drinking, his colleague the lecturer at Wakefield 'commended him excessively, especially for converting so many dissenters to the church'.[58]

During the eighteenth century some printed sermons were sharply
criticized. In 1708 White Kennett was lambasted for political time-
serving on account of his effusive praise of the duke of Devonshire.
He had only hinted at the duke's immorality while paying fulsome
tribute to his political career. A nobleman who had 'Wallow'd in
Fornications' had been washed clean by his chaplain 'With Funeral
Orations'.[59]

Before long, misuse of the funeral sermon caused controversy
among the Nonconformists too. Some Baptist ministers in particular
remained true to the tradition of vivid description of deathbed manifestations of faith. In 1729 one of them, John Gill, strongly criticized a
funeral sermon for Dame Mary Page recently preached by his colleague Thomas Harrison. Gill complained that Harrison had avoided
descriptions of the people of God taken from their faith, preferring

---

[58] Heywood, *Autobiography, Diaries*, ii. 260–1, 283.
[59] G. V. Bennett, *White Kennett, 1660–1728, Bishop of Peterborough: A Study in the Political and Ecclesiastical History of the Early Eighteenth Century* (1957), 98–100.

such insipid phrases as 'the sincerely good'. 'But I had almost forgot that this sermon was calculated for the polite part of the town, to whom those sounds, *believers, converted persons, regenerate ones*, &c. are as disagreeable, as the characters expressed by 'em are unsuitable.'[60] By the second quarter of the eighteenth century many Nonconformist sermons had fallen under the vitiating influence of the politeness of which Gill complained. In 1732 John Grant took to task Peter Belbin, a Berkshire Nonconformist minister, for the opinions which he had expressed in two funeral discourses. Men would receive rewards in the next world, Belbin had said, in proportion to their services in this one. Only a good life could make death comfortable. But eternal life was not a reward for our works. Belbin had said no word of 'the everlasting Love of God display'd in electing Grace, as the distinguishing Priviledge, of those who are, and shall be blessed, in and at their Death'.[61]

From around this time the numbers of Nonconformist funeral sermons appearing in print entered into a gradual decline. The printing of funeral sermons preached by the divines of the Established Church, having reached its highest point earlier, now underwent a veritable collapse. The delivery of such sermons had itself gone out of favour among the upper classes, according to George Lewis, vicar of Westerham in Kent. In 1726 he claimed that 'it is not the common Custom, or the Genteel Part of the degenerate Age we live in, to be attended to the Grave with a Funeral Sermon'. It was not difficult, he believed, to account for the disuse of such sermons. The good were buried in oblivion because the bad, who outnumbered them, did not deserve to be remembered.[62] The acceptability of funeral sermons depended upon a sometimes precarious reconciliation of individual example with general doctrine. Ministers provided reassurance and sealed the good name of the deceased when they were furnished with evidence of saving faith and its fruits, or of piety, devotion, and

[60] [J. Gill], *An Essay on the Original of Funeral Sermons, Orations, and Odes* (1729), 24. For sermons by a Baptist minister which contain powerful accounts of deathbed expressions of faith, see J. Brine *Covenant of Grace*, 39; id., *The Believer's Triumph over Death. Considered in a Sermon Occasion'd by the Decease of Mr. Hugh Lloyd* (1736), 36–7; and id., *The Chief of Sinners, saved thro' Jesus Christ: A Sermon, Occasioned by the Death of Mrs. Anne Wildman* (1747), 45–6.

[61] J. Grant, *An Essay, With Relation to the Gospel of our Lord Jesus Christ: Being a Friendly Examination of two Funeral Discourses: Publish'd by Mr. Peter Belbin* (1732), esp. 28; P. Belbin, *A Sermon Preach'd at the Funeral of Mr. George Elliott of Reading* (1730), esp. 26.

[62] G. Lewis, *A Sermon Preach'd . . . on the Occasion of the Death of Mrs. Paynter, Wife of Robert Paynter, Esq.* (1726), 5.

repentance. Eighteenth-century polite society put in the private sphere the sorts of evidence which had been laid out in the best funeral sermons of an earlier generation. The reluctance to speak of the deathbed, in particular, denied preachers their best evidence of faith. Some clergymen attempted to provide commendations of the dead which would answer the expectations of an urbane and reasonable age, but in doing so found themselves drawn into suave eulogies which consorted ill with any save the blandest expositions of doctrine. The results sometimes looked ridiculous. The weight of the lean-to was pushing the house down. Yet the need to fit commendations into a discourse designed for Christian edification did set bounds to the sorts of praise which might be given in a funeral sermon. These constraints help to explain the declining popularity of the funeral sermon among the upper classes of Georgian England.

The funeral sermon, usually combining doctrinal exposition with a reassuring testimonial, was especially characteristic and distinctive of the two centuries following the Reformation. Of all the public means of confirming the reputation of the dead it was probably the most widely valued. (In Germany, where they have been the subject of intensive study, funeral sermons were printed in vastly greater numbers than in England. Some 240,000 funeral sermons in German dating from 1570 to 1770 have been discovered. The trajectory of their popularity in the two countries, however, seems to have been broadly similar.)[63] A more permanent means of commemoration, the epitaph, also enjoyed its heyday during the early modern centuries.[64]

More closely related to the funeral sermon, but never anything like as popular, was the funeral oration (*oratio funebris*). In his sermon for Henry VII, John Fisher declared his intention of following the order of a secular funeral oration by in turn commending the deceased, stirring the audience to have compassion on him, and then comforting them again.[65] He dovetailed his chosen text Psalm 114

---

[63] R. Lenz (ed.), *Leichenpredigten: Eine Bestandsaufnahme: Bibliographie und Ergebnisse einer Umfrage* (Marburg, 1980); id. (ed.), *Leichenpredigten als Quelle historischer Wissenschaften* (3 vols.: Cologne, 1975; Marburg, 1979 and 1984). I am grateful to Prof. Dr Heide Wunder and Prof. Katalin Péter for kindly giving me offprints from these vols. In Frankfurt-am-Main alone, 409 funeral sermons and related texts are known to have been printed between 1550 and 1749. The years 1630–1719 stand out as the period of maximum production. See F. Lerner, 'Frankfurter Leichenpredigten als Quellen der Stadt- und Kulturgeschichte des 16. bis 19. Jahrhunderts', in Lenz (ed.) *Leichenpredigten als Quelle*, i. 238–9.

[64] See Ch. 11, below.   [65] Fisher, *English Works*, 268–9.

(116) with the oratorical sequence and facets of the dead king's experience rather than giving it separate exposition. English Protestant preachers seldom if ever attempted to marry form, text, and biography in this way. The *oratio funebris* remained a separate genre, successfully integrated into university funeral ceremonies in particular, but comparatively seldom printed. In a few cases a direct comparison between an *oratio* and a funeral sermon given for the same individual is possible. On the same day, 9 December 1613, Dr John Chadwich preached at the funeral of Sir George St Paul at Snarford in Lincolnshire, his home county, while Matthew Colmore delivered a Latin oration at Corpus Christi College in Oxford, of which St Paul had been a notable benefactor.[66] Colmore's *oratio* is an exuberantly allusive display of classical learning which celebrates St Paul's academic career, public service, and numerous benefactions. The part of Chadwich's sermon not devoted to the exposition of his text (Psalm 37: 37) also speaks of these things, but differs from the *oratio* in its description of St Paul's family life and private piety, and above all in its detailed account of his deathbed. In England there is relatively little evidence of the delivery of orations or eulogies of the recently dead, as distinct from funeral sermons, outside the academic context. (Ambrose Barnes, a famous former mayor of Newcastle upon Tyne, was the subject of a funeral oration heard by an assembly of gentlemen and friends the day after his burial in 1710. This ceremony may have been specially designed to allow Anglicans and Dissenters to join in paying tribute to a highly respected but Nonconformist member of the town's ruling class.)[67]

Less closely akin to the funeral sermon were the poetic tributes of elegy and ode, both traceable to ancient Greece. The ode was a 'poem intended to be sung', a 'rhymed . . . lyric, often in the form of an address; usually dignified or exalted in subject, feeling, and style'; the elegy a 'song of lamentation, especially a funeral ode'.[68] Praise, lament, consolation, and exhortation to follow good examples all played a part in funeral poetry, though the importance of any one of

[66] Chadwich, *Sermon*; M. Colmore, *Oratio funebris in obitum clarissimi viri et munificentissimi collegii Corporis Christi Oxon. benefactoris Georgii Sanctpaul equitis aurati* (Oxford, 1613). University funeral speeches or orations mentioned in Crosfield, *Diary*, 86; W. Wynne, *The Life of Sir Leoline Jenkins . . . and a Compleat Series of Letters . . .* (2 vols., 1724), vol. i. p. li; J. H. Monk, *The Life of Richard Bentley, D.D.* (2 vols., 1833), ii. 413.

[67] *Memoirs of the Life of Mr. Ambrose Barnes, late Merchant and sometime Alderman of Newcastle upon Tyne*, ed. W. H. D. Longstaffe (Surtees Soc. 50; 1867), 255.

[68] *Shorter Oxford English Dictionary*, s.v. 'Elegy', I; s.v. 'Ode', Ia, b.

them varied enormously from one composition to another. Laments had been a customary element of ancient funerals, and the writing of elegies and odes was greatly stimulated by the Renaissance exploration of classical antiquity. Verses were fixed to hearses and monuments; some elegies were employed as permanent memorial inscriptions. They also passed from hand to hand, and were often printed. Some odes and elegies were commissioned; many more were the unsolicited testimonies of friends, admirers, and young poets keen to make their names. In the late sixteenth and seventeenth centuries the deaths of widely respected public figures often released a torrent of such tributes. Several collections of funeral verse were published from 1551 onwards.[69] Elegies ranged in style and quality from stately Latin compositions designed for academic funerals to pedestrian broadsheet productions for mass circulation. The appearance in the eighteenth century of several journals designed for a polite readership provided a new vehicle of publication. The authors of elegies and odes included both the foremost poets and a man such as Leonard Wheatcroft (1627–1707), versatile yeoman craftsman and parish clerk of Ashover (Derby.), who eulogized several local worthies.[70] Such poetry was variously composed as a solace for private grief, for reading by selected friends, or for a large public. Elegies of the latter sort abounded with exhortations to grieve for men of note; it is in private elegies (or those which adopt a more intimate tone), that more restrained, more reflective, but also more powerful melancholy is to be found.[71] The commonest elegiac voice was one of Christian piety; but many poets adopted a secular or pagan tone. Of all forms of tribute to the dead, the elegy might be regarded as the most protean and versatile. Yet by the later eighteenth century the vein had been so thoroughly mined that the personal elegy had come to seem hackneyed, artificial, or extravagant in any save the most skilful hands. Writers found their work parodied and ridiculed. The

---

[69] J. W. Draper, *The Funeral Elegy and the Rise of English Romanticism* (New York, 1929), esp. 24–6, 49–52, 99–101; E. Smith, *By Mourning Tongues. Studies in English Elegy* (Ipswich, 1977), 1–21; G. W. Pigman III, *Grief and English Renaissance Elegy* (Cambridge, 1985), 40–127; D. Kay, *Melodious Tears: The English Funeral Elegy from Spenser to Milton* (Oxford, 1990), esp. 1–28.

[70] Wheatcroft's elegies are in his MS *The Art of Poetry*, pp. 81–133 which is in the Derbyshire Record Office, Matlock.

[71] Two of the most powerful English elegies are Ben Jonson's 'Epigram XLV: On My First Son' and Henry King's 'An Exequy to His Matchless Never to be Forgotten Friend', both in *The New Oxford Book of Seventeenth Century Verse*, ed. A. Fowler (Oxford, 1992), 125, 288–90. See G. W. Pigman's contrast between them in *Grief and Elegy*, 126–7.

best-known elegiac composition of the century refers, not to any specific dead individual, but to the 'rude forefathers of the hamlet' and the 'youth to fortune and to fame unknown'.[72]

An enduring invention of the eighteenth century which has assumed some of the functions of the funeral sermon, *oratio funebris*, elegy, and ode is the obituary notice. The word 'obituary' originally referred to a register of dates of death, especially of people to be prayed for. Only some time after the appearance of fuller death notices in journals and newspapers had become common was the word applied to them. Other antecedents of the modern obituary can be found in comments on the recently dead in journals and letters, even in the summary judgements on newly buried parishioners which the incumbent of Norton (Derby.) entered in his register in the late sixteenth and early seventeenth centuries. In 1585, for example, he commended Anne Blythe as a 'modesta, pia, et beneficientissima matrona'.[73]

From its inception in 1731, the *Gentleman's Magazine* printed death notices which may be regarded as forerunners of the modern obituary. The deaths of all sorts of men (and some women) were noticed, including public benefactors, politicians, lawyers, businessmen, scholars, artists, and centenarians. In February 1731 a scalemaker who had exported 27,000 pairs to Portugal the previous year appeared along with a noted sculptor of monuments in Westminster Abbey. Many notices were very concise. In 1740, for example, there died the 'Rev. Mr *Kidman*, aged 77, at *Dis*, *Norfolk*, remarkable for his generous Principles, and Love to Liberty. He introduc'd the reading of Mr *Locke* into the University of *Cambridge*.' Some notices, however, were much fuller. Henry Palmer 'an ancient and eminent' West India merchant, was commended that year for his professional skill, honourable dealing, beneficence, serenity of temper, and piety and temperance of life. The fully developed obituary would be relatively impersonal, aspiring to impartiality, free of poetic

---

[72] Draper, *Funeral Elegy*, 304–6; T. Gray, 'Elegy Written in a Country Churchyard' (1751), in *The New Oxford Book of Eighteenth Century Verse*, ed. R. Lonsdale (Oxford, 1984), 354–8.

[73] *Liber Vitae Ecclesiae Dunelmensis: nec non Obituaria duo ejusdem Ecclesiae*, ed. J. Stevenson (Surtees Soc. 13; 1841), 135–52; *The Obituary of Richard Smyth, Secondary of the Poultry Compter. London: being a Catalogue of all such Persons as he knew in their Life: extended from A.D. 1627 to A.D. 1674*, ed. Sir Henry Ellis (Camden os 44; 1849), a register of deaths with occasional biographical notes and comments; S. O. Addy, 'A Contribution towards a History of Norton, in Derbyshire', *Journal of the Derbyshire Archaeological and Natural History Society*, 2 (1880), 17.

emotion, concerned primarily with the public career rather than the domestic sphere, with the pattern of a lifetime rather than the last hours and the soul's prospects. It would satisfy the requirements of a more secular age and respect individuals' and families' desire for privacy.[74]

[74] *Gentleman's Magazine*, 1 (1731), 83–4; 10 (1740), 262, 469.

11

Burial and Commemoration

BURIAL

It was a Christian duty to bury the bodies of the dead. Burial of the poor was a meritorious work of mercy.[1] Prolonged exposure of the corpse was a mark of ignominy, rendered more horrible by the disbemberment of traitors' remains and the occasional disinterment of the bodies of notorious public enemies.[2] In the Roman world cemeteries had been located outside towns, but Pope Gregory I (590–604) authorized burial in the immediate vicinity of churches. The souls of the dead might benefit from the prayers of worshippers reminded of them as they passed their graves. The strong and enduring preference for burial on the south side of the church may be largely due to the fact that the church porch is normally situated there. The possession of a cemetery became an attribute of the great majority of parish churches.[3]

Early medieval Church councils forbade burial inside the church, except to members of the clergy and important lay people, such as monarchs, founders, and patrons. Gradually, however, this prohibition was relaxed, partly in order to raise money for church funds. The attractions of burial inside the church included social distinction, added protection for the corpse, and the supposed spiritual benefit of proximity to altars or the relics or images of saints. The striking growth of intramural burial during the later Middle Ages has been

---

[1] *ODCC* 349; J. Weever, *Ancient funerall monuments within the united monarchie of Great Britaine, Ireland, and the islands adjacent* (1631), 24–5; Duffy, *Stripping of Altars*, 357–8, 360; R. N. Swanson, *Catholic England: Faith, Religion and Observance before the Reformation* (Manchester, 1993), 55; P. Ariès, *The Hour of our Death* (Harmondsworth, 1983), 184–7.

[2] J. Foxe, *Acts and Monuments*, ed. J. Pratt (1877), vii. 91–2 (Bucer, Fagius, and Tooley); Pepys, *Diary*, i. 309; ii. 26–7, 31 (Cromwell, Bradshaw, and Ireton).

[3] E. Gibson, *Codex Juris Ecclesiastici Anglicani* (2 vols., Oxford, 1761), i. 453; *John Mirk's Instructions for Parish Priests*, ed. G. Kristensson (Lund Studies in English, 49; 1974), 146; J. Barrow, 'Urban Cemetery Location in the High Middle Ages', in S. Bassett (ed.), *Death in Towns: Urban Responses to the Dying and the Dead, 100–1600* (Leicester, 1992), 78–100 (showing that several urban churches lacked their own cemeteries).

confirmed by excavations, but the great majority, especially children and poorer adults, were still buried in churchyards.[4]

The conventional orientation of Christian burial was east–west, with the feet to the east. Corpses were laid on their backs. At the resurrection of the dead, Christians would at once see their risen Lord in the east. Relatively little is known about the organization of medieval cemeteries, partly because so many of them have remained in use down to the present day. However, more than two hundred skeletons discovered in the northern part of the now abandoned churchyard of Wharram Percy (N. Yorks.) had been buried in rows. Five layers were observed, which suggests that this part of the churchyard had been used in cycles. At Rivenhall (Essex) by contrast, medieval burials appear to have been grouped in tightly intersecting clusters which may represent 'repeated use by a single family group'. Here there was also a tendency to bury infants and young children close to the walls of the church itself.[5]

There was always more burial space in the countryside than in the towns. Urban mortality rates were higher than rural. The combination of limited space and high mortality led to far speedier reuse of the available urban ground. Largely to cope with this problem there developed the charnel or carnary. 'Clean' bones lifted from the churchyard soil were placed in a vault under the church or in a separate building specially set aside for the purpose. A number of institutions were founded in order to maintain intercessory masses for the souls of the departed Christians whose skeletal remains these were. Charnel-chapels were maintained by confraternities at Old St Paul's in London (which had the biggest charnel in England) and a number of

---

[4] [T. Lewis], *Churches no Charnel-Houses: being An Enquiry into the Profaneness, Indecency, and Pernicious Consequences to the Living, of Burying the Dead in Churches and Churchyards* (1726), 40–53; Ariès, *Hour*, 45–51; J. Le Goff, *The Birth of Purgatory* (1984), 276; V. Harding, 'Burial Choice and Burial Location in Later Medieval London', in Bassett (ed.), *Death in Towns*, 122–7, 130–4; B. Kjølbye-Biddle, 'Dispersal or Concentration: The Disposal of the Winchester Dead over 2000 Years', ibid. 233–4; N. P. Tanner, *The Church in Late Medieval Norwich, 1370–1532* (Toronto, 1984), 11–14, 189.

[5] *Popular Antiquities of Great Britain . . . from the Materials collected by John Brand F.S.A.*, ed. W. C. Hazlitt (3 vols., 1870), ii. 217; R. C. Finucane, 'Sacred Corpse, Profane Carrion: Social Ideas and Death Rituals in the later Middle Ages', in J. Whaley (ed.), *Mirrors of Mortality: Studies in the Social History of Death* (1981), 43; C. Daniell, *Death and Burial in Medieval England, 1066–1550* (1997), 148 (Christian explanations may have served to justify already established practice); J. G. Hurst and P. A. Rahtz, *Wharram: A Study of Settlement on the Yorkshire Wolds*, iii. *Wharram Percy: The Church of St Martin* (1987), 84; W. J. Rodwell and K. A. Rodwell, *Rivenhall: Investigation of a Villa, Church and Village, 1950–1977* (Council for British Archaeology Research Report 55; 1986), 99–100.

provincial towns. At Worcester, the chapel of the carnary, built early in the thirteenth century, was served by six chaplains from 1287 onwards. At Norwich, Bishop John Salmon (1299–1325) established a charnel where clean bones of people buried in the city might be 'decently reserved till the last day'. Four priests were attached to it. At least seven London parishes, and possibly many more, had charnels of their own. The use of charnels could under normal circumstances enable the urban parish to cope with a relatively high level of mortality reasonably efficiently. However, burial arrangements could break down during epidemics. The Black Death compelled urban communities in particular to find new burial space quickly. Two new cemeteries are known to have been established just outside London. One of these, at East Smithfield, probably received 2,400 corpses. All interments seem to have been carried out in an orderly fashion, but over half the individuals discovered had been laid in tightly packed trenches rather than graves, presumably because of the need for speed when mortality was at its height.[6]

The Reformation's repudiation of intercessory prayer had important implications for burial practices. No longer could the souls associated with the bones deposited in a particular ossuary benefit from masses celebrated on their behalf. The charnel (where it survived) became a simple bone-house. In Edward VI's reign the charnel-house and chapel of St Paul's were closed down. Over a thousand cartloads of bones were carried out and dumped in Finsbury Fields. Elsewhere charnel-buildings were sold and converted to other uses. In post-Reformation England, ancestral bones had no acceptable long-term resting-place comparable with the great ossuaries of Brittany, which were extensively rebuilt and embellished during the Counter-Reformation. Rites marking the transfer of clean bones were a very important part of Breton popular religion.[7]

Protestant rejection of prayer for departed souls and denial of any possible advantage from interment close to altars or shrines removed

---

[6] G. H. Cook, *Old St Paul's Cathedral* (1955), 67–8; id. *The English Medieval Parish Church* (1954), 128–30; F. M. Stenton, 'The City of Worcester', in *Victoria History of the County of Worcestershire* (1906–   ), iv. 411–12; F. Blomefield and C. Parkin, *An Essay towards a Topographical History of the County of Norfolk* (11 vols., 2nd edn., 1805–10), iv. 55–6; D. Hawkins, 'The Black Death and the New London Cemeteries of 1348', *Antiquity*, 64 (1990), 637–42.

[7] J. Stow, *A Survey of London*, ed. C. L. Kingsford (2 vols., Oxford, 1908), i. 293, 329–30; Blomefield and Parkin, *Norfolk*, iii. 261; E. Musgrave, 'Memento Mori: The Function and Meaning of Breton Ossuaries 1450–1750', in P. C. Jupp and G. Howarth (edd.), *The Changing Face of Death: Historical Accounts of Death and Disposal* (Basingstoke, 1997), 62–75.

important pretexts for burial in the church or churchyard. There could be no special spiritual benefit from burial in consecrated ground; certainly no greater benefit from burial in the church rather than the churchyard. However, only the most radical Protestants, such as the separatist Henry Barrow (d. 1593) rejected burial in consecrated ground as superstitious. Others, including conformable Puritans, continued to accept it. The presence of the remains of the dead still served the salutary purpose of reminding the living of their own mortality. Churchyard burial was also a means of showing proper respect for the residue of that body which had been the habitation of the soul and would be reunited with it at the resurrection. It was, thirdly, a testimony of proper affection towards the deceased.[8]

In 1563 a preacher called Turner solemnly requested the lord mayor of London to have the City's dead buried in the fields outside the walls. He probably had sanitary considerations in mind, for this was a year of especially heavy plague mortality. The Corporation later took up his idea, at least in part. The New Churchyard outside Bishopsgate, London's first extramural cemetery, was established in 1569. This extra-parochial site was favoured by the stauncher London Puritans of Elizabeth I's reign. Here they were able to put into practice their own preferences in conducting funerals. However, as time went by, the New Churchyard, from the first designed to ease the pressure on the overcrowded older cemeteries, increasingly became the last resting-place of poorer Londoners. In 1665–6, again as the result of a major outbreak of plague, a new burial-ground was established at Bunhill Fields. Its extra-parochial character made it, like the New Churchyard, a favourite place for Nonconformist burials, but in this case the connection with Dissent was stronger and lasted longer. [9]

Between the sixteenth and eighteenth centuries a number of London parishes acquired new ground for the extension of their churchyards or the creation of satellite cemeteries, especially on the edge of the city and in the suburbs. However, a widespread response to a growing shortage of space, especially in the inner city, seems to have been to pack the maximum possible number of corpses into the

---

[8] Greaves, *Religion and Society*, 697, 701–3; above, Ch. 5.

[9] *Three Fifteenth-Century Chronicles, with Historical Memoranda by John Stowe, the Antiquary, and Contemporary Notes of Occurrences written by him in the Reign of Queen Elizabeth*, ed. J. Gairdner (Camden NS 28; 1880), 125; V. Harding, ' "And one more may be laid there": The Location of Burials in Early Modern London', *London Journal*, 14 (1989), 118–19; ead., 'Burial of the Plague Dead in Early Modern London', in J. A. I. Champion (ed.), *Epidemic Disease in London* (Centre for Metropolitan History, Working Papers Ser. 1; 1993), 61.

available ground. Various parish registers record the multiple use of graves, with several bodies being placed together. Sheer lack of space compelled parishioners to make a much more intensive use of the ground inside churches than was ever necessary in the countryside. In so far as charnels were employed, it was in a more casual fashion than in medieval times. Where they did survive, their contents were probably treated with scant respect. An alternative to the charnel-house was a bone-pit like the one dug when the churchyard of St Margaret's, Westminster, was cleared in 1616. 'Our Bones in consecrated ground never lie quiet,' John Aubrey wrote; 'and in London once in ten yeares (or thereabout) the Earth is carried to the Dung-wharf' (presumably for use as fertilizer in the country outside London).[10]

During the repeated outbreaks of plague in post-Reformation London between 1563 and 1665, the overloaded metropolitan cemeteries could not cope with the additional demands on them, and many individuals had to be buried in pits both within and outside churchyards. The horror and pathos of the plague-holes, and the promiscuous mixing-up of all sorts of people, inspired some lurid passages in the works of Thomas Dekker and Daniel Defoe. The shame of pit-burial was to be avoided if at all possible. During the eighteenth century use of long-term burial-pits, gradually filled with the bodies of the poor, became necessary in some of the more crowded London parishes. The main expedients of more intensive use of available space, including the ground within the church itself or vaults underneath it, extension of churchyards where possible, and the occasional creation of new cemeteries, were also followed in provincial towns.[11]

Rising population exerted a pressure on burial space which was only offset to a very limited extent by exclusions from consecrated ground or deliberate avoidance of it. The penalty of excommunication, in theory entailing exclusion from burial in the churchyard, was employed by the Church courts against a growing number of people after the Reformation. Yet the courts seem to have shown relatively

---

[10] Harding, 'Location of Burials', 116–18; C. Gittings, *Death, Burial and the Individual in Early Modern England* (1984), 139; *Aubrey's Brief Lives*, ed. O. L. Dick (Harmondsworth, 1972), 103.

[11] Harding, 'Burial of the Plague Dead', 59–60, remarks that well-attested plague pits in unconsecrated ground were far less numerous than is often believed; Dekker, *Plague Pamphlets*, 28–9, 61, 72, 78, 132, 158–9; D. Defoe, *A Journal of the Plague Year*, ed. A. Burgess and C. Bristow (Harmondsworth, 1966), 77–81; Pepys, *Diary*, vi. 164–5; R. Richardson, *Death, Dissection and the Destitute* (Harmondsworth, 1989), 60–1; W. Andrews, *Burials without Coffins* (Hull, 1899), 6; Josselin, *Diary*, 521.

little interest in the burial of unreconciled excommunicates. In 1684 John Richardson, an excommunicated tanner and maltman of Durham, was expressly denied church burial by the bishop. He was interred in his own garden, where his wife joined him six years later. However, this unusual *cause célèbre* was brought to a head by the religious reaction of the 1680s and the personal interest of the bishop.[12]

Many descriptions of the customary highway burial of suicides survive. Yet much of the evidence comes from the years after 1700, when verdicts of unsound mind were being returned in a rapidly growing proportion of cases, and it may have been felt all the more important to enforce the full rigour of the law against the guilty minority. Earlier sources, especially parish registers, are disappointingly uninformative. Some suicides were certainly permitted churchyard burial during the sixteenth and seventeenth centuries. The friends of the dead occasionally made strenuous efforts to circumvent the ban by nocturnal interment or by going to some outlying chapelry.[13]

The majority of English Catholics were probably interred in family chapels or churchyards in the seventeenth and early eighteenth centuries. Sometimes these burials were recorded in the parish register. Discreet behaviour, such as choice of a nocturnal hour, was advisable. Some Catholic congregations had their own customary burial area in the parish churchyard. Burial with the deceased of earth previously blessed by a priest was one means of reconciling Catholic consciences to churchyard burial.[14]

Some Puritans made good use of the London extra-parochial burial-grounds. Yet most Presbyterians, Congregationalists, and Baptists were buried in churchyards until long after 1700, despite being permitted their own places of worship by the Toleration Act of 1689. As late as the 1740s the estimated total of interments in Nonconformist

[12] R. A. Marchant, *The Church under the Law: Justice, Administration and Discipline in the Diocese of York, 1560–1640* (Cambridge, 1969), 227; Gittings, *Death*, 76–7 (for some instances of exclusion); BRO D/A2/c60, fos. 325–6; 48–9, 54; *Six North Country Diaries*, ed. J. C. Hodgson (Surtees Soc. 118; 1910), 48–9, 54.

[13] M. MacDonald and T. R. Murphy, *Sleepless Souls: Suicide in Early Modern England* (Oxford, 1990), 16, 18–20, 44–9, 78, 138–9, 213–14, 357–8; Gittings, *Death*, 73–4; C. Kerry, 'Miscellanea', *Journal of the Derbyshire Archaeological and Natural History Soc.* 19 (1897), 101–3.

[14] J. C. H. Aveling, *The Handle and the Axe* (1976), 70, 144, 158, 310; J. A. Williams, *Catholic Recusancy in Wiltshire, 1660–1791* (Catholic Record Soc., Monograph Ser. 1; 1968), 3, 7, 68, 88–9; Gittings, *Death*, 77; H. Colvin, *Architecture and the After-Life* (New Haven, 1991), 257.

burial-grounds was under three thousand, 0.19 per cent of the 'Angli-can' national total. More important were the Quakers, who estab-lished their own burial-grounds as soon as possible. At the height of their strength in 1680, the Quakers may have made up 1.15 per cent of the population of England and Wales, but their numbers dwindled during the eighteenth century while the national population increased.[15]

A few people deliberately chose burial outside any cemetery. John Evelyn's brother-in-law asked to be buried at sea. Such committal to 'the deep' was normal for seamen who died during a voyage. The adapted burial service looked forward to resurrection 'when the Sea shall give up her dead'. In 1743 the Lancashire Nonconformist Richard Kay noted that his 'good and pious Uncle John', a wealthy bachelor, had, in accordance with his express wish, been buried 10 foot deep in his own garden.[16]

Although Protestants were taught that they derived no benefit from being buried in any particular spot, solicitude for the mortal remains and their preservation continued. It may indeed have been strength-ened by official rejection of intercession for the soul. Even a Puritan could cite biblical examples in order to justify care of the bodies of the godly.[17] A desire to protect the corpse may help to explain the con-tinuation of the practice of intramural interment after the Reforma-tion, the creation of larger areas of private burial space, and the spread of coffin burial. All three were inspired by a desire to demon-strate or maintain social status as well as a wish to protect the mortal remains. Probate accounts from Berkshire, Lincolnshire, and Kent suggest that intramural burial may have reached its peak at the end of the sixteenth century or early in the seventeenth in these predomin-antly rural counties.[18] The limited space available in many churches made it quite difficult to find room for a new grave. In some cases sex-tons were described as disturbing previously interred corpses or pushing them aside in order to make room for new burials.[19]

Creation of private burial space was a more effective means of

[15] E. A. Wrigley and R. S. Schofield, *The Population History of England 1541–1871: A Reconstruction* (1981), 89–96.

[16] Evelyn, *Diary*, v. 497; this 'made much discourse; he having no relation at all to the Sea'; Kay, *Diary*, 60.

[17] E. Reynolds, *Mary Magdalens Love to Christ Opened In a Sermon Preached at the Funeral of Mistris Elizabeth Thomason* (1659), 22–4.

[18] Gittings, *Death*, 241.

[19] Harding, 'The Location of Burials', 116–17; Pepys, *Diary*, v. 90; Bod. Lib. MS Eng. misc. f. 381, fo. 66ᵛ.

protecting the mortal remains. Separate burial vaults, often under family chapels, were first built in the later Middle Ages, but the great period of the private vault lasted from Elizabeth I's reign to Victoria's. Former charnels were sometimes converted into private vaults after the Reformation, but the great majority of the hundreds of English family vaults brought into use between the sixteenth and nineteenth centuries were purpose-built. Many were later improved and extended. Here were entombed successive generations of gentlefolk, including not just the current head of the family and his spouse, but many of their unmarried children, and, in some cases, even a few of their specially trusted servants. Some wealthy families even created separate mausoleums. Of these the most splendid is the rotunda at Castle Howard.[20]

Most urban families of middling rank had neither the resources nor the incentive to make the long-term provision represented by a vault. In many cases their needs were met by the simpler brick-lined shaft. Excavation of the church of St Augustine the Less in Bristol revealed over a hundred burial compartments under the floor. Some were vaults, but most were deep brick-lined shafts. These were designed to take up to six coffins separated from each other by iron bars. An alternative was to share in the security of vaults controlled by the parish vestry. All twelve churches completed under the terms of the Fifty New Churches Act of 1711 had extensive vaults which were used to accommodate coffins from an early stage. Those of Christ Church, Spitalfields, completed in 1729, had over a thousand coffins stacked in them during the following 130 years.[21]

Strong wooden coffins were used for some burials in England as early as Anglo-Saxon times. At least 30 per cent of the individuals found in the East Smithfield plague cemetery had been buried in coffins. Cist graves made of slabs of stone were also employed during the Middle Ages. However, there seems to have been an overall preponderance of earth burials in later medieval cemeteries and churchyards.[22] Evidence

---

[20] J. Litten, *The English Way of Death: The Common Funeral since 1450* (1991), 195–226; Colvin, *Architecture and After-Life*, 253–70, 295–363. Completion of Castle Howard mausoleum: 1736 (Colvin, *Architecture and After-Life*, 317); 1744 (Litten, *English Way of Death*, 226).

[21] Litten, *English Way of Death*, 221, 224; E. Boore, 'The Church of St Augustine the Less, Bristol: An Interim Statement', *Transactions of the Bristol and Gloucestershire Archaeological Soc.* 104 (1986), 211–13; M. Adams and J. Reeve, 'Excavations at Christ Church, Spitalfields, 1984–1986', *Antiquity*, 61 (1987), 247–56.

[22] W. Rodwell, *Church Archaeology* (2nd edn., 1989), 164; Kjølbye-Biddle, 'Dispersal or Concentration', 235–43; Rodwell and Rodwell, *Rivenhall*, 101; Hurst and Rahtz, *Wharram*, iii. 84, 96; Hawkins, 'Black Death and New London Cemeteries',

for the spread of coffin burial after the Reformation is found in probate accounts. Of course this evidence relates to people who owned at least some property. The process was an uneven one, and its extent varied from one county to another, but coffins, recorded in only a minority of detailed accounts before 1590, appeared in a substantial majority of them by the time of the Civil War. There were three major motives for coffin burial. The first was charitable solicitude for the corpse. Encasement in a coffin hid it from view, and gave it some protection against subsequent disturbance. The second was demonstration of social status. Coffin burial was always more expensive than earth burial. In 1580 the corporation of Rye forbade anybody below the degree of common councilman to be buried in a coffin unless they had been licensed by the mayor in return for a payment towards poor relief. A third was the sanitary concern which presumably inspired the decision taken in 1565 that no corpse should henceforth be buried within the church of St Helen's, Bishopsgate (London) unless coffined in wood.[23]

Between 1550 and 1750 a coffin came to be regarded as indispensable in a 'decent' burial. Plague-victims whose last request was that they be buried in coffins appear in Thomas Dekker's account of the visitation of 1603 and in a Norwich case of 1666. During the early eighteenth century even paupers were buried in coffins in many parishes. A cheaper alternative was the reusable parish coffin with a hinged underside which allowed the body to be dropped into the grave, but its use came to seem unacceptable.[24]

On the heels of the spread of coffin burial went the increasing elaboration of coffins themselves. Even the well-off were buried in relatively simple coffins in the sixteenth century, when coffin burial itself was still a mark of status. By the eighteenth century a much wider price range separated the cheapest coffins from the most expensive, and the latter had become very elaborate. Between 5s. and 7s. had been paid for most of the coffins mentioned in Berkshire probate accounts of the years 1590–1640. In the early eighteenth century coffin prices ranged from between 5s. and 9s. for a pauper to the £35. 15s. paid in 1723 for the duke of Richmond and Lennox. One suitable

638–40. For difficulties in detecting coffin traces in graves, see Daniell, *Death and Burial*, 162–3. Important people were often buried in stone coffins during the Middle Ages, but such burials made up a tiny fraction of all interments.

[23] Gittings, *Death*, 240; B. S. Puckle, *Funeral Customs: Their Origin and Development* (1926), 42; Andrews, *Burials without Coffins*, 4–5.

[24] Dekker, *Plague Pamphlets*, 39; NRO DN/DEP 48/52, fos. 28ᵛ–9ᵛ; Andrews, *Burial without Coffins*, 9–12.

for a member of the middling ranks of society could be bought for between £1 and £4. The use of lead greatly increased the cost of interment. Sealing the corpse in lead so as to prevent the escape of noxious odours and effluvia was common until the later seventeenth century both when a long interval was expected before burial and for intramural interment. Thereafter, a lead inner coffin, or a lead shell between inner and outer wooden coffins, replaced the earlier close sheathing of the body. By the second quarter of the eighteenth century there were four main types of coffin: the single case, the single case with a double lid, the double case, and finally the triple case 'comprising an inner wooden coffin, a lead shell and an outer wooden case'. The last sort was the most suitable for vault burial.[25]

The ornamentation of the most expensive coffins, as well as their structure, grew more elaborate with the passage of time. By the 1660s even a cheap deal coffin might bear the date and symbols of mortality composed of small nails. A more expensive coffin might have a cover of black fabric, 'grips' (handles) and grip-plates, angle-brackets, as well as nails arranged on the lid in the shape of the deceased's initials and date of death, and in a single row round the sides. During the early eighteenth century coffin-plates, lid decorations, and more elaborate grip-plates became common, all available in a variety of finishes. 'Depositum' plates gave the style of the deceased and his armorial bearings (if any). They might also be engraved with symbols or allegorical figures. Among Clarissa Harlowe's diversions on her deathbed was the sketching of no fewer than seven plates for her coffin-lid. The symbolic devices were common ones in funereal iconography: a winged hourglass; a crowned serpent forming a ring, the emblem of eternity (the principal device, enclosing her name, the date, and her

---

[25] BRO D/A1/173–7, 181–2; 18th-cent. overseers' accounts listed in Ch. 9 n. 75; F. W. Steer, 'The Funeral Account of the First Duke of Richmond and Lennox', *Sussex Archaeological Collections*, 98 (1960), 158; GL MSS 9182 (account of administration of estate of Margaret Leathwait, 1721); 9183 (John Levitt, 1714; Richard Smallpiece, 1712); 9185/3 (Francis Kercher, 1709); 9185/5 (Richard Freeman, 1725). In 1579 Sir Nicholas Bacon's elm coffin cost 15s., his lead coffin £5. 4s. 9d., an inscription on it £2. 3s. 4d. (Bod. Lib. MS Ashmole 836, pp. 33–4). In 1707 an elm coffin for John Egerton Esq. covered with fine cloth and set off with silver work cost £5, his leaden coffin £3 (BL MS Harley 1529/75); the same year £7 was paid for a large 6 foot double-lid elm coffin covered with fine cloth, four pairs of chased handles and a flower with a double plate, cherubim heads, and a coat of arms, all the work gilt with gold, for William Phelips Esq., while his large, thick leaden coffin cost £6 (SRO DD/PH 180); Litten, *English Way of Death*, 90–6, 100–1. The embalming of Prince Arthur's corpse in 1502 'was so sufficiently doon that it nedid noo leed [lead]': *The Receyt of the Ladie Kateryne*, ed. G. Kipling (EETS 296; 1990), 81.

age); the head of a white lily falling from the stalk; and an urn. Between the four devices, three suitable scriptural texts were to be placed. A London undertaker's purchase ledger of the 1740s records for 1746–7 prices ranging from £1. 12s. for an elaborate heraldic plate of brass to 8s. for the simplest white metal plate intended for an adult. The descriptions in executors' and undertakers' accounts convey a vivid impression of the rich outer covering, sumptuous lining, gilt nails, finely engraved plates, and chased handles of the splendid receptacles upon which so much money was lavished during the eighteenth century.[26]

Bodies normally went to the grave dressed in a shroud or winding-sheet. The winding-sheet originally covered the corpse completely and was tied at head and foot. Undershifts began to be used in the early seventeenth century. The wealthy were interred in both a shift (which came to be called a shroud) and a sheet. The development of grave-clothes, like that of coffins, was marked by a process of elaboration at the top of the range and widening price differentials. Burial in woollen was imposed by statutes of 1660 and 1678. The use of any other thread or fabric was forbidden. The Acts stimulated the ingenuity of manufacturers such as Mrs Potter who in 1678 claimed to have been the first to make 'Decent and fashionable laced Shifts and Dressings for the Dead made of Woollen'. Specially designed flannel shifts or shirts were sold in large numbers. The shirt was supposed to be at least 6 inches longer than the body so that it could be tied 'into a Kind of Tuft'. A cap was placed on the head, gloves on the hands, and a cravat round the neck. When the body was viewed by guests before the funeral 'the rich Equipage of the Dead' did 'Honour to the Living'. In 1714 William Phelips went to his grave in a 'superfine Norwich Crape sheet, shroud, gloues' (costing £1. 15s. together with a pillow). The upper classes readily paid the forfeiture to the use of the poor for their not being buried in woollen. Their ability to do so became one more mark of difference between them and the ranks below them in the social scale. The readiness to lavish money on an equipage which, once briefly admired, was designed to be buried for ever, was especially characteristic of the two centuries following the Civil War.[27]

---

[26] *Receyt*, 32, 99–100, 106; S. Richardson, *Clarissa or, The History of a Young Lady* (8 vols., Oxford, 1930), vii. 338–9; GL MS 5871 (purchase ledger of Richard Carpenter, undertaker; account with James Wigley, engraver, 1746–7).

[27] P. Cunnington and C. Lucas, *Costume for Births, Marriages and Deaths* (1972), 161; Litten, *English Way of Death*, 76–7, 143–4; Gittings, *Death*, 110–13; SRO DD/PH 180; cf. account of expenditure on Dame Hester Probert's funeral at Denham, 1743 (Aylesbury, Buckinghamshire Record Office, D/W 48/7).

The corpses of the wealthy were often embalmed. In Tudor England this involved removal of the soft organs, treatment of the body with resins, dressing with spices, and tight wrapping with waxed cloth. The recorded costs of preparation in three Elizabethan cases ranged from £3 to over £28. This span represented the difference between a local surgeon's basic job and the services of an expert who was paid for this one task more than most gentlefolk paid for an entire funeral. Some people disliked the mutilation of the body which embalming entailed. A new method of preservation, using spirits of wine, is mentioned in some eighteenth-century accounts.[28]

The overwhelming majority of corpses were buried with very little preparation. A well-constructed coffin, its joins thoroughly pitched, might minimize unpleasantness even when there was some delay before burial. 'Be pleas'd to take care of the inside for the Gentlewoman is not design'd to be buried this fortnight,' ran the instructions for Dorothy Wood's double coffin in 1704. Samuel Newton, alderman of Cambridge, dreaming in 1708 of his own burial, saw an old shoemaker nailing leather round the bottom of the coffin. Bran was often put in the coffin (three bushels of it in one case) to absorb effluents, and, by bedding the corpse more securely, to prevent inconvenient movement. Under favourable conditions, some close coffined corpses survived for very long periods.[29]

Burial usually occurred very soon after death. In a group of six mainly rural Yorkshire parishes over 95 per cent of interments took place on the day of death or the one following between 1647 and 1666. Even in the 'comparatively prosperous' parish of St Mary Woolnoth in London, which contained many highly skilled artisans and professional people, 70 per cent of all burials took place before the third day after death during the period 1653–1699, 86 per cent before the fourth day. According to Henri Misson, a three- or four-day interval was customary in the case of 'middling People'. He was probably writing about adults; over 40 per cent of the St Mary's interments

---

[28] Litten, *English Way of Death*, 35–44; BRO D/E Bt F34 (William Waite Esq. of Wymering, Hants, 1561); Bod. Lib. MS Ashmole, 836, p. 33 (Sir Nicholas Bacon, 1579); BL MS Harley 4774, fo. 141 (3rd earl of Huntingdon, 1596). See SRO DD/PH 180 (William Phelips, 1714) for 'A bed of Spices and Rich Sperits used about the body'; J. Hutchins, *The History and Antiquities of the County of Dorset* (3rd edn., 4 vols., 1861), i. 49 (coffin of James Thompson, merchant of Poole 'pitched and filled with spirit of wine', 1739).

[29] London, Greater London Record Office, Wood (Harrison) collection, no. 1689; *The Diary of Samuel Newton, Alderman of Cambridge (1662–1717)*, ed. J. E. Foster (Cambridge Antiquarian Soc. 23; 1890), 118; Litten, *English Way of Death*, 32–3, 144.

were of children or adolescents, who were buried sooner than adults. Misson thought that an important reason for delaying burial was to make sure that the individual had expired. Various stories illustrated the difficulty of ascertaining the moment of death. The fear of being buried alive gave edge to some of Dekker's plague anecdotes. In Samuel Newton's 1708 dream about burial he cried out, 'I am alive, I will not be buryed alive, stay till I am dead'.[30]

There were various popular rites or customs designed to speed the spirit on its way, but they were not underpinned by any coherent or generally held body of beliefs. In Lincolnshire there were two different traditional notions about the securing of the shroud: that it should be loosely tied, so as not to hinder resurrection, and tightly tied, so as to prevent the ghost from walking.[31] Before the Civil Wars, John Aubrey heard of a custom observed in what was then already 'the old time' in Wales and the north: putting a penny in the dead person's mouth to give to St Peter. Excavations have revealed miscellaneous small items in post-medieval graves, but the paucity and heterogeneity of these finds make it difficult to discern a consistent pattern of underlying beliefs or attitudes. A desire to preserve some shadow of individual identity in the impersonality of the grave may explain many of these deposits. The wedding rings found on some corpses buried in Spitalfields vaults in the eighteenth century seem to assert a union which continued beyond death. However, there is little evidence that artefacts placed in graves were expected to confer benefits or protection upon the deceased or survivors.[32]

COMMEMORATION

Monuments inside Churches

The commemoration of individuals by means of funeral monuments never died out entirely during the Middle Ages, but it was relatively

---

[30] S. Porter, 'Death and Burial in a London Parish: St Mary Woolnoth, 1653–1699', *London Journal*, 8 (1982), 76–80; Litten, *English Way of Death*, 144; Gittings, *Death*, 30, 108, 205–6; Bod. Lib. MS Eng. misc. f. 381, fo. 63ᵛ; Dekker, *Plague Pamphlets*, 61, 129–32; Newton, *Diary*, 118. See Gittings, *Death*, 30, for some requests for delayed burial in late medieval wills.

[31] H. Gutch and M. G. W. Peacock, *County Folklore, Printed Extracts, No. VII, Examples of Printed Folklore concerning Lincolnshire* (1908), 240, 243, cited in Gittings, *Death*, 112, 123.

[32] J. Aubrey, *Remaines of Gentilisme and Judaisme*, in id., *Three Prose Works*, ed. J. Buchanan-Brown (Fontwell, 1972), 172; Rodwell, *Church Archaeology*, 165; Daniell, *Death and Burial*, 149–51 (lack of grave goods in medieval cemeteries); Adams and Reeve, 'Excavations at Spitalfields', 251; Gittings, *Death*, 111.

rare until after *c*.1100. Three main developments may be discerned
during the following seven centuries: a gradual downwards diffusion
of the practice of erecting monuments from the uppermost ranks of
society to its middling strata; the increasing importance of commemoration, as distinct from the encouragement of intercession, as a function of monuments; and a long-term shift of emphasis from the visual
representation of the deceased to the epitaph. Much of the account
which follows is devoted to the monuments of a comparatively
wealthy minority, simply because they give beliefs and sentiments
the fullest visual and literary expression.

During the later Middle Ages the commemoration of important
people by means of permanent effigies in churches became increasingly common. In the fourteenth and fifteenth centuries it became
normal to show the deceased person at rest, lying on his or her back
on a tomb chest, hands held together in prayer.[33] We should imagine
these prayers directed to God, though to one eighteenth-century
observer it seemed that the ancient recumbent statues 'Devoutly
fix'd, with Hands uplifted high' were also 'Intreating Pray'rs of all the
passers-by'.[34] Effigies certainly presented to the faithful the images of
people who might benefit from their intercessions. Other motives for
such commemoration included a deep-rooted desire on the part of
the individual to be remembered with respect, and the hope of successors that they would benefit from their connection with a famous
ancestor or predecessor.

In the thirteenth century there appeared for the first time one-
dimensional commemorative monuments incised in stone or
engraved on plates of brass. 'Brasses' were usually cheaper to produce than effigies. The use of templates and master patterns facilitated large-scale production. The engravers grasped much earlier
than sculptors the possibility of reducing the scale of representations
of the deceased and removing them from the conventional tomb
chest. This occurred above all during the second half of the fifteenth
century. By then brasses far outnumbered carved effigies. Both the
supply of commemorative monuments and the demand for them
expanded rapidly at this time. Around 1300 most of the people portrayed were secular or ecclesiastical magnates. Two centuries later
the engravers' clientele included lesser gentry, merchants, lawyers,
parsons, and even some yeomen. Brass-engraving became the

---

[33] B. R. Kemp, *English Church Monuments* (1980), 22–3.
[34] John Dart, *Westminster* (*c*.1723), quoted in K. A. Esdaile, *English Church Monuments 1510–1840* (1946), 54.

medium in which compositional experiment and innovation were most marked. The engravers introduced standing and kneeling figures and groups of people, and brought together praying figures and the objects of their devotion. Such schemes were far easier to realize when drawn in two dimensions. The adoption of brass-engraving also facilitated the inclusion within the design of much more written text than had hitherto been common. This was a major step towards the ultimate triumph of the inscribed word as the most important element in funeral monuments.[35]

The earliest effigies represented individuals, but a high proportion of surviving funeral monuments commemorate more than one person. By far the commonest relationship portrayed is that of husband and wife. Hundreds of recumbent couples seem to await the resurrection together, vividly representing the central place which marriage occupied in medieval social life. A few of them convey the unique intimacy of the conjugal partnership by holding hands. This posture is 'peculiarly English'. It seems to have reached the height of its popularity around 1400. Several brasses dating from the late fifteenth and early sixteenth centuries show man and wife turned towards each other. Some of the monuments commemorate a man or woman and two successive partners, or, more rarely, even three.[36]

The walls of tomb-chests were often adorned with shields of arms representing the descents and alliances of the individual or couple commemorated. These vertical spaces might alternatively be decorated with figures reminiscent of the watchers keeping vigil round the bier before a magnate's funeral, or mourners in the funeral procession. Some were praying. 'And all a-bowt my tumbe', specified the countess of Warwick (d. 1439) in her will, 'to be made pore men and wemen In theire pore Array, with their bedys In theire handes.' In

[35] S. F. Badham, 'London Standardisation and Provincial Idiosyncrasy: The Organisation and Working Practices of Brass-Engraving Workshops in Pre-Reformation England', *Church Monuments*, 5 (1990), 3–25; M. Norris, 'Later Medieval Monumental Brasses: An Urban Funerary Industry and its Representation of Death', in Bassett (ed.), *Death in Towns*, 184–209; *Monumental Brasses: The Portfolio Plates of the Monumental Brass Society 1894–1984*, introd. M. W. Norris (Woodbridge, 1988), pls. 1–315 (covering 1301–1530); F. A. Greenhill, *Incised Effigial Slabs* (1976). For the increasing use of English in inscriptions on funeral monuments, see R. Rex, *Henry VIII and the English Reformation* (Basingstoke, 1993), 109–10.

[36] H. Tummers, 'The Medieval Effigial Tombs in Chichester Cathedral', *Church Monuments*, 3 (1988), 33, 35; Kemp, *English Monuments*, 54; *Monumental Brasses*, pls. 37, 81, 95, 96, 119, 121, 122, 199, 200, 226, 236, 245–7, 263–4, 269, 278, 290, 293, 297, 299, 303.

other cases these figures probably represent kinsfolk, especially children, of the deceased.[37]

The children of the couple commemorated appeared as subsidiary figures on a growing number of brasses from the early fifteenth century onwards. At first they were shown on a far smaller scale, below their parents. Eventually, during the later fifteenth century, they were often brought up to the same level, usually represented in profile, kneeling in male and female groups behind father or mother. On brasses of the last medieval decades, husband and wife sometimes face each other across a prayer desk. Representations of the family at prayer were combined on some sculpted monuments with representations of the Trinity, the Virgin Mary, the Annunciation, and the Resurrection.[38]

The inscriptions on family memorials seldom solicit prayers for the children as well as for their parents. Perhaps the portrayal of children was simply intended to demonstrate that God had made the marriage loving and fruitful. The fact that the whole family was joined in prayer conveyed the message that the children had been brought up in God's fear and were members of his household. Some memorials to children on their own were erected from the fourteenth century onwards, but they are rare. Children, who died innocent, or at least with a smaller burden of sins than adults, may not have been thought to stand in so great a need of intercession.[39]

One motif which may have been thought particularly effective in encouraging bystanders to pray for the departed soul was the image of the shrouded corpse. Originating in the early fifteenth century, this motif appeared first in sculpture, later in brasses. These images were intended to arouse horror and compassion: to bring home to the bystander the reality of man's common fate, to make him pity the

---

[37] Kemp, *English Monuments*, 26–30; *The Fifty Earliest English Wills in the Court of Probate, London*, ed. F. J. Furnivall (EETS 78; 1882), 117; P. M. King, 'The Cadaver Tomb in England: Novel Manifestations of an Old Idea', *Church Monuments*, 5 (1990), 28.

[38] J. Page-Phillips, *Children on Brasses* (1970), figs. 7–28; *Monumental Brasses*, pls. 238–9, 252, 290, 303–4; J. Bayliss, 'Richard Parker "the Alablasterman"', *Church Monuments*, 5 (1990), 43–6; Kemp, *English Monuments*, 64, 184; P. Hadfield, *Youlgreave Parish Church and Records* (Youlgreave, n.d.), back cover; N. Pevsner, *The Buildings of England, Herefordshire* (Harmondsworth, 1963), 130, 277–8.

[39] Page-Phillips, *Children on Brasses*, figs. 1, 29, 30. An undated incised alabaster slab of *c*.1480 at Croxall (Staffs.) nevertheless bears a prayer for God's mercy on John and Mary Curzon, children of Thomas Curzon Esq., even though they died 'in innocencia eorum': anon., 'Incised Slabs in Croxall Church', drawn by M. Ussher, *Journal of the Derbyshire Archaeological and Natural History Soc.* 2 (1880), 90; see also Norris, 'Later Medieval Brasses', 201.

plight of the dead person (which he would soon share), and then (contemplating his own mortality) pray for the deceased. Thomas Morys, grocer of London, stipulated in his will (1506) that he and his wife should be engraved 'like ij deade carkas as pitiouslye made as canne be thoughte'.[40]

Most later medieval memorial inscriptions follow certain established formulas. The commonest begins 'Hic iacet' (here lies), briefly identifies the deceased, supplies the date of death, and concludes with a plea for God's mercy on the soul. Many inscriptions of the fifteenth and sixteenth centuries begin with the appeal 'Orate pro anima' or 'Of your charite pray for the soule'. Sometimes scrolls issuing from the mouths of the dead bear pleas for divine grace or mercy or saintly intercession. A more explicit statement of faith is occasionally to be found. Job's ringing words of confident belief in his living redeemer, familiar from the office of the dead, appear in more than one late epitaph.[41] Several inscriptions sought to win the sympathy of the passer-by with a reminder that the fate of the dead will one day be his. 'Sum quod eris, fueramque quod es'; 'Hodie mihi, cras tibi': these were frequent refrains. Some more elaborate compositions dwell on such themes as the brevity of this life, the transitoriness of earthly possessions, the body's transformation into worms' food.[42] One purpose of such verses was to arouse pity for the dead; others were to stir up the living to work for their own salvation and prepare for death by contemplation of the afterlife.

Some epitaphs rehearsed the good deeds of the dead. Churchmen tended to receive the most elegant and fulsome eulogies, often in verse. An epitaph for a layman which is exceptional in its combination of eulogy and lament appears on John Cottusmore's brass at Brightwell Baldwin (Oxon., *c*.1445). In thirteen Latin couplets it celebrates his devotion to justice, tells of England's loss, and describes the grief of king, lords, people, and Church. His wife, with their children, lamented this blow most of all; eventually she joined her husband in the tomb. Their marriage, blessed by Providence, produced eighteen fair children. Nothing can avail against death, the epitaph to Thomas Grey Esq. at Cople (Beds.), *c*.1530, reminds the reader, but he and his

---

[40] King, 'Cadaver Tomb', 26–38; *Monumental Brasses*, pls. 279, 294; M. Norris, 'A List of Later Medieval Memorial Brasses which commemorate the Deceased as shrouded, as a Corpse or as a Skeleton', in Bassett (ed.), *Death in Towns*, 248–51; Norris, *Monumental Brasses: The Memorials* (2 vols., 1977), i. 206.

[41] T. F. Ravenshaw, *Antiente Epitaphes (from A.D. 1250 to A.D. 1800) collected and set forth in Chronologicall Order* (1878), 20; *Monumental Brasses*, pl. 315.

[42] Weever, *Funerall monuments*, 264, 368.

wife trusted to be remembered as long as the parish of Cople should last for the benefits they had done it.[43]

During the Reformation, 'superstitious' inscriptions and images suffered damage at the hands of enthusiastic iconoclasts, but in September 1560 Elizabeth I firmly forbade 'the breaking or defacing' of any sort of funeral monument. Her proclamation specified two legitimate reasons for the erection of such monuments. First, keeping alive 'the honourable and good memory of sundry virtuous and noble persons', especially public benefactors. Secondly, preservation of genealogical evidence.[44] With this unequivocal royal approval, the making of memorials of all sorts continued during Elizabeth's reign with renewed vigour. Separatists might disapprove of funerary monuments, but many Puritan gentlemen were clearly happy to pay substantial amounts for family memorials.

During the century following the Reformation, increased contact with the continental Renaissance brought about the widespread adoption of new styles and types of memorial. A growing number of sculptors, several of them immigrants, attempted more accurate and realistic portraiture, but continuity is also evident in the design of very many monuments. The conservatism of taste ensured that the recumbent effigy remained the most popular single design for larger monuments until the seventeenth century. The posture of the effigies, the canopies (sometimes similar to hearses in their design), and the prominence of carved and painted shields of arms, are all reminiscent of the heraldic funeral. There were, however, some changes. After 1610 the best recumbent effigies were shown as if asleep in death, their hands allowed to fall naturally to their chests or sides. Less successful was the reclining effigy, shown leaning on one elbow.[45]

In the portrayal of the family in sculpture, the most notable innovation of the later sixteenth century was to place in a central position the group of kneeling figures long familiar in brasses, the children placed behind mother or father according to their sex. Groups of this sort were suitable for wall monuments, especially of the 'hanging'

---

[43] *Funerall monuments*, 236–7 (to Thomas Goldstone and William Selling, priors of Canterbury; *Monumental Brasses*, pl. 168; Ravenshaw, *Epitaphes*, 21, cf. ibid. 14, inscription to Sir John Smith of Great Ilford, Essex, 1475; Duffy, *Stripping of Altars*, 332–3.

[44] *Tudor Royal Proclamations*, ed. P. L. Hughes and J. F. Larkin (3 vols., New Haven, 1964–9), ii. 146; M. Aston, *England's Iconoclasts*, i. *Laws against Images* (Oxford, 1988), 266–7, 269, 314–15, points out that this proclamation in effect strengthened a proviso of 3–4 Edward VI, cap. 10 (1550).

[45] Kemp, *English Monuments*, 65–82, 97; A. White, 'England *c*.1560–*c*.1660: A Hundred Years of Continental Influence', *Church Monuments*, 7 (1992), 34–74.

type which allowed a reduction in scale. Another development was the framing of the frontal demi-figure in a rectangular or oval recess as part of a wall monument. At first used to portray individuals, this format was adapted during the seventeenth century to accommodate married couples. The earliest free-standing effigies of a seated and a standing individual were erected in Westminster Abbey, that 'powerhouse of ideas' in 1602/3 and *c.*1631 respectively. Of the two, the sedentary posture was the more widely used. The seated effigy of Margaret, Lady Legh (1605), is a striking representation of a young mother holding her child. At Lydiard Tregoze (Wilts) the pensive seated figures of Sir Giles Mompesson (d. 1651) and his wife (d. 1633) face each other: 'the surviving husband contemplates, and seems almost to commune across the grave with, his deceased wife'.[46]

These were the main innovations in the presentation of effigies in the period between the Reformation and the Civil War. Elements of different types were combined in a number of compositions, as for example in Epiphanius Evesham's celebrated memorial to Lord Teynham (d. 1622) at Lynsted in Kent. The figure of Lady Teynham, kneeling by her recumbent husband, is an exceptionally successful evocation of the ideal of grief restrained by faith and prayer. Smaller sculptures in relief made it possible to capture a dramatic incident in which a number of people participated. The sculptor of the wall monument to Jane, Lady Crewe (d. 1639) in Westminster Abbey made unique use of a panel carved in relief to show a family gathered round the deathbed of a newly delivered mother. Brasses, too, were occasionally employed to depict mothers who died in childbed. Epiphanius Evesham engraved a dramatic allegorical representation of the demise of Edward West in 1618 (Marsworth, Bucks.). Death bears down on West's reclining figure with his spear, but carrying in his left hand the victor's circlet. The dying man's wife and children appear in various postures of prayer, surprise, and grief. As all these examples may suggest, a greatly extended range of feelings was given visual expression after the Reformation. Yet afterwards as well as beforehand, attitudes of serene contemplation and devout prayer were the ones most frequently depicted.[47]

[46] Kemp, *English Monuments*, 75, 80–2, 97–106; A. White, 'Westminster Abbey in the Early Seventeenth Century: A Powerhouse of Ideas', *Church Monuments*, 4 (1989), 16–53; Esdaile, *English Church Monuments*, pls. 15, 65 (Mompesson and Legh monuments).

[47] Kemp, *English Monuments*, 105, 107; White, 'England *c.*1560–*c.*1660', 39, 46, 61, 74; *Monumental Brasses*, pl. 405; J. Wilson, 'Icons of Unity', *History Today*, 43 (June 1993), 14–20.

Any religious imagery which might be stigmatized as idolatrous had now to be avoided. In practice this encouraged the adoption of ornamentation which was either not overtly Christian in character or was ultimately traceable to pagan antiquity. Angels, temporarily banished, were to some extent replaced by busy, versatile cherubs. Symbolic of immortality, and thus suitable associates of enduring fame, they turned their hands to all sorts of work, including supporting arms, blowing bubbles, putting out torches, and occasional digging. Burning lamps represented faith, obelisks eternity. The transitory character of earthly life was symbolized by hourglasses, scythes, withered garlands, bubbles, and spades. In more explicit reminders of death, corpses sometimes appeared naked or shrouded. Skeletons were shown as recumbent mortal remains, or, in a more active posture, as personifications of Death, sometimes wielding a dart.[48]

The prospect of the resurrection inspired a series of seventeenth-century monuments which show the reawakening of the dead. When John Donne posed for his monument by Nicholas Stone, his winding-sheet was folded back to 'shew his lean, pale, and death-like face, which was purposely turned towards the east, from whence he expected the second coming of his and our Saviour Jesus'. In a late variation of this theme, at East Carlton (Northants.) Sir Geoffrey (d. 1673) and Lady Palmer emerge from their tomb hand in hand, looking up expectantly. A chronologically parallel sequence of monuments shows the shrouded dead sitting up in, or beginning to rise out of, their coffins, often summoned by the trumpets of angels.[49]

As during the preceding period, so in the century following the Reformation, the relationship most often represented on monuments commemorating more than one person was the partnership of husband and wife, occasionally shown with hands linked. However, three-dimensional portrayals of family groups of parents and children were far commoner than they had been. By the closing decades of the sixteenth century even the less skilled sculptors were trying to differentiate between older and younger children. Those who had already died were commonly shown alongside their brothers and sisters, indicating that they had not been forgotten by survivors, but they were distinguished by symbols of mortality, especially skulls. The incorp-

---

[48] Kemp, *English Monuments*, 68, 70–1, 163–4, 172–7; Weever, *Funerall Monuments*, 11.

[49] Kemp, *English Monuments*, 164, 166–8; I. Walton, *The Lives of Dr John Donne, Sir Henry Wotton, Mr Richard Hooker, Mr George Herbert and Dr Robert Sanderson* (Oxford, 1824), 50; Litten, *English Way of Death*, 68.

oration of children in a family group was now a popular way of presenting them. Yet in many cases they still occupied a separate space, especially the walls of tomb chests. It was Epiphanius Evesham's unusual achievement to insert into this space relief panels poignantly depicting the grief of orphaned children. Physical contact between parents and children was rarely shown, but mothers, especially those who had died in childbed, were sometimes shown with their babies in their arms.[50]

The number of monuments devoted to infant children increased in the early seventeenth century, though the total remained small. Maximilian Colt's representation of Princess Sophia (d. 1606) in her cradle, said to have appealed especially strongly to female visitors to Westminster Abbey, probably gave a great impetus to this development. Several young children who had survived infancy were also commemorated in their own right.[51]

Epitaphs developed vigorously during the century after the Reformation, their audience increased by a general rise in literacy, the increasing familiarity of educated gentlemen with classical literature, and a new emphasis on the written word as a vehicle of religious instruction. Prose was commonly used to convey factual information concerning such things as careers, marriages, and numbers of children; but verse was especially favoured during this period, some of it by famous poets, most of it anonymous. The epitaph was usually shorter than the elegy. Brevity was encouraged by the need to gain an audience. It spoke especially to the unknown visitor pausing, perhaps only briefly, in the secluded aisle. It therefore had to seize attention and hold the reader long enough to drive a message home. All sorts of devices were used to this end: acrostics, anagrams, puns, paradox, metaphors, and similes. This period, and especially the first half of the seventeenth century, was the great age of the conceit, the 'fanciful, ingenious, or witty notion or expression'.

Beyond furnishing factual information, the chief functions of the epitaph, according to William Camden, were to show love to the deceased, preserve their memory, comfort their friends, and put

---

[50] Kemp, *English Monuments*, 72–83, 102–6; *Monumental Brasses*, pls. 354–419; Esdaile, *English Church Monuments*, pls. 8, 9, 11, 65, 81, 82; D. C. Missen, 'Children on Church Monuments in East Anglia', *East Anglian Magazine*, 39 (1980), 611–13.

[51] T. Fuller, *History of the Worthies of England*, ed. J. G. Nichols (2 vols., 1811), i. 490; White, 'Westminster Abbey', 29, 32–5; Page-Phillips, *Children on Brasses*, figs. 50–1, 56–60, and p. 89; Wilson, 'Icons of Unity', 18; Esdaile, *English Church Monuments*, 123; Missen, 'Children on Church Monuments', 612–13; N. Pevsner, *The Buildings of England, Cambridgeshire* (Harmondsworth, 1954), 237–8.

the reader in mind of human frailty.[52] Many writers also thought it important to set out a pattern of imitable virtue. All these were accommodated during this century within a broadly Protestant credal framework. Prayers for the dead were severely discouraged by the reformers. Some Catholic or crypto-Catholic families still authorized intercessory inscriptions in the seventeenth century, but over most of the country such prayers disappeared fairly swiftly after Elizabeth I's accession. A prayer of thanks might be considered a suitable substitute. The brass to Robert Cheyne of Chesham (d. 1552) exhorts all Christian people to give thanks for his godly death. One 1573 inscription echoes the old form so closely that it looks almost like a coded request for prayers: 'Of your charyte give thanks for the soules of Thomas Oken & Jone his wyff, on whose Soules Jesus hath mercy . . . Amen.'[53]

Many epitaphs imply or assert that the deceased's soul is in heaven. Several contrast the immediate destinations of body and soul: 'The earth his bones the Heavens possess his goste' (1570); 'Earth has his Bodye & Heaven his Soule' (1623). Such are the pithiest expressions of a notion dressed up in many an elaborate conceit. Our loss is the dead's gain: 'Waile not your losse, ne blame my present fate, | Which steers me hence into a blisse-full state' (1652). Charity and courtesy now allowed only one destination in the next life to be acknowledged in epitaphial verse. However, there was a danger that such confident assertions would be debased by overuse. The reunion of body and soul at the resurrection is another important theme. The death of the body is commonly likened to sleep. 'But drie thine eies, why wilt thou weep?', asks Mary Whiddon's epitaph at Chagford in Devon (1641): 'Such damsels doe not dye but sleep.' The dead are sometimes described as resting in their graves 'in thassuered hope of the Joyfull

---

[52] 'Of Epitaphes', 3 Nov. 1600, in T. Hearne (ed.), *A Collection of Curious Discourses written by Eminent Antiquaries upon Several Heads in our English Antiquities* (2 vols., 1771), i. 228. The discourse 'Of the Antiquity and selected Variety of Epitaphs in England' gives a list similar to Camden's, but deprecates attempts to lay down precise rules for the contents of epitaphs, praising the variety of English examples: ibid. 238–9. See also J. Scodel, *The English Poetic Epitaph: Commemoration and Conflict from Jonson to Wordsworth* (Ithaca, NY, 1991), an important and original study. As his title indicates, Prof. Scodel focuses on the work of the foremost poets, including some compositions which were never inscribed on monuments, but omitting prose inscriptions for the most part, whereas I am concerned with the 'common' epitaph and its recurrent themes. In my broader-brush treatment I play down some important differences in style and outlook between the later 17th and 18th cents. which Prof. Scodel discusses at length.

[53] *Monumental Brasses*, pl. 345 (contrast the surviving intercessory inscription below the figure of Elizabeth Cheyne, engraved c.1516); Ravenshaw, *Epitaphes*, 28.

Resurrection'. The resurrection presented an irresistible invitation to the devisers of puns and metaphors. The tomb is variously likened to a mother's womb or (in a baker's epitaph) to an oven in which the bodies of the faithful remain 'In hopes to Rise, and to be Drawn again'.[54]

The reader was repeatedly urged to prepare for death. 'I stood as yow, and yow as I to dust shall shortly come' (*c*.1580): this was an already ancient theme. To be able to face death with confidence was the great objective of life. (Some especially edifying deathbed performances received eloquent tributes, but most epitaphs did not dwell on the comportment of the dying.) Faith, some inscriptions indicate, is the basis of the happy death. 'Christ is to me as life on earth, and death to me is gaine | Because I trust thorowe him alone saluation to obteyne' was a popular couplet. 'His faith made way | to Heaven before,' asserts Richard Bluett's inscription at Holcombe Rogus in Devon (1614); 'his workes still day by day | now follow him.' However, good works bulk much larger in epitaphs than the faith which should have inspired them. 'Do well and die well' is the message they seem to convey. James and Elizabeth Hardy of Dagenham were described, *c*.1628, as a 'Thrice happy covple that doe now posses | The fruits of thine good works & holynes, | Now God rewards theire allmes & charitye, | Theire strict observinge of Saboath's pyetie.'[55]

Virtuous life and good deeds are also (many inscriptions proclaim) the surest basis of lasting fame. They give the deceased a sort of immortality, and make them worthy of imitation, a source of edification for succeeding generations. Almsgiving, often coupled with hospitality, was of all good works perhaps the most frequently praised. The peacemaker earned warm tributes. Men of different professions were lauded for virtues appropriate to their calling. The conscientious minister whose labours continued to bear fruit in his congregation after his death, the just and incorruptible lawyer, the skilled and enterprising merchant, the honest and faithful servant: all these received their due tribute. (In many cases, however, the epitaph includes telling details illustrative of individual character and achievement as well.)

[54] Norris, 'Later Medieval Brasses', 200, for a very early example (Elizabeth Horne, Shipton-under-Wychwood, 1548); Ravenshaw, *Epitaphes*, 27, 70, 79, 93, 94, 101; A. C. Bizley, *The Slate Figures of Cornwall* (1965), 171–2.

[55] A. B. Connor, *Monumental Brasses in Somerset* (Bath, 1970), 317 (96-line epitaph of Lady Magdalen Hastings, d. 1596, at Cadbury, with exceptionally full account of deathbed), 321; *Monumental Brasses*, 421 (deathbed expression of faith); Ravenshaw, *Epitaphes*, 28, 29, 33, 57, 69, 74–5, 86.

The frequent celebration of domestic virtues in these inscriptions, more especially by grateful husbands, was something new. Highest on the list of qualities valued in a wife came a loving or kind disposition, chastity, and a religious outlook. Obedience and good management of the household (though clearly thought important by some writers) were not the most frequently mentioned qualities. The great majority of intimate personal tributes were dedicated to marriage partners, but parents and children sometimes received them too. Children remembered their parents' 'tenderness' and 'indulgence'. Parents discerned in their young children virtues which had not yet had the opportunity of blossoming in the world.[56]

Love, and the grief which is caused when the ties of love are broken by death, were increasingly prominent themes in the epitaphs of this period. They had seldom appeared in medieval inscriptions, but post-Reformation desire to teach by example justified a fuller account of the individual's personal relationships. Loving spouses were worthy to be imitated. Looked at from another perspective, love and conjugal harmony were blessings from God for which those who had experienced them owed him thanks. Grief was a legitimate theme in the Protestant epitaph if it allowed for the demonstration of the power of faith: the greater the attachment, the more bitter the experience of grief; the more potent, therefore, the faith which could assuage such distress. The description of love and grief in the epitaphs of this period was on the whole distinguished by sobriety and restraint. However, a secular, even pagan, note crept into some compositions.[57]

Frequently encountered themes of inscriptions to husbands and wives are their steadfast affection during life, the pain of bereavement, the unwillingness of one partner to survive the other, the enduring memory of the loved one in the mind of the bereaved, the survivor's confidence that the departed spouse is happy, keen anticipation of reunion in heaven, and the mingling of mortal remains in the same grave. Love survived the grave; 'Corpora divisit Mors sociavit Amor'. The epitaph to Anne Gibson (1611) concludes, 'One Mind, one Faith, one Hope, one Graue: | In Life, in Death, they had, & still they haue. | *Amor coniugalis aeternus.*' Beyond the grave was the prospect of reunion. This oft-repeated idea is perhaps nowhere more

---

[56] Ravenshaw, *Epitaphes*, 70 (Tobie Waterhous, d. 1623, aged 4½, 'full of grace & truthe'), 78 (son of earl of Hertford, d. 1631: 'Speechless tho' yet he were, say all we can | that saw, he promise did a hopefvll man').

[57] *Monumental Brasses*, pl. 394.

eloquently expressed than in the inscription to Thomas and Anne Carew (who both died within two days in 1656) at Haccombe (Devon). 'One flame of love their lives did bvrne | Even to ashes in their vrne | . . . Therefore vnto one marble trvst | Wee leave their now vnited dvst | As rootes in earth embrace to rise | Most lovely flowers in paradise.' The survivor's duty of conjugal love survived the grave: 'Uxorem viuam amare voluptas est, Defunctam pietas'.[58]

Some of the strongest expressions of grief are conveyed by lines commemorating women who died in childbirth. Anne Savage's Latin epitaph (1605) tells us that her little son, her husband, and her father complained against the cruel fates who tore her away.[59] Children's epitaphs voice the pathos of the infant life cut short, of hopes blasted in the bud, and underline the uncertainty and transience of all earthly ties. The child's present happiness was the commonest source of consolation. As early as 1558 Christ's command to his disciples to let the little children come to him 'for to suche is the kingdome of heven' was inscribed on the memorial to the 15-month-old Margaret Sidney at Penshurst (Kent). The inscription at Northill (Corn.) to Richard Spoure, who died in 1623 in his third month, offered his tearful parents the consolation that his departure had freed him from future misery: 'instead of their Fond Dandling kisses' the infant now enjoyed 'A heaven of blisses'.[60]

During the century after the Restoration various monumental types and designs which had originated in the Middle Ages all but disappeared, and ones first introduced to England under Elizabeth and the early Stuarts were much more fully exploited. In themselves the changes had little to do with religious developments. Yet one consequence was a decided secularization of the appearance of funeral monuments. Many of them now sought to convey a sense of reposeful dignity, stoic composure, or heroic nobility. The recumbent or kneeling effigy with hands clasped in prayer was almost everywhere replaced by standing, reclining, or sitting figures, by busts, or by portrait medallions in low relief. The standing figure was judged particularly suitable for the courageous soldier, the barrister, or Member of Parliament, but occasionally used for married couples too. The reclining or semi-reclining figure was very popular. It could be used to

---

[58] H. T. Morley, *Monumental Brasses of Berkshire* (Reading, 1924), 213; Ravenshaw, *Epitaphes*, 51, 111; epitaph of Frances Thornehill, d. 1640, at Aston Rowant, Oxon. (author's transcription).

[59] *Monumental Brasses*, pl. 394; Ravenshaw, *Epitaphes*, 56, 115.

[60] Author's transcription; Bizley, *Slate Figures*, 122–3.

portray the dying, perhaps in the act of saying farewell, and also the dead, caught in the first stirrings of resurrection. It readily lent itself, too, to the representation of contemplative or visionary awareness of the divine. The bust or portrait in low relief was the most straight-forward way of representing the deceased, and often particularly effective in its classic simplicity.[61]

Classical influence over English church monuments reached a high level during the late seventeenth and early eighteenth centuries. The design of monuments, their symbolic and decorative elements, the posture and even in some cases the dress of the people commemor-ated, bore the stamp of pagan antiquity. The ruling classes' rejection of 'fanaticism' as well as 'superstition' after the Restoration militated against the ostentatious or exuberant manifestation of religious feel-ing. The canopied monument had disappeared, like the stationary funeral hearse which it often resembled. Instead, sculpted monu-ments now stood against a wall or hung from it, framed in a classical architectural surround, or backed by a pyramid. By far the common-est decorative element was the funeral urn, symbolic, according to its context, of either mortality or immortality. Allegorical figures were also introduced, especially ones personifying the virtues which were specially attributed to the deceased. Coats of arms usually occupied a less conspicuous position. Amid classical restraint or grandeur, they struck a slightly discordant note.[62]

Couples appeared with all their children in one group much less often after the Restoration. This development probably reflected autonomous stylistic changes rather than any alteration in the climate of family life itself, though it might be argued that it was a natural accompaniment of the decline of patriarchy in the upper-class family and the rise in respect for individual autonomy. Perhaps it was no longer felt appropriate to depict grown men and women kneeling behind their parents. The family conversation piece, so popular a genre of painting in the eighteenth century, had no exact counterpart in the field of memorial sculpture. However, moments of high emo-tional intensity in family life are shown on a number of monuments. The theme of the surviving spouse grieving by the reclining form of the dying partner was now infused with more overtly expressed feel-ing. Some monuments focus on the relationship between parents and a child or children. The best known of these, at Withyham in Sussex, commemorates the 12-year-old Thomas Sackville (d. 1677). It depicts

---

[61] Kemp, *English Monuments*, 108–17, 129–38, 168–9.
[62] Ibid. 108–11, 121–9.

his grief-stricken parents kneeling beside their son's semi-reclining form. His heavenward gaze conveys an intimation of his soul's destination. The inscription confirms that he 'liv'd and died well'.[63]

Children were sometimes portrayed without their parents on monuments of their own, but these were never very common. Among the finest English portrayals of a small child are John Dwight's stoneware figures of his little daughter Lydia (*c.*1674), though these, it seems, were never incorporated in a monument to her memory. One of them shows her, eyes shut, on her deathbed. She holds the bunch of flowers which, so eloquently symbolic of beauty, innocence, and transience, was thought to be especially suitable for inclusion in the designs of memorials to young children. The other perhaps depicts her resurrection. Among the fine monuments made for older children and adolescents are the low relief portrait at Brightwell in Suffolk of that 'gratious virgin' Anna Essington, who died in 1660 at the age of 17. At Great Barrington (Glos.) Jane (d. 1711) and Edward Bray (d. 1720), two smallpox victims, follow an angel across the clouds.[64]

The effect of the more ambitious eighteenth-century memorial sculpture was sometimes unintentionally comic. In *Clarissa*, Samuel Richardson had Lovelace ridicule the monument to Elizabeth Carteret in Westminster Abbey. This showed her being drawn up to heaven by a cherub ('a chubby fat little varlet . . . with wings not much bigger than those of a butterfly') which Lady Carteret seemed to be about to pull down about her ears. Such sculpture was also very expensive. None but the best likeness was now acceptable. Older types of memorial such as the brass and the incised stone had come to seem naïve and primitive. By 1750 the great majority of memorials focused on the inscription, grander ones hanging on the wall in architectural frames or cartouches, simpler ones, largely devoted to the memory of members of the middling ranks of society, on slabs set into the floor.[65]

The century after the Restoration was the great age of the English epitaph. The old perennial warnings of the transience of human life, the certainty of death, the uncertainty of its hour, and the need to prepare: all these persisted, but they were less conspicuous than they

[63] L. Stone, *The Family, Sex and Marriage in England 1500–1800* (1977), 239–57; Kemp, *English Monuments*, 112–14.

[64] N. Llewelyn, *The Art of Death: Visual Culture in the English Death Ritual c.1500–c.1800* (1991), 28–9, 44; N. Pevsner, *The Buildings of England, Suffolk* (2nd edn., rev. E. Radcliffe, Harmondsworth, 1979), 116; Esdaile, *English Church Monuments*, 125.

[65] Richardson, *Clarissa*, vii. 331; Kemp, *English Monuments*, 115, 118–20, 138–41.

had been. Themes emphasized during the previous century, including the expectation of meeting again in heaven, the contrast between
the immediate fates of body and soul, and the prospect of their ultimate reunion, remained quite prominent, but were now less central.
Many epitaphists focused firmly on the exercise of virtues, public and
private. Verse was often judged especially suitable for the expression
of grief and religious faith, but weighty, elegant, and carefully bal-
anced prose came to be preferred for the description of virtues and
personal achievements.

In 1740 Samuel Johnson published his 'Essay on Epitaphs' in the
Gentleman's Magazine. Honours are paid to the dead, he claimed, in
order to incite others to imitate their excellencies, and epitaphs are
principally intended to perpetuate examples of virtue. It is unnecessary to describe the achievements of the very greatest individuals.
'Next in Dignity to the bare Name is a short Character simple and
unadorned, without Exaggeration, Superlatives, or Rhetoric.' However, most people, not being well known, need to have their virtues
published by means of a longer encomium. It is in writing this that
skill is most required. An epitaph is a panegyric, and not confined to
'historical Impartiality'. Nobody should be commended for virtues
which he never possessed, but his faults may be passed over in
silence. 'The best Subject for EPITAPHS is private Virtue; Virtue exerted
in the same Circumstances in which the Bulk of Mankind are placed,
and which, therefore, may admit of many Imitators.'[66] Epitaphs continued to record public achievements, but they also celebrated more
fully than before qualities exercised in the private sphere, often by
people of comparatively humble status.

An elegantly concise summary listing of some of the foremost private virtues is to be found in the epitaph upon Thomas Fox of Wim-
borne Minster in Dorset (d. 1730). It describes him as 'In Conjugio
fidelis, Paternitate benignus, amicitia constans; | Socijs, Egenis,
Omnibus | Comis, Munificus, Supplex.'[67] Among the most often cele-
brated of all virtues were charitable beneficence and piety, partly
because they could be exercised by both sexes. Benevolence,
candour, integrity, and temperance were also frequently praised.
Marriage was the central relationship of the private sphere. Several
inscriptions record that a union was long (sixty years in one case) and

---

[66] Anon. [S. Johnson], 'An Essay on Epitaphs', *Gentleman's Magazine*, 10 (1740),
593–6, previously discussed, with different emphasis, by Scodel, *English Poetic
Epitaph*, 365–8.

[67] He was an apothecary and governor of the grammar school. Author's transcription.

happy. The commonest specific tribute paid to a husband was that he had been tender or loving. Husbands, too, appear to have placed the highest value on love and affection in their spouses. Also mentioned among the wifely virtues were prudence, discretion, modesty, fidelity, chastity, and frugality. Parents were commended as affectionate, indulgent, tender, or careful. One of the most eloquent tributes to a father is the epitaph to the Revd Robert Goodwin, vicar of Cleobury Mortimer (Shropshire), who died in 1691. 'In life to copy thee I'll strive, | And when I that resign, | May some good natur'd friend survive | To lay my bones by thine.'[68]

Several memorial inscriptions to children betray a strong sense of loss. The long-familiar themes of fragility, innocence, and unrealized early promise are prominent in them. The large number of epitaphs commemorating sons and daughters who died in later childhood or adolescence reflects in part the toll taken by smallpox during the century after the Restoration.[69] Many eloquent monumental inscriptions commemorate daughters. 'Know Reader', runs the inscription to the 15-year-old Judith Harris (d. 1674) in its elegant 'rural baroque' cartouche at Nettlebed (Oxon.), 'that if Piety, Prvdence Witt Innocence or Beavty covld rescve from the grave shee had been immortall. Since these are ineffectvall. Dvst and Ashes. Read thy own Destiny, and prepare to follow.' The physician Robert Awood was buried in 1734 together with his daughter Elizabeth, from whom he had caught a fatal fever while ministering to her. 'Here lies a Father with his offspring dear, | Joy of his Heart, & Solace of his Care,' their inscription says.[70]

Some epitaphs make special reference to exemplary courage and patience during terminal illness. Susanna Acworth (d. 1685) bore the cruellest torments of childbirth very piously for almost a week. Lady Bolingbroke set an example to both sexes through the manner of her death in 1751, 'with all the firmness that reason, with all the resignation that religion, can inspire'. Even children could be commended for their endurance. The 9-year-old Susan Pleydall (d. 1676) was said to have borne the tortures of dysentery with a patience beyond her age.[71]

---

[68] Transcribed by Margaret Houlbrooke.

[69] See inscription on Bray monument at Great Barrington (Glos.) in R. Bigland, *Historical, Monumental and Genealogical Collections relative to the County of Gloucester (1791–1899)*, ed. B. Frith (Bristol and Gloucestershire Archaeological Soc., Gloucestershire Record Ser. 2–3, 5, 8; 1989–95), i. 136, for smallpox mortality in one family.

[70] Author's transcription, and Ravenshaw, *Epitaphes*, 153–4 (Slimbridge, Glos.).

[71] Pyrton, Oxon. (author's transcription); D. Lysons, *The Environs of London: being an Historical Account of the Towns, Villages, and Hamlets, within Twelve*

The pain of bereavement is frequently mentioned. Spouses and parents are variously described as sad, weeping, mourning, or most sorrowful. The departed are said to have 'died lamented'. Such allusions were often incorporated in the epitaph in an unobtrusive fashion. In a minority of cases, however, the experience of loss became a major theme. Some inscriptions graphically record the psychological and physical effects of deep grief upon the bereaved.[72] Death and the fates are frequently characterized as cruel or hasty. Two great sources of consolation—the heavenly bliss enjoyed by the departed soul, and confident expectation of a future happy meeting—remained major themes of epitaphs during this period. Yet there was a tendency in the more urbane inscriptions for allusions to Christian hopes (sometimes described as the 'spes resurrectionis') to be expressed more concisely.[73] The record of virtuous action was frequently left to convey its own reassuring intimation.

Most eighteenth-century memorials carry no more than a simple inscription recording basic facts such as name, date of death or burial, status or occupation, and perhaps the names of spouse or parents. From the seventeenth century onwards there seems to have been an enormous increase in the numbers of enduring memorials of a comparatively simple sort: slabs set into the floor of the church, and ledgers or headstones in the churchyard. It was in towns that the largest numbers of inscribed slabs were set into the floors of churches, where extramural burial space was relatively limited. In the countryside, a higher proportion of monuments was placed in the churchyard.

Churchyard Memorials

The extent to which churchyard graves were marked before the seventeenth century is uncertain. Several medieval stone grave-markers, nearly all of which probably date from before 1300, have been discovered in Kent. Most are decorated with some form of cross,

Miles of that Capital (2nd edn., 4 vols., 1810–11), i. 31; Bigland, *Historical Collections*, i. 58. An exceptionally explicit epitaph which caused unintended mirth commemorates Dame Mary Page's patience in coping with dropsy before her death in 1729. 'In 67 months she was tapp'd 66 times. Had taken away 240 gallons of water without ever repining at her case or ever fearing the operation' (transcribed on the flyleaf of the Bod. Lib. copy of T. Harrison, *A Funeral Sermon Occasioned by the Death of Dame Mary Page* (1729)).

[72] Bigland, *Historical Collections*, i. 115 (William and Elizabeth Hynson, d. 1667, 1670, Badgeworth, Glos.); inscription to Elizabeth Lady Rous (d. 1692), at Rous Lench, Worcs.

[73] Bigland, *Historical Collections*, 130, 149, 181, 256, 307, 334–5.

but they carry no inscription, so that the identities of the individuals whose burial-places they marked would soon have been forgotten. Not much evidence survives from the period immediately preceding the Reformation.[74] In 1502 John Coote, a Suffolk testator, requested that wooden crosses be set up at the head and foot of his grave bearing his arms and a writing requesting people to pray for his soul. The earliest surviving head- and footstones commemorating a named individual may be those erected to Ann Davis at Broadway (Worcs) in 1516. During the 1530s two testators of Felsham (Suffolk) and Romney (Kent) left sums of 8*s.* and 10*s.* respectively for a pair of stone crosses to be set up on their graves. The Romney testator also left 33*s.* 4*d.* for a body-slab carved with arms and prayers, but such bequests are very rare in sixteenth-century wills.[75] An observation made by John Aubrey in about 1675 suggests that the low mounds over recently interred bodies were often sextons' principal means of deciding which areas of the churchyard to avoid in digging new graves. At Woking (Surrey), the gravedigger told him that the sandy soil of the churchyard was soon levelled by wind and boys playing on it, so that but for the presence of a plant which rooted itself in putrefying corpses, it would have been impossible to tell where they lay.[76]

In many churchyards some of the oldest surviving memorials, especially tomb chests, are quite large. People sufficiently wealthy to pay for a substantial monument may have had various reasons for choosing churchyard burial. There may no longer have been a convenient space in the church for a monument of the size desired. An attempt to erect a tomb in an area which had come to be regarded as the preserve of a long-established family could have created ill feeling. A prominent position in the churchyard might be considered preferable to a more sequestered one within the church. The erection of a substantial monument in a spacious churchyard offered a better means of establishing a family burial territory than an attempt to squeeze into a crowded church. Several groups of monuments

---

[74] B. Stocker, 'Medieval Grave Markers in Kent', *Church Monuments*, 1 (1986), 106–8, 114; Daniell, *Death and Burial*, 146–8.

[75] F. Burgess, *English Churchyard Memorials* (1963), 108, 147 n. 41; *Wills and Inventories from the Registers of the Commissary of Bury St Edmund's and the Archdeacon of Sudbury*, ed. S. Tymms (Camden os 49; 1850), 92. In 1557 Anthony Shalcrosse, a minor Derbyshire landowner, requested in his will burial in Taxal churchyard under the same stone as his father: W. H. Shawcross, 'The Owners of Shallcross', *Journal of the Derbyshire Archaeological and Natural History Soc.* 28 (1906), 96.

[76] J. Aubrey, *Observations*, in id., *Three Prose Works*, ed. J. Buchanan-Brown (Fontwell, 1972), 319, 448.

marking out such territory survive in churchyards like Painswick's (Glos.). There five table tombs set up between *c.*1667 and 1798 by the Poole family, first as yeomen, later as gentlemen, still stand in a commanding position on the left-hand side of the north door.[77]

During the seventeenth century, a number of churchmen opposed intramural burial as a profanation. Some laymen, too, argued for churchyard burial. 'He that lies under the Herse of Heaven', wrote Francis Osborne, in his immensely popular *Advice to a Son* (1656), 'is convertible into sweet Herbs and Flowers'. Sir Richard Browne (d. 1683) allegedly thought that 'making *Churches Charnel-houses*' was irreverent, insanitary, and structurally damaging. Browne's son-in-law John Evelyn not only wrote against intramural burial but also in 1689 urged the archbishop of Canterbury that it should be prohibited, and in 1692 spoke against it at his own parish vestry. The tract *Churches no Charnel Houses* (1726) asserted that many fatal diseases were spread imperceptibly by the 'Effluvia of the Dead', whose passage no stone or mortar was sufficient to contain, let alone flimsy coffins. Pestilential miasmata might enter through the pores of the skin. Lack of ventilation 'to disperse the Vapours that continually arise from the Graves' made intramural burial especially dangerous, though this author wanted churchyard burial prohibited as well. The current of disapproval of intramural burial which flowed through the seventeenth and early eighteenth centuries combined with the growing shortage of suitable space within the church itself to promote churchyard burial among people wealthy enough to wish to set up a monument over their own or their family's place of interment.[78]

The erection of substantial memorials in the churchyard seems to have been rare before 1600, somewhat commoner in the early seventeenth century, but widespread only from about 1650 onwards. The tomb-chest survived in the churchyard to enjoy another two centuries of outdoor life after its disappearance from the church. From the late seventeenth century onwards, there developed in Gloucestershire and Oxfordshire the variant type of the so called 'bale tomb'.

---

[77] Bigland, *Historical Collections*, iii. 972–3, lists some of these, though not all in the same place. They appear as nos. 14–18 in *Painswick Churchyard Tomb Trail* (1973), unpag., with map showing their present position.

[78] Gittings, *Death*, 141; E. Carpenter, *The Protestant Bishop* (1956), 370; *The Diary of the Rev. John Thomlinson*, in *Six North Country Diaries*, ed. J. C. Hodgson (Surtees Soc. 118; 1910), 88; F. Osborne, *Advice to a Son*, ed. E. A. Parry (1896), 132; Evelyn, *Diary*, iv. 304, 633–4, v. 119; *Churches no Charnel-Houses*, 56–60; Scodel, *English Poetic Epitaph*, 359–62 (pointing out, p. 360, that some people buried in the churchyard had memorials in the church).

A second type of monument, also medieval in origin, the coped stone, with or without plinth, the inscription running along it, is found in several parishes, especially in the East Midlands. Other forms of memorial stone akin to the coped stone, like the coffin-stone, were comparatively rare. Ledgers, commonly on a low base, were laid in Cheshire, Lancashire, and Yorkshire. A little later there developed another design, the table tomb, consisting of a ledger mounted on blocks or columns, which hardly spread outside the north of England. During the eighteenth century one more important form of church-yard monument appeared: the pedestal tomb, often capped by an urn or (less often) a sarcophagus. Enduring churchyard memorials were sometimes made of cast iron in areas of production such as Shropshire and the Weald. An early, crudely wrought example at Crowhurst in Surrey dates from 1591. Two series at Burrington (Here-fordshire, 1619–78) and Bridgnorth (Shropshire, 1679–1707), show finer workmanship.[79]

In one county, Gloucestershire, where some of the finest and oldest surviving churchyard memorials are to be found, the contents of churchyards were surveyed in the late eighteenth century by the antiquary Ralph Bigland and his assistants and continuators. With all their shortcomings, Bigland's massive collections give what is prob-ably the most reliable impression we can hope for of what existed in one county's churchyards on the eve of the Industrial Revolution. Only a minority of parishes had headstones bearing dates earlier than 1700. Some had none from before 1750, and not many had ones older than 1670. The oldest recorded 'tomb' usually antedated the first surviving headstone, and some parishes had tombs set up before the Civil Wars. Tomb chests often commemorated members of several generations of the same family.[80]

The headstone was the simplest form of churchyard monument. At Morton (Derby.) towards the end of the nineteenth century, the churchyard contained 'numerous small memorials of free stone not much more than eighteen inches in height'. These little stones bore no more information than the initials of the deceased and the year of death (ranging in this instance from 1673 to 1716). Such stones offered rudimentary but reasonably robust reminders of individuals'

[79] Burgess, *English Churchyard Memorials*, 128–34, 137, 139, 153 n. 70; Pevsner, *Herefordshire*, 96; id., *The Buildings of England: Shropshire* (1958), 80.

[80] Bigland, *Historical Collections*. Brian Frith's introd. to vol. iv., pp. xi, xx–xxvii, emphasizes the uniqueness of Bigland's interest in churchyard inscriptions and sets out what is known or can be deduced about his methods of compilation.

burial-places until their names had been forgotten. However, most of the headstones which survive in increasing numbers from the last quarter of the seventeenth century onwards bear the deceased's name in full, together with the date of death. In areas furthest from supplies of suitable stone, wood was used as a material for churchyard memorials until the nineteenth century. The larger wooden memorials consisted of a rail or board raised above ground level by two uprights. The oldest one still surviving, at Sidlesham (Sussex) dates from 1658.[81]

Early modern records which give some idea of the spatial distribution of interments within the churchyard are very rare. One is a list of burying-places in the church and churchyard at Ashover in Derbyshire. Dated 1722, it may have been compiled from earlier 'memoranda and recollections', but also mentions two inscriptions of 1729 and 1733. The character of the list can best be conveyed by setting out its first two entries.

ADAMS. This family lie buried at the head of Samuel Everard's stone.

ALLSOP of Martin Green, is buried by Richard Hopkinson's stone. A flat stone, with 'C' and 'A' on it.

This is a sexton's working guide, untidy and unsystematic. It includes very few dates or measurements, yet it refers to well over a hundred stones which appear to have been in the churchyard. This comparatively large number no doubt reflects the fact that Derbyshire is a county where stone is plentiful. Most of these memorials have since vanished. Over seventy of them are described as headstones or flatstones. Others are called 'stones' (sometimes 'little stones'), some 'tombstones', and a few 'long stones'. Over a quarter of the stones listed bore only the initials of the deceased. In many other cases the nature of the inscription is unclear. A few certainly had a name or even many names, one a verse. The Ashover list was being compiled at a time when the old style of rudimentary identification by initials was giving way to more detailed inscriptions.[82]

About three-quarters of the entries on the list are couched in the plural, indicating that members of the same family were buried together. However, long-lived parish dynasties which succeeded in establishing more than one branch seem very often to have had more

---

[81] C. Kerry, 'Miscellanea', *Journal of the Derbyshire Archaeological and Natural History Soc.*, 19 (1897), 106–7; Burgess, *English Churchyard Memorials*, 116–22.

[82] 'Burial Places, Ashover, shewing the Relative Position of the Graves in Ashover Church and Churchyard, 1722', in C. Kerry, 'Ashover, Memoranda by Titus Wheatcroft, A.D. 1722', *Journal of the Derbyshire Archaeological and Natural History Soc.* 19 (1897), 30–44.

than one burial-place. Men were occasionally buried among their wives' relatives. A number of children's interments are mentioned on the list, but they can have been only a small proportion of the total of such graves. A unique entry tells us that 'There are three little lime-stones for 3 of his children'. There was some tendency, but not a very pronounced or consistent one, for inhabitants of a particular outlying hamlet to be buried close to one another.

Sextons' registers, a rare and relatively little known type of record, enable one to follow the process of interment more closely than a survey of the churchyard taken at a particular time. One such register, begun in 1736, was kept in the parish of Alverstoke, near Portsmouth, a favoured place of residence for skilled craftsmen working in the dockyard. In 1750 some eighty-eight interments were recorded. Apart from burials in vaults, at least thirty-five of them (about 42 per cent) were close to relatives, most often a parent, spouse, or sibling, less frequently children or grandparents. However, in only five instances do the sites seem to have been determined by an existing family monument. Given the extent of early modern geographical mobility, haphazard patterns of mortality, and the exigencies of churchyard management, the proportion of people buried near relatives at Alverstoke seems quite a high one. Another Hampshire sexton's register, kept at Fordingbridge from 1731 onwards, is less detailed and precise, but it tends to corroborate the impressions given by the Alverstoke register: that efforts were made to bury individuals close to a relative, but that in the middle of the eighteenth century only a minority of families had a memorial (whether 'stones' or wooden 'rails' in the case of Fordingbridge).[83]

An unusually detailed map of the churchyard of Horley (Surrey), made in 1806, shows that in this Wealden parish there was a preference for burial near relatives, but that its effects were limited. Most of the burials of identified family members (well over 500) were grouped in clusters of two to five graves, though there were a few considerably larger ones. Prolific families which survived for some time in the parish tended to have more than one burial spot. The number of standing memorials, most of them wooden 'rails', was equivalent to not much more than a quarter of the number of identified burial sites. There were only about thirty-two gravestones and seven 'tombs', some of which probably commemorated extinct families.

[83] Winchester, Hampshire Record Office, M(icrofilm) 130 of 20M60/47, pp. 76–9, and M 72 of 24M82/PR23 (analysis of entries for 1731, 1741, and 1750, pp. 1–2, 9–11, 27–9).

One part of the churchyard was devoted to the unmarked burials of 'Travellars & People from the Workhouse'. These obscure dead were at the bottom end of a churchyard hierarchy whose upper ranks consisted of families like the Blundells, with over twenty identified graves in two burial clusters, four rails, and seven gravestones.[84]

The proliferation of memorials, a geographically uneven process influenced by a range of variables, the most important of which was the local social structure, gradually transformed the appearance of the churchyard, helping to change it into the numinous space beloved of the eighteenth-century funereal poets. Here, in 'A Night-Piece on Death' (1721), Thomas Parnell already distinguished the resting-places of the labouring poor, the middling sort ('half ambitious, all unknown') and the rich: the graves 'with bending osier bound, | That nameless heave the crumbled ground', the engraved but vulnerable 'flat smooth stones', and the 'marble tombs that rise on high'. The possible connections between the erection of increasing numbers of enduring memorials and longer term efforts to control indecorous activities in the churchyard would repay investigation.[85]

The oldest surviving churchyard monuments are generally very plain, but the decoration both of tomb-chests and, rather later and to a more limited extent, of headstones, tended to become more elaborate. With some notable exceptions, the men who worked on churchyard memorials had more limited repertoires and horizons than the best interior sculptors. They had local rather than national clienteles. The dominance of text and a limited range of conventional monumental shapes and forms usually restricted their roles to the cutting of letters and the provision of ancillary decoration, often of a fairly primitive sort. The reminders of death and time, such as the skull and crossbones, hourglass, taper, scythe, and mattock, appeared in large numbers in the churchyard after the peak of their popularity as motifs on intramural monuments had already passed. Sculptors of churchyard memorials were on the whole more conservative than those of intramural monuments. They were also eclectic in their choice of emblems and symbols. *Memento mori* imagery never vanished entirely from eighteenth-century headstones and monuments, but it

[84] Kingston upon Thames, Surrey Record Office, P30/1/18.

[85] *The New Oxford Book of Eighteenth-Century Verse*, ed. R. Lonsdale (Oxford, 1984), 117; J. W. Draper, *The Funeral Elegy and the Rise of English Romanticism* (New York, 1929), 275–82. One early 17th-cent. call for greater respect to be paid to churchyards, 'the *Dormitories* and sleeping places of the bodies of the saints', is in Oldmayne, *Lifes brevitie*, 73.

was often combined with gentler images which were increasingly popular after 1700. These alluded to the prospect of another life rather than warning of the approach of death. They included cherubs (for immortality), angels (divine messengers), doves symbolizing the Holy Spirit, and the hearts of abiding love.[86]

The majority of headstone inscriptions are very simple, giving the deceased's name, age, and date of death. Many specify his or her closest family relationship too. Information concerning family members who died at later dates was often added on when space permitted. At first the commonest opening words for inscriptions were 'Here lieth the body of', but in the course of time there was a gradual and uneven shift towards the form 'In memory of'. The commemoration of a departed individual replaced a concrete and immediate reminder of the presence of mortal remains, but the wider significance of the change remains obscure. It presents a seeming paradox: a reluctance to draw attention to the presence of the physical or 'natural' body at the very time when anxiety to protect it appears to have been more widespread than ever before.[87]

A minority of memorials were engraved with a few extra lines of text. Simple and conventional admonitory or hortatory verses were a frequent choice. 'All men to death must Tribute pay | The rich the poor the young the gay' (1714). 'Repent in time, do not delay, In my prime I was took away' (1733). Faith or hope might be expressed. The commonest way of doing this was simply to insert some such phrase as 'in hope of a joyful resurrection' after 'here lieth', though a few additional lines sometimes conveyed the message more emphatically. Some inscriptions anticipate reunion. 'My children dear the[y] lyeth hear my loveing Son and Daughter they are gon before and I am following after' (1726). Churchyard eulogies are relatively few and straightforward. Thus John Lane, gentleman, of Appleton (Berks.) 'Acquired a good character by his honesty, a Competent Estate by his Industry and a good share of Health by his Temperance and at last Resign'd his Breath [saying] Let the Will of the Lord be done'.[88]

---

[86] Burgess, *English Churchyard Memorials*, 132 (unusual decoration of tomb chest with weaving implements at Darley Dale, Derby.), 165–87, 190–1; H. Lees, *Hallowed Ground: Churchyards of Gloucestershire and the Cotswolds* (1993), esp. 44 (unusual carving of farmer and plough at Upper Cam), 77 (rich combination of different motifs on Knowles chest tomb—at Elmore, not Elkstone, cf. 78).

[87] See Llewellyn, *Art of Death*, 9, 46–59, for use of term 'natural' body, there contrasted with the 'social' body.

[88] Many county record offices or libraries hold collections of churchyard surveys. Among the seven I have consulted, Cambridgeshire's is the most outstanding in respect

Costs and Planning

The erection of an enduring memorial cost money. The most ostentatious monuments paid for by members of the nobility were erected between 1580 and 1625. Aristocratic tombs then cost roughly 250 per cent more in real terms than they had done in the years 1480–1500. Lasting commemoration had come to seem a better investment than funerary ostentation, and spending on monuments reached its height when investment in funerary theatre had already passed its peak. Later, the abandonment of the hearse-like canopy and the life-size recumbent effigy brought a fall in the average price of the grander monuments.[89] During the seventeenth century there was a much greater variety in the style and scale of monuments thought suitable for members of the nobility and upper gentry. One or two thousand pounds were paid for the most grandiose compositions, but several discriminating patrons preferred a simple portrait bust or an elegant inscription, either of which might cost well under £50.[90] The demand for monuments was always highest at the top of the social scale. In Elizabethan Essex, over half the noble testators made provision for memorials in their wills, just over a fifth of the knights, fewer than one in ten of the esquires, and 7.5 per cent of the 'mere' gentlemen, but it was in the middling ranks of society that the demand for memorials spread most rapidly after 1650. At the bottom end of the scale, simple headstones and rails might be put up for a pound or two.[91]

of detail and clarity. The cited inscriptions are in (*a*) Cambridge, Cambridgeshire County Record Office, 7050, Cottenham (Cottenham Village Soc., 1988), no. 387 (A); 7058, Dry Drayton (Michael Sekulla under auspices of Cambridgeshire Family History Soc., 1978), no. 127; (*b*) Aylesbury, Buckinghamshire Record Office, 'Memorial Inscriptions of South Bucks. The Churches of Wycombe Deanery' copied by W. T. Hall (1935), XX, Medmenham, no. 12; (*c*) Reading, Central Library, Local Studies Collection, B/TQF A5–2, Appleton monumental inscriptions (L. H. Chambers, 1933–4).

[89] L. Stone, *The Crisis of the Aristocracy 1558–1641* (Oxford, 1965), 579–81. The idea that money is better spent on an enduring memorial than a lavish funeral is well expressed in a letter from Sir Arthur Chichester, 2 Mar. 1614, in *Trevelyan Papers*, ed. J. Payne Collier, Sir W. C. Trevelyan, bart., and Sir C. E. Trevelyan (Camden os, 67, 84, 105; 1857–72), iii. 127. For the survival of older attitudes among the poor, see Scodel, *English Poetic Epitaph*, 363.

[90] Esdaile, *English Church Monuments*, 84–7.

[91] Emmison (ed.), *Elizabethan Life*, vol. iv. pp. vii, 1–48 (recorded provision ranged from £66. 13s. 4d. for a knight's widow's tomb to £4 for an engraved stone for an esquire and his widow: ibid. 36, 133). In 1694 Dr Claver Morris paid £9. 8s. 6d. for a black marble stone 6½' × 3¼', presumably for laying in an interior pavement, inscribed and 'emboss'd' with arms: *The Diary of a West Country Physician, A.D. 1684–1726*, ed. E. Hobhouse (1934), 149. An inscribed marble stone for the intramural grave of Thomas Skitch, yeoman of Tawstock, Devon, cost £5. 14s. 6d. in 1696 (SRO DD/WO

Monuments were conventionally seen as tributes by the living to the memory of the dead. In practice, however, many of them were set up by the people commemorated or in accordance with their detailed instructions. Several of these monuments commemorated the head of the family and his wife and children within a larger dynastic context. Tombs of this type were especially common during the reigns of Elizabeth I and James I. They may have been inspired in part by the desire to assert family status at a time when the ranks of the landed gentry were expanding faster than usual. After the Restoration the commissioning or planning of monuments during the lifetimes of the principal person commemorated was less common. The initiative of survivors inspired by personal affection, grief, or gratitude was correspondingly more important. As a consequence a higher proportion of monuments were erected to individuals, including wives, children, siblings, and even servants. The great majority of churchyard monuments were of a comparatively simple type, and set up to mark the graves of those already dead. Confirmation of a family's place and standing in the community, affection, and a sense of duty to the dead were all important motives for the erection of gravestones. Their function as a focus for personal grief may also have been significant.[92]

CONCLUSION

During this period major changes took place in the treatment of the mortal remains, in ways of expressing solicitude for the departed soul, and in attitudes to the commemoration of the dead. In the Middle Ages burial in church or chantry was the lot of a small minority. Most people might expect to be interred in the churchyard, where their bones would in course of time be mingled with those of succeeding generations. Where burial space was limited, 'dry' bones were later transferred to charnels, where masses might be said for the souls of those concerned. Before the close of the Middle Ages, an

---

36/8, p. 14). In 1726 Mrs Mary Field claimed to have paid £1. 1s. 'for posts and Rail' over her husband's grave at Bovington, Herts. (GL MS 9053 (32)). For some indications concerning early 18th-cent. gravestone prices, see Burgess, *English Churchyard Memorials*, 273. William Allwood's headstone at Glastonbury cost £1 c.1684; the cutting of the headstone for John Badman at Wrington c.1738 cost 13s. 6d. (SRO D/D/Ct, Administrators' Accounts, A 19, B 57).

[92] Esdaile, *English Church Monuments*, 87–90; Emmison (ed.), *Elizabethan Life*, iv. 1, 8, 12, 28, 39, 45, 81–2, 93, 96, 114, 150, 181, 189, 199, 212; J. Lord, 'Patronage and Church Monuments 1660–1794: A Regional Study', *Church Monuments*, 1 (1986), 99–101; *The Diary of Roger Lowe of Ashton-in-Makerfield, Lancashire, 1663–1674* ed. W. L. Sachse (1938), 29, 77.

increasing proportion of people from the middling ranks of society were seeking intramural burial. This demand may have been further stimulated by the Reformation, the unceremonious clearing of the charnels, and the heavier usage of urban burial space as a result of the resumption of strong population growth in the sixteenth century. However, in many places a shortage of desirable burial-places and a growing sense that burial in church was unseemly led before long to a gradual movement into the churchyard: a churchyard, however, where those who could afford to do so staked out their family burial spaces with monuments, some of which were quite large. Humbler folk also liked to be buried near recently deceased relatives, but most of the clusters of family graves which resulted were relatively small ones. The corpses of the wealthy were protected by ever more elaborate coffins. An increasing proportion of what was spent on the more lavish funerals went on coffin furniture and grave-clothes destined to be hidden for good once interment had taken place. Further means of ensuring an inviolate privacy were family vaults and shafts, which multiplied rapidly during the seventeenth and eighteenth centuries. It is tempting to ascribe this growing solicitude for the corpse to inability to intercede for the soul. Social emulation also played its part.

An important purpose of funeral monuments has always been to preserve the memory of the dead. However, during the later Middle Ages commemoration came to serve the paramount aim of securing intercessions. The deceased were depicted in a posture of prayer which invited the bystander's participation. Epitaphs warned readers to think of their own ends, so that they might pity the dead and pray for them. The content of epitaphs changed in response to the doctrinal revolution of the Reformation. Prayer for the departed had been repudiated; hell was an unthinkable destination for the loved or honoured dead. Many inscriptions expressed confidence that departed souls had been received into heaven and supplied grounds for doing so. At a deeper psychological level, the functions of late medieval and post-Reformation epitaphs may have been similar. Despite the differences of form and content, they articulated the common desire of survivors to work for the dead and provided tangible evidence that something had been done on their behalf. Personal loss and grief were now more widely and openly recognized, but the pain of bereavement did not manifest itself in a solely plaintive grief. Rather did it offer opportunities for the exercise of faith and hope.

The effects of the Reformation on monumental forms and iconography were less profound. The recumbent effigy and the kneeling family group, both shown in prayer, survived the religious changes. New forms and styles, nearly all of them mediated through continental examples, but ultimately derived from antiquity, appeared from the later sixteenth century onwards, but not for another century did they finally displace the inherited models. After the Restoration, ideas of urbanity, dignity, and balance played for several decades an increasing part in shaping both epitaphs and effigial representations. By the eighteenth century the gentry and the professional classes relied above all on the epitaph to commemorate their dead. A recital of virtues and achievements, an account of the life well led, furnished grounds for confidence in a future about which little was said.

In the churchyard, simple markers and temporary memorials gave way, especially during the seventeenth and eighteenth centuries, to more enduring monuments. Headstones or ledgers marked the burial-places of the middling sort, more substantial tombs those of a growing number of clergy, gentry, and men of wealth. The erection of churchyard monuments by people of substance afforded opportunities of emulation and imitation to a gradually widening circle of people who would never have aspired to an intramural memorial. Outside, under the sheltering sky,[93] the predominant tone was altogether more conservative than it was within the church. Long-established iconographical elements were sometimes assembled in startlingly eclectic combinations by rustic craftsmen. In epitaphs, gloomy themes familiar since the Middle Ages competed with more optimistic hopes and sentimental expressions of affection, often in execrable verse. However, most of these memorials maintained a decent reticence. They all expressed two aims shared by an increasing proportion of the population: those of preserving a little longer the memory of individuals and families, and of delaying the ultimate disturbance of their remains.

---

[93] Borrowed from Paul Bowles, *The Sheltering Sky* (1949). Cf. Francis Osborne's metaphor 'the Herse of Heaven' (n. 78 above).

Conclusion

The time has come to try to set the developments described in this book in a broader spatial and chronological perspective and to assess the importance of different causes of long-term change in the 'culture of death'. Some investigators of the social history of death have turned to the work of anthropologists and sociologists for help in setting their findings in a larger context. These scholars in related disciplines have constructed conceptual frameworks which facilitate comparisons between the beliefs, customs, and rituals of different societies and epochs. No concept has been more influential in this respect than that of 'rites of passage', expounded by the anthropologist Arnold van Gennep (1909). Each stage of human life, van Gennep held, is marked by such rites: the last of the series, and often the most important, accompany the passage from life to death. Within rites of passage, van Gennep distinguished three phases: separation, transition, and incorporation. He considered this scheme broadly applicable to a wide range of different human societies. The newly deceased are separated from the living and incorporated into the world of the dead. The transitional or liminal (threshold) phase between separation and final incorporation is one of varying length and ritual elaboration. Survivors close to the deceased go through a transitional period of mourning which they enter through rites of separation and from which they emerge through rites of reincorporation into society. Some of the best-known work done by Robert Hertz, a contemporary of van Gennep's, was devoted to human societies which see death as a gradual process, and in which the liminal phase is particularly important.[1]

[1] A. van Gennep, *The Rites of Passage*, trans. M. B. Vizedom and G. L. Caffee, introd. S. T. Kimball (1960), esp. pp. vii–viii, xvi–xviii (probable value of transition ceremonies in maintaining individual mental health), 11, 146–65; R. Hertz, 'A Contribution to the Study of the Collective Representation of Death', in id., *Death and the Right Hand*, trans. R. and C. Needham, introd. E. E. Evans-Pritchard (1960), 25–86. Among the Indonesian peoples mentioned by Hertz, reburial occurred after the disintegration of the flesh, finally liberating the soul. The superficially similar practice of reinterment of 'clean' bones buried in crowded English medieval cemeteries had no such underlying significance.

'Van Gennep's notion that a funeral ritual can be seen as a transition that begins with the separation of the deceased from life and ends with his or her incorporation into the world of the dead is merely a vague truism unless it is positively related to the values of the particular culture.'[2] The warning is a salutary one, yet many aspects of death ritual in late medieval England fit van Gennep's scheme.[3] The process of separation began on the deathbed through will-making, signalling the dying person's recognition of the imminence of death and his readiness to relinquish earthly goods. Extreme unction and the viaticum prepared him for his last journey, and the commendation of the soul at the point of death included the valedictory words 'go forth, Christian soul, out of this world'. The period during which the body remained above ground (often prolonged in the case of the upper classes) may be envisaged as a liminal one. During this time it was prepared for the grave, watched, and viewed for the last time. In the case of the soul, the most obvious threshold was the moment of its departure from the body: a moment often prolonged by onlookers' uncertainty about the precise moment of death. The chief difficulty in applying van Gennep's scheme to Catholic rites lies in deciding when the liminal period should be deemed to have ended. The soul's fate and the time of its release from purgatory were normally unknowable. The period after death during which intercessory services were celebrated varied enormously according to the wealth and personal preferences of the deceased individual. For survivors, there were various rites and customs which assisted the process of reincorporation. The elaborate ceremonies of the heraldic funeral underlined the successor's assumption of the role and responsibilities of the dead man,

[2] P. Metcalf and R. Huntington, *Celebrations of Death: The Anthropology of Mortuary Ritual* (2nd edn., Cambridge, 1991), 112. Cf. Metcalf's remark that in the hands of the widely admired anthropologist Victor Turner, the category of rite of passage 'is fantastically expanded, to the point where it is hard to describe a ritual (or much else) that is not in some sense a rite of passage. Influenced by his writings, historians, literary critics, and dramatists press the concept into service. Its appeal is the universal symbolism of the liminal' (ibid. 11).

[3] A number of historians have applied van Gennep's and Hertz's ideas to late medieval and early modern English death rites. Problems are apparent in nearly every case. D. Cressy, 'Death and the Social Order: The Funerary Preferences of Elizabethan Gentlemen', *Continuity and Change*, 5 (1989), 99–119 (the most comprehensive); R. Dinn, 'Death and Rebirth in Late Medieval Bury St Edmunds', in S. Bassett (ed.), *Death in Towns: Urban Responses to the Dying and the Dead, 100–1600* (Leicester, 1992), 151–69; C. Gittings, *Death, Burial and the Individual in Early Modern England* (1984), 19–20, 23. For seventeenth-century New England, see D. Stannard, *The Puritan Way of Death: A Study in Religion, Culture, and Social Change* (New York, 1977), 126–7.

replacing a broken link in the social chain. Neighbours, friends, and kinsfolk joined with the relatives of the deceased both in funeral respect and in convivial celebration which emphasized continuing life. However, the widow's year of mourning distinguished a longer period of transition before her reincorporation.

The changes in death rituals which took place after the Reformation make them more difficult to fit into van Gennep's interpretative scheme. Most obviously, the elements of liminality were curtailed. Most Protestants believed that the souls of the newly dead went straight to heaven or to hell. Funeral sermons offered reassurance concerning the destinations of some of the departed, but there was no longer any scope for helping them thereafter. In the long run the wealthy expressed a sense of liminality above all by adopting increasingly elaborate mourning-dress and accessories, by distinguishing phases within mourning, and by specifying periods of mourning appropriate to different degrees of relationship. Separation (of the dying individual from friends and family, of soul from body, of the body from the physical world of the living) had hitherto been, so to speak, encased in a ritual framework which veiled, channelled, even to some extent sublimated, personal grief. Changes in the last rites and funeral ceremonies left both the dying and the survivors with much-diminished ritual support. In the longer run the restriction of conviviality and the exclusion of the poor tended to reduce the value of funerals as rites of incorporation, though older ways of doing things persisted lower down the social scale and in remoter areas of the country. Those who could afford to do so had the bodies of their dead dressed and coffined in increasingly elaborate fashion before committal to the grave. One can only speculate how far these practices were due to the sublimation or transferral of impulses of solicitude previously expressed by care for the soul. The deceased were also incorporated into a realm of memory: inscriptions in stone recorded the span of their existence, their closest relationships, and often their status, occupation, and character. A dwindling proportion of epitaphs referred to the presence of a mortal corpse which would one day be reunited with an immortal soul, in part, perhaps, because conceptions of the resurrection had grown more nebulous and spiritual, less literal and corporal. They were 'in memory of' the departed.

The social history of death in England after 1750 lies outside the scope of this book, but some important changes may be briefly sketched. The main elements now considered especially characteristic of the Victorian way of death nearly all had roots in the eighteenth century or earlier: the family farewell, charged with emotion; the observance of a comparatively elaborate mourning etiquette; the sombre pomp of the funeral; the investment in the coffin and its furniture; the erection of enduring monuments, and the development of great municipal and private cemeteries. All these things, though not in themselves specifically Christian, were still underpinned by a Christian belief. The ideal of the good death enjoyed a strong revival among Evangelical Christians, who also derived powerful consolation from the prospect of future reunion. However, the extent to which Christian hopes were shared by the majority of the population is uncertain, and during the later Victorian decades, the framework of belief was somewhat loosened by heterodoxy and agnosticism.[4]

The practices of the nineteenth century were to be criticized in the twentieth as epitomizing some of the worst faults supposedly characteristic of the Victorian way of life: hypocrisy, formality, social conformism, tasteless ostentation, and morbid emotionalism. The undertakers' 'dismal trade' was blamed for maintaining a needlessly high level of expenditure on funerals. The demand for simpler, 'quieter', and more private funerals, the growing popularity of cremation, the hospitalization of an increasing proportion of the dying, and growing vagueness or uncertainty about the hereafter, reduced the 'rites of passage' attending death to a shrivelled husk of what they had once been.[5]

The foremost English critic of this mid-twentieth-century 'way of death' was Geoffrey Gorer. His thesis has recently been summed up (perhaps with some pardonable exaggeration) as follows.

Modern death is terrifying. The dying are isolated in hospital wards from their family and friends, dependent on the impenetrable medical knowledge of doctors and subject to impersonal hospital routines. The old are shunted off to residential homes, where they are ignored until they die. People who are bereaved, like those who are dying, are treated as lepers and are not supported in coming to terms with their loss.[6]

---

[4] J. Morley, *Death, Heaven, and the Victorians* (1971); J. S. Curl, *The Victorian Celebration of Death* (Newton Abbot, 1972); P. Jalland, *Death in the Victorian Family* (Oxford, 1996), 17–58, 265–83.

[5] P. Jalland, 'Death, Grief and Mourning in the Upper-Class Family, 1860–1914', in R. Houlbrooke (ed.), *Death, Ritual and Bereavement* (1989), 171–2, 233 n. 1; B. S. Puckle, *Funeral Customs: Their Origin and Development* (1926); Morley, *Death, Heaven and Victorians*; D. Cannadine, 'War and Grief, Death and Mourning in Modern Britain', in J. Whaley (ed.), *Mirrors of Mortality: Studies in the Social History of Death* (1981), 191–5, 218–19; G. Gorer, *Death, Grief and Mourning in Contemporary Britain* (1965).

[6] Gorer, *Death, Grief and Mourning*; T. Walter, *The Eclipse of Eternity: A Sociology of the Afterlife* (1996), 50.

Gorer regretted the passing of customs and conventions observed before the First World War. His work possibly did more than that of any other single scholar to make the study of changing attitudes to death fashionable among sociologists and historians. Philippe Ariès acknowledged that Gorer's ideas gave a decisive twist to his own investigations. Around 1965, he wrote, helped by Gorer's *Death, Grief and Mourning in Contemporary Britain*, he had suddenly discovered a great change.

When I began my research, I thought I was starting with a contemporary phenomenon: the cult of the cemetery, the pilgrimage to the tomb. But the phenomenon that I believed to be contemporary had been at least partly outmoded before my eyes. The prohibitions that were born in the United States and northern Europe in the twentieth century were now invading France.[7]

If one idea stands out from the tangled skein of Ariès's argument, it is that of the journey from the 'Tame Death' of the early Middle Ages to the 'Invisible Death' of the mid-twentieth century, and the formulation of that idea surely owes something to Gorer's influence. However, by the time Ariès came to write the preface to *The Hour of Our Death* in the middle of the 1970s, death was being so much discussed by the practitioners of a great range of different disciplines that he felt he was merely adding his voice to a 'large chorus of "thanatologists" '. In the past twenty-five years this lively interest has borne fruit not only in numerous studies of the behaviour of the dying and those around them, but also in the growth of the hospice movement, the development of counselling for the terminally ill and the bereaved, the promotion of 'open awareness situations' in which the dying and their families can express their feelings more fully, much more vigorous discussion of the hereafter, and experiments with new forms of funeral which reflect individual beliefs and preferences.[8]

What were the most important motors of change in attitudes and practices concerned with death? Five in particular may be singled out: new religious beliefs, levels of mortality, the development of the social structure, the spread of literacy, and the rise of individualism. Each of them has been assigned a key role by at least one scholar, but the influence of each of them naturally varied from one period to another.

---

[7] P. Ariès, *The Hour of Our Death* (Harmondsworth, 1983), p. xii.
[8] A good introd. to the developments of the last twenty-five years is provided by Walter's *Eclipse of Eternity* and *The Revival of Death* (1994).

This book has focused on the complex effects of religious change. The Protestant reformers drastically reduced the role of sacraments in helping the dying and repudiated intercessory prayer as a means of helping the dead. Radical Puritans complained that far too many undesirable 'relics of popery' had in fact survived: deathbed Communion and absolution; elements of prayer for the dead, reinforced by the tolling of bells; funeral doles; superstitious and hypocritical mourning-garb; and intramural burial. Funeral sermons had replaced trentals of masses. During the seventeenth century there was a strong counter-current of opinion, largely but never exclusively High Church, in favour of the viaticum and deathbed confession. Among people of religious outlook there was an interest in the last hours which transcended doctrinal differences and grew if anything more intense during the decades following the Reformation. Some old habits were very slow to change, notably the tendency to postpone until the deathbed the making of the last will.

The Reformation none the less initiated a series of fundamental if sometimes gradual changes, especially in the pattern of pious bequests and in the means of commemorating the dead. Despite the complaints of radical Puritans, there seems little doubt that the clergy's ministrations to the dying lost much of their former potency and influence. The divisions within the Church of England prevented the imposition of a coherent and uniform system of deathbed ministry to replace the one which had existed in late medieval times. Individuals and their families were largely free to choose their own 'way of dying'. Lack of agreement about how to tell good deaths from bad tended to assist the process whereby the focus of attention slowly shifted from the last hours. The abolition of purgatory made the prospect of suffering in the next life less immediate and credible for the many who could not accept that a loving God would condemn them to hellfire. By the end of our period the very concept of eternal punishment was being called in question. Thereafter there was to be no 'smooth attrition of belief' in the Christian scheme of the hereafter. Religious revivals renewed a vivid sense of heaven and hell among sections of the population. However, by the late nineteenth century the 'melancholy, long, withdrawing roar' of the tide of faith was clearly audible. Today it is estimated that only about a quarter of the population believes in hell.[9]

[9] G. Rowell, *Hell and the Victorians* (Oxford, 1974); id., review of Walter, *Eclipse* and Walter, *Revival*, *Mortality*, 1 (1996), 242–4; Matthew Arnold, 'Dover Beach' (1851), l. 25; Walter, *Eclipse*, 19–20, 32–3, 35–6.

The sociologist Robert Blauner argued in an influential article published in 1966 that a diminished concern with death and the dead is a natural outcome of the decline of mortality.[10] A society in which the death rate is high, and in which many people die in the prime of life, their work in family and community unfinished, is usually one in which the dead are relatively close to the living, and are served by them. However, when most people die in old age, their work finished, their social roles fulfilled, death is naturally a much less prominent concern for society at large. This model has an elegant simplicity and logic which make it very appealing. Although Blauner certainly deprecated some consequences of 'death control' in modern society, his thesis does not exaggerate the modern 'concealment' of death. One may add that though death is nearly always distressing, it is, according to a long-established conventional belief, comparatively merciful to the old. There is a natural span for worn-out bodies, and of all deaths, those of the aged have seemed in general to be the easiest, as well as the least disruptive of social networks.[11]

Blauner's thesis cannot, however, be accepted without qualifications, at least so far as England is concerned. It plays down the autonomous role of ideas, as against that of the material environment. Investment in the service of the dead may have reached its peak during the long aftermath of the demographic catastrophe of the Black Death (though all the most important forms of such investment had been developed beforehand). Yet the doctrines which underpinned efforts to help the departed were repudiated by the Protestant reformers at a time when demographic recovery was barely under way, and mortality crises were still frequent and severe. A much more costly culture of death was to survive in countries which remained loyal to Roman Catholicism.[12] There is a better fit between the major decline in mortality which began in the second half of the nineteenth century and the movement towards more modest funerals from the 1880s onwards. However, declining death rates played little part in the arguments of those who advocated greater simplicity and

---

[10] R. Blauner, 'Death and Social Structure', *Psychiatry: Journal for the Study of Interpersonal Processes*, 29 (1966), 378–94.

[11] Ibid. 391–2; S. B. Nuland, *How We Die* (1994 edn.), 70–85; Gataker, *Certaine sermons*, ii. 268. An optimistic article written during the dramatic late 19th-cent. decline in mortality which anticipates some of Blauner's arguments is J. Jacobs, 'The Dying of Death', *Fortnightly Review*, 72 (1899), 264–9, quoted at length by Cannadine, 'War and Grief, Death and Mourning', 194.

[12] C. M. N. Eire, *From Madrid to Purgatory: The Art and Craft of Dying in Sixteenth-Century Spain* (Cambridge, 1995).

reticence. Indeed, the casualties of the First World War, all the more terrible because they followed a long period of falling adult mortality, brought about a curtailment of mourning.[13]

Changes in the culture of death have sometimes been explained in terms of social structure. According to V. Gordon Childe's bold thesis, formulated over fifty years ago, investment in grave-goods and funeral monuments tends to decline in proportion to total wealth in a stable society.[14] The history of English death rites since the Middle Ages suggests that there is some truth in Childe's argument (broadly interpreted to apply to all forms of funeral expenditure), at least so far as the upper classes are concerned. In the long run, the higher ranks of society have set the upper limit of acceptable expenditure, and that has indeed fallen with the growth of social and political stability. The elaborate displays of power and lordship which were such important elements of the obsequies of late medieval magnates had largely become redundant by the eighteenth century. However, there have been many exceptions to the general trend. Both individuals and groups or classes within society have at different times used relatively ostentatious funeral rites as a means of asserting or confirming their status. Emulation and imitation in the ranks of the relatively large middle strata of society help to explain several developments which were especially marked from the seventeenth century onwards: the increasing number of funeral tokens and accoutrements, the elaboration of coffins, the expansion of private burial space, and the proliferation of inscribed memorials. The middling sort also emphasized the growing distance between themselves and the poor by an insistence on decorum which limited funeral conviviality. In the nineteenth century the respectable poor in turn devoted a comparatively large proportion of their resources to funerals in order to distinguish themselves from paupers.[15]

The spread of literacy, itself the result of developments in religion as well as in society and the economy, was enormously important.[16]

[13] Jalland, 'Death, Grief and Mourning', 185–6; Cannadine, 'War and Grief, Death and Mourning', 192–4, 218–225 (emphasizing, however, the inauguration of the collective rites of Remembrance Day); Gorer, *Death, Grief and Mourning*, 6–7.

[14] V. G. Childe, 'Directional Changes in Funerary Practices during 50,000 Years', *Man: A Record of Anthropological Science*, 45 (1945), 13–19. See Stannard, *Puritan Way of Death*, 122–34 for a detailed and ingenious but (to my mind) unconvincing application of Childe's model to later 17th-cent. New England.

[15] R. Richardson, *Death, Dissection and the Destitute* (Harmondsworth, 1989); ead., 'Why was Death so Big in Victorian Britain?', in Houlbrooke (ed.), *Death, Ritual and Bereavement*, 105–17.

[16] D. Cressy, *Literacy and the Social Order: Reading and Writing in Tudor and Stuart England* (Cambridge, 1980). K. Thomas, 'The Meaning of Literacy in Early

This account has emphasized in particular the enhanced autonomy of the literate testator. The ability to read created a potential audience for all sorts of text commemorating the dead or communicating ideas about death, ranging from funeral sermons and tracts expounding the *ars moriendi* to elegies and epitaphs. It gave people a means of condoling with the bereaved and expressing a sense of their own loss. It could even be argued that the communication of ideas in writing gave individuals a much more concrete and clearly defined awareness of their own feelings. However, the historian must as always avoid falling into the trap of concluding that feelings or attitudes had not existed before their first appearance in writing.

The concept of individualism has loomed large in recent discussion of the social history of death, especially as a result of the work of Philippe Ariès.[17] For him, it manifested itself above all in a growing concern about one's own fate (during the later Middle Ages), and a sense of the uniqueness and irreplaceability of loved ones (during the eighteenth century). Individualism has meant many different things to other historians, and the protean character of the concept makes it difficult to define its role as an agent of historical change. Is it to be regarded on the one hand primarily as an idea, or set of ideas, or on the other as a human propensity, present to differing degrees in all of us, but developed by external opportunities or stimuli? Christianity is a strongly individualistic religion in so far as it teaches that all human beings are equal in the sight of God, and responsible for their actions, and that all souls are immortal, alike destined for an eternity of bliss or torment. It is quite conceivable that, as Ariès suggests, these doctrines were more effectively assimilated, especially by the wealthy and educated, in the later Middle Ages, but they had been present in Christianity from the start. His picture of the calm acceptance of death in the early Middle Ages is based on very few examples,[18] and in fact we know little about the experience of death among the majority of the population at that time. Ariès's belief that a sense of the irreplaceability of loved ones first became widespread in early modern times results from his rather partial reading of the evidence. The grief of the family round the deathbed may indeed become more visible in the eighteenth-century sources, but careful perusal of earlier materials

Modern England', in G. Bauman (ed.), *The Written Word: Literacy in Transition* (Oxford, 1986), 97–131 takes a more sceptical view of the importance of literacy than the one presented here. I am grateful to Sir Keith Thomas for giving me an offprint of this article.

[17] Ariès, *Hour*, 95–139, 409–74, 605–8, 609–11.   [18] Ibid. 5–28.

shows that it was present long beforehand. In the seventeenth-century narratives, however, it was often mentioned only in order to throw into higher relief the Christian courage and faith of the dying person. A great mass of intimate testimony in the form of letters, diaries, and autobiographies gives us a vivid sense of the intense feelings of personal loss suffered by many seventeenth-century people. These feelings were not new even then, but hitherto such effective media of expression had been either unknown or much less familiar.

The term 'affective individualism', favoured by Lawrence Stone,[19] refers to the curbing of the individual's self-centred drives by affection for other human beings as distinct from (for example) an inculcated sense of duty. Stone and other historians have argued that the nuclear family became the dominant focus of such affection only during early modern times. Yet it was accepted as axiomatic long before then that the individual had a natural propensity to love his closest relatives most. Christianity has often shown a somewhat ambivalent attitude towards the family. Christ himself reportedly insisted that anyone who wished to be his disciple must 'hate' his closest relatives (Luke 14: 26). While in many ways strengthening and upholding marriage and the family, the Church also sought to channel individual wealth from families into its own hands and to develop social ties outside the family. The paramount temporal concern of those later medieval testators who had wives and children was to provide for them. However, their wills also bore the imprint of Catholic teaching in their abundant pious bequests, especially to the parish church. The Reformation weakened the parish as the site of voluntary pious co-operation. The descendants of guild brethren became ratepayers. As other voluntary obligations and other forms of association disappeared, so the proportion of wealth bequeathed outside the family declined. Because of the curtailment of priestly ministrations, the family also bulks larger in the poignant narratives of the good deathbed in the sixteenth and seventeenth centuries. The 'centrality' of the family in eighteenth-century accounts of death was not the result of sudden or recent developments.[20]

This book took as its starting-point a set of beliefs and practices which, despite some anomalies, was remarkably coherent, powerful, and pervasive. It has charted that structure's disintegration and the failure to replace it with any system of equal consistency or social

[19] L. Stone, *The Family, Sex and Marriage in England 1500–1800* (1977).
[20] The word is used by R. Porter, 'Death and the Doctors in Georgian England', in Houlbrooke (ed.), *Death, Ritual and Bereavement*, 86.

power and influence. Putting it like that may strike a rather too negative note which it is important to correct. It would be ridiculous to
envelop the late medieval Church in a rosy haze of nostalgia. Its eschatology held out the prospect of unimaginable happiness for the saved,
but forecast with equal certainty an eternity of excruciating torment
for the damned. A long though indeterminate period of terrible suffering in purgatory seemed likely for the majority. Yet a dangerous
impression was created that the personal balance sheet could largely
be corrected by investment in indulgences and intercessory prayers.
The thousands of masses mechanically celebrated for wealthy
donors, 'mumbled, murmured and piteously puled forth' were to be
an easy target for the reformers' subsequent attacks.[21] A high proportion of later medieval pious giving was driven by selfish anxieties and
intended to benefit the souls of the rich and powerful. It proved a considerable burden on succeeding generations. The neglect of obligations and the misuse of endowments were already widespread before
the break with Rome.[22] The Reformation and the accompanying orgy
of plunder and destruction were deeply disruptive. However, it is
hard to resist the conclusion that they liberated energies and
resources for ends which were (at least in terms of this world) more
fruitful and constructive.

No attempt to achieve a sympathetic understanding of the death rituals and customs of the past five centuries should blind us to the fact
that they always attracted some criticism from contemporaries.
Erasmus caricatured the parasitic greed of priest and friars around
the deathbed with stinging wit.[23] Thomas More ridiculed the self-
regarding snobbery of the wealthy parvenu's funeral plans and evidently
overlooked the value of the funeral meal as a social rite of incorporation when he angrily compared it to a bride-ale.[24] More was only one
of a long line of observers, Catholic and Protestant, who condemned
or satirized the hypocrisy of mourning practices which all too often
concealed indifference or even pleasure. (The anthropologist might

[21] William Marshall's *Prymer in Englyshe*, quoted by Duffy, *Stripping of Altars*,
382.
[22] A. Kreider, *English Chantries: The Road to Dissolution* (Cambridge, Mass.,
1979), 89.
[23] *The Colloquies of Erasmus*, trans. C. R. Thompson (Chicago, 1965), 360–9.
[24] *A Treatise (unfinished) upon these Words of Holy Scripture. Memorare novissima, & in aeternum non peccabis. 'Remember the last things, & thou shalt never
sin'—Ecclus*. 7., in id., *The English Works of Sir Thomas More*, ed. W. E. Campbell
et al. (2 vols., 1927, 1931), i. 470; id., *The Supplication of Souls*, ed. G. Marc'hadour, in
id., *The Complete Works of St Thomas More* (New Haven, 1963–), vii (1990), 220.

retort that death rites have always served social purposes much larger than the expression of individual emotion, and that the 'psychic process of grieving only partially intersects with the performance' of such rites,[25] but these perfectly valid responses would not alter the fact that in all relatively complex societies whose culture is shaped by a number of distinct influences, customary rituals are liable to be criticized from different points of view.)

Individual behaviour may seldom have matched the ideal patterns prescribed or advocated in the literature of Christian counsel which has bulked so large in this volume. The world pays no great attention to any individual's death, be he never so high, or rich, or good; 'even to die well, the prise of it is not considerable in the world, compared to the many in the world that know not nor make anything of it'.[26] Samuel Pepys's sobering observation cautions us against overestimating the influence of the *ars moriendi*. For every man or woman of his day who died after making an inspiring declaration of faith or after receiving absolution and the viaticum, there were probably scores who passed out of the world suddenly, confused, prostrated by fever, or slipped into oblivion without full awareness of their approaching end. Most writers of the *ars moriendi* agreed that the great majority of people preferred not to think about death in advance, much less prepare for it; some of these authors complained of widespread disbelief in hell or eternal punishment.

Although a substantial minority of the present-day British population still believes in a life after death, conceptions of it appear to be very varied and often vague.[27] The decline of concrete, vivid, and unquestioning belief in official teaching concerning man's eternal fate has been a long process. Belief in the afterlife was the linchpin of Christian 'ways of death' whether Catholic or Protestant. Without it, Christian rites of passage in their old form are an empty shell for the majority of people.

The 'eclipse of eternity' has a number of implications for our society's attitudes to death. The majority approach death without seeing a prospect of eternal life beyond it. However, that prospect, deeply sustaining and comforting for some in early modern times, was troubling, perhaps even frightening, for others. Hell has probably lost its horror for most people today, and that is no bad thing. For centuries, churchmen who wrote and preached about death portrayed it as the

---

[25] Metcalf and Huntington, *Celebrations of Death*, 4–5.
[26] Pepys, *Diary*, iv. 338–9.   [27] Walter, *Eclipse of Eternity*, 30–5.

king of terrors. However, it was what followed death, rather than death itself, that terrified. Many Christians today are strongly hostile to the idea of a morality founded on fear of everlasting punishment. One has gone so far as to say that 'It is spiritually important that one should *not* believe in life after death.' This means working out 'ethics without eternity'.[28] However, focusing on life in this world rather than eternity certainly does not mean ignoring death. As we approach the end of the second millennium, dying, death, grief, mourning, and the commemoration of the dead, are being discussed more openly than ever before.

---

[28] Walter, *Eclipse of Eternity*, 160, quoting Don Cupitt, and 161–71.

APPENDIX 1: BERKSHIRE AND
NORFOLK WILLS

Note: Statements in the text concerning wills or testators in the archdeacon-ries of Berkshire or Norwich rest only on wills specified in this appendix, not (unless otherwise stated) on all the wills made or proved in a given year or longer period.

Six hundred manuscript wills dating from between *c*.1500 and the 1740s were analysed in detail in order to gain some idea of key long-term trends in testamentary practice. Three hundred of them were proved in the arch-deaconry of Berkshire, three hundred in that of Norwich. Archdeaconry wills were chosen for analysis in the hope of penetrating the lower strata of testa-tors. All classes of society between the nobility and the propertyless poor are represented in the resulting selection.

Berkshire Archdeaconry Wills in the Berkshire Record Office

Thirty-two registered wills made between 1509 and 1520. Thereafter, surviv-ing wills made by testators with names beginning with letters A–D in each twentieth year (1540, 1560, 1580, 1600, 1620, 1640, 1660, 1680, 1700, 1720, 1740). The numbers made by the specified group of testators varied from year to year. One hundred and forty-eight of the wills dated from 1509–1620, 152 from 1640–1740. All the wills dating from after 1540 are either originals or probate copies, not ones entered in registers. Reference numbers for the Berkshire will series all include the prefix D/A1/. The wills analysed came from register 1A, volume 2 ('Dandridge', bound wills), and files 35–41, 43–5, 47–9, 51–9, 61–4.

Norwich Archdeaconry wills in the Norfolk Record Office

Fifty wills from each of six ANW will registers, at roughly fifty-year intervals, as follows (dates given are those of probate):

Fuller alias Roper, fos. 293^v–314^v (1497–1500).
Aleyn, fos. 212b^v–262^v (1549).
Bastard, fos. 24^v–74^v (1600).
Moore, fos. 106^r–184^r (1649).
Register 74, fos. 18^r–199^v (1699, last fifty wills proved).
Registers 96, fos. 225^r–249^v, and 97, p. 1–fo. 44^v (1746, first fifty wills proved).

APPENDIX 2: NUMBERS OF FUNERAL
SERMONS PUBLISHED

In 1989–90 I made provisional estimates of the numbers of funeral sermons published between 1600 and 1749 based on a count of entries in the following sources: (1) A. F. Herr, *The Elizabethan Sermon: A Survey and a Bibliography* (Philadelphia, 1940); (2) W. Crowe, *The Catalogue of our English Writers On the Old and New Testament, Either in Whole, or in Part: Whether Commentators, Elucidators, Adnotators, Expositors, At large, or in Single Sermons. Corrected and Enlarged with three or four thousand Additionals* (2nd impression, 1668); (3) S. Letsome, *An Index to the Sermons published since the Restoration, pointing out the texts in the order they lie in the Bible, shewing the Occasion on which they were preached, and directing to the Volume and Page where they occur* (1751); (4) J. Cooke, *The Preacher's Assistant, (After the Manner of Mr. LETSOME), containing a Series of the Texts of Sermons and Discourses published either singly, or in volumes, by Divines of the Church of England, and by the Dissenting Clergy, since the Restoration to the present Time* (2 vols., Oxford, 1783); (5) The catalogue of sermons in Dr Williams's Library; (6) The list of sermons in the bibliography of J. L. McIntosh, 'English Funeral Sermons 1560–1640: The Relationship between Gender and Death, Dying, and the Afterlife', M.Litt. thesis (Oxford, 1990). Certain categories of sermon, including funeral sermons, are distinguished by letters or abbreviations in (2), (3), and (4). The Dissenting clergy are distinguished by italics in (4). Of these three indexes, (4) is much the best, and (2) the least reliable.

The advent of computerized catalogues has made it possible to improve on my earlier statistics. For the period 1650–99 I have relied on the *Eureka* on-line English Short Title Catalogue, using the search term 'funeral sermons'. However, at present this means of exploiting the *Eureka* on-line ESTC seems to be quite inadequate for the years before 1641 and after 1699, yielding very meagre results. For the years after 1699 I have relied almost entirely on the Eighteenth-Century Short Title Catalogue on CD-Rom, using the key words 'sermon and funeral' and 'sermon and death'. For the period before 1641 I have drawn on (1), (2) and (3) as well as the ESTC. I have tried to exclude reprints and sermons printed outside England, but some will undoubtedly have escaped notice.

The resulting totals are: 1600s 10, 1610s 38, 1620s 38, 1630s 32, 1640s 50 (or 96 if all the sermons in the 1640 collection *Threnoikos* are counted individually), 1650s 119, 1660s 61, 1670s 83, 1680s 110, 1690s 161, 1700s 150, 1710s 132, 1720s 121, 1730s 85, 1740s 76.

The figures for 1700–49 are somewhat lower than my own earlier estimates but close to them, those for 1640–99 substantially higher. Most of my decadal totals for 1600–99 are lower than the corresponding figures published by Professor David Cressy in his *Birth, Marriage and Death: Ritual, Religion, and the Life-Cycle in Tudor and Stuart England* (Oxford, 1997), 572 n. 39. This is largely because his statistics include reprints as well as some 'related' publications which are not funeral sermons. The proportional differences are biggest in the case of the years 1600–40, suggesting that my own figures for those decades are too low.

Professor F. B. Tromly estimated that 'fewer than twenty' funeral sermons were printed during Elizabeth I's reign: see '"Accordinge to Sounde Religion": The Elizabethan Controversy over the Funeral Sermon', *Journal of Medieval and Renaissance Studies*, 13 (1983), 306. Professor Cressy's note refers to twenty-four items for the years 1560–99.

I am very grateful to Dr Stephen Taylor for introducing me to the Eighteenth-Century Short Title Catalogue on CD-Rom, as well as to Cooke's invaluable *Preacher's Assistant*, and to Professor Cressy for discussing with me his use of the on-line ESTC. He has pointed out that the amount of information retrievable from that catalogue is growing all the time. Certainly none of the figures here presented should be regarded as anything but provisional. They appear to establish certain long-term trends, but they will no doubt be superseded by more precise statistics before long.

BIBLIOGRAPHY

Primary Sources

Manuscript

London

British Library
Additional MSS 6303, 12514, 27353, 27356.
Arundel MS 26.
Harleian MSS 295, 304, 1301, 1368, 1529, 3881, 4774, 5176.
Lansdowne MSS 23, 50, 82, 88.

Greater London Record Office
Acc 1017/908: description of the death of John Eliot in 1735.
Wood (Harrison) collection, no. 1689.

Guildhall Library
MS 5871: Purchase ledger of Richard Carpenter, undertaker, starting in 1746.
MSS of the Diocese and Archdeaconry of London: 9053, London Arch-
    deaconry, Papers appertaining to Wills; 9065A/1–11, Bishop's Commissary
    Court, Deposition Books in Testamentary Causes; 9182/1–2, Miscellan-
    eous Papers; 9183, Bishop's Commissary Court, Miscellaneous Cause
    Papers and Exhibits in Testamentary Proceedings; 9185/1–7, Bishop's
    Commissary Court, Exhibits; 9186/1, 4, Miscellaneous Cause Papers.

Public Record Office
STAC 5: Star Chamber Proceedings, Elizabeth I.

Other Locations

Aylesbury, Buckinghamshire Record Office
D/W 48: Way MSS, Miscellaneous Executorship and Annuity Accounts.
MS Accounts of Overseers of the Poor: PR 140/12/1–2, Marlow; PR 227/11/1,
    3, West Wycombe.
'Memorial Inscriptions of South Bucks. The Churches of Wycombe Deanery'
    copied by W. T. Hall (typescript, 1935).

Bristol Record Office
MS AC/F9/2a: Accounts for the Funeral of the Earl of Suffolk and Bindon,
    1723.

Cambridge, Cambridgeshire County Record Office
Monumental Inscriptions (typescripts): 7050, Cottenham; 7058, Dry
    Drayton.

Durham, Prior's Kitchen
Will register 1734–52.

Exeter, Devon Record Office
MS Accounts of Overseers of the Poor: 2141A/PO 1–5, Ashburton; 2922A/PO 1–3, Hennock; (no parish number) PO 1–4, Chudleigh.

Kingston-upon-Thames, Surrey Record Office
P30/1/18: Plan of Horley Churchyard, 1806.

Manchester, Chetham's Library
MS Mun.A.2.137: Edmund Harrold's Diary.

Norwich, Norfolk Record Office
Archdeaconry of Norwich (ANW) Wills (see App. 1 for fuller details): Fuller alias Roper; Aleyn; Bastard; Moore; Registers 74, 96, and 97.
Consistory Court Deposition Books (all prefixed DN/DEP): 2/3, 3/4A, 4/4B, 5/5A, 6/5B, 7/6A, 8/7B, 8/7C, 8/7E, 28/30B, 36/39, 38/43, 44/48A, 48/52, 51/55, 53/58A, 61/65.
MS Accounts of Overseers of the Poor: PD 5/31, Guestwick; PD 382/33–8, Hilgay; PD 461/57, Norwich St. John Maddermarket; PD 533/15, Breckles; PD 553/54, Wighton.

Oxford Bodleian Library
Ashmolean MSS 818, 836, 1109.
MS Eng. misc. f. 381: Diary of Samuel Woodforde.
MS Sancroft 133.

Reading, Berkshire Record Office
Archdeaconry of Berkshire.
    Wills (prefix D/A1/). Many of these contain depositions: 1A, 2, 4, 5, 35–69, 73, 80–2, 87, 90, 94, 98, 102, 107–8, 113, 120–2, 128, 137, 139.
    Probate Accounts (prefix D/A1/): 173–225.
    Act and Deposition Books (prefix D/A2/): c40, c60, c154, c155.
D/E Bt: Belson and Barrett Family Papers.
MS Accounts of Overseers of the Poor: T/F 41 and D/P 2 12/1, Abingdon; D/P 10 12/1, Aston Tirrold; D/P 16 12/1, Beenham; D/P 26 12/2, Brimpton; D/P 27 11/1 12/4, Buckland; D/P 43 12/1, Cookham; D/P 45 12/1, Cumnor; D/P 96 12/1–10, Reading St. Giles; D/P 109 12/1, Shellingford; D/P 156 12/1, Woolhampton.

Reading Central Library
Local Studies Collection.
B/TQF: Berkshire Monumental Inscriptions.

Taunton, Somerset Record Office
Diocese of Bath and Wells.
    D/D/Cd 71, 77, 97, 117: Consistory Court Deposition Books.
    D/D/Ct: Administrators' Accounts.
DD/ES Box 18: The Manner of the Solemnisation of the Funeral of Sir John Stawell, 1662 (transcript).

DD/PH/180, 224, 238, 239: Phelips Family Papers.
DD/SAS c/127 6/3: Will of Henry Selleck, Gent., 1741.
DD/WO 36/8: Bill for the Funeral of Thomas Skitch of Tavistock, 1695.
MS Autobiography of John Cannon.

Warwick, Warwick County Record Office
CR 1291/289: Greswold Family Accounts.
CR 1886: Greville Family Accounts.
MS Accounts of Overseers of the Poor: Dr 296/43–6, Kenilworth; Dr 404/87, Fillongley.

Winchester, Hampshire Record Office
Winchester Diocesan Records, Register Fox iv.
M(icrofilm) 130 of 20M60/47: Alverstoke Sextons' Register.
M 72 of 24M82/PR23: Fordingbridge Sextons' Register.

York, Borthwick Institute
PROB. EX. 1607–46: Executors' and Administrators' Accounts.

Printed

Titles of books published before 1641 are normally given as they appear in the *Short Title Catalogue*, but sometimes in fuller form.

ABBOT, G., *A sermon preached at Westminster May 26, 1608. At the funerall solemnities of Thomas earle of Dorset* (1608).

AINSWORTH, S., *A Sermon Preached . . . At the Fvnerall of Mr Andrew Pern* (1655).

ALLET, T., *The Christian's Support under the Loss of Friends. A Sermon Occasion'd by the Death of Mr. Henry Clements, of London Bookseller* (1720).

ANDERSON, A., *A sermon of sure comfort, preached at the funerall of master Robert Keylwey esquire* (1581).

ANDREWES, L., *Works*, ed. J. P. Wilson and J. Bliss (LACT, 11 vols., 1841–54).

The Ars Moriendi. Editio Princeps, c.1450. A Reproduction of the Copy in the British Museum, ed. W. H. Rylands (Holbein Soc. 6, Fac-simile Reprints, 1881).

ASHE, S., *Gray Hayres crowned with Grace, A Sermon Preached . . . At the Funerall of . . . Mr. Thomas Gataker* (1655).

ASHMOLE, E., *The Diary and Will of Elias Ashmole*, ed. R. T. Gunther (Oxford, 1927).

ASSHETON, N., *The Journal of Nicholas Assheton of Downham, in the County of Lancaster, Esq.*, ed. F. R. Raines (Chetham Soc. OS 14; 1848).

ASSHETON, W., *A Theological Discourse of Last Wills and Testaments* (1696).

ATKINSON, D. W. (ed.), *The English* ars moriendi (New York, 1992).

ATTERBURY, F., *Sermons and Discourses on Several Subjects and Occasions* (2 vols., 1820).

AUBREY, J., *Remaines of Gentilisme and Judaisme*, in id., *Three Prose Works*, ed. J. Buchanan-Brown (Fontwell, 1972).

Aubrey's Brief Lives, ed. O. L. Dick (Harmondsworth, 1972).

AUGUSTINE, St, *De Cura gerenda pro Mortuis*, in id., *Œuvres*, ii. *Problèmes moraux*, ed. G. Combès (Paris, 1948).

BABINGTON, G., *A funerall sermon [on 2 Sam. x. 1]. Preached by G. Babington [at] (the funerall of maister T. L. esquire.)* (1595).

BAILLIE, R., *The Letters and Journals of Robert Baillie A.M. Principal of the University of Glasgow* (3 vols., Edinburgh, 1841–2).

Barlow's Journal of his Life at Sea in King's Ships, East & West Indiamen & Other Merchantmen from 1659 to 1703, ed. B. Lubbock (2 vols., 1934).

BARLOW, J., *Hieron's last fare-well. A sermon* (1618).

—— *The true guide to glory. A sermon preached at Plympton Mary in Devon, at the funerals of the lady Strode of Newingham* (1619).

Barrington Family Letters, 1628–1632, ed. A. Searle (Camden, 4th ser. 28; 1983).

BARROW, H., *A Brief Discoverie of the False Church* (1590), in id., *The Writings of Henry Barrow 1587–1590*, ed. L. H. Carlson (Elizabethan Nonconformist Texts, 3; 1962).

BARTHOLOMAEUS ANGLICUS, *On the Properties of Things: John Trevisa's Translation of Bartholomaeus Anglicus 'De Proprietatibus Rerum'. A Critical Text*, ed. M. C. Seymour (3 vols., Oxford, 1975–88).

BATES, W., *A Funeral Sermon preached Upon the Death of . . . Dr. Thomas Manton* (1678).

BAXTER, R., *The Practical Works of the Rev. Richard Baxter*, ed. W. Orme (23 vols., 1830).

BAYES, J., *A Funeral Sermon occasioned by the Death of the late Reverend Mr. Christopher Taylor* (1723).

BAYLY, L., *The practise of pietie: directing a christian how to walke* (11th edn., 1619).

BEARD, T., *The Theatre of Gods Judgements* (4th edn., 1648).

BEAUMONT, G. F., *A History of Coggeshall, in Essex with an Account of its Church, Abbey, Manors, Ancient Houses &c.* (1890).

BECON, T., *The Catechism of Thomas Becon, S.T.P. . . . with other pieces written by him in the Reign of King Edward the Sixth*, ed. J. Ayre (Parker Soc., 1844).

—— *The Sicke mannes Salue, wherein the faithfull Christians may learne both how to behaue themselues paciently and thankefully in the tyme of sickenes, and also vertuously to dispose their temporall goods, and finally to prepare themselues gladly and godly to dye*, in id., *Prayers and other Pieces of Thomas Becon, S.T.P.*, ed. J. Ayre (Parker Soc., 1844).

BEERMAN, W., *Sorrow upon Sorrow: or, The much Lamented Death of the worthy Mr. Ralph Venning* (1674).

BELBIN, P., *A Sermon Preach'd at the Funeral of Mr. George Elliott of Reading* (1730).

BIRCH, T., *The Life of the Right Honourable Robert Boyle* (1744).

BLOMEFIELD, F., *The History of the Ancient City and Burgh of Thetford* (Fersfield, 1739), app. viii.

BLUNDELL, N., *The Great Diurnal of Nicholas Blundell of Little Crosby, Lancashire*, ed. F. Tyrer and J. J. Bagley (Record Soc. of Lancashire and Cheshire, 110, 112, 114; 1968, 1970, 1972).

The Book of the Knight of the Tower, ed. M. Y. Offord (EETS, suppl. ser. 2; 1971).

Boswell's Life of Johnson, ed. R. W. Chapman (Oxford Standard Authors, 1953 edn.).

BOWLE, J., *A sermon preached at Flitton in the countie of Bedford, at the funerall of Henrie earle of Kent* (1615).

BRADBURY, T., *Winning Christ, and being found in him, considered: In two Sermons on the Death of the Reverend Mr. Robert Bragge* (1738).

BRAMHALL, J., *Works*, ed. A. W. Haddan (LACT, 5 vols., 1842–5).

BRAY, T., *The good Fight of Faith, in the Cause of God against the Kingdom of Satan, Exemplified, in a Sermon Preach'd at the Parish-Church of St. Clements Danes, Westminster, on the 24th of March, 1708/9, at the Funeral of Mr. John Dent* (1709).

Brief Narratives of the Lives of Gilbert Latey, Christopher Storey and John Banks (Friends' Library, 9; 1834).

BRIGHTMAN, F. E., *The English Rite* (2 vols., 1915).

BRINE, J., *The Covenant of Grace open'd in a Sermon Occasioned by the Death of Mrs. Margaret Busfield* (1734).

—— *The Believer's Triumph over Death. Considered in a Sermon Occasion'd by the Decease of Mr. Hugh Lloyd* (1736).

—— *The Chief of Sinners, saved thro' Jesus Christ: A Sermon, Occasioned by the Death of Mrs. Anne Wildman* (1747).

BROOKS, T., *A String of Pearles: Or The best things reserved till last. Discovered, In a Sermon Preached . . . At the Funeral of . . . Mris. Mary Blake . . . with an Elegy on her Death* (1657).

BROWNE, Sir THOMAS, *Works*, ed. G. Keynes (4 vols., 1964).

—— *The Religio Medici & other Writings of Sir Thomas Browne* (1906).

BUNYAN, J., *The Life and Death of Mr. Badman. Presented to the World in a Familiar Dialogue Between Mr. Wiseman, and Mr. Attentive*, ed. J. F. Forrest and R. Sharrock (Oxford, 1988).

BURCHES, G., *A Sermon preached . . . at the Funerall of . . . M^{ris} Margaret Elmes* (1641).

BURNETT, G., *A Sermon Preached at the Funeral of Mr. James Houblon . . .* (1682).

—— *The Lives of Sir Matthew Hale, Kt. . . .; Wilmot, Earl of Rochester; and Queen Mary* (1774 edn.).

BURNET, T., *A Treatise Concerning the State of Departed Souls Before, and At, and After the Resurrection* (1733).

BURTON, R., *The Anatomy of Melancholy*, ed. T. C. Faulkner, N. K. Kiessling, and R. L. Blair (Oxford, 1989–94).

BYROM, J., *The Private Journal and Literary Remains of John Byrom*, ed. R. Parkinson (Chetham Soc., OS 32, 34, 40, 44; 1854–7).

CALAMY, E., *The Doctrine of the Bodies Fragility: with A Divine Project, discovering how to make these vile bodies of ours glorious by getting gracious Souls* (1655).

CAVENDISH, G., *The Life and Death of Cardinal Wolsey*, in *Two Early Tudor Lives*.

The Cely Letters, 1472–1488, ed. A. Hanham (EETS 273; 1975).

Certain Sermons or Homilies, ed. G. E. Corrie (Cambridge, 1850).

CHADWICH, J., *A sermon preached at Snarford at the funerals of sir George Sanct-Paule. Together with a briefe relation of his life and death* (1614).

CHAMBERS, R., *Sarahs sepulture: or a funerall sermon preached for the countesse of Northumberland* (1620).

CHARDON, J., *A comfortable sermon for all such as thirst to be ioined with Jesus Christ. Preached at the funerals of syr Gawen Carew in Exeter the two and twentieth of April. 1584* (Oxford, 1586).

Cheshire and Lancashire Funeral Certificates, A.D. 1600 to 1678, ed. J. P. Rylands (Lancashire and Cheshire Record Soc. 6; 1882).

CLARKE, M., *A Funeral Sermon occasioned by the much lamented Death of the Reverend Mr. Jeremiah Smith* (2nd edn., 1723).

—— *A Funeral Sermon on the Death of the Late Reverend Mr. Thomas Mitchell* (1722).

CLARKE, S., *The Lives of Sundry Eminent Persons in this Later Age* (2 pts. in 1 vol., 1683).

—— *The Marrow of Ecclesiastical History* (3rd edn., 1675).

—— *The Second Part of the Marrow of Ecclesiastical History* (2 bks. in 1 vol., 2nd edn., 1675).

—— *A Collection of the Lives of Ten Eminent Divines* (1662).

CLIFFORD, Lady ANNE, *The Diary of the Lady Anne Clifford*, ed. V. Sackville-West (1923).

COLLINS, A., *The Life of William Cecil Lord Burghley* (1732).

COLMORE, M., *Oratio funebris in obitum clarissimi viri et munificentissimi collegii Corporis Christi Oxon. benefactoris Georgii Sanctpaul equitis aurati* (Oxford, 1613).

COOKE, E., *A Sermon Preach'd in the Parish Church of Braden, in Northamptonshire, On April 19, 1719. . . . at the Funeral of William Ives, Esq.* (2nd edn., 1719).

COSIN, J., *Works*, ed. J. Sansom (LACT, 5 vols., 1843–55).

The Courts of the Archdeaconry of Buckingham, 1483–1523, ed. E. M. Elvey (Buckinghamshire Record Soc. 19; 1975).

COVERDALE, M., *Remains of Myles Coverdale, Bishop of Exeter*, ed. G. Pearson (Parker Soc., 1846).

CROMPTON, W., *A lasting jewell, for religious woemen. In the summe of a sermon, preached at the funerall of mistris Mary Crosse of Barnestaple and now published with some additions* (1630).

CROSFIELD, T., *The Diary of Thomas Crosfield*, ed. F. S. Boas (Oxford, 1935).

CROSS, M. C., 'The Third Earl of Huntingdon's Death-bed: A Calvinist Example of the *Ars Moriendi*', *Northern History*, 21 (1985), 80–107.

CRUSO, T., *The Period of Humane Life determined by the Divine Will. A Funeral Sermon on the Death of Mr. Henry Brownsword* (1688).

CUTTS, E. L., 'Curious Extracts from a MS Diary, of the time of James II and William and Mary', *Transactions of the Essex Archaeological Soc.* (1858), 117–19.

D., J., *A Sermon Preached at the Funeral Of that incomparable Lady, the Honourable, the Lady Mary Armyne* (1676).

Darlington Wills and Inventories 1600–1625, ed. J. A. Atkinson, B. Flynn, V. Portass, K. Singlehurst, and H. J. Smith (Surtees Soc. 201; 1993).

DAY, A., *The English Secretary* (1599), ed. R. O. Evans (facsimile edn., Gainesville, Fla., 1967).

DEE, J., *The Private Diary of Dr. John Dee*, ed. J. O. Halliwell (Camden OS 19; 1842).

DEFOE, D., *A Journal of the Plague Year*, ed. A. Burgess and C. Bristow (Harmondsworth, 1966).

—— *The King of Pirates, Being an Account of the Famous Enterprises of Captain Avery with Lives of other Pirates and Robbers*, ed. G. A. Aitken (1895).

DEKKER, T., *The Plague Pamphlets of Thomas Dekker*, ed. F. P. Wilson (Oxford, 1925).

DELANY, M., *The Autobiography and Correspondence of Mary Granville, Mrs. Delany*, ed. Lady Llanover (3 vols., 1861).

DELAVAL, Lady ELIZABETH, *The Meditations of Lady Elizabeth Delaval, written between 1662 and 1671*, ed. D. G. Greene (Surtees Soc. 190; 1978).

DENT, E., *Everlasting Blessedness. A Sermon preached at The Funerall of . . . Mr. William Baker, who Left this Vale of Tears, and was received to Heavenly Joyes, the 14th. Day of October, 1691* (1692).

Depositions and other Ecclesiastical Proceedings from the Courts of Durham, extending from 1311 to the Reign of Elizabeth, ed. J. Raine (Surtees Soc. 21; 1845).

A Description of the State, Civil and Ecclesiastical, of the County of Lancaster about the Year 1590, ed. F. R. Raines, in *Chetham Miscellany*, v (Chetham Soc., OS 96; 1875).

D'EWES, Sir SIMONDS, *The Autobiography and Correspondence of Sir Simonds D'Ewes, Bart*, ed. J. O. Halliwell (2 vols., 1845).

DILLINGHAM, W., *A Sermon at the Funeral of the Lady Elizabeth Alston, wife of Sir Thomas Alston, . . . Septemb. 10. 1677* (1678).

A Directory for the Publique Worship of God, Throughout the Three Kingdoms (1645).

Dives and Pauper, ed. P. H. Barnum (EETS 275, 280; 1976, 1980).

Documentary Annals of the Reformed Church of England, ed. E. Cardwell (2 vols., Oxford, 1844).

Documents Illustrative of English Church History, ed. H. Gee and W. J. Hardy (1896).

Documents of the English Reformation, ed. G. Bray (Cambridge, 1994).

DODDRIDGE, P., *Practical Reflections on the Character and Translation of Enoch* (Northampton, 1738).

DODSON, J., *A Sermon preached at the Funeral Obsequies of Jacob Lucie Esq: Late Alderman of the City of London* (1688).

DODWELL, W., *The Eternity of future Punishment asserted and vindicated. In answer to Mr. Whiston's late Treatise on that Subject* (Oxford, 1743).

DONNE, J., *The Sermons of John Donne*, ed. G. R. Potter and E. M. Simpson (10 vols., Berkeley and Los Angeles, 1953–62).

—— *Devotions upon Emergent Occasions*, ed. A. Raspa (New York, 1987).

DUGDALE, Sir WILLIAM, *The Life, Diary, and Correspondence of Sir William Dugdale, Kt, sometimes Garter Principal King of Arms*, ed. W. Hamper (1827).

DUNTON, J., *An Essay Proving We shall Know our Friends in Heaven* (1698).

EATON, R., *A sermon preached at the funeralls of Thomas Dutton of Dutton, esquire* (1616).

EDMUNDSON, W., *A Journal of the Life of William Edmundson* (Friends' Library, 4; 1833).

EDWARDS, T., *Gangraena; or a . . . Discovery of Many Errours, Heresies, Blasphemies and Pernicious Practices* (1646).

An Elegie upon The much lamented Death, of . . . Elizabeth Hoyle (York, 1644).

ELLESBY, J., *The Great Danger and Uncertainty of a Death-Bed Repentance* (1693).

EMMISON, F. G. (ed.), *Elizabethan Life*, iv. *Wills of Essex Gentry and Merchants Proved in the Prerogative Court of Canterbury* (Chelmsford, 1978).

ERASMUS, D., *The Colloquies of Erasmus*, trans. C. R. Thompson (Chicago, 1965).

—— *Preparation to deathe, a boke as deuout as eloquent* (1538).

Essex Wills, 1558–1603, ed. F. G. Emmison (Chelmsford, 1982–).

EVELYN, J., *The Diary of John Evelyn*, ed. E. S. de Beer (6 vols., Oxford, 1955).

—— *The Life of Mrs. Godolphin*, ed. H. Sampson (Oxford, 1939).

EYRE, R., *A Sermon Preach'd at the Funeral of . . . Sir Stephen Fox* (1716).

—— *A Sermon preached . . ., At the Funeral of Thomas Pitt Esq.* (1726).

F., I., *A sermon preached at Ashby De-la-zouch at the funerall of the lady Elizabeth Stanley late wife to Henrie earle of Huntingdon* (1635).

FANSHAWE, ANN Lady, *The Memoirs of Ann Lady Fanshawe*, ed. H. C. Fanshawe (1907).

FARINDON, A., *LXXX Sermons preached at the Parish-Church of St Mary Magdalene Milk-street, London* (2nd edn., 2 vols., 1672).

FEATLEY, D., *A sermon preached at the funerall of sir Humphrey Lynd. At Cobham, June the 14th 1636*, in H. Lynde, *A case for the spectacles, or, a defence of Via tuta, together with Stricturae in Lyndomastygem* (1638).

FEREBE, G., *Lifes farewell. Or a funerall sermon. At the funerall of John Drew gentleman* (1615).

The Fifty Earliest English Wills in the Court of Probate, London, ed. F. J. Furnivall (EETS 78; 1882).

The First and Second Prayer Books of Edward VI (1910).

FISHER, J., *The English Works of John Fisher*, ed. J. E. B. Mayor (EETS extra ser. 27; 1876).

FITZ-GEFFREY, C., *Death's sermon unto the living. Delivered at the funerals of the ladie Philippe, late wife unto Sir A. Rous* (1620).

FLEETWOOD, W., *A Compleat Collection of the Sermons, Tracts, and Pieces of all Kinds, That were Written by . . . Dr. William Fleetwood, Late Lord Bishop of Ely* (1737).

FORTESCUE, T. (Lord Clermont), *A History of the Family of Fortescue in all its Branches* (1880).

FOXE, J., *Acts and Monuments*, ed. J. Pratt (8 vols., 1877).

FREKE, E., *Mrs. Elizabeth Freke her Diary 1671–1714*, ed. M. Carbery (Cork, 1913).

FULLER, T., *History of the Worthies of England*, ed. J. G. Nichols (2 vols., 1811).

GABRIELI, V., *Sir Kenelm Digby: Un inglese italianato* (Rome, 1957).

GATAKER, T., *Certaine sermons first preached and since published* (Two parts in one vol., 1637).

Gentleman's Magazine, 1 (1731), 9 (1739), 10 (1740), 20 (1750).

GERARD, J., *John Gerard: The Autobiography of an Elizabethan*, trans. P. Caraman (1951).

GEREE, S., *The Ornament of women or, A description of the true excellency of women, Delivered in a Sermon at the Funerall of M. Elizabeth Machell* (1639).

GIBSON, E., *Codex Juris Ecclesiastici Anglicani* (2 vols., Oxford, 1761).

GIFFORD, G., *A briefe discourse of certaine points of the religion, which is among the common sort of christians which may be termed the countrey divinitie. With a confutation of the same, after the order of a dialogue* (1581).

[GILL, J.], *An Essay on the Original of Funeral Sermons, Orations, and Odes* (1729).

GOUGE, W., *Of domesticall duties eight treatises* (1622).

GRAILE, J., *Vigorous Longevity; or, A good old age, And the best Way, both to Attain it: and to Improve it . . .* (1720).

GRANT, J., *An Essay, With Relation to the Gospel of our Lord Jesus Christ: Being a Friendly Examination of two Funeral Discourses: Publish'd by Mr. Peter Belbin* (1732).

GRIFFITH, E., *A Sermon preached . . . At the Funerall of Sir Matthew Hale K^t late Chief Justice of His Majestie's Court of the King's Bench* (1677).

GROSVENOR, B., *Observations on Sudden Death. Occasion'd by the late fre-quent Instances of it, both in City and Country* (1720).

—— *Precious Death. A Sermon On Occasion of the Death of M^rs· Susannah Rudge* (1716).

HALKETT, Lady ANNE, *The Autobiography of Anne Lady Halkett*, ed. J. G. Nichols (Camden NS 13; 1875).

HALL, E., *A Sermon Preached at Stanton-Harcourt Church. . . . At the Funer-all of the Honourable the Lady Ann Harcourt* (Oxford, 1664).

HALL, T., *A Sermon Preached . . . At the Funeral of Robert Huntington Esq.* (1684).

HAMMOND, H., *The Miscellaneous Theological Works of Henry Hammond*, ed. N. Pocock (LACT, 3 vols., 1847–50).

HARCOURT, J., *A Sermon Preach'd . . . Upon the Death of Edward Colston, Esq.* (1721).

HARDY, N., *Death's Alarum: or, Security's Warning-Piece. A Sermon preached . . . at the Funerall of M^rs· Mary Smith* (1654).

HARRIS, R., *The workes . . . Revised, and in sundrie places corrected. With an addition of two sermons, not formerly extant. As also two tables* (1635).

—— *Abners Funerall, or, A Sermon Preached at the Funerall of . . . Sir Thomas Lvcie* (1641).

HARRIS, W., *Funeral Discourses. In Two Parts: containing, I. Consolations on the Death of our Friends. II. Preparations for our Death* (1736).

HARRISON, T., *A Funeral Sermon Occasioned by the Death of Dame Mary Page* (1729).

HASTINGS, Sir FRANCIS, *The Letters of Sir Francis Hastings, 1574–1609*, ed. C. Cross (Somerset Record Soc. 69; 1969).

HEARNE, T. (ed.), *A Collection of Curious Discourses written by Eminent Antiquaries upon Several Heads in our English Antiquities* (2 vols., 1771).

HERBERT, G., *Works*, ed. F. E. Hutchinson (Oxford, 1941).

Here begynneth a lityll treatise shorte and abredged spekynge of the arte & crafte to knowe well to dye (1490).

HEYWOOD, O., *The Rev. Oliver Heywood, B.A. 1603–1702: his Autobiog-raphy, Diaries, Anecdote and Event Books*, ed. J. Horsfall Turner (4 vols., Brighouse, 1882–5).

HICKES, G., *The Life and Death of David. A Sermon Preached at the Funer-alls of that Worthy Member of the Honourable House of Commons, William Strode Esquire* (1645).

Historical Register, 21/81 (1736).

HOADLY, B., *A Sermon Preach'd at the Funeral of Mrs. Elizabeth Howland* (1719).

HOBY, Lady MARGARET, *Diary of Lady Margaret Hoby, 1599–1605*, ed. D. M. Meads (1930).

HOOKE, R., *The Diary of Robert Hooke, F.R.S., 1672–1680*, ed. H. W. Robin-son and W. Adams (1935).

HOOKER, R., *Of the Laws of Ecclesiastical Polity*, in id., *The Works of that Learned and Judicious Divine, Mr. Richard Hooker* (2 vols., Oxford 1841).

HOOPER, J., *Early Writings of John Hooper, D.D.*, ed. S. Carr (Parker Soc., 1843).

HORNECK, A., *A Sermon, Preached at the Solemnity of the Funeral of M^{rs}. Dorothy St. John, Fourth Daughter of the late Sir Oliver St. John* (1677).

HOULBROOKE, R. (ed.), *English Family Life, 1576-1716: An Anthology from Diaries* (Oxford, 1988).

HUDSON, S., *David's Labour and Rest: or, a Discourse . . . Preached at the Funeral of Mr. Richard Shute* (1689).

HUGHES, G., *The saints losse and lamentation. A sermon at the funerall of captaine Henry Waller* (1632).

HUTCHINSON, L., *Memoirs of the Life of Colonel Hutchinson, with the Fragment of an Autobiography of Mrs Hutchinson*, ed. J. Sutherland (1973).

HUTTON, W., *The Life of William Hutton, and the History of the Hutton Family*, ed. L. Jewitt (1872).

I., W., *A Sermon Preached at the Fvnerall of M^{rs}. Alice Bray* (1646).

IDLEY, P., *Peter Idley's Instructions to his Son*, ed. C. D'Evelyn (Modern Language Association of America, Monograph Ser. 6; 1935).

JANEWAY, J., *A Token for Children: being an Exact Account of the Conversion, Holy and Exemplary Lives, and Joyful Deaths, of Several Young Children* (1676 edn.).

JEAKE, S., *An Astrological Diary of the Seventeenth Century: Samuel Jeake of Rye 1652-1699*, ed. M. Hunter and A. Gregory (Oxford, 1988).

JENNY, J., *A Sermon preached At the Funeral of the Right Honble the Lady Frances Paget. The religious Consort of the right Honble William Lord Paget* (1673).

JOCELINE, E., *The mothers legacie, to her unborne childe* (6th impression, 1632; repr. 1894).

JOHNSON, S., *Lives of the English Poets*, ed. G. B. Hill (3 vols., Oxford, 1905).

JOLLY, T., *The Note Book of the Rev. Thomas Jolly, A.D. 1671-1693*, ed. H. Fishwick (Chetham Soc., NS 33; 1894).

JONES, J., *The Mysteries of Opium Reveal'd* (1700).

JOSSELIN, R., *The Diary of Ralph Josselin, 1616-1683*, ed. A. Macfarlane (Records of Social and Economic History, NS 3, 1976).

KAY, R., *The Diary of Richard Kay, 1716-1751, of Baldingstone, near Bury, a Lancashire Doctor*, ed. W. Brockbank and K. Kenworthy (Chetham Soc., 3rd ser. 16; 1968).

KENNEDY, W. P. M., *Elizabethan Episcopal Administration: An Essay in Sociology and Politics* (Alcuin Club Collections, 26-7; 1924).

KENNETT, W., *A Sermon Preach'd at the Funeral of the . . . Duke of Devonshire, . . . on Friday Septemb. 5th MDCCVII* (1708).

KIDDER, R., *The Life of Richard Kidder, D.D., Bishop of Bath and Wells, written by himself*, ed. A. E. Robinson (Somerset Record Soc. 37; 1924).

KIDDER, R., *A Sermon Preached at the Funeral of Mr William Allen* (1686).

KILBIE, R., *A sermon preached . . . in Oxford at the funeral of Thomas Holland* (Oxford, 1613).

KING, R., *A funerall sermon that was prepared to have bene preched, by Robert King doctour in divinite for a certein honourable Lady then almoste deade, but afterward recouered* (1552).

KNAGGS, T., *A Sermon Preach'd . . . the Sunday after the Death of . . . Dr. John Sharp, Lord Arch-bishop of York* (1714).

KNIGHT, S., *A Sermon Preached at the Funeral of . . . Laetitia, Lady Dowager Russel* (1722).

The Ladies' Dictionary (1694).

Lancashire Funeral Certificates, ed. T. W. King (Chetham Soc., os 75; 1869).

LATIMER, H., *Sermons by Hugh Latimer*, ed. G. E. Corrie (Parker Soc., 1844).

LAUD, W., *Works*, ed. W. Scott and J. Bliss (LACT, 7 vols., 1847–60).

LAYFIELDE, E., *The soules solace. A sermon preached at the solemn funerall of William Fawcit Gent.* (1632).

L'ESTRANGE, H., *The Alliance of Divine Offices* (4th edn., LACT, 1846).

LEWIS, G., *A Sermon Preach'd at Westram in Kent, on the Occasion of the Death of Mrs. Paynter, Wife of Robert Paynter, Esq.* (1726).

[LEWIS, T.], *Churches no Charnel-Houses: being, An Enquiry into the Profaneness, Indecency, and Pernicious Consequences to the Living, of Burying the Dead in Churches and Churchyards* (1726).

Liber Vitae Ecclesiae Dunelmensis: nec non Obituaria duo ejusdem Ecclesiae, ed. J. Stevenson (Surtees Soc. 13; 1841).

Lincoln Wills, i. *A.D. 1271 to 1526*, ed. C. W. Foster (Lincoln Record Soc. 5; 1914).

The Lisle Letters, ed. M. St Clare Byrne (6 vols., Chicago, 1981).

Lollard Sermons, ed. G. Cigman (EETS 294; 1989).

London Consistory Court Wills 1492–1547, ed. I. Darlington (London Record Soc. 3; 1967).

LOVE, B., *A Sermon Preach'd at the Funeral of Nathanael Symonds, Esq.* (1721).

LOWE, R., *The Diary of Roger Lowe of Ashton-in-Makerfield, Lancashire, 1663–1674*, ed. W. L. Sachse (1938).

MACHYN, H., *The Diary of Henry Machyn, Citizen and Merchant-Taylor of London, from A.D. 1550 to A.D. 1563*, ed. J. G. Nichols (Camden os 42; 1848).

Manuale ad vsum percelebris ecclesie Sarisburiensis, ed. A. J. Collins (Henry Bradshaw Soc. 91; 1960).

The Manuscripts of His Grace the Duke of Rutland, G.C.B., preserved at Belvoir Castle (Historical Manuscripts Commission, 4 vols., 1888–1905).

MARSHALL, J., *A Sermon Preach'd . . . Opon [sic] Occasion of the much Lamented Death of . . . Robert Nelson Esq.* (1715).

MARSHALL, N., *A Sermon Delivered... Upon Occasion Of the much Lamented Death of the Rev^d. John Rogers, D.D.* (1729).

MARTINDALE, A., *The Life of Adam Martindale, written by himself*, ed. R. Parkinson (Chetham Soc., os 4; 1845).

A Memoir of the Life, Travels and Gospel Labours of George Fox (1839).

Memoirs of the Life of Mr. Ambrose Barnes, late Merchant and sometime Alderman of Newcastle upon Tyne, ed. W. H. D. Longstaffe (Surtees Soc. 50; 1867).

MILLER, W., *A sermon preached at the funerall of Gilbert Davies esquire* (1621).

MIRK, J., *John Mirk's Instructions for Parish Priests*, ed. G. Kristensson (Lund Studies in English, 49; 1974).

MISSON, H., *Memoirs and Observations in his Travels over England* (1719).

MONTAGU, H., *Death and Immortality*, ed. E. Waterhouse (1906).

MONTAGU, Lady MARY WORTLEY, *The Complete Letters of Lady Mary Wortley Montagu*, ed. R. Halsband (3 vols., Oxford, 1965–7).

MOORE, G., *The Journal of Giles Moore*, ed. R. Bird (Sussex Record Soc. 68; 1971).

MORE, Sir THOMAS, *The Correspondence of Sir Thomas More*, ed. E. F. Rogers (Princeton, 1947).

—— *The Supplication of Souls*, ed. G. Marc'hadour, in id., *The Complete Works of St Thomas More* (New Haven, 1963–), vii (1990).

—— *The English Works of Sir Thomas More*, ed. W. E. Campbell, A. W. Reed, R. W. Chambers, and W. A. G. Doyle-Davidson (2 vols., 1927, 1931).

MORRIS, C., *The Diary of a West Country Physician, A.D. 1684–1726*, ed. E. Hobhouse (1934).

MUNBY, L. M. (ed.), *Life & Death in Kings Langley: Wills and Inventories 1498–1659* (Kings Langley, 1981).

The New Oxford Book of Eighteenth Century Verse, ed. R. Lonsdale (Oxford, 1984).

The New Oxford Book of Seventeenth Century Verse, ed. A. Fowler (Oxford, 1992).

NEWCOME, H., *The Autobiography of Henry Newcome, M.A.*, ed. R. Parkinson (Chetham Soc., os 26 and 27; 1852).

NEWTON, S., *The Diary of Samuel Newton, Alderman of Cambridge (1662–1717)*, ed. J. E. Foster (Cambridge Antiquarian Soc. 23; 1890).

North, R., *The Autobiography of the Hon. Roger North*, ed. A. Jessopp (1887).

Norwich Consistory Court Depositions, 1499–1512 and 1518–1530, ed. E. D. Stone (Norfolk Record Soc. 10; 1938).

Obsequies of Certain of the Family of Blackett of Newcastle, ed. M. A. Richardson, in *Reprints of Rare Tracts and Imprints of Antient Manuscripts &c. chiefly illustrative of the History of the Northern Counties* (Newcastle, 1846).

OGLANDER, Sir J., *A Royalist's Notebook: The Commonplace Book of Sir John Oglander Kt of Nunwell*, ed. F. Bamford (1936).

The Oglander Memoirs: Extracts from the MSS of Sir J. Oglander Kt., ed. W. H. Long (1888).

OLDMAYNE, T., *Lifes brevitie and deaths debility. Evidently declared in a sermon preached at the funerall of E. Lewkenor* (1636).

OSBORNE, F., *Advice to a Son*, ed. E. A. Parry (1896).

PARKHURST, J., *The Letter Book of John Parkhurst, Bishop of Norwich, 1571-1575*, ed. R. A. Houlbrooke (Norfolk Record Soc. 43; 1974–5).

PARKHURST, N., *The Redeemer's Friend; or, a Sermon . . . Preached at the Funeral of the Reverend, Learned, and Faithful Minister of the Gospel, Mr. Samvel Fairclough* (1692).

PARSLEY, H., *A Sermon Preached at the Funeral of M^r. Thomas Whitchurch. October the 15th. 1691* (1692).

PARSONS, R., *A Sermon preached at the Funeral of the . . . Earl of Rochester* (Oxford, 1680).

Paston Letters and Papers of the Fifteenth Century, ed. N. Davis (2 vols., Oxford, 1971, 1976).

PEARSON, R., *A Sermon Preached at the Funeral of the Reverend Doctor Ambrose Atfield. Late Minister of St. Leonard Shoreditch* (1684).

PECK, F., *Desiderata Curiosa: or, a Collection of divers Scarce and Curious Pieces, relating chiefly to Matters of English History* (2 vols., 1779).

PECK, S., *A Sermon preached at the Funeral of Sir Henry Johnson K^t.* (1684).

PEPYS, S., *The Diary of Samuel Pepys: A New and Complete Transcription*, ed. R. Latham and W. Matthews (11 vols., 1970–83).

—— *Private Correspondence and Miscellaneous Papers of Samuel Pepys, 1679-1703*, ed. J. R. Tanner (2 vols., 1926).

PERKINS, W., *A salue for a sicke man, or, a treatise containing the nature, differences, and kindes of death: as also the right manner of dying well* (edn. of *c.*1638, STC 19747.3).

PHILLIPS, J., *The way to heaven* (1625).

PIERS, H., *True Wisdom from Above: or, Christianity the Best Understanding. A Sermon Preach'd . . . at the Funeral of Mary Godden* (1746).

POTTER, B., *The baronets buriall, or a funerall sermon at Sr Edward Seymours buriall* (Oxford, 1613).

POUNDS, N. J. G., 'William Carnsew of Bokelly and his Diary, 1576-1577', *Journal of the Royal Institution of Cornwall*, NS 8/1 (1978), 14–60.

PRESTON, J., *A sermon preached at the funerall of J. Reynel* (1615).

—— *A sermon preached at the funeral of M^r. Arthur Upton* (1619).

PRICKE, R., *A verie godlie and learned sermon, treating of mans mortalitie and of the estate both of his bodie, and soule after death* (1608).

Puritan Manifestoes, ed. W. H. Frere and C. E. Douglas (1954).

RANBY, J., *A Narrative of the Last Illness of the Right Honourable the Earl of Orford* (1745).

RAVENSHAW, T. F., *Antiente Epitaphes (from A.D. 1250 to A.D. 1800) collected and set forth in Chronologicall Order* (1878).

READ, H., *Be Ye also ready. A Funeral-Discourse, Occasion'd by the Much lamented Death of Mr Thomas Adams, Who Died in the 23d Year of his Age* (2nd edn., 1737).

The Receyt of the Ladie Kateryne, ed. G. Kipling (EETS 296; 1990).

The Recusancy Papers of the Meynell Family, ed. J. C. H. Aveling, in *Miscellanea*, ed. E. E. Reynolds (Catholic Record Soc. 56; 1964).

RERESBY, Sir JOHN, *Memoirs of Sir John Reresby: The Complete Text and a Selection from his Letters*, ed. A. Browning (Glasgow, 1936).

REYNOLDS, E., *Mary Magdalens Love to Christ Opened In a Sermon Preached at the Funeral of Mistris Elizabeth Thomason* (1659).

RICH, M., *The Autobiography of Mary, Countess of Warwick*, ed. T. C. Croker (Percy Soc. 76; 1848).

RICHARDSON, S., *Clarissa or, The History of a Young Lady* (8 vols., Oxford, 1930).

—— *One Hundred and Seventy-Three Letters written for Particular Friends, on the most Important Occasions* (7th edn., 1764).

ROGERS, D., *Matrimoniall Honovr: Or the mutuall Crowne and comfort of godly, loyall, and chaste Marriage* (London, 1642).

ROGERS, S., *The Comfort, Certainty, and Blessedness of the Christian Hope: in a Sermon Preach'd at the Funeral Of . . . Baptist, Earl of Gainsborough* (1714).

—— *A Sermon Preach'd at the Funeral Of the Honourable Susanna Noel* (1715).

ROPER, W., *The Life of Sir Thomas More*, in *Two Early Tudor Lives*.

ROWE, E., *Friendship in Death, in Twenty Letters from the Dead to the Living* (1814 edn.).

RUSSELL, Lady RACHEL, *The Letters of Lady Rachel Russell: From the Manuscript in the Library at Wooburn Abbey* (4th edn., 1792).

RYDER, D., *The Diary of Dudley Ryder, 1715–1716*, ed. W. Matthews (1939).

RYMER, T., *Foedera* (The Hague, 1739–45).

SCOTT, C., *The Saints Priviledge, or Gain by Dying* (1673).

SCOTT, J., *A Sermon Preach'd at the Funeral of Sir John Buckworth . . . December 29, 1687* (1688).

—— *A Sermon Preached at the Funeral of Sir John Chapman Late Lord Mayor of London* (1689).

Selby Wills, ed. F. Collins (Yorkshire Archaeological Soc. Record Ser. 47; 1912).

Sevenoaks Wills and Inventories in the Reign of Charles II, ed. H. C. F. Lansberry (Kent Archaeological Soc., Kent Records, 25; 1988).

A Seventeenth Century Doctor and his Patients: John Symcotts, 1592?–1662, ed. F. N. L. Poynter and W. J. Bishop (Bedfordshire Historical Record Soc. 31; 1951).

SHERLOCK, W., *A Practical Discourse concerning Death* (23rd edn., 1739).

SISSON, C. H. (ed.), *The English Sermon*, ii. *1650–1750* (Cheadle, 1976).

Six North Country Diaries, ed. J. C. Hodgson (Surtees Soc. 118; 1910).

SLINGSBY, Sir HENRY, *The Diary of Sir Henry Slingsby, of Scriven, Bart.*, ed. D. Parsons (1836).

SMYTH, J., *The Lives of the Berkeleys*, in *The Berkeley Manuscripts*, ed. J. Maclean (Gloucester, 1883).

SMYTH, R., *The Obituary of Richard Smyth, Secondary of the Poultry Compter, London: being a Catalogue of all such Persons as he knew in their Life: extended from A.D. 1627 to A.D. 1674*, ed. Sir Henry Ellis (Camden OS 44; 1849).

SPARKE, R., *A Sermon preached . . . at the Funeral of that Pious and Worthy Gentlewoman. Mrs Frances Fenn* (1679).

The Spectator, ed. D. F. Bond (5 vols., Oxford, 1965).

SPENCER, B., *Aphonologos. A Dumb Speech. Or, A Sermon made, but no Sermon preached, at the Funerall of . . . Mrs Mary Overman* (1646).

SPINCKES, N., *The Sick Man visited: And Furnish'd with Instructions, Meditations, and Prayers* (1712).

STANHOPE, G., *Death just Matter of Joy to good Men. A Sermon Preach'd . . . At the Funeral of Mr. Richard Sare, of London, Bookseller* (2nd edn., 1724).

STEELE, R., *The Funeral: or, Grief A-la-Mode*, in id. *The Plays of Richard Steele*, ed. S. S. Kenny (Oxford, 1971).

STEER, F. W., 'The Funeral Account of the First Duke of Richmond and Lennox', *Sussex Archaeological Collections*, 98 (1960).

STEPHENS, G., *The amiable quality of goodness as compared with Righteousness, considered. In a Sermon Preach'd . . . the Sunday after the funeral of . . . Elizabeth, Lady Onslow* (1731).

STEPHENS, L., *A Sermon Preached . . . At the Funeral of . . . Dr. Charles Trimnel, Late Lord Bishop of Winchester* (1723).

STONE, W., *A curse become a blessing: or, a sermon preached at the funerall of Paul Cleybrooke esquire* (1623).

STOUT, W., *The Autobiography of William Stout of Lancaster, 1665–1752*, ed. J. D. Marshall (Chetham Soc., 3rd ser. 14; 1967).

STOW, J., *A Survey of London*, ed. C. L. Kingsford (2 vols., Oxford, 1908).

STUBBES, P., *A christal glasse for christian women. Contayning an excellent discourse, of the life and death of Katherine Stubbes* (1592 edn.).

—— *Christal glasse*, repr. with some omissions in *Philip Stubbes's Anatomy of the Abuses in England in Shakspere's Youth, A.D. 1583*, ed. F. J. Furnivall (New Shakspere Soc., 6th ser. 4, 6, 12; 1877–82).

SUTTON, C., *Disce Mori: Learn to Die* (1843, repr. from 1st edn. of 1600).

SWINBURNE, H., *A briefe treatise of testaments and last willes* (1590).

Synodalia: A Collection of Articles of Religion, Canons, and Proceedings of Convocations, ed. E. Cardwell (2 vols., Oxford, 1842).

TAYLOR, J., *The Whole Works of the Right Reverend Jeremy Taylor, D.D.*, ed. C. P. Eden (10 vols., 1847–54).

THOMLINSON, J., *The Diary of the Rev. John Thomlinson*, in *Six North Country Diaries*, ed. J. C. Hodgson (Surtees Soc. 118; 1910), 64–167.

THORNDIKE, H., *Works*, ed. A. W. Haddan (LACT, 6 vols., 1844–54).

THORNE, E., *A Funeral Sermon Upon the much lamented Death of Col. Edward Cook* (1684).

THORNTON, A., *The Autobiography of Mrs Alice Thornton, of East Newton, Co. York*, ed. C. Jackson (Surtees Soc. 62; 1875).

Three Fifteenth-Century Chronicles, with Historical Memoranda by John Stowe, the Antiquary, and Contemporary Notes of Occurrences written by him in the Reign of Queen Elizabeth, ed. J. Gairdner (Camden NS 28; 1880).

—— *Threnoikos. The house of mourning. Delivered in XLVII sermons, preached at funeralls* (1640).

TILLOTSON, J., *Sermons on several Subjects and Occasions*, in id., *Works* (12 vols., 1757).

TOMKINS, J., FIELD, J., BELL, J., and WAGSTAFFE, T., *Piety Promoted, in Brief Memorials, of the Virtuous Lives, Services, and Dying Sayings, of some of the People called Quakers* (3 vols., 1789).

TONG, W., *A Funeral Sermon Upon Occasion of the Death of Mrs. Ann Warner* (1708).

TOY, J., *A Sermon preached . . . at the funerall of M^{ris} Alice Tomkins wife unto Mr Thomas Tomkins one of the Gentlemen of his Majesties Chappell Royall* (1642).

Trevelyan Papers, ed. J. Payne Collier, Sir W. C. Trevelyan, bt., and Sir C. E. Trevelyan (Camden OS 67, 84, 105; 1857–72).

A true reporte of the honourable buriall and funerall solempnities, of George, earle of Shrewsburie, the thirteenth of January, 1590 (1591).

Tudor Royal Proclamations, ed. P. L. Hughes and J. F. Larkin (3 vols., New Haven, 1964–9).

TURNER, T., *The Diary of Thomas Turner 1754–1765*, ed. D. Vaisey (Oxford, 1985).

Two Early Tudor Lives, ed. R. S. Sylvester and D. P. Harding (New Haven, 1962).

Two East Anglian Diaries 1641–1729: Isaac Archer and William Coe, ed. M. Storey (Suffolk Records Soc. 36; 1994).

Two Elizabethan Puritan Diaries, ed. M. M. Knappen (Chicago, 1933).

Two Elizabethan Women: Correspondence of Joan and Maria Thynne 1575–1611, ed. A. D. Wall (Wilts. Record Soc. 38; 1982).

UTIE, E., *Mathew the publican. A funerall sermon* (1616).

Village Life from Wills and Inventories: Clayworth Parish 1670–1710, ed. E. R. Perkins (Centre for Local History, Univ. Nottingham, Record Ser. 1; 1979).

Visitation Articles and Injunctions of the Early Stuart Church, i, ed. K. Fincham (Church of England Record Soc. 1; 1994).

Visitation Articles and Injunctions of the Period of the Reformation, ed. W. H. Frere and W. P. M. Kennedy (Alcuin Club Collections, 14–16; 1910).

Visitations in the Diocese of Lincoln, 1517–1531, ed. A. Hamilton Thompson (Lincoln Record Soc. 33, 35, 37; 1940, 1944, 1947).

WALKER, A., *Leez Lachrymans, sive Comitis Warwici Justa: A Sermon, Delivered at the Funeral of the Right Honourable Charles, Earl of Warwick* (1673).

WALL, J., *A sermon preached at Shelford in Nottinghamshire: on the death of M. John Stanhope* (1623).

WALTON, I., *The Lives of Dr John Donne, Sir Henry Wotton, Mr Richard Hooker, Mr George Herbert and Dr Robert Sanderson* (Oxford, 1824).

WARD, S., *Woe to drunkards. A sermon* (1622).

WARREN, J., *Domus ordinata. A funerall sermon, preached in Bristoll, at the buriall of mistresse Needes* (1618).

WARWICK, Sir PHILIP, *Memoires Of the Reign of King Charles I . . . Together with A Continuation to the Happy Restauration of King Charles II* (1702).

WEBB, J., *A Sermon preach'd . . . At the Funeral of the Reverend Mr. John Hinton* (1720).

—— *The Duty of serving our Generation. Set forth in a Sermon Preached at the Funeral Of . . . Mr. Isaac Milles*, in T. Milles, *An Account of the Life and Conversation of . . . Isaac Milles* (1721).

WEEVER, J., *Ancient funerall monuments within the united monarchie of Great Britaine, Ireland, and the islands adjacent* (1631).

Wentworth Papers 1597–1628, ed. J. P. Cooper (Camden 4th ser. 12; 1973).

WERGE, R., *A Sermon preached . . . at the Funeral of George Johnson, Gent.* (1683).

WESLEY, J., *The Journal of the Rev. John Wesley A.M., sometime Fellow of Lincoln College, Oxford*, ed. N. Curnock (8 vols., 1909–16).

WEST, W., *Symbolaeographia. Which may be termed the art, description or image of instruments, covenants, contracts &c.* (1590).

WESTON, W., *William Weston: The Autobiography of an Elizabethan*, trans. P. Caraman (1955).

WHITELOCKE, B., *The Diary of Bulstrode Whitelocke, 1605–1675*, ed. R. Spalding (Records of Social and Economic History, NS 13; 1990).

WHYTHORNE, T., *The Autobiography of Thomas Whythorne*, ed. J. M. Osborn (Oxford, 1961).

WILFORD, J., *Memorials and Characters, together with the Lives of divers Eminent and Worthy Persons* (1741).

WILLAN, R., *Eliah's wish: a prayer for death. A sermon preached at the funerall of viscount Sudbury, lord Bayning* (1630).

WILLIAMSON, T., *A comfortable meditation of humane frailtie, and divine mercie: in two sermons* (1630).

The Will of Horbury, ed. K. S. Bartlett (3 vols., Wakefield, 1979–81).

Wills and Inventories from the Registers of the Commissary of Bury St. Edmund's and the Archdeacon of Sudbury, ed. S. Tymms (Camden OS 49; 1850).

Wills and Inventories from the Registry at Durham, pt. iv, ed. H. M. Wood (Surtees Soc. 142; 1929).

Wills from Doctors' Commons: A Selection from the Wills of Eminent Persons proved in the Prerogative Court of Canterbury, 1495–1695, ed. J. G. Nichols and J. Bruce (Camden OS 83; 1862).

The Wills of the Archdeaconry of Sudbury 1630–1635, ed. N. Evans (Suffolk Records Soc. 29; 1987).

WILSON, T., *The practise of the saints* (1609).

WILSON, T., *Works*, with life by J. Keble (LACT, 7 vols., 1847–63).

WOODCOCK, T., *Extracts from the Papers of Thomas Woodcock (Ob. 1695)*, ed. G. C. Moore Smith, in *Camden Miscellany*, xi (Camden 3rd ser. 13; 1907).

WREN, C., *Parentalia* (1750).

WROE, R., *Righteousness Encouraged and Rewarded with an Everlasting Remembrance. In a Sermon at the Funeral of the Right Worshipful Sir Roger Bradshaigh of Haigh, Knight and Baronet* (1684).

WYNNE, W., *The Life of Sir Leoline Jenkins . . . and a Compleat Series of Letters . . .* (2 vols., 1724).

Yorkshire Diaries and Autobiographies in the Seventeenth and Eighteenth Centuries (Surtees Soc. 65; 1877).

Yorkshire Writers: Richard Rolle of Hampole and his Followers, ed. C. Horstmann (2 vols., 1895–6).

YOUNG, E., *Night Thoughts*, ed. S. Cornford (Cambridge, 1989).

Selected Secondary Sources

ADAMS, M., and REEVE, J., 'Excavations at Christ Church, Spitalfields, 1984–1986', *Antiquity*, 61 (1987), 247–56.

ADDY, J., *Death, Money and the Vultures: Inheritance and Avarice 1660–1750* (1992).

ALMOND, P. C., *Heaven and Hell in Enlightenment England* (Cambridge, 1994).

ALSOP, J. D., 'Religious Preambles in Early Modern English Wills as Formulae', *Journal of Ecclesiastical History*, 40 (1989), 19–27.

ALTER, G., and RILEY, J. C., 'Frailty, Sickness, and Death: Models of Morbidity and Mortality in Historical Populations', *Population Studies*, 43 (1989), 25–45.

AMUSSEN, S. D., *An Ordered Society: Gender and Class in Early Modern England* (Oxford, 1988).

ANDREW, D. T., *Philanthropy and Police: London Charity in the Eighteenth Century* (Princeton, 1989).

ANDREWS, W., *Burials without Coffins* (Hull, 1899).

ANON., 'Incised Slabs in Croxall Church', drawn by M. Ussher, *Journal of the Derbyshire Archaeological and Natural History Soc.* 2 (1880), 90–1.

ARCHER, I. W., *The Pursuit of Stability: Social Relations in Elizabethan London* (Cambridge, 1991).

ARIÈS, P., *The Hour of Our Death* (Harmondsworth, 1983).

—— *Western Attitudes towards Death: From the Middle Ages to the Present* (Baltimore, 1974).

ASTON, M., *England's Iconoclasts*, i. *Laws against Images* (Oxford, 1988).

ATKINSON, D. W., '*A Salve For A Sicke Man*: William Perkins' Contribution to the *ars moriendi*', *Historical Magazine of the Protestant Episcopal Church*, 46 (1977), 409-18.

—— 'The English ars morendi [*sic*]: Its Protestant Transformation', *Renaissance and Reformation*, NS 6, OS 18 (1982), 1-9.

ATTREED, L. C., 'Preparation for Death in Sixteenth Century Northern England', *Sixteenth Century Journal*, 13/3 (1982), 37-66.

BABB, L., *The Elizabethan Malady: A Study of Melancholia in English Literature from 1580 to 1642* (East Lansing, 1951).

BADHAM, S. F., 'London Standardisation and Provincial Idiosyncrasy: The Organisation and Working Practices of Brass-Engraving Workshops in Pre-Reformation England', *Church Monuments*, 5 (1990), 3-25.

BAILEY, M., 'Demographic Decline in Late Medieval England: Some Thoughts on Recent Research', *Economic History Review*, 49 (1996), 1-19.

BARRY, J., 'Piety and the Patient: Medicine and Religion in Eighteenth Century Bristol', in Porter (ed.), *Patients and Practitioners*, 145-75.

BASSETT, S. (ed.), *Death in Towns: Urban Responses to the Dying and the Dead, 100-1600* (Leicester, 1992).

BAYLISS, J., 'Richard Parker "the Alablasterman"', *Church Monuments*, 5 (1990), 39-56.

BEATY, N. L., *The Craft of Dying: A Study in the Literary Tradition of the Ars Moriendi in England* (New Haven, 1970).

BEAVER, D., ' "Sown in Dishonour, raised in Glory": Death, Ritual and Social Organization in Northern Gloucestershire, 1590-1690', *Social History*, 17 (1992), 389-419.

BEIER, L. M., 'The Good Death in Seventeenth-Century England', in Houlbrooke (ed.), *Death, Ritual and Bereavement*, 43-61.

—— 'In Sickness and in Health: A Seventeenth Century Family's Experience', in Porter (ed.), *Patients and Practitioners*, 101-28.

—— *Sufferers and Healers: The Experience of Illness in Seventeenth-Century England* (1987).

BERNSTEIN, A. E., *The Formation of Hell: Death and Retribution in the Ancient and Early Christian Worlds* (1993).

BIGLAND, R., *Historical, Monumental and Genealogical Collections relative to the County of Gloucester (1791-1899)*, ed. B. Frith (Bristol and Gloucestershire Archaeological Soc.: Gloucestershire Record Ser. 2-3, 5, 8; 1989-95).

BINSKI, P., *Medieval Death: Ritual and Representation* (1996).

BITTLE, W. G., and LANE, R. T., 'Inflation and Philanthropy in England: A Re-Assessment of W. K. Jordan's Data', *Economic History Review*, 2nd ser. 29 (1976), 203-10.

BIZLEY, A. C., *The Slate Figures of Cornwall* (1965).

BLAUNER, R., 'Death and Social Structure', *Psychiatry: Journal for the Study of Interpersonal Processes*, 29 (1966), 378-94.

BLOMEFIELD, F., and PARKIN, C., *An Essay towards a Topographical History of the County of Norfolk* (11 vols., 2nd edn., 1805-10).

BOASE, T. S. R., *Death in the Middle Ages: Mortality, Judgment and Remembrance* (1972).

BOGGIS, J. E., *Praying for the Dead: An Historical Review of the Practice* (1913).

BONFIELD, L., 'Normative Rules and Property Transmission: Reflections on the Link between Marriage and Inheritance in Early Modern England', in Bonfield, Smith, and Wrightson (edd.), *World We have Gained*, 155-76.

—— SMITH, R. M., and WRIGHTSON, K. (edd.), *The World We have Gained: Histories of Population and Social Structure, Essays presented to Peter Laslett on his Seventieth Birthday* (Oxford, 1986).

BOORE, E., 'The Church of St Augustine the Less, Bristol: An Interim Statement', *Transactions of the Bristol and Gloucestershire Archaeological Soc.* 104 (1986), 211-13.

BOWLBY, J., *Attachment and Loss*, iii. *Loss: Sadness and Depression* (Harmondsworth, 1981).

BRANDON, S. G. F., *The Judgment of the Dead: An Historical and Comparative Study of a Post-Mortem Judgment in the Major Religions* (1967).

BRIGDEN, S., *London and the Reformation* (Oxford, 1989).

BROCE, G., and WUNDERLI, R. M., 'The Funeral of Henry Percy, Sixth Earl of Northumberland', *Albion*, 22 (1990), 199-215.

BRODSKY, V., 'Widows in Late Elizabethan London: Remarriage, Economic Opportunity and Family Orientations', in Bonfield, Smith, and Wrightson (edd.), *World We have Gained*, 122-54.

BURGESS, C., '"A Fond Thing vainly invented": An Essay on Purgatory and Pious Motive in later Medieval England', in S. J. Wright (ed.), *Parish Church and People: Local Studies in Lay Religion 1350-1750* (1988), 56-84.

—— '"By Quick and by Dead": Wills and Pious Provision in Late Medieval Bristol', *EHR* 102 (1987), 837-58.

BURGESS, F., *English Churchyard Memorials* (1963).

BURNS, N. T., *Christian Mortalism from Tyndale to Milton* (Cambridge, Mass., 1972).

CAIGER-SMITH, A., *English Medieval Mural Paintings* (Oxford, 1963).

CAPP, B., 'Will Formularies', *Local Population Studies*, 14 (1975), 49-50.

CARLSON, E. J., 'The Historical Value of the Ely Consistory Probate Records', in C. and D. Thurley (comp.), E. Leedham-Green and R. Rodd (edd.), *Index of the Probate Records of the Consistory Court of Ely 1444-1858*, i. *A-E* (Index Library, 103, British Record Soc., 1994), pp. xvii–lix.

CARLTON, C., *Going to the Wars: The Experience of the British Civil Wars, 1638-1651* (1992).

CARTER, T. T., *The Doctrine of Confession in the Church of England* (1865).

CHAUNU, P., *La Mort à Paris: 16ᵉ, 17ᵉ, 18ᵉ siècles* (Paris, 1978).

CHILDE, V. G., 'Directional Changes in Funerary Practices during 50,000 Years', *Man: A Record of Anthropological Science*, 45 (1945), 13–19.

CLARKSON, L., *Death, Disease and Famine in Pre-Industrial England* (Dublin, 1975).

COLDICOTT, D. K., *A Long Sutton Miscellany, including a Study of the Wills (1502-1856) and Probate Inventories (1558-1709) from the Parish of Long Sutton and Well, Hampshire* (1979).

COLLINS, M., 'A Little Known "Art of Dying" by a Brigittine of Syon: *A Daily Exercise and Experience of Death* by Richard Whitford', in J. H. M. Taylor (ed.), *Dies Illa: Death in the Middle Ages* (Vinaver Studies in French, 1; 1984), 179–93.

COLLINSON, P. (ed.), '"A Magazine of Religious Patterns": An Erasmian Topic transposed in English Protestantism', in id., *Godly People: Essays on English Protestantism and Puritanism* (1983), 499–525.

COLVIN, H., *Architecture and the After-Life* (New Haven, 1991).

CONNOR, A. B., *Monumental Brasses in Somerset* (Bath, 1970).

COOK, G. H., *The English Medieval Parish Church* (1954).

COPEMAN, W. S. C., *Doctors and Disease in Tudor Times* (1960).

COPPEL, S., 'Willmaking on the Deathbed', *Local Population Studies*, 40 (1988), 37–45.

—— 'Wills and the Community: A Case Study of Tudor Grantham', in Riden (ed.), *Probate Records and the Local Community*, 71–90.

COSTER, W., *Kinship and Inheritance in Early Modern England: Three Yorkshire Parishes* (Borthwick Papers, 83; 1993).

CRAIG, J., 'Margaret Spitlehouse, Female Scrivener', *Local Population Studies*, 46 (1991), 54–7.

—— and Litzenberger, C., 'Wills as Religious Propaganda: The Testament of William Tracy', *Journal of Ecclesiastical History*, 44 (1993), 415–31.

CRESSY, D., *Birth, Marriage, and Death: Ritual, Religion, and the Life-Cycle in Tudor and Stuart England* (Oxford, 1997).

—— 'Death and the Social Order: The Funerary Preferences of Elizabethan Gentlemen', *Continuity and Change*, 5 (1989), 99–119.

—— 'Kinship and Kin Interaction in Early Modern England', *Past and Present*, 113 (1986), 38–69.

—— *Literacy and the Social Order: Reading and Writing in Tudor and Stuart England* (Cambridge, 1980).

CROSS, C., 'The Development of Protestantism in Leeds and Hull, 1520-1640: The Evidence from Wills', *Northern History*, 18 (1982), 230–8.

CROSS, F. L., and LIVINGSTONE, E. A. (edd.), *The Oxford Dictionary of the Christian Church* (2nd edn., 1974).

CUNNINGTON, P., and LUCAS, C., *Costume for Births, Marriages and Deaths* (1972).

CURL, J. S., *The Victorian Celebration of Death* (Newton Abbot, 1972).

DANIELL, C., *Death and Burial in Medieval England 1066-1550* (1997).

D'AVRAY, D., *Death and the Prince: Memorial Preaching before 1350* (Oxford, 1994).

DEBUS, A. G., *The English Paracelsians* (1965).

—— (ed.), *Medicine in Seventeenth Century England* (Berkeley and Los Angeles, 1974).

DELUMEAU, J., *Sin and Fear: The Emergence of a Western Guilt Culture 13th-18th Centuries* (New York, 1990).

DENDY, D. R., *The Use of Lights in Christian Worship* (Alcuin Club Collections, 41; 1959).

DICKENS, A. G., *Lollards and Protestants in the Diocese of York, 1509-1558* (1959).

DINN, R., 'Death and Rebirth in Late Medieval Bury St Edmunds', in Bassett (ed.), *Death in Towns*, 151-69.

DISLEY, E., 'Degrees of Glory: Protestant Doctrine and the Concept of Rewards Hereafter', *Journal of Theological Studies*, NS 42 (1991), 77-105.

DOBSON, M. J., 'The Last Hiccup of the Old Demographic Regime: Population Stagnation and Decline in Late Seventeenth and Early Eighteenth-Century South-East England', *Continuity and Change*, 4 (1989), 395-428.

—— 'Malaria in England: A Geographical and Historical Perspective', *Parassitologia*, 36 (1994), 35-60.

DOEBLER, B. A., *'Rooted Sorrow': Dying in Early Modern England* (Rutherford, 1994).

DRAPER, J. W., *The Funeral Elegy and the Rise of English Romanticism* (New York, 1929).

DUFFY, E., *The Stripping of the Altars: Traditional Religion in England c.1400-c.1580* (New Haven, 1992).

DYER, A., 'Epidemics of Measles in a Seventeenth-Century English Town', *Local Population Studies*, 34 (1984), 35-45.

EARLE, P., *The Making of the English Middle Class: Business, Society and Family Life in London, 1660-1730* (1989).

EIRE, C. M. N., *From Madrid to Purgatory: The Art and Craft of Dying in Sixteenth-Century Spain* (Cambridge, 1995).

ERICKSON, A. L., *Women and Property in Early Modern England* (1993).

ESDAILE, K. A., *English Church Monuments 1510-1840* (1946).

EVANS, N., 'Inheritance, Women, Religion and Education in Early Modern Society as Revealed by Wills', in Riden (ed.), *Probate Records and the Local Community*, 53-70.

FINLAY, R. A. P., *Population and Metropolis: The Demography of London, 1580-1650* (Cambridge, 1981).

FINUCANE, R. C., *Appearances of the Dead: A Cultural History of Ghosts* (1982).

—— 'Sacred Corpse, Profane Carrion: Social Ideas and Death Rituals in the later Middle Ages', in Whaley (ed.), *Mirrors of Mortality*, 40–60.

FLEMING, P. W., 'Charity, Faith, and the Gentry of Kent 1422–1529', in J. Pollard (ed.), *Property and Politics: Essays in Later Medieval English History* (Gloucester, 1984), 36–58.

FORBES, T. R., 'By what Disease or Casualty: The Changing Face of Death in London', in Webster (ed.), *Health, Medicine and Mortality*, 117–39.

FRITZ, P., 'From "Public" to "Private": The Royal Funerals in England, 1500–1830', in Whaley (ed.), *Mirrors of Mortality*, 61–79.

—— 'The Undertaking Trade in England: Its Origins and Early Development, 1660–1830', *Eighteenth-Century Studies*, 28 (1994–5), 241–53.

GENTLES, I., 'Political Funerals during the English Revolution', in S. Porter (ed.), *London and the Civil War* (1996), 205–24.

GIBSON, W. C. (ed.), *British Contributions to Medical Science* (1971).

GITTINGS, C., *Death, Burial and the Individual in Early Modern England* (1984).

GORER, G., *Death, Grief and Mourning in Contemporary Britain* (1965).

—— 'The Pornography of Death', *Encounter*, 5/4 (1955), 49–52.

GOTTFRIED, R. S., *Epidemic Disease in Fifteenth-Century England* (Leicester, 1978).

GREAVES, R. L., *Society and Religion in Elizabethan England* (Minneapolis, 1981).

GREENHILL, F. A., *Incised Effigial Slabs* (1976).

HADFIELD, P., *Youlgreave Parish Church and Records* (Youlgreave, n.d.).

HAIGH, C., *English Reformations: Religion, Politics and Society under the Tudors* (Oxford, 1993).

HAIR, P. E. H., 'Deaths from Violence in Britain: A Tentative Secular Survey', *Population Studies*, 25 (1971), 5–24.

HALLAM, E. A., 'Turning the Hourglass: Gender Relations at the Deathbed in Early Modern Canterbury', *Mortality*, 1 (1996), 61–82.

HARDING, V., ' "And one more may be laid there": The Location of Burials in Early Modern London', *London Journal* 14 (1989), 112–29.

—— 'Burial Choice and Burial Location in Later Medieval London', in Bassett (ed.), *Death in Towns*, 119–35.

—— 'Burial of the Plague Dead in Early Modern London', in J. A. I. Champion (ed.), *Epidemic Disease in London* (Centre for Metropolitan History, Working Papers Ser. 1; 1993), 53–64.

HARVEY, B., *Living and Dying in England 1100–1540: The Monastic Experience* (Oxford, 1993).

HATCHER, J., *Plague, Population and the English Economy, 1348–1530* (Basingstoke, 1977).

Hatchments in Britain, v., *Kent, Surrey and Sussex*, ed. P. Summers and J. Titterton (1985).

HAWKINS, D., 'The Black Death and the New London Cemeteries of 1348', *Antiquity*, 64 (1990), 637–42.

HERTZ, R., 'A Contribution to the Study of the Collective Representation of Death', in id., *Death and the Right Hand*, trans. R. and C. Needham, introd. E. E. Evans-Pritchard (1960).

HOLLINGSWORTH, T. H., 'The Demography of the British Peerage', suppl. to *Population Studies*, 18 (1964).

HOULBROOKE, R., *Church Courts and the People during the English Reformation 1520–1570* (Oxford, 1979).

—— (ed.), *Death, Ritual and Bereavement* (1989).

—— ' "Public" and "Private" in the Funerals of the Later Stuart Gentry: Some Somerset Examples', *Mortality*, 1 (1996), 163–76.

HOUSTON, R. A., *The Population History of Britain and Ireland 1500–1750* (Basingstoke, 1992).

HOWELL, D., *Sir Philip Sidney, the Shepherd Knight* (1968).

HUNTER, D., *The Diseases of Occupations* (1955 edn.).

HURST, J. G., and RAHTZ, P. A., *Wharram: A Study of Settlement on the Yorkshire Wolds*, iii. *Wharram Percy: The Church of St Martin* (1987).

HUTCHINS, J., *The History and Antiquities of the County of Dorset* (3rd edn., 4 vols., 1861).

JALLAND, P., *Death in the Victorian Family* (Oxford, 1996).

JAMES, M. E., 'Two Tudor Funerals', *Transactions of the Cumberland & Westmorland Antiquarian and Archaeological Soc.* NS 66 (1966), 165–78.

JOHNSTON, J. A., 'The Probate Inventories and Wills of a Worcestershire Parish 1676–1775', *Midland History*, 1 (1971–2), 20–33.

—— 'Social Change in the Eighteenth Century: The Evidence in Wills from Six Lincolnshire Parishes, 1661–1812', *Lincolnshire History and Archaeology*, 27 (1992), 27–33.

JORDAN, W. K., *Philanthropy in England, 1480–1660* (1959).

—— *The Charities of Rural England 1480–1660* (1961).

KAY, D., *Melodious Tears: The English Funeral Elegy from Spenser to Milton* (Oxford, 1990).

KEMP, B. R., *English Church Monuments* (1980).

KERRY, C., 'Ashover, Memoranda by Titus Wheatcroft, A.D. 1722', *Journal of the Derbyshire Archaeological and Natural History Soc.* 19 (1897), 30–44.

KING, P. M., 'The Cadaver Tomb in England: Novel Manifestations of an Old Idea', *Church Monuments*, 5 (1990), 26–38.

KJØLBYE-BIDDLE, B., 'Dispersal or Concentration: The Disposal of the Winchester Dead over 2000 Years', in Bassett (ed.), *Death in Towns*, 210–47.

KRAMER, J. C., 'Opium Rampant: Medical Use, Misuse and Abuse in Britain and the West in the 17th and 18th Centuries', *British Journal of Addiction*, 74 (1979), 377–89.

KREIDER, A., *English Chantries: The Road to Dissolution* (Cambridge, Mass., 1979).

KÜBLER-ROSS, E., *On Death and Dying* (1973).

LAKE, P., 'Popular Form, Puritan Content? Two Puritan Appropriations of the Murder Pamphlet from Mid-Seventeenth-Century London', in A. Fletcher and P. Roberts (edd.), *Religion, Culture and Society in Early Modern Britain: Essays in Honour of Patrick Collinson* (Cambridge, 1994), 313–34.

LANDERS, J., *Death and the Metropolis: Studies in the Demographic History of London, 1670–1830* (Cambridge, 1993).

—— and Mouzas, A., 'Burial Seasonality and Causes of Death in London 1670–1819', *Population Studies*, 42 (1988), 59–83.

LANGFORD, P., *Public Life and the Propertied Englishman, 1689–1798* (Oxford, 1991).

LAQUEUR, T. W., 'Crowds, Carnival and the State in English Executions, 1604–1868', in A. L. Beier, D. Cannadine, and J. M. Rosenheim (edd.), *The First Modern Society: Essays in English History in Honour of Lawrence Stone* (Cambridge, 1989), 305–55.

LAURENCE, A., 'Godly Grief: Individual Responses to Death in Seventeenth-Century Britain', in Houlbrooke (ed.), *Death, Ritual and Bereavement*, 62–76.

LEBRUN, F., *Les Hommes et la Mort en Anjou aux 17ᵉ et 18ᵉ siècles* (Paris, 1971).

LEES, H., *Hallowed Ground: Churchyards of Gloucestershire and the Cotswolds* (1993).

LEGG, J. W., *English Church Life from the Restoration to the Tractarian Movement* (1914).

LE GOFF, J., *The Birth of Purgatory* (1984).

LENZ, R. (ed.), *Leichenpredigten: Eine Bestandsaufnahme: Bibliographie und Ergebnisse einer Umfrage* (Marburg, 1980).

—— (ed.), *Leichenpredigten als Quelle historischer Wissenschaften* (3 vols: Cologne, 1975; Marburg, 1979 and 1984).

LEVINE, D., and WRIGHTSON, K., *The Making of an Industrial Society: Whickham 1560–1765* (Oxford, 1991).

LITTEN, J., *The English Way of Death: The Common Funeral since 1450* (1991).

LITZENBERGER, C., 'Local Responses to Changes in Religious Policy based on Evidence from Gloucestershire Wills (1540–1580)', *Continuity and Change*, 8 (1993), 417–39.

LLEWELLYN, N., *The Art of Death: Visual Culture in the English Death Ritual c.1500–c.1800* (1991).

LORD, J., 'Patronage and Church Monuments 1660–1794: A Regional Study', *Church Monuments*, 1 (1986), 95–105.

MCDANNELL, C., and LANG, B., *Heaven: A History* (New York, 1990).

MACDONALD, M., *Mystical Bedlam: Madness, Anxiety and Healing in Seventeenth-Century England* (Cambridge, 1981).
—— and Murphy, T. R., *Sleepless Souls: Suicide in Early Modern England* (Oxford, 1990).
MACFARLANE, A., *The Family Life of Ralph Josselin, a Seventeenth-Century Clergyman: An Essay in Historical Anthropology* (Cambridge, 1970).
MCINTOSH, J. L., 'English Funeral Sermons 1560–1640: The Relationship between Gender and Death, Dying, and the Afterlife', M.Litt. thesis, (Oxford, 1990).
MCMANNERS, J., *Death and the Enlightenment: Changing Attitudes to Death in Eighteenth-Century France* (Oxford, 1985).
MADDERN, P., 'Friends of the Dead: Executors, Wills and Family Strategy in Fifteenth-Century Norfolk', in R. S. Archer and S. Walker (edd.), *Rulers and Ruled in Late Medieval England: Essays presented to Gerald Harriss* (1995), 155–74.
MARCHANT, R. A., *The Church under the Law: Justice, Administration and Discipline in the Diocese of York, 1560–1640* (Cambridge, 1969).
MAYHEW, G. J., 'The Progress of the Reformation in East Sussex 1530–1559: The Evidence from Wills', *Southern History*, 5 (1983), 38–67.
METCALF, P., and HUNTINGTON, R., *Celebrations of Death: The Anthropology of Mortuary Ritual* (2nd edn., Cambridge, 1991).
MISSEN, D. C., 'Children on Church Monuments in East Anglia', *East Anglian Magazine*, 39 (1980), 611–13.
Monumental Brasses: The Portfolio Plates of the Monumental Brass Society 1894–1984, introd. M. W. Norris (Woodbridge, 1988).
MORLEY, H. T., *Monumental Brasses of Berkshire* (Reading, 1924).
MORLEY, J., *Death, Heaven, and the Victorians* (1971).
NORRIS, M., 'Later Medieval Monumental Brasses: An Urban Funerary Industry and its Representation of Death', in Bassett (ed.), *Death in Towns*, 184–209.
—— *Monumental Brasses: The Memorials* (2 vols., 1977).
NULAND, S. B., *How We Die* (1994 edn.).
O'CONNOR, M. C., *The Art of Dying Well: The Development of the Ars Moriendi* (New York, 1942).
OLIVER, T. (ed.), *Dangerous Trades* (1902).
PAGE-PHILLIPS, J., *Children on Brasses* (1970).
PARKES, C. M., *Bereavement: Studies of Grief in Adult Life* (2nd edn., Harmondsworth, 1986).
PARRY, E., 'Helmdon Wills 1603–1760', *Northamptonshire Past and Present*, 5 (1975), 235–41.
PAXTON, F. S., *Christianizing Death. The Creation of a Ritual Process in Early Medieval Europe* (Ithaca, NY, 1990).
PIGMAN, G. W., *Grief and English Renaissance Elegy* (Cambridge, 1985).

PLATT, C., *King Death: The Black Death and its Aftermath in Late-Medieval England* (1996).

POLLOCK, L., *Forgotten Children: Parent–Child Relations from 1500 to 1900* (Cambridge, 1983).

—— *With Faith and Physic: The Life of a Tudor Gentlewoman, Lady Grace Mildmay 1552–1620* (1993).

POLLOCK, Sir F., and MAITLAND, F. W., *The History of English Law before the Time of Edward I* (2 vols., 2nd edn. reissued, Cambridge, 1968).

POOLE, E., 'Will Formularies', *Local Population Studies*, 17 (1976), 42–3.

PORTER, D. and R., *Patient's Progress: Doctors and Doctoring in Eighteenth-Century England* (Cambridge, 1989).

PORTER, R., 'Death and the Doctors in Georgian England', in Houlbrooke (ed.), *Death, Ritual and Bereavement*, 77–94.

—— *Disease, Medicine and Society in England 1550–1860* (Basingstoke, 1987).

—— (ed.), *Patients and Practitioners: Lay Perceptions of Medicine in Pre-Industrial Society* (Cambridge, 1985).

PORTER, S., 'Death and Burial in a London Parish: St Mary Woolnoth, 1653–1699', *London Journal*, 8 (1982), 76–80.

POWELL, S., and FLETCHER, A. J., '"In Die Sepulture Seu Trigintali": The Late Medieval Funeral and Memorial Sermon', *Leeds Studies in English* NS 12 (1981), 195–228.

PUCKLE, B. S., *Funeral Customs: Their Origin and Development* (1926).

RAINE, J., *The History and Antiquities of North Durham* (1852).

RAWCLIFFE, C., *Medicine & Society in Later Medieval England* (Stroud, 1995).

RAZZELL, P., *The Conquest of Smallpox* (Firle, 1977).

—— *Essays in English Population History* (1994).

REX, R., *Henry VIII and the English Reformation* (Basingstoke, 1993).

RICHARDSON, R., *Death, Dissection and the Destitute* (Harmondsworth, 1989).

RICHARDSON, R. C., 'Wills and Will-Makers in the Sixteenth and Seventeenth Centuries: Some Lancashire Evidence', *Local Population Studies*, 9 (1972), 33–42.

RIDEN, P. (ed.), *Probate Records and the Local Community* (Gloucester, 1985).

RILEY, J. C., *The Eighteenth-Century Campaign to avoid Disease* (Basingstoke, 1987).

RODWELL, W., *Church Archaeology* (2nd edn., 1989).

—— and RODWELL, K. A., *Rivenhall: Investigation of a Villa, Church and Village, 1950–1977* (Council for British Archaeology Research Report, 55; 1986).

ROSENTHAL, J. T., *The Purchase of Paradise: Gift Giving and the Aristocracy 1307–1485* (1972).

ROWELL, G., *Hell and the Victorians* (Oxford, 1974).

—— *The Liturgy of Christian Burial* (1977).

SCARISBRICK, J. J., *The Reformation and the English People* (Oxford, 1984).

SCHIESARI, J., *The Gendering of Melancholia: Feminism, Psychoanalysis and the Symbolics of Loss in Renaissance Literature* (Ithaca, NY, 1992).

SCHOFIELD, R., 'Did the Mothers Really Die? Three Centuries of Maternal Mortality in "The World We Have Lost"', in Bonfield, Smith, and Wrightson (edd.), *World We have Gained*, 231–60.

—— and WRIGLEY, E. A., 'Infant and Child Mortality in England in the Late Tudor and Early Stuart Period', in Webster (ed.), *Health, Medicine and Mortality*, 61–95.

SCODEL, J., *The English Poetic Epitaph: Commemoration and Conflict from Jonson to Wordsworth* (Ithaca, NY, 1991).

SEAVER, P. S., *Wallington's World: A Puritan Artisan in Seventeenth-Century London* (1985).

SHARPE, J. A., *Crime in Early Modern England, 1550–1750* (Harlow, 1984).

—— '"Last Dying Speeches": Religion, Ideology and Public Execution in Seventeenth-Century England', *Past and Present*, 107 (1985), 144–67.

SHEEHAN, M. M., *The Will in Medieval England: From the Conversion of the Anglo-Saxons to the End of the Thirteenth Century* (Toronto, 1963).

SHEPPARD, E., 'The Reformation and the Citizens of Norwich', *Norfolk Archaeology*, 38 (1981–3), 44–56.

SHREWSBURY, J. F. D., *A History of Bubonic Plague in the British Isles* (Cambridge, 1970).

SLACK, P., *The English Poor Law, 1531–1782* (Basingstoke, 1990).

—— *The Impact of Plague in Tudor and Stuart England* (Oxford, 1985).

—— 'Mortality Crises and Epidemic Disease in England 1485–1610', in Webster (ed.), *Health, Medicine and Mortality*, 301–34.

SMITH, E., *By Mourning Tongues: Studies in English Elegy* (Ipswich, 1977).

SMITH, L. B., 'English Treason Trials and Confessions in the Sixteenth Century', *Journal of the History of Ideas*, 15 (1954), 471–98.

SMITH, R. M., 'Population and its Geography in England 1500–1730', in R. A. Dodgshon and R. A. Butlin (edd.), *An Historical Geography of England and Wales* (1978), 199–237.

SPENCE, R. T., 'A Noble Funeral in the Great Civil War', *Yorkshire Archaeological Journal*, 65, (1993), 115–23.

SPENCER, T., *Death and Elizabethan Tragedy: A Study of Convention and Opinion in the Elizabethan Drama* (Cambridge, Mass., 1936).

SPUFFORD, M., *Contrasting Communities: English Villagers in the Sixteenth and Seventeenth Centuries* (Cambridge, 1974).

—— 'Peasant Inheritance Customs and Land Distribution in Cambridgeshire from the Sixteenth to the Eighteenth Centuries', in J. Goody, J. Thirsk, and E. P. Thompson (edd.), *Family and Inheritance in Western Europe 1200–1800* (Cambridge, 1976), 156–74.

SPUFFORD, M., *Small Books and Pleasant Histories: Popular Fiction and its Readership in Seventeenth-Century England* (1981).

STAFFORD, W. S., 'Repentance on the Eve of the English Reformation: John Fisher's Sermons of 1508 and 1509', *Historical Magazine of the Protestant Episcopal Church*, 54 (1985), 297–337.

STANNARD, D., *The Puritan Way of Death: A Study in Religion, Culture, and Social Change* (New York, 1977).

STONE, L., *The Crisis of the Aristocracy, 1558–1641* (Oxford, 1965).

—— *The Family, Sex and Marriage in England 1500–1800* (1977).

STRANKS, C. J., *Anglican Devotion: Studies in the Spiritual Life of the Church of England between the Reformation and the Oxford Movement* (1961).

STRONG, R., *The English Icon: Elizabethan & Jacobean Portraiture* (1969).

SWANSON, R. N., *Catholic England: Faith, Religion and Observance before the Reformation* (Manchester, 1993).

TAKAHASHI, M., 'The Number of Wills proved in the Sixteenth and Seventeenth Centuries', in G. H. Martin and P. Spufford (edd.), *The Records of the Nation* (Woodbridge, 1990), 185–213.

TANNER, N. P., *The Church in Late Medieval Norwich, 1370–1532* (Toronto, 1984).

TAYLOR, L., *Mourning Dress: A Costume and Social History* (1983).

THOMAS, K., *Religion and the Decline of Magic: Studies in Popular Beliefs in Sixteenth- and Seventeenth-Century England* (1971).

—— 'The Meaning of Literacy in Early Modern England', in G. Bauman (ed.), *The Written Word: Literacy in Transition* (Oxford, 1986), 97–131.

THOMSON, J. A. F., 'Piety and Charity in Later Medieval London', *Journal of Ecclesiastical History*, 16 (1965), 178–95.

TRANTER, N. L., *Population and Society, 1750–1940: Contrasts in Population Growth* (1985).

TROMLY, F. B., ' "Accordinge to Sounde Religion": The Elizabethan Controversy over the Funeral Sermon', *Journal of Medieval and Renaissance Studies*, 13 (1983), 293–312.

TRUMBACH, R., *The Rise of the Egalitarian Family: Aristocratic Kinship and Domestic Relations in Eighteenth-Century England* (1978).

TUMMERS, H., 'The Medieval Effigial Tombs in Chichester Cathedral', *Church Monuments*, 3 (1988), 33–5.

TURNER, A. K., *The History of Hell* (1995).

TYACKE, N., *Anti-Calvinists: The Rise of English Arminianism c.1590–1640* (Oxford, 1986).

VALE, M. G. A., *Piety, Charity and Literacy among the Yorkshire Gentry, 1370–1480* (Borthwick Papers, 50; 1976).

VAN GENNEP, A., *Rites of Passage*, trans. M. B. Vizedom and G. L. Caffee (1960).

VANN, R. T., 'Wills and the Family in an English Town: Banbury, 1550–1800', *Journal of Family History*, 4 (1979), 346–67.

WAGNER, Sir ANTHONY, *Heralds of England: A History of the Office and College of Arms* (1967).

WALKER, D. P., *The Decline of Hell: Seventeenth-Century Discussions of Eternal Torment* (1964).

WALTER, J., and SCHOFIELD, R., *Famine, Disease and the Social Order in Early Modern Society* (Cambridge, 1989).

WALTER, T., *The Eclipse of Eternity: A Sociology of the Afterlife* (1996).

—— 'Emotional Reserve and the English Way of Grief', in K. Charmaz, G. Howarth, and A. Kellehear (edd.), *The Unknown Country: Experiences of Death in Australia, Britain and the U.S.A.* (Basingstoke, 1997), 127–40.

—— *The Revival of Death* (1994).

WATT, T., *Cheap Print and Popular Piety, 1550–1640* (Cambridge, 1991).

WEAR, A., 'Puritan Perceptions of Illness in Seventeenth Century England', in Porter (ed.), *Patients and Practitioners*, 55–99.

WEBSTER, C. (ed.), *Health, Medicine and Mortality in the Sixteenth Century* (Cambridge, 1979).

—— 'Alchemical and Paracelsian Medicine', ibid. 301–34.

WHALEY, J. (ed.), *Mirrors of Mortality: Studies in the Social History of Death* (1981).

WHITE, A., 'England c.1560–c.1660: A Hundred Years of Continental Influence', *Church Monuments*, 7 (1992), 34–74.

—— 'Westminster Abbey in the Early Seventeenth Century: A Powerhouse of Ideas', *Church Monuments*, 4 (1989), 16–53.

WHITING, R., *The Blind Devotion of the People: Popular Religion and the English Reformation* (Cambridge, 1989).

WILSON, J., 'Icons of Unity', *History Today*, 43 (June 1993), 14–20.

WRIGHTSON, K., and LEVINE, D., *Poverty and Piety in an English Village: Terling, 1525–1700* (1979).

WRIGLEY, E. A., and SCHOFIELD, R. S., *The Population History of England 1541–1871: A Reconstruction* (1981).

WUNDERLI, R., and BROCE, G., 'The Final Moment before Death in Early Modern England', *Sixteenth Century Journal*, 20 (1989), 259–75.

WYLIE, J. A. H., and COLLIER, L. H., 'The English Sweating Sickness (Sudor Anglicus): A Reappraisal', *Journal of the History of Medicine*, 36 (1981), 425–45.

ZALESKI, C., *Otherworld Journeys: Accounts of Near-Death Experience in Medieval and Modern Times* (New York, 1987).

ZELL, M. L., 'The Social Parameters of Probate Records in the Sixteenth Century', *Bulletin of the Institute of Historical Research*, 57 (1984), 107–13.

INDEX

Abbot, George 126 n., 209, 273, 275 n.
Abingdon, Berks. 102, 276
Abner 310
Abraham 30, 41, 45, 189, 222, 241
absolution 149, 152, 155-6, 168-73,
    377, 383
accidents 24, 208
Acle, Norfolk 103
Acworth, Susanna 359
Adam 29
Adams, Robert 108
Addison, Joseph 52, 76, 217
Alborowe, William 102
Alby, Norfolk 115
Allen, William 67
Allington, Richard 200
Allsop family 364
Alverstoke, Hants. 365
Ambrose, St 222
Amery, Roland 99
Anderson, Anthony 304
Andrewes, Lancelot 21, 39, 166
Andrews, James 112
Angier, Elizabeth 189, 193
Angier, John 185, 189
Anne of Denmark 169
apoplexy 18, 199, 208, 209
Appleton, Berks. 367
Arbuthnot, Dr John 67, 248
Archer, Isaac 235
Archer, Mary 235
Ariès, Phillipe 1, 59, 218, 376, 380
Aristotle 62, 226
Ars Moriendi 151, 157, 200
Arthur, Prince 237, 261
Ashburton, Devon 288
Ashe, Simeon 299
Ashford, Andrew 95
Ashford, Richard 154
Ashmole, Elias 174
Ashover, Derby. 328, 364
Assheton, William 51, 92, 131, 133
Astley, Sir Jacob 79
Atterbury, Francis 64, 299
Aubrey, John 39, 76, 148, 266, 335, 343,
    361
Augustine, St 32-5, 47, 49, 222, 289-90
Augustus 217

Awood, Elizabeth 359
Awood, Robert 359
Axminster, Devon 181
Ayloffe, Margaret 127

Babington, Gervase 319
Bacon, Sir Nicholas 268
Bacon, Roger 20
Bailey, Mark 6 n.
Baker, William 303
Banbury, Oxon. 85, 87
Banckes, Miles 103
Banks, John 179
baptism 49, 52-3
Baptists 40, 324, 336
Baret, John 257
Barett, Elizabeth 86 n.
Barlow, Anna 239
Barlow, Edward 239
Barlow, John 43, 204, 302
Barnes, Ambrose 177, 327
Barney, Norfolk 118
Barnstaple, Devon 302
Baron, Joseph 189
Baron, Lippy 187
Barrington, Sir Francis 247
Barrington, Joan, Lady 68, 247
Barrow, Henry 156, 266 n., 297, 334
Barton, Thomas 108
Barwis, John 281
Basildon, Berks. 134
Bassett, Richard 108
Bates, Dr William 44
Baxter, Richard 46, 55, 65, 175-6, 202,
    206
Bayes, Joshua 302
Bayly, Lewis 100 n., 102 n., 170-1, 176
Bayning, Paul, 1st viscount Bayning of
    Sudbury 272, 318, 320
Beard, Thomas 207
Beauchamp, Isabel, countess of Warwick
    345
Beaufort, Lady Margaret 69, 152, 258,
    296, 311
Beckenham, Kent 51, 131
Becon, Thomas 49, 135, 157-9, 166,
    173
bede-roll 113